The Stuarts in Italy, 1719–1766

A Royal Court in Permanent Exile

Edward Corp

CAMBRIDGE UNIVERSITY PRESS
Cambridge, New York, Melbourne, Madrid, Cape Town,
Singapore, São Paulo, Delhi, Tokyo, Mexico City

Cambridge University Press
The Edinburgh Building, Cambridge CB2 8RU, UK

Published in the United States of America by
Cambridge University Press, New York

www.cambridge.org
Information on this title: www.cambridge.org/9780521513272

First published 2011

Printed in the United Kingdom at the University Press, Cambridge

A catalogue record for this publication is available from the British Library

Library of Congress Cataloging-in-Publication Data

Corp, Edward T.
The Stuarts in Italy, 1719–1766: a royal court in permanent exile /
Edward Corp.
    p. cm.
Sequel to: A court in exile: the Stuarts in France, 1689–1718, published by
Cambridge University Press in 2004.
Includes bibliographical references and index.
ISBN 978-0-521-51327-2 (Hardback)
1. James, Prince of Wales, 1688–1766–Homes and haunts–Italy–Rome.
2. Great Britain–Court and courtiers–History–18th century.   3. British–Italy–
Rome–History–18th century.   4. James, Prince of Wales, 1688–1766–Exile.
5. Great Britain–Foreign relations–Italy.   6. Italy–Foreign relations–
Great Britain.   7. Princes–Great Britain–Biography.   8. Stuart, House of.
9. Jacobites.   10. Exiles–Great Britain.   I. Title.
DA814.A3C676 2011
941.07092–dc22   2011008589

ISBN 978-0-521-51327-2 Hardback

Contents

Illustrations

The illustration credits in the list above detail the locations of the
paintings featured in the book. The author would like to thank the
institutions below for supplying photographs of the paintings, and for
granting permission to reproduce them. Where no photographic credit is
listed below, the photographs have been reproduced from the author's
collection.

Archivio di Stato di Roma: 5
Scottish National Portrait Gallery, Edinburgh: 8, 10, 11, 13,
    14, 17, 18, 23–7
Pinacoteca Cantonale Giovanni Zust, Rancate: 9
Musée National du Louvre: 19
National Portrait Gallery, London: 21, 22

Acknowledgements

The study of any royal court during the eighteenth century involves research into the history of painting and music as well as politics, religion and society. I am indebted to the many people from different academic disciplines who have generously shared information with me during the years when this book was in preparation.

I wish particularly to thank Alastair Laing and James Holloway, who have encouraged and supported my work during the past twenty years. My most important acknowledgement, however, must go to the Paul Mellon Centre for the Study of British Art, which awarded me a fellowship to spend four months in residence at the British School at Rome during the academic year 2004–5. This book could not possibly have been written if I had not lived and researched in Rome for an extended period, and I am extremely grateful to the Director and Council of the Paul Mellon Centre for making this possible.

The permanent staff and research fellows of the British School at Rome made the time I spent there as profitable and enjoyable as possible. If I only mention Dr Susan Russell, Maria Pia Malvezzi and Dr Carol Richardson, I do not forget the kindness and stimulating company provided by the other fellows and scholars, nor the unfailingly warm welcome I received from everyone there.

On specific aspects of Stuart portraiture I must acknowledge the help and stimulation given me by Simona Capelli, Bendor Grosvenor, Nicola Kalinsky, David Marshall, Robin Nicholson and Karin Wolfe, as well as by Richard Sharp, the leading authority on Jacobite engravings. My research into the musical life of the exiled Stuart court has been enormously helped over many years by Jane Clark. I am also very grateful to Professor Michael Talbot. I owe a special debt of gratitude to Professor Xavier Cervantes, whose knowledge both of Grand Tour portraiture and of *opera seria* has been of inestimable value.

For my research in Bologna I am greatly indebted to Dr Maurizio Ascari, who guided me into both the Biblioteca Universitaria and the Archivio di Stato. Most of my Italian research was carried out in Rome and the Vatican City, but the chapters dealing with Bologna rely very heavily on the material he enabled me to discover in that city.

The Stuart court in exile was the headquarters of the Jacobite movement in England, Scotland and Ireland, as it was also of the Jacobite communities in continental Europe. I am heavily indebted to the work of the leading authorities on the various aspects of Jacobitism, notably Professor Jeremy Black, Professor Jonathan Clark, Dr Eveline Cruickshanks, Professor Howard Erskine-Hill, Professor Paul Monod, Professor Murray Pittock, Abbot Geoffrey Scott, Professor Daniel Szechi and the late Professor Edward Gregg. I have also been helped by Mary Jane Cryan, William Eisler, Tim Llewellyn and Dr Steve Murdoch, among many others.

Most of my research within Great Britain was carrried out in the British Library, the National Archives, the National Library of Scotland and the Scottish Catholic Archives. It is a pleasure to work in all four places, but nothing can equal the extraordinarily warm welcome I have always received in the last of them, where the archivists have treated me with the very greatest kindness and generosity. I have also had a most helpful reception from the archivists at Windsor Castle, where the papers of James III are preserved among the Royal Archives. I am grateful to Her Majesty Queen Elizabeth II for permission to use and make frequent reference to the Stuart Papers.

My research in Rome was mainly in the Archivio Storico Vicariato, which contains the parish registers of the Church of Santi Apostoli, and in the papal archives, now divided between the Archivio di Stato di Roma and the Archivio Segreto Vaticano. All historians need to make use of catalogues, and the ones in the Archivio Segreto are often inadequate. I therefore acknowledge (though I doubt if he will ever read this) the help of the assistant there who discreetly guided me from the *Sala studio vecchia* to the *Torre dei venti* and allowed me to wander freely among the bookshelves to identify volumes concerning the Stuarts which I could not otherwise have discovered. I would also like to pay tribute to Michael Erwee for his generosity in sharing with me his knowledge of the Archivio Segreto.

I am particularly indebted to Jonathan Corp for the help he gave me in preparing some of the illustrations. Finally I must acknowledge once again the moral support and practical assistance given me by my wife, who has read, discussed and improved every chapter. This book is dedicated to her, with love and gratitude.

Abbreviations

Archives

ASB.	Archivio di Stato di Bologna
ASR.Cam I:	Archivio di Stato di Roma: Camerale I
CDG	Conti della Depositeria Generale
GT	Giustificazione di Tesoriere
RMC	Registro de' Mandati Camerale
ASV.	Archivio Segreto Vaticano
PAC	Palazzo Apostolico Computisteria
SS: Ingh	Segretario di Stato: Inghilterra
ASVR.	Archivio Storico Vicariato di Roma
BAV.	Biblioteca Apostolica Vaticana
BL. Add	British Library, Additional
Bod. Lib.	Bodleian Library
BSR	British School at Rome
Ghiselli	Biblioteca Universitaria di Bologna, Avisi di Ghiselli
NA. SP	National Archives, State Papers
NLS.	National Library of Scotland
RA. SP	Royal Archives, Stuart Papers
SCA. BL	Scottish Catholic Archives, Blairs Letters
VEC.	Venerable English College
WDA.	Westminster Diocesan Archives
WSRO.	West Sussex County Record Office

Publications

Benoît XIV	*Correspondance de Benoît XIV*
HMC	Historical Manuscripts Commission
JCR	*The Jacobite Court at Rome in 1719*
SPW	*The Stuart Papers at Windsor*

Introduction

For three-quarters of a century following the Glorious Revolution of 1688–9 King James II and then his son James III maintained a royal court in exile. At first it was based in France at Saint-Germain-en-Laye. After 1719 it was situated in Rome. This book, which concerns the second phase, provides a sequel to *A Court in Exile: The Stuarts in France, 1689–1718*, published by Cambridge University Press in 2004 (paperback reissue 2009).

The Stuart or Jacobite court in Italy has been one of the most misunderstood and misrepresented aspects of British history in the early modern period. There are several reasons for this, and the most obvious is that no previous historian has ever subjected it to serious study. Many books have been written about the exiled Stuarts, but no attention has been given to the court over which they presided.

Contemporary Hanoverian propaganda sought to misrepresent the court as impoverished, deadly dull and, for a Protestant audience, dominated by intolerant Catholic bigots. The aim was to undermine residual support for the Stuarts within the British Isles, and to deter people from going abroad to serve James III and his family.

The Whig historical tradition regarded the Stuarts as an obstruction to progress and treated their failure to regain their thrones as virtually inevitable. The Jacobites were therefore depicted as unattractive reactionaries who had very little support, except among the most backward peoples of the Highlands and Catholic Ireland. If their failure was inevitable, then the exiled court was not worth studying. Indeed the court was bound to be the insignificant and despicable little institution described in Hanoverian propaganda.

Support for this point of view became available during the 1870s when a series of letters describing the court was found among the State Papers in the Public Record Office.[1] They were written by a Prussian

---

[1] The references are NA. SP 85/14 (1722–3), 15 (1724–5), 16 (1726–9), and NA. SP 98/32

antiquarian living in Italy called Baron von Stosch, who was paid to spy
on the court by successive secretaries of state in London. The letters of
Stosch, written at least once a week from 1722 until his death in 1757,
provide an enormous amount of information about the court, and
indeed constitute one of our most important sources about it. But they
were used selectively to support the prevailing Whig interpretation.

Stosch, who clearly hated James III and his supporters, and who knew
what would please his readers and paymasters in London, sprinkled his
letters with hostile and dismissive comments. But examined objectively,
with no preconceived attitude towards the court, the letters actually
present a very different picture. The court which they discuss is surprisingly large and influential, very well connected and maintained on a
lavish scale. Stosch regarded the Stuarts as posing a very serious threat
to the stability of Hanoverian Great Britain, and went to great lengths to
study their court and alert the Whig ministers to its activities. He
disliked the Stuarts as people, but did not minimise their importance.
A small proportion of his letters do seem to support the Whig interpretation, but the majority contradict it. Very full use of the letters has been
made throughout the present study.

Another reason why the court has been misrepresented stems from the
belief that it can be properly understood in purely British terms. This is
not the place to reopen the old debate about the prospects of Jacobitism
within England and Scotland. Some historians have concluded that the
movement enjoyed very considerable support in both kingdoms and
might well have succeeded in overthrowing the Hanoverian monarchs,
George I and George II. Many have denied this, while others have
suggested a more nuanced interpretation between the two extreme positions.[2] Yet the argument of the present book is that the debate is actually
irrelevant to any study of the exiled court. For what mattered in Rome
was what the people *there* judged to be the prospects of a Jacobite
restoration. So long as the Italians, French and Spanish in the papal city
believed that a restoration was a serious prospect – which they did until
the end of the 1740s – then the exiled court assumed an importance

(1730–4), 37 (1734–6), 38 (1735), 41 (1737–9), 43 (1740–1), 46 (1742–3), 49
(1744–6), 53 (1747–50), 58 (1751–2), and 61 (1753–7). Except where shown, all the
information in this introduction has been taken from these weekly letters. To avoid
unnecessary repetition, the reference of each letter will be restricted to the folio
number in the relevant volume. The letters were used for the first time in A.C. Ewald,
The Life and Times of Charles Edward Stuart, 2 vols. (London, 1875). It should be noted
that Stosch wrote in French, and that all quotations from his letters in the main text are
translations. The original French has been retained for the footnotes.
[2] See the introduction to Daniel Szechi, *The Jacobites: Britain and Europe, 1688–1788*
(Manchester, 1994), which remains as valid today as when originally published.

which might well have surprised some people in eighteenth-century England and amazed the Whig historians of the nineteenth and twentieth centuries.

There is another misconception which has hindered our understanding of the court. After the failure of the Jacobite rising of 1715–16 James III was forced to leave both France and Lorraine and take refuge within the Papal States. This second exile, or exile within an exile, was unquestionably a very serious blow for the Jacobite cause, and for the prospects of a restoration, because it pushed the king further and then still further away from England and made his kingdoms less accessible. Moreover, it associated him more than ever before with popery as well as Catholicism, and thus diminished the attraction of the court. Yet in another way it actually greatly benefited it.

The return of peace in 1713–14, after a lengthy period of major wars, witnessed a dramatic increase in the number of people travelling away from the British Isles on a Grand Tour to Italy.[3] Because there were no diplomatic relations between the court in London and the papacy, and because successive popes refused to give even *de facto* recognition to Queen Anne, King George I or King George II, there was no British embassy in Rome, at precisely the moment when one was most needed. The Stuart court filled this gap, providing the Grand Tourists with a substitute or surrogate embassy where they could obtain passports, diplomatic protection, an Anglican chapel and various other services. The court was used in this way by Protestants and Catholics, by Whigs and Tories, by Hanoverians as well as Jacobites. King James III was personally more influential at the papal court than any ambassador could have been. This reason alone makes it imperative to revise our perception of the exiled court.

According to Stosch, the British and Irish Grand Tourists who arrived in Rome were immediately met and helped by the Jacobite courtiers already there.[4] 'Les Anglois', as he called them, always preferred to mix with each other than with foreigners, so they naturally socialised with the Jacobites.[5] Most of them were young, a long way from home, and surrounded by people unable to speak their language. Stosch wrote in November 1723 that it made no difference whether they were or were not supporters of King George. They put politics on

---

[3] John Ingamells, *A Dictionary of British and Irish Travellers in Italy, 1701–1800, Compiled from the Brinsley Ford Archive* (New Haven and London, 1997), 1070 pp.

[4] Stosch, 1 December 1722 (f. 181). The same point was made over thirty years later, in November 1756 (Ingamells, *Dictionary*, p. 615).

[5] Stosch, 12 January 1723 (f. 228).

one side and regularly met the Jacobites, some of whom were relations or old friends, whilst others were merely good company.[6] As he put it in January 1725, James III exercised 'protection and domination . . . over all the English'.[7]

One thing the Stuart court did was to help obtain a passport for any Grand Tourist who wanted to return home through France and had failed to obtain one before leaving England. At least one of the French ambassadors refused to give any passports without a recommendation from James III.[8] In 1734, when the Bourbons captured Naples from the Emperor, the same applied to anyone wanting a passport to go there.[9] Also, any British Grand Tourists who approached the papal authorities were said to be badly treated if they did not do so via the court.[10] In one letter Stosch added that the best way to obtain any favour even from the court of Madrid was to get a recommendation from James III.[11]

The Stuart court, like an embassy, contained an Anglican chapel, to which all Protestants were admitted.[12] The Anglican chaplains were particularly active in helping the Grand Tourists[13] and attracting them to visit the court.[14] There are no surviving registers of Anglican baptisms, marriages and burials, but we do know of at least one marriage and eight burials.[15]

Very little information has survived concerning the activities of the doctors attached to the court. One of them seems to have attended the Duke of Hamilton in 1729,[16] while another is known to have been

---

[6] Stosch, 27 November 1723 (f. 520).   [7] Stosch, 30 January 1725 (f. 265).

[8] Stosch, 7 and 28 November 1733 (ff. 586, 594); 15 May 1734 (f. 93).

[9] Ingamells, *Dictionary*, p. 110; John Doran, *Mann and Manners at the Court of Florence, 1740–1786* (2 vols., London, 1876), vol. I, p. 190, Mann to H. Walpole, 9 March 1745. This can be compared with BL. Add MSS 312645, f. 192; and Add MSS 31266, f. 185, undated letters from Hay (before 1726) in which he asked Cardinal Gualterio to obtain for him some passports for Naples from the Imperial ambassador.

[10] Stosch, 16 February 1730 (f. 27), 26 May and 5 June 1731 (ff. 201, 211), 27 November 1734 (f. 182), 16 April 1751 (f. 32); Ingamells, *Dictionary*, p. 206. The Roman customs officers apparently passed on to the Stuart court the names of all the British and Irish tourists who arrived in the city (*ibid.*, p. 310).

[11] Stosch, 24 September 1735 (f. 273). For an example, see Chapter 12, p. 254.

[12] Stosch, 15 August 1726 (f. 118).   [13] Stosch, 16 December 1724 (f. 228).

[14] Stosch, 12 September 1726 (f. 139).

[15] For the marriage in April 1721, see Ingamells, *Dictionary*, p. 49. The burials, all of which are referred to below, were of James Graham and Lord Linlithgow (April 1723), Balthazar Guidet (July 1726), Alan Cameron (November 1730), Sir William Ellis (August 1732), Revd Daniel Williams (August 1733), Mark Carse (February 1736) and David Fotheringham (November 1747). By contrast, the 2nd Duke of Buckingham's body was returned to England in 1735 and buried in Westminster Abbey (Ingamells, *Dictionary*, p. 151).

[16] Stosch, 7 April 1729 (f. 521). The doctor was Robert Wright.

on friendly terms with many of the Grand Tourists[17] and to have looked after the Duke of Buckingham when he died in 1735.[18] A third diagnosed and treated James Boswell in 1765.[19] It is only reasonable to assume that any visitor who became ill preferred to be treated by one of his own countrymen, speaking his own language, rather than by an Italian.

Another service provided by the court was the provision of good quality French wines. The yeoman of the king's wine cellar built up a 'considerable' business importing additional wines so that he could sell them to the Grand Tourists.[20] In 1729 Stosch explained that neither burgundy nor champagne were normally available in Rome, but that they could be and were bought from the king's *cave*.[21]

Some Grand Tourists visited the court secretly, while others did so openly.[22] Some met the king and his two sons at favourite places like the Villa Borghese and pretended that it was by accident.[23] The Tories argued that there was no Act of Parliament which made it illegal to pay their respects to the Stuart princes (born in 1720 and 1725), so they had no compunction in doing so, even if the king was present.[24] But Whigs as well as Tories socialised with the Jacobites, by giving each other dinner and supper parties,[25] and by frequenting the same evening balls, concerts and assemblies, called *conversazioni*.[26] In 1731 Stosch noted that the *conversazione* of the Countess of Newburgh (married to the attainted Earl of Derwentwater) was particularly brilliant, and that more and more Grand Tourists were going there to meet the Jacobite courtiers.[27] Hanoverians and Jacobites mixed there 'pele mele', and discovered

---

[17] Dr James Irwin appears with many Grand Tourists in Joshua Reynolds's *Parody of the School of Athens* of 1751 (National Gallery of Ireland).

[18] Stosch, 19 November 1735 (f. 291).

[19] Ingamells, *Dictionary*, p. 107. The doctor was James Murray.

[20] RA. SP 102/87/134, Ellis to Helen Macarty, 20 March 1728; RA. SP 143/150, Lewis to Ellis, 13 March 1731.

[21] Stosch, 24 November 1729 (f. 606). Thirty years later a Grand Tourist who wanted to buy some wine was told that the only wines available at the court were 'Burgundy, Champagne and Spanish, which are directly imported from the places' (NLS. MS 14260, p. 28, Lumisden to Duff, 29 December 1759).

[22] Stosch, 31 March 1725 (f. 326), 6 and 20 July 1726 (ff. 104, 108), 19 May 1729 (f. 538), 16 February 1737 (f. 16). Anon. (Viscount Rialton), *A Letter from an English Traveller at Rome to His Father of the 6th of May 1721* (London, 1721), pp. 2–6.

[23] E.g. Stosch, 12 May and 11 August 1729 (ff. 536, 571).

[24] Stosch, 13 April 1730 (f. 55), 13 September 1739 (f. 342). See also 6 January 1725 (f. 243) in which he says that the Tories liked to drink 'Punch' with the Jacobites.

[25] Stosch, 20 July 1726 (f. 108), 12 May 1729 (f. 536), 4 January, 21 April and 1 December 1731 (ff. 140, 183, 307).

[26] Stosch, 23 February 1732 (f. 343), 17 January 1733 (f. 477).

[27] Stosch, 24 February 1731 (f. 159).

where the king and his sons would be the next day so that they could arrange to meet them and kiss hands 'in one garden or another'.[28]

In one particularly revealing letter Stosch wrote that when 'English travellers' arrived in Rome they were met by the Anglican chaplain, the Protestant doctor and another Protestant from the court, and quickly introduced to Lady Newburgh's *conversazione*. There they became friendly with all the Jacobite courtiers, and conversed with so little constraint that it was impossible to distinguish those who were loyal to King George from those who were loyal to King James: 'People are mentioned to me whose principles I know to be firmly Whig, but who have been swept along with the others.'[29] In another letter he noted the presence among the Jacobite courtiers of at least one person whom he described as an 'out and out' Whig.[30]

The visiting Whigs and other Hanoverians also needed introductions to the concerts and *conversazioni* of the princely families. So long as Naples was ruled by the Habsburgs, Roman society was divided between the Imperialist and Spanish factions, and Grand Tourists could enter the houses of the former without introductions from the court. But that changed when the Bourbons reconquered Naples in 1734. Virtually all the Roman families then declared themselves to be pro-Spanish and pro-Jacobite, and it became impossible for British and Irish visitors to attend any of the important concerts and *conversazioni* without encountering the king, the princes or their courtiers.[31] The task of providing introductions was delegated by the court to the Agent of the Scottish Catholic Clergy.[32] Even as late as the 1760s 'the families to whom the English commonly have Letters' were among those which were closest to James III, the Borghese, the Barberini, the Corsini and particularly the Giustiniani.[33]

---

[28] Stosch, 11 July 1731 (f. 225).   [29] Stosch, 23 November 1731 (f. 303).

[30] Stosch, 12 April 1732 (f. 361).

[31] Stosch, 27 November 1734 (f. 182), 8 December 1736 (f. 426), 17 January 1740 (f. 6).

[32] William Patoun, 'Advice on Travel in Italy', c.1766, in Ingamells, *Dictionary*, p. xlvi. Until 1737 the agent was William Stuart. He was succeeded in January 1738 by Peter Grant (SCA. BL 3/45/12, Mayes to G. Innes, 23 January 1738). The Agent of the English Clergy was a salaried member of the court, which is why the task of giving introductions was given to the Scottish agent.

[33] James III was especially close to the Giustiniani family, and was instrumental in arranging the marriage between principe Benedetto Giustiniani and Cecilia Mahony, the granddaughter of Lady Newburgh (RA. SP 371/170, James III to Cecilia Mahony, 6 June 1757; RA. SP 372/5, James III to Anne (née Clifford), Countess Mahony, 7 June 1757). The description by Patoun (see note 32) of the prince as a man 'of good character' and of the princess as 'a genteel Woman and a safe Acquaintance' provides a good illustration of the fact that Hanoverians mixed freely with pro-Jacobites in Rome.

One of the most important ways in which the court helped the Grand Tourists – and for us today this is of particular significance – was to provide introductions to the portrait painters working in Rome. In this case it is the pictures themselves rather than any letters which provide us with the evidence.

There are relatively few surviving portraits of British and Irish Grand Tourists, as distinct from Jacobite courtiers, painted in Rome before 1750. It is noticeable, however, that most of them are by Antonio David, who was well known to be the official painter to the court until his death in 1737. In fact there are about as many portraits by David as there are by all the other painters in Rome put together. The portraits are of young men of all political persuasions.[34]

Three other painters who owed their British commissions to the Stuart court were Francesco Trevisani, Giovanni Paolo Panini and Domenico Dupra.[35] But the most important and prolific of all the Grand Tour portraitists in Rome was Pompeo Batoni, who was in very close contact with the Stuart court. It was the court which launched his career, yet most of his early patrons were Whigs, and virtually all of them were loyal Hanoverians,[36] which demonstrates that the court served in effect as a cultural forum as well as a surrogate embassy. In the 1750s, when the court was in decline, it was the king's assistant secretary who provided introductions for young Scottish painters to train in the work-shop of Anton Raphael Mengs.[37] And it was to the Stuart court that Frederick the Great of Prussia turned when he wanted to buy paintings by Batoni and Placido Costanzi.[38]

This is not the kind of information which Stosch knew about or chose to report. His letters are enormously valuable because they record the day-to-day social life of the Stuart court, and contain information which has not otherwise survived. But they tell us very little about the court as a surrogate embassy.

This distinction is important. For example, the historian Alice Shield, who wrote extremely influential lives of both James III and his son Cardinal York, wrote in 1908 that 'everything known in Rome was

---

[34] Edward Corp, 'The Stuart Court and the Patronage of Portrait-Painters in Rome, 1717–1757', pp. 39–53 in D.R. Marshall, S. Russell and K. Wolfe (eds.), *'Roma-Britannica': Art Patronage and Cultural Exchange in Eighteenth-Century Rome* (London and Rome, 2011), at p. 46.

[35] *Ibid.*, pp. 44–5.   [36] *Ibid.*, pp. 46–7.

[37] Ingamells, *Dictionary*, p. 617. The court also obtained permission for English and Scottish painters to copy pictures in the collections of the Roman princely families. For examples, see BL. Add MSS 31266, f. 6, and BL. Add MSS 31264, f. 187, both Hay to Gualterio, undated; and Ingamells, *Dictionary*, p. 850.

[38] Corp, 'Patronage of Portrait-Painters in Rome', p. 47.

known to the British government', and that 'the daily doings' of the king are 'minutely chronicled' in the 'volumes of letters [from Stosch] in the Public Record Office'.[39] Most historians have adopted this line, and assumed that Stosch was able to inform London of everything which happened at the court. In fact that was far from being the case. Stosch was able to report those of its activities which were in no way secret, but complained during the 1720s that he was unable to identify the British and Irish people who made clandestine visits there.[40] His spies were arrested, expelled and even assassinated,[41] and he himself was constantly watched.[42] In 1731 he was expelled from Rome, after which he had to rely on his 'correspondents' to gather information from any Italian lower servant who could be bribed.[43]

Stosch's espionage activities were then severely curtailed at the end of 1733 when the Pope decided to put guards around the court and close off the adjacent streets and piazzas every evening and night. As a result even watching the court became impossible,[44] and five and a half years later Stosch noted that the situation had not improved. He could easily report the social activities of the court during the day, including the names of the Italian cardinals and princes who visited it. But it was impossible to discover who visited the court in the evenings.[45] This meant that British and Irish people could go there without any real fear of being identified, and that the activities of the surrogate embassy could continue undisturbed.[46] An appreciation of the role and importance of the exiled court is essential for anyone studying the Grand Tour.

---

[39] Alice Shield, *Henry Stuart, Cardinal of York and His Times* (London, 1908), p. 131.

[40] Stosch, 12 January and 26 June 1723 (ff. 228, 382), 11 November 1724 (f. 212).

[41] Stosch, 17 and 21 November 1722 (ff. 162, 166), 31 August 1723 (f. 430), 17 and 24 February 1729, 3 and 11 March 1729 (ff. 502, 504, 506, 510), 17 March 1731 (f. 169), 23 January 1732 (f. 331), 21 November 1733 (f. 590).

[42] Stosch, 13 January 1725 (f. 247), 11 August 1729 (f. 571).

[43] Stosch, 17 April 1731 (f. 179).

[44] Stosch, 2 January 1734 (f. 16): 'On ne pourra plus a l'avenir, sans courir un visible risque, sçavoir les visites nocturnes . . . [Jacques III] pourra aussi partir de Rome de nuit, sans que mes amis, chargés de l'observer pourront le sçavoir; je ne trouve personne qui veuille hazarder de se trouver dans le voisinage du Palais le soir.'

[45] Stosch, 9 August 1739 (f. 332): 'Il est . . . difficile de sçavoir au juste les Etrangers, qui y vont depuis que les Avenues sont guardés au soir de pres par des soldats, et de loin par les Sbirris. Ailleurs on n'ose pas se fier sur les Rapports des Italiens, sur le Chapitres des Etrangers, a cause qu'ils estropient tellement les noms Anglois, qu'ils les rendent inintelligibles.'

[46] Any servants even suspected of speaking to Stosch's 'correspondent' were immediately dismissed (15 and 22 December 1736 (ff. 428, 430), 13 April 1737 (f. 33)) and in 1739 the unidentified 'correspondent' was himself arrested and imprisoned (21 and 28 June, 5 July and 2 August 1739 (ff. 314, 316, 318, 328)). His successors died in 1740 and 1744 (27 March 1740 (f. 27), 18 and 25 January 1744 (ff. 20, 22)), by which time Stosch's letters had come to resemble a modern court circular. The Hanoverian Horace

There are other ways in which the present book breaks new ground and provides a much needed reassessment. For example, none of the many biographies of the Stuarts in exile – James III, Prince Charles (Bonnie Prince Charlie) and Prince Henry (Cardinal York) – has correctly identified the building in which the court was situated, or attempted to explain how it was used. Indeed, there has not been a genuinely original biography of James III or Prince Henry published for over a hundred years, while even the major biography of Prince Charles is incomplete and even unreliable for his early years in Rome.[47] The present study includes entirely new information concerning the lives of each of the members of the family.

This is especially true as regards James III's wife, Queen Clementina. It is well known that the relations between James and Clementina were not good, and that the queen left the court in 1725, taking refuge in one of the Roman convents. One of the arguments of the book is that the reasons for this separation, which had such a significant impact on the entire Jacobite movement, and such a profound psychological effect on both Stuart princes, have never been properly explained. Only by understanding how the court actually operated can we comprehend the reasons for this development.

James III lived at Saint-Germain-en-Laye with his mother, Mary of Modena, until 1712. As explained in *A Court in Exile: The Stuarts in France, 1689–1718*, the Stuart court was then divided. The queen mother remained at Saint-Germain until her death in 1718, while the king experienced a relatively peripatetic existence. From 1713 to 1715 he and his courtiers were in Lorraine. After the Jacobite rising in Scotland they were then based at Avignon in 1716–17, at Pesaro in the spring of 1717, and at Urbino from the summer of 1717 to the autumn of 1718.[48] After the death of Mary of Modena there was a Jacobite community at Saint-Germain, but the court was to be found exclusively within the Papal States.

Urbino was a relatively remote city, and it has recently been argued that the papacy gave James III the Palazzo Ducale there to keep him 'at arm's length'.[49] This is completely wrong. James himself asked to be

---

Walpole wrote in May 1743 about 'Stosch's intelligence; nobody regards it but the King [George II]; it pleases him – *e basta!*' (Martin Haile, *James Francis Edward, The Old Chevalier* (London, 1907), p. 295, H. Walpole to Mann, 4 May 1743).

[47] The major biography (an exceptionally good book) is Frank McLynn, *Prince Charles Edward Stuart* (London, 1988).

[48] Corp, *A Court in Exile*, chapters 12 and 13.

[49] According to Leo Gooch (*Recusant History*, 29:3 (May 2009), pp. 441–2), 'while there were a number of palazzi at its disposal closer to Rome suitable as a royal residence, none was

given the palazzo at Urbino, and he did so because it had originally been built for an independent prince and reflected that status. It was also large enough to accommodate his entire court. He subsequently discovered that it suffered from an unfavourable climate, and even became virtually inaccessible during part of winter. In the autumn of 1718, when planning to marry Princess Maria Clementina Sobieska, he asked the Pope to let him have a temporary residence in or near Rome. The Pope agreed.

After some negotiation the building selected was a medium-sized palazzo at the north end of the Piazza dei Santi Apostoli, near the Quirinale. It became the Palazzo del Re. But it was never intended to be a permanent residence because James himself was to go to Spain and join a planned invasion of England. Indeed, if everything had gone according to plan he would never have returned to the Papal States and would never have set foot in the palazzo. But it did not, and the invasion fleet was destroyed by a storm. The princess arrived in Rome during the spring of 1719, and James returned from Spain during the summer. They were married at Montefiascone at the beginning of September 1719 and moved into the Palazzo del Re two months later.[50] Rome became the permanent residence of the exiled Stuart court for the next forty-six years.

The present book follows a broadly chronological plan, from the arrival of the court in Rome in 1719 until the death of James III on the first day of 1766. Part I covers the years 1719 to 1729, and Part III the years 1729 to 1766. The separation of the king and queen resulted in the division of the court between Rome and Bologna from 1726 to 1729, and this turning point is the subject of Part II.

Some of the chapters are thematically linked and can be read as pairs. Chapters 1 and 11 consider the relations between James III and the successive popes who reigned while he was living in the Papal States, without whose generosity and active assistance there could have been no Stuart court in Rome. One important feature of these chapters is that they make considerable use of papal archives which have never been used before, providing a much more authoritative account than has been available hitherto. This applies even more to Chapter 2, which describes the building in which the court was situated and explains where its principal apartments were located. That building is, for the first time,

---

offered him except that in a distant backwater of the Papal States'. Apart from the one at Castel Gandolfo, which the Pope used himself as his summer residence, it is hard to think of a single *palazzo apostolico* which would have been suitable.

[50] Edward Corp, *The Jacobites at Urbino: An Exiled Court in Transition* (Basingstoke, 2009).

given its correct name, the Palazzo del Re, the name by which it was known to contemporaries.

Chapters 3 and 12 concern the relations between the Stuarts and Roman society. Stuart biographers have tended to ignore the people with whom the royal family mixed in Rome, concentrating too exclusively on the English, Irish and particularly Scottish Jacobites in exile. These chapters argue that the court cannot be understood unless it is taken to encompass all those people, mainly of foreign nationality, who chose freely to join it, and who thus considerably enhanced its prestige. As the years went by, James III relied more and more on these courtiers, the unpaid members of his entourage, rather than on his salaried servants.

It has been almost entirely overlooked that the Stuart court played a very significant part in Italian operatic life, and that it employed some of the leading musicians and singers in Rome to provide concerts within the Palazzo del Re. Chapters 4 and 13 discuss this important aspect of the life of the court, and show how James and Clementina, and later their sons, influenced the development of *opera seria*. They also reveal (to take just two examples) that an important serenata by Antonio Vivaldi was written in honour of James III, and that the then celebrated composer and cellist Giovanni Costanzi was employed on a regular basis and for many years to provide music for the court.

James III attached considerable importance to commissioning original portraits of himself and his family, to be distributed in multiple copies and engraved, to thank influential friends in continental Europe and to inspire the loyalty of the people within the British Isles. Chapters 5 and 14 identify all the portrait painters who worked for the Stuarts, and explain the circumstances of each commission, with the dates and the prices paid. The chronology of the Stuart portraits, which has confused so many art historians, is thus clarified, with consideration also given to the surviving portraits of the Jacobite courtiers.

The rest of the book focuses on the composition and organisation of the court. Chapters 6 and 15 identify all the people receiving salaries and pensions, and consider their national origins, their religious affinity, their marital status, and how they were recruited. These chapters also explain the structure of the court, and identify the people holding each post. By the time the court reached Rome in 1719 it had already been in exile for thirty years and was no longer organised as it had been at Whitehall. These chapters consider the evolution and gradual Italianisation of the departments of the household.

Any organisation is likely to experience tensions between its members, and the Stuart court was no exception. There were two principal reasons for this during the early 1720s. The first was the partiality shown by the king towards his Scottish favourites: John Hay, created Earl of Inverness; and James Murray, created Earl of Dunbar. The second cause of dissent was the refusal of the king to grant his wife her own independent household, containing servants of a sufficiently elevated rank to reflect her status as a queen. Chapter 7 explains how these two factors interacted, while Chapter 8 considers the impact of the separation on the household.

In 1726 James III went to live in Bologna, leaving some of his servants in the Palazzo del Re, while the queen remained in a convent. Chapter 9 examines the life of the court in Bologna, and the negotiations to persuade Clementina to rejoin her husband. There were two developments which made this possible. The first was the departure of one of the king's favourites, Lord Inverness. The second was the complete reorganisation of the household, which is described in Chapter 10.

Yet the king's other Scottish favourite, Lord Dunbar, remained at the court, and his continued presence was the principal cause of tension during the 1730s and 1740s. Chapter 16 discusses the attempts made by the other courtiers to bring about his downfall. New light is shed on the mysterious Order of Toboso, and the significance of the Jacobite Lodge of Freemasons is revealed.

The prestige of the exiled court depended to a great extent on the perceived prospects of a restoration in England and Scotland. By the end of the 1740s public opinion in Rome finally realised that the Stuarts never would be restored to their thrones. Yet this coincided with the promotion of Prince Henry to be a cardinal, and the beginning of what would become a most successful ecclesiastical career. The slow but steady decline of the court is the subject of Chapter 17, which finishes with the death of James III at the beginning of 1766.

The extended exile of the Stuarts is unique in modern European history. Many royal and princely families have been overthrown and exiled to make way for republics or as a result of national unification. Elected rulers have also been deposed and forced into exile. But the Stuarts were hereditary monarchs, replaced by a rival dynasty. The same fate awaited the Bourbons in 1804 and 1830, yet Louis XVIII was soon restored in 1814–15, and Charles X saw his rival Louis-Philippe overthrown by a republic in 1848. Only the Stuarts had to endure an extended exile, during which they could neither renounce their inheritance nor even depend on the support and sympathy of the monarchists within their own kingdoms. James III endured this growing burden with dignity. Prince Henry sought solace in a successful ecclesiastical career. Prince Charles, the dashing elder son who believed he had come so close to victory in 1745–6, was destroyed by it. Fearing the ignominy of becoming irrelevant, he brought upon himself a different kind of disgrace by his wild and dishonourable conduct, with the result that he was never recognised anywhere as a legitimate king. The Stuart court in exile simply ceased to exist. It was no longer royal and it no longer contained any political exiles other than Charles himself. The conclusion to this book explains what happened to the Palazzo del Re before and after the death of Prince Charles in 1788.

Part I

Rome, 1719–1729

1 The Stuarts and the papacy: I

King James III was the guest in Rome of six successive popes. Clement XI welcomed him in 1719 and Clement XIII authorised his state funeral in 1766. During the 1720s his hosts were Innocent XIII and Benedict XIII. The Pope during the 1730s was Clement XII; his successor during the 1740s and a large part of the 1750s was Benedict XIV.

Most of these men were considerably older than James. Clement XI, Innocent XIII, Benedict XIII and Clement XII had all been born between 1649 and 1655, and grown up when England was ruled by Charles II. They had been in their thirties when James had himself been born in 1688 and the Stuarts had first gone into exile in the winter of 1688–9. Consequently, although James had dealings with four different popes between 1719 and the 1730s they were all of the same generation. Their relationship with him might be likened to that of an affectionate – or angry – father. It was not until 1740 that this changed. Benedict XIV was only thirteen years older than James, and treated him with the kindness and care of an older brother. He also took a strong paternal interest in Charles and Henry, the young Stuart princes. Clement XIII, by contrast, was four and a half years younger than James, and was not created a cardinal until the Stuart court had already been in Rome for eighteen years. He took a kindly interest in James and his son Henry, but he had grown to maturity in the changed world of the Hanoverian succession. It was he who decided not to recognise Prince Charles as the legitimate king of Great Britain and Ireland.

This last point is important because it emphasises that what these six popes all had in common was their willingness to support James III and afford him full royal honours. From 1719 until 1766 the papacy provided the exiled Stuart king with a regular quarterly pension and a residence for his court near the Quirinale in the centre of Rome. For nearly all of this period it also provided James with a secondary residence at Albano. The king was afforded social precedence, outranking all the princes of the Church and the foreign ambassadors. He was also given the special political privilege of nominating cardinals. He was allowed to have Protestant services performed within his court, and was given a plot of land within the city where his Protestant subjects could be given public burial. The story of the Stuart court in Rome logically begins with a brief examination of the personal, financial and social relations between James III and the papacy.

Clement XI, 1700–1721

Clement XI had already been Pope for many years before James III and his new bride, Queen Clementina, came to live in Rome in November 1719. It was he who had originally welcomed James and the Stuart court to the Papal States, following their expulsion from Avignon in 1717. He had given James an annual pension of 10,000 *scudi*, paid at the end of each quarter, and guaranteed from the profits of the *luoghi di monte* belonging to the *Camera Apostolica*. He had allowed James to occupy the Palazzo Ducale at Urbino from 1717 to 1718, and had then agreed to provide him with a palazzo at the north end of the Piazza dei Santi Apostoli. This property was rented from the marchese Giovanni Battista Muti and renamed the Palazzo del Re. The rent, the decoration, the furniture and all the maintenance costs were to be paid, on the Pope's orders, by the *Camera Apostolica*.[1]

By 1719 Clement XI was seventy years old, and no longer in good health. He was naturally timid, and worried about the political implications of supporting James III against his Hanoverian rival, King George I, who was an ally of the Emperor Charles VI. With the British fleet in the Mediterranean, and the Imperialists in the Kingdom of Naples, he felt he had to be cautious in the support he gave to the exiled king. There was also the position of the Catholics in England and Scotland to be considered. Taking these various factors into account, the result was a compromise. Clement XI never wavered in the support he provided for James III, but the latter felt frustrated that papal support was not more far-reaching or more active.

One problem facing the king was a shortage of money. The annual pension of 10,000 *scudi* was just sufficient to maintain his court, but it was not enough to enable James to support the many exiled Jacobites living in France. The Regent had promised to give him a secret annual pension of 300,000 *livres*, but had stopped paying it in 1718.[2] James therefore came under considerable financial pressure during 1720, and

---

[1] Edward Corp, *The Jacobites at Urbino: An Exiled Court in Transition* (Basingstoke, 2009). For the pension, see pp. 20, 162, 170. For the palazzo, see chapter 11.
[2] Corp, *Jacobites at Urbino*, pp. 162, 192.

urged Clement XI to give him more money. The Pope refused, but eventually agreed to give him a small amount in cash. James wrote to his treasurer at Saint-Germain in April 1720 that 'you will I am sure be . . . not a little scandaliz'd when I tell you that I receiv'd 3000 Crowns yesterday from the Pope's own hand'.[3]

By the autumn of 1720 Queen Clementina was pregnant, and the birth of a prince or princess was bound to increase the size and expense of the royal household. Yet James felt he had no hope of getting any more money from the Pope, and commented to his treasurer at Saint-Germain that he could only just live on the pension he was already receiving.[4] He therefore resolved to do what he could to persuade the Regent to resume the payment of his French pension.

The Regent's chief minister was Guillaume Dubois, recently appointed Archbishop of Cambrai. Dubois was keen to become a cardinal, so a plan was formed whereby James III would nominate him in return for the payment of his French pension.

Dubois's mistress, Alexandrine de Tencin, had previously been the mistress of Lieutenant-General Arthur Dillon who was now, as Lord Dillon, James III's official representative in France. Alexandrine de Tencin persuaded Dubois to send her brother, the abbé Pierre de Tencin, to support the French chargé d'affaires in Rome, and suggest to the king that Dubois would be willing to secure the resumption of James's French pension in exchange for his nomination.[5]

By the autumn of 1720 Clement XI was ill and not expected to live very much longer. He had been pope for over twenty years, and his family had benefited enormously from his papacy. But his nephews, Cardinal Annibale and don Carlo Albani, had also made enemies, particularly at the Imperial court. They were now keen to obtain support to protect themselves against the possible hostility of a future pope. If, then, they could persuade their uncle to make Archbishop Dubois a cardinal, they would obtain the gratitude of both James III and the French government.[6]

During December 1720 it was not clear if Clement XI would agree to make Dubois a cardinal.[7] Yet Queen Clementina was expected to give birth at the end of the month. James wrote cryptically to Dillon on the 9th that 'I can expect nothing [i.e. no money] from the Pope, and

[3] RA. SP 46/57, James III to Dicconson, 14 April 1720.
[4] RA. SP 50/6, James III to Dicconson, 10 November 1720.
[5] René de la Croix, duc de Castries, *La scandaleuse Madame de Tencin, 1682–1749* (Paris, 1986), pp. 62, 106, 109.
[6] BL. Add MSS 31262, f. 50 and f. 62, Murray to Gualterio, 20 and 29 November 1720.
[7] BL. Add MSS 31262, f. 69, Murray to Gualterio, 7 December 1720.

whether I shall get a new supply at the years end from the Regent is more than I know as matters now stand. And in the meantime my expense here is increasing.'[8]

It seems that the Pope deliberately waited until the queen had safely given birth. On 31 December Charles, Prince of Wales, was born in the Palazzo del Re. Two days later Don Carlo Albani brought a message to the king that his uncle had at last agreed to accept his nomination to make Dubois a cardinal at the next promotion.[9] In addition, Cardinal Annibale Albani brought a present from his uncle of 10,000 *scudi*, the equivalent of an entire year's pension, to celebrate the birth of the prince.[10] For the little prince himself, the Pope commissioned a jeweller in Rome to make twenty-four gold buttons decorated with diamonds, to be stitched on to his clothes.[11]

Unfortunately for James III, Pope Clement XI died in March 1721, before he had had time to make the necessary arrangements for the next promotion of cardinals. This meant that he did not immediately receive the French pension which he had been promised.

In addition to trying to help James improve his finances, Clement XI allowed him to bring his two Protestant chaplains from Urbino, and permitted them to inaugurate the celebration of Anglican services within the Palazzo del Re. These services were not only for the king's own household servants, but for any Protestants in Rome who wanted to attend them.[12] It was also Clement XI who set aside a plot of land beside the Pyramid of Cestius to be used as a Protestant cemetery.[13]

Clement XI did James III one more good turn before his death in March 1721: he arranged for the king to be given permanent use of the Palazzo Apostolico at Albano for his *villeggiature* in the Alban hills, when Rome itself became too hot. James and Clementina had stayed at Albano in June 1720 with Cardinal Aquaviva, who had a villa there,[14] and they asked the Pope to let them have a residence of their own. Clement

[8] RA. SP 50/84, James III to Dillon, 9 December 1720.
[9] BL. Add MSS 31262, f. 77, Murray to Gualterio, 2 January 1721; BL. Add MSS 31263, f. 45, Murray to Gualterio, undated.
[10] Chracas, *Diario ordinario*, no. 544, 4 January 1721, p. 11.
[11] ASR. Cam I: RMC b. 1068, ff. 179–80. The jeweller was Pietro Paolo Gelpi, and the buttons cost 91 *scudi*.
[12] NA. SP 85/16/f. 118, Stosch to Newcastle, 15 August 1726.
[13] NA. SP 85/14/f. 310, Stosch to Carteret, 3 April 1723, in which he said that the land had been destined for the cemetery 'depuis quelques annees'. The cemetery was opened in 1716, while the court was at Avignon (HMC *Stuart*, III, p. 92, Kenyon to Mar, 17 October 1716).
[14] BL. Add MSS 31255, f. 205, James III to Gualterio, 7 June 1720; BL Add MSS 31262, f. 25, Murray to Gualterio, 20 June 1720.

generously agreed, and let James select whichever of the papal properties he liked best. James Murray wrote to Cardinal Gualterio in the autumn of 1720 that 'the King is determined to go ... to Albano to see the houses he might have there and choose one of them'.[15] James selected the most important palazzo at Albano, which had originally belonged to the Savelli family and which had been known as the Palazzo Apostolico since 1696.[16] On 6 March 1721, thirteen days before Clement XI died, a visiting Jacobite recorded that James 'went to see the House fitting up for him at Albano by the Pope, and returned that night'.[17]

Innocent XIII, 1721–1724

Cardinal Conti was elected pope in May 1721, and crowned in St Peter's Basilica on the 18th of that month.[18] A Jacobite who observed the ceremony noted that a special 'gallery of crimson' had been erected to give James III and Queen Clementina a position of honour 'on the left hand of the altar'. Once the ceremony was over they were invited to join the new pope 'in the Vatican palace', where 'they and their court were treated with a handsom desert of frescos, sweetmeats wet and dry, chocolat, coffee etc at the Pope's expence'.[19]

Innocent XIII confirmed all the arrangements concerning the Stuart court made by his predecessor, including the use of the Palazzo del Re in Rome and the Palazzo Apostolico at Albano. He formally continued the Stuart pension on 9 July[20] and inaugurated a practice which would be continued by his successors: he gave James III a present of 8000 *scudi* to celebrate his election.[21] He also promoted Guillaume Dubois to be a cardinal. At first the promised French pension was still not forthcoming, and the abbé de Tencin, now appointed French chargé d'affaires in Rome, had to persuade Cardinal Dubois to honour his part of the bargain. It was not until May 1722 that he was able to tell James that Dubois had at last agreed to pay the pension. It was backdated to 1 April 1721,[22] and

[15] BL. Add MSS 31263, f. 123, Murray to Gualterio, undated.
[16] Chiara Bugliosi, *Itinerario Storico Archeologico Artistico di Albano Laziale* (Albano, 1989), p. 15.
[17] Bod. Lib. Rawlinson MSS D.1180, p. 311, Rawlinson's diary, 6 March 1721.
[18] Marcello Fagiolo (ed.), *Corpus delle feste a Roma*, vol. II, *Il settecento e l'ottocento* (Rome, 1997), p. 39.
[19] Bod. Lib. Rawlinson MSS D.1181, pp. 376–7, Rawlinson's diary, 18 May 1721.
[20] ASV. SS: Ingh 21, p. 246; ASR. Cam I: GT b. 438/f. 6; ASR. Cam I: RMC b. 1069/f. 70. The subsequent payments are recorded in ASR. Cam I: GT b. 438 and ASR. Cam I: RMC b. 1069.
[21] ASR. Cam I: RMC b. 1069/f. 63; ASV. SS: Ingh 21, p. 255.
[22] BL Add MSS 31266, f. 141, Tencin to James III, undated but late May 1722.

continued to be paid until Dubois died in the summer of 1723.[23] It amounted to 48,000 *scudi* per annum, nearly five times the papal pension of 10,000 *scudi*.[24]

Meanwhile James III had been falling into debt, because of the additional expenditure on his household after the birth of the Prince of Wales. He wrote to his treasurer at Saint-Germain on 17 May 1722 that 'the truth is I never was in so low nor destitute a way as to money matters'.[25] Shortly afterwards the French pension was finally resumed.

During 1722 the Atterbury Plot was being planned in England and France. According to the recently published definitive study of the plot,

> The time appointed for the rising was the early autumn of 1722 when the camp at Hyde Park was expected to have broken up and before George I's return from Hanover for the opening of Parliament. Some hundreds of officers in the Jacobite regiments in France and Spain were to be brought over to discipline those taking part in the rising, together with an appropriate supply of arms and ammunition. In addition, soldiers from George I's army in England as well as English sailors were recruited with remarkable success in James III's name ... There were three other groups of armed men, who were to take part in the rising ... Measures were taken to enable Scotland to assist England.[26]

Three ships were assembled at Genoa to take James III to England so that he could join the rising:

> the *Revolution*, which was to carry James III to England, was manned with 40 guns, with 120 officers on board ... The *Lady Mary* ... had 14 guns ... was loaded with great quantities of arms and could carry several thousand men. Also in Genoa was the *Fortune* ... carrying 1000 muskets, 1000 carbines, 2000 bayonets and 300 barrels of powder.
>
> The Jacobites in Britain and in continental Europe had made a Herculean effort in collecting money, buying arms and recruiting soldiers and sailors for the cause. By the summer of 1722 everything was ready.[27]

James needed an excuse to get away from Rome without causing suspicion, and he needed to be able to reach Genoa very quickly when the time came. He therefore devised an ingenious plan which even the authors of *The Atterbury Plot*, the definitive study of the conspiracy, failed

[23] BL. Add MSS 31264, f. 151, Hay to Gualterio, 28 April 1724.
[24] BL. Add MSS 31265, f. 233, Hay to Gualterio, undated; BL. Add MSS 31264, f. 150, Hay to Gualterio, 27 April 1724.
[25] RA. SP 59/117, James III to Dicconson. See also RA. SP 58/26, James III to Higgons, 23 February 1722: 'at present, I am worse than ever I was in my life as to money matters'.
[26] Eveline Cruickshanks and Howard Erskine-Hill, *The Atterbury Plot* (Basingstoke, 2004), pp. 132–3.
[27] *Ibid.*, p. 152.

to fathom. He determined to send Queen Clementina to take the waters at the Baths of Lucca for the sake of her health. He himself would remain in Rome, but would then change his mind and decide to join her, informing everyone that he and Clementina would then go directly from Lucca to Albano, and come back to Rome in November. Once he was with his wife at Bagni di Lucca he would be able to make a dash for Genoa when the time was right.

At the beginning of July James informed Innocent XIII that he had decided to send Queen Clementina to take the waters at Lucca. The Pope, suspecting nothing, responded by giving him 3000 *scudi* to help finance her visit.[28] James then spoke to Gian Giacomo Fatinelli, the Lucchese minister in Rome, and told him to notify his government. The queen would be coming to Lucca incognito as the Duchess of Cornwall, accompanied by a very small suite. She set out on 19 July, stopped at Montefiascone, Siena and Pisa, and reached Lucca on the 22nd. On the following day she continued her journey for the remaining twelve miles up into the hills to Bagni di Lucca, where accommodation had been prepared in the Villa Buonvisi.[29]

James remained in Rome until the beginning of August. On the 2nd he 'announced after dinner that he would go to join the Queen at Lucca'. In the letter which reported this news, Sir David Nairne added: 'after the Queens baths are over, theyl return both back and go straight to Albano towards the beginning of next month without stoping in Rome because of the air in that season'.[30] James left Rome on the 4th and travelled north with a similarly small suite, reaching Lucca on the 7th. From there he wrote to Innocent XIII that he had only gone to get some exercise and to have a change of air, and said that he intended to return to Rome with the queen at the end of November.[31]

By the time James reached Bagni di Lucca on 8 August[32] the Jacobite plans had been discovered in England by Sir Robert Walpole. Various people were arrested and interrogated, and the Jacobite leaders gradually identified, resulting in further arrests. Francis Atterbury, Bishop of Rochester, was himself arrested on the 15th, and by the time Parliament met in October he had been followed by Lord North and Grey, Lord Orrery and even the Duke of Norfolk. The imprisonment of the

[28] ASR. Cam I: RMC b. 1069/f. 200.
[29] E.E. Whipple, *A Famous Corner of Tuscany* (London, 1928), pp. 133–4.
[30] WDA. Paris Seminary Papers/477, Nairne to Ingleton, 2 August 1722. See also SCA. BL 2/247/7, Stuart to T. Innes, 4 August 1722.
[31] H.C. Stewart, 'The Exiled Stewarts in Italy, 1717–1807', *The Scottish Historical Society Miscellany*, VII (Edinburgh, 1941), p. 97, James III to Innocent XIII, 7 August 1722.
[32] Whipple, *Famous Corner of Tuscany*, p. 134.

Jacobites was not legal, and Walpole did not yet have sufficient evidence to risk bringing them to trial, but by keeping them for an extended period in prison he was able to put a stop to the Atterbury Plot. By December 1722 even the ship waiting at Genoa to carry James III to England had been seized by the Mediterranean fleet.[33]

It took some time for the news to reach Bagni di Lucca, and a little longer for the seriousness of the situation to become apparent. The king sent John Hay on a fact-finding mission to Florence and Leghorn to obtain what information he could,[34] and when Hay returned on 20 August he brought the depressing news that the Jacobite rising in England had had to be cancelled. On the following day the Lucchese senator who had been appointed to attend the king at Bagni di Lucca reported back to his colleagues in Lucca that he had asked one of the Jacobites if Hay had brought back good news. 'What good news would you that there could be now?' he replied. 'The time is not yet.'[35] James realised that he could no longer think of sailing for England, and on the 23rd sent a letter to Innocent XIII saying that he and Queen Clementina would be leaving Bagni di Lucca as planned during September.[36]

Four days later the news arrived that Queen Clementina's mother had died,[37] thereby adding formal mourning to the gloom which had already descended on the king and queen. To make up for Clementina's bereavement and her bitter disappointment at the cancellation of the uprising, James then organised for her a tour of central Italy. They left Bagni di Lucca on 20 September and slept at Florence, Bologna, Ferrara, Ravenna, Rimini, Pesaro, Urbino, Sinigallia, Ancona and Loreto, before returning down the Via Flaminia via Foligno to Rome. All the papal legates offered them accommodation in the *palazzi apostolici*, but James preferred 'to stay in a private house wherever he could find one that was suitable, and to travel completely incognito'.[38] They were back in Rome before the end of October.

The failure of the Atterbury Plot put an end to any hopes for an imminent restoration, and therefore prolonged the period during which the Stuarts would have to remain in Rome as the guests of the papacy.

---

[33] Cruickshanks and Erskine-Hill, *Atterbury Plot*, chapter 6.

[34] BL. Add MSS 31264, f. 62, Hay to Gualterio, 20 August 1722. John Hay had been created Earl of Inverness in October 1718, and had used the title for a short time. It was not publicly recognised until March 1725.

[35] Whipple, *Famous Corner of Tuscany*, p. 136.

[36] Stewart, 'Exiled Stewarts in Italy', p. 99, James III to Innocent XIII, 23 August 1722.

[37] BL. Add MSS 31264, f. 68, Hay to Gualterio, 27 August 1722.

[38] BL. Add MSS 31264, f. 90, Hay to Gualterio, 9 October 1722. See also same reference, f. 83 and f. 93, Hay to Gualterio, 19 September and 19 October 1722.

Innocent XIII remained friendly, and formally blessed James and Clementina at San Giovanni Laterano the following May, in front of all the assembled cardinals 'and a numerous concourse of people in the piazza'.[39]

The prolonged exile of James III in Rome had one more consequence during the papacy of Innocent XIII. Of limited significance in itself, it would nevertheless become socially important in future years. It was in 1723 that the Protestant cemetery beside the Pyramid of Cestius was first used. A burial took place in January,[40] followed by two more in April.[41]

Benedict XIII, 1724–1730

Even before the election of Cardinal Orsini as Pope in May 1724, James III's finances began to improve. During the conclave the French government sent another instalment of the king's pension, amounting to 12,000 *scudi*, so that he would use his influence in favour of a pro-French candidate.[42]

Benedict XIII soon made it very clear that he was extremely well disposed to the exiled Stuarts. One of his first acts was to send a strongly worded Apostolic letter to the Emperor and to the kings of France and Spain urging them to do what they could to bring about the restoration of James III.[43] He then set about providing James with more money.

The Pope gave the king an audience in the gardens of the Vatican on 7 June and promised that he would increase his pension from 10,000 to 16,000 *scudi* per annum as soon as the necessary funds could be allocated to the *Camera Apostolica*.[44] He also gave him an immediate present of 10,000 *scudi* to celebrate his election,[45] 2000 more than his predecessor had given in 1721. The increased pension, now 4000 *scudi* each quarter, started in January 1725.[46]

---

[39] Bod. Lib. Rawlinson MSS D.1183, p. 1569, Rawlinson's diary, 6 May 1723.
[40] NA. SP 85/14/f. 244, Stosch to Carteret, 23 January 1723.
[41] NA. SP 85/14/f. 310 and f. 318, Stosch to Carteret, 3 and 6 April 1723; Bod. Lib. Rawlinson MSS D. 1183, p. 1555, Rawlinson's diary, 6 April 1723.
[42] BL. Add MSS 31264, f. 150 and f. 151, Hay to Gualterio, 27 and 28 April 1724.
[43] Haile, *James Francis Edward, The Old Chevalier*, pp. 305–6.
[44] ASV. SS: Ingh 21, p. 247; NA. SP 85/15/ff. 137, 149, 151, Stosch to Newcastle, 10 and 24 June 1724, 1 July 1724.
[45] ASV. SS: Ingh 21, p. 255; ASR. Cam I: RMC b. 1070/f. 21.
[46] The payments before and after January 1725 are recorded in ASR. Cam I: RMC b. 1070, with the increase shown at f. 133. Also NA. SP 85/15/f. 265 and f. 291, Stosch to Newcastle, 30 January and 24 February 1725.

Benedict XIII also paid a compliment to James III by personally consecrating one of his leading supporters in Rome. The abbé de Tencin had done all he could, as French chargé d'affaires, to persuade his government to pay James the pension he had been promised. As Montesquieu once commented, 'he never left the king's apartments',[47] an observation confirmed by Baron von Stosch, who wrote that Tencin spent 'all day, every day', in the Palazzo del Re.[48] In May 1724 he was appointed Archbishop of Embrun, and 'to demonstrate his liking for the new archbishop, the Pope himself consecrated him on July 2 1724, in the church of San Filippo Neri'. This was a privilege normally reserved for cardinals. The ceremony took place in the presence of James III, Queen Clementina, all the cardinals, the ambassadors and (as Tencin himself put it) 'a vast crowd thronging the nave'.[49]

Benedict XIII then considered improving the accommodation provided for the Stuart court in the Palazzo del Re. James initially asked if he might move into another, more suitable building, but the Pope persuaded him to remain where he was, and promised to have the entire palazzo renovated.[50] Leaving aside the annual rent of 1632 *scudi*, the *Camera Apostolica* had spent 14,630 *scudi* having the palazzo prepared for the Stuart court in 1719, but since then no further money had been spent on it.[51] In the autumn of 1724 James and Clementina went away for an extended period to Albano, to allow far-reaching building works and redecoration to be carried out in the Palazzo del Re, at a total cost of 4580 *scudi*.[52] When they returned in November the queen was pregnant. It was noted that 'the Pope did her the extraordinary and unprecedented favour of sending his own litter to meet her'.[53]

Benedict XIII had meanwhile decided that 1725 should be celebrated as an *anno santo*, or jubilee year. The year ran from Christmas Eve 1724 to Christmas Eve 1725, and began with the opening of the Holy Door at St Peter's by the Pope himself. The door had been walled up with masonry since the previous *anno santo* in 1700, and was now opened in an elaborate ceremony in which the Pope hammered on the door and made the masonry fall away. As usual James III and Queen Clementina were given

[47] Castries, *Scandaleuse Madame de Tencin*, p. 106, quoting Montesquieu's *Voyage en Italie*, p. 40.
[48] NA. SP 85/14/f. 382, Stosch to Carteret, 26 June 1723.
[49] Castries, *Scandaleuse Madame de Tencin*, p. 123.
[50] See below, Chapter 2, pp. 54–5.
[51] ASR. Cam I: CDG b. 2017 bis/13/8 and 10. Innocent XIII had, however, authorized the expenditure of 1138 *scudi* on the Palazzo Apostolico at Albano: ASR. Cam I: CDG b. 449/f. 18, b. 457/f. 4, b. 458/f. 11, b. 459/f. 3, b. 460/f. 17.
[52] ASV. PAC 983/nos. 62–6, 68–70, 73, 75.
[53] NA. SP 85/15/f. 218, Stosch to Newcastle, 25 November 1724.

the positions of honour. Stosch, who observed the ceremony, recorded that the king and queen 'watched . . . from a high gallery that had been specially constructed . . . Another gallery had been put up for the foreigners, to be entered only by those English recommended by [the king].'[54]

By the end of 1724, when this ceremony took place, the relations between Pope Benedict XIII and James III were excellent, and showed no signs of deteriorating. Queen Clementina was due to give birth to her second child in early March, and the Pope sent her a message to say that he would like to baptise the baby himself, in the Chapel Royal of the Palazzo del Re.[55]

Prince Henry, Duke of York, was born on the morning of 6 March 1725. That afternoon the Pope arrived at the palazzo, where he was met at the foot of the grand staircase by James III himself:

the Pope descended from his chair and went up the staircase on foot with him; and when they arrived at the apartment, [the King] presented the child to him . . . Then the Pope baptised him giving him the names Henry Benedict . . . Afterwards the Pope went to the [Queen's] Bedchamber, where he conversed with her for a short while, and then returned to the Vatican.[56]

The Pope then sent 14,000 *scudi* as a present for the queen,[57] followed by some 'consecrated linen' for the baby, which apparently cost 3000 *pistoles*.[58] It was, as one can see in retrospect, the high point in the relations between Benedict XIII and James III.

All continued well during the summer of 1725. In June it was announced that Louis XV was to marry the daughter of King Stanislas, and the Pope showed his usual consideration for the Stuarts. Hearing the news, Benedict 'sent a priest [to the king], offering his congratulations, because the new Queen of France was a relation' of Queen Clementina's.[59] At the beginning of September 1725 the king and queen were asked by the Pope to advise him how to settle a quarrel which had broken out between the French and the Imperial ambassadors.[60] Then,

---

[54] Francesco Valesio, *Diario di Roma*, vol. IV, *1708–1728*, ed. Gaetano Scana (Milan, 1978), p. 449, 24 December 1724; BSR. Revillas MSS F/84/3, Revillas's diary, 24 December 1724; NA. SP 85/15/f. 235, Stosch to Newcastle, 26 December 1724.

[55] NA. SP 85/15/f. 233, Stosch to Newcastle, 23 December 1724.

[56] NA. SP 85/15/f. 314, Stosch to Newcastle, 10 March 1725. See also Valesio, *Diario di Roma*, IV, p. 479; and BSR. Revillas MSS F/84/3, Revillas's diary, 6 March 1725. According to the parish register, the Pope also confirmed Prince Charles while he was in the Palazzo del Re (ASVR. Santi Apostoli vol. 12, p. 171).

[57] NA. SP 85/15/f. 326, Stosch to Newcastle, 31 March 1725.

[58] NA. SP 85/15/f. 330, Stosch to Newcastle, 7 April 1725.

[59] NA. SP 85/15/f. 388, Stosch to Newcastle, 9 June 1725.

[60] *Diario ordinario*, no. 1263, p. 12, 8 September 1725; NA. SP 85/15/f. 436, Stosch to Newcastle, 15 September 1725.

suddenly, the whole situation changed and the relations between the Pope and the king collapsed.

In September 1725 James III took the young Prince of Wales out of the hands of women and entrusted his future upbringing and education to men. He also appointed a Protestant to be his governor. This was James Murray, who was now publicly recognised by his Jacobite title as Earl of Dunbar. The women objected very strongly to having to hand over control of the four-year-old prince to a group of men, and the queen herself had a strong antipathy towards Dunbar. But what really enraged Clementina was the fact that Dunbar was a Protestant. She demanded that her son's governor should be a Catholic. The king refused. She then demanded, on 11 November, that the leading Protestants at the court (Dunbar, his sister Lady Inverness, and his brother-in-law Lord Inverness) should all be sent away, to ensure that her son should be brought up a good Catholic.[61] When the king again refused, she decided to leave the court. On 15 November she suddenly took refuge in the Convent of Santa Cecilia, on the other side of the river in Trastevere, and refused to return to the Palazzo del Re until the three Protestants had been dismissed and her son had been entrusted to a Catholic governor.[62]

The Pope, like his predecessors, had been willing to allow James to have Protestant services conducted in the Palazzo del Re. He was also reluctant to interfere with the management of the Stuart court. But whereas James regarded the appointment of a Protestant governor for his son as a purely domestic matter, Benedict XIII regarded it as a question of public importance. He therefore made it clear that he supported the queen in her determination to remain in the convent.[63] James was furious. He had absolutely no intention of bringing up his son as a Protestant, but was making a deliberate gesture towards Protestant opinion in England and Scotland. He wrote to Bishop Atterbury in December: 'It has been talked in town as if the Pope might take from me the pension he gave me, but neither threats of this kind, nor any want of regard the Pope might show me will induce me to alter my conduct and will only serve to afford me an opportunity of showing my subjects that nothing can make me alter a conduct which I think right or just.'[64]

---

[61] HMC *10th Report* (London, 1885), p. 161, James III to Queen Clementina, 11 November 1725; NA. SP 85/15/f. 460, Stosch to Newcastle, 17 November 1725.

[62] Valesio, *Diario di Roma*, IV, p. 605, 15 November 1725; BSR. Revillas MSS F/84/3, Revillas's diary, 15 November 1725; BAV. Fondo Borgia Lat MS 565, f. 333, Foucquet to Ramsay, 20 November 1725; same reference, Foucquet's diary, 29 November 1725.

[63] NA. SP 85/15/f. 490, Stosch to Newcastle, 22 November 1725; Frank McLynn, *Prince Charles Edward Stuart* (London, 1988), pp. 17–18.

[64] James III to Atterbury, December 1725, cited in McLynn, *Charles Edward Stuart*, p. 18.

The Pope, however, felt equally strongly, especially after all the kindness he had shown James since his election the previous year. At the end of December he reduced James's quarterly pension from 3000 to 2500 *scudi*, and instructed the *Camera Apostolica* to give only 2000 *scudi* to the king, and the remaining 500 *scudi* to the queen.[65] He also decided to prohibit all Protestant services in the Palazzo del Re. When this decision reached the king he insisted on receiving the order in writing.[66] The two Protestant chaplains were allowed to remain in Rome for the time being, but they were ordered to leave the following September.[67]

It was a sad ending to the *anno santo* which had started in such a promising manner. On 24 December James returned to St Peter's to see the Pope ceremonially close up the Holy Door. The king 'accompanied by . . . his whole suite and his elder son attended with great devotion in a gallery made especially for them'.[68] But of course the queen was noticeably absent. The following week James rewarded Lord Dunbar and Lord Inverness by investing them as Knights of the Thistle.[69]

There was stalemate during 1726, with neither side willing to give way. The king refused to dismiss Dunbar and Lord and Lady Inverness, and the queen refused to leave the convent. Various cardinals tried and failed to negotiate a settlement. Meanwhile Pope Benedict maintained his support for the queen, and it was very apparent that most people in Rome, and at the Catholic courts of Europe (notably in Spain), thought that James should give way.[70]

During the summer James decided that he would withdraw from Rome and rent a palazzo in Bologna, where he was popular and where the cost of living was cheaper. He would take the two princes with him, and perhaps return after a few months. Before leaving he had a farewell audience with the Pope and took with him the Prince of Wales and Lady Nithsdale, the only Catholic noblewoman attached to the court.[71]

During September 1726 James made arrangements to rent the Palazzo Fantuzzi. The two princes, accompanied by Lord Dunbar and Lady

---

[65] ASR. Cam I: GT b. 509/f. 16, Paulucci to Collicola, 17 December 1725; ASR. Cam I: RMC b. 1070/f. 290.

[66] Valesio, *Diario di Roma*, IV, 15 January 1726; BL. Add MSS 31265, f. 128, Inverness to Gualterio, undated; BL. Add MSS 20313, f. 225, Paulucci to Gualterio, 24 January 1726.

[67] NA. SP 85/16/f. 137 and f. 139, Stosch to Newcastle, 7 and 12 September 1726.

[68] NA. SP 85/15/f. 520, Stosch to Newcastle, 29 December 1725.

[69] Marquis de Ruvigny et Raineval, *The Jacobite Peerage* (Edinburgh, 1904), p. 194. The original of Dunbar's warrant is RA. SP 88/148.

[70] McLynn, *Charles Edward Stuart*, pp. 19–21.

[71] NA. SP 85/16/f. 145, Stosch to Newcastle, 19 September 1726; McLynn, *Charles Edward Stuart*, p. 21.

Inverness, left Rome on the 30th, and travelled slowly via Loreto, Pesaro and Rimini. The king then left with Lord Inverness two days later, and travelled the more direct route via Florence. The king's party arrived on 9 October, and were joined by the princes twelve days later.[72]

The Pope was not pleased, in part because the Palazzo del Re, rented and recently renovated by the *Camera Apostolica*, was left unoccupied, with only a small staff of servants to look after it. The longer the king stayed away, the more displeased Benedict became. The Pope felt obliged to go on renting the palazzo because the building would be needed when the queen eventually decided to leave the convent. However, the new situation made him reconsider the pension which was still being paid to the king every quarter.

In October Cardinal Gualterio tried to persuade the Pope to restore the money which he had deducted from the pension, but Benedict refused.[73] Instead the Pope threatened to reduce the pension a second time and increase the amount given to the queen.[74] In December Cardinal Collicola, the treasurer of the *Camera Apostolica*, informed Sir William Ellis, the treasurer at the Palazzo del Re, that the Pope had decided to reduce the pension to 10,000 *scudi* per annum, the amount it had previously been during the pontificates of Clement XI and Innocent XIII.[75] Shortly afterwards he specified that the Pope wanted only 1500 *scudi* paid each quarter to the king, and the remaining 1000 *scudi* to the queen.[76] There was nothing for the king to do but observe a profound silence.[77] The new arrangement came into force when the pension for the first quarter of the year was paid at the beginning of April 1727.[78]

The reduction of his pension made James decide to remain at Bologna, and not return to Rome after a few months as originally intended. The Pope meanwhile showed his support for the queen by giving her extra money and making her more comfortable in the convent. On 10 December Clementina attended a ceremony for the canonisation

---

[72] NA. SP 85/16/f. 153, Stosch to Newcastle, 3 October 1726; BL. Add MSS 31264, f. 226, Inverness to Gualterio, 23 October 1726; McLynn, *Charles Edward Stuart*, p. 22.

[73] BL. Add MSS 31267, f. 45 and f. 46, Ellis to Gualterio, 8 and 11 October 1726; BL. Add MSS 31264, f. 217, Inverness to Gualterio, 12 October 1726.

[74] BL. Add MSS 31264, f. 226, Inverness to Gualterio, 23 October 1726.

[75] BL. Add MSS 31264, f. 250, Inverness to Gualterio, 7 December 1726.

[76] BL. Add MSS 31267, f. 57, Ellis to Gualterio, 7 December 1726; BL. Add MSS 31264, f. 268, Inverness to Gualterio, 7 January 1727.

[77] BL. Add MSS 31264, f. 261, Inverness to Gualterio, 21 December 1726.

[78] ASR. Cam I: RMC b. 1074/f. 46; BL. Add MSS 31267, f. 62, Ellis to Gualterio, undated but early April 1727; BL. Add MSS 31262, f. 203, Dunbar to Gualterio, 28 September 1727.

of new saints, at the end of which Benedict gave her 1000 *scudi*.[79] During January he sent extra furniture to her apartment in the convent, and then gave orders that various building works should be undertaken to increase its size.[80]

During the same month, January 1727, there occurred the death of Giuseppe Sacripanti, the Cardinal Protector of Scotland. This immediately raised the question of whether or not James III would be allowed to nominate his successor. James had nominated Cardinal Gualterio to be Protector of England in 1717, but prior to that all cardinal protectors had been selected by the Pope, without consulting either James himself or his father, James II.[81] The king regarded his nomination of Gualterio as setting a precedent which would enable him to select all future cardinal protectors, but no new vacancy had been created until now. If Sacripanti had died in 1725, or perhaps even when James had still been in Rome, James would almost certainly have been allowed to nominate his successor. But under the changed circumstances of his residence in Bologna, Pope Benedict XIII appointed a new cardinal protector for Scotland without consulting him. The king wanted the post to be given to Cardinal Gianantonio Davia, but the Pope gave it to Cardinal Alessandro Falconieri and refused to change his mind when James protested.[82]

The reduction of his pension and his inability to nominate the new cardinal protector convinced the king that he would have to make some concession to persuade the queen to leave the convent and rejoin the court. At the beginning of April Lord and Lady Inverness, two of the three Protestants to whom the queen objected, left Bologna and went to live at Pistoia.[83] Lord Dunbar remained, but by now it was known that the prince's tutors were all Catholic, and opinion began to turn in the king's favour. The King and Queen of Spain, who had hitherto given Clementina their full backing, sent a strongly worded letter advising her

[79] Valesio, *Diario di Roma*, IV, p. 756, 10 December 1726; NA. SP 85/16/f. 185, Stosch to Newcastle, 12 December 1726.

[80] ASV. PAC 983, numerous entries starting at no. 83; ASR. CDG b. 2017 bis/13/12/ pp. 6–8; NA. SP 85/16/f. 199 and f. 201, Stosch to Newcastle, 11 and 18 January 1727.

[81] RA. SP 105/7, Innes to James III, 17 March 1727.

[82] BL Add MSS 31255, f. 285, James III to Gualterio, 8 January 1727; BL. Add MSS 31264, ff. 272, 274, 277 and 282, Inverness to Gualterio, 8, 11, 15 and 22 January 1727; SCA. BL 2/305/1, Inverness to Stuart, 15 January 1727; SCA. BL 2/309/7, Stuart to T. Innes, 12 February 1727; Scots College Rome, vol. 4, varia no. 5, Revd Paul McPherson, unpublished 'History of the Scots College Rome, 1600–1793', pp. 191–2.

[83] BL. Add MSS 31255, f. 303, James III to Gualterio, 26 March 1727; BL. Add MSS 31264, f. 327, Inverness to Gualterio, 4 April 1727.

to rejoin her husband and accept his concession,[84] and she realised that she had no real choice but to give way.

At the end of June 1727 Clementina finally agreed that she would leave the convent and join her husband at Bologna. She was due to leave on 8 July, but while the necessary preparations were being made for her journey the news reached Rome that George I had just died at Osnabrück, and that James III had hastily left Bologna in an attempt to reach England and claim the throne. Pope Benedict visited the convent and told her that she should still go to Bologna, and gave her 4000 *scudi* for her journey.[85] But at the same time he cancelled the payment of the pension (1500 *scudi* for the king; 1000 *scudi* for the queen) which was due to be paid at the beginning of July to cover the second quarter of the year.[86]

When James III reached Lorraine he received the news that George II had peacefully succeeded his father and that Sir Robert Walpole had been confirmed in office as prime minister. All thoughts of an immediate restoration had to be put aside. James remained in Lorraine for three weeks, and then withdrew to the papal enclave at Avignon, where he arrived on 19 August. His hope was that he would be allowed to remain there, that the queen would travel from Bologna to join him, and that he would not therefore need to return to Rome.[87]

Pope Benedict XIII evidently shared these hopes. In the middle of July he ordered that prayers should be said for James in the Basilica of Santa Maria Maggiore,[88] and in August gave his agreement for James to remain at Avignon.[89] But he quickly came under pressure from the Whig government in London, which threatened naval action against Civita Vecchia and renewed persecution of the Catholics in England. Faced with this uncertainty, Clementina refused to leave Bologna and join her husband in Avignon,[90] and Benedict again stopped the payment of the Stuart pension when the third quarter of the year became due at the beginning of October.[91]

---

[84] Haile, *James Francis Edward*, pp. 320–5; McLynn, *Charles Edward Stuart*, pp. 24–5.
[85] Valesio, *Diario di Roma*, IV, pp. 826–7, 3, 5, 6, 7 and 8 July 1727; NA. SP 85/16/ff. 277, 279 and 281, Stosch to Newcastle, 3, 5 and 10 July 1727.
[86] ASR. Cam I: RMC b. 1074, which shows that no payment was made in July 1727; BL. Add MSS 31262, f. 178, Dunbar to Gualterio, 30 July 1727.
[87] Haile, *James Francis Edward*, pp. 325–8.
[88] Valesio, *Diario di Roma*, IV, p. 831, 16 July 1727.
[89] BL. Add MSS 31262, f. 194, Dunbar to Gualterio, 6 September 1727; NA. SP 85/16/ f. 305, Stosch to Newcastle, 13 September 1727.
[90] Haile, *James Francis Edward*, p. 327; McLynn, *Charles Edward Stuart*, pp. 25–6.
[91] ASR. Cam I: RMC b. 1074, which shows that no payment was made in October 1727; BL. Add MSS 31262, f. 212, Dunbar to Gualterio, 25 October 1727.

The French government under Cardinal Fleury now also joined the government of Walpole in putting pressure on the Pope to make James leave Avignon. With no papal pension, and still separated from Clementina, he had little choice but to agree.[92] At the end of December James told the Pope that he would return to Bologna. Benedict responded by ordering that the pension should be resumed in January 1728, and that all the arrears, with an additional 1500 *scudi*, should be paid at the same time.[93] James reached Bologna on 7 January and was reunited with the queen after a separation of nearly twenty-six months.[94]

From this point onwards the papal pension was paid regularly. It remained at the reduced level of 10,000 *scudi* per annum, but it was all now paid to the king, to distribute as he wished.[95] Moreover an additional 4000 *scudi* was settled on the queen as a temporary measure during Benedict's own life time, bringing the annual Stuart pension for the time being to 14,000 *scudi*.[96] The improved relations between the king and the Pope were soon put to the test, because Cardinal Gualterio died in April, and once again it was necessary to select a new cardinal protector, this time for England. To the king's relief, the Pope was prepared to accept his nomination, and Cardinal Davia was appointed.[97]

At the beginning of 1729 James III decided that he would return to Rome and again take up residence in the Palazzo del Re. The Pope ordered that the building should be thoroughly cleaned, painted, decorated and repaired, all at the expense of the *Camera Apostolica*.[98] James himself arrived at the beginning of February.[99] The Prince of Wales joined him at the end of April, followed by the queen and the Duke of York at the beginning of June.[100] Shortly afterwards the Stuart family, at

---

[92] It should be added, however, that Cardinal Fleury gave James III 12,000 *écus* in July, when the news reached Versailles that George I had died and before it was known that George II had peacefully succeeded his father (RA. SP 108/66, Ellis to Gualterio, 12 July 1727).

[93] ASR. Cam I: RMC b. 1074/f. 152 records that 9000 *scudi* were paid to Girolamo Belloni, James III's banker, on 20 December 1727.

[94] NA. SP 85/16/f. 358, Stosch to Newcastle, 17 January 1728.

[95] The payments are all recorded in ASR. Cam I: RMC b. 1074.

[96] RA. SP 108/76, Dunbar to James III, 14 July 1727; RA. SP 108/111, Ellis to James III, 21 July 1727.

[97] RA. SP 116/96, Innes to James III, 24 May 1728.

[98] ASV. PAC 983/nos. 110–13, 119, 125, 132–5, 139; ASR. Cam I: CDG b. 2017 bis/13/12/pp. 12–13.

[99] Valesio, *Diario di Roma*, v, *1729–1736*, ed. G. Scana (Milan, 1979), p. 16, 6 February 1729; NA. SP 85/16/f. 500, Stosch to Newcastle, 10 February 1729.

[100] Valesio, *Diario di Roma*, v, p. 67, 5 June 1729; NA. SP 85/16/f. 552, Stosch to Newcastle, 9 June 1729.

last permanently reunited, had a successful audience with the Pope at the Vatican. Benedict agreed to James's request that he should confirm the Prince of Wales, now eight and a half years old and educated as a good Catholic. James then gave him as a present one of the most precious relics which his parents had brought from England to Saint-Germain in the winter of 1688–9. It is described in one of the Stuart inventories as 'a cross and chain found in St Edward's tomb in ye year 1685'.[101] Stosch noted that the relic was received 'with great Devotion and respect by His Holiness'.[102]

Two and a half weeks later, on 4 July, Benedict confirmed the Prince of Wales in the Sistine Chapel, and gave him 'several gifts'.[103] They included a bas-relief made of silver representing the Holy Family.[104] The breach between the king and the Pope had at last been healed. In September James had an audience during which he was received 'with exceptional marks of distinction'.[105] And when the queen announced that she was expecting a visit from her father, and that she needed more furniture, 'the Pope ordered his Maggiordomo to provide her gratis . . . with everything she asked for'.[106]

By the end of 1729 the Pope was nearly eighty-one years old and his life was drawing to a close. His final gesture of goodwill towards James III was to let him nominate a new cardinal. James chose Archbishop de Tencin, who had consistently supported him during his recent difficulties, and had tried to persuade the French government to let him remain at Avignon. But Tencin's support had made him enemies at Versailles, and Louis XV, on the advice of Cardinal

---

[101] RA. SP Box 4/2/1, 'an inventorie of w. was in y. strong box sent to Rome', 26 September 1718 (for the date, see RA. SP 36/141); Corp, *Jacobites at Urbino*, pp. 100, 188; Valesio, *Diario di Roma*, v, p. 72, 17 June 1729: 'Ebbe questa mattina udienza da S. Beatitudine il re con la regina sua sposa ed il re portò a donare a S. Santità una croce d'oro con un crocefisso di smalto da una parte e dall'altra un santo con alcune reliquie incognito dentro, con alcune lettere, e questa croce era attaccata ad una catena d'oro ed era stata ritrovata già sopra il corpo di S. Eduardo re d'Inghilterra.'

[102] NA. SP 85/16/f. 548, Stosch to Newcastle, 23 June 1729.

[103] NA. SP 85/16/f. 552, Stosch to Newcastle, 7 July 1729. The Pope had previously confirmed Prince Charles on 6 March 1725 (see above, note 56).

[104] ASV. PAC 854/no. 248, 5 November 1729. The silversmith was Francesco de Martini, and the bas-relief cost 100 *scudi*.

[105] NA. SP 85/16/f. 588, Stosch to Newcastle, 22 September 1729. Also Valesio, *Diario di Roma*, v, p. 113, 16 September 1729.

[106] NA. SP 85/16/f. 600, Stosch to Newcastle, 27 October 1729. The details are shown in ASV. PAC 983/no. 124; and ASR. Cam I: CDG b. 2017 bis/13/14/p. 1. The queen was given new wall hangings of red damask, twenty-four red velvet 'siede all'Imperiale', and nine large tapestries 'di buona qualità' representing stories from the Old Testament, at a total cost of 1535 *scudi*.

Fleury, made it clear that his nomination would be unwelcome.[107] James therefore withdrew it and instead nominated his old friend Alamanno Salviati, whom he had met at Avignon, and who had been the *presidente* at Urbino since 1717.[108] Salviati was created a cardinal on 8 February 1730, in a consistory attended by the king, the queen and both princes.[109] Thirteen days later Pope Benedict XIII died.

[107] Castries, *Scandaleuse Madame de Tencin*, pp. 106, 161, 169; Pierre-Maurice Masson, *Madame de Tencin, 1682–1749* (Paris, 1909; new edn Geneva, 1970), p. 77.
[108] Edward Corp, 'Maintaining Honour during a Period of Extended Exile: The Nomination of Cardinals by James III in Rome', in Martin Wrede and Horst Carl (eds.), *Zwischen Schande und Ehre: Erinnerungsbrüche und die Kontinuität des Hauses* (Mainz, 2007), p. 164; Corp, *Jacobites at Urbino*, pp. 19–20, 37.
[109] Valesio, *Diario di Roma*, v, p. 173, 8 February 1730; NA. SP 98/32/f. 25, Stosch to Newcastle, 9 February 1730.

2   The Palazzo del Re

The Stuart court in Rome was housed in a medium-sized palazzo at the north end of the Piazza dei Santi Apostoli. Previously known as the Palazzo Muti, after 1719 it was called the Palazzo del Re.

There has been considerable confusion concerning the location of the court because, until very recently, all books on Jacobitism, and indeed all the biographies of James III and his two sons, have referred to the building by its former name, the Palazzo Muti. In recent years this confusion has been increased because there was an adjacent building which really was called by that name. Thus some works have appeared in which the court has been given the wrong location as well as the wrong name. We need to begin by clearing away this confusion. Briefly stated, in the years after 1719 King James III and the Stuart court occupied the Palazzo del Re at the north end of the Piazza dei Santi Apostoli, while an Italian nobleman called the marchese Muti occupied the other building, which was called the Palazzo Muti, on the west side of the adjacent Piazza della Pilotta.[1]

Correctly distinguishing between these two buildings is not simply a question of historical accuracy. It also has implications for our understanding of the exiled Stuart court, and thus of the role it played in the Jacobite movement. Unless we can identify and describe the palazzo in which the court was located, we cannot understand how it was used by the Stuarts and their household, nor estimate the influence that its architecture had on court ceremonial. And without this we cannot appreciate the impact it made on Roman society and on the many

---

[1] The reasons why there has been so much confusion concerning both the name and the location of the Stuart court in Rome are analysed in Edward Corp, 'The Location of the Stuart Court in Rome: The Palazzo del Re', in Paul Monod, Murray Pittock and Daniel Szechi (eds.), *Loyalty and Identity* (Basingstoke, 2009), pp. 180–205. Baron von Stosch, the Hanoverian spy, who naturally referred to James III as the Pretender, always called it the *Palais du Prétendant*, though in one of his letters he described it as the *Palais Royal* (NA. SP 85/16/f. 112, Stosch to Newcastle, 3 August 1726).

British and Irish Grand Tourists who visited the papal city during
the eighteenth century.

The name given to the building occupied by the Stuart court was also
important because it reflected the status given to James III by the Pope,
the cardinals and the Roman aristocracy. James was always treated
in Rome as the King of England, and given full royal honours, and
therefore his home was naturally called the Palazzo del Re. If it
had really been called the Palazzo Muti after 1719 that would have
implied that James did not enjoy royal status. Contemporaries were
well aware of this, and knew that the name given to the building was
politically significant.

To understand why the Palazzo del Re was previously known as the
Palazzo Muti, and why the adjacent building in the Piazza della Pilotta
continued to be called by that name, we need to know something about
the Muti family during the previous hundred years. The family had risen
to prominence by holding municipal and papal offices, and by the
beginning of the seventeenth century it owned two distinct but adjacent
buildings, separated by a street which is now called the Via dell'Archetto.
The plots on which these buildings stood were described for convenience in the parish registers in Latin as the 'Insula Maior de Mutis' and
the 'Insula Minor de Mutis', or in Italian as the 'Isola Maggiore' and the
'Isola Minore'. The former was the site of the future Palazzo del Re, the
latter of the future Palazzo Muti (Fig. 1). Both buildings were then
owned by the senior member of the family, Girolamo Muti, who provided accommodation for his many relations, including his brothers,
stepbrothers, uncle, aunt and first cousins.[2]

Because the family as a whole was prosperous and becoming more
important, Girolamo Muti set about improving both buildings. In 1626
he bought land on the east side of the *isola minore*, which enabled him to
build a larger palazzo for himself and his children in the Piazza della
Pilotta. As a result he gave the *isola maggiore*, and the buildings on it at
the north end of the Piazza dei Santi Apostoli, to his first cousin,

---

[2] For the history of the *isola minore* in the Piazza della Pilotta, see Giuseppe Marinelli,
'L'architettura palaziale romana tra Seicento e Settecento. Problemi di linguaggio. Un
approccio filologico: la testimonianza delle incisioni dello "Studio d'Architettura Civile";
una verifica sistematica: il palazzo Muti Papazzurri alla Pilotta' (Universita Sapienza di
Roma, doctoral thesis, no date shown but after 1990), particularly pp. 146–7, 152–3
(notes 11 and 12), 157–61 and 250–3. For the history of the *isola maggiore* in the Piazza
dei Santi Apostoli, see Aloisio Antinori, 'Il palazzo Muti Papazzurri ai Santi Apostoli nei
secoli XVI e XVII: Notizie sull'attività di Giovanni Antonio de Rossi, Carlo Fontana e
Carlo Francesco Bizzaccheri', in *Architettura: Processualità e trasformazione*, proceedings
of the international conference, Rome, Castel Sant'Angelo, 24–7 November 1999, ed.
Maurizio Caperna and Gianfranco Spagnesi (Rome, 2002), pp. 439–46.

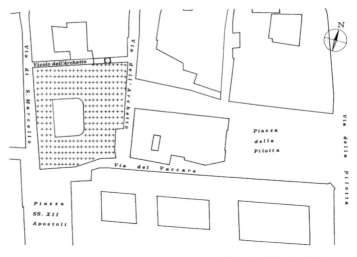

Figure 1. The location of the Palazzo del Re, beside the Palazzo
Muti. The 'Isola Maggiore' (Palazzo del Re) can be seen shaded on
the left, with the 'Isola Minore' (Palazzo Muti) on the right.

Giovanni Battista Muti, in 1632.[3] This meant that there were thenceforth two branches of the Muti family, the senior branch in the expanded
isola minore, and the junior branch in the *isola maggiore*. Girolamo died in
1662 and left all his property to one of his sons, Pompeo. Giovanni
Battista died in 1667 and bequeathed his to one of his sons, Marcello.[4]
Both Pompeo and Marcello, who were second cousins, had noble status
and were known as marchese Muti. By the time that the Stuart court
arrived in 1719, marchese Pompeo Muti had been succeeded as the
owner of the *isola minore* by his son, marchese Girolamo Muti; and
marchese Marcello Muti as the owner of the *isola maggiore* by his son,
marchese Giovanni Battista Muti. At the beginning of 1719 there were
therefore two adjacent but totally distinct buildings, both confusingly
referred to by the names of their owners as the Palazzo Muti. The
owners were third cousins. When the Pope rented the Palazzo Muti on
the *isola maggiore* for King James III and the Stuart court it was only

---

[3] Marinelli, 'Il palazzo Muti Papazzurri alla Pilotta', pp. 162–3, 185–6 (note 49).
[4] Details concerning the members of the Muti family, often called Muti Papazzurri to
distinguish it from another family called Muti Bussi, are given by Marinelli and Antinori.
Whenever they differ, as they frequently do, I have followed Marinelli because his
reconstruction of the family tree is based on the parish registers of the Church of Santi
Apostoli and various notarial archives (pp.157–9, 183). Moreover Antinori, to judge by
his footnotes, seems to have been unaware of Marinelli's thesis.

natural that the name should be changed, no doubt to the relief of the local inhabitants, to become the Palazzo del Re. Thereafter there was only one Palazzo Muti, in the Piazza della Pilotta, occupied by marchese Girolamo Muti.

There is no need to give here the history of the building on the *isola minore*, which continued to be called the Palazzo Muti,[5] but one point needs to be made. When James III arrived in Rome it had recently been expanded, with a completely new east façade and entrance. Much admired at the time, the new east side became the subject of two contemporary engravings,[6] which are of interest because they both show, in the background on the right-hand side, part of the building on the adjacent *isola maggiore* (Fig. 2).[7]

The palazzo on the *isola maggiore*, owned by Giovanni Battista Muti from 1632 until his death in 1667, and thereafter by his son, Marcello, needs to be considered in rather more detail. In reality this building, regarded then and now as a single palazzo, contained several distinct residences. This was partly because the north side of the *isola* was actually split into two parts by a little alley, known as the Vicolo dell'Archetto, which ran through the property beneath a connecting

[5] The building had recently been expanded a second time. In 1665 Pompeo Muti, who had succeeded his father, Girolamo, purchased an additional plot of land immediately to the east of the 'isola minore', and decided to provide his palazzo with a completely new façade and entrance, and with a modernised and redecorated interior. The man employed to do this was Mattia De Rossi, a former pupil of Bernini, who had become the most fashionable architect employed by the aristocratic families of Rome. Building work started in 1678, was interrupted more than once because of financial difficulties, and was not completely finished until 1703 (Marinelli, pp. 168–74, 191–200, 202–3). Apart from a particularly fine frescoed gallery which still exists (Marinelli, pp. 175–7; Danuta Batorska, 'Grimaldi and the Galleria Muti–Papazzuri', *Antologia di belli arte*, 7:8 (1978), pp. 204–15), the most impressive feature of the new Palazzo Muti was its remodelled east façade. A central courtyard, which separated the north and the south wings of the palazzo, was entered through a gate between two pairs of doric columns. The wall containing the gate extended up to the second floor only, so that the recessed portion of the façade, at the back of the courtyard, was clearly visible above it from the Piazza della Pilotta. An internal balcony with a marble balustrade went around the front three sides of the courtyard, and could also be seen from the piazza, giving the illusion that the balcony might perhaps extend back to the recessed part of the façade (Marinelli, pp. 192–3, 200).

[6] The better-known engraving was published in Alessandro Specchi, *Il nuovo teatro delle fabbriche et edifici in prospettiva di Roma moderna* (Rome, 1699), as plate no. 45 'nel disegno et intaglio'. The other engraving, by Freicenet after a drawing by Jean Barbault, was published separately in the 1750s. There is also an engraving by Giovanni Carlo Alet, which shows the entrance only, which was published in Domenico De Rossi, *Studio d'architettura civile, libro primo: Sopra gli ornamenti di porte e finestre* (Rome, 1702), illustration 142.

[7] These engravings are also of interest because they have been erroneously reproduced since 1988 as showing the Stuart court (see note 1).

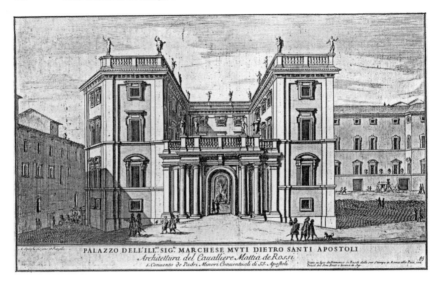

PALAZZO DELL'ILL. SIG: MARCHESE MVTI DIETRO SANTI APOSTOLI
Architettura del Caualliere Mattia de Rossi.

Figure 2. Part of the east façade of the Palazzo del Re, facing the
Piazza della Pilotta: an engraving by Alessandro Specchi, 1699.
The Palazzo del Re can be seen in the background on the right,
behind the Palazzo Muti.

covered bridge (the *archetto*). It was partly also because the entire west
side, running along the Via di San Marcello from the Piazza dei Santi
Apostoli in the south to the Vicolo dell'Archetto in the north, had been
rebuilt in a different architectural style and with rooms on a different
level. The new building, called the *palazzo grande*, was finished at the
beginning of 1638, and can be seen in an engraving published that year
by Giambattista De Rossi.[8] The most important rooms had ceilings
painted by Charles Mellin,[9] though Giuseppe Passeri and Claude Lorrain
were said to have contributed to the decoration.[10] This prestigious west
side was regarded as separate, but was nevertheless joined to the east side

---

[8] Giambattista De Rossi, *Palazzi diversi nel'alma città di Roma* (Rome, 1638), plate 30.
This engraving, despite the fact that it has an inscription on it, was accidentally
published by De Rossi in reverse, and therefore gives a completely misleading
impression of the palazzo as it was at that time. It also shows a row of shops on the
ground floor which were no longer there after 1719.

[9] Rossella Pantanella, 'Palazzo Muti a piazza SS. Apostoli residenza degli Stuart a Roma',
Storia dell'arte, 1995, no. 84, pp. 307–15.

[10] Lione Pascoli, *Vite de' pittori, scultori, ed architetti moderni* (Rome, 1730, facsimile edn
1933), pp. 220: 'In casa Muti a Santiapostoli [Giuseppe Passeri painted] la soffita della
sala, ed un gran quadro, ed in una stanza la soffita d'un alcova.' The involvement of
Claudio 'Gellee' [Claude Lorrain] is referred to on p. 25.

of the building around a spacious central courtyard. The east side was itself divided into two parts, described as *palazzetti* or small palaces, though with a common principal staircase. One was situated in the north-east corner, on the angle of the Vicolo and the Via dell'Archetto, the other in the south-east corner, on the angle of the Via dell'Archetto and a street called the Via del Vaccaro (which led from the Piazza della Pilotta to the Piazza dei Santi Apostoli).[11] These two *palazzetti* were separated on the ground floor by an entrance which was situated opposite the back of the adjacent Palazzo Muti on the *isola minore* (Fig. 3).

The *palazzetti* contained three storeys above the ground floor, whereas the *palazzo grande* (with higher ceilings in the principal rooms) contained only two. There were various mezzanines in all three parts of the *isola maggiore*, mainly on the north side or overlooking the *cortile*, with those above the third floor of the *palazzetti* on the same level as the ones above the second floor of the *palazzo grande*. As one walked about the Palazzo del Re these different levels were a constant reminder that it was composed of three distinct buildings joined together.[12]

After 1660 the *palazzo grande* was rented out by Giovanni Battista and then by Marcello Muti, who themselves occupied one of the two *palazzetti*.[13] Their tenants included (after 1682) Cardinal Nicolò Ludovisi Albergati[14] and (in 1708) conte Luigi Ferdinando Marsili, the famous naturalist who founded the Institute of Sciences and Arts in Bologna.[15] The principal entrance to the *palazzo grande* was situated between two ionic columns and beneath a balcony on the narrow south side of the building, on the Piazza dei Santi Apostoli,[16] (Fig. 4) but there was a second entrance in the middle of the long façade running along the Via di San Marcello.

Conscious that their property had now effectively been divided into two main parts (the *palazzo grande* in the west and the *palazzetti* in the east), Giovanni Battista and Marcello Muti did what they could to improve the appearance of the east side of the *isola maggiore*. Because the north-east corner projected further into the Via dell'Archetto than the rest of the building, Giovanni Battista straightened the façade at

---

[11] Antinori, 'Il palazzo Muti Papazzurri ai Santi Apostoli', p. 444.

[12] The different levels can easily be seen today by walking around the outside of the Palazzo del Re. The positions of the mezzanines can be seen in ASR. Collezione Disegni e piante I, c. 87, n. 562, 'Palazzo Muti-Papazzuri', tipi I–VII.

[13] Antinori, 'Il palazzo Muti Papazzurri ai Santi Apostoli', pp. 443–4.

[14] Marinelli, 'Il palazzo Muti Papazzurri alla Pilotta', p. 186 (note 49); Antinori, 'Il palazzo Muti Papazzurri ai Santi Apostoli', p. 443.

[15] Valesio, *Diario di Roma*, IV, pp. 116, 119, 135, 20 July and 13 August 1708.

[16] Paul-Marie Letarouilly, *Les edifices de Rome moderne* (Paris, 1860, rev. edn Novara, 1992), plate 28.

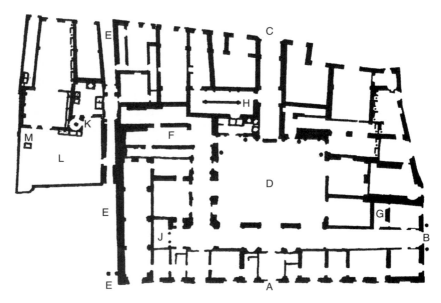

Figure 3. Plan of the ground floor of the Palazzo del Re
A Front entrance from the Via di San Marcello
B Side entrance from the Piazza dei Santi Apostoli
C Back entrance from the Via dell'Archetto (opposite the back of the Palazzo Muti)
D Courtyard (*cortile*)
E Vicolo dell'Archetto
F Grand staircase
G Secret staircase, from 1724
H Princes' staircase
J Chapel staircase, from 1724
K Spiral staircase
L Garden
M Fountain

ground level in 1661, with a spacious *loggetta*, or balcony, above, which extended outside the two *palazzetti* on the first floor or *piano nobile*.[17] It can be seen in the background of the engravings of the other Palazzo Muti on the *isola minore*, which have already been referred to. In 1685

---

[17] ASR. Presidente delle Strade b. 45, f. 174, has a drawing dated 7 October 1661 showing the new *loggetta* on the east façade of the Palazzo Muti on the *isola maggiore*, with the Vicolo dell'Archetto on the right-hand side.

Figure 4. The south façade of the Palazzo del Re, facing the Piazza dei
Santi Apostoli: an engraving by Giuseppe Vasi, 1754. The entrance
to the *palazzo grande* (subsequently the entrance for carriages to
the Palazzo del Re) can be seen in the distance.

Marcello placed two columns on either side of what had originally been
the back entrance on the east side beneath the *loggetta*, to reflect its
enhanced status as the only entrance to the two *palazzetti*.[18]

The legal agreement between the *Camera Apostolica* and Giovanni
Battista Muti (the son of Marcello), whereby the entire *isola maggiore*

---

[18] Antinori, 'Il palazzo Muti Papazzurri ai Santi Apostoli', p. 444.

was to be rented on behalf of James III and the exiled Stuart court, is dated 22 December 1718.[19] It refers specifically both to 'the palace of Marchese Giovanni Battista Muti in the Piazza dei Santi Apostoli' (the *palazzo grande*) and 'the two other small palaces [*palazzetti*] adjoining it'.[20] It states that the *palazzetta* in the south-east corner was then occupied by conte Musignani, and that the one in the north-east corner was occupied by both Giovanni Battista Muti himself and his nephew, abbate (later Cardinal) Mario Mellini. Muti (with his wife and daughter, Ginevra) occupied the 'lower part' (presumably the ground and first floors, which gave access via the *archetto* to an enclosed garden) and Mellini the 'upper part' (presumably the second and third floors). When the Stuart court moved in during 1719 the *palazzo grande* and the two *palazzetti* were joined up to form a single large residence. James III and Queen Clementina occupied what had been the *palazzo grande*. When their children were born they were given apartments in what had previously been the *palazzetta* in the north-east corner.

The rental agreement, however, also refers to two 'adjoining small houses with their appurtenances' which Giovanni Battista Muti had previously been renting for his own use, and both of which were 'included in the lease'. One of these houses was rented from Giovanni Battista Muti's cousin, marchese Girolamo Muti, the other from a relation called Giacinto Manni.[21]

It is not possible to identify with any certitude where these two houses were located, but they both seem to have been on the north side of the Piazza della Pilotta, on the corners of the Monastery of the Humiltà and of the Palazzo Ciogni.[22] The two houses are still

---

[19] ASR. Cam I: GT, b. 444, f. 9, *istromento rogito*, 22 December 1718.

[20] Marchese Giovanni Battista Muti's letter of 22 December 1718 to the *Camera Apostolica*, in which he confirmed the details of the rental agreement, was published in English translation in HMC *Stuart*, VII, p. 662.

[21] The annual rent for the *isola maggiore* (the *palazzo grande* and the two *palazzetti*) was 1536 *scudi*, of which marchese Giovanni Battista Muti received 1036 *scudi*, and his mother (marchesa Alessandra Mellini Muti) received 500 *scudi*. The two houses rented from marchese Girolamo Muti and Giacinto Manni cost, respectively, 60 *scudi* and 36 *scudi*, making a total annual rent of 1632 *scudi*. The rent was paid in advance every six months by the *Camera Apostolica*. The payments for 1719 to 1730 are recorded in ASR. Cam I: CDG b. 2017 bis/13/8 (January 1719 to January 1721), 13/10 (July 1721 to July 1724), and 13/12 (January 1725 to January 1730). They are also all recorded in ASV. PAC 5044, pp. 15–70 (January 1719 to January 1730).

[22] In 1683 Giovanni Battista Muti was said to have owned two houses in the Piazza della Pilotta, one beside a palazzo which occupied part of the north side of the piazza, described as a 'casino posto incontro la Casa delli Sig.ri Ciogni', the other beside a monastery which occupied the rest of the north side, described as a 'casino posto incontro il Muro di fianco del Monastero dell'humiltà' (Antinori, 'Il palazzo Muti Papazzurri ai Santi Apostoli', p. 444). It is possible that Giovanni Battista Muti had

shown as separate properties on the nineteenth-century *Catasto Gregoriano*.[23]

The property belonging to Giovanni Battista Muti was chosen to be the new residence of the exiled Stuart court because the *palazzo grande* happened to be available in December 1718, and because Muti and his two tenants (Musignani and Mellini) were prepared to vacate the *palazzetti*. It was never intended, or even expected, to become a permanent residence. Nevertheless it was well situated and perfectly suitable in the short term. The Piazza dei Santi Apostoli was also the location of the Palazzo Colonna, the home of James III's cousins, and was conveniently close both to the Quirinale (where the popes normally lived during the eighteenth century), and to the Corso, where Cardinal Gualterio, the Protector of England, had his residence.[24] The entire building was cleaned, painted, decorated and furnished during 1719, under the supervision of the architect Alessandro Specchi.[25] In particular an entirely new ceiling was painted, in what was to become the king's gallery on the first floor, by Giovanni Angelo Soccorsi.[26]

---

sold these two properties, and subsequently rented them. A document of 1724, referring to building works carried out for the Stuart court, includes the 'Stalla incontro al Palazzo de Sig.r Cionni [sic]', which might be the house by then owned by Giacinto Manni (ASV. PAC 983, no. 63/10, payments made by the *Camera Apostolica* for King James III, 15 October 1724). An inventory drawn up in 1713 after the death of Pompeo Muti refers to a 'casa incontro il Monastero del l'Humiltà', which might well be the house rented for the Stuart court from Pompeo's son Girolamo (Marinelli, 'Il palazzo Muti Papazzurri alla Pilotta', p. 241). Although there are other possibilities, these seem the most likely.

[23] Reproduced between pp. 164 and 165 in Marinelli, 'Il palazzo Muti Papazzurri alla Pilotta'.

[24] James III originally hoped to be lent the Palazzo Cibò, on the west side of the Piazza dei Santi Apostoli, immediately opposite the Palazzo Colonna: see Corp, *Jacobites at Urbino*, chapter 11. The Palazzo Gualterio was on the west side of the Corso, immediately to the south of the Palazzo Ruspoli, and was rented by Gualterio from the family of Cardinal Ottoboni.

[25] James III would have been familiar with the work of Alessandro Specchi because the architect had previously worked for the Albani family at Urbino (Anna Fucili Bartolucci, 'Urbino e gli Albani', pp. 441–8 in Franco Battistelli (ed.), *Arte e cultura nella provincia di Pesaro e Urbino dalle origini a oggi* (Venice, 1986), at p. 443).

[26] ASV. PAC 982 (mainly but not completely reproduced in Pantanella, 'Palazzo Muti a piazza SS. Apostoli', pp. 317–28); ASR. Cam I: CDG b. 2017 bis/f. 13/7 (partly reproduced in Pantanella, pp. 316–17) and f. 13/8/pp. 1–11 (not reproduced). The previous ceiling, painted by Charles Mellin, presumably included the arms of the Muti family, and would have been inappropriate for the residence of the Stuart court. The redecoration of the gallery in the king's apartment therefore symbolised the change in the building's status from the Palazzo Muti to the Palazzo del Re. The total cost of preparing the palazzo for the Stuart court during 1719 was 14,559 *scudi* (ASR. Cam I: CDG b. 2017 bis/f. 13/8/pp. 1–2).

Figure 5. The west façade of the Palazzo del Re, in the Via di San Marcello, a nineteenth-century drawing.

There were three entrances to the Palazzo del Re. The main one was now in the Via di San Marcello, in the centre of the *palazzo grande*,[27] but the narrowness of the street made it easier for carriages to enter through the decorated entrance from the Piazza dei Santi Apostoli on the south side. Passing under the king's apartment, they turned right into the central courtyard, dropped off their passengers, and then departed through the entrance on the east side, between the two former *palazzetti*, towards the Palazzo Muti.

The façade of the *palazzo grande*, running along the Via di San Marcello, contained thirteen windows on the first and second floors. These windows, however, were not regularly spaced. The four on the left (north) were separated by a wider gap from the nine on the right (south). This was significant because the nine on the right provided light for the royal apartments, whereas the four on the left opened into rooms used for other purposes (Fig. 5).

There was another irregular feature, this time on the first floor only: a row of smaller windows between the first and the second floors. The six on the left (north) were taller that the seven on the right (south). This is because there was a mezzanine floor on the left, whereas the rooms on the right had much higher ceilings. Given that the king's apartment on the first floor contained nine windows overlooking the Via di San

---

[27] This was the entrance guarded by the head of the Swiss Guards, known as the *guarda portone*. From 1719 to 1746 this position was held by Bernhardt Nieriker.

Marcello, and that two of these nine were taller than the other seven, it meant that the apartment had some rooms with, and others without, mezzanines above.[28]

The grand staircase was situated in the middle of the north wing and led directly up to the king's guard chamber overlooking the central courtyard. Beyond the guard chamber, extending around the courtyard on the inside, and along the Via di San Marcello on the outside, the apartment then consisted of four antechambers, a bedchamber and a gallery. The first two antechambers had low ceilings because of the mezzanines above, and led to the other rooms through a sequence of doors placed *enfilade* on the San Marcello side. The third and fourth antechambers and the bedchamber had impressive high painted ceilings. The gallery had the high ceiling painted by Giovanni Angelo Soccorsi. Beyond the gallery there was a cabinet, situated in what had been the south-eastern *palazzetta*. It was on a different level, and probably not decorated until after 1719 (Fig. 6).

The rooms in the king's apartment were described in 1726–7 as follows (with the Italian numbers in reverse order): guard chamber (*Sala*), 1st antechamber 'next ye Sala' (*camera passato li accanto*), 2nd antechamber, 'where ye King eats' (*camera dove mangiare il Rè*), 3rd antechamber (*2e anticamera*), 4th antechamber (*anticamera*), 'Great Bedchamber below' (*camera del Rè*), gallery, closet (*1e gabinetto*), '2nd little room' (*2e gabinetto*), 'inward little room' (*3e gabinetto*). There were also two rooms which were possibly the mezzanines overlooking the *cortile*: wardrobe (*guardaroba del Rè*) and 'where pages wait' (*stanza delli carabinieri nella guardaroba del Rè*).[29]

These rooms are all in very bad condition today, and only small parts of their ceilings have survived. The third antechamber, which had a little balcony immediately above the entrance, had a large painting within a heavy gilded frame, showing an angel appearing before a kneeling Virgin Mary and sleeping child. The fourth antechamber had a frescoed ceiling by Charles Mellin showing *La Fama* blowing a trumpet, between a pair

---

[28] These windows can easily be seen today, because the façade has not been significantly changed above the ground floor. The appearance of the façade as it was in the nineteenth century can be seen in ASR. Collezione disegni e piante I, c. 87, n. 562, 'Palazzo Muti-Papazzuri', tipo VII.

[29] RA. SP 98/131 and 106/79, inventories of the Palazzo del Re, October 1726 and April 1727. The contents of the king's bedchamber were listed as: 'Tappisseria di seta rossa, 2 tavolini, un crocifesso, 10 sedie di tabino bianco, et una di corame, uno scabello, un ecran du chemini, 2 piedi per potere li candelieri, un letto di rosso d'imbroccado, 2 bianchi, 4 tavole di letto, 3 matarazzi, un capezzale, un letto di riposo vaccamato dentro il cammino, 2 capofochi, le molle, una paletta, un tira brascia, et un soffietto' (RA. SP 106/79).

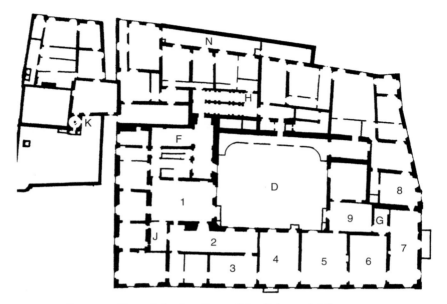

Figure 6. Plan of the first floor of the Palazzo del Re

D Courtyard (*cortile*)
F Grand staircase
G Secret staircase, from 1724; back staircase (connecting the
   bedchambers)
H Princes' staircase
J Chapel staircase, from 1724
K Spiral staircase
N Balcony (*loggetta*)

The king's apartment

1 Guard Chamber
2 First antechamber
3 Second antechamber
4 Third antechamber
5 Fourth antechamber
6 Bedchamber
7 Gallery
8 Closet
9 Private secretary's room

of sphinxes on either side (placed above the interior walls). Above the
windows overlooking the courtyard Mellin had also painted some large
seated male nudes on top of an antique bas-relief. The bedchamber
contained a framed painting by Mellin showing the legendary hero

Marcus Curtius, whom the Muti family regarded as an ancestor, fully armed and on horseback, leaping down into the chasm (effectively formed by the bedchamber itself) which had opened in the Forum.[30] These three rooms all overlooked the Via di San Marcello, and were therefore shaded from the sun, but the bedchamber had a view down the Via dei Santi Apostoli, across the Corso, towards the Collegio Romano.[31]

The king's gallery, which had a balcony above the carriage entrance, looked due south down the Piazza dei Santi Apostoli towards the Palazzo Bonelli (which, from 1732 to 1740, was the French embassy).[32] The Church of Santi Apostoli and the Palazzo Colonna were on the left, and the Palazzo Chigi and the Palazzo Cibò on the right. Only part of the ceiling of the gallery has survived, but the papal archives contain a brief description of Soccorsi's overall design. In the centre there was a framed oval painting containing two *putti*, one holding a sceptre, the other the royal crown of England. At the west end of the gallery there was a seated lady, dressed in white, who represented *la Religion Cattolica*, and at the east end, beneath a white dove, there was another seated lady, also dressed in white but with a yellow cloak, representing *la Fede*. The eventual triumph of the exiled King of England would thus be brought about with the help of the Catholic religion and faith. The ceiling also contained, in small round painted frames, more references to Marcus Curtius, the saviour of Rome. The only painting from that series which has survived happens to be another one in which the mounted hero is shown leaping on his horse into the chasm. It was placed at the east end of the gallery, near the picture representing *la Fede*.[33]

---

[30] When a deep chasm opened in the Forum in 362 BC it was believed that it would not close until Rome's most valued possession had been thrown into it. Marcus Curtius, believing this to be a brave citizen, leaped fully armed on horseback into the chasm, which immediately closed.

[31] There are no existing ground plans showing how the floors of the palazzo were arranged during the eighteenth century. The ones in the Archivio di Stato di Roma (see note 28, tipi I–VII), which show how it was arranged in the second half of the nineteenth century, need to be corrected as far as that is possible by careful comparison both with the inventories in the Stuart Papers and with the descriptions in the papal archives of the building works carried out by the *Camera Apostolica* for James III. Parts of the ceilings are shown in Pantanella, 'Palazzo Muti a piazza SS. Apostoli', pp. 311–14. Restoration work was in progress when I inspected and photographed the king's apartment in July 2005.

[32] It was used as the French embassy by the duc de Saint-Aignan, the younger half-brother of the duc de Beauvilliers.

[33] ASV. PAC 982, reproduced in Pantanella, 'Palazzo Muti a piazza SS. Apostoli', pp. 319–20. The gallery was decorated while James III was in Spain, and it is unlikely that he had anything to do with its design.

The king's cabinet, beyond the east end, was in the adjacent *palazzetta* rather than the *palazzo grande*, and consequently on a different (higher) level. An opening had to be made in the connecting wall, with a short flight of four steps, in order to reach it. This cabinet, which was probably decorated for James III a little later, was a delightful room. The rounded ceiling, which is in surprisingly good condition, was painted to be open to the sky, and showed several birds fluttering above. *Putti* could be seen within a delicate floral design, supported by a wooden rococo trellis frame.[34] It was beneath this attractive ceiling that James III conducted his business, receiving and despatching the Stuart Papers, which are now preserved at Windsor Castle.

The queen's apartment was situated on the second floor, immediately above the king's, with a small inner staircase connecting the two bed-chambers. It was accessed by continuing further up the grand staircase, and contained exactly the same sequence of rooms (Fig. 7). Unfortunately none of its decoration has apparently survived. When Prince Charles was born in December 1720 he too was given an apartment on the second floor, on the north side of the *palazzetta* overlooking the Vicolo dell'Archetto.[35] It consisted of a '1st room' (*sala*), three rooms described as the '2nd, 3rd and 4th rooms' (*stanza dei cammerieri; guardarobba; stanza dove dormire il servitore*), a '5th room' (*stanza accorso alla guardarobba*), a bedchamber (*cammera*), and a closet (*gabinetto*). There was also a *camera dove si vestiva il Principe* and a kitchen (*cucina*).[36]

Prince Henry's apartment was in the same *palazzetta*, also on the second floor, but overlooking the Piazza della Pilotta from above the *loggetta*.[37] It was referred to as the nursery, and contained a room for the prince's nurse, described variously as '1st room backwards' or 'darkroom' (*stanza della balia*), and three others called the '2nd room' (*stanza dove dormire il cameriere*), '3rd room' (*2e stanza*) and '4th room next to ye Prince's lodging' (*3e stanza*).[38] Prince Henry slept in this fourth room immediately beside Prince Charles's bedchamber, with a double connecting door.[39]

---

[34] Notes and photographs taken during my visit to the palazzo in July 2005.

[35] ASV. PAC 983, no. 63/10, payments made by the *Camera Apostolica* for King James III, 15 October 1724.

[36] RA. SP 98/131 and 106/79, inventories of the Palazzo del Re, October 1726 and April 1727.

[37] Numerous references in ASV. PAC 983–87, payments made by the *Camera Apostolica*, 1724–43.

[38] RA. SP 98/131 and 106/79, inventories of the Palazzo del Re, October 1726 and April 1727.

[39] RA. SP 131/7, James III to Inverness, 1 October 1729; RA. SP 131/29, Edgar to Ellis, 5 October 1729.

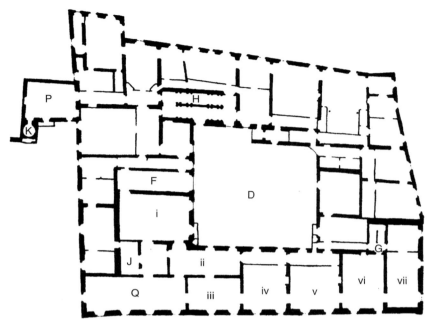

Figure 7. Plan of the second floor of the Palazzo del Re

D Courtyard (*cortile*)
F Grand staircase
G Back staircase (connecting the Bedchambers)
H Princes' staircase
J Chapel staircase, from 1724
K Spiral staircase
P First chapel, 1719–24
Q Second chapel, from 1724

The king and queen's apartment

i Guard Chamber
ii First antechamber
iii Second antechamber
iv Third antechamber
v Fourth antechamber
vi Bedchamber
vii Gallery

The Chapel Royal was originally above the *archetto* which connected the main part of the *isola maggiore* with the smaller part (including the garden) on the other side of the Vicolo dell'Archetto. Beneath the *archetto*, in the little lane outside but protected by the bridge, the Muti family had created a small shrine dedicated to the Virgin Mary. It was properly called the shrine of 'La Madonna dell'Archetto', and contained a picture of the Virgin, painted in oil on stone by Domenico Muratori in 1690.[40] Because of its small size, it was referred to as 'La Madonella'. When the *isola maggiore* was rented by the *Camera Apostolica* for James III this shrine was specifically excluded from the lease. Muti wrote that 'one dark room is reserved to the lessor, which is under the Arch of the Madonna in the lane under the house at present inhabited by him, which room is used for the furniture of the said sacred image, to which his family have a particular devotion'.[41]

Muti had had his own chapel built on the second floor directly above the arch, accessible from both sides of the *isola maggiore*, and this was the chapel which was used by the Stuart court after 1719. Situated immediately beside the apartment destined for the king's first child, it was the place where Prince Charles was baptised at the end of 1720.

The chapel contained a painting given to the king by Pope Clement XI in 1719. It showed *La navicella di san Pietro con la virtù Teologali*, and had been painted the previous year by Giuseppe Chiari. The painting, which is now at Frascati, measures 170 × 122 cm. It shows St Peter steering a small boat during a storm at sea, accompanied by Faith, Hope and Charity (the theological virtues), observed and protected from above by the Holy Trinity.[42] At the end of 1722, in front of this picture, James III gave the orders of the Garter and the Thistle to the little Prince of Wales.[43]

In the autumn of the following year James ordered that the six large gold candlesticks in the little chapel at Saint-Germain-en-Laye, which had remained there after the death of Mary of Modena, should be sent to Rome and placed on the altar of the Chapel Royal in the Palazzo del Re.[44] He also purchased another (but unknown) painting to be placed

---

[40] Information taken from the notice displayed (in 2005) on the wall of the Madonna dell'Archetto.

[41] HMC *Stuart*, VII, p. 662, G.B. Muti to *Camera Apostolica*, 22 December 1718.

[42] ASV. PAC 982, reproduced in Pantanella, 'Palazzo Muti a piazza SS. Apostoli', p. 317. The painting itself is reproduced in colour in *Il settecento a Roma*, catalogue of the exhibition in the Palazzo di Venezia, edited by Anna Lo Bianco and Angelo Negro (Rome, 2005), no. 91, pp. 206–7.

[43] NA. SP 85/14/f. 207, Stosch to Carteret, 26 December 1722.

[44] Corp, *Court in Exile*, p. 102; NA. SP 85/14/f. 498, Stosch to Carteret, 30 October 1723. The rich prie-dieu, which Louis XIV had given to Mary of Modena in May 1689, was also brought from the Château de Saint-Germain at this time (Corp, *Court in Exile*, p. 101; RA. SP 69/113, Ellis to Hay, 18 October 1723).

above the altar,[45] possibly because the candlesticks obscured the bottom of the large one by Chiari.

Unfortunately this chapel posed a major problem for the Stuart court. There was no direct communication between the first floor of the Palazzo del Re and the private garden on the north side of the arch. In order to reach the garden, without going out into the street, or perhaps through the mezzanines, one had to go up to the second floor and through the chapel, and then down a spiral staircase. The chapel there-fore presented an obstacle to free circulation within the palazzo, and must, at least occasionally, have been used as a kind of connecting corridor.

By 1724, after the failure of the Atterbury Plot, it became clear that James III would have to remain in Rome for much longer than originally expected. This prompted him to reconsider the suitability of the Palazzo del Re as the location of the exiled court. It certainly had some positive advantages: it was well situated, it had a private garden, and it did not contain any shops running around the outside of the ground floor. Yet by 1724 James was perhaps more conscious of its disadvantages. The chapel was inconveniently positioned; it was not possible to go for long walks, as had been the case at Saint-Germain, without travelling out to the Borghese gardens, or those of some other villa on the edge of the city; and there was no secret staircase. This last point was particularly import-ant. A steady stream of British visitors to Rome wanted to see the king without being observed, but could not easily do so because of the need to go up the grand staircase, and then through the four antechambers. There was no other convenient way of reaching the gallery or the cabinet of the king's apartment.[46]

---

[45] RA. SP Misc 34, 'To Father Brown for a picture for ye altar in ye Ma.ties Chappel … 131 livres', November 1723. It is possible that the king had his own small chapel, or oratory, on the first floor and that this painting was purchased to be placed there rather than in the Chapel Royal. The available archives are insufficiently precise for any definite conclusions to be drawn. An inventory of 1727 shows that the Chapel Royal then contained 'un gran quadro con il baldachino' (RA. SP 106/79, 'an inventory of the King's Palaces in Rome in ye month of April 1727').

[46] In the absence of contemporary ground plans, it is very hard to be absolutely sure about the distribution of space within the Palazzo del Re. It seems that there was a 'scaletta segreta' which led up to the apartment with the *loggetta* on the east side of the palazzo, within one of the *palazzetti*: 'la Scaletta segreta, dove … è … la Loggia' (ASV. PAC 983, no. 63/10 and no. 64/9, payments made by the *Camera Apostolica* for King James III, 15 and 20 October 1724). James Murray referred to it in an undated letter to Cardinal Gualterio, in which he told the cardinal that the king had agreed to meet someone secretly in Murray's own apartment: 'ainsi si V.E. le trouve a propos je viendray le trouver un demy heure auparavant, et nous viendrons icy ensemble, et pendant que V.E. monte a l'appartement du Roy je meneray a Mons.r chez moy, en attendant que le Roy et V.E. pourront nous venir trouver par un passage secrete' (BL. Add MSS 31263,

Perhaps the most important problem was the growing shortage of space. At first the palazzo contained enough accommodation for all the members of the royal household, but the birth of Prince Charles resulted in an increase in the number of servants employed, and it was obvious that as he grew older more would have to be taken on. Then, in the summer of 1724, the queen became pregnant for a second time. The birth of another child would eventually increase the size of the household even more. It was this that prompted James to ask for an alternative, larger residence.

He cannot have been very optimistic about obtaining one. Nevertheless the timing seemed propitious. Pope Benedict XIII was elected in May 1724, and had already shown himself to be particularly well disposed towards James and Clementina. One of his first acts was to give to the queen all the rich furnishings which had been recently purchased for the private apartments of his predecessor, Innocent XIII. The latter were said to be worth 12,000 *scudi*, the equivalent of seven and a half times the annual rent paid by the *Camera Apostolica* for the Palazzo del Re.[47]

In June 1724, a few weeks after the papal election, James III asked Benedict XIII to let him move to the Palazzo Riario in Trastevere.[48] It had once been occupied by Queen Christina of Sweden, and had more space to accommodate his expanding household. Although it was inconveniently situated on the other side of the river Tiber, it had a large and spacious garden, offering easy access to agreeable walks. It also offered the important advantage, because of its location away from the centre of the city, of making it easier for Jacobites and other British Grand Tourists to visit him discreetly.

Benedict XIII considered the matter during that summer, but eventually decided (probably because of pressure from the Imperial ambassador) that the Stuart court should remain where it was. He did, however, come up with a compromise proposal. James III should go away for several months to Albano, where he had the permanent use of the Palazzo Apostolico, so that the entire Palazzo del Re could be refurbished and made more suitable.[49] James accepted this offer, and

---

f. 24, undated, but between October 1719 and February 1721). Stosch also referred to this 'scaletta segreta' in a letter dated 6 April 1723 which reported that it had been used by William Bromley (NA. SP 85/14/f. 318, to Carteret).

[47] NA. SP 85/15/f. 149 and f. 151, Stosch to Newcastle, 24 June and 1 July 1724. See note 21 for the rent.

[48] NA. SP 85/15/ff. 137, 161, 163 and 171, Stosch to Newcastle, 10 June, 22 and 25 July, and 5 August 1724.

[49] BL. Add MSS 31264, f. 159, Hay to Gualterio, 20 September 1724; NA. SP 85/15/ ff. 194, 210, 212, Stosch to Newcastle, 16 September, 4 and 11 November 1724; SCA. BL 2/270/13, Stuart to T. Innes, 23 November 1724.

the building works were carried out during a period of a little over three months, from September to November.[50] When the court returned from Albano one of the Jacobites observed that 'our Palazzo is quite an other thing than it was'.[51]

The changes cannot all be analysed here, but two points might conveniently be made. A new secret staircase was created, giving direct access from beside the south entrance to the king's gallery and cabinet. A visitor could thus enter discreetly on foot through one of the other two entrances, leaving the one for carriages closed, and could see the king without the need to go up the grand staircase and pass through the guard chamber and antechambers.[52] The second change concerned the chapel, which was deconsecrated and replaced by an entirely new one in a much more convenient position. Its construction involved using some of the space in the queen's apartment, and indeed the new chapel is listed as part of that apartment in the inventories of 1726–7.[53]

---

[50] ASV. PAC 983, payments made by the *Camera Apostolica* for King James III. The principal references are nos. 63/10, 64/9, 62/6 and 64/10, respectively 15 October, 20 October, 30 November and 15 December 1724. The total cost of the building works was 5064 *scudi* (ASR. Cam I: CDG 2017 bis/f. 13/12/pp. 1–2).

[51] NA. SP 85/13/f. 118, Edgar to Clephane, 28 November 1724. One change involved supplying the Palazzo del Re with a regular supply of water. To achieve this, pipes were laid through the streets of Rome linking the building with the gardens of the Quirinale. The papal accounts include payments for digging the necessary trench, laying down the lead pipes, and replacing all the cobblestones, to bring 'l'acqua alla Botte del Organo nel Giardino del Palazzo Quirinale a la porta nel Palazzo ... dove sta Sua Maestà' (ASV PAC 983/nos. 70/21 and 76/5; ASR. Cam I: CDG b. 2017 bis/13/12/p. 5).

[52] Stosch reported on 30 December 1724 that two masked men (believed to be John Guise, MP, and Christopher Milles) had been brought up 'l'Escalier secret' into the king's bedchamber by John Hay (NA. SP 85/15/f. 237, to Newcastle). If Stosch is to be believed, a secret door was later made which gave direct access to the secret staircase from the Via del Vaccaro: 'Mes Emissaires m'assurent que plusieurs nuits consecutives, ils ont vû entrer dans une maison contigue a celle du Prétendant des Etrangers. J'ay decouvert depuis que dite maison a été louee expres et que au travers de la Muraille on a ouvert le passage, par où on peut commodement passer, jusques dans l'Apartement du Prétendant par un escalier derobé' (NA. SP 85/16/f. 104, Stosch to Newcastle, 6 July 1726). Visitors who used the secret staircase were received in the king's cabinet, which they reached by passing through one end of the gallery.

[53] The queen's apartment was described in the inventories of 1726–7 as containing: guard chamber (*Cammera della guardia*), antechapel (*Cammera acanto alla Cappella*), chapel (*Cappella*), two antechambers (*1a e 2a Anticamera*), bedchamber (*Grand Cammera del Rè, e delle Regina*), gallery (*Stanza accorso alla scala secreta*) and closet (*Gabinetto della Regina*). The queen also had an additional chapel on the shaded side looking north over the *cortile*: *stanza della cappella per Estate* and *stanza accante alla cappella dell'Estate* (RA. SP 98/131 and 106/79, inventories of the Palazzo del Re, October 1726 and April 1727). The contents of the king and queen's bedchamber were listed as: 'due grandi spechij, un cantarene, un ripostino con li christalli, un tavolino, un altro tavolino piccolo, un prie dieu, e sopra tre libri, due bianchi di ferro, 4 tavole di letto, e li legni del cielo del'letto, una sedia d'appreggia negra, 11 sedie di velluto, un piede per potare il candeliere, un baso della china, con alcuni fiori' (RA. SP 106/79). A document of 1725

The new chapel was situated on the second floor, overlooking the Via di San Marcello, behind the four windows on the left-hand side. It was adjacent to the apartment of the queen, and was provided with its own staircase, which enabled people to reach it without having to pass through her apartment. It contained the six great gold candlesticks, and probably the two paintings, which had been in the previous chapel, and some additional rich furnishings which were given as a present by Benedict XIII.[54]

Three months later, in March 1725, the queen gave birth to her second son, Henry, created Duke of York, and the Pope, who had not yet seen the new chapel, decided to visit the palazzo and baptise the little prince himself.[55] The king then commissioned his principal painter, Antonio David, to produce a large picture showing the interior of his new chapel. James decided, however, that the picture should not show the baptism of his second son by the Pope, but rather the baptism of his heir, the Prince of Wales, by the Bishop of Montefiascone. That ceremony had in reality taken place four years earlier in the previous chapel, but David was ordered to show it in the new one.[56] The six large gold candlesticks from Saint-Germain can be seen on the altar, with the rich red damask hangings decorated with gold, the gift of Benedict XIII, in the background (Fig. 8). Neither of the two paintings is visible, so if they were retained for the new chapel, as was probably the case, they were no doubt displayed on one of the other walls.

It was thus the decision of Pope Benedict XIII to refurbish the entire Palazzo del Re, rather than to let James III move elsewhere, which ensured that it became the permanent residence of the Stuart court in Rome. Although James moved his court to Bologna in October 1726, following Clementina's retirement into the Convent of Santa Cecilia in Trastevere, the palazzo continued to be rented for him by the *Camera*

specifies that there were 'pictures made by ye P[rin]cess of Piombino, which hung by ye Bed in ye great Bedchamber above stairs' (RA. SP Box 4/2/12, 'a list of the Queen's goods remaining in the Kings Palace, November 1725').

[54] Bod. Lib. Rawlinson MSS D. 1185, p. 2077, Rawlinson's diary, 20 September 1724; NA. SP 85/15/f. 233, Stosch to Newcastle, 23 December 1724. The rest of the plate used in the Chapel Royal belonged to the Pope (RA. SP 105/140, James III to Ellis, 9 April 1727), and included 'quattro candelieri, un crucifio, un tondo, un calice con patena, [e] un sechietto con l'aspersori'. There was also 'una Madonna con cornice d'argento' (RA. SP 106/24, 'nota dell'Argentaria', 18 April 1727).

[55] See Chapter 1, p. 27.

[56] David was paid 603 *livres* (approximately 120 *scudi*) for the picture in November 1725 (RA. SP Misc 34). The picture, now in the Scottish National Portrait Gallery (no. 2511), measures 243.9 × 350.3 cm.

Figure 8. The Chapel Royal: *The Baptism of Prince Charles,
31 December 1720*, 1725 (243.9 × 342 cm), by Antonio David. From
left to right: Cardinal Giuseppe Renato Imperiali, Cardinal Giuseppe
Sacripanti and Cardinal Filippo Antonio Gualterio (the Cardinal
Protectors of Ireland, Scotland and England), behind Cardinal
Annibale Albani; James III; Lord Richard Howard (English), Lord
William Drummond (Scottish), Antonio Ragazzi (parish priest of Santi
Apostoli) and Father John Brown (Irish) with two boys, behind
Sebastiano Bonaventura (Bishop of Corneto and Montefiascone);
contessa della Torre (better known as the princesse des Ursins)
kneeling and holding Charles, Prince of Wales; six Roman and Jacobite
ladies (two of whom are kneeling); Ippolita Boncampagni (principessa
di Piombino) and three Roman ladies; four Roman and Jacobite
gentlemen; Cardinal Francesco Aquaviva, Cardinal Francesco
Barberini, Cardinal Fabrizio Paulucci and Cardinal Pietro Ottoboni,
standing behind don Carlo Albani.

Apostolica, and therefore remained available whenever he chose to go
back.[57] It was in the Palazzo del Re that the Stuart court was reestablished when the king and queen returned to Rome in the spring of 1729,
following their reconciliation.

[57] ASR. Cam I: CDG b. 2017 bis/f. 13/12; ASV. PAC 5044, 'Rincontro del Banco in conte
a parte delle spese che p. ordine di N.tro Sig.re si fanno p. la Maestà di Giacomo 3° Rè
d'Inghilterra', 1719–33.

When the Stuarts returned in 1729 the entire palazzo was thoroughly cleaned and refurnished by the *Camera Apostolica* at a cost of 4379 *scudi*.[58] The king, the queen and the Prince of Wales reoccupied their old apartments, but Prince Henry, now four years old, was moved out of the nursery and given a larger apartment overlooking the Piazza della Pilotta and the north wing of the adjacent Palazzo Muti.[59]

---

[58] ASV. PAC 983, payments made by the *Camera Apostolica* for King James III. The principal references are nos. 110/10, 111/11, 113/16 and 135/14, 2 February to 31 March 1729, and no. 124/11, 24 November 1729.

[59] RA. SP 131/7, James III to Inverness, 1 October 1729; RA. SP 131/29, Edgar to Ellis, 5 October 1729. Prince Henry was moved out of the nursery at that time because it was believed that the queen was pregnant and that it would be needed for her next child.

3 James III, Queen Clementina and Roman society

The Palazzo del Re was not a centre of government and administration, but rather a court where (to use the definition in the *Oxford English Dictionary*) 'a sovereign resided and held state, attended by his retinue'. It is the nature of this retinue which now needs to be examined. It consisted, as also defined by the *OED*, of two separate groups of people. There was 'a number or company of persons retained in [his] service'. These people, who formed the royal household, were all exiled British and Irish Jacobites, or servants who had been recruited in France or the Papal States. There was also 'a number or company of persons ... attached to and following' the king. These counsellors and attendants included a small number of exiled Jacobites, but most of them were people of foreign nationality already resident in Rome who chose to attach themselves to the court of James III and Queen Clementina. The Palazzo del Re contained and attracted an international community.

This was not necessarily what James III himself wanted. Like most exiled monarchs, the Stuarts had difficulty in attracting to their court a sufficient number of noblemen and women of the highest rank from among their own subjects. At Saint-Germain they were fortunate to have been followed into exile by a duke, a marquess and several earls, with their wives, as well as some ladies of a similar rank in the service of the queen. Nevertheless, it had been necessary to elevate some of them to a higher rank in the peerage to help maintain the prestige of the court,[1] and as time went by several had died or left without being replaced.

Frequent meetings with Louis XIV and the French royal family, and the close proximity of Saint-Germain to both Versailles and Paris, had provided the young James III with a substitute group of aristocrats with whom he could socialise. The exiled English court had regularly entertained, and been entertained by, the leading French

[1] Corp, *Court in Exile*, pp. 173–4.

courtiers, thus enabling James to develop close relationships with people of an appropriate rank.

This balance between Jacobite and French nobles had been upset by the time the Stuart court was established at Rome in the autumn of 1719. There were no longer any peers employed in the royal household or the secretariat, and only four Scottish lords (three of whom were unmarried) among the small group of pensioners attached to the court. James III in Rome was obliged to turn to the cardinals and the local princely families for social companionship.

This point needs to be emphasised. James, like any other king, had friendly relations with some of the members of his household, but they were the relations of a master with his servants. The most important of them, James Murray, John Hay and the latter's wife Marjory (née Murray), were the younger children of Scottish peers, but they were nevertheless commoners when they joined the court, and not at all of the same status and prestige as the most senior servants who had been employed at Saint-Germain.

Any study of the Stuart court in Rome must therefore identify the members of Roman society who attended the Palazzo del Re and with whom James III and Queen Clementina socialised. Some of them, like the leading French courtiers, were no more than friends and acquaint-ances. Others, however, were particularly associated with the Stuart court and indeed became virtual members of it. Their position was more like that of the English aristocrats who had frequented the Stuart court at Whitehall without obtaining or indeed wanting a salaried office.

During 1720 James III continued to cultivate the small group of cardinals associated with the Jacobite cause. In addition to Filippo Gualterio (Fig. 9), with whom he had particularly friendly relations, they included the protectors of his other kingdoms (Giuseppe Sacripanti and Giuseppe Imperiali), the Protector of France and *vice-cancelliere* (Pietro Ottoboni), the Spanish ambassador (Francesco Aquaviva),[2] the secretary of state (Fabrizio Paulucci), and the *camerlengo*, who was one of the Pope's nephews (Annibale Albani). James also socialised with the Ruspoli family, who lived next door to the Palazzo Gualterio on the Corso, and with the Colonna family, his cousins, who lived in the Piazza

---

[2] Cardinal Aquaviva understood English (SCA. BL 2/269/8, Stuart to T. Innes, 29 February 1724) and seems to have wanted to replace Gualterio as James III's chief adviser. See BL. Add MSS 20308, f. 203, Gualterio to Bourke, 5 August 1721, in which he explained that he and Aquaviva were not as friendly as they used to be: 'lorsque le Roy d'Angleterre passa en Espagne quoique c'est été moy qui l'eut introduit dans la confiance de S.M.B. mais encore il tachâ tout a fait de me lever la main auprès de ce prince et de me supplanter.'

Figure 9. *Cardinal Filippo Antonio Gualterio*, *c.*1720 (90 × 70 cm), by Antonio David. Having served as papal nuncio to France (1700–6), Gualterio became James III's unofficial ambassador at Rome (1711–17) and then his principal minister. He was also Cardinal Protector of England from 1717 until his death in 1728. His brother was created Earl of Dundee.

dei Santi Apostoli. James had helped sponsor the marriage of principe Fabrizio Colonna to Catterina Teresa Salviati, a niece of his friend Alamanno Salviati, the *presidente* at Urbino.[3] The duca and duchessa Salviati were also in James's circle of friends.

The other people most closely associated with the Stuart court at this time were don Carlo Albani (another of the Pope's nephews) and

---

[3] Corp, *Jacobites at Urbino*, p. 91.

the principessa di Piombino. Albani and his wife donna Teresa (née Borromeo) had visited James at Urbino,[4] and were now regular visitors to the Palazzo del Re. Ippolita Boncampagni (née Ludovisi) was James's closest female friend. She had been the ruler of the small independent principality of Piombino since 1701, and was twenty-four years older than him, but they developed a very warm friendship and she also provided advice and companioniship to Queen Clementina. Among the undated letters sent by Murray to Gualterio in 1720 there are several which refer to the use of the principessa di Piombino's home (the Villa Ludovisi) as a meeting place. In one of them Murray informs Gualterio that the king would like to see him that evening 'at the small house in the middle of Princess [sic] Piombino's garden at 11p.m.'.[5] The princess had six daughters, four of whom with their husbands, principe Giustiniani, principe Barberini di Palestrina, the duca di Fiano and duca Salviati, also formed part of James's social circle.

At the end of 1720 the court was joined by the princesse des Ursins, who was then seventy-eight years old. She had first met James in 1705, when she had stayed at the Château de Saint-Germain, and had spent many years in Spain at the court of Philip V.[6] She returned to live in Rome that autumn and rented the Palazzo Cibò (opposite the Palazzo Colonna) in the Piazza dei Santi Apostoli. She told Cardinal Gualterio, in a letter dated 6 November, that she had been extremely well received by the king and the queen.[7] Two weeks later she told him that she had decided to attach herself to the Stuart court because, as she herself put it, that would be an honourable thing for her to do.[8] Living only a few yards away from the Palazzo del Re, she was in regular attendance on James and Clementina, but had neither official duties nor salary.

The birth of the Prince of Wales at the end of 1720 provides us with an ideal opportunity to observe the social relations between James, Clementina and Roman society. During November, we are told, the

---

[4] *Ibid.*, pp. 83–4, 184.
[5] BL. Add MSS 31262, f. 98, Murray to Gualterio, undated.
[6] NLS. MS 14266, Nairne's diary, 6 February 1705: 'La Pr.sse Ursini came to see ye Q(ueen) and lay at La(dy) Perths.' Anne-Marie de la Trémoille had married Flavio Orsini, the duca di Bracciano, in 1675. After his death in 1698 she was popularly referred to as the principessa Orsini, and known in France and Spain as the princesse des Ursins. Her correct title in Rome was actually the contessa della Torre. The principessa di Piombino had been in the entourage of the Queen of Spain when the latter had peremptorily dismissed her from the Spanish court in December 1714. See Marcel Loyau (ed.), *Correspondance de Madame de Maintenon et de la princesse des Ursins* (Paris, 2002), particularly pp. 22–42.
[7] BL. Add MSS 20533, f. 419, princesse des Ursins to Gualterio, 6 November 1720. See also BL. Add MSS 31262, f. 72, Murray to Gualterio, undated.
[8] BL. Add MSS 20533, f. 421, princesse des Ursins to Gualterio, 20 November 1720.

principessa di Piombino and the midwife decided that the baby would be born during the following month.[9] It was necessary to decide who should be invited to the birth. The entire Albani family had already been invited in July, when the queen's pregnancy had first been announced,[10] as no doubt had James's other close friends. The princesse des Ursins recorded that she was invited shortly after her arrival, at the beginning of November.[11] The king, however, knew that he should also invite the leading members of the papal court, and consulted Cardinal Gualterio about who should be included.[12]

Acting on Gualterio's advice, James invited the governor and magistrates of the city of Rome. That, however, raised important questions of protocol, because the governor (Alessandro Falconieri) expected to be received in his official capacity *en cérémonie*. James had so far always made a point of receiving everyone, even the cardinals, without any ceremonial, and wanted to keep the occasion as informal as possible. So Sir David Nairne was sent to sound out the secretary of state, Cardinal Paulucci.[13] The latter agreed, and the governor was persuaded that it would be more convenient to drop all ceremonial, particularly as the queen might go into labour suddenly and give birth during the middle of the night.[14]

There was, however, another important point to be resolved. It was customary for the birth of a royal prince to be witnessed by a large number of people assembled in the queen's Bedchamber, and it was well known that aspersions had been cast upon James's own legitimacy because his father, James II, had reduced the number of people present at his birth. James III, however, decided to spare Clementina the ordeal of having a large crowd of people in her Bedchamber, believing that it was not necessary to see the actual birth. As Murray put it to Gualterio, 'as for the room in which we are to wait, the nature of the affair requires that everyone should be in the one that is beside the Queen's bed [chamber] such that they can hear her in labour'.[15]

As the queen's pregnancy neared its end the people who were expected to attend the birth were asked to be ready to come to the Palazzo del Re at short notice.[16] There was a false alarm on 30 December, and one Jacobite noted that several cardinals, the principessa di Piombino and three of her daughters, and some of the magistrates of

[9] *Ibid.*   [10] BL. Add MSS 31262, f. 50, Murray to Gualterio, 20 November 1720.
[11] BL. Add MSS 20533, f. 419, princesse des Ursins to Gualterio, 6 November 1720.
[12] BL. Add MSS 31262, f. 42, Murray to Gualterio, undated.
[13] BL. Add MSS 31262, f. 70, Murray to Gualterio, undated.
[14] BL. Add MSS 31262, f. 65, Murray to Gualterio, 4 December 1720.
[15] *Ibid.*   [16] McLynn, *Charles Edward Stuart*, p. 7.

Rome all arrived and had to be sent away again.[17] They all returned on the following day, and in the early evening the queen gave birth to a son named Charles, immediately created Prince of Wales.[18]

The account which was published in Rome a few days later gives the names of the more important people who assembled in the Palazzo del Re to hear the queen give birth. In effect it contains a list of all the people whom James and Clementina met socially at the Stuart court and elsewhere at this time. They include, in the order presented in the *Diario ordinario* (the weekly news pamphlet), don Carlo and donna Teresa Albani, the princesse des Ursins, the principessa di Piombino, four of her married daughters with their husbands, Cardinals Paulucci, Barberini (*primo prete*), Sacripanti, Aquaviva, Gualterio, Pamphili (*primo diacono*), Ottoboni, Imperiali and Albani, the Governor of Rome, Sebastiano Bonaventura (Bishop of Montefiascone) and members of many of the most important Roman families, including the Colonnas and the Ruspolis. The number of these people, when added to that of the Jacobite courtiers also present, amounted to about one hundred in all. An hour after the birth they all reassembled in and outside the Chapel Royal, where Bishop Bonaventura, specially summoned to Rome for the occasion, performed the sacrament of baptism.[19]

By February 1721 Queen Clementina had resumed her social life as the first lady of Rome. She was observed at the Aliberti opera house with her husband on the 11th. The people they had invited to join them included, as one might expect, principe Fabrizio Colonna, the principessa di Piombino and the princesse des Ursins.[20]

During 1721 the death of Clement XI brought many cardinals to Rome to attend the conclave which elected Innocent XIII. Among them was Cardinal de Rohan, whom James had known in France, and whom he now entertained at Albano.[21] French visitors were always made particularly welcome at the Stuart court, and this was the time when the abbé de Tencin began regularly to attend the Palazzo del Re.[22]

[17] Bod. Lib. Rawlinson MSS D. 1180, p. 193, Rawlinson's diary, 30 December 1720.
[18] McLynn, *Charles Edward Stuart*, p. 8.
[19] *Diario ordinario*, no. 544, 4 January 1721, pp. 2–8. The four married daughters of the principessa di Piombino who attended the birth were Costanza (wife of Vincenzo Giustiniani, principe di Bussano, called principe Giustiniani), Teresa (married to Urbano Barberini, principe di Palestrina), Giulia (married to Marco Ottoboni, duca di Fiano) and Anna (married to Gian Vincenzo Salviati, duca di Giuliano, called duca Salviati).
[20] Bod. Lib. Rawlinson MSS D. 1180, p. 270, Rawlinson's diary, 11 February 1721. Prince Colonna's wife had died of smallpox the previous August (SCA. BL 2/232/12, Stuart to Smith, 20 August 1720).
[21] BL. Add MSS 31264, f. 4, Hay to Gualterio, 29 July 1721.   [22] Chapter 1, p. 19.

In other respects, 1721 was a relatively uneventful year. James and Clementina went to Albano in the summer and autumn for their *villeggiatura*, and visited Nettuno in October to watch the fishing.[23] The end of the year, however, brought two important social occasions. On 31 December a large group of people, including twenty cardinals, visited the Palazzo del Re to compliment the king and queen on the first birthday of the Prince of Wales.[24] On the following day James and Clementina attended the celebrations in Rome of the betrothal of the Prince of Asturias (elder son of Philip V) to Princess Elisabeth of Orléans.[25] The rest of the carnival season was taken up with regular visits to the opera houses of Rome.[26]

During 1722 James III was increasingly preoccupied with the organisation of the Atterbury Plot, and his plan to disguise his own departure by sending Clementina to Bagni di Lucca. In May he took her to Albano, where they were joined by the princesse des Ursins, 'several Cardinals, Ministers and other people of rank'.[27] Back in Rome, they were able to witness the *Festa della Chinea*. This annual fête had been abandoned twenty years earlier, at the beginning of the War of the Spanish Succession, but was now revived on 28 and 29 June. It involved the payment by the Grand Constable of Naples of 'a white mare named *Chinea*' as feudal tribute from the King of Naples to the Pope.[28] The grand constable was James III's cousin and neighbour, principe Fabrizio Colonna:

A great procession accompanied him from the piazza dei Santi Apostoli to St. Peter's ... On the piazza dei Santi Apostoli ... facing the palazzo Colonna, was mounted a large 'machine', holding the fireworks that were to be let off once darkness fell ... After the spectacle, the fireworks were let off and the machine was set alight, applauded by the spectators. After that the people danced and ate sorbets all night long in the piazza, during which time in the brightly illuminated Colonna gardens a magnificent reception was organised, the most brilliant in the entire Roman season.[29]

The 'machine' was erected in the piazza immediately in front of the Palazzo Colonna, and therefore immediately in front of the galleries of the king and the queen in the Palazzo del Re. The annual *festa* was held during June in 1722, 1723, 1725 and 1726, though delayed until

[23] BL. Add MSS 31264, f. 17, Hay to Gualterio, 7 October 1721.
[24] *Diario ordinario*, no. 696, 3 January 1722, p. 12.
[25] Fagiolo, *Corpus delle feste a Roma*, vol. II, p. 42.   [26] Chapter 4, p. 84.
[27] NA. SP 85/14/f. 75, Stosch to Carteret, 30 May 1722.
[28] Fagiolo, *Corpus delle feste a Roma*, vol. II, p. 43.
[29] Maurice Andrieux, *La vie quotidienne dans la Rome pontificale au XVIIIe siècle* (Paris, 1962), pp. 167–8.

September in 1724 because of the death of Innocent XIII and the election of Benedict XIII.[30]

Queen Clementina left Rome for Bagni di Lucca in July 1722, and James followed her there in August, hoping to travel on to England and never return to Rome again. Their tour of central Italy, following the failure of the Atterbury Plot, provides us with another opportunity to observe their social relationships.

Having visited Florence, Bologna, Ferrara, Ravenna and Rimini,[31] James took Clementina to see Pesaro and Urbino, the cities in which he had lived when he first arrived in Italy. At Pesaro they stayed in the Palazzo Ducale with Alamanno Salviati. Then, on 14 October, they travelled up to Urbino with Salviati to stay in the Palazzo Albani with Cardinal Annibale Albani. That evening they went to the theatre in the Palazzo Ducale for a concert, consisting of 'a cantata by a composer from Bologna', sung by Paolo Mariani (called Paulino),[32] followed by the setting of a motet 'by another composer who was invited to come from Rome'. On the following morning James showed Clementina the apartment and rooms which he and the court had occupied on the first floor of the Palazzo Ducale, and then took her via the inner staircase to see the cathedral.[33] After lunch there was a concert in the Palazzo Albani, and in the evening they returned to the theatre for another performance organised by Cardinal Albani and the *Accademia Pascolini*. This time there was a play entitled *Nicomede*, preceded by the intermezzo *Le forze di Ercole*, which had been performed for the Stuart court in 1718.[34] It was followed by a ball, attended by the Electoral Prince of Saxony (the future King Augustus III of Poland), who was travelling in Italy and was specially invited by Cardinal Albani to meet James III.[35]

---

[30] Fagiolo, *Corpus delle feste a Roma*, vol. II, pp. 45, 49, 55 and 58.

[31] BL. Add MSS 31264, ff. 83 and 90, Hay to Gualterio, 19 September and 9 October 1722. During their visit to Bologna on 4 October, James and Clementina attended a solemn service in the Church of San Petronio to celebrate the festival of the city's patron. The occasion was recorded in a small painting by Leonardo Sconzani, reproduced as plate 6 in Maurizio Ascari, 'James III in Bologna: An Illustrated Story', *Royal Stuart Papers*, LIX (London, 2001).

[32] Paolo Mariani had previously performed for James III in 1718. See Corp, *Jacobites at Urbino*, p. 79.

[33] *Ibid.*, p. 39.   [34] *Ibid.*, pp. 80–1.

[35] Biblioteca Universitario d'Urbino, Fondo del Comune, b. 167, f. XI, pp. 291–3, 'La venuta in Urbino di Giacomo III Stuardi Re della Gran Brettagna, sua permanenza, et partenza; di poi suo ritorno di Passagio con la Regina sua Consorte. Malamente il tutto descritto da me Gio. Fortuniano Gueroli Pucci, bèn si la pura verità narrata, e senza alcuna alterazione descritta.' (For details of the surviving contemporary copies of the manuscript, see Corp, *Jacobites at Urbino*, p. 168, note 22).

On 16 October James and Clementina returned to Pesaro with Salviati, and then continued their journey via Sinigallia to stay with Cardinal Aquaviva at Ancona and with Cardinal Imperiali at Foligno.[36] By then the queen was keen to get back to Rome to see Prince Charles, so James cancelled a planned visit to Assisi and they returned directly to Rome. Meanwhile the elderly princesse des Ursins, who was not in good health, was expressing her hope that the king and queen would soon return so that she could 'pay court to them'.[37]

At the beginning of December the princesse des Ursins died, and James bought some of her *argenterie* and furniture to keep as a souvenir of her attendance at court.[38] He consoled his wife by taking her to Assisi.[39] It was at this time that he decided to give both the Garter and the Thistle to the Prince of Wales on the occasion of his second birthday.[40] The ceremony was held in the Chapel Royal of the Palazzo del Re on Christmas Day, attended by virtually all the cardinals resident in Rome.[41]

By 1723 it was clear that the Stuart court would have to remain in Rome for much longer than originally expected, and the lives of James and Clementina settled into a regular pattern. That year, opera performances during the carnival season were followed by Lent, and then by the first of many hunting trips to the estates of Prince Rospigliosi: to Macarese near Civita Vecchia in the spring,[42] and to Zagarolo to the east of Rome (south of Tivoli) in the autumn.[43] At the end of May the king and queen went to Albano and planned to go from there to visit Cardinal Gualterio at his villa at Corgniolo, near Orvieto. Their plans were upset by the news of the death of Clementina's elder sister Casimira,[44] so James left his wife at Albano and went to Corgniolo without her.[45] Passing through Viterbo he was met by don Carlo Albani and his brother Cardinal Annibale, who had come from their estates nearby. Don Carlo announced that his wife had given birth to a son, and

[36] BL. Add MSS 31264, f. 93, Hay to Gualterio, 19 October 1722.
[37] BL. Add MSS 20533, f. 428, princesse des Ursins to Gualterio, 14 October 1722.
[38] BL. Add MSS 31266, f. 194, Hay to Gualterio, undated (December 1722).
[39] ASV. Fondo Benedetto XIV 23, p. 234, 'Ricevimento delle Maesta Reali d'Inghilterra', September 1747.
[40] RA. SP 64/58, James III to Lansdowne, 27 December 1722.
[41] NA. SP 85/14/f. 207, Stosch to Carteret, 26 December 1722. The only cardinals in Rome who did not attend were Cienfuegos (the Imperial ambassador) and Alberoni.
[42] Bod. Lib. Rawlinson MSS D. 1183, pp. 1565–6, Rawlinson's diary, 19 and 22 April 1723; NA. SP 85/14/ff. 324 and 328, Stosch to Carteret, 20 and 24 April 1723.
[43] NA. SP 85/14/f. 502, Stosch to Carteret, 6 November 1723.
[44] BL. Add MSS 31265, f. 4, Hay to Gualterio, 3 June 1723.
[45] NA. SP 85/14/f. 362, Stosch to Carteret, 8 June 1723.

James agreed that he might be baptised in the Chapel Royal in the Palazzo del Re.[46] The ceremony took place on the 17th. The king and queen returned from Albano to hold the baby at the font, after which James gave a dinner for all the guests.[47]

The *Festa della Chinea* took place at the end of the month, and James added to the splendour of the occasion by having the south side of the Palazzo del Re illuminated by twenty torches.[48] On 4 July there was another important social occasion which allows us to appreciate the important role played by the exiled king and queen in Roman society. This was the wedding of the principessa di Piombino's remaining unmarried daughter to the principe di Santobuono, in the presence of 'all the Cardinals, Priests, and Ministers of the Spanish and French Factions'.[49] Once again, the official report in the *Diario ordinario* gives us the names of those members of Roman society closest to the Stuarts, and allows us to imagine James and Clementina holding court in the papal city, surrounded by their retinue. The service was conducted by Cardinal Aquaviva, and attended by Gualterio, Ottoboni and many other (unnamed) cardinals. In addition to the families of the bride and groom, we are specifically told that the Salviatis were present. James and Clementina hosted the marriage and provided them all with a meal after the ceremony, and in the evening accompanied them as guests of honour to the gardens of the Villa Ludovisi for the performance of a serenata *a tre voci*, followed by a supper illuminated by torches.[50]

The hot month of August found the Stuarts once more in the position of honour at one of the major Roman festivities. Each Sunday the Piazza Navona was flooded with water and transformed into a lake, through which people rode their horses and drove their carriages, and where the common people could enjoy a *gala nautique*.[51] The Spanish church was situated on the south-east side of the piazza, and was used on this occasion by Cardinal Aquaviva to pay tribute to the Stuarts. We have the following description:

the Piazza Navona had been flooded with water for the people's amusement, as happened every Sunday in August in Rome. In front of a house belonging to the

[46] BL. Add MSS 31264, f. 108, Hay to Gualterio, 12 June 1723.
[47] BL. Add MSS 31264, f. 111, Hay to Gualterio, 19 June 1723; NA. SP 85/14/f. 374, Stosch to Carteret, 19 June 1723.
[48] *Diario ordinario*, no. 925, 3 July 1723, p. 19.
[49] NA SP 85/14/ff. 388 and 394, Stosch to Carteret, 3 and 10 July 1723. The principessa di Piombino's youngest daughter, Lavinia, married Marino Caracciolo, principe di Santobuono.
[50] *Diario ordinario*, no. 926, 10 July 1723, pp. 6–8.
[51] Andrieux, *Vie quotidienne dans la Rome pontificale*, p. 170.

Spanish national Church of Saint James two magnificent thrones covered in red damask and trimmed with gold braid had been erected for [the king and queen], on a Royal dais of the same fabric.

James and Clementina sat on their thrones on the balcony surveying the scene below, and occasionally joined the crowd by getting into their coach and being driven around the piazza.[52]

Late summer was spent *en villeggiatura* at Albano with the principessa di Piombino, exchanging hospitality with the cardinals and other princes who had villas in the area.[53] Then in the autumn, during the hunting season, there were two more social events. On All Saints' Day, as reported in the *Diario ordinario*, the parish church of 'S. Ivo della Nazione Britannica' at the Sapienza was lavishly decorated for a solemn sung mass 'with excellent music, and numerous instruments'.[54] This was followed on 13 December by the annual dinner for 150 people at the French embassy to celebrate the conversion of James III's great-grandfather, Henri IV.[55]

Mention might also be made here of two priests who joined the circle of people associated with the Stuart court during 1723. The first was Diego de Revillas, 'physicist, meteorologist, human physiologist, cartographer, metrologist and classical topographer', who lived in a monastery on the Aventine Hill.[56] He recorded in his diary that James and Clementina visited him there in April 1723 to see his globes, and invited him back to the Palazzo del Re in July. Further visits followed, including one in November when James took Cardinal Ottoboni and the abbé de Tencin to see Revillas's scientific instruments.[57]

The other priest whom James met was François Foucquet, a French Jesuit who had served as a missionary in China from 1699 to 1722, and who was now living in the Palazzo di Propaganda Fide on the Piazza di Spagna.[58] They were introduced by Cardinal Gualterio, who invited

[52] NA. SP 85/15/f. 422, Stosch to Newcastle, 18 August 1725. This description was actually written two years later, but the thrones were erected for James and Clementina every August.

[53] NA. SP 85/14/f. 463, Stosch to Carteret, 25 September 1723.

[54] *Diario ordinario*, no. 979, 13 November 1723, pp. 2–3.

[55] Andrieux, *Vie quotidienne dans la Rome pontificale*, p. 182.

[56] Mary Pedley, 'The Manuscript Papers of Diego de Revillas in the Archive of the British School at Rome', *Papers of the British School of Rome*, LIX, pp. 319–24 (London, 1991), at p. 319.

[57] BSR. Revillas MSS F/84/2, 'Diario in Roma', 3 April, 11 July and 6 November 1723, 23 January 1724.

[58] Bruno Neveu, 'A Contribution to an Inventory of Jacobite Sources', pp. 138–58 in Eveline Cruickshanks (ed.), *Ideology and Conspiracy* (Edinburgh, 1982), at p. 142. See SCA. BL 2/275/5, T. Innes to Rokeby, 27 February 1725: 'P. Foucquet a French birly [code word for Jesuit] who hath passed many years in Chin and is one of the greatest masters of that language and customs. This man is quite opposite to his brother birlies and is therefore entertained by [the Pope] in the Prop[agan]da, and not in birly house.'

them both to dine with him in October. Foucquet's diary contains the following description: 'The dinner was served, we were only four at table: His Majesty, His Eminence, one of the King's gentlemen – an Irishman called Captain John O'Brien – and myself.' The conversation must presumably have been mainly in French, but nevertheless 'I noticed that the King speaks Italian very well and very fluently. Nothing could have been more agreeable and relaxed than his manner after the meal.' Coffee was served and the four men continued talking for another forty-five minutes. Then, 'the King discovered that I had never seen San Giovanni di Laterano or Santa Maria Maggiore and said that he would like to take me there'. Gualterio wanted to accompany them, and 'he was humble enough to wait outside these churches because he was wearing a short soutane and cardinals only enter these basilicas in long ones'.[59]

At the beginning of June 1724 James III lost one of his best friends and supporters when don Carlo Albani died.[60] However the conclave following the death of Pope Innocent XIII brought to Rome another man with whom he was to establish very close relations. This was Melchior de Polignac, whom James had nominated to be a cardinal in 1712.[61] He arrived in April,[62] and was appointed French ambassador to replace Tencin in June.[63] Stosch reported to London that the appointment of Polignac had been greeted at the Stuart court with 'extreme joy ... because he is believed to be more knowledgeable than Tencin about English affairs, and more likely to indulge in intrigues beyond the mountains, being imbued with maxims from the reign of Louis XIV'.[64] Even before the departure of Tencin in October, it was noticed that cardinals Aquaviva and de Polignac were now cooperating very closely with cardinals Gualterio, Ottoboni and Alberoni to further the interests of James and Clementina.[65] By the beginning of December Stosch noted that 'the close links with them [the Jacobites] enjoyed by the Spanish and French Ministers are becoming more evident every day, almost as if they were trying to make a point'.[66]

---

[59] BAV. Fondo Borgia Lat MS 565, f. 189, Foucquet's diary, 8 October 1723.
[60] BSR. Revillas MSS F/84/2, 'Diario in Roma', 2 June 1724; NA. SP 85/15/f. 129, Stosch to Newcastle, 3 June 1724.
[61] Corp, 'Nomination of Cardinals by James III', p. 162.
[62] BAV. Fondo Borgia Lat MS 565, f. 249, Foucquet's diary, 21 April 1724; Bod. Lib. Rawlinson MSS D. 1185; p. 2005, Rawlinson's diary, 24 April 1724.
[63] BSR. Revillas MSS F/84/2, 'Diario in Roma', 26 June 1724.
[64] NA. SP 85/155/f. 185, Stosch to Newcastle, 2 September 1724.
[65] NA. SP 85/15/ff. 190, 208 and 214, Stosch to Newcastle, 9 September, 28 October and 18 November 1724.
[66] NA. SP 85/15/f. 222, Stosch to Newcastle, 2 December 1724.

There was one other important social event during the second half of 1724. In September, a week after the *Festa della Chinea*, Benedict XIII consecrated the new church of the Santi Apostoli. James and Clementina missed the *festa* because the Palazzo del Re was being renovated at the time, but James came from Albano 'to see part of the function from a gallery in the Church', and then dined with Gualterio before returning.[67]

At the beginning of January 1725 the death of Cardinal Aquaviva deprived James and Clementina of another of their most active supporters.[68] Early in March, Queen Clementina gave birth to her second child, Prince Henry, Duke of York. The timing was unfortunate because the cardinals had gathered at the Vatican for a memorial service for Innocent XIII, and could not immediately come to the Palazzo del Re. It was noted that cardinals Gualterio, Imperiali, Albani and Alberoni, together with the Governor of Rome (Antonio Banquieri) and the treasurer of the *Camera Apostolica* (Carlo Collicola), broke away from the memorial service to be present at the birth. The principessa di Piombino was already there,[69] and we may assume that her daughters and sons-in-law, the Salviatis, and members of the Colonna, Ruspoli and Rospigliosi families were among the people gathered in the queen's antechamber. Cardinal Albani arranged for the cannons of the Castel Sant'Angelo to be fired[70] and, as already described, Pope Benedict XIII visited the Palazzo del Re later in the day to baptise the newly born prince in the Chapel Royal.[71]

In May, when Clementina had fully recovered from the birth, James took her to see Gualterio's villa at Corgniolo. They stayed en route at Caprarola,[72] and then travelled to Orvieto via Montefiascone,

---

[67] BAV. Fondo Borgia Lat MS 565, f. 271, Foucquet's diary, 17 September 1724; Bod. Lib. Rawlinson MSS D. 1185, p. 2075, Rawlinson's diary, 17 September 1724; NA. SP 85/15/f. 196, Stosch to Newcastle, 23 September 1724.

[68] Valesio, *Diario di Roma*, IV, p. 455, 8 January 1725; NA. SP 85/15/f. 247, Stosch to Newcastle, 13 January 1725. According to Valesio, James III visited him before he died and was seen crying as he left. According to Stosch, Aquaviva had employed spies to keep an eye on his (Stosch's) activities.

[69] Valesio, *Diario di Roma*, IV, p. 479, 6 March 1725.

[70] NA. SP 85/15/f. 314, Stosch to Newcastle, 10 March 1725.

[71] Chapter 1, p. 27. James III celebrated the birth by going with the Prince of Wales 'e tutte le Dame di suo corte' to the Irish Dominican Church of San Clemente to hear a sung *Tè Deum*, 'in rendimento di grazie all'Altissimo, per aver concessio alla Maestà Sua il Secondogenito Maschio' (*Diario ordinario*, no. 1191, 24 March 1725, pp. 13–14). A few days later the Holy Week 'grande procession de St. Marcello passa exprés devant le Palais ... (quoique cela fut hors du chemin) par ordre exprés de la Cour', i.e. the papal court (NA. SP 85/15/f. 326, Stosch to Newcastle, 31 March 1725).

[72] NA. SP 85/15/ff. 366, 370, 380, Stosch to Newcastle, 12, 17 and 26 May 1725.

where they had been married.[73] They were back in Rome for the *Festa della Chinea* in June.

During that summer James and Clementina began to anticipate that the pro-Hanoverian foreign policy conducted by the duc d'Orléans and his successor, the duc de Bourbon, might at last be about to change. They were encouraged by Cardinal de Polignac to believe that there might be a return to the foreign policy of Louis XIV, which would allow the Stuarts to return to France, which they felt would facilitate an eventual restoration to England.

The change seemed to be imminent because Louis XV was to marry Princess Maria Leszczynska, who was not only a cousin of Queen Clementina, but also the daughter of Stanislas Leszczynski, the exiled King of Poland. Polignac and the pro-Jacobite cardinals therefore hoped that she would use her influence to support the claims of the two exiled kings (her cousin's husband, and her own father) and to have the duc de Bourbon dismissed. Many people expected that Polignac, who had previously been French ambassador to Poland, would then be recalled from Rome to take charge of the new French government. He would reverse France's foreign policy and invite James III to return to his former home at Saint-Germain.

This new development was carefully watched by Baron von Stosch, the Hanoverian agent. In June 1725 he wrote that Polignac had informed Pope Benedict XIII of the marriage concluded between Louis XV and Maria Leszczynska, and that the Pope had immediately sent a messenger to congratulate James.[74] The possibilities which this opened up were seized upon by the Jacobites, and by August their hopes were running high. Stosch wrote that on 24 August, 'the eve of the Feast of St. Louis', James was at the Church of San Luigi dei Francesi, 'and he stayed for more than an hour talking to Cardinal de Polignac'. Stosch found it difficult to reconcile the apparently good relations between Versailles and London 'with the sincere and close friendship' between Polignac and James III.[75]

Stosch also reported the attitude of Queen Clementina: '[she] has told her close friends that very soon she and her husband will be living elsewhere . . . I think these are hopes raised by Cardinal de Polignac of their going soon to France, something that the Princess passionately longs for'.[76] By the beginning of September Stosch sounded seriously alarmed: 'I have learned that the marriage of the King of France to

[73] BL. Add MSS 31265, f. 50, Inverness to Gualterio, undated.
[74] NA. SP 85/15/f. 388, Stosch to Newcastle, 9 June 1725.
[75] NA. SP 85/15/f. 426, Stosch to Newcastle, 25 August 1725.   [76] *Ibid.*

the Polish Queen who is a relation of Princess Sobiesky has considerably raised the hopes of [James III] and his supporters,' and that the new Queen of France might be inspired with 'antipathy towards Monsieur le Duc Chief Minister of the same sort as that which was inspired in the new Parmesan Queen of Spain towards Madame des Ursins'.[77]

It was at this precise moment that a seemingly petty dispute arose between Cardinal de Polignac and the Imperial ambassador, Cardinal Cienfuegos. The reason for the dispute was a demand made by Polignac that he should be given a second box in the opera houses of Rome. The Imperial ambassador had two boxes because the Emperor Charles VI claimed also to be the *de jure* King of Spain, and Polignac demanded that there should be parity between the representatives of the Emperor, the King of France and King Philip V of Spain: either one box or two boxes each.[78] During the late summer of 1725 this became a major issue, and it was felt that only James III, who (as King of England, Scotland and Ireland) had the right to have three boxes, had sufficient influence to settle the dispute. James, however, had no formal diplomatic relations with the Imperial ambassador, so he entrusted the negotiation to his wife who, as a Sobieski princess, was closely related to the Holy Roman Emperor and was held in high esteem in Vienna. Stosch noted on 8 September that '[she] has gone to great pains to solve the differences between Cardinals Cienfuegos and Polignac'.[79] Clementina openly supported Polignac and rejected the arguments of Cienfuegos. On 7 September James and Clementina had a private audience with Benedict XIII, and a few days later Cienfuegos, 'seeing that the French succeed in obtaining everything they ask for, and that the Emperor is refused every request', apparently spoke to the Pope 'in a very angry tone'.[80]

While the issue hung in the balance Cardinal de Polignac and Cardinal Ottoboni (the Protector of France) decided to celebrate the anticipated political changes in France by commissioning the composition and performance of two serenatas. The wedding of Louis XV would be celebrated by Polignac with a serenata entitled *Senna, Fama, Amore e Imeneo* by the Venetian composer Francesco Gasparini. Polignac's appointment as chief minister, bringing about James III's return to Saint-Germain, would then

[77] NA. SP 85/15/f. 428, Stosch to Newcastle, 1 September 1725. See above, note 6.
[78] NA. SP 85/15/f. 422, Stosch to Newcastle, 18 August 1725.
[79] NA. SP 85/15/f. 432, Stosch to Newcastle, 8 September 1725.
[80] NA. SP 85/15/f. 436, Stosch to Newcastle, 15 September 1725.

be celebrated by Ottoboni with another work entitled *La Senna festeggiante* by another Venetian, Antonio Vivaldi.[81]

The first of the two planned celebrations took place on 25 September. James and Maria Clementina joined Cardinal de Polignac at the Church of San Luigi dei Francesi for a *Te Deum* and sung mass, after which 'the Minister of France offered large quantities of wine, and gave this famous Serenade, to which came [James III], his wife and 18 Cardinals and all the Roman nobility'.[82] According to Francesco Valesio, who described the celebration in his diary, the serenata by Gasparini 'was requested by the queen of England'.[83]

Everything was now ready for a performance of the second serenata by Vivaldi, once Polignac's appointment was announced. This, according to Stosch, seems to have been regarded as imminent. Then, at the beginning of October, very bad news was received in Rome. A new alliance had been signed between the governments of Great Britain and France, confirming that French foreign policy would remain pro-Hanoverian and anti-Jacobite. The new Queen of France had not acquired any significant political influence, the duc de Bourbon was not to be replaced, and Cardinal de Polignac was not to return to Versailles as the new chief minister. Stosch noted the surprise and disappointment felt in Rome: 'The court at Rome is at present seriously alarmed by the alliance signed in Hanover by the Kings of Great Britain, France and Prussia; Cardinal de Polignac has been spoken to most seriously.'[84] Under these circumstances Vivaldi's *La Senna festeggiante*, which celebrated the return of James III to a royal palace beside the river Seine, was no longer appropriate, and consequently Ottoboni's plans to perform it in the Palazzo della Cancelleria were quashed.

The social and political repercussions in Rome were significant. Although Cardinal de Polignac was nominated by Louis XV to the vacant archbishopric of Auch, by way of compensation, and retained as ambassador in Rome, Pope Benedict XIII was very angry with him for having misled so many people. He immediately showed his displeasure by supporting Cardinal Cienfuegos in the dispute concerning opera boxes.[85]

[81] Edward Corp, '*La Senna festeggiante* Reconsidered: Some Possible Implications of Its Literary Text', in Francesco Fanna and Michael Talbot (eds.), *Antonio Vivaldi, passato e futuro* (Venice, 2009), pp. 231–8.

[82] NA. SP 85/15/f. 440, Stosch to Newcastle, 29 September 1725. Also Fagiolo, *Corpus delle feste a Roma*, II, p. 57.

[83] Valesio, *Diario di Roma*, IV, pp. 582–3, 25 September 1725.

[84] NA. SP 85/15/f. 444, Stosch to Newcastle, 4 October 1725.

[85] NA. SP 98/32/f. 391, Stosch to Newcastle, 31 May 1732.

The impact on Clementina was even greater. She had become increasingly dissatisfied with the organisation of the royal household within the Palazzo del Re, and was bitterly opposed to the appointment of a Protestant to be the governor of her son. She had therefore longed to escape from an unsatisfactory situation in Rome by moving to France. Her hopes were now dashed, and she had to suffer the added disappointment of seeing the Pope reject her advice and support the Imperial ambassador in the dispute over opera boxes. She was so bitterly disappointed that she left her husband, withdrew from public life and took refuge in the Convent of Santa Cecilia in Trastevere.[86]

Roman society was inevitably divided in its attitude to the royal separation. The Pope actively supported the queen, as also did Cardinal Alberoni. The king's principal supporters were Cardinal Gualterio and Cardinal de Polignac. Meanwhile Cardinal Imperiali and the principessa di Piombino did everything they could to bring about a reconciliation, though to no avail.[87] At the end of November the abbé Foucquet, who had become an intimate friend,[88] had a long conversation with James, in which the latter spoke of 'the pain he felt at the decision of the Queen to retire to the convent of St. Cecilia'. Foucquet recorded in his diary that 'the King spoke with a moderation and wisdom that surprised me'.[89] But James was concerned about public opinion, and he cultivated good relations with his friends by increasing his entertaining. In December, for example, he gave a magnificent dinner to the duca di Cellamare, and it was noted that there were now 'very frequent entertainments at his palace'.[90]

It was at this time that Cardinal Alberoni advised Clementina that she would get more public support if she were to argue that her objection to Lord Dunbar's appointment as her son's governor was not so much because he was a Protestant, but because he, his sister Lady Inverness and his brother-in-law Lord Inverness were personally objectionable.[91] The tactic was successful, and it helped spread an unfounded rumour that James III was having an affair with Lady Inverness.

Christmas and the New Year gave Roman society the opportunity to show the king how much support he still had. A long list of '59 letters

---

[86] See above, Chapter 1, p. 28.
[87] NA. SP 85/15/ff. 460, 490, 510, 514, Stosch to Newcastle, 17 and 22 November, 6 and 15 December 1725; Valesio, *Diario di Roma*, IV, p. 607, 20 November 1725; BAV. Fondo Borgia Lat MS 565, f. 338, Foucquet to Ramsay, 2 January 1726.
[88] See particularly BAV. Fondo Borgia Lat MS 565, f. 317 and f. 322, Foucquet's diary, 22 March and 20 April 1725.
[89] BAV. Fondo Borgia Lat MS 565, f. 333, Foucquet's diary, 29 November 1725.
[90] NA. SP 85/15/f. 514, Stosch to Newcastle, 15 December 1725.
[91] NA. SP 85/15/f. 510, Stosch to Newcastle, 6 December 1725.

containing compliments and good wishes for the New Year received in December 1725 and at the beginning of 1726' has survived in the handwriting of Sir David Nairne.[92] Stosch reported to London in January that 'there is one thing I never will understand: the close and loyal friendship' between the king and Cardinal de Polignac, 'which goes beyond the limits of political dissimulation so natural to the French'.[93] Subsequent letters referred to their frequent 'secret meetings'.[94]

In May 1726 James paid another visit to Cardinal Gualterio at Corgniolo,[95] and invited him back to Albano the following month.[96] As Polignac was staying at Frascati at the same time there was plenty of opportunity for reciprocal entertaining.[97] The festivities continued after James returned to Rome, when the *Festa della Chinea* took place as usual in the Piazza dei Santi Apostoli. It was noted that the Palazzo del Re 'was illuminated at every window with torches of white wax, on the occasion of the festival ... given by the Constable (whose palace is adjacent to his own)'.[98]

By this time, however, the reduction in his papal pension was beginning to have a serious impact on James's finances. The summer of 1726 was spent planning the move to Bologna. It was significant that when the Stuarts finally left Rome they were joined for the first stage of the journey by two of James's closest friends who, though not salaried servants, should nevertheless be regarded as members of his court. The princes left on 30 September and were accompanied up the Via Flaminia as far as Civita Castellana by the principessa di Piombino and her son-in-law principe Giustiniani.[99] James himself left Rome two days later, having said farewell to Cardinal de Polignac, and also travelled to Civita Castellana. There he found his two sons waiting for him with the principessa and Giustiniani.[100] The principessa di Piombino returned to Rome, where she remained in regular contact with Queen Clementina, described by Stosch as 'her intimate friend'.[101]

Once James III was established in Bologna a new group of Italians began to attach itself to his court – as we shall see in Part II. Yet his Roman courtiers remained in contact and would again frequent his

[92] RA. SP 89/4.   [93] NA. SP 85/16/f. 18, Stosch to Newcastle, 19 January 1726.
[94] NA. SP 85/16/f. 28, Stosch to Newcastle, 16 February 1726.
[95] BL. Add MSS 31264, ff. 205, 206, Inverness to Gualterio, 1 and 11 May 1726.
[96] BL. Add MSS 31264, f. 215, Inverness to Gualterio, undated (June 1726).
[97] NA. SP 85/16/f. 81, Stosch to Newcastle, 18 May 1726.
[98] NA. SP 85/16/f. 104, Stosch to Newcastle, 6 July 1726.
[99] NA. SP 85/16/f. 151, Stosch to Newcastle, 28 September 1726.
[100] NA. SP 85/16/ff. 153, 157, Stosch to Newcastle, 3 and 5 October 1726.
[101] NA. SP 85/16/f. 380, Stosch to Newcastle, 27 March 1728.

court after his return in 1729. The principessa di Piombino even visited James III in Bologna on three occasions: in May and June 1727,[102] and in the spring of 1728, after James had returned from Avignon, when she and principe Giustiniani joined the king and queen there for two months.[103]

---

[102] Ghiselli, 15 May and 29 June 1727.
[103] Ghiselli, 10, 14, 21, 24 and 25 April, 22 May, 5 and 12 June 1728.

4   The Stuarts and Italian operatic life

A few references scattered through the surviving archives make it clear that musical concerts were organised at the Stuart court in Rome, as they had previously been at Saint-Germain-en-Laye.[1] The most famous of these is the comment by Charles de Brosses that 'once a week they have an exquisite concert: it's the best music in Rome'.[2] That comment, however, was written in 1739 or 1740, and will be discussed in a later chapter. We know very little about the concerts which took place between 1719 and 1726.

The Stuart accounts show that musicians, particularly singers, were employed at the court during these years. But the only musician who was paid on a regular basis was Innocenzo Fede, previously master of the music at Saint-Germain. He had remained with Mary of Modena until her death in May 1718, and never went to Urbino, but once he heard that the court had settled in Rome he quickly rejoined it. At that time he was fifty-nine years old. He was paid a monthly pension throughout the 1720s, and continued to receive it until his death in December 1732.[3] It is possible, even probable, that Fede was responsible for organising the concerts in the Palazzo del Re during these years.

Fede's family was well established in Rome, where two of his uncles had been castrati in the papal choir. His father, Antonio Maria, was a friend and agent of Arcangelo Corelli, with an estate at Tivoli, and had been made a *conte* by the Grand Duke of Tuscany.[4] Three of Fede's

---

[1] For the concerts at Saint-Germain, see Corp, *A Court in Exile*, pp. 204–5.

[2] Charles de Brosses, *Lettres d'Italie*, ed. Frédéric d'Agay (2 vols., Paris, 1986), vol. II, letter XL, p. 81.

[3] Fede's monthly pension is shown in RA. SP Misc 34 (1722), Box 3/81 (1726), 123/21 (1729), 136/53 (1729–30), 137/39 (1730), 151/107 (1731–2) and 158/41 (1732). A certificate of his death on 25 December 1732, signed by his cousin, Father Ippolito Desideri, SJ, is at RA. SP 158/41/16.

[4] Hans Joachim Marx, *Arcangelo Corelli, Historisch-Kritische Gesamtausgabe des Musikalischen Werke* (Cologne, 1980), pp. 30–2; Jean Lionnet, 'Innocenzo Fede', in *The New Grove Dictionary of Music and Musicians*, 2nd edn, ed. Stanley Sadie and John

surviving musical manuscripts can probably be dated to the early 1720s, shortly after his return to Rome.[5]

In a letter of December 1725 Baron von Stosch recorded that 'in the evening' James III 'gave a fine concert of music', and he added that 'there are very frequent entertainments in his palace'.[6] We may assume that the music performed during these concerts was whatever was fashionable in Rome at the time. It is easy to mention the sonatas and concerti of Corelli, and the cantatas of Alessandro Scarlatti, which had also been performed at Saint-Germain. But that is not very helpful. We need to look more closely at James III's musical taste, and also that of Queen Clementina, and our only information concerns opera.

The singer most favoured by James III at this time was the castrato Pasqualino Tiepoli, generally called Pasqualino or Pascolino, whom he had first heard at Fontainebleau in 1703, and again at Castel Gandolfo in 1717.[7] Since then the singer had been living as a hermit at Monteluco, near Spoleto, but James called him out of retirement in September 1719 to perform during his wedding celebrations at Montefiascone.[8] He then brought him to Rome. The court accounts contain payments to Pasqualino throughout 1720 and 1721.[9] The last payment in which he is named was for ten Spanish *pistoles* in January 1723, a substantial amount which was, for example, the amount of money paid to Girolamo Pesci a year earlier for his double portrait of the queen and the Prince of Wales.[10]

A few other singers are mentioned by name in the accounts, such as Jovanini (Tiburzio Giovanini), Formilino and don Angelico,[11] but unfortunately individual names were no longer included after 1723. In February 1722 an entry merely records that ten *pistoles* were 'given to musick two nights';[12] another of February 1724 mentions forty-one and

---

Tyrrell (London, 2001), vol. VIII, pp. 634–5; Edgar Peters Bowron, *Pompeo Batoni* (London, 1985), p. 49.

[5] BL. Add MSS 31476, ff. 26–7, *Laudate pueri Dominum* in A minor for four choirs; BL. Add MSS 31480, ff. 15–18, *Exurgat Deus* in D major for soprano, contralto, tenor and bass; BL. Add. MSS 31502, ff. 174–7, 'Vieni, ò caro', an aria for soprano.

[6] NA. SP 85/15/f. 514, Stosch to Newcastle, 15 December 1725. In March 1721 Viscount Rialton attended a concert in the Palazzo del Re, and described it as follows: 'a bright Assembly of the prime Roman Nobility, the Consort compos'd of the best Musicians in Rome, a plentiful and orderly collation served' (*A Letter from an English Traveller at Rome to His Father, of the 6th of May 1721. O.S.* (London, 1721), p. 9).

[7] Corp, *Jacobites at Urbino*, pp. 27, 138.

[8] RA. SP 45/71, James III to Sheldon, 26 October 1719.

[9] RA. SP Misc 32, account book, 1 January 1720 (8 *pistoles*), 23 May 1720 (5 *pistoles*), 27 June 1720 (5 *pistoles*), 2 October 1720 (6 *pistoles*), 29 October 1721 (10 *pistoles*).

[10] RA. SP Misc 34, account book. See Chapter 5, note 30.

[11] RA. SP Misc 32, account book, 23 May 1720 for Jovanini and Formilino; and 29 January 1721 for Don Angelico.

[12] RA. SP Misc 32, account book, February 1722.

a half *scudi* 'for Musitians'.[13] One outside source, however, records that in April 1723 Faustina Bordoni sang in the Palazzo del Re, 'where the usual audience was present, and she was given a gold medal, on one side of which was a portrait [of James III], and on the other a portrait of his wife'.[14] This was the medal struck by Ottone Hamerani to celebrate the king and queen's proxy marriage, worth fifty *scudi*.

In addition to these vocal or operatic concerts within the palazzo, there are occasional references to concerts attended by James and Clementina elsewhere. When the king first arrived in Rome we are told that he attended a *festa musicale* in his honour at the Palazzo Albani,[15] followed by a very good concert at the English College.[16] Rawlinson saw both the king and queen at the Church of the Jesù in December 1721 for a concert of very fine instrumental and vocal music.[17] Living so close they were probably present in April 1723 'at the primi vespri at the Church of Santi Apostoli, where sung the famed Cecchini and Pasqualini'.[18] They were probably also present in March 1725, two weeks after the birth of Prince Henry, at the Seminario Romano, where an oratorio entitled *Sant' Ermenegildo*, with music by Domenico Sarro, was 'sung by Paschalino, Farinelli, Domenichino and two others of base voice', accompanied by 'the best musick to be had in the city [including] the chief Violin, Base and Flute'.[19] During the same week James went with Prince Charles 'and all the ladies of his court' to the Church of San Clemente, where the Irish Dominicans organised a choral *Tè Deum* to thank God for the birth of a second Stuart prince.[20] These are merely examples, and perhaps others could be given, but they are enough to demonstrate how important musical entertainment was in the life of the Stuart court in Rome, both in and out of the Palazzo del Re. What they do not tell us is the style of music favoured by the king and queen, and performed in the palazzo.

James III had begun to appreciate Italian opera while he was at Urbino in 1718, and when the Stuart court arrived in Rome at the beginning of

---

[13] RA. SP 72/140, 'Form of a paper for the King to sign for his accomptant', February 1724.

[14] NA. SP 85/14/f. 320, Stosch to Carteret, 10 April 1723.

[15] Franco Piperno, '"Su le sponde del Tebro": eventi, mecenati e istituzioni musicali a Roma negli anni di Locatelli. Saggio di cronologia', pp. 793–877, in Albert Dunning (ed.), *Intorno a Locatelli: Studi in occasione del tricentenario della nascita di Pietro Antonio Locatelli (1695–1764)* (2 vols., Lucca, 1995), vol. II, at p. 849.

[16] BL. Add. MSS 31261, f. 300 and f. 303, Nairne to Gualterio, 28 December 1718 and 4 January 1719.

[17] Bod. Lib. Rawlinson MSS D. 1181, p. 692, Rawlinson's diary, 3 December 1721.

[18] *Ibid.*, D. 1183, p. 1568, 30 April 1723.

[19] *Ibid.*, D. 1185, p. 2137, 21 March 1725. This was part of a season of oratorios organised by Cardinal Ottoboni (Piperno, '"Su le sponde del Tebro"', pp. 873–4).

[20] *Diario ordinario*, no. 1191, 24 March 1725, pp. 13–14.

1719 it brought with it a considerable quantity of operatic music in manuscript. The composers represented were the ones who were then fashionable in Venice and Bologna, notably Francesco Gasparini, Giuseppe Maria Orlandini and Antonio Vivaldi.[21] The first two were already well known in Rome, because operas composed by them had been performed there in 1717 and 1718.[22] On the other hand, no opera by Vivaldi had been performed in Rome, and it is possible that it was the Stuart court which introduced his operatic (as opposed to his instrumental) music to the city.

The court also arrived in Rome at a particularly significant time, because Pope Clement XI had only recently agreed to allow operas to be performed in public theatres. The Teatro Capranica had reopened in 1717 with two operas by Gasparini, and the Teatro della Pace had reopened the same year with a pasticcio. In the following year a newly built theatre had been opened, to the north of the Piazza di Spagna, in the Via Margutta, immediately below the Villa Medici. Owned and managed by conte Antonio Alibert, it was called the Teatro Alibert or, more commonly, the Aliberti.[23] It was the biggest and the best of the three opera houses that now entered into rivalry to attract the favour of the Roman audiences.

It was agreed that the theatres would each put on two operas during future carnival seasons. In 1718, while James was at Urbino, the Capranica had staged one work by Alessandro Scarlatti (*Telemaco*), and another jointly composed by both Domenico Scarlatti and Nicola Porpora. These composers were associated at that time with the well-established and perhaps old fashioned Neapolitan style. The new Aliberti had compromised with one work in the 'old' Neapolitan style by Francesco Mancini and one in the 'new' Venetian style by Gasparini; and the Pace had followed suit with one work by Alessandro Scarlatti and one by Orlandini. The question which faced the Roman impresarios was which of these styles would prevail, and the debate was rife when James III and the Stuart court arrived in Rome.

The 1719 carnival season had, of course, been planned before it was known that James would bring his court to Rome. The Aliberti had prepared two new works by Gasparini, and the Pace had again followed suit with two works by another northern Italian composer, Giovanni

---

[21] Corp, *Jacobites at Urbino*, chapter 7.

[22] All information about the operas performed in Rome and elsewhere is taken from Claudio Sartori, *I Libretti italiani a stampa dalle origini al 1800*, six volumes and two volumes of Indici (Cuneo, 1990–4).

[23] Alberto De Angelis, *Il teatro Alibert o Delle Dame, 1717–1863* (Tivoli, 1951).

Bononcini. This time it was the Capranica which had compromised, with one opera by Alessandro Scarlatti to be followed later on with another by Carlo Francesco Pollarolo. The arrival of such a prestigious royal patron was bound to have an effect on public opinion, and James's reaction was awaited with some interest.

During January 1719 James went to all three opera houses on several occasions,[24] but it soon became clear that he preferred the Aliberti, as did 'most of Rome'.[25] The king's presence at the carnival, however, was cut short in February when he suddenly departed for Spain. It was the failure of the Spanish expedition, and his return to Rome in the autumn of that year with his new bride, Queen Clementina, which meant that the Stuarts became regular patrons of the Roman opera houses. There was thenceforth to be a symbiotic relationship, in which the Stuarts influenced the repertory of the Roman opera houses, but were themselves influenced in return by the style of music performed.

Soon after his arrival James became a formal patron of the Teatro Aliberti, where he chose three adjacent boxes for his permanent use.[26] This was an important political statement because foreign ambassadors were granted one box each in honour of the monarchs they represented. James's three boxes were not only a public acknowedgement of his royal status, but also a tribute to the fact that he was the legitimate monarch of the three kingdoms of England, Scotland and Ireland. Gratified, Count Antonio Alibert arranged that the libretto of every opera performed in his theatre should be dedicated either to James or to Clementina.[27]

---

[24] RA. SP Misc 32 records numerous payments for opera boxes and 'opera books' (i.e. libretti).

[25] BL. Add MSS 31261, f. 314, Nairne to Gualterio, 18 January 1719. See also *ibid.*, f. 311, Nairne to Gualterio, 11 January 1719; and BL. Add MSS 20298, f. 116, Nairne to Gualterio, 14 January 1719. Trevisani's portrait of the Duchess of Mar, in which an aria from Bononcini's *Erminia* is clearly visible on the harpsichord, suggests that she might have preferred the Pace.

[26] RA. SP 102/31, Ellis to Inverness, 27 January 1727. In an undated letter to Cardinal Gualterio, Murray explained that 'le Roy . . . ne s'embarrasse pas beaucoup si les loges qu'on propose luy donner sont vis a vis le theatre ou non', but added that 'S.M. les aimeroit mieux vis a vis le theatre qu'autrement, sans avoir egard a la situation de l'appartement' (BL. Add MSS 312363, f. 67, *c.*1720). The king liked to have an apartment in addition to his boxes. In one of the other theatres, where he only had one box, he gave priority to having his box beside the apartment. See BL. Add MSS 20292, f. 248, James III to Gualterio, undated: 'Je prends une loge a l'Opera au 3ᵉ etage pour le comodité d'un apartement qui en est a plein pied.' In this same letter James asked Gualterio to take the box beside his. For letters inviting Gualterio and other cardinals to join him *in* his box, see BL. Add MSS 31263, f. 175; 31265, ff. 167, 172; and 31266, f. 190, all undated.

[27] The operas dedicated to James III were Gasparini, *Amore e Maestà* (1720); Lotti and Porpora, *Artaserse* (1721); Predieri, *Sofonisba* (1722); Pollarolo, *Cosroe* (1723); Vinci,

James was invited to attend rehearsals and bring with him the English from the nearby Piazza di Spagna.[28]

James and Clementina were frequently to be seen at the opera. Half way through the 1720 carnival season James wrote to the Duke of Mar that 'the operas are mighty fine this year'.[29] At the end of that season he wrote again that he had seen 'no less than 21' performances of the six operas.[30] Clementina seems to have been equally enthusiastic.[31] Indeed, in December 1720, a few days before she gave birth to Prince Charles, Alibert even arranged for a special performance of Gasparini's *Faramondo* to be performed for her in the Palazzo del Re.[32]

James's royal status was publicly acknowledged in two privileges denied to others. No performance that he was expected to attend could start before his arrival, and once in his box he was permitted to sup. Baron von Stosch observed both of these on a single evening in January 1726: 'The overture had already been played, when an order was received from the Officer of the Guard that we shouldn't start until [the king] had arrived ... [He] later had supper in his box during the second act ... a prerogative accorded to him alone, and otherwise prohibited to all.'[33]

It was not only in the Teatro Aliberti that James was given such royal honours. Rawlinson has left us with a description of a performance of *Griselda* by Alessandro Scarlatti at the Teatro Capranica in February 1721:

Went this day to the Theater of Capronica, where we saw the opera of Griselida, played without any life or action, the songs sung so low as to be hardly heard, and the whole received without any extraordinary marks of satisfaction from the auditory: as soon as [James III] and his spouse entred a front box ... a young child representing a naked angel descended from the clouds or top of the Theater

---

Farnace (1724); Vinci, *Didone abbandonata* (1726); and Vinci, *Gismondo re di Polonia* (1727). Those dedicated to Clementina were Gasparini, *Faramondo* (1720); Porpora, *Eumene* (1721); Porpora, *Flavio Anicio Olibrio* (1722); Porpora, *Adelaide* (1723); Predieri, *Scipione* (1724); Sarro, *Il Valdemaro* (1726); and Porpora, *Siroe re di Persia* (1727).

[28] NA. SP 85/15/f. 520, Stosch to Newcastle, 29 December 1725; Valesio, *Diario di Roma*, IV, p. 620, 27 December 1725.

[29] RA. SP 46/7, James III to Mar, 3 February 1720.

[30] RA. SP 46/16, James III to Mar, 26 February 1720.

[31] NA. SP 85/16/f. 18, Stosch to Newcastle, 19 January 1726.

[32] Bod. Lib. Rawlinson MSS D. 1180, p. 192, Rawlinson's diary, 26 December 1720. According to the *Diario ordinario*, 4 January 1721, no. 544 (quoted in De Angelis, *Il teatro Alibert*, p. 137), 100 people were invited to attend the performance. One copy of the specially reprinted libretto has survived in a private collection, with a Spanish provenance.

[33] NA. SP 85/16/f. 18, Stosch to Newcastle, 19 January 1726.

holding a silver plate in which were two books of the opera, and papers of verse in favour of the author, which he presented to [James III] and his spouse who returned a present of gold into the plate: immediately after ... the curtain was drawn up by two more angels from the top of the stage. I could not but observe the respect paid to [James III] and his spouse, so that the opera began on their entry, and the curtain was lett down upon their exit.[34]

During the 1720s James III's musical taste began to evolve. At first he continued to prefer the northern Italian style, as represented by Gasparini. It is interesting to note that Vivaldi received his first commission from a Roman theatre (the Pace) immediately after the king's return from Montefiascone. As Vivaldi only provided the music for one act of a three act opera (*Tito Manlio*) which he had already set in its entirety elsewhere, it is possible that it was a last minute commission. After the 1720 season, when there had been two works by Gasparini at the Aliberti, a work by Orlandini and the one mentioned with music by Vivaldi at the Pace, and two by Alessandro Scarlatti at the Capranica, James wrote that 'there was four of the 6 that were really very fine'.[35]

From 1721 onwards, however, the Teatro Aliberti began to mount operas written in the new *galant* style from Naples.[36] As the libretti were all dedicated to James and Clementina, we may assume that was done with their approval, and it seems that James now enjoyed equally the northern Italian and the new Neapolitan styles. In 1721 there was a work by Nicola Porpora, then in 1722 one by Porpora and one by Luca Antonio Predieri. These two composers then took it in turns. In 1723 there was an opera by Porpora, followed in 1724 by another from Predieri. But the 1724 season at the Aliberti was special because it also included the first work to be performed in Rome by Leonardo Vinci, the greatest and most popular of all the composers working in the Neapolitan *galant* style. Another attraction was that all the four works at the Aliberti during 1723 and 1724 were performed by the rising star from Naples, the castrato Farinelli.

The other theatres responded by concentrating on the composers from northern Italy, notably Orlandini and Vivaldi at the Capranica.

---

[34] Bod. Lib. Rawlinson MSS D. 1180, p. 271, Rawlinson's diary, 12 February 1721.
[35] RA. SP 46/16, James III to Mar, 26 February 1720. According to Lowell Lindgren, 'Rome 1680–1730', *New Grove Dictionary of Opera*, ed. Stanley Sadie (4 vols., London, 1992), vol. IV, p. 26, until 1722 the Capranica 'featured works ... in an old-fashioned Baroque style'.
[36] In the '*galant*' style ... an unobtrusive orchestra supports (and often doubles) a virtuosic vocal line. This ... replaced the texture which had predominated at Rome in 1670–1722 and had featured polarised vocal and continuo lines, with motivic interplay frequently added by treble instruments' (Lowell Lindgren, 'Rome', *New Grove Music*, vol. XXI, p. 629).

Thus the highlights of the 1724 season were Vinci and the *galant* style at the Aliberti, and Vivaldi and his so-called 'Lombard' style at the Capranica. The Pace, which had actually been closed during the two previous seasons, reopened in 1724 with two new works dedicated to the Stuarts (so that four of the six works that year carried Stuart dedications). One of them, set by Philipo Falconi and dedicated to James, was significantly entitled *Ginevra principessa di Scozia*.[37]

There were no operas performed in Rome during the following carnival season because the new Pope, Benedict XIII, declared that 1725 should be an *anno santo*. It was feared that Benedict might go further and ban all future opera performances from public theatres, as had happened before 1717. This possibility was increased in the summer of that year when the quarrel about the allocation of opera boxes broke out between Cardinal de Polignac and Cardinal Cienfuegos.[38] On 7 September James and Clementina had a private audience with Benedict XIII, during which the queen 'gave to His Holiness a memorial supporting the opera entrepreneurs',[39] and shortly afterwards the Pope agreed that the 1726 carnival season should be allowed to take place.[40]

These events provide the background to an important episode in the career of Antonio Vivaldi, which has escaped the attention of all his biographers, and indeed of all those musicologists who have analysed his work. It concerns Vivaldi's serenata entitled *La Senna festeggiante*, which was composed in homage to James III and planned for performance in Rome during the autumn of 1725.[41]

Vivaldi had been commissioned by the Teatro Capranica to compose an opera for the 1723 season, but it was in 1724 that his music had a major impact in Rome. That year the Capranica performed not only one of his finest operas, *Il Giustino*, but also another for which Vivaldi had composed one of the three acts.[42] Johann Quantz, who was in Rome that spring, recorded that 'the latest novelty of which everyone

---

[37] The other work at the Pace, dedicated to Clementina, was Sarro, *Partenope*.

[38] See Chapter 3, p. 73.

[39] NA. SP 85/15/f. 436, Stosch to Newcastle, 15 September 1725. Stosch gives an incorrect date for this audience, which was also recorded in the *Diario ordinario*, no. 1263, 8 September 1725, p. 12.

[40] NA. SP 98/32/f. 391, Stosch to Newcastle, 31 May 1732.

[41] See Chapter 3, p. 74. Until now it has been assumed that *La Senna festeggiante* was probably composed for a performance in Venice in 1726. See Michael Talbot and Paul Everett, 'Homage to a French King: Two Serenatas by Vivaldi (Venice, 1725 and ca. 1726)', the introduction to Antonio Vivaldi, *Due serenata*, facsimile edition (Venice, 1995), pp. ix–lxxxvii.

[42] The opera was *La virtù trionfante dell'amore e dell'odio*. Vivaldi composed the second act, entitled *Il Tigrane*.

speaks is what has been called the "Lombard" style, which was quite new to me, and which was introduced to Rome some little time before by Vivaldi in one of his operas. The public was so enthusiastic that it virtually refused to hear anything that did not resemble this style.'[43] This was an exaggeration, because 1724 was also the year which witnessed Leonardo Vinci's first success in Rome. But Vivaldi also composed instrumental music, and 1724 saw the publication of his Opus 8 violin concerti, *Il cimento dell'armonia e dell'invenzione*, including the overwhelmingly successful 'Quattro stagioni'.[44] Although there is a total lack of documentation, it would seem very likely that the Teatro Capranica would have commissioned another opera from Vivaldi if Benedict XIII had not declared 1725 an *anno santo* and closed all the opera houses. It was under these circumstances that Cardinal de Polignac decided to commission Vivaldi to compose a serenata in honour of James III.[45]

The text, divided into two acts, contains three allegorical characters. Apart from La Senna (the river Seine), they are L'Età dell'Oro (the Golden Age of Louis XIV) and La Virtù (Virtue). Virtue, of course, represents James III.

Virtue and the Golden Age have been forced to wander far and wide, but they now return in Act One to be greeted by the Seine in a royal palace (*reggia del piacer*) beside the river – an obvious reference to the Château de Saint-Germain. In the second act they decide to go to see Louis XV (*il gran regnante*) at Versailles (*il bel ricco edificio ove risiede*). The text, superficially a work of homage to Louis XV, has been carefully written to avoid any possible confusion as to its true intent. The audience at the time would have known perfectly well that there were only two royal palaces beside the Seine, Saint-Germain and the Tuileries (connected to the Louvre), which had been abandoned in favour of Versailles by Louis XV in 1722. Therefore, the Seine celebrating the return of Virtue and the Golden Age to a royal palace on its banks, followed by a visit to Louis XV at Versailles, could only be referring to a revival of the traditional pro-Jacobite foreign policy, which would allow James III to return to Saint-Germain.

---

[43] Frédéric Delaméa, 'Giustino, Vivaldi's Last Roman Triumph', booklet to accompany the recording of *Il Giustino* by Il Complesso Barocco, conducted by Alan Curtis (EMI Records, Virgin Classics, 2002), pp. 10–11.

[44] There is very little documentary evidence concerning Vivaldi's visits to Rome, but it is known that he performed for James III's cousin, principessa Diana Colonna, at the Palazzo Colonna in the Piazza dei Santi Apostoli. See Roland de Candé, *Vivaldi* (Paris, 1967, 2nd edn 1994), p. 76.

[45] See Chapter 3, p. 74.

The serenata has been described as 'Vivaldi's grandest and best secular vocal work', with an 'unusually heavy concentration in it of French (or supposedly French) stylistic traits'.[46] But the libretto was never printed, and the serenata was never performed, because of the news that France and Great Britain had signed a new alliance.[47] It is for this reason that its origins have remained unknown until now.

Vivaldi never returned to Rome, and none of his operas was ever performed there again, but the 1726 carnival opera season went ahead as planned. As usual the Aliberti dedicated both its operas to James and Clementina (though she had just retired to the convent in Trastevere). It was noticeable that of the four works performed at the Aliberti and the Capranica (the Pace remained closed) three, including both at the Aliberti, were new works in the Neapolitan 'galant' style, by Vinci, Sarro and Leonardo Leo.

It is clear, then, that by 1726 the Stuarts had had a significant impact on operatic life in Rome, though James III's own taste had evolved in the process. The operas performed in Rome were, of course, attended by the many Grand Tourists, Jacobite or Hanoverian, who visited the city during the carnival seasons. We therefore need to consider what influence these works might have had on the Royal Academy of Music in London, which was founded in 1719 and which continued to mount operas during most of the period covered by the present chapter.[48]

No organisation that mounted Italian operas in Protestant England during the 1720s could avoid being influenced by what was happening in Rome. 'In its early years, the Academy had two internal, political factions: the opposition party – Jacobite, Catholic and Italian, represented by composer Giovanni Bononcini and librettist Paolo Rolli – and the court party, represented by Handel and the librettist Nicola Haym.'[49] Although Bononcini and Rolli were both dismissed from the

---

[46] Michael Talbot, booklet to accompany the recording of *La Senna festeggiante* and *Gloria e Imeneo* by the King's Consort, conducted by Robert King (Hyperion Records, 2002), p. 10.

[47] Edward Corp, '*La Senna festeggiante* Reconsidered: Some Possible Implications of Its Literary Text', in Francesco Fanna and Michael Talbot (eds.), *Antonio Vivaldi, passato e futuro* (Venice, 2009), pp. 231–8.

[48] Elizabeth Gibson, *The Royal Academy of Music, 1719–1728: The Institution and Its Directors* (New York and London, 1989).

[49] Ellen T. Harris, 'With Eyes on the East and Ears in the West: Handel's Orientalist Operas', *Journal of Interdisciplinary History*, 36:3 (Winter, 2006), pp. 419–43, at p. 429. See also Carole M. Taylor, 'Italian Operagoing in London, 1700–1745' (Syracuse University Ph.D. thesis, 1991), p. 133: 'Political issues were obviously more dilute for the opera house than for Parliament, yet the Jacobite/Whig divide was a fact of life and Bononcini and Handel landed into the two respective camps, albeit in a quasi-political fashion.'

company in 1722, for political reasons, and Handel ultimately became the academy's dominant composer, it has recently been argued that 'the directors probably selected many, if not most of [their] librettos with an eye toward analogies with events in the news ... opera audiences (like theater audiences) were ready to make connections'.[50] The libretti did not necessarily reflect the political opinions of the composers, but they *were* intended to be topical and to attract attention or even notoriety.

It is therefore worth observing that nine of Handel's operas from the period 1722–37 were settings of libretti previously performed in Rome in 1719–27, seven of which had been specifically dedicated to James III and Clementina.[51] In addition Handel arranged a pasticcio based on works by Leonardo Vinci which had been first performed in Rome.[52] Of these ten works (nine new compositions and one pasticcio), six had been performed at the Teatro Aliberti. To this list we might also add six works by Ariosti and Bononcini, including the latter's *Erminia* (shown in Trevisani's portrait of the Duchess of Mar), which had previously been performed in Rome.[53]

The subject matter of these libretti was important. During the 1718 carnival season a Jacobite wrote from Rome that the operas were mainly concerned with 'dethroning usurpers and restoring lawful kings'.[54] Recent research on the subject has revealed the following, as summarised by Ellen Harris:

two-thirds of the librettos written between 1640 and 1740 depict western, principally Roman, themes. The remaining one-third, about 270 librettos, has Persian or eastern settings ... [and can be divided] into two categories. The chronologically earlier group consists of fictional ... stories set in ancient Medea ... and Persia, as well as in ... bordering countries ... they tend to

---

[50] Harris, 'With Eyes on the East and Ears in the West', p. 434.

[51] The seven operas previously dedicated to the Stuarts were *Flavio* (1723), *Scipione* (1726), *Siroe* (1728), *Lotario* [i.e. *Adelaide*] (1729), *Partenope* (1730), *Ariodante* [i.e. *Ginevra principessa di Scozia*] (1735) and *Faramondo* (1738): see above, note 27. The other operas were *Arminio* (1737; A. Scarlatti, 1722) and *Giustino* (1737; Vivaldi, 1724). Handel also set operas previously performed in Rome after 1727: see Chapter 13, p. 275.

[52] *Didone abbandonata* (Vinci, Rome, 1726; Handel, London, 1737). Handel also created pasticcios based on operas previously set by Vinci in Rome after 1727: see Chapter 13, p. 275.

[53] The list of operas performed in London is given in Taylor, 'Italian Operagoing in London', pp. 340 ff. See also *ibid.*, p. 129: 'Three of Bononcini's eight operas new to London were revivals of continental works by him first heard in Rome ... These works, completely new to non-travellers, functioned in some sense also as revivals for those who had heard the works abroad.' For a letter sent to the Duchess of Mar in 1723 by her sister, who had just seen Bononcini's *Erminia* in London, see Gibson, *Royal Academy of Music*, pp. 171–2, 180.

[54] HMC *Stuart*, v, p. 405, Redmond to Mar, 26 January 1718.

feature a heroine or Amazon protagonist and focus on the consolidation or restoration of a legitimate regency through marriage. The group that followed comprises semihistorical ... stories of a later period largely about dynastic succession and just lineage in Asiatic and Mediterranean monarchies.[55]

Both of the categories with Persian or eastern settings, but particularly the second, lent themselves to a Jacobite interpretation, and the operas dedicated to the Stuarts in the last twenty years covered by this survey naturally fall mainly within this group.[56] It is interesting to observe that Handel's operas for the Royal Academy of Music concentrate on eastern settings, for example *Scipione* (Predieri, Rome, 1724; Handel, London, 1725–6) and *Siroe* (Porpora, Rome, 1727; Handel, London, 1727–8).

If the general theme of operas performed at the Aliberti was the triumph of good over evil, the reward for patience and the restoration of legitimate monarchy, the best examples in Handel's work for London are *Floridante* (1721–2) and *Lotario* (1729). The latter concerns the usurpation of a crown, the defeat of the usurper and the restoration of a rightful monarch. Entitled *Adelaide*, the same libretto had been dedicated to Clementina, set by Porpora and performed at the Aliberti in 1724. *Floridante* had been set by Vivaldi as *La constanza trionfante*, and performed for James at Fano in 1718. It concerns the imprisonment of the rightful king by a usurper, and was specially requested by the Jacobite faction of directors of the Royal Academy for the 1721–2 season, following the South Sea Bubble. The printed libretto carried an epigraph which stated that the 'arguments are drawn not merely from admitted fact, but from fictitious suppositions'! We have a contemporary description of one of the first performances in a letter dated 19 December 1721, the very week that Hamerani's 'Unica Salus' medal arrived in London:

Some things have happened at a new opera which have given great offence. It is called *Floridante*. There happens to be a right heir in it, that is imprisoned. At last the right heir is delivered and the chains put upon the oppressor. At this last circumstance, there happened to be a very great and unseasonable clapping, in the presence of the great ones.[57]

Until 1726 the reigning prima donna in London was Francesca Cuzzoni, but that year the Royal Academy also hired Faustina Bordoni, the singer who had been given a gold medal by James III for a performance in the Palazzo del Re. The presence of these two women in London,

---

[55] Harris, 'With Eyes on the East and Ears in the West', p. 428.   [56] *Ibid.*, pp. 428–9.
[57] Gibson, *Royal Academy of Music*, pp. 155–6. See also Eveline Cruickshanks and Howard Erskine-Hill, *The Atterbury Plot* (Basingstoke, 2004), p. 85, for a similar report to Paris from the French diplomat Chammorel.

and the overt rivalry between them, emphasised the connection between the Stuarts and Italian opera. An anti-Jacobite pamphlet, which refers to James III as 'the Pretender', was published in London to draw attention to the dangers being run by the Royal Academy in inviting these Catholic Italian opera singers:

1. They come from Rome:
2. The Pope lives at Rome:
3. So does the Pretender.
4. The Pope is a notorious Papist;
5. So is the Pretender,
6. So is Madam Faustina,
7. And so is Madam Cuzzoni.
8. King George ... is a Protestant;
9. The Papists hate the Protestants;
10. The Pope hates King George;
11. The Pretender can't abide him.
12. But Madam Cuzzoni and Madam Faustina love the Pope, and in all Probability the Pretender.

The conclusion, as the author of the pamphlet pointed out, was 'that it is not safe to have Popish Singers tolerated here, in England',[58] and that the involvement of the Stuarts with Italian opera had ramifications which went well beyond Rome and the Jacobite court. This last point was to be made even more clear by the career of the castrato Farinelli.

When James III decided to move from Rome to Bologna in the autumn of 1726 the opera seasons for the carnival of 1727 had already been planned,[59] and the king's boxes had already been reserved.[60] The Teatro Aliberti had commissioned new operas from Vinci (*Gismondo re di*

---

[58] *The Devil to Pay at St. James's*, quoted in Gibson, *Royal Academy of Music*, p. 427. Cuzzoni and Faustina sang in Handel's *Alessandro* with the castrato Senesino. In June 1726, just before the planned last performance, Senesino announced that he was unwell and would return to Italy to recover his health. He was still in Venice when James III and his court moved from Rome to Bologna that October. He had been given a letter by the Hanoverian Princess of Wales to deliver to the principessa Violante (sister-in-law of the Grand Duke of Tuscany), but disobliged her by not doing so, even though he passed through Florence on at least two occasions. He had also been asked to return to London in the autumn for the new opera season of the Royal Academy, but could not be persuaded to leave until December, because he claimed that he did not yet feel well enough. It was noted, however, that he was well enough to visit Bologna on 6 November. See David Hunter, 'Senesino Disobliges Caroline, Princess of Wales, and Princess Violante of Florence', *Early Music*, 30 (May 2002), pp. 215–23, at p. 219; and Gibson, *Royal Academy of Music*, pp. 239–42, 370.

[59] Gibson, *Royal Academy of Music*, McSwiny to Richmond, 31 May 1726: 'I think I told your Grace in my last letter that He [Farinelli] was engaged to Sing in one of the Theatres of Rome.'

[60] RA. SP 102/31, Ellis to Inverness, 27 January 1727.

Polonia) and Porpora (*Siroe re di Persia*), dedicated respectively to the king and the queen.[61] The Capranica had commissioned new works by Giovanni Costanzi (*L'amor generoso*) and Leonardo Leo (*Il Cid*). Farinelli, who had performed in all four operas dedicated to the Stuarts at the Aliberti in 1723 and 1724, had this time been engaged to sing in both the operas at the Capranica. It promised to be another successful season.

Bologna, by contrast, had a much less interesting programme on offer. The city contained five theatres, of which only two, the Formigliari and the Marsigli-Rossi, had planned opera seasons for the forthcoming carnival. According to the diary of Antonio Francesco Ghiselli, none of the operas was well received.[62] An attempt was then made by the Teatro Formigliari to please James III by adding a new intermezzo by Orlandini. This was a setting of Molière's *Monsieur de Pourceaugnac*, entitled *Monsieur di Porsugnacco* but sung in French.[63] During May the theatre engaged a troupe of 'Ballarini da Corda [Rope] Francesi e Inglesi' as another obvious tribute to the Stuart court.[64] It is interesting to note that conte Girolamo Formigliari was given an appointment at the court a few weeks later.

Neither of these spectacles was a substitute for the top-quality operas starring Farinelli and others that James III would have experienced if he had remained in Rome. During March 1727, therefore, the Teatro Malvezzi in Bologna commissioned a new opera by Orlandini to be performed for the king during the early summer, and engaged Farinelli to come from Rome to take one of the leading parts.

The directors of the theatre were conte Sicinio Pepoli, who was married to James's cousin Eleonora Colonna, marchese Marcantonio Ranuzzi and conte Angelo Ranuzzi, whose wife was also given an appointment at the Stuart court. Letters have survived from both Constable Fabrizio Colonna and Cardinal Carlo Colonna, who lived beside the Palazzo del Re in the Piazza dei Santi Apostoli, asking Pepoli to take

---

[61] RA. SP 104/57, Ellis to Inverness, 26 February 1727. In this letter Ellis stated that he had written 'to thank March.se Macarani for the new Aliberti opera, and letter, which he sent to His Ma.tie'.

[62] Biblioteca Universitaria di Bologna MS 770, vol. 91, unpaginated, the diary of Antonio Francesco Ghiselli (hereafter Ghiselli), 28 December 1726, 11 and 15 January 1727. The operas at the Formigliari were Francesco Pistocchi, *La risa di Democrito* (first performed at Vienna in 1700), and Giuseppe Maria Buini, *Albumazar* (Corrado Ricci, *I teatri di Bologna nei secoli XVII e XVIII* (Bologna, 1888), p. 430). It is not known which work or works were performed at the Marsigli-Rossi.

[63] According to Sartori, the intermezzo was also performed in Venice and Milan during 1727, but he makes no mention of the performances in Bologna, where James III would not himself have needed a libretto. Ghiselli noted that the singing in French was full of mistakes (29 January 1727).

[64] Ghiselli, 17 and 31 May 1727.

Farinelli under his protection.[65] What was so special about the opera was that, as a special compliment to James III, the other leading role was taken by another great castrato, the Bolognese Antonio Bernacchi, who had been performing in Munich and returned at Pepoli's special request.[66]

The opera, entitled *La fedeltà coronata*, opened in the Teatro Malvezzi at the beginning of June 1727. The appearance of two such great singers in the same work was exceptional. As one historian put it, 'the public went in their hundreds to the Malvezzi theatre to watch the confrontation between one singer who was adulated by his fellow citizens and who had fifteen years of success behind him, and the young Farinelli, twenty years his junior and still at the beginning of his career though already a legend'.[67] James III, for whom the opera had been commissioned, had been about to leave Bologna for his *villeggiatura* at the nearby Villa Alamandini, but he decided to attend every performance. This meant delaying his *villeggiatura*, and then returning to the city in the evening whenever the work was put on.[68] The run of performances was still continuing when James heard of the death of George I at the beginning of July and hastily left for Lorraine.[69]

For Farinelli, 'the trip to Bologna marks the great turning-point in his career ... the leap forward which carried his reputation beyond the Italian frontiers'.[70] Thenceforth Pepoli remained permanently his protector and then his friend, which meant that Farinelli, who now lived in Bologna when not performing elsewhere, was drawn into the politics of Jacobitism.[71] This had an impact on the Royal Academy of Music in London, which was closed for the 1728–9 season. Because Senesino refused to return to London, Handel had to go to Italy to recruit a new castrato. Hearing that James III had just returned to Rome, Handel visited Bologna in March 1729 hoping to persuade Farinelli to come to London. The singer refused even to see him.[72] Handel then travelled to

---

[65] Carlo Vitali, 'Da "schiavottielo" a "fedele amico": Lettere (1731–1749) di Carlo Broschi Farinelli al conte Sicinio Pepoli', *Nuova rivista musicale italiana*, 26:1 (1992), pp. 1–36, at pp. 33–4.

[66] Ghiselli, 31 May 1727.

[67] Patrick Barbier, *Farinelli: Le castrat des lumières* (Paris, 1994), p. 36.

[68] Ghiselli, 4, 14 and 21 June, and 5 July 1727.

[69] The opera was performed until the end of July (Ghiselli, 26 July 1727).

[70] Barbier, *Farinelli*, p. 36.

[71] Edward Corp, 'Farinelli and the Circle of Sicinio Pepoli', *Eighteenth Century Music*, 2:2 (September 2005), pp. 311–19.

[72] Gibson, *Royal Academy of Music*, p. 283, Burges to Newcastle, 20 January 1730. Antonio Bernacchi, on the other hand, agreed to meet Handel and accepted his invitation to become the *primo uomo* at the Royal Academy.

Rome, where he in turn declined an invitation from Fabrizio Colonna because he knew that James III would be with his cousin.[73] A few years later Farinelli would join the Opera of the Nobility with Senesino in a conscious attempt to break Handel's monopoly of opera in the Hanoverian capital.

Farinelli's patron Sicinio Pepoli was particularly friendly with a Bolognese family named Albergati, which included the composer Francesco Albergati Capecelli (1663–1735). Pepoli's first cousin Eleonora, with whom he was described as an 'inseparable couple', was married to marchese Luigi Albergati, and it is worth noting that the latter's nephew marchese Fabio Albergati was also given an appointment at the Stuart court in the summer of 1727. The symbiotic relationship therefore continued, with James's presence in Bologna having a significant influence on the performance of opera in the city, yet with the musical connections which were thereby formed resulting in the recruitment of three Italians (Formigliari, Ranuzzi and Albergati) to join the Stuart court.[74]

James III's departure from Bologna meant that nothing special was planned for the 1728 carnival season: two new operas by Buini at the Teatro Marsigli-Rossi, and a revival of an old pastorale by Giuseppe Aldrovandini at the Teatro Angelelli.[75] His unexpected return therefore had exactly the same effect as his arrival the previous year. Farinelli was brought back to sing for the king and queen in San Petronio during Easter week,[76] and additional productions[77] had to be prepared for a spring opera season: a new work by Albinoni at the Formigliari and another by Buini at the Marsigli-Rossi.[78] While the season continued in Bologna,[79] the Duke of Parma arranged for Farinelli to sing in a new work by Vinci (*Medo*), staged in the Teatro Nuovo Ducale. The king attended several performances with

[73] Christopher Hogwood, *Handel* (London, 1984), pp. 91–2.

[74] For these appointments, see Chapter 10, pp. 189–90.

[75] The operas by Buini were *Il Malmocor* and *Il Filendo* (dedicated to Sicinio Pepoli's wife), with an intermezzo entitled *La serva astuta*; and the pastorale by Aldrovandini was *Gl'inganni amorosi scoperti in villa* (Ghiselli, 10, 24 and 29 January 1728; Ricci, *Teatri di Bologna*, pp. 431–2).

[76] Ghiselli, 31 March 1728.

[77] The Accademia del Corto Naviglio and the Collegio dei Nobili both put on operas which were attended by James III and Prince Charles. The two works (the names of their composers were not recorded) were *La Didone* and *Il Celso*, the latter dedicated to Prince Charles (Ghiselli, 31 January, 7 and 11 February 1728; Ricci, *Teatri di Bologna*, pp. 296, 431).

[78] Ghiselli, 26 May 1728; Ricci, *Teatri di Bologna*, pp. 431–2. The works were Albinoni, *L'incostanza schernita* and Buini, *La forza del sangue*.

[79] The king attended performances of both works (Ghiselli, 5 and 12 June, 10 July 1728).

Prince Charles in June.[80] A few weeks later, in July, James took his son to Faenza, where the local Accademia dei Remoti had engaged the castrato Nicolini to sing in a new setting by Orlandini of *Arsace*, dedicated to James III. As a further compliment they had arranged a revival of Orlandini's intermezzo *Monsieur di Porsugnacco*.[81] When both the Formigliari and the Marsigli-Rossi provided further operatic entertainment in Bologna during the autumn,[82] the king could feel that he had been very well entertained throughout the year.

Nevertheless the general standard of performances in Bologna was well below that to which James had been accustomed in Rome, and the 1729 carnival season offered nothing of any great interest: two more works by Buini at the Marsigli-Rossi, and two pasticcios at the Teatro Pubblico.[83] The king saw one opera in each theatre,[84] but then left Bologna on 30 January to return to Rome before the first performances of the other two works.[85]

By 1729 James III and Clementina had been reunited and living together for a year, and the king's papal pension had been restored. There was no longer any obvious reason why the Stuart court should remain in Bologna. One reason for James's decision to go back to the Palazzo del Re in Rome during the middle of the carnival season must surely have been his growing feeling that, from a musical point of view, Bologna was decidedly provincial when compared with the papal capital. He was certainly not disappointed. Shortly after his arrival he was able to attend performances of new works by Vinci and Costanzi.[86]

Later that same year it was those two composers who were selected to celebrate the birth of the Dauphin. Cardinal de Polignac (the French

[80] NA. SP 85/16/ff. 416, 422, Stosch to Newcastle, 22 May and 12 June 1728; Ghiselli, 12, 19, 23 and 26 June 1728.
[81] Ghiselli, 30 June 1728; NA. SP 85/16/f. 437, Stosch to Newcastle, 8 July 1728.
[82] Ghiselli, 16, 20, 22, 27 October, 6, 10 November 1728; Ricci, *Teatri di Bologna*, pp. 90–1, 431–3. The operas at the Formigliari were Buini, *Il Teodorico* and Giovanni Battista Mancini, *L'Endimione*. The work at the Marsigli-Rossi was a pastorale entitled *Le vicende amorose*. The name of its composer was not recorded, but *Le vicende amorose* was previously given a special performance for James III at San Giovanni di Persiceto, north of Bologna (Ghiselli, 2 October 1728).
[83] Buini, *Il diporti d'amore in villa*, then *Chi non fa, non falla*, described respectively as a 'scherzo rusticale' and a 'divertimento comico'. The pasticcios were *Il finto chimico*, then *Il don Chischiotte* (Ghiselli, 24 December 1728; Ricci, *Teatri di Bologna*, p. 433).
[84] Ghiselli, 5, 8, 19 January 1729.   [85] Ghiselli, 5 February 1729.
[86] Vinci, *Semiramide riconosciuta* at the Aliberti; and Costanzi, *Rosmene* at the Pace. The other works were Auletta, *Ezio* (Aliberti), Leo, *Arianna e Teseo* (Pace), and Fischetti, *La Costanza* and *La somiglianza* (Capranica). Stosch recorded that at a performance of *Semiramide riconosciuta* one of the English Grand Tourists kissed the king's hand 'dans sa loge dans le Theatre public d'Aliberti, à vue de tous les Anglois' (NA. SP 85/16/f. 504, to Newcastle, 24 February 1729).

ambassador) and Cardinal Ottoboni (the Protector of France) repeated in the autmn of 1729 what they had planned in the autumn of 1725 following the marriage of Louis XV and Maria Leszczynska. On the earlier occasion they had commissioned serenatas from Gasparini and Vivaldi. This time Polignac commissioned a serenata from Vinci entitled *La contessa de' numi*, and Ottoboni commissioned an opera from Costanzi entitled *Carlo Magno*. When the former was performed at the French embassy in November Polignac had a box specially constructed, to be occupied by King James and his entourage.[87] When the latter was performed in the theatre of the Palazzo della Cancelleria in December Ottoboni gave James the keys to all the boxes in the theatre so that he could personally invite the people he wanted to the performances.[88]

A few weeks later, just before Christmas, a new carnival season opened as usual. It was particularly spectacular, with two new works by Porpora at the Capranica, new works by Francesco Feo and Costanzi at the recently opened Teatro Valle[89] and two new works by Vinci at the Aliberti. Of the latter, the first was *Alessandro nell' Indie*, dedicated to James III. The second was *Artaserse*, dedicated to Queen Clementina. It was during the run of performances of the second work that Pope Benedict XIII died, and all the theatres were immediately closed.

Both *Alessandro nell' Indie* and *Artaserse* had libretti written by Metastasio, who had lived in Rome until his departure for Vienna in September 1729. Between 1726 and 1730 seven of Metastasio's libretti were set to music for the first time at the Aliberti, and four of them were dedicated to the Stuarts.[90] The three others were composed while the Stuart court was at Bologna and would no doubt otherwise have also been dedicated to them.[91] As these libretti became extremely famous and were set to music by numerous composers throughout the eighteenth century, it is worth reflecting that they were originally written for James III and his wife. If one assumes that the poet tried to please the patrons to whom he dedicated his libretti, then we may say that in this respect the taste of the exiled Stuarts had a marked impact on the nature of drama represented on the operatic stage throughout much of the eighteenth century.

---

[87] NA. SP 85/16/ff. 604, 608, Stosch to Newcastle, 17 November and 1 December 1729. According to Chracas, *Diario ordinario*, no. 1924, 3 December 1729, p. 4, there was an orchestra of 130 players for this serenata.

[88] NA. SP 98/32/f. 15, Stosch to Newcastle, 5 January 1730. James III's copy of the libretto, *Carlo Magno, festa teatrale in occasione della nascita del Delfino* (Rome, 1729), is now in the Biblioteca Apostolica Vaticana (Bindelli, *Enrico Stuart*, p. 136).

[89] Porpora, *Mitridate* and *Siface*; Feo, *Andromaca*; Costanzi, *L'Eupatra*.

[90] The other two works were *Didone abbandonata* and *Siroe re di Persia*.

[91] *Catone in Utica*, *Ezio* and *Semiramide riconosciuta*.

5   The portraits of the Stuarts and their courtiers: I

Throughout the period when the exiled court was at Saint-Germain-en-Laye the Stuarts had commissioned a large number of portraits, partly to decorate their own apartments, partly to be sent away as diplomatic gifts and partly to be distributed in multiple copies to the Jacobites in England, Scotland and France. The royal family had employed several painters, but by 1706 Alexis-Simon Belle was recognised as their official portraitist.[1] Belle had even followed the court to Bar-le-Duc in Lorraine, where he had continued to produce portraits of James III and some of his courtiers.[2] But when James was forced to leave Lorraine and move to Avignon in 1716, and then to cross the Alps and settle at Pesaro in 1717, Belle had remained in Paris. The court had needed to find a new portrait painter.

During his first visit to Rome in the spring and early summer of 1717 James was painted by Antonio David, on the recommendation of Cardinal Gualterio.[3] The king was pleased with the portrait, and when he reached Urbino he ordered David to produce eleven copies, for distribution among his friends and supporters in Rome and elsewhere. As a result David was given a royal warrant in March 1718, appointing him to be James's official portrait painter in Italy.[4]

It was while David was making copies in Rome that the Duke of Mar rejoined the court at Urbino. Mar had spent the previous months in and near Paris, where he had probably met Belle and seen his work. When one of his Jacobite contacts in England had asked him to send a portrait of James III, so that he could present it to his wife, Mar had employed Belle to produce a copy. In a letter of July 1717 he explained that it was not an original portrait, but that it was 'by the best hand at Paris, and done from an original by the same hand'.[5] Mar probably ordered other

---

[1] Corp, *King over the Water*, part 1; Corp, *Court in Exile*, chapter 7.
[2] Corp, *Court in Exile*, pp. 292–3.   [3] Corp, *Jacobites at Urbino*, pp. 23–5.
[4] *Ibid.*, pp. 68, 87–91.
[5] HMC *Stuart*, IV, pp. 414, Mar to Caesar, 3 July 1717; HMC *Stuart*, V, p. 122, Mar to Caesar, 9 October 1717. The portrait was for Caesar's wife, Mary, who kept it hidden, but showed it on one occasion to Lord Cowper (*The Journal of Mary Frewan Caesar*, ed.

copies, and several miniatures, because the accounts of Mary of Modena's treasurer show substantial sums paid to Belle and Jacques-Antoine Arlaud that December.[6] Not surprisingly, when his own wife travelled to join the court at Urbino in the autumn of 1718, and stopped in Paris en route, Mar arranged that she should have her portrait painted by Belle.[7]

It is clear, then, that Mar had a high opinion of Belle's work. It is equally clear that he had a low opinion of the first portrait of the king painted by David in Rome. In July 1718 he wrote that it was 'by no means a good picture', which did 'no honour to the original', and that he felt that too many copies had been made and distributed.[8] Mar therefore determined to find an alternative painter to replace David and, in the spring of 1718, went to Rome with this as one of his objectives.

The painter selected by Mar was Francesco Trevisani, who was not in fact primarily a portraitist, but who was probably recommended by both David Nairne and the Scottish painter John Alexander. Nairne had met Trevisani on many occasions when he had accompanied Lord Melfort to Rome in 1689–91, and might well have mentioned his name to Mar at Urbino.[9] Alexander had been in Rome for several years and, in the spring of 1717, worked for Thomas Coke of Holkham at the same time as the latter's portrait was painted by Trevisani.[10] In any event, while Mar was in Rome he commissioned Trevisani to paint his portrait.[11] He was sufficiently pleased with it to order a miniature copy, and he returned to Urbino and advised James III that Trevisani should replace David as the portrait painter to the Stuart court.[12]

Dorothy B.T. Potter (Lampeter, 2002), p. 30). James was obliged to employ a local artist to copy an old portrait by Belle for the Palazzo Ducale at Pesaro: see Corp, *Jacobites at Urbino*, p. 21.

[6] HMC *Stuart*, v, p. 424, accounts of Dicconson, 31 January 1718.

[7] HMC *Stuart*, vii, p. 337 and p. 392, Duchess of Mar to Mar, 2 and 15 October 1718.

[8] HMC *Stuart*, vii, p. 1, Mar to Dillon, 1 July 1718. See also HMC *Stuart*, v, pp. 499, 511, G. Hamilton to Mar, 21 and 26 February 1718.

[9] NLS. MS 14266, the Journal of David Nairne. Nairne met Trevisani on at least seventeen occasions between 16 January and 1 September 1691. Trevisani had painted a portrait of Lady Melfort, which Mar probably saw in Paris (Corp, *Court in Exile*, p. 198).

[10] Alexander had been in Rome since at least 1712 (SCA. BL 2/176/12, T. Innes to Stuart, 30 May 1712). See also Ingamells, *Dictionary*, p. 13 and p. 226.

[11] The painting is in the collection of the Earl of Mar and Kellie at Alloa Tower, and is reproduced in Corp, *Jacobites at Urbino*, p. 64, illustration 11.

[12] The miniaturist selected by Trevisani was Giovanni Felice Ramelli, who had finished his copy by June (HMC *Stuart*, vi, p. 517, Alexander to Mar, 11 June 1718: 'Your picture remains safe at Trevisani's, till I receive new orders'). See also *ibid.*, p. 517, Ramelli to Mar, June 1718. In July 1718 Alexander wrote to Mar that Trevisani 'desired me to present his duty to you' (HMC *Stuart*, vii, p. 50, Alexander to Mar, 16 July 1718).

When James and Mar arrived in Rome at the end of 1718 Trevisani was therefore given two commissions. The first was to paint James half-length in his Garter robes, with a closed crown on a table beside him.[13] The second was to paint the Duchess of Mar and her daughter beside a harpsichord, on which can be seen an aria from Giovanni Bononcini's opera *Erminia*, first performed at the Teatro della Pace in January 1719.[14] The portrait of James was entrusted to Cardinal Gualterio, to be given to Princess Maria Clementina Sobieska at the first opportunity. That of the duchess was presumably intended for Mar himself.

In February 1719 both James and Mar left Rome. While they were away Clementina made her daring escape from Innsbruck, and was married to James by proxy in Bologna. There she was presented with Trevisani's portrait of her new husband.[15] A month later she arrived in Rome, where Gualterio arranged that she too should be painted by Trevisani. She was shown as the new Queen of Great Britain, with a closed crown placed beside her, in a composition intended to be hung beside that of the king.[16] The picture was finished at the end of July.[17]

For the rest of 1719, and into 1720, Trevisani continued to work for the Stuart court. As his portrait of Clementina was immediately despatched to James in Spain, where it remained,[18] he simultaneously painted a copy to be displayed beside his portrait of the king in the Palazzo del Re. This portrait of Clementina was then copied by an unnamed painter (perhaps David), and the new copy sent away to the Duke of Mar.[19]

In 1720, after James had formally married Clementina at Montefiascone, he commissioned two more paintings from Trevisani. The first was a replica of his own portrait in the robes of a Garter Knight, the second a new portrait of Clementina wearing a gold bejewelled dress and a blue ermine lined cloak, but without the crown or any other royal regalia.[20]

---

[13] Corp, *King over the Water*, p. 58, fig. 38: the painting is at Holyroodhouse, Edinburgh. See also Corp, *Jacobites at Urbino*, p. 116, illustration 17.

[14] The painting is in the collection of the Earl of Mar and Kellie at Alloa Tower, and is reproduced in Corp, *Jacobites at Urbino*, p. 115, illustration 16.

[15] Peggy Miller, *A Wife for the Pretender* (London, 1965), p. 141.

[16] Corp, *King over the Water*, p. 56, fig. 36: the painting is in the Prado, Madrid, where it is wrongly attributed to Largillière. A miniature portrait of the princess, presumably originally painted at Ohlau, had already been sent to England the previous year. See HMC *Stuart*, VII, p. 467, Ogilvie to Mar, 29 October 1718.

[17] RA. SP 44/57, Murray to Mar, 19 August 1719.

[18] RA. SP 44/26, Murray to Mar, 1 August 1719. It arrived after James had left, and was kept by Elisabeth Farnese, the Queen of Spain, who sent a portrait of herself in exchange.

[19] RA. SP 44/57, Murray to Mar, 19 August 1719.

[20] Corp, *King over the Water*, p. 59, fig. 39.

The former was sent to the Duke of Mar in April 1720,[21] so that he and James now each had a pair of portraits by Trevisani. The latter was to be engraved in Paris.[22] Trevisani was paid fifty *pistoles* (837 *livres*, 5 *sols* 0 *deniers*) for these two works in September of that year.[23]

Trevisani was no doubt pleased to be given these prestigious commissions but, not being primarily a portraitist, it is most unlikely that he had any desire to become the new official painter to the Stuart court. He was asked by Cardinal Ottoboni to paint replicas of his companion portraits of the king and the queen, to be displayed in the Palazzo della Cancelleria,[24] and he agreed to paint James Murray and his sister Marjory Hay.[25] But in the second half of 1720 he decided to pass over any future commissions to someone else.

It was the birth of Prince Charles at the end of December 1720 which prompted James to commission a new set of portraits. There was to be one of James himself, a second of Clementina and a third, when the prince was old enough, of mother and son together. The painter selected was Girolamo Pesci, a former pupil of Trevisani, and presumably recommended by him.

Pesci's portrait of James was finished in January 1721.[26] It is not a good likeness. The king is shown three-quarter length in armour, standing by the sea. He is accompanied by a page and rests his left hand on a map of England. His right holds a baton which points across an invading army towards the water.[27] The original picture was to be kept in the Palazzo del Re, but a smaller copy was sent to Bayonne for the Queen Dowager of Spain, who was one of Clementina's aunts.[28]

---

[21] RA. SP 46/64, James III to Mar, 20 April 1720.

[22] Corp, *The King over the Water*, p. 60.

[23] RA. SP Misc 32, account book, 9 September 1720. There is no trace of payments to Trevisani for the earlier works.

[24] Armando Schiavo, *Il Palazzo della Cancelleria* (Rome, 1963), p. 196.

[25] Both paintings are at Scone Palace (respectively 101.6 × 76.2 cm and 101.6 × 74.9 cm), and are reproduced in Corp, *Jacobites at Urbino*, p. 124, illustration 19, and p. 58, illustration 10. Trevisani also painted a portrait of David Murray, later 6th Viscount Stormont (Scone Palace, 101.6 × 76.2 cm), who visited his brother and sister in Rome in March 1719 (*JCR*, p. 164).

[26] RA. SP Misc 32, account book, 28 January 1721: 'Paid Peché for the original of the Kings Picture to the knee: 67 [*scudi*] 0. 0' (i.e. 335 *livres*).

[27] Corp, *King over the Water*, p. 60, fig. 41: the painting is at Stanford Hall.

[28] RA. SP 57/97, Hay to L. Innes, 27 January 1722. Three other copies by Pesci are recorded: RA. SP Misc 32, account book, 5 February 1721: 'Paid Peché for a small picture of the Kings for Mr Murray: 13 [*scudi*] 4. 0' (i.e. 66*l*. 5*s*. 0*d*.); 25 May 1721: 'Paid Peché for a Picture of the Kings promised me [Ellis]: 40 [*scudi*] 2. 0' (i.e. 200*l*. 10*s*. 0*d*.); Bod. Lib. Rawlinson MSS D. 1180, pp. 337–8, Rawlinson's diary, 3 April 1721: 'received my picture from Signore Hieronymi Peschi, and paid him two pistols [33*l*. 10*s*. 0*d*.], to the single one [16*l*. 15*s*. 0*d*.] paid formerly'. Rawlinson's copy was a miniature.

In April 1721, once the queen had recovered from the birth, Pesci painted two identical portraits of her, one to be sent to Bayonne, the other for the Duchess of Mar.[29] These were in effect preparatory works, while the prince was still too young to be painted. At the end of 1721 Pesci finally produced a double portrait of Clementina and the prince. The image of Clementina herself is very similar, but the canvas is much larger, with exactly the same dimensions as Pesci's portrait of James. Both were kept in the Palazzo del Re, and neither was engraved.[30]

In the original composition Clementina is shown standing three-quarter length. On her left side there is a table, where she rests her left hand near her crown. Her right hand holds some flowers across her bosom (Fig. 10).[31] The larger double portrait shows her sitting on a throne with the baby prince at her side in place of the table and crown. There is now a table on her right side, from which she is taking flowers and handing them to the prince.[32] The queen is radiantly beautiful, looking more poised and confident than in the earlier portraits by Trevisani (Fig. 11).

From 1719 to 1721, while Trevisani and Pesci were painting these portraits, David had continued to work for the Stuart court, mainly producing copies. He did, however, paint an original portrait of Clementina. An engraved portrait of the new queen was urgently needed in the spring of 1719 to send to England, but there seemed little prospect of getting a copy of Trevisani's portrait to Paris in time for it to be engraved there. Mar would probably not have employed David, but he had left the court and, in his absence, James Murray commissioned David to produce an alternative half-length portrait, including a crown, for immediate despatch to Paris.[33] There it was engraved by Drevet and sent to England.[34]

---

[29] Bod. Lib. Rawlinson MSS D. 1181, pp. 353–4, Rawlinson's diary, 25 April 1721: 'This day the Princess satt a third time for her picture to Signore Hierolymo Peschi'; RA. SP 57/97, Hay to L. Innes, 27 January 1722. Two other copies by Pesci are recorded: RA. SP Misc 32, account book, May 1721: 'Given Peché for a little picture done for Mr Murray of ye Queen: 13 [*scudi*] 4. 0' (i.e. 66*l*. 5*s*. 0*d*.); Bod. Lib. Rawlinson MSS D. 1181, p. 338, diary, 3 April 1721: 'paid him [Pesci] one more [*pistole* = 16*l*. 15*s*. 0*d*.] in earnest for a ristretto of my Lady'. This was also a miniature.

[30] RA. SP Misc 32, account book, February 1722: 'Paid Peché for the Queens picture with ye Princes: 33 [*scudi*] 5. 0' (i.e. 166*l*. 5*s*. 0*d*.). Rawlinson saw a sketch for this double portrait as early as May 1721 (Bod. Lib. Rawlinson MSS D. 1181, p. 388, diary, 27 May 1721), and recorded that a preliminary version of the portrait of the prince was given to Hay at the end of April 1721 (*ibid.*, p. 354, diary, 25 April 1721).

[31] Corp, *King over the Water*, p. 61, fig. 42: the painting is in the Prado, Madrid.

[32] *Ibid.*, p. 61, fig. 43: the painting is at Stanford Hall.

[33] *Ibid.*, p. 60, fig. 40: the painting is at Chiddingstone Castle; RA. SP 44/57, Murray to Mar, 19 August 1719: 'being of opinion that the matter press'd I sent a great while ago a little one done by David which I cou'd command at my own time'.

[34] Two other engravings were made after this portrait, one by Dupuis, the other anonymous, and wrongly attributed to Trevisani. See Corp, *The King over the Water*, p. 60.

Figure 10. *Queen Clementina*, 1721 (*c.*102 × *c.*80 cm), by Girolamo Pesci.

Apart from this original portrait David was paid for painting copies. In January 1720 he received ten *pistoles* (166*l.* 5*s.* 0*d.*) 'for 10 Pictures',[35] and three months later he was given a further two *pistoles* (33*l.* 5*s.* 0*d.*), probably for two more copies.[36] We do not know how many copies he made of his own portraits of the king and queen, and whether he also copied Trevisani's first portrait of the queen. We do, however, know that Clementina showed her appreciation of his work by giving him a

[35] RA. SP Misc 32, account book, 12 January 1720.   [36] *Ibid.*, 5 April 1720.

Figure 11. *Queen Clementina with Prince Charles*, 1721 (167.6 × 116.8 cm), by Girolamo Pesci.

medal in the spring of 1721,[37] so he was perhaps mainly employed in copying her portraits.

We also know very little about the recipients of the copies. In June 1718 Sir Peter Redmond, then in Madrid, wrote to Mar that he had brought for Lady Arthur (the wife of the banker Sir Francis Arthur), 'the

---

[37] *Ibid.*, 28 May 1721.

King's picture from Rome'.[38] Given the early date, this must have been a copy of the portrait by David. We also know that Robert Pigott, MP, was given a portrait of the king when he was in Rome in 1720.[39] It is tempting to assume that this copy was also painted by David, and it probably was. But other artists had by then begun to make copies of these portraits of the king and queen by David, Trevisani and Pesci. One such artist was John Smibert, who was in Rome on and off from November 1720 to June 1721, and then again in December 1721. We know, for example, that he was allowed to copy on to a single canvas the two new portraits by Pesci.[40]

Richard Rawlinson took a strong interest in the new portraits, and his diary is a valuable source of information. In December 1720, for example, he visited both the English and the Scots colleges in Rome. In the English College he saw portraits of James III ('the best likeness I have ever seen') and Clementina. In the Scots College, on the other hand, he saw 'three different pictures' of the king and one of the queen: 'Two of the former when young [in France] were tolerable, but the latter, and that of his spouse very bad.'[41] His most interesting observations were made in February 1721, when he saw 'two different pictures' of James and Clementina 'in the palace of Cardinal Gualtieri [sic] and in the lodgings of his Maitre d'Hotel, both very ill done as well for resemblance as the beauty of the colours, much faded'. Who were these pictures by, and why had they already faded? They cannot have been by David, because Rawlinson recorded that 'afterwards' he saw the portrait of the king 'at full length at the house of Signior Antonio David, which is inferiour to none but that done by Sign. Hieronymo Peche', which, he misleadingly wrote, was also 'at full length, with his spouse also in the same manner'.[42]

These paintings, and the engravings made after them, were not the only portraits of James and Maria Clementina produced in Rome during these years. Mention should also be made of five medals, struck by

---

[38] HMC *Stuart*, VI, p. 584, Redmond to Mar, 27 June 1718.
[39] Ingamells, *Dictionary*, p. 768.
[40] RA. SP 173/118, Cockburne to Edgar, 23 September 1734: Smibert, 'at my desire, procured an original picture of the King and Queen which he copyed and gave me. They are both on one canvas. This I have lent to several of the King's friends which they cause copy and have them in their house.' One copy has survived (in a private collection) and shows that the portraits were the ones by Pesci. See also RA. SP 174/171, Edgar to Cockburne, 3 November 1734: 'I remember very well the time of Mr Smibert's doing you the pictures you have of their Ma.ties.'
[41] Bod. Lib. Rawlinson MSS D. 1181, pp. 171–2, Rawlinson's diary, 15 December 1720; *ibid.*, p. 176, 22 December 1720.
[42] *Ibid.*, pp. 296–7, 25 February 1721.

Ottone Hamerani and his elder brother Ermenegildo. Members of the Hamerani family had worked for the papal mint in Rome since the early seventeenth century, and in 1719, while James was in Spain, Ottone Hamerani struck a medal celebrating Clementina's escape from Innsbruck and safe arrival in Rome. The medal shows a profile of Clementina, who is described as Queen of Great Britain, France and Ireland, with a pearl necklace, looking to the left. The reverse carries the legend *Fortunam Causamque Sequor* (I follow his fortune and his cause).[43] This medal was commissioned by Pope Clement XI, and Rawlinson noted in his diary that copper copies of the medal were still being sold by Hamerani two years later.[44]

Before the end of 1719 two other medals had been struck by the Hamerani brothers. There was one engraved by Ottone, which celebrated James and Clementina's proxy marriage at Bologna, and another by Ermenegildo, which celebrated their real wedding at Montefiascone. The former was probably struck on Ottone Hamerani's own initiative. The obverse shows the king in profile facing right, while the reverse has a new image of the queen facing left, with pearls draped over her bodice and no pearl necklace. The image of the king was copied by Hamerani from the Jacobite coinage produced by Norbert Roettiers in 1716, which also showed James facing right.[45] The medal by Ermenegildo Hamerani, which was struck after James's return to Rome, shows conjoined busts of the king and queen. The reverse shows Hercules taking the hand of Venus, attended by Cupid holding a caduceus, with the legend *Regium Connubium* (the royal nuptials).[46] The Stuart accounts contain several references to these medals. For example thirty-eight silver ones were purchased in September 1720 for 152 *livres*, and three gold ones in October 1720 for 150*l*. 7*s*. 5*d*.[47] During that month Ottone Hamerani was given a warrant to be the king's engraver.[48]

During 1721 Ermenegildo Hamerani's medal was reissued to celebrate the birth of Prince Charles, with a new reverse showing Providence holding a child in her arms, and pointing to a globe marked 'Ing Sc Irl'. The legend is *Providentia Obsterix* (Providence, helper in childbirth).[49] This medal, according to Richard Rawlinson, who heard it from

[43] N. Woolf, *The Medallic Record of the Jacobite Movement* (London, 1988), p. 78, no. 36; Michael Sharp, 'Jacobite and Anti-Jacobite Medals', *Royal Stuart Papers*, LXXIV (2008), p. 8; Neil Guthrie, '"A Polish Lady": The Art of the Jacobite Print', *1650–1850: Ideas, Aesthetics and Inquiries in the Early Modern Era*, 14 (2007), pp. 287–312, at pp. 289, 292.

[44] Bod. Lib. Rawlinson MSS D. 1181, p. 662, Rawlinson's diary, 27 October 1721.

[45] Woolf, *Medallic Record*, p. 79, no. 37; Corp, *A Court in Exile*, p. 298.

[46] Woolf, *Medallic Record*, p. 80, no. 37.

[47] RA. SP Misc 32, account book, 9 September 1720 and 5 October 1720.

[48] Woolf, *Medallic Record*, p. 76.   [49] *Ibid.*, p. 81, no. 38.

Hamerani himself, was not for general sale, and only available directly from the Palazzo del Re.[50] But Hamerani also told Rawlinson that he was making another which would be more generally available. This was the famous South Sea Bubble medal, which was finished at the beginning of December 1721. The obverse carries a new profile of James, still looking right, wearing armour, with a sun at his neck. James's royal titles are not included. He is simply identified as *Unica Salus* (the only security). The reverse shows the captivity of the British people, as a Hanoverian horse tramples on a lion and a unicorn, with London in the background.[51] One hundred silver and two hundred brass medals were sent for distribution in England,[52] and more copies were struck in March 1722.[53]

In the autumn of that year James III decided he wanted another three-quarter-length portrait of himself, possibly to replace the one by Pesci, and a new bust of Clementina. This time he gave both commissions to David. The new portrait of James showed him three-quarter length wearing armour, with his left hand placed on the crown. In the background David included a view of the Tower of London, closely based on an engraving published in *Britannia Illustrata* (1707) by Knyff and Kip (Fig. 12).[54] This picture was displayed in the Palazzo del Re. The new portrait of Clementina showed her wearing an ermine-lined dress, with a double string of pearls attached to her right shoulder and elegantly falling towards her left hip. On the front of her dress there is a delicate floral design, while beside her left shoulder there is a crown.[55] This portrait was probably also kept in the Palazzo del Re. Both pictures were finished by January 1723 when David was paid twenty-nine *pistoles* (485*l.* 15*s.* 0*d.*).[56]

Neither image was engraved, but James was constantly being asked by his supporters in Great Britain and elsewhere for portraits of himself and his wife.[57] In 1723–5 he agreed to send several sets of paired portraits. He ordered David to make copies of the bust of his own new portrait.

---

[50] Bod. Lib. Rawlinson MSS D.1181, p. 662, Rawlinson's diary, 27 October 1721.
[51] Woolf, *Medallic Record*, p. 83, no. 40.
[52] RA. SP 56/41, Hay to Freebairne, 9 December 1721.
[53] NA. SP 85/14/f. 23, Stosch to Carteret, 14 March 1722.
[54] Corp, *King over the Water*, p. 62, fig. 44: the painting was until recently at Stanford Hall.
[55] This portrait was not included in Corp, *King over the Water*. It is reproduced in the *I David* exhibition catalogue, p. 82. The painting is in the Walters Art Gallery, Baltimore.
[56] RA. SP Misc 34, account book, January 1723: 'for a picture of ye King at full length and a buste of ye Queen'.
[57] For a British request, see RA. SP 56/13, J. Hamilton to James III, 27 November 1721; RA. SP 56/86, James III to J. Hamilton, 21 December 1721. These letters refer to portraits of the queen for the Duchess of Hamilton, Lord Cowper, Lady Orkney and Lady Fortescue. For an Italian request for a portrait of the queen, see RA. SP 44/131, James III to contessa Molza, 18 September 1719; RA. SP 46/22, contessa Molza to James III, 12 March 1720.

Figure 12. *James III*, 1722 (134 × 96 cm), by Antonio David.

But that of Clementina had never been intended as a pair, and was unsuitable, because she was not shown at a similar angle. James therefore commissioned David to produce another new bust, which could be copied for hanging alongside his own portrait. This time David omitted the pearls and the floral design on the front of the queen's dress, and turned the composition so that the angle of the body matched that of the king, the queen looking left, and the king looking right.[58]

---

[58] Corp, *King over the Water*, p. 63, fig. 45: one copy of this painting is at Hawarden Castle. RA. SP Misc 34, account book, March 1724: 'To David painter: 19 Spa. pist/318*l*. 5*s*. 0*d*.'; *ibid.*, September 1724: 'To Sig.re David penteur: 21 Spanish pistoles/351*l*. 15*s*. 0*d*.'.

The accounts of the payments to David during these years are too unspecific for a detailed chronology to be established. There is also a problem of interpretation. An interesting entry of September 1723 records the payment 'to David painter for a picture at length of ye Ma.ties and the Prince: 30 Span pistoles (502*l*. 10*s*. 0*d*.)'.[59] If this refers to a new double portrait, then the picture has been lost without trace. If, however, it refers to two separate pictures, then it is easier to explain. At this time David made an improved copy of Pesci's portrait of James with a page. In David's version James now points with his baton to the map rather than the sea. The face of the page remains the same, but the features of James himself have been softened to make him much more handsome.[60] David also painted a small portrait of Prince Charles, who had been given both the Garter and the Thistle on the previous Christmas Day.[61] This portrait was never engraved, but David continued to supply copies and miniatures for the next two years.[62]

By the end of 1723 it is clear that David had reestablished himself as the official portrait painter of the Stuart court in Italy. The Duke of Mar's criticism of his work might have been unjust, but it had at least resulted in the commissioning of important portraits during the years 1719–21 from Trevisani and Pesci. However, David continued to have his critics. In 1723 he painted two similar portraits of Marjory Hay, one for her husband showing her holding some flowers, the other for her brother showing her with a bow and arrow (Fig. 13).[63] After finishing these pictures David began work on two copies of a companion portrait of her husband, but before they could be finished the latter was sent by James on a mission to Paris. Deprived of the sitter, David's likeness was then judged by a group of courtiers to be unrecognisable, so that he was totally discouraged from continuing. Marjory Hay explained to her husband that 'David

---

[59] *Ibid.*, September 1723.

[60] Corp, *King over the Water*, p. 63, fig. 46: the painting is at Blair's College, Aberdeen.

[61] *Ibid.*, p. 63, fig. 47: the painting is in a private collection. RA. SP 67/73, Ellis to Nairne, 12 June 1723: 'Adjoynd I send the Princes Picture, left with me this forenoon by Mr David'. This was only three months before the payment to David in September 'for a picture at length of ye Ma.ties and the Prince'. See Chapter 2 for giving Prince Charles the Garter and the Thistle.

[62] See note 58.

[63] Corp, *The King over the Water*, p. 104. The paintings are, respectively, in the collection of Lord Kinnoul (96.5 × 76.2 cm) and at Scone Palace (97.7 × 76.2 cm). There is a copy of the portrait with a bow and arrow in a private collection at Crarae, Argyllshire. It was possibly painted by David in 1727 (see below, notes 98, 101 and 104).

Figure 13. *Marjory Hay, Countess of Inverness, as Diana,* 1723
(97.7 × 76.2 cm), by Antonio David. Marjory Hay, the sister of
James Murray, Earl of Dunbar, was lady of the Bedchamber from
1719 to 1722.

was so much ashamed to see in a company of ten or twelve people
that no body imagined that one that he did to be so much as designed
for you in great rage he throw it out at ye window'.[64] When Hay
returned to Rome in 1724 the commission to paint his portrait was
accepted by Trevisani (Fig. 14).[65]

In 1725 David was given the most important commission he ever
received from the Stuart court. It was to paint a group portrait

---

[64] RA. SP 69/87, Marjory Hay to Hay, 5 October 1723.
[65] The painting is in the collection of Lord Kinnoull (96.5 × 76.2 cm).

Figure 14. *John Hay, Earl of Inverness*, 1724 (96.5 × 76.2 cm),
by Francesco Trevisani. John Hay was groom of the Bedchamber
(1717–18), then *maggiordomo* (1718–22), acting secretary of state
(1721–5) and secretary of state (1725–7). He was created Earl
of Inverness in 1718, but the title was not officially recognised
until 1725.

showing the baptism of Prince Charles, which had taken place four
and a half years earlier, at the end of December 1720. This painting,
now in the Scottish National Portrait Gallery, used to be attributed
to Agostino Masucci and Pier Leone Ghezzi, and dated 1735.[66] In
fact it was painted by David in 1725. He was given thirty-six *pistoles*

[66] Corp, *King over the Water*, p. 73, fig. 61.

(603*l*. 0*s*. 0*d*.) for it in November 1725, with a further small payment in January 1726 (see Fig. 8).[67]

David's painting does not attempt to provide an accurate re-creation of the baptism of Prince Charles, which he had anyway not attended. As already explained in Chapter 2, the original chapel in the Palazzo de Re had been destroyed in 1724, and replaced by a new one situated on the second floor overlooking the Via di San Marcello. The scene is therefore set in the second chapel. James III is wearing the Garter and the Thistle, and stands on the first step leading to the altar, on which can be seen the six great candlesticks which had previously been in the little chapel of the Château de Saint-Germain. To James's left, on the second step, is Bishop Sebastiano Bonaventura, who had officiated at his marriage with Clementina in the cathedral at Montefiascone. Standing behind James on his right, but on the left side of the canvas, are four cardinals: Annibale Albani, nephew of Clement XI and *camerlengo* of the Church, with his right arm raised; and the three protectors of England, Scotland and Ireland, Filippo Gualterio, Giuseppe Sacripanti and Giuseppe Renato Imperiali. Bishop Bonaventura is assisted by Antonio Ragazzi, the parish priest of the Church of Santi Apostoli, and three much younger chaplains, each representing one of James's kingdoms: Lord Richard Howard (brother of the 8th and 9th Dukes of Norfolk), Lord William Drummond (son of the 1st Duke of Melfort), and Father John Brown (the king's confessor). The symbolism of the groups surrounding James and the bishop could hardly have been more apparent.

In the centre of the painting the elderly contessa della Torre (better known as the princesse des Ursins) kneels on the first step leading to the altar. She is dressed in black and holds in her arms the newly born Prince of Wales, whom she presents to the bishop for baptism. Behind her are: two ladies kneeling; two groups of four ladies standing; four gentlemen in the far background; and (in the foreground on the right) four more cardinals, with a nobleman holding a three-cornered hat. It is not difficult to identify who most of these people are, and James obviously intended that they should be immediately recognisable. The two ladies kneeling can be assumed to represent the Countess of Nithsdale and Marjory Hay, the two most senior ladies at the Jacobite court. The first group of ladies standing are probably principessa Giustiniani, principessa Barberini di Palestrina, the duchessa di Fiano and duchessa Salviati. The second group of ladies probably includes the principessa di Piombino, donna Teresa Albani (the wife of don Carlo Albani),

---

[67] RA. SP Misc 34, account book, November 1725; RA. SP 90/55, household accounts, January 1726: 'David, Painter: 22. 0. 0' (i.e. 1 *pistole* and 1 *filippo*).

principessa Colonna and principessa Pamphili. The four gentlemen in the far background are difficult to identify and can be assumed to represent either some of the Jacobite peers, or the husbands of the ladies present at the ceremony. There is no doubt, however, about the identities of the figures on the right. Don Carlo Albani stands at the front, in equipoise to his brother Annibale, so that the two nephews of Pope Clement XI occupy the dominant positions on each side of the picture. Behind Albani are Cardinal Francesco Aquaviva (the Spanish ambassador), Cardinal Francesco Barberini (*primo prete* of the Church), Cardinal Fabrizio Paulucci (*segretario di stato*), and Cardinal Pietro Ottoboni (*vice-cancelliere*, and Cardinal Protector of France). With the exception of Marjory Hay, all these people and about seventy-five others were present at the birth and the baptism.[68]

David's portrayal of the *Baptism of Prince Charles* is the most important painting produced for the Stuart court in Rome, and the only one which shows the interior of the Palazzo del Re. Apart from five pictures painted later by Giovanni Paolo Panini, it is also the only one which allows us to see James III surrounded by the people who are so often mentioned in the Stuart Papers and other archival sources. For the historian it is thus of inestimable value, but it is not entirely satisfactory as a composition, and David's portrait of James himself seems a little lifeless. It may be for this reason that the painting did not meet with the king's entire approval. In August 1729 James replied to a Jacobite who had asked for a double portrait of his children that 'I could not send them to you both in one, without spoiling the likeness ... since there are none here who could paint such a picture as you desire well, that draws pictures like'.[69] Presumably David was included in this condemnation.

In 1725, when David was occupied painting *The Baptism*, James commissioned a new pair of portraits of himself and Clementina. The artist selected was Martin van Meytens (the Younger), who was briefly in Rome at that time. Why Meytens was chosen, and how he was introduced to the Stuart court, remains completely unknown. The portraits were intended as mutual presents between James and Clementina, to mark the birth of her second son.[70] They are busts and make an

---

[68] *Diario ordinario*, no. 544, 4 January 1721, pp. 2–8. The Jacobite peers present at the ceremony were Lord Nithsdale (Catholic) and Lords Linlithgow, Southesk, Winton and Kilsyth (all Protestants).

[69] RA. SP 130/85, James III to Anne Oglethorpe, 23 August 1729.

[70] RA. SP Misc 34, account book, April 1725: 'Mr Mytens ye Sweedish painter on 2nd May z[*ecchini*] 200/1000 [*livres*]'; RA. SP 101/119, Inverness to Ellis, 15 January 1727: 'Her M.ty has ... [the King's picture], and the Queens picture used to be in the Kings low apartment.'

Figure 15. *James III*, 1725 (73.2 × 61 cm), copy of 1730
by Antonio David, after Martin van Meytens.

excellent pair. Each wears an ermine-lined red cloak, James looking to
his left, Clementina to her right. James is shown wearing the Garter and
the Thistle as usual over armour, which has a gorgoneion at the neck
(Fig. 15).[71] His orders are then nicely balanced in the portrait of Maria
Clementina, who has a strip of blue material falling from her right
shoulder to her left hip and a large jewelled brooch pinned to the front
of her bodice (Fig. 16).[72] Sir William Ellis said that the pictures showed
the king and queen 'fuller in the face than their Ma.ties are, and consequently less resemble them, than they should have done'.[73] Nevertheless
the portrait of Clementina was the most successful image of her ever
painted, and eventually became her official portrait, to be seen by
millions of people in its reproduction as part of her monument in
St Peter's. Meytens left Rome for Vienna in 1726, and never painted

---

[71] Corp, *King over the Water*, p. 65, fig. 50. The original by Meytens has not been
identified.

[72] *Ibid.*, p. 65, fig. 51.   [73] RA. SP 104/57, Ellis to Inverness, 26 February 1727.

Figure 16. *Queen Clementina*, 1725 (73.2 × 61 cm), copy of 1730 by Antonio David, after Martin van Meytens.

another Stuart portrait. Until now the artist who originally created the image has remained unknown.

When David had finished *The Baptism* he was available to accept the next Stuart commissions. This time it was Queen Clementina rather than James III who asked him for new portraits. She had recently left the Palazzo del Re and entered the Convent of Santa Cecilia in Trastevere, and she wanted portraits of her two children to hang in her new apartment.[74] The first was a large full-length of the five-year-old Prince of Wales.[75] The second showed the one-year-old Duke of York, full length,

[74] NA. SP 85/16/f. 104, Stosch to Newcastle, 6 July 1726.
[75] Corp, *King over the Water*, p. 64, fig. 49: the painting is at Stonyhurst College; RA. SP Box 4/4/166: 'Per il ritratto intero del Principe intela di sette e cinque con abito di velluto racamato: d[oppie] 40' (i.e. 670 *livres*).

sitting on a cushion with ermine and flowers.[76] The latter has been lost, but the former, of which several full-length and three-quarter-length copies were made,[77] was sent to Paris in June 1726 and engraved by Edelinck in the winter of 1726–7.[78]

Shortly after David painted these two portraits James III left Rome and went to live with his two sons in Bologna. This had important consequences for the commissioning of Stuart portraits, because James now wanted copies of the recent pictures of himself, Maria Clementina and Prince Charles to be sent to him. Lord Inverness wrote to Sir William Ellis in Rome: 'The King desires that you would order to be made out of hand copies of the King and Queens pictures done by the Suede on oyl cloth, and a copy of the Princes picture by David. It represents the Prince at full length, but the copy ought to be made of the same bigness wt the other two wtout the legs.'[79] James also felt obliged to reassure his friends and supporters by commissioning and distributing a large number of portraits of himself and his wife. He quickly decided, however, that the painters in Bologna were not good enough,[80] so all of these additional copies had to be painted by some-one in Rome. Inverness specified that the copies should be obtained as cheaply as possible: the set of three for the king should cost no more than five Spanish *pistoles* (83*l*. 15*s*. 0*d*.), and 'in proportion for the two others' of the king and queen which were for distribution.[81]

It was left to Ellis to select a suitable painter willing to work within the available budget. All he was told was that 'the King wants they should be soon done and well done', and that the painter should 'copy the pictures he is adoing exactly from the original, for if he pretends to change anything, he'll probably spoil them'.[82] The painter chosen

[76] *Ibid.*: 'Per un ritratto del Sig.r Duca intiero a sedere sopra un cuscino con pelle bianca, e fiore: d[oppie] 12' (i.e. 201 *livres*).

[77] David was paid 4 *pistoles* (67 *livres*) in September 1726, and again in December 1726, for a copy of his portrait of Prince Charles (notes of Clare Stuart Wortley, preserved with the Stuart Papers, part one, p. 36; RA. SP 99/61, Inverness to Ellis, 22 November 1726; RA. SP 103/154, notes by Ellis, 19 February 1727).

[78] RA. SP 94/75, Inverness to Innes, 5 June 1726; RA. SP 95/95, Innes to Inverness, 15 July 1726. The portrait was taken to Paris by a man named Andrew Ramsay (i.e. not the chevalier Ramsay), who arranged for it to be engraved (RA. SP 102/34, Ramsay to Inverness, 26 January 1727). The first three hundred prints were sent to England in June 1727 (RA. SP 107/128, Ramsay to Inverness, 30 June 1727), the remainder during August (RA. SP 102/87/61, Ellis to Waters, 9 September 1727).

[79] RA. SP 101/119, Inverness to Ellis, 15 January 1727.

[80] RA. SP 99/84, Dunbar to O'Bryen, 26 November 1726: 'les peintres soient bien mauvais ici'.

[81] RA. SP 105/78, Ellis to Inverness, 29 March 1727.

[82] RA. SP 101/119, Inverness to Ellis, 15 January 1727; RA. SP 102/93, same to same, 1 February 1727. Ellis had suggested that 'the Perriwig which the Suede drew for the

was an Englishman who had been resident in Rome for several years and who was called E. Gill. His christian name is still unknown, and indeed until now no information about him of any kind has come to light.

This is actually rather surprising, because the division of the court between Bologna and Rome meant that it was necessary to correspond about matters which had previously been settled in conversation, and therefore left unrecorded. Despite this, the surviving correspondence tells us no more than the painter's name. It has now been established that Ellis knew of Gill because the latter had been in the entourage of Lord Richard Howard, who had enabled the painter to live and study in Rome by giving him a monthly pension of six *scudi* (30 *livres*).[83] After Howard's death in 1723 this pension had at first been continued by the Duke of Norfolk,[84] but after five months had been terminated. In November 1723 Gill had been given a final payment of fifty *scudi* (83*l.* 10*s.* 0*d.*), and told that 'he must depend no more on this benevolence'.[85] He had presumably been struggling to maintain himself in Rome for the previous three and a half years, and was available when Ellis wanted a painter to make all the necessary copies at a low price.[86]

The three copies for the king were finished in February 1727, and sent to Bologna. Ellis felt that 'they seem to be well copied from the originals',[87] but in reply he was told to give 'the painter notice, to make ye green riband, on the King's picture, of a deeper dye'.[88] Gill was then ordered to make sixteen more copies, ten of Clementina, five of James and one of Prince Charles. Most of them were to be given away as presents, but one copy of the queen's portrait was to be sent to Alexis-Simon Belle, so that further copies could be made in France.[89]

King is thought to be too light coloured, and its thought would be more agreeable to those His Ma.tie wears if it were ye colour of chestnut' (RA. SP 102/31, Ellis to Inverness, 27 January 1727).

[83] WDA. Epist. Var. 8/26, Philip Howard to Mayes, 6 June 1723. Gill must have been a Catholic. According to *Bishop Leyburne's Confirmation Register of 1687* (Wigan, 1997) there were Catholics called Gill living on the estates of William Dicconson at Wrightington (pp. 156–7, 164) and Lord Molyneux at Euxton (pp. 147, 150), both in Lancashire.

[84] WDA. Epist. Var. 8/31, P. Howard to Mayes, 24 July 1723.

[85] WDA. Epist. Var. 8/42, P. Howard to Mayes, 28 October 1723.

[86] RA. SP 102/76, Inverness to Ellis, 29 January 1727. In a letter of 27 January 1727 Father Lawrence Mayes in Bologna asked Father William Stuart in Rome to remember him to 'Mr Gill, when you see him' (SCA. BL 2/305/12).

[87] RA. SP 104/57, Ellis to Inverness, 26 February 1727. Ellis commented that 'those of the King and Queen, are fuller in the face than their Ma.ties are, and consequently less resemble them, than they should have done'.

[88] RA. SP 104/141, Ellis to Inverness, 12 March 1727.

[89] In 1724 Belle had painted Clementina's sister, Maria Charlotte, and signed the picture 'Pictor Regis Britann.' (Walters Art Gallery, Baltimore; copy in the Royal Palace,

Gill continued to work on these pictures for the rest of 1727 and until March 1728. At first he was supervised by Ellis, who paid him as he produced each copy,[90] but when Ellis joined the court at Bologna this task was entrusted to Girolamo Belloni. Gill made very slow progress[91] and in March 1728, when he had only finished six of the sixteen copies required, he was told to stop.[92] James III had meanwhile found a painter in Bologna to produce portraits, and all the remaining copies of the pictures by Meytens were postponed.

The painter employed by James III in Bologna was Lucia Casalini Torelli. Between January and May 1727 she produced portraits of both the Prince of Wales and the Duke of York.[93] They were sent away to Paris in May,[94] but it is not known what then happened to them, and they have been lost without trace. Torelli made copies of both portraits for one of the Bolognese senators, and they also have disappeared.[95]

Madrid). RA. SP Box 4/2/8, a list by Ellis of pictures promised but not yet finished, March 1727. The pairs of portraits were to be given to Cardinal Gualterio, the Bishop of Montefiascone, Louis, comte de Béthune, in France (first cousin of Clementina's father), and an unnamed person at Lucca. The separate portraits of the queen were for contessa Sardi at Lucca, contessa Molza at Modena, the Duchess of Melfort in France, Colonel O'Rourke in Lorraine, and Randall MacDonnell in Spain. Inverness added to this list 'a small Picture of the King' for James Hamilton, and 'a Picture of ye Prince for Sir Luke O'Tool'. There is a second 'List of Pictures promised but not yet furnished' by Ellis in RA. SP 104/139.

90 RA. SP Misc 34, account book, February and March 1727.

91 It is not known why Gill made slow progress, nor is it known where he lived. In June 1727 Father Mayes considered letting him occupy his apartment in Rome, because his servant there was ill, and he thought he might need someone else to look after it: 'Sometimes I think of Mr Gill, to putt him there, I believe he's an honest Lad: but I cann't satisfy myself, nor know wt to resolve on' (SCA. BL 2/305/16, Mayes to Stuart, 7 June 1727). Mayes's servant recovered, and it seems that Gill did not move into his apartment (SCA. BL 2/305/18, Mayes to Stuart, 2 August 1727).

92 RA. SP 112/127, Belloni to Ellis, 20 December 1727; RA. SP 102/87/36, Ellis to Belloni, 24 March 1728. Two lists of 'pictures promised', undated but June and July 1730, show that the only people who had by then received their copies were Alexis-Simon Belle, Cardinal Gualterio, the comte de Béthune and the Duchess of Melfort (RA. SP Box 4/2/11 and 9).

93 According to the notes of Clare Stuart Wortley, preserved with the Stuart Papers (part one, p. 25, taken from RA. SP Misc 35), Torelli was paid 40 *livres* in January 1727 for the portrait of the prince. Both portraits are recorded in M. Oretti, 'Notizie de' Professori del Dissegno cioè Pittori, Sculptori ed Architetti bolognesi e de' forestieri di sua scuola', 1760–80 (Biblioteca Comunale dell'Archiginnasio di Bologna, MS B. 131, c. 69) and L. Crespi, *Felsina pittrice. Vite de' pittori bolognesi* (Bologna, 1769), p. 267.

94 RA. SP 102/87/21, Ellis to Waters, 27 May 1727.

95 Irene Graziani, *La bottega dei Torelli: Da Bologna alla Russia di Caterina la Grande* (Bologna, 2005), p. 259, nos. 86 and 87. The two portraits are included among the pictures at one time in the 'Casa di Giuseppe Bianchi'. Ghiselli noted that James III went to see the portrait of Prince Charles on 28 June 1727.

While Torelli was at work on these portraits Sir William Ellis wrote from Rome to say that he was having problems with Antonio David. Ellis was under strict instructions 'to pay no pictures that are bespoke by the Queen after her going into the Convent' in November 1725,[96] yet David was now, in March 1727, painting a new portrait of Clementina for the Duchess of Melfort, which the queen was alleging the king had agreed to pay for.[97] To make matters worse, the queen had refused to pay for several other pictures, notably the full-length ones of the prince and the duke, which she had commissioned in 1726. David was understandably worried, and in April 1727 presented Ellis with a bill for eight finished portraits, amounting to ninety-nine *pistoles* (1485 *livres*).[98]

Ellis informed the king that he had refused to pay for the new portrait, and that five of the eight portraits mentioned in David's bill were the responsibility of the queen. He went further, and advised that David's prices were anyway much too high.[99] By this time James III was trying to persuade Clementina to leave the convent and join him in Bologna, so he agreed to pay David five *pistoles* (84 *livres*) for the new portrait, which was subsequently sent to the Duchess of Melfort in France.[100] He also instructed Ellis to pay David twelve *pistoles*, instead of the eighteen demanded, for the three pictures in his bill not commissioned by the queen.[101] But he refused to give way and pay anything for the remaining five.

In July, therefore, when James III went to Lorraine and then settled at Avignon, and when Queen Clementina left the convent and

[96] RA. SP 92/150, James III's orders to Ellis before he left for Bologna, 18 September 1726.

[97] RA. SP 104/141, 105/78, Ellis to Inverness, 12 and 29 March 1727; RA. SP 106/12, Ellis to James III, 16 April 1727.

[98] RA. SP Box 4/4/166, 'Copie of Mr. David ye Painter's Bill'. The bill was dated April 1727, but the copy was made by Domenico Arnoux in July 1727. It included two miniatures of the queen, each in a bracelet (8 *pistoles* each), the full-length of the prince (40 *pistoles*), two three-quarter-length copies of the prince (6 *pistoles* each), one bust copy of the prince (also 6 *pistoles*), the full-length of the duke on a cushion (12 *pistoles*), and a copy of the duke for Prince James Sobieski (10 *pistoles*). There was also a portrait of Lady Inverness for her husband (10 *pistoles*). With some incidental travel expenses, the overall total was 109 *pistoles* (1635 *livres*). The two miniatures were probably painted for David by Georg Andreas Wolfgang (NA. SP 85/16/f. 275, Stosch to Newcastle, 28 June 1727).

[99] RA. SP 106/12, Ellis to James III, 16 April 1727.

[100] RA. SP 102/87/14, Ellis to Belloni, 30 April 1727; RA. SP 102/87/67, Ellis to W. Drummond, 30 September 1727.

[101] RA. SP 112/162, receipt drawn by Belloni's clerk to be signed by David, undated but April 1727. The king agreed to pay for the three copies of the portrait of the prince, but at 4 instead of 6 *pistoles* each (RA. SP Box 4/4/166, notes by Ellis on David's bill). In addition Lord Inverness told Ellis to give David 5 instead of 10 *pistoles* for the portrait of his wife (RA. SP 102/87/14, Ellis to Belloni, 30 April 1727).

rejoined the court at Bologna, David had still not been paid anything for most of the pictures. The king now found himself in a weak bargaining position. He was keen to persuade the queen to join him in Avignon, so he ordered Ellis to tell her that he was willing to accept responsibility for all the pictures.[102] But he was much less conciliatory towards David himself, and told Ellis (who was still in Bologna) to reduce the painter's overall bill from the original ninety-nine *pistoles* (1485 *livres*) to sixty-eight *pistoles* (1020 *livres*).[103] David was extremely annoyed, so the king tried to appease him by paying an extra *pistole* for two of the three pictures which he had previously bought,[104] but Belloni wrote from Rome that he could do nothing to pacify him.[105]

Queen Clementina, who had no intention of joining her husband in Avignon, took full advantage of her strong position. In the autumn of 1727 she commissioned two religious paintings and a new portrait of herself from Lucia Casalini Torelli.[106] She also commissioned David to make several copies of his recent portrait of her, two of which were given to the Convents of Santa Cecilia and Sant' Ursula in Rome.[107] The portrait by Torelli and a copy of the one by David were given to Maria Laura Chiarini, a nun in the Convent of San Pietro Martire with whom the queen became particularly friendly. Unfortunately the one by Torelli, like those which she did of the two princes, has not survived.[108] The one by David shows her modestly dressed and as if in mourning, holding a breviary beside her crown. She seems to have lost weight under the strain

---

[102] RA. SP 111/80, 69, James III to Ellis, enclosing 'the king's orders relating to Her Ma.ts journey' [to Avignon], 16 October 1727.

[103] RA. SP Box 4/4/169, reduced account of David, 21 July 1727. The prices were reduced as follows (see note 98): 8 *pistoles* down to 6, 40 down to 30, 12 down to 6, and 10 down to 6.

[104] The king agreed to pay an extra *pistole* for each of the three-quarter-length copies of the portrait of the prince (5 instead of 4), thus making them more expensive than the bust, and Inverness also agreed to pay an extra *pistole* for the portrait of his wife (6 instead of 5).

[105] Notes of Clare Stuart Wortley with the Stuart Papers, part one, p. 19, Belloni to [Ellis], 14 January 1728.

[106] The religious paintings, now lost, were 'una Nostra Donna Addolorata, ed un Ecce Homo' (G.P. Cavazzoni Zanotti, *Storia dell'Accademia Clementina* (Bologna, 1739), vol. I, p. 88). Copies, or perhaps the originals, were later in the 'Casa di Giuseppe Bianchi' (Graziani, *la bottega dei Torelli*, p. 259, no. 86).

[107] RA. SP 117/53, Belloni's accounts, April 1728. David was paid 1 *pistole* for each copy. A copy given to the Irish Dominicans of San Clemente in Rome (73.7 × 61 cm) can still be seen in one of the private rooms of the religious house beside the church.

[108] Lodovico Frati, *Il Settecento a Bologna* (Bologna, 1923), p. 186: 'suor Laura volle due ritratti della principessa [sic], uno dei quali si conservò nel monastero fino alla sua soppressione'.

of the separation and her face, so full and beautiful in Meytens's portrait of 1725, is now pinched and thin.[109]

James III returned from Avignon to Bologna, and was finally reunited with the queen, in January 1728. During the next few months no new portraits were commissioned. Then, in June, he received requests for new portraits of the two princes from both the Dowager Duchess of Parma and Prince James Sobieski.[110] As he did not want to use Torelli again, he invited Giovanna Fratellini to come from Florence, where she was employed at the court of the Grand Duke of Tuscany. Fratellini was primarily a pastellist, but when she arrived in July the king asked her to paint portraits of himself and Clementina in oils. If he liked them he would then ask her to paint portraits in oils of his two sons.[111] And if they were good enough they might also become possible replacements for the portraits by Meytens which Gill had been copying until March of that year.

Fratellini's portraits were finished in September 1728, and cost twenty *pistoles* each.[112] James was apparently disappointed with them, but he decided to commission five pastels from her: original portraits of the prince and the duke, a copy of the one of the prince, and copies of the oil portraits of himself and the queen. They were all finished in Florence by January 1729, when the king left Bologna and returned to Rome, but they were judged to be no better than the previous ones in oils.[113] James sent the set of four as a present for Admiral Thomas Gordon,[114] recently promoted to be the commander-in-chief of the Russian Baltic Fleet. The fifth pastel, which showed Prince Charles, was probably sent to Bishop Atterbury in France.[115] All five pastels, and both the oils, have disappeared without trace.

In 1729, when the court returned permanently to the Palazzo del Re in Rome, Prince Charles was eight and a half years old, and Prince Henry was just four. Both boys had changed a great deal since they had been painted by David in 1726, and new portraits of them were badly needed. In addition, James still needed copies of the portraits by Meytens, which had been promised to several people. The obvious

---

[109] Corp, *King over the Water*, p. 67, fig. 53.
[110] Notes of Clare Stuart Wortley with the Stuart Papers, part one, p. 24.
[111] RA. SP 117/137, James III to Innes, 28 June 1728.
[112] RA. SP 120/157, instructions of James III for Ellis, after 17 September 1728; notes of Clare Stuart Wortley with the Stuart Papers, part one, p. 25.
[113] Notes of Clare Stuart Wortley with the Stuart Papers, part one, p. 25.
[114] HMC, *10th Report*, p. 162, James III to Gordon, 5 March 1729.
[115] Atterbury had been promised the next available portrait of Prince Charles (RA. SP 117/137, James III to Innes, 28 June 1728).

person to provide both the new portraits and the copies was David, who could therefore be appeased for his recent disappointments by being generously paid for these commissions. This was clearly in the king's mind when he agreed to pay the large bill which Fratellini presented in January 1729. All five of her pastels were to be paid as though they were originals, at eight *pistoles* each, with a further forty *pistoles* to cover her expenses in providing the glass-fronted frames and in sending them from Florence to Bologna.[116] As Edgar wrote to Ellis from Rome on 19 February, 'H.M. seems to think that it is not worth the while to give the Paintress occasion to complain, when probably he wont have further occasion to employ her.'[117]

[116] RA. SP 124/160, James III to Ellis, 29 January 1729; RA. SP Box 4/4/3, payments to Fratellini 'per no. 5 ritratti' and for 'spese fatte per i ritratti', January 1729; RA. SP Misc 35, account book, 11 February 1729; RA. SP 126/68, receipt by Fratellini, 29 March 1729.
[117] RA. SP 125/52, Edgar to Ellis, 19 February 1729.

6   The Jacobite courtiers, 1719–1726

At the beginning of 1720, shortly after James III and Queen Clementina moved into the Palazzo del Re, the Stuart court employed eighty-three people, of whom sixty-five had lodgings in the palazzo. In addition to these salaried household servants there were also nineteen exiled Jacobites who received pensions from the king and were regarded as attached to the court. In the following years the numbers fluctuated. By 1725 there were eighty-seven salaried servants and thirteen pensioners.[1] The increase in the number of servants was occasioned by the births of the Prince of Wales in December 1720 and of the Duke of York in March 1725. The reduction in the number of pensioners was mainly caused by the departure of some of the Scots.

Most of the Jacobite courtiers were unmarried or widowed, though some of them had left their wives behind at Saint-Germain. In 1720 only fifteen of the salaried servants were living in Rome with their spouses. There were four couples of which both the husband and the wife were employed,[2] all of them with lodgings in the palazzo. There were seven other servants living in the palazzo with their wives,[3] whose presence

---

[1] See Appendix A. The list of the salaried servants and pensioners at Urbino in 1718 is given in Corp, *Jacobites at Urbino*, pp. 152–5. There is no list in the Stuart Papers for 1720, so it has been created (1) by comparing the 1718 list with the list in RA. SP Misc 34, which shows all the courtiers (except those employed in the household and stables) in November 1722, (2) by extracting the names mentioned both in the accounts for 1720–2 (also in RA. SP Misc 34) and various letters and diaries, (3) by examining the lists of servants still employed in 1726 and later (e.g. RA. SP Box 3/81) and (4) by examining the registers of baptisms, marriages and burials for the parish of Santi Apostoli (ASVR. vols. 12, 22 and 41). The list of people who had accommodation in the Palazzo del Re in 1720 is shown in the *Stati d'Anime* for the parish of Santi Apostoli (ASVR. vol. 57, pp. 36–7). Two people who were possibly omitted by mistake are shown in a supplementary list of 1723 (same reference, p. 92).

[2] Richard and Margaret Baines, Gerald and Mary Fitzgerald, John and Marjory Hay, Nicolas and Anne Prévot.

[3] Antoine and Elisabeth Brun, Nicholas and Mary Anne Clark, Henry and Elizabeth Kerby, Bernard and Maria Anna Nieriker, Gottfried and Angela Rittel, Michele and Anna Vezzosi, Joseph and Katherine Weber.

increased the relatively small number of women at the court. On the other hand there were very few children: only eight in 1720, including an eighteen-year-old girl.[4] Between 1720 and 1726 one of these children died,[5] but ten more were born.[6] Child mortality, however, was high: three of the ten died before their first birthday.[7] During these years there were only two recorded marriages among the servants, and one of them was clearly a special case. The eighteen-year-old girl, daughter of the king's chairman (recruited at Avignon), married one of the English footmen in 1721 and gave birth to a baby boy less than three months later.[8] Among the pensioners there was only one married couple, the Earl and Countess of Nithsdale. The rest were all single men, though not necessarily unmarried.

Approximately half of the salaried servants had originally been employed at Saint-Germain and Bar-le-Duc. Ten had joined the court at Avignon and six at Urbino. Of the eighty-three working in the Palazzo del Re in 1720, twenty-six had been recruited in Rome, mainly to serve the queen or to work in the stables. There were twenty-three Irish, eighteen French, seventeen English, ten Scots, eight Italians, five Germans and two Swiss. Fifteen out of the seventeen English were Catholic. The Irish, French, Italians, Germans and Swiss were all Catholic. Six out of the ten Scots were Protestant. There were consequently only eight Protestants, and this small number included the two chaplains.[9] In the following six years, up to 1726, twenty-one new servants were recruited, of whom only one (an Englishman) was Protestant.[10] Seven were English, five were French and four were Italian. Three were Irish and only two were Scottish.[11] A trend was therefore set, which would be continued in the years to come. Except in the stables, the

---

[4] One Brun, 3 (Henry) Kerbys, 1 Prévot, 2 Rittels, 1 Raffa. (Maria Raffa was a widow.) The 18-year-old girl was Thérèse Brun.

[5] A son of the Rittels.

[6] One (James) Kerby, 4 Nierikers, 2 Prévots, 1 Rittel, 2 Vezzosis.

[7] All three were children of the Nierikers.

[8] James Kerby married Thérèse Brun on 17 February 1721 (ASVR. Santi Apolstoli vol. 22, p. 93). Their son was baptised on 8 May 1721 (ASVR. Santi Apostoli vol. 12, p. 135). The other marriage was between two of the queen's German servants. Her tailor (Joseph Weber) married one of her chambermaids (Katherine Kloppelin) in January 1720 (ASVR. Santi Apostoli vol. 22, p. 89).

[9] The English Protestants were the Revd Patrick Cowper and Sir William Ellis. The Scottish Protestants were the Revd George Barclay, John Hay, Marjory Hay, Francis Kennedy, Dr Charles Maghie and James Murray.

[10] Thomas Forster. Some of the new servants were probably already living in Rome, but others were invited to come from the Jacobite community at Saint-Germain and Paris.

[11] See note 1.

Stuart court would remain English,[12] but its Irish and Scottish servants would gradually be replaced by French and Italians.

The pensioners, by contrast, were mainly Scottish and all had gone into exile following the unsuccessful rising in 1715–16. In 1720 there were fifteen Scots, two English (including Winifred, née Herbert, the wife of the Scottish Earl of Nithsdale) and two Irishmen. The balance between nationality and religion was similar to that among the servants: all the Scots were Protestant except Lord Nithsdale, whereas all the English and Irish were Catholic except Thomas Forster.

While the court was at Urbino there had been friction between these groups, notably the old servants from Saint-Germain (mainly English and Catholic) and the new exiles (mainly Scottish and Protestant), but by 1720 these differences had been largely overcome. In part this was the result of the passing of time. When the court was established in Rome in the winter of 1719–20 even the new exiles had been abroad for nearly four years. In part it was because most of the senior servants and several of the new exiles, including the Duke of Mar, had left the court to live elsewhere. But mainly it was because the various national and religious groups were brought together by their shared hostility towards the king's three favourites, John Hay, his wife, Marjory Hay, and particularly the latter's brother James Murray. As these three were also detested by Queen Clementina, the factions which had divided the court at Urbino were now also drawn together by their shared loyalty to the young, attractive and popular queen.

The salaries and pensions paid to the Jacobite courtiers in Rome remained the same as they had been at Urbino, though the cost of living was obviously much higher.[13] The king continued to provide food for the more senior servants,[14] but the most important factor which determined the standard of living of the courtiers was whether or not they had accommodation in the palazzo. The pensioners were all obliged to find and rent their own lodgings in the surrounding area. Lord Nithsdale commented on one occasion that 'my Master allowes both my wife and me as much as he dos to any of our companions', but explained that

---

[12] It is not easy to distinguish the Welsh from the English servants, but there is evidence that they were conscious of their separate national identity. See Bod. Lib. Rawlinson MSS 1180, p. 303, Rawlinson's diary, 1 March 1721: 'This being St. David's Day was observed here by the Welch in the [king's] service who wore their leeks, as did the [king] and his spouse themselves, and their son was dressed accordingly.'

[13] RA. SP Misc 34 and SP Box 3/81. The salaries and pensions were paid in Bolognese rather than French *livres*. For the salaries and pensions at Urbino, also paid in Bolognese *livres*, see Corp, *Jacobites at Urbino*, pp. 152–3.

[14] RA. SP 103/29, Ellis to Inverness, 5 February 1727.

'thos that has lodgings and diet in the house can afford to goe more desent in their cloaths than wee'.[15] He had a monthly pension of 200 *livres*, but had to spend nearly half of it (about 90 *livres*) on his lodgings, leaving only 110 *livres* 'for cloathing and diet to myself and servant, which in this place are both very dear, especially cloathing'.[16] As the available accommodation in the palazzo was reserved for the household servants, it is not surprising that several of the pensioners, notably the Nithsdales, were keen to obtain a salaried post in the royal household.[17] What they particularly wanted was to serve the queen and to be involved in the upbringing of the Stuart princes.

Those exiled Jacobites who were able to have money sent to them from England or Scotland inevitably enjoyed a higher standard of living. The Earl of Southesk received money from his relations but not enough to maintain him in the house he rented from the duca di Gaetani in the Strada Vittoria. By the beginning of 1723 he was seriously in debt and had to ask James III to give him enough money to cover the rent and escape his creditors by going to France.[18] He returned a few months later accompanied by his Protestant wife, Margaret (née Stuart),[19] and with a sufficient income from Scotland to move into the Palazzo Vidaschi.[20] Lady Southesk was soon pregnant and gave birth to a baby girl named Clementina in September 1724.[21] She, like Lady

[15] H. Tayler, *Lady Nithsdale and Her Family* (London, 1939), p. 177, Nithsdale to Lady Traquair, 14 April 1723.

[16] *Ibid.*, p. 179, Nithsdale to Lady Traquair, 28 September 1723.

[17] The Nithsdales lived in the third of three apartments in a building named the 'Fabbrica nova de Luchesi'. At first they employed a valet, a chambermaid, a servant and a cook (from Urbino), but by 1723 they had reduced their staff to a chambermaid (Cecilia Evans) and two servants (ASVR. Santi Apostoli vol. 57, p. 88; vol. 59, unpaginated; vol. 60, unpaginated, *Stati d'Anime* for 1721, 1723–5). James Edgar and Charles Forbes shared the second of seven lodgings in a house called 'Il Palazzaccio' and had no servants (ASVR. Santi Apostoli vol. 57, pp. 17, 63; vol. 58, unpaginated, *Stati d'Anime* for 1720–2). None of the other pensioners is shown in the *Stati d'Anime* for the parish of Santi Apostoli, so they presumably all lived around the Piazza di Spagna. Lord Southesk and Colonel William Clepham lived in the Strada Vittoria (Ingamells, *Dictionary*, pp. 216, 879).

[18] BL. Add MSS 20310, p. 327, Southesk to Gualterio, 22 April 1723; NA. SP 85/14/ff. 320, 328, 336, 362, 366, 374, Stosch to Carteret, 10 and 24 April, 22 May, 8, 12 and 19 June 1723; BL. Add MSS 31265, pp. 27, 38, Hay to Gualterio, both undated (June 1723).

[19] SCA. BL 2/252/7, T. Innes to W. Stuart, 20 September 1723; NA. SP 85/14/ff. 471, 488, 498, 502, Stosch to Carteret, 9, 23 and 30 October, 6 November 1723. His wife was a daughter of the 5th Earl of Galloway.

[20] ASVR. Santi Apostoli vol. 59, unpaginated, *Stati d'Anime* for 1724.

[21] ASVR. Santi Apostoli vol. 60, unpaginated, *Stati d'Anime* for 1725–6. The Southesks employed a valet, a chambermaid, two servants and a cook.

Nithsdale (though with less financial need), became a candidate for a post in the service of the queen.

The fact that nearly all the pensioners were Protestant made it easier for the Stuart court to take on the role of a surrogate British embassy for the Grand Tourists visiting Rome during these years, including the provision of church services. As Baron Stosch reported to London, 'the Pope had given his permission and actually allowed ... that the divine service be publicly celebrated according to the Protestant rite' in the Palazzo del Re. This was not only for the king's household servants but 'for all those Protestants who wished to attend'.[22]

The king's two Protestant chaplains and the Protestant pensioners, like his English speaking doctors, played a very important role in welcoming Grand Tourists and helping them during their visits to the city.[23] As Stosch also observed, 'the nature of the English being to prefer the company of those belonging to their own nation rather than that of the local inhabitants, they are unwittingly led into the company of the [Jacobites]'.[24] The Jacobite pensioners included five peers (the earls of Linlithgow, Nithsdale, Southesk and Winton, and Viscount Kilsyth) as well as several gentlemen (Colonel Alan Cameron, Colonel William Clepham, Major John Cockburne, Captain Collier, James Edgar and Charles Forbes), and they went out of their way to greet their fellow countrymen, particularly the Scots. They frequented 'all the cafés in the piazza di Spagna, where the foreigners live and ... latch on to them with their offers of assistance, and make themselves agreeable to the young people in hundreds of different ways'.[25] They helped them find accommodation, they showed them the major sites of Rome, they recommended portrait painters, they introduced them to Roman society, and they helped provide diplomatic protection. Referring to James III in one of his letters, Stosch regretted 'the protection and domination' that he exercised over 'all the English who come into the Papal States'.[26]

The key point, of course, was the fact that the king could provide protection for Protestants. In April 1721 Richard Rawlinson noted in his diary that the Episcopalian chaplain at the court had conducted a marriage service for one of the visiting Grand Tourists.[27] A particularly important question was what would happen if a Protestant, whether a household servant, a Jacobite pensioner or a visiting Grand Tourist, were

[22] NA. SP 85/16/f. 118, Stosch to Newcastle, 15 August 1726.
[23] NA. SP 85/15/f. 228, Stosch to Newcastle, 16 December 1724.
[24] NA. SP 85/14/f. 228, Stosch to Carteret, 12 January 1723.
[25] NA. SP 85/14/f. 181, Stosch to Carteret, 1 December 1722.
[26] NA. SP 85/15/f. 265, Stosch to Newcastle, 30 January 1725.
[27] Bod. Lib. Rawlinson MSS D. 1181, p. 353, Rawlinson's diary, 25 April 1721.

to die while in Rome. Would he be allowed to have a proper Christian burial? Before he arrived in the city James III had persuaded the Pope to set aside an area to be used in the future as a Protestant cemetery.[28] It was not needed by the court at first, but then a Grand Tourist died in March 1723, followed by one of the Scottish pensioners, the Earl of Linlithgow, in April. The latter was thus the first courtier to be buried in the cemetery. Stosch reported that 'a Scotsman named Graham died here last week, a relation of Mylord Linlitgou, and was buried beside the sepuchral Pyramid of Cajus Cestius, a place designated to be the grave-yard for the English (not the Roman Catholics) with the connivence of the government for the last few years'.[29] Lord Linlithgow, who presum-ably died of the same illness as his relation, was buried in the new cemetery beside the Pyramid of Caius Cestius a few days later.[30] The next Protestant to be buried there was another Grand Tourist who died in July 1726.[31] It was not until 1732 that one of the Protestant house-hold servants (Sir William Ellis) died and was also buried there.[32]

The departments

James III was served in his Bedchamber by a small staff of seven people. He had a French yeoman of the robes (James Rodez), two valets who were also barbers, one of whom was French (Thomas Saint-Paul), the other Irish (Gerald Fitzgerald), two other valets who were French (Felix Bonbled and Pierre Bouffer), a French servant to help the valets, and an Irish washerwoman. By 1726 he had reduced the number of his valets from four to three. In 1722 or 1723 (the precise date is uncertain) Gerald Fitzgerald died and Pierre Bouffer was replaced by another Frenchman (François Delaux). This modest team of Frenchmen then continued to serve the king in his Bedchamber for many years, which means that James began and ended each day speaking French to his servants.

What had once been the Chamber was now reduced to a skeleton staff of four people. They included the king's Irish Dominican confessor, Father John Brown; his two Protestant chaplains, the Episcopalian George Barclay and the Anglican Patrick Cowper; and his Scottish personal physician, Dr Charles Maghie. A second physician, who was

---

[28] See Chapter 1, p. 20.   [29] NA. SP 85/14/f. 310, Stosch to Carteret, 3 April 1723.
[30] Bod. Lib. Rawlinson MSS D.1180, p. 1555, Rawlinson's diary, 6 April 1723.
[31] NA. SP 85/16/f. 104, Stosch to Newcastle, 6 July 1726.
[32] Valesio, *Diario di Roma*, v, p. 504, 4 August 1732; NA. SP 98/32/f. 424, Stosch to Newcastle, 12 August 1732.

Scottish (Dr Robert Wright), had joined the court as a pensioner by 1721, and a French servant (Pierre Arnoux) was employed to look after the Chapel Royal. As there was neither a lord chamberlain nor a vice-chamberlain, the king needed someone to deal with the ceremonial of receiving important visitors in his apartment. This task was entrusted to John Hay as *maggiordomo*. In October 1722 he was replaced by Thomas Forster, who until then had been one of the unemployed pensioners.[33]

The household below stairs and the stables were much larger, and were both supervised by the *maggiordomo*. The former was divided, as it had been at Urbino, into four sub-departments: the kitchen, the confectionary, the bakehouse and the wine cellar. The clerk of the kitchen, now referred to as the *maestro di casa*, was an Irishman, Jeremiah Broomer. He was supported by three cooks, an assistant cook and three kitchen boys. The yeoman confectioner, now known as the *confetiere*, was French and had his own personal servant as well as an assistant, but the French baker worked by himself.[34] The yeoman of the wine cellar (the *bottigliere*), Charles Macarty, was another Irishman. He had an assistant, a scourer and his own personal servant. These twelve lower servants included four Englishmen, four Italians, three Frenchmen and an Irishman, but no Scots. When one of the English cooks died in 1720 he was replaced by a Frenchman. All these servants were Catholic.

The stables employed twenty-six people, most of whom had previously served at Urbino. The king had an Irish coachman (*primo cocchiere*: Edmund Butler), two chairmen, six footmen, four grooms, who themselves had two helpers, and a harbourer of the deer. There were also seven postillions, who seem to have been recruited after the court's arrival in Rome. The most important servants, however, were the French equerry (James Delattre) and the Irish riding purveyor (John Sheridan). The people employed in the stables were mainly Irish, but also included some English, some French and one Swiss. There were no Scots and only one Italian, but another Italian joined the household in 1722 when the king decided to employ a third chairman. Like the servants in the household below stairs, they were all Catholic.

The presence of all these servants of different national origins and backgrounds, speaking a variety of languages, must have given the Stuart

---

[33] BL. Add MSS 31264, p. 98, Hay to Gualterio, 31 October 1722; RA. SP 62/151, Hay to Mar, 3 November 1722. The Italian title *maggiordomo* had been introduced at Pesaro and Urbino to describe the official in charge of the household below stairs, the table and the stables. Hay had held the post since April or May 1718 (Corp, *Jacobites at Urbino*, pp. 17, 60–6).

[34] Unlike the kitchen, the confectionary and the wine cellar, the bakery was not actually situated within the Palazzo del Re (ASVR. Santi Apostoli vol. 57, pp. 36–7).

court in Rome a very cosmopolitan atmosphere. As time went by the royal household inevitably became increasingly Italian, but in these early years it continued to be primarily English, French and Irish. The salaries of all these servants were paid by a Protestant Englishman, Sir William Ellis, who had already served for many years as controller and treasurer.[35] He was subordinate to the *maggiordomo* until 1722, after which he was given independent responsibility for receiving and spending the king's papal pension and other sources of revenue.[36] He was supported by an English assistant.

The secretariat

In 1720 James III's political secretariat contained only four people. There was no secretary of state because the Duke of Mar had resigned the seals in 1719 and had not been replaced. The unpopular James Murray was therefore serving in a temporary capacity as acting secretary of state, supported by a Scottish under-secretary. This was Francis Kennedy, whom the king had met while he was in Spain and brought back with him, and who had previously been with the Duke of Ormonde.[37] Neither of these two men could understand Italian, and it seems that their French was not very good either.[38] James therefore continued to employ Sir David Nairne, who had previously had independent responsibility for all the king's Catholic correspondence, but was now effectively demoted and made subordinate to Murray.[39] At the beginning of 1721 a second under-secretary was employed, who was fluent in French. This was Thomas Sheridan, an Irishman who had previously lived for many years at Saint-Germain.[40] Finally the Agent of the English Clergy in Rome, Father Lawrence Mayes, was employed as Latin secretary.[41]

As we shall see in the next chapter, James Murray left the court in February 1721 and was replaced as acting secretary of state by John Hay, who continued also to serve as *maggiordomo* until October 1722. Hay was formally appointed secretary of state in March 1725.[42]

[35] Corp, *Court in Exile*, pp. 360, 362–3; Corp, *Jacobites at Urbino*, p. 66.
[36] BL. Add MSS 31264, p. 98, Hay to Gualterio, 31 October 1722.
[37] H. Tayler, *The Seven Sons of the Provost* (London, 1949), pp. 16–17.
[38] In a letter to Gualterio dated 13 November 1720 Murray wrote that 'je supplie V.E. d'avoir la bonté d'excuser mon françois' (BL. Add MSS 31262, f. 44).
[39] Corp, *Jacobites at Urbino*, pp. 142–3.
[40] *SPW*, p. 62, Hay to Murray (not to Edgar as printed), 16 December 1720.
[41] BL. Add MSS 31263, f. 190, Murray to Gualterio, undated; RA. SP 89/4, note by Nairne, January 1726.
[42] Ruvigny, *Jacobite Peerage*, p. 215.

The king's three favourites

Many people at the time, and since, have wondered why James III showed so much favour to John Hay, his wife, Marjory Hay, and the latter's brother James Murray. The history of the Stuart court in Rome would have been very different if the king had not placed so much confidence in people who were disliked and distrusted by most of the other household servants and pensioners, and indeed by virtually all the Jacobites in France and Spain.

Some people have speculated that James had an affair with Marjory Hay after his marriage to Queen Clementina. However, there is no evidence to support this idea, which was a rumour deliberately invented by the king's enemies.[43]

John Hay, who was the brother-in-law of the Duke of Mar, had joined the exiled court at Avignon in 1716, but was not included among the Jacobites invited to follow the court to Pesaro at the beginning of the following year. He must, however, have made a favourable impression on the king, because the latter soon regretted his decision and asked him to rejoin the court. James wrote to Mar that 'you know the kindness I have for him'.[44]

The king became particularly friendly with Hay during his first visit to Rome, from May to July 1717.[45] Immediately after that visit the court moved to Urbino, and James informed Mar that Hay 'hath my favour and he knows it, and nobody shall be able to take it from him ... 'tis a pleasure to be attended by such a one'.[46] Hay was then rapidly promoted. In August 1717 he was appointed groom of the Bedchamber, in the spring of 1718 he was promoted to be *maggiordomo*, and in October 1718 he was created Earl of Inverness.[47]

James III and John Hay were of approximately the same age, and appear simply to have liked each other – and no one then or later has ever hinted at any homosexual attraction. Hay had married Marjory Murray in July 1715, shortly before the Jacobite rising of that year, and had left his wife behind in Scotland. Thus the favour shown by the king to John Hay pre-dated Marjory Hay's arrival at the court. In March 1718 James III stated that he would not allow any women to join the court until he himself was married, but a few months later, as a special favour

---

[43] The question is considered in Bryan Bevan, *King James the Third of England* (London, 1967), pp. 132–3.
[44] HMC *Stuart*, IV, p. 140, James III to Mar, 27 March 1717.
[45] Corp, *Jacobites at Urbino*, chapter 2.
[46] HMC *Stuart*, IV, p. 445, James III to Mar, 13 July 1717, with postscript of 16 July.
[47] Corp, *Jacobites at Urbino*, pp. 60–6.

to John Hay, he made an exception and allowed the latter to invite his wife, Marjory, whom he had not seen for two and a half years. She arrived at Urbino in July 1718, accompanied by her brother James Murray.[48]

Murray was extremely ambitious and used his connection with Hay to gain the confidence and favour of the king. At the end of 1718 the court left Urbino and moved to Rome, but James then left for Spain with Hay in February 1719 to join a Spanish fleet being assembled to invade England. As the Duke of Mar also left the court at the same time, the king entrusted the entire management of the court to Murray.[49] No doubt James had a high opinion of the latter's abilities, but we may assume that his chief recommendation was his close relationship with John Hay. Marjory Hay remained in Rome with her brother and did not accompany her husband and the king.

It was during 1719 that the close friendship between James III and Hay was further consolidated, because they shared a series of experiences which involved danger, triumph and deep despair. Accompanied by only three servants, they sailed together in a small French ship from Nettuno to Villefranche, avoiding the British fleet patrolling the area, and risking imminent shipwreck because of terrible storms. After a day at Villefranche the two men travelled on to one of the islands opposite Hyères, where they stayed incognito in a tavern and were obliged by the landlady to dance with her. They then sailed to Marseille, where they hid for three days in a house owned by the master of the ship, before continuing their journey to Catalonia. They landed safely in March 1719.[50]

These bonding experiences were followed by a state entry into Madrid and residence as the honoured guests of King Philip V in the Buen Retiro palace. The king and Hay then travelled to Corunna in Galicia to join the invasion force, but when they arrived there in April were told that the fleet had been destroyed in a storm and that the invasion of England could not therefore be contemplated.

A small diversionary force, meanwhile, had succeeded in sailing for Scotland, so the king decided to remain in Galicia in the hope of going to Scotland to join a Jacobite rising there. For three whole months James III and John Hay lived in the small and remote town of Lugo.[51] How they spent their time we do not know. No doubt they went to Santiago de Compostela together; perhaps they took walks and went hunting. They must have talked and talked. What matters is that the two

---

[48] *Ibid.*, p. 57.   [49] *Ibid.*, chapter 12.   [50] Bevan, *King James the Third*, pp. 115–16.
[51] Corp, *Jacobites at Urbino*, p. 130.

men shared the experience of living together from April to July 1719, thrown upon each other's company, two close friends living without ceremony, and sharing all their hopes and fears. When the Jacobite defeat at Glenshiel obliged them to return to Italy they had become intimate friends for life. The visit to Spain in 1719 needs to be constantly borne in mind if we are to understand the favouritism shown by James III to John Hay, his wife and his brother-in-law.

The king and Hay met Queen Clementina and Murray at Montefiascone in September. James III was thirty-one years old; Clementina was only seventeen. James had experienced several military campaigns and endured both hardship and danger; Clementina was inexperienced and lacking in education. It was hardly surprising that the king felt closer to his friend than to his new wife. At Montefiascone James began to hear criticisms of the way Murray had behaved during his absence. As Murray was defended by his sister, Marjory, and the latter was supported by her husband, the king was not willing to give any credence to what was said.[52]

James III also regarded as a threat to his own authority any criticism of the man whom he had appointed. And it was this which was to be the king's chief motivation in the years to come. James was determined to maintain absolute control over his own court and household – which, after all, was in the last resort all that remained of an exiled king's authority. Criticism of Hay and of Hay's brother-in-law was regarded by the king as tantamount to the undermining of his authority.

James needed to appoint a new secretary of state, to replace the Duke of Mar, but the only possible candidates (notably Lord Lansdowne, then Bishop Atterbury) made it clear that they would not join the court so long as Hay remained there.[53] The king would not be dictated to in the management of his court, so he preferred to keep Hay and do without a secretary of state.

Similarly, the new queen expected to have the management of her own household. But she was young and regarded as irresponsible, so that giving her any independent authority – as Hay pointed out – would threaten to undermine the king's own authority.[54] The king was not willing to run this risk, at least while the queen was still relatively young, so he preferred to maintain his absolute control and accept that she would become increasingly dissatisfied.

By 1720 it had become virtually impossible to attract any nobleman to leave Great Britain voluntarily to join the court, so James III had to

---

[52] *Ibid.*, Chapter 13.   [53] See below, Chapter 7, p. 139, and Chapter 10, p. 199.
[54] See below, Chapter 7, p. 144.

employ people who were already in exile. Both Hay and Murray were the sons of Scottish peers, a reason in itself for not wanting to lose them. Moreover they were Protestants, so their presence at the court was symbolically important. They were tactless and even overbearing towards the other courtiers, and were detested by the queen, but they appeared devoted to the king and keen to maintain his absolute control over the court, so James regarded them as indispensable.

Marjory Hay, whom Baron von Stosch described as 'blind in one eye' and in danger of 'losing the second one also',[55] was merely the link between her husband and her brother. Of course we may assume that the king liked her, and that the favour shown to her husband and brother made her as haughty as them. But just as the king's principal friendship was with John Hay, so her own principal loyalty was to her husband. She was the wife of the king's favourite, and for that reason was resented by the queen, but there is nothing to indicate that she was the king's mistress.[56]

The queen's servants

The queen had servants, but she had no independent control over them. Just as her apartment on the second floor was referred to as the 'King and Queen's Apartment',[57] so her servants were in reality members of the king's household and answerable to him. She had a very small staff attached to her Bedchamber and an even smaller one attached to her Chamber, but she was totally dependent on the servants of her husband in the household below stairs and the stables.

In 1720 the queen had one Scottish lady of the Bedchamber, one Irish Bedchamber woman, two Scottish chambermaids, four general servants (English, Irish, Italian and French), two washerwomen (Irish and English) and a 'mender and marker of linen' (Irish). Most of these people were merely the wives of some of the king's servants. Thus the lady was Marjory, wife of John Hay, one of the chambermaids was Mary, wife of Gerald Fitzgerald (*valet de chambre* and barber), one of the servants was Margaret, wife of Richard Baines (cook), one of the washerwomen was Anna, widow of Lawrence Doyle (helper in the stables)[58] and the mender was Anne, wife of Nicolas Prévot (footman). The second chambermaid

[55] NA. SP 85/16/f. 95, Stosch to Newcastle, 15 June 1726.
[56] Stosch began to insinuate this in the autumn of 1724 (NA. SP 85/16/f. 218, Stosch to Newcastle, 25 November 1724).
[57] RA. SP 98/131, an 'inventory of the King's Palace at Rome', October 1726.
[58] Lawrence Doyle died in December 1719, followed by Richard Baines in May 1720 (ASVR. Santi Apostoli vol. 41, pp. 133, 135).

was Mary Fitzgerald's unmarried sister, Isabella Gordon. One of the other servants was Sarah Maguirk, whose husband had been one of the king's grooms. The only woman attached to the queen who could be regarded in any real sense as belonging to her was her Bedchamber woman, Eleanor, Lady Misset, whose husband had been one of the three Irishmen who had rescued her from house arrest at Innsbruck.

The queen was also served by a small group of five men. She had two valets, a servant, a confessor and a secretary. One of the valets was Michele Vezzosi, previously one of the king's valets. The servant was Alexander Gordon, brother of Mary Fitzgerald and Isabella Gordon. Her confessor was Father John Brown, who was also the king's confessor. Her secretary was Robert Creagh, an Irishman who had previously worked for the Duke of Mar and James Murray. The only man attached to the queen who really belonged to her was her senior valet, called Gottfried Rittel.

Rittel was one of a small staff of servants appointed by Clementina's mother to accompany her to Italy and remain with her once she was married. It is not clear how many of them there were, but they certainly included two chambermaids, a tailor and his wife and another valet, as well as Rittel. Even before the king's return from Spain in August 1719 Murray had argued that they should all be sent back to the Sobieski estate at Ohlau in Silesia.[59] At some point in 1720, probably during the spring, he had his way. All the German servants were dismissed, with the single exception of Rittel.[60] As the queen could not yet speak English, Rittel was therefore the only person with whom she could converse in her own language. She could, of course, speak French, which created a divide between those of her servants who could and those who could not speak that language. The wives of the old servants, and any others who had been at Saint-Germain, were thus distinguished from Marjory Hay, who primarily spoke English.

The situation was very unsatisfactory, but it was not only the result of James III's determination to maintain absolute control over the household. There were several other reasons. There was limited accommodation in the Palazzo del Re, so it was convenient to employ the wives of servants who were already lodged there. James wished to economise by having as small a household as possible. It was not easy to recruit suitable British and French servants in Rome. But the essential

---

[59] Corp, *Jacobites at Urbino*, p. 136.
[60] BL. Add MSS 31263, f. 196, Murray to Gualterio, undated (1720). The German servants are shown in the list of people living in the Palazzo del Re at Easter 1720 (ASVR. Santi Apostoli vol. 57, pp. 36–7).

reason seems to have been because the king had abolished formal waiting in his own Bedchamber and Chamber and decided that his wife should live in the same way. He was content to be served by his valets, so he felt that she should similarly be served by no servants more elevated than chambermaids and valets.[61] But there was an essential difference. When the king received visitors or went out he could be accompanied by his *maggiordomo* or his secretary of state, or by one of his pensioners. The queen needed some ladies of sufficient rank to attend her, and in 1720 only one of the pensioners, Lord Nithsdale, had been joined in Rome by his wife. As James distrusted Lady Nithsdale, he imposed on the queen the wife of his favourite John Hay as an informal lady of the Bedchamber, and allowed her to take Lady Misset as a Bedchamber woman. But the queen resented the fact that someone of her rank, both by birth and by marriage, was not properly attended and served. She wanted her own separate and independent household, and she wanted a staff of several ladies of the Bedchamber and several gentlemen. The king's refusal to grant her them meant that his relationship with her was bound to become seriously strained.

During 1720 there was little that the queen could do, but she set about cultivating the loyalty of Lady Misset, her chambermaids and her valets, so that they would support her in the event of any future rupture. Sooner or later she would become pregnant, and if she gave birth to a child, particularly a boy, it would be necessary to appoint a new team of women. Who was to choose these women, how many should there be, and what should be their social status? To whom should they feel primarily responsible, the queen or the king? In the summer of 1720 it was announced that the queen was pregnant, and the courtiers began to wait with growing anticipation to see what arrangements the king would make.

The allocation of space

When the Stuart court moved into the palazzo at the beginning of 1719 it was necessary to decide where the most important courtiers should be accommodated. At that time they included the Duke and Duchess of Mar, John and Marjory Hay, James Murray, Sir David Nairne and Sir William Ellis. The king and queen occupied the first and second floors of the *palazzo grande*, so it was the principal two floors of the two *palazzetti* on the east side which needed to be allocated.

---

[61] Tayler, *Lady Nithsdale*, p. 145, Lady Nithsdale to Lady Traquair, 18 May 1720.

James III decided that Mar, Hay, Murray and Nairne should all be given apartments on the first floor. As Mar and Hay had come to Rome with their wives, their accommodation had to be large enough for two people. Mar was given the apartment with the *loggetta* on the east side of the north-east *palazzetto*, overlooking the Piazza della Pilotta. It contained a private inner staircase which connected it to the second floor, so the apartment above was given to the Duchess of Mar.[62]

There were no other private staircases, so that John Hay's wife had to be accommodated with him on the first floor. The architecture of the Palazzo del Re therefore dictated that, whereas the queen, the Duchess of Mar and the more important female servants (such as Lady Misset) were accommodated on the second floor, Marjory Hay exceptionally lived with her husband on the first floor.

It is difficult to ascertain the usage of each room, but it seems that Murray and Nairne both lived in the south-east *palazzetto*, which also contained the secretariat; that Murray's apartment was beside that of the king, overlooking the church and buildings of Santi Apostoli;[63] and that Nairne's was between those of Murray and Mar, facing the back of the Palazzo Muti.[64] The Hays lived on the other side of the palazzo in a sequence of rooms overlooking the Vicolo dell'Archetto in the north wing, which connected the *palazzo grande* and the north-east *palazzetto*.[65] Those rooms were selected to become the apartment of the *maggiordomo* and his wife because there were enough of them and because they were beside both the grand staircase and the king's Guard Chamber. Sir William Ellis was given an apartment on the second floor above the back entrance facing the Palazzo Muti.[66]

Because Mar had left the court in February 1719 his apartment was actually vacant, as was the one above when in October the duchess also left. This meant that throughout 1720, and so long as the king hoped that Mar and his wife might return, the best of the available apartments for courtiers in the Palazzo del Re were unoccupied. It was no wonder

---

[62] RA. SP 62/151, Hay to Mar, 3 November 1722; ASV. PAC 983, no. 64/9, payments made by the *Camera Apostolica* for King James III, 20 October 1724. The staircase can be seen in ASR. Collezione Disegni et Piante I, c. 87, n. 562, 'Palazzo Muti-Papazzuri', tipo II.

[63] BL. Add MSS 31263, f. 24, Murray to Gualterio, undated (1720).

[64] ASV. PAC 983, no. 63/10, no. 64/1, no. 135/14, payments made by the *Camera Apostolica* for King James III, 15 October 1724, 15 December 1724, 4 February 1729; RA. SP 77/127, Nairne to Ellis, 30 October 1724.

[65] ASV. PAC 983, no. 135/14, 4 February 1729; RA. SP 131/7, James III to Inverness, 1 October 1729.

[66] ASV. 983, no. 135/14, 4 February 1729.

that some of the Scottish pensioners, particularly Lord and Lady Niths-dale, resented having to pay rent for their accommodation elsewhere.

During 1720, when the queen's pregnancy was confirmed, a nursery was established on the second floor of the north-east *palazzetto*. It was beside the vacant apartment of the Duchess of Mar,[67] which would now provide accommodation for whoever was appointed to take care of the infant. The court waited to be told who these women were to be.

---

[67] RA. SP 62/151, Hay to Mar, 3 November 1722; RA. SP 131/7, James III to Inverness, 1 October 1729; RA. SP 131/29, Edgar to Ellis, 5 October 1729.

7 Tensions within the royal household, 1719–1724

Between 1720 and 1725 the relations between the king and the queen steadily deteriorated until, in November 1725, the queen left the Palazzo del Re and took refuge in the Convent of Santa Cecilia in Trastevere. The reason for this separation was the king's refusal to give his wife a separate household and his unwillingness to let her control the upbringing of their children.

In order to understand what happened we need to emphasise the unfortunate favour shown by the king towards the Hays and Murray. During 1719, when the king was in Spain with Hay, Murray and his sister, Marjory, were able to take complete control over the court, offending and alienating by their arrogance and rudeness the old household servants, the Scottish pensioners, the Duchess of Mar and, of greatest consequence, Queen Clementina. The refusal of James III to listen to the almost unanimous complaints against Murray and his sister, and the obvious preference which he continued to show towards them and towards Hay, then alienated the majority of the Jacobite courtiers.[1] The situation was made worse by the irresponsible and arrogant behaviour of the three favourites.

To understand what happened, however, we also need to appreciate that by 1720 the exiled Jacobite community was not only based within the Stuart court. In particular the Jacobites in France remained important. Situated much closer to the British Isles, and in regular contact with the pro-Jacobite faction at the court of France, James III's representative at Paris and Saint-Germain was able to exercise considerable influence on the king's supporters in England, Scotland and Ireland. Since 1717 this position had been occupied by General Lord Dillon, an Irishman who commanded his own regiment within the French army. In June 1720 Dillon was joined in Paris by Lord Lansdowne, a leading Tory who had been involved in planning the West Country Jacobite rising in 1715.

---

[1] Corp, *Jacobites at Urbino*, particularly chapters 12 and 13.

Then, in October 1720, he was joined by the Duke of Mar. The new triumvirate of Dillon, Lansdowne and Mar provided James III with an important and influential group of advisers, bringing together the original Jacobite community in France, the Tory party in England and the post-1715 Scottish exiles. In particular the new triumvirate in France represented the reconciliation between the old Saint-Germain servants and the new Scottish exiles, whose rivalry had so divided the court at Urbino. This development was a direct result of the hostility these groups felt towards the three favourites in Rome. It also, by extension, provided Queen Clementina with an important group of supporters in her attempts to establish her own household and to have influence in the upbringing of her children.

The hostility felt towards Murray and Hay had significant political implications. Dillon informed James in January 1720 that 'by many informations I had these four months past, I should naturally infer that friends both of this and the other side of the water are prepossessed that the King has so entire a confidence in Mr Murray and Mr Hay that he communicates the most secret affairs to them, preferably to all others'. He wrote that the Jacobites in England and Scotland were therefore reluctant to have any secret correspondence with the king. Hay as *maggiordomo* dominated the court and was the king's confidant. Murray was the acting secretary of state. Therefore unless Mar could be persuaded to return to Rome and resume his control of the correspondence, contact with the Jacobites in England and Scotland was likely to be interrupted. Yet Mar's return was improbable because of 'several ill offices' done to him by Murray and 'incivilities beyond measure' done by Murray to the Duchess of Mar while she was in Rome.[2]

What particularly shocked and discouraged the Jacobites in France and elsewhere was the way the king, after his return from Spain, had supported Murray and shown extreme displeasure when Lord Pitsligo and others had complained of Murray's rudeness and high-handed behaviour. One Scottish Jacobite who visited Rome in August 1720 informed the king that 'all honest men and good subjects' believed that Murray's 'misrepresentations' concerning Pitsligo, and his rudeness 'to the Duchess of Mar and to the nobilitie and gentrie at Rome', had 'discouraged your subjects at Rome, so that none of them would ventar ever after to inform you of Mr Murray's Insolences to themselves and the Duchas of Mar', and to the Duke of Mar himself. He warned

---

[2] *JCR*, p. 192, Dillon to James III, 22 January 1720.

the king that 'Mr Murray's being continued to be employed ... cannot but be of very ill consequences'.[3]

By September 1720 James III realised that this situation could not continue: he could neither employ Murray as his secretary of state, nor continue using him for much longer as acting secretary. Mar had made it clear that he and his wife had no intention of returning,[4] and it was obvious that no one else would be prepared to accept the post so long as Murray remained at the court in Rome.

At the end of the month the king informed the Jacobites in England and Scotland that he needed someone to come to Rome to be his new secretary of state, just as Lord Middleton had gone to Saint-Germain in 1693. He also allowed Murray to send a personal apologia to the Duke of Ormonde in Spain, and an open letter to the leading Jacobites in Scotland. Murray's letter to Ormonde claimed that people had been telling lies about him: 'I need not mention ... the situation I was in here during the King's absence and the extraordinary treatment I receiv'd.' He could no longer 'struggle ... against this torrent of difficultys', and therefore needed to be replaced by a new secretary of state, who should be sent over from England to fill the post.[5] His 'Letter to Scotland' went further. In it he complained of 'the treatment I have receiv'd by the injurious discourses and Letters of some of my Country men abroad', and hoped that the new secretary of state would be used 'with the respect which is due to one who has the honour' to serve the king. 'I cannot but regret,' he added, that people 'shou'd from a certain perverse disposition of mind, be creating continued uneasiness to the King himself, and make it impossible for any man to serve him in his business, while they are utterly uncapable of doing it themselves.'[6]

This letter was intercepted in Paris by Dillon and Mar, who refused to send it on to Scotland. In October, by which time Queen Clementina was seven months pregnant, James therefore sent Hay to Paris to discuss the situation with them. Hay arrived there at the beginning of November, and ordered Dillon and Mar to send on Murray's letter to Scotland. But he was quickly convinced that no one would agree to become the king's new secretary of state until Murray had actually left Rome. With reluctance he therefore advised James to send Murray away.[7]

[3] *Ibid.*, pp. 192–3, Campbell of Glendarule to James III, August 1720.
[4] *SPW*, p. 62, Hay to Murray (not Edgar as printed), 16 December 1720.
[5] *JCR*, pp. 195–7, Murray to Ormonde, 28 September 1720.
[6] *Ibid.*, pp. 198–9, Murray's Letter to Scotland, 28 September 1720.
[7] *Ibid.*, pp. 194–5, Hay to James III, 5 November 1720.

By the end of November, to the relief of the Jacobite courtiers, it was agreed that Murray would leave Rome shortly after the queen had given birth.[8] He himself commented that this 'is, I may say, a loss to the King, but to me it is none', and looked forward to 'managing a paper war with my Lord Mar in England'.[9] In one sense his departure would indeed be a loss for the king, as it would leave the secretariat understaffed. James therefore asked Hay to bring Thomas Sheridan with him when he returned to Rome, as 'there is nobody but Nairn [sic] that can serve for the French language'.[10]

Once all this had been agreed, Murray asked the king to give him a peerage, to show that his departure from Rome 'did not proceed from any dissatisfaction you had personally at me'. He added that 'I know that your Majesty has layd down a general rule against promotions while you are abroad', but argued that 'there is no rule without an exception'.[11] The king had the good sense to refuse this request.[12]

Queen Clementina was now within a few weeks of her delivery, and the attention of the court naturally turned to the arrangements which had been made for looking after her baby. There had been a false alarm back in March 1720 which had made it clear how things were likely to develop. Lady Nithsdale explained in a letter to her sister-in-law in Scotland that she was deliberately kept away from the queen, who was believed to be pregnant only because Marjory Hay, 'that has never had any children', thought she could feel a baby move: 'tho' I have had occasion to be better versed in those things, having been so long married, and had so many children, yet they prefer one who has had noe experience of that kind'.[13]

By May 1720 the queen really was pregnant, so Lady Nithsdale asked the king to appoint her to be the child's governess. James refused to do this, but explained that 'I have taken long agoe a resolution to give noe places whilst abroad and therefore intend to make noe Governess nor Under Governess for the Queen. My wife has little to do and will look to it herself. It is true she cannot always be there but when she is not Lady Misset will stay with it.'[14] The baby, therefore, like the king and queen, was to be mainly looked after by servants of a lower social status.

---

[8] *Ibid.*, pp. 116, 200, 204, Murray to Hay, 20 October, 26 November and 3 December 1720; BL. Add MSS 31262, f. 56, Murray to Gualterio, 27 November 1720.

[9] *JCR*, p. 200, Murray to Hay, 20 November 1720.

[10] *Ibid.*, p. 201, James III to Hay, 24 November 1720.

[11] *Ibid.*, pp. 201–4, Murray to James III, undated (November 1720).

[12] BL. Add MSS 31262, p. 79, Murray to Gualterio, undated (December 1720).

[13] Tayler, *Lady Nithsdale*, pp. 141–2, Lady Nithsdale to Lady Traquair, 9 March 1720.

[14] *Ibid.*, p. 145, Lady Nithsdale to Lady Traquair, 18 May 1720.

A small group of three servants had been appointed by December 1720. There was an English wet nurse, an English chambermaid and a French 'necessary woman'. The wet nurse, the wife of a nonjuring clergyman, was Lois Hughes, specially selected by an eminent physician in London (Dr John Freind, MP), and sent out to Rome.[15] The chambermaid was Mrs Grace Appleton, who had previously worked at Saint-Germain for Theresa Stafford (née Strickland).[16] The necessary woman is simply referred to in the court accounts as Bahores.[17]

Contrary to what he had assured Lady Nithsdale, the king had wanted to appoint an under-governess. His choice had been Mary Plowden, the daughter of his own under-governess, Mary Stafford, and widow of his under-governor Francis Plowden. She had for many years been a Bedchamber woman to Mary of Modena, and in 1720 James III had written that there were 'few women I have had a greater esteem for'.[18] His invitation reached her at Saint-Germain in October shortly after Dillon and Mar intercepted Murray's letter to Scotland, when any prospect of joining the court seemed particularly unattractive. Mary Plowden sent a polite refusal, arguing that her health would not permit her to make the journey, that she could not take her children with her, and she was not prepared to leave them behind.[19] Things might have developed very differently at the court in Rome if the king's favouritism for Murray and the Hays had not deterred Mary Plowden from accepting this invitation to look after the Prince of Wales.

It is possible that the king might have invited Theresa Stafford, the daughter of one of his mother's Bedchamber women, and widowed second wife of Mary Plowden's father. But she had recently remarried an Irish officer at Saint-Germain.[20] Failing these ladies James was unable to find a suitable under-governess, so he decided that Lady Misset should be given overall responsibility for the prince's upbringing, but without any formal title. Mrs Hay was not to be directly involved, but was meant to look after the queen. On 10 December Marjory Hay wrote to her husband, then in Paris, that 'Her Majesty grows bigger every day'. Because she had never had any children of her own she was understandably worried: 'I do assure you I tremble many times, when I think of the danger she must be in, tho' I don't imagine her Maj. shall

[15] Cruickshanks and Erskine Hill, *Atterbury Plot*, p. 92.
[16] C.E. Lart, *The Parochial Registers of Saint-Germain-en-Laye: Jacobite Extracts*, vol. II (London, 1912), p. 81.
[17] RA. SP Misc 34, household accounts, November and December 1722.
[18] RA. SP 45/121, James III to Dicconson, 1 January 1720.
[19] RA. SP 48/75, Mary Plowden to James III, 21 October 1720.
[20] She married Daniel O'Donnell in 1719.

suffer more than other people do . . . and when I look upon myself as the only body that is to have care of her, it gives me all the pain in the world.'[21] Of course there was to be a locally employed midwife, as well as the principessa di Piombino, Lady Misset and Lois Hughes, who had had children of their own.

Prince Charles was born in the Palazzo del Re on 31 December 1720, John Hay rejoined the court with Sheridan during January,[22] and James Murray left on 6 February.[23] Almost immediately a struggle started for control of the baby. Hay was keen that his wife should be given the honour of looking after the prince, and it was known that Lady Nithsdale was resentful at being passed over. Lady Misset confided to her brother during February 1721 that it was a great honour to be given overall responsibility for the baby, 'but when I consider the importance of the task compared to the very little merit that I have, and that I am occupying the post instead of several other people far more worthy than myself, the honour puts me more in a state of embarrassment than of vanity'.[24] Lady Misset was perfectly correct that she did not have sufficient social status to assume the position which had been given to her, and she now found herself confronted by the concerted opposition of the Hays.

Queen Clementina had been rescued from Innsbruck in 1719 by Charles Wogan, Richard Gaydon and John Misset, who was accompanied by his wife, Eleanor. The three Irishmen had all been officers in Dillon's Regiment, and looked to Lord Dillon as their patron. Dillon, with Mar and Lansdowne, had now become the leading critic of the Hays.

Murray, and it seems James III also, disliked Wogan, Gaydon and Misset, whereas Queen Clementina understandably had a high regard for them. Wogan had been rewarded with a baronetcy, and both Gaydon and Misset with knighthoods, but commissions had also been found for them in the Spanish army to remove them from the court.[25] Only Lady Misset had remained, at the request of the queen, though partly also because she had just given birth to a baby girl (named Maria Clementina) in September 1719.[26] The wife of an obscure captain in Dillon's

[21] *SPW*, pp. 63–4, Marjory Hay to Hay, 10 December 1720.
[22] *Ibid.*, p. 62, Hay to Murray (not Edgar as printed), 16 December 1720; *JCR*, p. 205, Hay to James III, 16 December 1720.
[23] *JCR*, p. 120, James III to Hay, 8 February 1721.
[24] Ushaw College, Tyrrell Papers OS 2/B.4, Lady Misset to Gealeagh, February 1721.
[25] For the king's low opinion of Wogan, and the obtention of his Spanish commission to get him out of the way, see *JCR*, pp. 210–14, Mar to Hay, 19 April 1722 (N.B. 'Morton', the code name in the letter for Wogan, is wrongly deciphered by Tayler as referring to Murray).
[26] ASVR. Santi Apostoli vol. 12, p. 124. Although the entry is in the register for the parish of Santi Apostoli, the baby was born on 10 September 1719 and baptised by Father John

Regiment, she had suddenly been elevated to become the queen's only Bedchamber woman and now the person responsible for the upbringing of the Prince of Wales. She was out of her depth, and she knew it.

It seems that Lois Hughes, the wet nurse, was appreciated by the king and Hay, but not by the baby prince.[27] Meanwhile Lady Misset made it all too clear that she disliked the Hays and felt her primary loyalty was to the queen rather than to the king and his two favourites. At the end of February the prince was given a new wet nurse called Francesca Battaglia,[28] but Lois Hughes was not sent back to England. Instead she was retained at the court and given overall charge of the prince in place of Lady Misset. The latter was humiliated, particularly when it was stated in Jacobite circles that she had been disrespectful towards the king.[29] James III wrote to Mar:

> The qualities of a person for so important a charge are obvious, the better born she be, the better, but what is above all requisite is prudence, a reasonable knowledge of the world and a principle of obedience, attachment and submission to me, which may put her above private envies of faction. I know by experience these qualities are rare ... Till he [the prince] is a year old, our English woman [Lois Hughes] will do and she doth mightily well, but after that she will not be big enough, I mean she will be of too low a rank.[30]

This was all very well, but it seems that the change was made without the agreement of the queen. Lady Misset complained to Lord Dillon, who assured her that he approved of all that she had done, but warned her to be cautious. She also wrote to Sir Charles Wogan in Spain to let him know about 'the revolution that has occurred here as to my position'.[31] Wogan promptly left Spain and returned to Rome to complain to the queen. He had always resented the way he had been pushed aside by Murray and his sister, and he now determined to use his influence to help Lady Misset against the Hays. As Mar put it,

> it was naturall to believe that Queen Clementina wou'd have a favourable ear to those two who had so eminently assisted her and brought her out of her difficultys ... Wogan and Lady Misset's services to the King and the Queen are now well knowen to every body and people generally think the Queen has a kindness for the Lady not only upon her own account, but in

    Brown on 11 February 1720 in the Church of San Lorenzo in Luchina. The godparents were the king and the queen, represented at the font by Lord and Lady Nithsdale.

[27] BL. Add MSS 31262, f. 84, Murray to Gualterio, 5 March 1721.

[28] *Ibid.*; McLynn, *Charles Edward Stuart*, p. 9; Bod. Lib. Rawlinson MSS D. 1180, p. 310, Rawlinson's diary, 6 March 1721.

[29] Ushaw College, Tyrrell Papers OS 2/B.6, Lady Misset to Gealeagh, April 1721.

[30] RA. SP 53/44, James III to Mar, 21 April 1721.

[31] Ushaw College, Tyrrell Papers OS 2/B.7, Lady Misset to Wogan, April 1721.

odium tertii [i.e. Mrs Hay] who is belived to be imposed on her and to give her great and dayly vexation and trouble.[32]

Hay's responsibility for the dismissal of Lady Misset is clearly revealed in a letter that he wrote to Mar in April 1721. The queen merely wanted to be able to manage her own household, but Hay encouraged the king to regard this as completely undermining his royal authority at the court. In Hay's own words, the queen, whom he described as 'passion [and] youth ingrafted by a little mean education', had 'the desire of governing', while the king had 'the dread of being governed':

should the Queen have cunning enough to get the better of the King ... matters will go on at a very strange rate, everything will be governed by whim and fancy, without any manner of difference made betwixt the advice of a chambermaid and that of a man of sense ... and adieu all thoughts of a restoration.

On the other hand, shall they fall out together, what a noise must that make, where will be our prospect of a Succession ...

The Queen has not found out the way to please the King, and would have the direction of everything without taking that trouble ... It will be the dismallest sight for the King's adherents when the Queen getts the management.[33]

The rest of 1721 was a period of waiting. The queen did what she could to cover her resentment, and looked to Wogan and Lady Misset in Rome, and Dillon and Mar in Paris, for support against her husband and the Hays. Meanwhile the baby Prince of Wales was looked after by Lois Hughes, Francesca Battaglia and Grace Appleton. The king had decided that his son would be weaned, and given a nurse of a higher social status to replace Lois Hughes, in April 1722.

The king then made a mistake that he would bitterly regret. A Jacobite invasion of Scotland and England was being planned, and Lord Dillon was to command the Irish troops to be sent to Scotland. In June James promoted Dillon from viscount to earl.[34] More particularly he agreed to appoint one of Dillon's nieces to be the prince's new nurse. She was Dorothy, daughter of Ralph Sheldon, who had served both James II and James III as an equerry for many years. In a way hers was an ideal appointment. She was unmarried, middle-aged, and had lived at Saint-Germain since at least 1714, and possibly ever since 1689.[35] But, given that she was Dillon's niece, she was bound to support the queen against

---

[32] *JCR*, pp. 210–14, Mar to Hay, 19 April 1722.

[33] *Ibid.*, p. 120, Hay to Mar, 21 April 1721. This letter is given in full in Haile, *James Francis Edward*, pp. 289–90, where it is dated 1722.

[34] Ruvigny, *Jacobite Peerage*, p. 40.

[35] She is not mentioned in the parish registers of Saint-Germain-en-Laye before 1714. All Stuart biographies (e.g. Haile, *James Francis Edward*, p. 294; McLynn, *Charles Edward Stuart*, pp. 10–11) describe her as Dillon's sister-in-law. In fact she was the daughter of

the Hays. And because she had lived so long at Saint-Germain she knew how that court had been organised, and that Mary of Modena had had her own independent household, with complete control over the upbringing of James III himself when he had been a little child.

Dorothy Sheldon arrived in Rome in March 1722,[36] and shortly afterwards the Prince of Wales was weaned. Lois Hughes returned to England and Francesca Battaglia was converted from wet nurse to dry nurse.[37] At the same time the king ordered Sir Charles Wogan and Lady Misset to leave Rome.[38] The result was what one would expect: the queen was furious. She had lost her only Bedchamber woman, and was now more than ever dependent on Marjory Hay, who was the only lady of any status left in her service. She naturally turned to Dorothy Sheldon for comfort and support, and became increasingly withdrawn from her husband.

Hay then made matters worse by presuming to speak to the queen and by trying to reconcile her to her husband – as Mar put it, by 'medling in things between the King and the Queen'. When Hay told Mar what had happened he received a frank reply, written in the third person:

I am afraid that Hay, like one playing at chess, does not see the game so clearly in this as a bystander and I know not one this side the sea who wish him well ... What makes me still the more concerned for Lady Misset's going away is that the Queen will have so few about her, that tho Hay should find it for his interest that Mrs Hay should go away, he can scarce propose it when the Queen wou'd be in a maner quitt left alone. And it will be said I know, that she is left so on purpose that Mrs Hay's stay comes to be absolutely necessary.[39]

At this point Queen Clementina received support from Francesco Bianchini, a *cameriere d'onore* in the *Camera Apostolica*. Bianchini was a renowned scholar and astronomer whose famous meridian, marking noon with a beam of sunlight, had been placed in the Basilica of Santa Maria degli Angeli in Rome. Bianchini had been on good terms with James III since 1717, when he had shown the king his meridian. He had also visited James at Urbino in the autumn of 1717 to observe two

---

his brother-in-law Ralph Sheldon, who died at Saint-Germain in April 1723 at the age of ninety. At first Stosch spelt the name Sheldon as 'Lelido' (NA. SP 85/14/f. 37, to Carteret, 28 March 1722), a mistake which has caused much confusion. See, e.g., McLynn, *Charles Edward Stuart*, pp. 9–10, where the name 'Lelido' is given instead of Mrs Hughes as the name of the prince's original wet nurse.

[36] NA. SP 85/14/f. 37, Stosch to Carteret, 28 March 1722.

[37] *SPW*, p. 81, James III to Cardinal Albani, 19 April 1722: 'Je viens de sevrer mon fils et je suis (très) content des services de sa nourice.'

[38] BL. Add MSS 20303, f. 198, Hay to Gualterio, undated (March or April 1722); NA. SP 85/14/f. 45, Stosch to Carteret, 11 April 1722.

[39] *JCR*, pp. 210–14, Mar to Hay, 19 April 1722.

eclipses of the moon, and had traced a second meridian in the Palazzo Ducale there at the king's request.[40] He had helped David Nairne select the Palazzo del Re as the residence for the Stuart court, and had been particularly hospitable to the Jacobites while James had been in Spain.[41] At the beginning of 1721 he had 'placed a marble stone to mark the point where the sun's light struck the pavement of Santa Maria degli Angeli on the moment and hour of the King's birth'.[42]

Bianchini, however, disliked Murray and the Hays and now put himself forward to champion the queen's cause at the papal court. In particular, he suggested that he himself should join the royal household as the prince's tutor. The king had no intention of entrusting the prince's education to a Catholic priest, and was very annoyed, particularly when Bianchini actually announced publicly that he had been appointed. The question blew over, and Stosch reported in March 1722 that 'the whole matter has been calmed down' by the queen, and that 'that priest continues to visit the palace as before'.[43]

It was during the summer of 1722 that James and Clementina visited Lucca. The queen arrived first, in July, accompanied by Marjory Hay, Mary Fitzgerald, Isabella Gordon, Gottfried Rittel, Robert Creagh, a cook and two footmen. The king arrived two and a half weeks later, in August, accompanied by Hay, Thomas Forster, Captain O'Brien, Father Brown, Dr Maghie, Thomas Saint-Paul and various lesser servants from the household below stairs and the stables.[44] They remained at Lucca until the second half of September, and then returned slowly to Rome via Florence, Bologna, Pesaro, Urbino and Loreto, reaching the Palazzo del Re at the end of October.[45]

It was while the king and queen were at Lucca that Francesco Bianchini attempted to change the arrangements at the Stuart court concerning the upbringing of the Prince of Wales. The details are obscure, but he seems to have collaborated with Dorothy Sheldon and Lady Misset, who returned to Rome after the king's departure. He also tried to contact the queen by writing to a lady at Lucca, contessa Sardi, who had previously been a lady-in-waiting to Clementina's mother.

[40] William Eisler, 'The Construction of the Image of Martin Folkes (1690–1754): Art, Science and Masonic Sociability in the Age of the Grand Tour', *The Medal*, 58 (Spring 2011) pp. 4–29, at pp. 10–11.

[41] Corp, *Jacobites at Urbino*, pp. 193, 196.

[42] Eisler, 'Construction of the Image'.

[43] NA. SP 85/14/f. 37, Stosch to Carteret, 28 March 1722.

[44] Whipple, *Famous Corner of Tuscany*, pp. 133–4; BL. Add MSS 31264, f. 71, Hay to Gualterio, 3 September 1722.

[45] See Chapter 3, p. 66.

Bianchini's letter was seen by the king (it is not known how), with the result that Robert Creagh was ordered by James to send a letter 'to forbid him to come ever again to my household in Rome'. James assumed that the Pope was not 'behind this plot', but told Cardinal Gualterio that the Pope would have to answer before God if he showed any support for what Bianchini and his accomplices had been doing. He also told him that he would now 'take away Madame Misset's pension and ... make her disgrace public'.[46] The letter in which he wrote this made no mention of Dorothy Sheldon.

At the end of September 1722, before the royal party left Lucca, Hay received a letter from the Duke of Mar in which he was advised to send his wife away from the court. Hay described Mar's letter as follows:

After a pritty long preamble showing the reasonableness of sending Mrs Hay from Rome, the writer says 'The Queen's dislike to Mrs Hay is now known almost to everybody' and the letter runs so much upon the notion, as I cannot but construct it of a jealousie which people believe the Queen to have with relation to the King's conduct with Mrs Hay, which is confirmed by another expression where he says that 'the Queen should be made easy with regard to Mrs Hay'.[47]

Hay should either have kept this letter to himself or sent his wife away from court. Better still, he should have left the court with her. Instead he had the effrontery to show the letter to the queen. Clementina hated the Hays, as she had hated Murray, because they dominated the court and, in her opinion, helped prevent her from having her own independent household, with servants selected by herself. Mrs Hay had been imposed on her and, now that Lady Misset had been sent away, she had no other servants of any elevated status. These were the reasons why the queen wanted Mrs Hay sent away and replaced by other ladies. Hay's insinuations were unnecessary and insulting:

I was not ignorant Madam, even before your Maj.tie had been six weeks married, of endeavours then used to raise jealousie in yr Maj. as to ye king's Conduct in relation to Mrs Hay. I was so much persuaded then of the King's virtue as well as of Mrs Hay's, who I did believe would not throw away her reputation upon any King or Prince in the World, and seeing yr Majesty's goodness towards Mrs Hay continue, I then believed that those were only assertions and contrivances of some people by which they might be enabled to gett att their own ends and that they had no manner of impression upon yr Maj.te. But since the same story is renewed again, I beg yr Maj.te would lett me know what would be agreable to you yt I should do to remove uneasiness ... There is nothing that I'll stick at one

[46] BL. Add MSS 31255, f. 246, James III to Gualterio, 29 August 1722.
[47] *JCR*, p. 217, summarised in Hay to Queen Clementina, undated (September 1722).

moment to make ye union with the King flourish. I most humbly beg of your
Maj.ty that this letter may be seen by nobody . . . Your Maj.tie may easily perceive
that I have calculated my letter for *yourself alone* . . . This is a subject the King is
intirely a stranger to and I hope yr Maj.tie wont mention it to him. You'll do me a
particular favour if you are so generous as to return me the letter yt I may putt it
in the fire . . . I shall only add, that the King has not these 6 weeks past mentioned
the least thing to me of any family uneasiness.[48]

The fact that this letter has survived suggests that Queen Clementina,
now twenty years old, must have showed it to her husband and
demanded that some action should be taken against Hay. We only have
the latter's version of what happened next. Hay wrote nonchalantly to
inform Gualterio on 31 October that he was no longer the king's
maggiordomo:

I no longer occupy myself with the domestic affairs of the King. His Majesty
however continues to give me his confidence . . . Mr Forester [sic] is now
responsible for everything to do with ceremonials and Mr Ellis with
expenditure, so I will have far less bother than I had before.

He pretended that the change had been made at his own request and
that 'nobody is happier than I am at the change'. But he added a very
significant point: 'Mrs Hay is no longer in the service of the Queen as
she was'.[49]

Yet Hay's wife now enjoyed direct access to the Prince of Wales,
because the change of *maggiordomo* involved a reallocation of the apartments on the first floor of the Palazzo del Re. Thomas Forster moved
into the apartment beside the grand staircase, previously occupied by the
Hays, who themselves moved into the apartment with the *loggetta* which
had been kept vacant for the Duke of Mar. At the same time the prince
was moved out of the nursery into the apartment kept vacant for the
Duchess of Mar above, connected to the new apartment of the Hays by
the inner staircase.[50] The move also gave Hay direct access on the east
side to the apartment of the king, without having to walk through the
public rooms. Since Murray's departure his apartment in the south-east
palazzetto had been used by the king himself as an 'apartment . . . for
recreation'. One of the rooms, described as the 'stanze grande', was

---

[48] *Ibid.*, pp. 217–19, and *SPW*, pp. 66–8, Hay to Queen Clementina, undated (September
1722).
[49] BL. Add MSS 31264, f. 98, Hay to Gualterio, 31 October 1722. See also RA.
SP 62/151, Hay to Mar, 3 November 1722.
[50] RA. SP 62/151, Hay to Mar, 3 November 1722; ASV. PAC 983, no. 64/9 and no. 135/
14, payments made by the *Camera Apostolica* for King James III, 20 October 1724 and
4 February 1729.

'beside the Anticamera' of the Hays,[51] so the king and Hay could meet informally in these *cabinets intérieurs* whenever they wished. In their daily lives the Hays were now brought closer to the king than they had been before the revelation of the insulting letter.

The relations between the king and the queen never really recovered from this incident. Clementina demanded that both the Hays should be expelled from the court, and the king refused. So the queen shut herself up in her apartment for most of the time and could hardly bring herself to look at or even to speak to her husband.[52] Lady Nithsdale recorded in July 1723 that 'our Mistress . . . is here, but in a monastery, and noebody permited to goe in'. The queen now had neither a lady of the Bedchamber nor a Bedchamber woman, and no one except Dorothy Sheldon above the rank of chambermaid and valet. Lady Nithsdale, as a Catholic, tried to fill the gap but it was clear that she was not welcome. The queen, she wrote, 'comes out every day to take the aire . . . but I have noe opportunity of speaking one word but in publick; far from going in, as it was once thought, and even at times when others cannot goe, because not of her profession, she does not seem to desire me'.[53]

Hay's evil influence now began to have an unfortunate effect on the secretariat. Since the departure of Murray in February 1721 the king had failed to persuade anyone to come to Rome to be his new secretary of state. He had particularly wanted Lord Lansdowne to accept the post, but the latter was not prepared to join the court so long as Hay remained there, and the king was not prepared to send his favourite away. So the post remained unfilled. James III explained on one occasion that he really needed a new secretary of state, 'for I cannot hold out long with the drudgery I must now have on my hands',[54] and in one of his letters he even described himself as 'a commis'.[55]

Most of the work of the secretariat was performed by David Nairne and the two under-secretaries, Francis Kennedy and Thomas Sheridan, though Hay had been used as an unofficial acting secretary. This situation could not go on indefinitely. In August 1722, while the king and queen were at Lucca, Nairne, who had been left behind in Rome, asked to be allowed to retire: 'I have scribbled enough for these 33 years past, and being now enterd in my 68 I find I am not able to undergo much toyl or fatigue, and therefore . . . I should be glad the King (to whom you see

[51] ASV. PAC 983, no. 64/10, payments made by the *Camera Apostolica* for King James III, 15 December 1724.
[52] HMC, *10th Report*, p. 161, James III to Queen Clementina, 11 November 1725.
[53] Tayler, *Lady Nithsdale*, pp. 190–1, Lady Nithsdale to Lady Traquair, 11 July 1723.
[54] *JCR*, p. 205, James III to Ormonde, 19 January 1721.
[55] *Ibid.*, p. 120, James III to Murray, February 1721.

I am of very little or no use at all here), would give me leave in the next spring to go and end my old days with my daughters' in France.[56] The king was not willing to let Nairne go, because he still had not found a new secretary of state. But when Hay was relieved of his post as *maggiordomo* in October 1722 he was able to devote much more time to being acting secretary of state. Within a very short time, however, he managed to alienate Francis Kennedy.

We only have Hay's version of what happened, but it is enough to show that Kennedy, like virtually everyone else at the court, disliked the king's favourite, and resented the fact that he was now more active in the secretariat:

Frank [Kennedy] has been ... uneasy and melancholy to a degree ... He has desired ... leave to return [to Scotland] ... He has said to some people that I was his enemy, and indeed his dryness and shieness of me this while past has perswaded me that he thought so ... the King is a good deal out of humour to see one he looked upon entirely his own and in whom he had an intire confidence, act the part Frank has done.'[57]

The new friction in the secretariat must have been apparent, because there is a letter written by Stosch during the same month which states that considerable rivalry had developed between Kennedy and Hay.[58]

It seems that Kennedy was not the only person that Hay managed to offend during the summer of 1723. He made fun of Thomas Forster because he was overweight and, in his new role as *maggiordomo*, was not very good at making a graceful bow.[59] And some of the lesser servants were said to be interested in finding new employment 'due to the bad treatment that ... Hay gives to everyone'.[60] Nothing, however, seemed to lessen the king's warm feelings towards him.[61]

The tensions in the secretariat, and in the court as a whole, were relieved in the autumn of 1723 when James III sent Hay on a mission to consult with the exiled Jacobite leaders in Brussels and Paris.[62]

---

[56] RA. SP 61/145, Nairne to Hay, 29 August 1722.

[57] Tayler, *Seven Sons of the Provost*, pp. 105–7, Hay to D. Kennedy, 21 August 1723. See also *ibid.*, p. 105, James III to D. Kennedy, 17 August 1723.

[58] NA. SP 85/14/f. 416, Stosch to Carteret, 7 August 1723.

[59] NA. SP 85/14/f. 382, Stosch to Carteret, 26 June 1723. In an earlier letter to Carteret of 7 November 1722 Stosch had described Forster as 'gros et gras' (NA. SP 85/14/f. 150). See also RA. SP 62/151, Hay to Mar, 3 November 1722 announcing Forster's appointment: 'Moving up and down will do Tom a great deal of good.'

[60] NA. SP 85/14/f. 434, Stosch to Carteret, 28 August 1723.

[61] Hay was also openly critical of the daughters of the principessa di Piombino (BL. Add MSS 31264, f. 186, Hay to Gualterio, undated).

[62] NA. SP 85/14/ff. 447, 451, Stosch to Carteret, 7 and 11 September 1723; SCA. BL 2/257/14, W. Stuart to T. Innes, 27 September 1723.

Informing them of Hay's journey, the king told them he trusted Hay 'wt every thing without reserve and desired (them) to do so too'.[63] Hay was absent from September 1723 to January 1724.

The investigations following the failure of the Atterbury Plot in 1722 had revealed the fact that the Duke of Mar, keen to secure a pardon and the return of his Scottish estates, had betrayed to the Whig government in London the names of the leading conspirators.[64] Francis Atterbury, Bishop of Rochester, had been banished from Great Britain and was living in Brussels, and Hay met him there in November.[65] Atterbury explained to Hay how Mar had effectively given the plot away, and Hay then moved on to Paris to confront Mar himself. The two men had an angry quarrel, during which Mar denied all the accusations made against him. But Mar then counter-attacked, with the support of Dillon and Lansdowne, telling Hay that he and his wife should leave the court in Rome. In a letter to the king, Mar accused Hay of 'playing so falss a part to me' and 'endeavouring to do me such injurys' by his accusations. He alleged that Hay had made them up because Mar had told him to leave the court:

The whole was upon the account of my having, with some others, advised him, upon his own asking of us, what he should do upon the Queen's displeasure wt him, To retire some time wt his wife from Court.

We conceived that to be the only way to restore tranquility and peace in yr family and that it was the more necessary then that the ill agreement there, upon his account ... was become the publick talk over Europe ... So it is more properly the Queen's quarrel than mine.

Mar added that Hay had even said things 'to lessen the good opinion people had generally of the Queen'.[66] As the king remained determined to keep John and Marjory Hay at his court, this incident merely weakened the position of the triumvirate in Paris, and made him dislike the growing intimacy between the queen and Dorothy Sheldon.

While Hay was in Paris the duc d'Orléans, the Regent of France, died. One of his last acts was to recommend to James III that he should employ Andrew Ramsay in some capacity at the Stuart court.[67]

[63] *JCR*, pp. 219–21, Mar to James III, 6 March 1724.
[64] Cruickshanks and Erskine-Hill, *Atterbury Plot*, p. 129; Edward Gregg, 'The Jacobite Career of John, Earl of Mar', in Eveline Cruickshanks (ed.), *Ideology and Conspiracy: Aspects of Jacobitism, 1689–1759* (Edinburgh, 1982), pp. 190–1.
[65] SCA. BL 2/252/10, T. Innes to W. Stuart, 2 November 1723.
[66] *JCR*, pp. 219–21, Mar to James III, 6 March 1724. See also RA. SP 79/46, Mar to James III, 15 January 1725.
[67] BL. Add MSS 31255, f. 404, James III to Gualterio, undated.

Ramsay had been a disciple of François de Salignac de La Motte-Fénelon, the celebrated Archbishop of Cambrai, who had converted him to Catholicism. From 1718 to 1722 he had been employed as tutor to the son (born 1704) of the Regent's *premier gentilhomme de la chambre* (the comte de Sassenage), but for the past year had been without regular employment. The Regent had made him a *chevalier de l'Ordre de Saint-Lazare*, and the suggestion now was that he should join the court in Rome and eventually become tutor to the Prince of Wales.

Ramsay's qualifications were good. In 1721 he had published an *Essai philosophique sur le gouvernement civil*, which had been translated into English and published in both London and Edinburgh the following year. In the *Essai* Ramsay 'praised the virtues of monarchy [and] condemned rebellion'. He had followed this in 1723 with his *Histoire de la vie de Fénelon* (translated the same year as the *Life of Fénelon*), which gave an account of James's visit to the archbishop in 1710. The book recorded both the sensible advice which Fénelon gave James on religion and the favourable opinion which he had formed of the exiled king.[68]

During 1722, while he was writing this book, Ramsay had met in Paris the two daughters of Sir David Nairne, and obtained for them a pension from Cardinal de Rohan.[69] Nairne and Ramsay did not know each other, but they corresponded,[70] and on one occasion Nairne had forwarded one of Ramsay's letters to Hay to be shown to the king: 'I cannot forbear sending you this inclosed from Mr Ramsay, in wch he expresses his duty to the King in so zealous a manner.'[71] As Hay had already met Ramsay in 1720 and had a high opinion of him[72] it is not surprising that James III agreed to the Regent's suggestion and instructed Hay to bring Ramsay with him when he returned to Rome.[73]

Ramsay was friendly with the Duke of Mar, but that was not at all the reason why he was appointed. If anything, by the end of 1723 that might have been a reason for *not* appointing him. Some people believed that he would be employed in the secretariat, but the king made it clear that 'Ramsay is not to be anyways concerned in writing or politics'.[74] It was

[68] Scott Mandelbrote, article on 'Sir Andrew Ramsay' in the *Oxford Dictionary of National Biography*; Cruickshanks and Erskine-Hill, *Atterbury Plot*, pp. 85–6, 265.
[69] RA. SP 61/70, Ramsay to James III, 1 August 1722; RA. SP 61/145, Nairne to Hay, 29 August 1722.
[70] SCA. BL 2/264/1, T. Innes to W. Stuart, 3 January 1724.
[71] RA. SP 61/97, Nairne to Hay, 12 August 1722.
[72] RA. SP 61/145, Nairne to Hay, 29 August 1722.
[73] SCA. BL 2/264/1, T. Innes to W. Stuart, 3 January 1724; BL. Add MSS 31255, f. 425, James III to Gualterio, undated (January 1724); NA. SP 85/15/f. 20, Stosch to Carteret, 25 January 1724.
[74] *JCR*, p. 229, James III to Murray, 3 April 1724.

not at all clear what Ramsay *would* do in the immediate future. The intention was that he would eventually become the prince's preceptor, but as the child was still only three years old that plan could not be put into operation for several more years.

As a celebrated man of letters Ramsay made his mark in Roman society, and became particularly friendly with the abbé Foucquet.[75] Within the court he struck up a close friendship with Sir David Nairne.[76] But his relations with Hay quickly deteriorated, as they did also with Thomas Forster, the *maggiordomo*. In April 1724 Hay told Gualterio that Forster and Ramsay 'had a dispute that went as far as the drawing of swords, and the latter was wounded'.[77]

During the summer of 1724 Queen Clementina became pregnant for the second time, but her relations with the king did not improve. The return of the Earl of Southesk with his wife, while Hay was in Paris, at last provided her with a Jacobite companion of a sufficiently elevated rank whom she liked, but her hostility towards the Hays remained undiminished. Then Bishop Atterbury sent a letter to James from Paris in which he revealed that he had discovered positive proof that Mar had betrayed the Jacobite plans to the Whig government.[78] Mar denied everything and was supported by Dillon and Lansdowne, so James formally withdrew his confidence from the triumvirate in Paris.[79] 'Apart from the Bishop of Rochester [Atterbury],' he wrote in December 1724, 'there is no one in France whom I can trust with my affairs.'[80] The queen and Dorothy Sheldon had lost their influential supporters in Paris.

This development, which took place while the Palazzo del Re was being renovated and the court was at Albano, also undermined the position of Andrew Ramsay. His relations with both Hay and Forster

[75] BAV. Fondo Borgia Lat MS 565, f. 253, Foucquet's diary, 7 June 1724.

[76] RA. SP 79/47, Mar to Nairne, 15 January 1725; BAV. Fondo Borgia Lat MS 565, f. 333, Foucquet to Ramsay, 20 November 1725: 'Nos livres seront a Paris dans peu . . . M. Nairne avoit reglé cette affaire . . . Il sort de ma chambre bien affecté, mais vraiment notre ami. Il vous salue.'

[77] BL. Add MSS 31264, f. 145, Hay to Gualterio, 23 April 1724. Stosch described the incident in a letter to Newcastle of 6 May 1724: '[Hay, Forster et Ramsay] retournant de l'auberge au logis eurent de grosses paroles ensemble l'un ayant objecte à l'autre son peu de conduite dans le management des affaires du Maitre a peine furent ils descendus du Carosse dans la cour du Palais . . . que Forster donna un Coup d'Epée dans le Corps à Ramsay le quel ayant tiré aussi la sienne desarma Forster lui rompit l'Epée et l'aurait tué sur la place si le Colonel Haye et un autre des Gentilhommes ne les eussent separés a tems.'

[78] Gregg, 'Jacobite Career of John, Earl of Mar', p. 192.

[79] *JCR*, p. 133, James III to Dillon, 28 August 1724, and to Ormonde, 7 September 1724. For Hay's commentary, see BL. Add MSS 31264, f. 67, Hay to Gualterio, undated.

[80] RA. SP 78/100, James III to Torcy, 15 December 1724. Also RA. SP 78/178, James III to the *curé* of Saint-Sulpice, 31 December 1724.

had become worse and worse, and it was known that he had previously been a friend of Mar. Some people began to regard him, like Dorothy Sheldon, as a supporter of the discredited triumvirate. Hay informed Gualterio on 1 November:

The letters have been sent to remove Mr Dillon from [the king's] confidence . . . Mr Ramsay desires strongly to go to Paris; he has made a protest in which he declares that his three friends in Paris wish him to return, to counter the calomny surrounding them that they advised him to go to Rome; he says he will return when everyone is satisfied.[81]

Stosch, writing three weeks later, was more realistic:

Ramsay asked for leave of absence on the pretext of certain letters he had received from the Bishop of Fréjus [Fleury], who was asking for him to return to France to look after his interests, and because of the tender age of his Pupil; who had more need of women's care, than of a man's teaching. He has promised to return here whenever he is asked . . . The real reason for his departure is that he couldn't in any way get on with Haye [sic] and Foster [sic].[82]

Cardinal de Rohan, who was in Rome at the time, suggested that the king might like to employ Ramsay in France, but James was not prepared 'to employ him in any way whatsoever'.[83] As James himself put it, 'Ramsay is an odd body. He exposed himself strangely here to myself and others, but as yet I will be charitable enough to think him a madd man.'[84] There was no longer any question of his returning as the prince's preceptor.

These developments inevitably had an impact on the secretariat. Nairne had wanted to retire since 1722 but Kennedy's desire to leave meant that he could not be spared. Hay had been away for several months, making Nairne's continued presence still more necessary. His friendship with Ramsay during 1724, however, made the king and Hay extremely displeased with him. Shortly after his arrival back in Paris, Ramsay proposed marriage to the elder of Nairne's two daughters.[85] She turned him down, because she wanted eventually to become a nun.[86]

---

[81] BL. Add MSS 31264, f. 180, Hay to Gualterio, 1 November 1724.

[82] NA. SP 85/15/f. 216, Stosch to Newcastle, 21 November 1724. See SCA. BL 2/270/12, W. Stuart to T. Innes, 20 November 1724: 'Chev.r Ramsay parted three dayes agoe for Amsterdam [sic] hel tell you himselfe his errand.'

[83] BL. Add MSS 31266, f. 205, Hay to Gualterio, undated (November or December 1724).

[84] JCR, p. 135, James III to Murray, undated (1725).

[85] RA. SP 80/107, Nairne to Hay, undated (February 1725).

[86] BL. Add MSS 20298, f. 133, 'extraits de quelques lettres ecrittes de Paris au Chev.r Nairne au sujet de sa fille la Religieuse', 1719; RA. SP 108/108, F. Nairne to James III, 21 July 1727; RA. SP 178/83, Nairne to James III, 7 March 1735.

Nairne sent a friendly message to Ramsay via a friend in March 1725: 'he knows that my writing regularly to him in his and my present circumstances could be of no service to him ... but he shall always find me incapable of ingratitude'.[87]

As Nairne was not allowed to retire and join his daughters in France, he now asked to be allowed to let them live with him in Rome. Nearly seventy years old, he sent a humble letter to Hay:

Upon your last advice to me I have given over all thoughts of attempting any more to have leave to go and end my old days in quiet with my poor daughters in France, especially upon your assuring me that the King is not now displeased with me, but if I could by your means have his Mat.ys leave to bring my daughters here to live with me and take care of me it would be the greatest of comforts to me.[88]

This request was rejected,[89] and there was probably a very simple reason. The queen's two chambermaids, Mary Fitzgerald and Isabella Gordon, were Nairne's first cousins,[90] and his daughters had known them and Dorothy Sheldon at Saint-Germain.[91] Allowing the Nairne sisters to come to the court in Rome risked strengthening the small entourage of women serving the queen. And at the precise moment that Nairne made this request James III was about to do something which would result in the collapse of his marriage and the queen's decision to leave the court.

---

[87] SCA. BL 2/277/9, Nairne to T. Innes, 21 March 1725.

[88] RA. SP 80/107, Nairne to Hay, undated (February 1725).

[89] The request was apparently granted at first, but then rejected. Louis Innes thanked Hay in a letter of 29 July 1725 in which he wrote that 'honest Sr. Da. Nairne' was very grateful for 'the Kings consent for his sending for his daughters to live with him at Rome; he thinks that will be such a comfort to him in his old age, that he longs for it beyond what I could have imagind' (RA. SP 84/149). Yet there is a letter to the king of 9 September 1726 from Nairne's elder daughter begging him to allow her to go to Rome, as she has wanted to do for a long time, 'assister par mes soins un pere dans sa vieillesse' (RA. SP 97/18).

[90] Hôtel de Ville de Saint-Germain-en-Laye, parish registers, marriage certificate of Gerald Fitzgerald and Mary Gordon, 6 November 1710, witnessed by David Nairne, 'Secrétaire du conseil d'Etat de Marie d'Este, et cousin de l'épouse'. The description is omitted in Lart, *Parochial Registers of Saint-Germain-en-Laye*, vol. II, pp. 10–11, but included in Jacques Dulon, *Jacques II Stuart, sa famille et les Jacobites à Saint-Germain-en-Laye* (Saint-Germain, 1897), p. 97.

[91] Dorothy Sheldon was present when Nairne's elder daughter took the habit as a novice at the convent of the English Augustinian nuns in Paris (BL. Add MSS 20298, f. 133, F. Nairne to Nairne, 9 May 1719).

The separation of the king and the queen,
        1725–1726

Since the Stuart court had settled in Rome at the end of 1719 the king
had refused to allow the queen to have her own independent household.
As we have seen, she had very few servants, and they were all appointed –
and dismissed – by the king. By 1724 Clementina had neither a lady of
the Bedchamber nor even a Bedchamber woman. All she had was a small
staff of chambermaids and valets. She evidently disliked Lady Nithsdale,
so the only Jacobite women to whom she could turn for support were
Dorothy Sheldon, whom the king had placed in charge of the little
Prince of Wales, and Lady Southesk. The latter was not a member of
the royal household, but her husband was one of the Scottish pensioners
attached to the court.

The queen's second pregnancy raised some important questions for
the management of the court. The new baby would need an additional
staff of women, who would need to be recruited, paid, and accommodated within the Palazzo del Re. The presence of these women might
perhaps provide the queen with an additional group of supporters
against the Hays. More importantly, it might strengthen the queen's
arguments for being given an independent household. Clementina was
now twenty-two years old and increasingly annoyed that she was not
being treated like other married princesses. As François Foucquet put it,
'she wants to be treated as a Queen, to have a household and to be in
command of it'.[1]

There was another factor to be considered. When Prince Charles
reached the age of seven, in December 1727, the time would come for
him to be taken out of the hands of women, and have his upbringing and
education entrusted to men. So the timing of the queen's second pregnancy was a little inconvenient. She was due to give birth in March
1725. At that time a new team of women would need to be recruited, but
two and three-quarter years later, in December 1727, the original team

---

[1] BAV. Fondo Borgia Lat MS 565, f. 345, Foucquet to Ramsay, 20 January 1726.

would have to be dismissed and replaced by a team of men. This would not have been a problem for a normal court, established in its home country. Nor would it have been a problem for the Stuart court when it had been in exile at Saint-Germain, where the Jacobite community was much larger, and access to England much easier. But for a court experiencing a second exile, a long way away from England, with some difficulty in recruiting suitable servants, it seemed unnecessarily wasteful. James III therefore made a very practical but extremely unfortunate decision. It was to bring forward from 1727 to 1725 the moment when the Prince of Wales would be taken away from the women and entrusted to men.

In 1725 the prince would be only four years old. The women at the court were bound to be unanimously against this decision, and the queen was certain to feel personally outraged. Nevertheless the king decided to go ahead with his plan. There was to be a short period of six months after the birth of the second baby during which the women would look after both children. Then the handover would take place, and the women would care for the second child only. Prince Henry was born in March 1725 and given his own wet nurse, Mrs Teresa Keller.[2] In September 1725 Prince Charles was given a governor, an under-governor and a *valet de chambre*.[3] The following July he was also given a gentleman and two equerries, one of whom also served as his riding master.[4] In addition to these he had a dancing master[5] and various tutors, but (in the absence of Ramsay) the under-governor served as preceptor. The only woman who continued to serve him was his former wet nurse, Francesca Battaglia, who was not needed to look after Prince Henry, and who was retained as a necessary woman.[6]

The six men placed in charge of the four-year-old prince were all unmarried. The under-governor was Thomas Sheridan, who was replaced in the secretariat by James Edgar. The valet was Michele Vezzosi, who had previously served the queen.[7] The gentleman was

---

[2] Teresa Keller (née Giobbi) had given birth in February 1725 to a boy who died in October of the same year (ASVR. Santi Apostoli vol. 12, p. 169, and vol. 41, p. 157).

[3] NA. SP 85/15/f. 438, Stosch to Newcastle, 22 September 1725.

[4] NA. SP 85/16/f. 112, Stosch to Newcastle, 3 August 1726.

[5] This was Jean Arnaux, who was first employed in April 1725 (RA. SP Misc, household accounts, 18 July 1725) and continued to teach Prince Charles and then Prince Henry until at least 1742 (RA. SP 135/81, 214/15, 246/111, 'Gages du Roy', 1730, 1739, 1742).

[6] RA. SP Box 3/81, a list of salaries, October 1726.

[7] Vezzosi was replaced by François Decelles, twenty-five years old, who came from Tours (ASVR. Santi Apostoli vol. 65, p. 180, *Stati d'Anime*, 1737). It is not known how he was recruited.

John Stewart, younger half-brother of the Earl of Bute.[8] The first equerry and riding master was an Irish *chevalier de l'Ordre de Malte* named Nicholas Geraldin,[9] and the other equerry was Captain John O'Brien.[10] These men, three Irish, one Scottish and one French, were all Catholic, but they were to be placed under the control of a governor who was to be Protestant. The prince would be brought up a good Catholic,[11] but his Protestant governor would encourage him to follow his father and grandfather in advocating religious toleration. The queen, a devout Catholic, was further outraged. When, however, she discovered who the new governor was to be her feelings of resentment towards her husband turned to hatred. For the man to be placed in charge of her four-year-old son was someone she loathed, James Murray, the brother of Marjory Hay.

Since leaving the court in February 1720 Murray had lived in Lorraine, France and the Austrian Netherlands, and continued to receive a pension from the king.[12] He had maintained a regular correspondence with both John and Marjory Hay, as well as the king himself, thereby keeping in touch with developments at court and the revelations concerning his enemy Mar's treachery.[13] At the beginning of 1724, shortly after Hay's return from his trip to Brussels and Paris, James III finally agreed to give Murray a peerage.[14] It was to be kept secret, but it

---

[8] Stewart had been living at Saint-Germain since 1718 (HMC *Stuart*, VI, p. 87, Lady Bute to Mar, 5 March 1718; HMC *Stuart*, VII, p. 434, 24 October 1718; BL. Add MSS 31260, f. 133, F. Nairne to Nairne, 9 May 1719). He had visited the court in Rome in 1721 (Bod. Lib. Rawlinson MSS D. 1181, p. 398, Rawlinson's diary, 4 June 1721; SCA. BL 2/237/1, Lady Bute to W. Stuart, 21 July 1721).

[9] Geraldin was made a *chevalier de l'Ordre de Malte* in 1715 on the recommendation of Gualterio, as a favour to the Duke of Perth (BL. Add MSS 31256, f. 137, Perth to Gualterio, undated). He had visited the court in Rome in 1725 (NA. SP 85/16/f. 95, Stosch to Newcastle, 15 June 1726).

[10] O'Brien was already living in Rome with a small pension from the king. Hay explained his situation in a letter of 18 May 1724 to Gualterio: 'Mr Obrien qui est de long tems dans le service du Roy estoit autrefois dans le service d'Angleterre mais ayant eté decouvert d'etre Catholique et partisans du Roy il a eté obligé de quitter ce service, et le Roy l'a employé toujours depuis dans des affaires d'importance ou il s'est acquitté toujour bien, sans que Sa Ma.té pourtant peut rien faire pour le recompenser; il ne veut pas absolument quitter le service du Roy mais souhatteroit d'avoir quelque employ qui pourroit l'aider de subsister pendant que le Roy est en Italie' (BL. Add MSS 31264, f. 156).

[11] An unnamed Irish priest was employed to teach the prince his catechism (BAV. Fondo Borgia Lat MS 565, f. 333, Foucquet's diary, 29 November 1725).

[12] Murray's letters to Gualterio in BL. Add MSS 31262 show where he lived after he left Rome. For the continuation of his pension, see *JCR*, pp. 209–10, James III to Murray, 13 December 1721; and *ibid.*, p. 223, Murray to Hay, 19 March 1724.

[13] Their correspondence can be studied in *JCR*, pp. 121, 131–2, 207–10, 215–16 and 221–9.

[14] *JCR*, p. 222, Hay to Murray, 22 February 1724.

was backdated at Murray's request to 1 February 1721, just before he had left Rome. The title he chose was Earl of Dunbar.[15] During the summer of 1724, when Mar's dealings with the Whig government were finally proved by Atterbury, Murray was thinking of returning to Scotland.[16] At that time the queen was not yet known to be pregnant, so the king agreed to his going,[17] and there seemed very little prospect of Murray's ever rejoining the court.

The situation changed in the autumn of 1724. James III had not found anyone who was willing to leave England to become his secretary of state. He therefore decided that he would have to give the post to John Hay, and publicly recognise him as Earl of Inverness, the title originally given him at Urbino in 1718.[18] Hay, however, wanted his wife to visit Scotland to discuss financial affairs with his family, so the king decided to defer the announcements until her return.[19]

Hay's decision that his wife should go to Scotland was very ill-judged. To make matters worse the Hays decided that she should travel through France, and then cross from Calais to Dover. This was simply provocative. When she reached Calais she was warned that she would be arrested if she went ahead and crossed the Channel.[20] She ignored the warning and, on landing at Dover, was taken into custody and escorted to London. She was subsequently interrogated by the Privy Council at Windsor, and then imprisoned as a common criminal in Newgate prison.[21] After four months she was given a pardon, on condition that she left the country.[22] The whole episode was unnecessary and, under the circumstances, she was lucky to be allowed to return abroad. Its importance for the Stuart court in Rome is that it persuaded James Murray, her brother, that it would be much too dangerous for him ever to think of returning to Scotland. He remained in France, and was therefore available to be recalled to Rome if the king wanted him.

---

[15] *JCR*, p. 222, Murray to Hay, 12 March 1724.

[16] *JCR*, pp. 225–6, Murray to Mrs Hay, 10 April 1724; BL. Add MSS 31262, ff. 146, 148, Murray to Gualterio, 16 June and 2 August 1724.

[17] *JCR*, pp. 226–7, James III to Murray, 21 August 1724.   [18] See above, p. 129.

[19] *JCR*, pp. 226–7; BL. Add MSS 31264, f. 159, Hay to Gualterio, September 1724.

[20] BL. Add MSS 31264, f. 166, Hay to Gualterio, 7 October 1724. Hay's brother, the Earl of Kinnoull, had recently taken the oaths of loyalty to George I, and she believed he would be able to protect her (Haile, *James Francis Edward*, pp. 304–6).

[21] BL. Add MSS 31264, ff. 171, 175, Hay to Gualterio, 11 and 18 October 1724; NA. SP 85/15/f. 212, Stosch to Newcastle, 11 November 1724.

[22] BL. Add MSS 31262, ff. 152, 153, Murray to Gualterio, 22 December 1724 and 5 February 1725; *JCR*, pp. 227–8, James III to Murray, 6 January 1725. To obtain her release, Queen Clementina was obliged to write to the duchesse de Bourbon to ask her husband to get the French ambassador to plead her cause with George I (Haile, *James Francis Edward*, p. 306).

On 5 March 1725, when it was known that Marjory Hay was safely back in France, James III formally recognised her husband as Earl of Inverness and appointed him secretary of state. Prince Henry was born the following morning and baptised by the Pope.[23] The king was delighted with his second son, and told Foucquet, who was now an intimate friend, that the birth 'had given him even more pleasure in a way than that of his elder son'.[24]

James had already, on 20 February, written to Murray and asked him to accept the post of governor to the Prince of Wales. The letter arrived in Paris while Murray's sister was still there,[25] so they must have discussed it together. Murray's reply has not survived, and perhaps he asked his sister to speak to the king on his behalf when she returned to Rome. He confided to Gualterio that he was surprised and embarrassed by the offer, and that he felt completely unqualified for the post. As an unmarried man who had never had any children of his own, he wrote that 'I know no more about this job than I do about medicine and it seems to me that I might just as well have been named chief doctor as to be given this responsibility'.[26] He asked Gualterio to support him in declining the offer. Gualterio, however, told him that it was his duty to accept, and in April Murray wrote that he had agreed to do so.[27]

It is not certain, but the evidence suggests that the queen was not at this point informed of what the king was planning. Foucquet, who visited the Palazzo del Re on 20 April, found her in the king's Bedchamber, and noted that 'she told me that she was making a ribbon to put on the King's cane'.[28] But trouble was brewing. Shortly after her return to Rome, Mrs Hay, now Lady Inverness, was again placed in attendance on the queen.[29] Cardinal Alberoni, who had decided to make himself the queen's champion, seems to have spoken out against this, and Stosch noted that 'disagreements between Haye [sic] and Cardinal Alberoni increase every day'.[30]

During May the king and queen visited Gualterio at Orvieto and Corgniolo,[31] and in June they spent two weeks at Albano. On both occasions they left the two princes in Rome with Dorothy Sheldon,

[23] NA. SP 85/15/f. 310, Stosch to Newcastle, 6 March 1725.
[24] BAV. Fondo Borgia Lat MS 565, f. 317, Foucquet's diary, 22 March 1725. See also the entry for 19 February 1725 (f. 311).
[25] SCA. BL 2/279/4, W. Stuart to T. Innes, 8 March 1725.
[26] BL. Add MSS 31262, f. 155, Murray to Gualterio, 19 March 1725.
[27] BL. Add MSS 31262, f. 157, Murray to Gualterio, 7 May 1725.
[28] BAV. Fondo Borgia Lat MS 565, f. 322, Foucquet's diary, 20 April 1725.
[29] NA. SP 85/15/f. 318, Stosch to Newcastle, 17 March 1725; JCR, pp. 228–9, James III to Murray, 28 March 1725.
[30] NA. SP 85/15/f. 326, Stosch to Newcastle, 31 March 1725.
[31] NA. SP 85/15/ff. 366, 380, Stosch to Newcastle, 12 and 26 May 1725.

Grace Appleton, Francesca Battaglia and Teresa Keller, and took with them only Lord and Lady Inverness, Captain John O'Brien, Alan Cameron and their personal domestic servants.[32] The false calm continued during August when they were back in Rome to watch the flooding of the Piazza Navona as usual from the thrones erected on the balcony outside the Spanish Church.[33] This was the period when Cardinal de Polignac encouraged them to expect a change of French foreign policy and when they were asked by the Pope to help negotiate a settlement between Polignac and Cienfuegos concerning their opera boxes.[34]

The first sign of trouble came in July when Francis Kennedy decided he could no longer work in the secretariat with Lord Inverness. His precise motives are not entirely clear. Perhaps he simply detested Inverness. Perhaps he knew that Murray was about to return, and that Sheridan was to be replaced in the secretariat. At any rate, he spoke to the king in 'a violent manner' and asked to be allowed to leave the court and go to France. The king eventually agreed to his first request, but told him that if he wanted to keep his salary he had to stay in Italy, so he went to live in Siena.[35] The rumour which reached Stosch was only half true, but it pointed to the unpopularity of Inverness and correctly identified Kennedy as a supporter of the Jacobites in Spain and France: 'The dismissal of Kennedy ... was the result of Hayes' requests, the latter having found a means to get rid of his enemy and the Duke of Ormond's chief supporter permanently, making him seem suspect.'[36]

In July 1725, just before Kennedy left the court, James III wrote to Murray to tell him that everything was now settled for him to return to the Palazzo del Re:

I desire to put my son among men, when I go to Albano next Autumn ... I would have you here about the middle of Sept ... It will be proper that you take your title [Earl of Dunbar] upon you at that time ... I wish you a good journey with all my heart and shall be impatient to have you here, to make my son a good Englishman.[37]

There was no suggestion that the appointment had the approval of the queen.

Murray arrived in Rome in the middle of September, was recognised by the king as Earl of Dunbar and appointed Governor of the Prince of

[32] NA. SP 85/15/ff. 392, 396, Stosch to Newcastle, 14 and 30 June 1725.
[33] NA. SP 85/15/f. 422, Stosch to Newcastle, 18 August 1725.
[34] See Chapter 3, pp. 72–3.
[35] RA. SP 84/165, Kennedy to Inverness, 31 July 1725; BL. Add MSS 31265, f. 112, Inverness to Gualterio, undated; Tayler, *Seven Sons of the Provost*, p. 123, Inverness to Kennedy, 17 May 1726.
[36] NA. SP 85/15/f. 418, Stosch to Newcastle, 4 August 1725.
[37] *JCR*, pp. 134–5, James III to Murray, July 1725.

Figure 17. *James Murray, Earl of Dunbar*, 1719 (101.6 × 76.2 cm),
by Francesco Trevisani. James Murray was acting secretary of state
(1719–21), then governor of both the Prince of Wales (1725–38) and
the Duke of York (1729–43). He was created Earl of Dunbar in 1725.

Wales (Fig. 17). He was given an apartment on the east side of the
Palazzo del Re, beside the one occupied by Prince Charles on the second
floor. On the following day, 16 September, James III took Queen Clementina to Albano, and Stosch reported to London that 'the elder son . . .
has been taken out of the care of women'.[38]

---

[38] NA. SP 85/15/f. 438, Stosch to Newcastle, 22 September 1725.

We can only imagine what the queen's feelings must have been while she was at Albano, and the friction which must have developed in her absence between the women still looking after Prince Henry and the unmarried men now looking after Prince Charles. It seems reasonable to assume that the queen was pinning all her hopes on Cardinal de Polignac and on the prospect of a removal of the court from Rome back to Saint-Germain. The women, however, had to watch as Lord Dunbar, Thomas Sheridan and the valet Michele Vezzosi, assisted by Francesca Battaglia, took charge of the little four-year-old prince. Shortly after the news of the Treaty of Hanover between England and France reached Rome in October, thereby dashing all hopes of a move to Saint-Germain, Stosch wrote that 'there has been a great dispute ... between Lord Dunbar the Governor of the elder son and the women who have brought the boy up until now and who were still trying to play a part in his education'. When the queen visited the Palazzo del Re to see her two children she not only had to listen to the complaints of Dorothy Sheldon, but found herself unable to see Prince Charles without Dunbar remaining in the room with her.[39]

James was very angry when he heard that Dorothy Sheldon had questioned Dunbar's authority, and decided to dismiss her. The queen, however, dissuaded him, perhaps because of the shortage of available Jacobite women to replace her. But when the court returned to Rome on 5 November[40] Dorothy Sheldon was openly rude to the king and was summarily dismissed.[41] She was ordered to return to France, but instead flouted his authority by taking refuge in the Convent of Tor de' Specchi.[42] Lady Misset was recalled temporarily to take Dorothy Sheldon's place,[43] but it seemed possible that Lady Inverness might also become involved in the care of Prince Henry. This, for the queen, was the last straw.[44]

---

[39] NA. SP 85/15/f. 450, Stosch to Newcastle, 20 October 1725; HMC, *10th Report*, p. 161, James III to Queen Clementina, 11 November 1725.

[40] NA. SP 85/15/f. 470, Stosch to Newcastle, 10 November 1725.

[41] McLynn, *Charles Edward Stuart*, pp. 15–17.

[42] NA. SP 85/15/f. 460, Stosch to Newcastle, 17 November 1725. Charles Forbes supported Dorothy Sheldon and was ordered to return to France (NA. SP 85/16/f. 24, Stosch to Newcastle, 9 February 1726), where he was described as 'a very fowll mouth'd gentleman' (RA. SP 92/120, L. Innes to Inverness, 8 April 1726). Many of the other pensioners sympathised with Dorothy Sheldon, and Lord Winton was 'a leur tete' (NA. SP 85/15/f. 495, Stosch to Newcastle, 24 November 1725).

[43] BAV. Fondo Borgia Lat MS 565, f. 333, Foucquet's diary, 20 November 1725; RA. SP Box 3/81, a list of salaries, October 1726.

[44] BAV. Fondo Borgia Lat MS 565, f. 332, Foucquet's diary, 14 November 1725.

On 11 November the king and queen had a furious argument in front of their servants in the Palazzo del Re, during which Clementina demanded that Lord and Lady Inverness should be sent away from the court, and threatened to leave it herself if they remained. She also complained that Dunbar was preventing her and her Catholic women from seeing the Prince of Wales. When James refused to give way she went to bed, refused to take supper and announced that she wanted to sleep by herself.[45] That evening the king sent her a letter in which he repeated that he was not prepared to send the Invernesses away, but asked her to accept this and remain at the court. In his own defence he said that he had suffered in silence her angry looks for the last two years, during which she had hardly looked at or spoken to him. Ignoring the insulting letter which his favourite had sent her in the autumn of 1722, he claimed that he did not know how Lord and Lady Inverness had offended her, and argued with some justice that his correspondence would fall into confusion if he were now to dismiss his recently appointed secretary of state. He admitted that he had issued a general order that the governor and under-governor should remain with the prince at all times, but said that that was to prevent the child's escaping among the lower servants, 'where children learn nothing good'.[46]

The queen sent no reply to this letter, and remained in seclusion for the next three days. Then, on the morning of the 15th, she went out in her coach with Lady Southesk and took refuge in the Convent of Santa Cecilia in Trastevere, claiming that her husband was intending to bring her children up as Protestants by entrusting them to Lord Dunbar and Lady Inverness.[47] This, of course, was an argument which was intended to appeal to Pope Benedict XIII.[48] Clementina stated that she would not leave the convent, which she had chosen because it was under the protection of Cardinal Gualterio,[49]

---

[45] NA. SP 85/15/f. 460, Stosch to Newcastle, 17 November 1725.

[46] HMC, *10th Report*, p. 161, James III to Queen Clementina, 11 November 1725.

[47] Valesio, *Diario di Roma*, IV, p. 605, 15 November 1725; BSR. Revillas MSS F/84/3, 'Diario di Roma', 15 November 1725; NA. SP 85/15/f. 460, Stosch to Newcastle, 17 November 1725; BAV. Fondo Borgia Lat MS 565, f. 333, Foucquet's diary, 20 November 1725.

[48] See Chapter 1, p. 28. See also HMC, *10th Report*, appendix, part VI, p. 217, James III to Queen Clementina, 20 February 1726, in which he wrote that she had originally never pressed for anything except the dismissal of Lord Inverness, and had never explained her reason for distrusting him. James argued that if she had anything to urge against Inverness she ought to have urged it before going into the convent.

[49] BAV. Fondo Borgia Lat MS 565, f. 332, Foucquet's diary, 14 November 1725. The queen occupied an apartment which she knew was vacant, but which had previously

until both Inverness and Dunbar had been dismissed, and until Dorothy Sheldon had been reinstated.[50]

James III was outraged, particularly when the Pope and various cardinals took her side against him, and he refused to accept any of the queen's terms. The most he would do was to agree to send her a small staff of personal servants to attend her, and enough plate for her to eat and drink.[51] The servants included Mary Fitzgerald and Isabella Gordon (two of her chambermaids) and Catherina Rittel (daughter of her valet Gottfried Rittel).[52] The king was furious to discover that they were then joined by Dorothy Sheldon, who was escorted to Trastevere by Cardinal Alberoni himself.[53] James issued an order to the members of his court forbidding them to have any contact either with the queen or with any of her servants in the convent.[54] It was understood, of course, that this could not apply to Lord and Lady Southesk, but Southesk agreed not to visit his wife openly at the convent.[55]

It is important to keep in mind what this dispute between the king and the queen was actually about, and not to confuse the symptoms with the cause. The queen wanted to control her own household, to appoint and dismiss her servants and to retain control over the upbringing of her elder son until he was seven years old. Her servants would all have been Catholic, which would automatically have eliminated the Protestant Lady Inverness, and kept all other Protestants away from Prince Charles. The reason why Clementina hated Lord and Lady Inverness was because she believed – rightly – that they had advised the king not to let her have her own household, and because she considered that they enjoyed too much influence with the king. She attributed to them the king's decision to entrust her four-and-a-half-year-old son to a Protestant bachelor, Lord Dunbar, whom she already disliked. Only by forcing her husband to make the Invernesses leave the court could she remove their evil influence, recover control over Prince Charles and invite Dorothy Sheldon to return. James, who felt that such decisions were

---

been occupied by Cardinal Aquaviva's mother (same reference, f. 336, Foucquet to Ramsay, 19 December 1725).

[50] BAV. Fondo Borgia Lat MS 565, f. 333, Foucquet to Ramsay, 20 November 1725.

[51] Valesio, *Diario di Roma*, IV, p. 606, 16 November 1725; RA. SP 87/83, receipt from Gordon, 16 November 1725; RA. SP 87/104, receipt from Read, 22 November 1725.

[52] Valesio, *Diario di Roma*, IV, p. 606, 16 November 1725; BAV. Fondo Borgia Lat MS 565, f. 333, Foucquet's diary, 20 November 1725, and Foucquet to Ramsay, 20 November 1725; NA. SP 85/15/f. 490, Stosch to Newcastle, 22 November 1725.

[53] Valesio, *Diario di Roma*, IV, p. 607, 20 November 1725; NA. SP 885/15/f. 490, Stosch to Newcastle, 22 November 1725.

[54] BAV. Fondo Borgia Lat MS 565, f. 333, Foucquet to Ramsay, 20 November 1725.

[55] NA. SP 85/16/f. 18, Stosch to Newcastle, 19 January 1726.

his to make as man, husband and king, denied that he was under the influence of the Invernesses, was determined to bring up his sons as Catholics, and was therefore not prepared to give way.

Clementina originally intended to send Lady Southesk away from the convent because she was Protestant. But Alberoni advised her that she would alienate Jacobite opinion if she were to appear openly anti-Protestant. He therefore persuaded her to keep Lady Southesk with her and allege that her quarrel with Inverness and Dunbar was not because they were Protestants, but simply because they were personally objectionable. This was dishonest and deliberately misleading. But it coincided with the opinion of most people, especially in Jacobite circles, and Alberoni persuaded her that she would thereby command widespread public sympathy and make her husband give way.[56] Some people inevitably wondered why the queen found Lord and Lady Inverness so objectionable, so rumours began to spread (actively encouraged by Baron von Stosch) that James III was having an affair with Lady Inverness. This made certain Jacobites – for the first time – move on from criticising the king's favourites to criticising the king himself.

James countered by at last giving employment to Lady Nithsdale, a Catholic to whom neither Pope Benedict XIII nor Cardinal Alberoni could object. She was now given charge of the upbringing of Prince Henry in place of Dorothy Sheldon and Lady Misset.[57] James also announced that Lord Nithsdale would be appointed Prince Henry's governor when he was old enough to be handed over to men.[58] To emphasise the point, the king invested Nithsdale as a Knight of the Order of the Thistle at the end of the year.[59]

James III's attitude at this moment of crisis has been preserved in the diary of François Foucquet, who had a long conversation with him on 29 November. 'He had me ... brought to his bedchamber, and after a few minutes, when everyone else had left, he began to tell me how hurt he was at the actions of the Queen in her withdrawal to the convent of Santa Cecilia.' James began by saying that the queen had been given bad advice. He made no mention of Alberoni, but suspected that Lady Southesk was partly to blame, and should not be allowed by the Pope to remain in the convent.[60] He then told Foucquet that the queen

[56] NA. SP 85/15/f. 510, Stosch to Newcastle, 6 December 1725.
[57] BAV. Fondo Borgia Lat MS 565, f. 333, Foucquet to Ramsay, 20 November 1725.
[58] NA. SP 85/15/f. 490, Stosch to Newcastle, 22 November 1725.
[59] Ruvigny, *Jacobite Peerage*, p. 194; BAV. Fondo Borgia MS 565, f. 338, Foucquet to Ramsay, 2 January 1726.
[60] See also BL. Add MSS 31266, f. 23, Inverness to Gualterio, undated (November or December 1725).

wanted two things, the dismissal of Lord Inverness and the dismissal of Lord Dunbar. There was no mention of Lady Inverness:

On the first point, that the Queen desired the minister to be sent away, the King said that she had given no reason at all. He repeated this twice. On the second, that the governor should be sent away because he is a Protestant, the king said that this was a pretext, as he had provided for the Prince's religious education, giving him a good man, a Catholic, who was always with him, and that the Governor was there only to give the boy a general view, that he was an honourable man, a man of quality (he repeated this on two different occasions) incapable of instilling bad maxims in the Prince, and very capable of inspiring him with beneficial ones, that he knew him well ... and that he had put in a young Irishman from the Irish College to teach the Prince his catechism.

After this explanation James then came to the real problem between him and the queen, which concerned whether or not Clementina was to have her own household:

he had known the Queen's views for some time, but had never wanted to aquiesce in the matter, for to grant her wishes would be making her the mistress, and ceasing *to be the master for the rest of his days*, that these matters were not women's affairs, and that it was up to him to make such decisions.[61]

James, of course, was well aware of the rumours which were beginning to circulate concerning his alleged conduct with Lady Inverness.[62] He therefore called together all the members of his court to explain the situation to them. He also instructed Lord Inverness to write to William Dicconson at Saint-Germain and Lewis Innes at Paris to reassure them that there had been nothing wrong in his conduct despite the queen's action.[63] Dicconson and Innes were given a memorandum written by Thomas Sheridan, which included a copy of the king's long letter to his wife and laid much of the blame on Dorothy Sheldon. They were asked to do what they could to counter the malicious rumours.[64]

Dicconson wrote back to say that he had done his best to carry out his instructions by calling a meeting in the Château de Saint-Germain and

[61] BAV. Fondo Borgia Lat MS 565, f. 333, Foucquet's diary, 29 November 1725 (Foucquet's emphasis). Foucquet had been Bishop of Eleutheropolis *in partibus* since March 1725.

[62] Lady Inverness was in bad health at this time because of her experiences at Newgate, and reported to be going blind (*JCR*, p. 227, James III to Murray, 6 January 1725; NA. SP 85/16/f. 95, Stosch to Newcastle, 15 June 1726).

[63] Even before the news arrived that the queen had taken refuge in the convent, opinion in France was critical of Lord Dunbar's appointment. See WDA. Epist Var vol. 8, no. 118, Ingleton to Mayes, 22 October 1725.

[64] RA. SP 87/103, Inverness to Dicconson, 21 November 1725; 89/53, Inverness to L. Innes, 9 January 1726; 87/130, memorandum by Sheridan.

reading the papers to them.[65] But the unpopularity of the Invernesses and Dunbar was such that many people, perhaps even most, were not prepared to believe what they were told.

The social life of the Jacobite community at Saint-Germain was particularly active during the winter of 1725–6. In addition to Lord Dillon and the many others who lived in the Château-Vieux, the town was visited by various Jacobites from Paris, and also by the Duke of Mar, who was living nearby at Chatou.[66] Moreover the eighteen-year-old 3rd Duke of Beaufort was in Paris at the start of his Grand Tour. Early in January 1726 Beaufort invited all the Jacobites to a great ball in the château,[67] thus providing a particularly good opportunity for the latest developments in Rome to be fully discussed. Stimulated by letters written from Rome which have not survived, and possibly also by Mar and Ramsay, who had been there, the general verdict seems to have been against the king and his favourites. Lord Dillon sent the following protest to Cardinal Gualterio on 13 January, blaming Lord Inverness for all the problems at the court in Rome:

I am told that in Rome they are trying to implicate me in a plot along with Miss Sheldon, my sister-in-law [Mrs Ralph Sheldon] and others, to cause the unfortunate separation that has befallen the Royal family. The character imputed to me is so evil, and inspires such horror, that I would do anything to defend myself. I have seen public documents that Lord Inverness has had published here, in which I can recognize perfectly clearly that he intended to designate me without actually naming me; he even dares use the King's authority to transmit his calumnies to the world.[68]

Another letter written from Saint-Germain the following day goes even further, and accuses 'those two villainous traitors' Inverness and Dunbar of working for George I. It states that the paper read out by

---

[65] RA. SP 88/64, Dicconson to Inverness, 17 December 1725.
[66] HMC, *9th Report*, part II, appendix (London, 1884), p. 217, Atterbury to Keith, 7 November 1725; SCA. BL 2/287/1, T. Innes to W. Stuart, 1 July 1726; *SPW*, p. 78, Mar to James III, 5 May 1727. Mar was living at Chatou in one of the 'vastes demeures entourées de grands parcs ... de part et d'autres de la route de Saint-Germain-en-Laye' (Laurent Robert, *Chatou et Croissy-sur-Seine: Villégiatures en bordure de Seine* (L'inventaire générale des monuments et des richesses artistiques de la France, Paris, 1993), p. 5). It was there that he befriended and employed the gardener Claude Richard and was the first person to introduce greenhouses ('serres chaudes') into a French garden (Gabriella Lamy, 'Des Jardiniers Saint-Germanois au service de Louis XV puis de Marie-Antoinette au Petrit Trianon: Claude (1705–1784) et Antoine (1734–1807) Richard', *Bulletin des amis du vieux Saint-Germain*, no. 44 (2007), pp. 103–15, at p.104. When this article was published, 'ni la localisation de ce jardin, ni le nom de cet anglais [*sic*] n'ont été retrouvés').
[67] Corp, *A Court in Exile*, p. 340.
[68] BL. Add MSS 20310, f. 370, Dillon to Gualterio, 13 January 1726.

Dicconson 'excuses the Kings conduct in regard of Hays [sic] and Murray ... but very poorly', and argues that 'those two sparks Hays and Murray desire his restauration as much as I desire to hang myself'. If it reflects Saint-Germain opinion, as it probably does, it shows how much damage had been done by the rumours circulating among the Jacobites in France:

> The poor Queen is so virtuous and good that none can git anything from her but that those three persons must be sent away or that she cannot live with the King, without giving any reason, but the dainger of her children being perverted, but that is but a small part of the reasons that several persons ... of the family [in Rome] ... write ... [The Queen] found by all the proceedings of Lord Inverness towards her, by in a manner making love to her by dumb signs and gestures as squeesing of hand, and amorous loocks and gestures, that he had a desirer eyther to attempt her honor, or at least to make her servants and others believe that there was ... [a] familiarity between him and the Queen ... And so the Queen to preserve her Honor thought it necessary to retire to a convent.[69]

If this is what some people at Saint-Germain and at the Palazzo del Re thought, then the king's determination to defend Lord Inverness was bound to alienate many Jacobites both in France and at Rome.

The salaried servants at the court in Rome, and the other exiled Jacobites living there on a pension from the king, were in no position to express their feelings and publicly criticise Inverness and Dunbar. They therefore attached considerable importance to the anticipated arrival of the Duke of Beaufort on his Grand Tour. The enormous prestige conferred on him by his rank and family connections, and by his independent financial means, suggested that he would be able to say what others could only think. He could express the opinion of the community at Saint-Germain, headed by Mar and Dillon and represented in Rome by Dorothy Sheldon. He could also speak for those like Francis Kennedy at Siena who had been patronised by Beaufort's great-uncle the Duke of Ormonde.

The one person in Rome who dared express himself, and then only guardedly, was Lord Southesk, whose wife had remained in the convent with the queen. In March he gave the king a paper in which he admitted that 'Your Majesty is certainly the best Judge as well as absolute Master as to your servants', but reminded him that 'the eyes of all mankind are

---

[69] BL. Add MSS 21896, f. 1, W. Connock to T. Connock, 14 January 1726. There is another letter of 11 February 1726 (f. 3) containing similar criticisms. Colonel William Connock was a cousin of the poet Jane Barker. His son, Sir Timon Connock, was a brigadier in the Spanish army serving as under-governor to the infante Philip, later Duke of Parma (RA. SP 106/84, a list of Jacobite officers in the Spanish army, May 1727; RA. SP 132/78, L. Innes to James III, 28 November 1729).

still upon the actions of Princes and the best of Ministers have not thought it a matter of indifference what the general opinion was concerning them'. His message was not difficult to decipher. If Inverness and Dunbar were really 'such as they ought', they would resign and leave the court so that other, better men could be sent for.[70] The king was not willing to let his favourites leave the court, but he did offer to provide Lord and Lady Inverness with accommodation outside the Palazzo del Re if that would persuade the queen to return.[71] She, however, was equally intransigent, though she let Lady Southesk rejoin her husband every evening and only wait on her during the day.[72]

The Duke of Beaufort left France at the end of March 1726 and continued his Grand Tour by visiting some of the cities of northern Italy.[73] In Siena he listened to the complaints of Francis Kennedy and encouraged him to return to Rome.[74] Meanwhile he contacted the king and told him that he would himself reach Rome in May. The king instructed Captain John O'Brien to find him accommodation,[75] and arranged to meet him secretly in the countryside before he arrived in the city.[76] Beaufort entered Rome on 6 May, accompanied by his governor (William Philips) and Sir Charles Wogan's younger brother, Nicholas, a lieutenant in Dillon's Regiment. As if to emphasise his connection with the Jacobite community in France, he also brought with him his new steward, Dominique Dufour, who had previously been employed as a page of the Bedchamber to Mary of Modena, and had first hand experience of the management of the queen's household at Saint-Germain.[77]

Three days after Beaufort's arrival, James III withdrew to Albano with Inverness, Dunbar, Prince Charles and most of the court, leaving Lady Inverness, Lady Nithsdale and all the women with Prince Henry in the Palazzo del Re.[78] He did not return until 23 June,[79] so for six and a half

[70] *JCR*, pp. 44–5, Southesk to James III, 25 March 1726.
[71] NA. SP 85/16/f. 65, Stosch to Newcastle, 27 April 1726.
[72] NA. SP 85/16/ff. 63, 139, 141, Stosch to Newcastle, 20 April, 12 and 14 September 1726.
[73] Ingamells, *Dictionary*, pp. 67–9.
[74] Tayler, *Seven Sons of the Provost*, Inverness to O'Bryen, 29 May 1726.
[75] NA. SP 85/16/f. 63, Stosch to Newcastle, 20 April 1726.
[76] Beaufort travelled down the Via Aurelia from Leghorn. James III pretended that he was going to visit Gualterio at Orvieto, and left Rome on the Via Cassia. Lake Bracciano lies between the two roads, and that is where they met. Beaufort then went to the Via Cassia to make his entry into Rome, while James returned to the city on the Via Aurelia (NA. SP 85/16/ff. 71, 87, Stosch to Newcastle, 4 May and 1 June 1726).
[77] Corp, *A Court in Exile*, p. 340; NA. SP 85/16/f. 73, Stosch to Newcastle, 8 May 1726.
[78] NA. SP 85/16/f. 75, Stosch to Newcastle, 11 May 1726.
[79] NA. SP 85/16/f. 101, Stosch to Newcastle, 29 June 1726.

weeks Beaufort and his party were left to do as they pleased in Rome. It was noted that Beaufort became particularly friendly with Lord South-esk and all those who disliked Inverness,[80] and that he went to visit the queen at the convent in Trastevere.[81]

Beaufort also provided the Jacobites with entertainment, as he had previously done at Saint-Germain. On 9 June (30 May Old Style), to mark the restoration of Charles II, he gave a 'large party, with dinner and music',[82] followed twelve days later by a 'large supper'.[83] The Jacobites invited included Lord Bulkeley, an old school friend on the Grand Tour whose cousins lived in the Château de Saint-Germain,[84] and Francis Kennedy.

The presence of Kennedy in Rome was resented by James III, who was continuing to pay his salary though he was without employment. When Kennedy had returned from Siena, the king had assumed that he wanted to resume his work in the secretariat, so had ordered him to accompany the court to Albano. Kennedy went to Albano, but then returned to Rome the next day without permission so that he could escape from Inverness and be with Beaufort. Kennedy was ordered to return to Siena, but he refused to go.[85] Sir William Ellis reported to Inverness from Rome on 23 May that the Duke of Beaufort had been to see him 'and expressed the great interest he took in Francis Kennedy and that his returning from Albano without leave was not sufficiently serious for the King to order him to Siena'.[86] A few days later it was observed that the duke had made Kennedy 'one of his constant companions'.[87]

This episode reveals very strikingly the vulnerability of a king managing a court during a period of extended exile, in a country where he had no control over the central administration. It also provides further evidence of the increasingly unfortunate consequences of James III's

[80] NA. SP 85/16/ff. 79, 81, 99, Stosch to Newcastle, 15 and 18 May, and 22 June 1726.
[81] NA. SP 85/16/f. 85, Stosch to Newcastle, 25 May 1726.
[82] NA. SP 85/16/f. 93, Stosch to Newcastle, 13 June 1726.
[83] NA. SP 85/16/f. 99, Stosch to Newcastle, 22 June 1726.
[84] Richard, 5th Viscount Bulkeley, was the same age as Beaufort and had also been educated at Westminster. His great-grandfather, the 2nd viscount, was the brother of Henry Bulkeley (master of the household to James II), whose wife, Lady Sophia, was a lady of the Bedchamber to Mary of Modena at Saint-Germain and was still living in the Château-Vieux with three of her daughters. Her other daughter was married to the Duke of Berwick and had an apartment in the château, as did her son Lieutenant-General Francis Bulkeley (Corp, *A Court in Exile*, pp. 337–9, 346).
[85] Tayler, *Seven Sons of the Provost*, pp. 122–4, Kennedy to James III, 14 May 1726; Inverness to Kennedy, 17 May 1726; Ellis to Inverness, 17 and 21 May 1726.
[86] *Ibid.*, pp. 124–5, Ellis to Inverness, 23 May 1726. In another letter of the same day Ellis told Inverness that Philips had been to see him to explain that Beaufort had actually told Kennedy to come back from Albano (RA. SP 94/27).
[87] Tayler, *Seven Sons of the Provost*, p. 125, Inverness to O'Bryen, 29 May 1726.

friendship with Inverness and Dunbar. As he could expect no help from the Pope, there was nothing that the king could do but forbid Kennedy to enter the Palazzo del Re, and even then he was not obeyed until he had issued the order in writing.[88] Because James could not risk a breach with Beaufort, he also felt obliged to continue paying Kennedy his salary, which was now regarded as a pension.[89]

It would be wrong, however, to doubt Beaufort's continued Jacobite loyalty. It was merely that he strongly disapproved of the king's favourites and could afford to show his support for the queen. In July he celebrated Clementina's birthday by giving 'a magnificent supper with 25 dishes of meat ... at which all the English Jacobites and many of [the king's] servants were present'.[90] He nevertheless met James III and Prince Charles 'almost every day' at the Villa Borghese[91] and frequently used the secret staircase in the Palazzo del Re to see the king in his apartment.[92]

It is probable that Beaufort's continued presence in Rome had become a major source of embarrassment and that it contributed to the king's decision to transfer his court temporarily to Bologna. The duke was planning to leave Rome for Venice before the end of the year, and James seems to have felt that it would be more convenient to absent himself and not return until Beaufort had actually gone. The duke's presence, with Kennedy in his entourage, was a constant reminder that his authority over his own subjects had been openly flouted. In August Stosch noted that the duke 'gave a large dinner and supper ... for his usual companions', that he continued 'on several days of this week to give similar examples of his generosity', and that 'one of the most assiduous visitors to the Duke's palace is Kennedy'.[93] A few days later James III announced his intention to go to Bologna for an extended *villeggiatura* of three or four months. The reason given was that the Pope had reduced his pension and allocated part of it to the queen,[94] but it seems clear that Beaufort's presence in Rome was an important contributory factor.

[88] *Ibid.*, p. 125, Ellis to Inverness, 3 and 4 June 1726; RA. SP 94/70, Ellis to Inverness, 5 June 1726.

[89] Tayler, *Seven Sons of the Provost*, p. 125.

[90] NA. SP 85/16/f. 108, Stosch to Newcastle, 20 July 1726. In another letter Stosch informed Newcastle that the guests included both Thomas Forster and Lord Bulkeley (same reference, f. 110, 27 July 1726).

[91] NA. SP 85/16/ff. 106, 112, Stosch to Newcastle, 13 July and 3 August 1726.

[92] Alice Wemyss, *Elcho of the '45* (Edinburgh, 2003), Elcho's journal for October 1740 (written in 1781–3), p. 26.

[93] NA. SP 85/16/f. 116, Stosch to Newcastle, 10 August 1726.

[94] NA. SP 85/16/f. 124, Stosch to Newcastle, 24 August 1726. See also SCA. BL 2/289/9, Nairne to T. Innes, 21 August 1726, and BL 2/294/9, W. Stuart to T. Innes, 12 September 1726.

Part II

Bologna, 1726–1729

James III had already visited Bologna three times: in March 1717, when he first arrived in the Papal States; in October 1718, when he had gone there to await Clementina's arrival from Ohlau;[1] and in October 1722, when he had taken her there after leaving Bagni di Lucca.[2] On each occasion he had stayed in the Casa Belloni, the recently built home of his banker, Giovanni Angelo Belloni,[3] and had been very well received by the leading senators of the city.

Bologna was within the Papal States and was very close to his mother's birthplace at Modena. Some of the families who had served her had come from Bologna and were still living there.[4] Another important connection was with the leading Bolognese senator, conte Sicinio Pepoli, who had married James's cousin Eleonora Colonna in Rome in 1720.[5] The city was also the home of Cardinal Davia, brother-in-law of the Countess of Almond, his mother's lady of the Bedchamber. The king knew that he would be well received in Bologna.

The city was governed by the Papal Legate, Cardinal Tommaso Ruffo, and it retained, as a reminder of its former independence, a senate composed of sixty members, headed by an elected *gonfalonier* and eight *anziani* (elders).[6] At the beginning of September 1726 James sent Thomas Forster (his *maggiordomo*) and François Delaux (one of his

---

[1] Corp, *Jacobites at Urbino*, pp. 13–15, 105–12.   [2] See Chapters 1, 3 and 7.

[3] For the Belloni family, see Alberto Caracciolo, *L'albero dei Belloni: una dinastia di mercanti del Settecento* (Bologna, 1982). Giovanni Angelo Belloni was given the title of marchese by James III (p. 52).

[4] For James III's links with Bologna, see Edward Corp, 'Farinelli and the Circle of Sicinio Pepoli: A Link with the Stuart Court in Exile', *Eighteenth Century Music*, 2:2 (September 2005), pp. 311–20, at pp. 311–13. Joseph Ronchi, gentleman usher of the King's Privy Chamber at Whitehall and Saint-Germain, had been created a baronet on 24 July 1715. He wrote to Nairne from Bologna on 1 March 1721 that he was as loyal to James III as if he had been born in the middle of England: 'I do like as little to be an Italian as possible, but I cannot help it' (RA. SP 52/74).

[5] Corp, 'Farinelli and the Circle of Sicinio Pepoli,' p. 312.

[6] Maurizio Ascari, 'James III in Bologna'.

valets de chambre) on a mission to speak to the leading senators and select a building within the city which could be rented for the use of the court. Forster and Delaux chose the Palazzo Fantuzzi in the Via San Vitale, and its owner (conte Filippo Gaetano Fantuzzi) agreed to make it available. It was arranged that the king should live temporarily in the Casa Belloni, and then move to the Palazzo Fantuzzi when he had seen it for himself and when an apartment had been prepared for him.[7]

The month of September was spent making all the necessary arrangements.[8] As the move was regarded at this stage as no more than an extended *villeggiatura*,[9] followed by a return to the Palazzo del Re at the end of the year,[10] decisions had to be taken concerning what furniture, plate and linen should go to Bologna and what should be left in Rome.[11] It was also necessary to decide which servants should be left behind in Rome to look after the palazzo and its contents.

On 19 September James had an audience with Pope Benedict XIII and informed him of his plans. He took with him the two princes and Lady Nithsdale,[12] and told the Pope that he had appointed Father Lawrence Mayes, the Agent of the English Catholic Clergy in Rome, to accompany the court to Bologna as Prince Charles's preceptor.[13] On 29 September, shortly before their departure, James took the two princes to see their mother at the convent in Trastevere. It was hoped that this might persuade Clementina to rejoin the court, but she remained determined to stay where she was until the king had agreed to give her a separate household and to send Inverness and Dunbar away from the court.[14]

The royal household was now formally divided between the servants of the king in the Palazzo del Re, who might accompany him to Bologna,

[7] ASB. Ass. di Mag: Affari Diversi, b. 118/c. 19/pp. 630, 632–7, 646–9, proposals presented to the *magistrati* explaining the terms on which the owners of palazzi would make them available to 'a distinguished person', undated (August to September 1726); NA. SP 85/16/ff. 135, 139, Stosch to Newcastle, 5 and 12 September 1726; Biblioteca Universitaria di Bologna MS 770, vol. 91, unpaginated, the diary of Antonio Francesco Ghiselli, 22 and 28 September, 16 October 1726; WSRO. Goodwood MS 105/407, 408, McSwiny to Richmond, 11 and 18 October 1726.

[8] NA. SP 85/16/ff. 126, 132, 137, 141, 147, 151, Stosch to Newcastle, 29 and 31 August, 7, 14, 21 and 28 September 1726.

[9] SCA. BL 2/294/9, 10, Stuart to T. Innes, 12 and 26 September 1726; NA. SP 85/16/ f. 145, Stosch to Newcastle, 19 September 1726.

[10] BL. Add MSS 31264, f. 226, Inverness to Gualterio, 23 October 1726. The Palazzo Apostolico at Albano was also retained by James III, and looked after for him by Giovanni Evangelista, the *guardarobbe*.

[11] The inventories of the plate taken to Bologna are in RA. SP 97/67, and 99/114–17, 119. The inventory of the plate left in Rome is in RA. SP 99/118.

[12] NA. SP 85/16/f. 145, Stosch to Newcastle, 19 September 1726.

[13] SCA. BL 2/289/11, Nairne to Stuart, 2 November 1726.

[14] SCA. BL 2/294/11, Stuart to T. Innes, 30 September 1726.

and the servants of the queen who had joined her in the Convent of Santa Cecilia.[15] James also selected from among the former group several people to remain in the Palazzo del Re. Most of them were old servants who had originally joined the court at Saint-Germain-en-Laye. They included the yeoman of the robes (James Rodez), the yeoman of the wine cellar (Charles Macarty), the clerk of the kitchen (Jeremiah Broomer), the riding purveyor (John Sheridan), a chairman, a footman and a groom (respectively Henry Kerby, Andrew Simms and Mark Manning).[16] In addition to these, there were the three servants whose duties were to look after parts of the palazzo: the Swiss Guard (Bernhardt Nieriker), the chapel keeper (Pierre Arnoux) and the sweeper (Pietro Pezzi). These servants were placed under the authority of Sir William Ellis, the controller and treasurer of the household, another old servant from Saint-Germain.[17] All the other servants were ordered to prepare themselves for the journey to Bologna.[18]

Ellis felt himself to be in a potentially difficult position because he might receive orders from Queen Clementina after the king had left. He therefore asked James for specific instructions. There is a document containing twenty questions which Ellis submitted to the king on 18 September. The paper contains the king's answers in the margin. The first question concerns 'the Table Plate, the Backstairs Plate, Candlesticks etc which the Queen has of Yr Ma.ties in the Convent. The Table linen. Sheets for the Queens own use. Sheets for the servants.' The king comments: 'The Queen to have the use of these things, without any addition being made to them.'[19] The other questions concern

---

[15] RA. SP 98/47, Ellis to Inverness, 19 October 1726. The women in the service of the queen were summoned to the Palazzo del Re on 20 September, and it was probably on this occasion that they were told they were no longer to be paid by the king (NA. SP 85/16/f. 147, Stosch to Newcastle, 21 September 1726).

[16] These servants had been employed for many years at the court of Saint-Germain: Rodez since at least 1692, Macarty since 1689, Broomer since 1689, Sheridan since 1707, Kerby since at least 1693, Simms since at least 1695, and Manning since at least 1699.

[17] The lists of salaries paid in Rome after the court had left for Bologna are in RA. SP Box 3/81 (October 1726), 103/150 (February 1727), Box 4/4/39 (March 1727), and 105/92 (March 1727). The two nurses (Mrs Francesca Battaglia and Mrs Teresa Keller) were also allowed to remain in Rome, as was the scourer (Magdalen Rebout). Sir William Ellis, who had been employed at Saint-Germain since 1695, was assisted in Rome by William Watkins, whose mother, Elizabeth (daughter of Jeremiah Broomer), lived at Saint-Germain with her second husband, William Crane, previously a gentleman usher of Queen Mary of Modena's Privy Chamber (RA. SP 62/151, Hay to Mar, 3 November 1722; RA. SP 66/24, Crane to James III, 1 February 1723).

[18] NA. SP 85/16/f. 137, Stosch to Newcastle, 7 September 1726.

[19] An inventory of 16 November 1726 in RA. SP 98/83 shows that a significant amount of plate was sent back from Bologna in November 1726 for the use of the queen. There is also an inventory dated 28 November 1726 which shows the plate which by then 'Her Majesty uses in ye Convent' (RA. SP 99/120).

clothes, plate, furniture, jewels, pictures, chocolate, tea, wine, beer, wood and salt, and the use of a coach or sedan chair. The king's replies are consistent: nothing should be given to the queen except those items which were her own property. The three key questions are found near the end of the document:

In case the Queen should come to the Pallace, or go to Albano, and order lodgings for any others, Her Ma.ties servants or others.
    No lodging to be given to the Queen's order.
    If Her Ma.tie should order me to remove out of the Palace.
    not to go
    If Her Ma.tie remaining in the nunnery or out of it should send for me at any time.
    not to go.[20]

It is clear that at this stage the king had no intention of making any compromises.

By the end of September all the necessary preparations had been made for the journey. First to leave were the lesser servants with all the packing cases and furniture, starting on the 27th and arriving at the Casa Belloni on 5 October.[21] They were followed on Monday 30 September by the two princes and their servants, led by Lord Dunbar, Lady Inverness, Thomas Sheridan, the chevalier Geraldin and Lady Nithsdale. On the following day Sir David Nairne set off with a group of people including Charles Fleming. Finally, on Wednesday 2 October the king himself left Rome, accompanied by Lord Inverness, Thomas Forster, Alan Cameron and John Stewart.[22]

The princes and their party travelled by short stages to Loreto, and then up the Via Emilia from Ancona. The king's party took the shorter route up the Via Aurelia to Leghorn, and then via Lucca and Pistoia. Nairne and Fleming travelled via Florence. One reason for dividing the members of the court into three groups was so that they would not all arrive at the same time. This was to relieve the pressure on the Casa Belloni, which was not large enough to accommodate all the court. The king reached Bologna on Wednesday 9 October,[23] followed the next day

[20] RA. SP 92/150, 'Orders by the King in HM's own hand, yt is answ[eri]ng to my Q.ries sometime before H. Mat.y went to Bologna', 18 September 1726.
[21] NA. SP 85/16/ff. 149, 151, Stosch to Newcastle, 26 and 28 September 1726; Ghiselli, 5 October 1726; WSRO. Goodwood MS 105/408, McSwiny to Richmond, 18 October 1726.
[22] SCA. BL 2/294/11, Stuart to T. Innes, 30 September 1726; BAV. Fondo Borgia Lat MS 565, f. 351, Foucquet's diary, 2 October 1726; NA. SP 85/16/f. 153, Stosch to Newcastle, 3 October 1726.
[23] BL. Add MSS 31264, f. 217, Inverness to Gualterio, 12 October 1726; Ghiselli, 12 October 1726; BL. Add MSS 31264, f. 226, Inverness to Gualterio, 23 October 1726.

by Nairne and Fleming.[24] It was not until the king moved to the Palazzo Fantuzzi on Saturday 19 October[25] that there was room in the Casa Belloni for the princes, who had meanwhile been entertained by Alamanno Salviati at Pesaro. They arrived on Monday 21 October.[26] It was noted that Lady Inverness had left the princes at Rimini and arrived in Bologna four days earlier.[27]

The Palazzo Fantuzzi was larger than the Casa Belloni, but it was too small to house the entire court. James III therefore successfully negotiated to rent the Palazzo Ranuzzi-Cospi, which was immediately beside it in the Via San Vitale.[28] The king would occupy the Palazzo Fantuzzi, and the princes the Palazzo Ranuzzi-Cospi once an arch had been constructed to permit communication between the two.[29] In the hope of placating Queen Clementina, it was arranged that Lord and Lady Inverness should find their accommodation elsewhere in a completely separate building. This was the Casa Pistorini, which was rented from a doctor of that name who had fallen into debt.[30] Describing the arrangement to Cardinal Gualterio, Inverness added that he particularly liked the house because he had a small apartment from which he could go 'in a sedan chair directly to the King's apartment'.[31] According to the diary of Francesco Ghiselli, the Palazzo Fantuzzi was rented for 800 *scudi* per annum, the Palazzo Ranuzzi-Cospi for 400 *scudi* and the Casa Pistorini for 120 *scudi*.[32]

It was not until 23 November that the building works at the Palazzo Ranuzzi-Cospi were finally terminated, and the princes were able to move there from the Casa Belloni.[33] They were not the only ones who had been waiting for the works to be completed. Sir David Nairne had been living near the Casa Belloni in the Palazzo Monti with Father

---

[24] SCA. BL 2/289/10, Nairne to Stuart, 16 October 1726.

[25] Ghiselli, 23 and 26 October 1726.

[26] BL. Add MSS 31264, f. 221, Inverness to Gualterio, 16 October 1726; Ghiselli, 21 October 1726; BL. Add MSS 31262, f. 162, Dunbar to Gualterio, 23 October 1726.

[27] BL. Add MSS 31264, f. 223, Inverness to Gualterio, 19 October 1726; Ghiselli, 19 October 1726.

[28] Ghiselli, 12 October 1726. Conte Ferdinando Vincenzo Ranuzzi, who had inherited the palazzo from his grandmother (née Dorotea Cospi), had died in 1726, and neither of his two sons needed it. See Giancarlo Roversi, *Palazzi e case nobili del '500 a Bologna* (Bologna, 1986), pp. 184, 187.

[29] BL. Add MSS 31264, f. 217, Inverness to Gualterio, 12 October 1726; Ghiselli, 16 and 19 October 1726; WSRO. Goodwood MS 105/408, McSwiny to Richmond, 18 October 1726.

[30] *SCW*, p. 80, Inverness to Ormonde, 29 October 1726.

[31] BL. Add MSS 31264, f. 230, Inverness to Gualterio, 30 October 1726.

[32] Ghiselli, 21 and 27 October 1726.

[33] BL. Add MSS 31264, f. 235, Inverness to Gualterio, 6 November 1726; Ghiselli, 27 November 1726.

Lawrence Mayes (Prince Charles's preceptor).[34] They also now joined the princes in the Palazzo Ranuzzi-Cospi.[35]

The Palazzo Fantuzzi was one of the most distinguished senatorial buildings in Bologna, and provided a suitably impressive temporary home for the Stuart court.[36] It contained an important *sala* with frescoes by Angelo Michele Colonna, and a *salone d'onore* with a famous perspective painted by Francesco Galli-Bibiena. But its most celebrated feature was a monumental staircase which, as Inverness put it, 'most of the strangers that pass this way, come to see'.[37] Unfortunately, no information seems to have survived concerning the precise allocation of space within the palazzo, the nature of the apartment occupied by the king, or the one intended to be occupied by the queen.[38]

When James III arrived in Bologna he received a series of formal visits. On 9 October the eight *anziani* came to pay him compliments 'acting as Ambassadors in the name of the public'.[39] On the following day he was welcomed by Cardinal Ruffo, the Papal Legate, followed by Cardinal Giacomo Boncampagni (Archbishop of Bologna), Cardinal Ulisse Gozzadini (Archbishop of Imola) and Cardinal Davia (Legate of the Romagna).[40] Given the hostility of the Pope, it was particularly gratifying that he quickly established good relations with Cardinal Ruffo.[41]

---

[34] SCA. BL 2/289/10, Nairne to Stuart, 16 October 1726; SCA. BL 2/289/2, 3, 3/2, Mayes to Stuart, 2, 6 and 16 November 1726.

[35] James III gave marchese Monti two Spanish horses to thank him for making these rooms available (Ghiselli, 2 November 1726).

[36] For a detailed description of the Palazzo Fantuzzi, see Roversi, *Palazzi e case nobili del '500 a Bologna*, pp. 82–97. See also Charles de Brosses to Neuilly, 15 September 1739: 'Au palais Fantuzzi, une façade magnifique d'ordres dorique et ionique, et, qui pis est, les colonnes sont toutes taillées en espèce de pointes de diamants, ce qui produit un effet fort singulier' (*Lettres d'Italie*, ed. Frédéric d'Agay (2 vols. (Paris, 1986), vol. I, p. 265).

[37] *SPW*, p. 80, Inverness to Ormonde, 29 October 1726. Also BL. Add MSS 31264, f. 217, Inverness to Gualtiero, 12 October 1726: 'Le grand palais est du Senateur ffantuzzi ou est le fameux escallier qui est l'objet de la curiosité de toutes les etrangeres qui passent par cette ville.' When the Duke of Mar saw it in 1718 he was so impressed that he asked conte Fantuzzi to let him have detailed architectural drawings of the staircase (HMC *Stuart*, VII, p. 678, W. Drummond to Mar, 28 December 1718).

[38] BL. Add MSS 31264, f. 217, Inverness to Gualtiero, 12 October 1726 makes it clear that there was a separate apartment for the queen.

[39] ASB. Senato Diari vol. 12, pp. 63–4, 'Arrivo del Re d'Inghilterra Giacomi III', 9 October 1726, and 'Ringraziamento del Rè', 12 October 1726. When the prince and the duke arrived they were also formally visited by eight of the *anziani* (ASB. Senato Diari vol. 12, pp. 64–6, for the *ambasciate* to the prince and duke, 22 October 1726, and the *ringraziamento* of the prince, 23 October 1726). Angelo Michele Tosi's miniature painting recording these visits is included as plate 8 in Ascari, 'James III in Bologna', p. 25. See also the description in Ascari, pp. 16–17.

[40] BL. Add MSS 31264, f. 217, Inverness to Gualtiero, 12 October 1726; WSRO. Goodwood MSS 105/408, McSwiny to Richmond, 18 October 1726.

[41] BL. Add MSS 31264, f. 244, Inverness to Gualtiero, 23 November 1726.

Once these formal visits had been concluded the king began to enjoy himself. On 19 October Inverness wrote to Gualterio that the king 'is enjoying himself here. He has been to the theatre and to some *conversazioni* which please him greatly'.[42] A few days later he added that 'His Majesty continues to enjoy himself in this town to which the nobility is returning every day from the countryside'.[43]

The diary of Francesco Ghiselli contains the details of the various social activities which James III enjoyed at Bologna during the autumn and winter of 1726–7.[44] He visited the most important houses in and around Bologna, including the Villa Ranuzzi (called Mirabello) outside the Porta Lame, and the Palazzo Albergati at Zola Predosa.[45] He regularly attended performances at the Teatro Pubblico and, during the carnival season, at the opera houses. He frequently went to the balls given by the senators in their palazzi, and always danced with several of the ladies. He generally took with him the Prince of Wales, who had been having dancing classes with Jean Arnaux for over a year and a half. Perhaps the most notable was the 'magnificent' ball given by marchese Marescotti to mark the prince's sixth birthday.[46] There is a small painting which shows him dancing with one of the ladies, watched by his father and the assembled company.[47] At another ball the prince particularly danced with his cousin the contessa Pepoli.[48] In addition to these social occasions, the king regularly attended private musical evenings. Ghiselli recorded that one of them was given by Lord Inverness in the Casa Pistorini. There were at least twenty ladies present, and the music was followed by dancing and refreshments.[49]

During November 1726 James III considered making a visit to Venice because Cardinal Ottoboni was there with the duchessa di Fiano (one of the daughters of the principessa di Piombino).[50] In the event he decided not to go, so the duchess visited him in Bologna instead.[51] Inverness informed Gualterio that James had gone out of his way to entertain her

---

[42] BL. Add MSS 31264, f. 223, Inverness to Gualterio, 19 October 1726.

[43] BL. Add MSS 31264, f. 230, Inverness to Gualterio, 30 October 1726.

[44] Biblioteca Universitaria di Bologna MS 770, 'Avisi Secreti di Bologna dall' Abate Ant. Francesco Ghiselli' in 93 volumes. Vol. 91 covers the years 1725–7.

[45] Ghiselli, 16 and 19 October 1726.　　[46] Ghiselli, 1 and 4 January 1727.

[47] It was painted by Leonardo Sconzani, and is reproduced as plate 9 in Ascari, 'James III in Bologna', p. 26.

[48] Ghiselli, 7 December 1726; Ludovico Frati, *Il Settecento a Bologna* (Bologna, 1923), p.133.

[49] Ghiselli, 11 December 1726.

[50] BL. Add MSS 31264, f. 243, Inverness to Gualterio, 20 November 1726; RA. SP 99/77, 78, Inverness to Graeme, 23 November 1726; WSRO. Goodwood MS 105/414, McSwiny to Richmond, 29 November 1726; BL. Add MSS 31264, ff. 248, 250, 258, Inverness to Gualterio, 30 November, 7 and 14 December 1726.

[51] BL. Add MSS 31264, f. 240, Inverness to Gualterio, 16 November 1726.

with as much honour as possible, in order to show his friendship and esteem for the family of the principessa di Piombino.[52]

There was an important social event in January 1727 when marchese Giacomo Gualterio married Vittoria Albergati.[53] The marchese was the son of the Jacobite Earl of Dundee (the brother of Cardinal Gualterio).[54] Vittoria Albergati's sister later married a son of contessa Veronica Molza, who had been a Bedchamber woman to Mary of Modena at Saint-Germain.[55] The Albergati family now became increasingly associated with the Stuart court.

James III, meanwhile, was assiduous in his religious observations. He regularly attended services both at the Church of Santi Vitale e Agricola in Arena, situated opposite the Palazzo Ranuzzi-Cospi,[56] and at the Basilica of San Petronio in the Piazza Maggiore.[57] Within the Palazzo Fantuzzi (temporarily renamed the Palazzo del Re by the Bolognese)[58] he instructed Father Lawrence Mayes to start saying Mass in a specially decorated Chapel Royal. Sir David Nairne recorded at the beginning of November that, although Mayes 'officiats chiefly as Precepteur to the Prince, and gos twice a day to teach him his Christian Doctrine', he now also 'says mass' for the king.[59] Mayes himself, in a letter written the same day, wrote that 'I have had ye hon.r to say Mass twice, and to communicate his Majesty both times'.[60] What Mayes did not record, but fortunately Ghiselli did, is that the king invited people suffering from scrofula (the king's evil) to come to the Chapel Royal so that he could perform the ceremony of touching them. It seems that he did this on the last Thursday of each month, giving to each person a silver touch-piece.[61]

---

[52] BL. Add MSS 31264, f. 244, Inverness to Gualterio, 23 November 1726.
[53] BL. Add MSS 31264, ff. 274, 280, Inverness to Gualterio, 11 and 18 January 1727.
[54] Ruvigny, *Jacobite Peerage*, p. 46.
[55] Ghiselli, 5 February 1729. For contessa Veronica Molza, see Corp, *A Court in Exile*.
[56] Ghiselli, 8 February 1727.   [57] Ghiselli, 15 March 1727.
[58] Fedora Servietti Donati, 'Sua Maestà britannica a Bologna e il Palazzo del Rè, anno 1728', *Strenna storica bolognese*, 30 (1980), pp. 332–46, at p. 342.
[59] SCA. BL 2/289/11, Nairne to Stuart, 2 November 1726.
[60] SCA. BL 2/289/2, Mayes to Stuart, 2 November 1726.
[61] Ghiselli, 30 October 1726: 'Giovedi Sua Mta fece celebrare messa nella Reale Cappella del suo Palazzo, e fatte le sacramentali penzioni fece la funzione di segnare la scrofe a buon numero d'infermi alli quali al solito diedonna medaglia d'argento.' Also 30 November 1726: 'In tutti li giovedi fatto le sacramentali divozioni nella cappella del suo Palazzo segna molte Persone opresse dal male di scroffe, facedogli à tutte il noto regallo d'una medaglia d'Argento, e si sente, che molte ne guariscono.' Also 21 April 1728. The king had also touched many Italians suffering from the king's evil when he had been at Lucca in 1722. See Janet Ross and Nelly Erichsen, *The Story of Lucca* (London, 1912), pp. 343–4; and Whipple, *Famous Corner of Tuscany*, pp. 143–8. See also Noel Woolf, *The Medallic Record of the Jacobite Movement* (London, 1988), p. 77, for the Italian touch-pieces. For an example of touch-pieces being sent from Italy to Saint-Germain-en-Laye, see RA. SP 54/111, Margaret Nugent to Nairne, 16 August 1721.

The king had originally intended his visit to Bologna to be no more than an extended *villeggiatura*, but in January 1727, by which time the queen had still not returned to him, he decided to remain there for an indefinite period. One reason was clearly that he was enjoying himself there, and looking forward to the rest of the carnival season. Another was no doubt the inconvenience of moving out of the palazzi Fantuzzi and Ranuzzi-Cospi after all the building works had been achieved. But this was also the moment when the Pope reduced the quarterly Stuart pension to 2500 *scudi*, and ordered that James himself should only receive 1500 *scudi*, the remaining 1000 being reserved for the queen so that she could pay her servants at the convent. It was also in January 1727 that the Pope ignored James's nomination of Cardinal Davia to be the new Protector of Scotland.[62]

The reduction in the papal pension obliged the king to consider making some concession to persuade Clementina to return to the court. The queen's demands had remained the same. She wanted to have her own household, she wanted Dunbar to be dismissed as the governor of Prince Charles, and she wanted Lord and Lady Inverness (whom she regarded as her enemies) to be sent away from the court.

By 1727 most people had begun to regard the dismissal of Lord Dunbar as no longer necessary. Prince Charles's other servants, including his preceptor, were all Catholic, and at the end of the year he would be seven years old, the normal age to be entrusted to men. Moreover there were very few Protestants, and no Protestant clergymen, attached to the court. Indeed, the only Protestants at the court in Bologna, apart from Dunbar, were Thomas Forster (*maggiordomo*), James Edgar (under-secretary), Alan Cameron and Lord and Lady Inverness. James realised with deep regret that if Lord and Lady Inverness were to leave he might be able to persuade Clementina to return.

The decision was finally taken on 26 March 1727, on which day both the king and Inverness sent letters to Cardinal Gualterio to give him the news. Inverness explained that the queen had agreed that Dunbar might remain, but no mention was made of her demand to have her own independent household.[63] The king was clearly very saddened to lose his favourite – the man with whom he had spent three months at Lugo in 1719 – and wrote to Lewis Innes in Paris that 'I never knew anybody in my life of more principles of honor and veracity than he; he was void of all ambition, but that of serving me usefully, I could never discover in

[62] See Chapter 1, p. 31.
[63] BL. Add MSS 31255, f. 303, James III to Gualterio, 26 March 1727; BL. Add MSS 31264, ff. 318, 320, Inverness to Gualterio, two letters of 26 March 1727.

him a selfish thought'.[64] James showed his appreciation by giving Inverness an English peerage as Baron Hay and (though secretly) creating him Duke of Inverness in the peerage of Scotland.[65] The couple left the court on 5 April and went to live at Pistoia.[66]

The departure of Lord and Lady Inverness was greeted with relief and hope by the Jacobites in Bologna,[67] in Rome[68] and in France,[69] because it was assumed that the queen would now leave the convent in Trastevere and rejoin the court. Clementina, however, had not yet obtained what she mainly wanted. She agreed to give way over Dunbar, but still insisted on having her own household.[70] It was only when the king finally agreed to this condition in the second half of June, after he had received a visit from the principessa di Piombino and the duchessa di Fiano,[71] that she consented to come to Bologna.[72]

The departure of Lord Inverness meant that the king needed to appoint a new secretary of state. The man he selected was Sir John Graeme, one of the Scottish pensioners whom he had previously sent from Rome to be his representative in Vienna.[73] As Graeme did not actually arrive in Bologna until the end of May,[74] the change inevitably put pressure in the secretariat on Nairne and Edgar, as well as the king himself.

There was another consequence to the resignation of Inverness. The salaries and pensions of all the people attached to the court had for

---

[64] RA. SP 105/125, James III to L. Innes, 7 April 1727.
[65] Ruvigny, *Jacobite Peerage*, p. 68; BL. Add MSS 31264, f. 322, Inverness to Gualterio, 29 March 1727.
[66] BL. Add MSS 31264, f. 327, Inverness to Gualterio, 4 April 1727; Ghiselli, 5 April 1727; NA. SP 85/16/ff. 241, 243, Stosch to Newcastle, 10 and 12 April 1727; HMC, *9th Report*, part II, appendix, p. 218, Atterbury to Keith, 21 April 1727; BL. Add MSS 31255, f. 334, James III to Gualterio, 28 May 1727. It was perhaps at this time that the king gave the 'title and interest in the Salts of Brouage and in the Isle of Rhé or elsewhere in France and all rents and revenues thence arising' to Lord and Lady Inverness and Lord Dunbar, 'to be enjoyed during their lives and the longest of them three' (ASV. SS: Ingh 25, pp. 109–12, the Last Will and Testament of James III, 21 November 1760). The annual income was 1000 *livres* (see Chapter 10, p. 203).
[67] SCA. BL 2/306/6, Nairne to T. Innes, 8 April 1727; SCA. BL 2/313/10, Mayes to Stuart, [8] April 1727.
[68] RA. SP 105/161, Ellis to James III, 12 April 1727.
[69] *JCR*, pp. 231–2; and *SCW*, pp. 78–9, Mar to James III, 5 May 1727.
[70] BL. Add MSS 31264, f. 329, Inverness to Gualterio, 22 April 1727.
[71] Ghiselli, 15 May 1727.
[72] BL. Add MSS 31255, f. 342, James III to Gualterio, 28 June 1727; BL. Add MSS 31264, f. 342, Inverness to Gualterio, 30 June 1727.
[73] BL. Add MSS 31264, f. 324, Inverness to Gualterio, 2 April 1727; HMC, *9th Report*, part II appendix, p. 218, Atterbury to Keith, 21 April 1727. It is not clear when Graeme went to Vienna, but it seems to have been before November 1722. Inverness merely stated that he had been there 'pour quelque tems'. He had been knighted and promoted minister on 6 September 1726 (Ruvigny, *Jacobite Peerage*, p. 6).
[74] BL. Add MSS 31255, f. 334, James III to Gualterio, 28 May 1727.

many years been paid by Sir William Ellis, but he had been left behind
in Rome, so a new servant named Pietro Marsi had been recruited in
Bologna to act as a temporary substitute.[75] Ellis continued to pay the
people who remained in Rome and Marsi now paid all those (the great
majority) who had accompanied the king to Bologna. The accounts of
Marsi, who was presumably recommended by Giovanni Angelo Belloni,
were supervised and checked by Inverness. The latter's departure therefore obliged the king to summon Ellis to Bologna and reconsider the
arrangements he had made for the Palazzo del Re in Rome.[76]

Since the departure of the court the previous October, Ellis had ensured
that the building and contents of the Palazzo del Re remained safe. To this
end Ellis had drawn up a detailed inventory of everything which still
remained in the palazzo belonging both to the royal family and to the
household servants,[77] including all the books and pictures belonging to
Lord Inverness and Lord Dunbar.[78] As treasurer of the household he had
been in charge of receiving the reduced papal pension, and, to make ends
meet, had been authorised to sell part of the king's plate, including some
gilt items and others felt to be 'not of ord[ina]ry use, as being too large a
size'.[79] Now, at the end of March 1727, he was ordered to hand over his
responsibilities to Girolamo Belloni, the nephew of Giovanni Angelo
Belloni and head of the family's bank in Rome, and to resume his role
as paymaster in Bologna. The Palazzo del Re was to be placed in the
charge of John Sheridan, the riding purveyor, under the general direction
of Belloni.[80] Before leaving on 21 April Ellis had another complete
inventory drawn up of 'all the furniture, yt is left in the appartments',
and handed over all the remaining plate to be looked after by Belloni.[81]

[75] RA. SP 98/62, Inverness to Ellis, 19 October 1726.

[76] Ellis took the opportunity to dismiss William Watkins, his assistant in Rome, and have
him sent back to Saint-Germain (RA. SP 102/87/33, Ellis to Broomer, 14 June 1727),
replacing him with Pietro Marsi. Ellis disliked Watkins, and had apparently treated him
very badly, provoking a series of strongly worded complaints from his family at Saint-
Germain (RA. SP 67/65, 73/70 and 76/54, Crane to Hay, 7 June 1723, 2 April and
20 August 1724; RA. SP 141/129, Elizabeth Crane to Inverness, 15 January 1731).

[77] RA. SP 98/47, Ellis to Inverness, 19 October 1726; RA. SP 98/131, 'an inventory of
goods in the King's Palace at Rome', October 1726; RA. SP 99/118, 'a list of the King's
Plate in the Custody of Sir William Ellis', 18 November 1726.

[78] RA. SP Box 4/2/28, 29.

[79] RA. SP 98/11, Forster to Ellis, 12 October 1726; RA. SP 98/47, 82, Ellis to Inverness,
19 and 23 October 1726.

[80] RA. SP 105/111, Ellis to Inverness, 2 April 1727. The Belloni family tree is shown in
Caracciolo, L'albero dei Belloni, p. 10. Girolamo Belloni (1688–1760) was the son of the
elder brother of Giovanni Angelo Belloni (c. 1650–1729).

[81] RA. SP 105/111, Ellis to Inverness, 2 April 1727; SP 105/140, James III to Ellis, 9 April
1727; SP 106/12, Ellis to James III, 16 April 1727; SP 106/24, 'Nota dell'Argentaria del

The decision to summon Ellis from Rome to Bologna enabled James III to hold a Garter investiture in the *sala* of the Palazzo Fantuzzi. His nephew James FitzJames, Earl of Tynemouth and Duke of Liria in Spain, of whom he was particularly fond,[82] had recently been appointed Spanish ambassador to the Court of St Petersburg. When the news had first reached Bologna in January, and it was known that Liria intended to visit the Stuart court en route to Russia, James III determined to give him the Garter.[83] The king's own Garter robes and collar, however, had been left behind in Rome. Ellis, therefore, was instructed to bring them with him.[84] The Duke of Liria arrived by sea at Genoa towards the end of April[85] and then travelled via Milan to Bologna, where he arrived on Tuesday 29 and was given accommodation in the Palazzo Fantuzzi.[86] He was invested with the Garter on the following day,[87] and remained with the king until 4 May.[88]

Meanwhile the Duke of Beaufort, who had left Rome as planned in December, had been in Venice and was now returning to France to complete his Grand Tour. On 30 April (the same day as the Garter investiture) he also arrived in Bologna to see James III. He stayed in an *albergo*, and on 1 May entertained the Jacobites with 'una serenata' given by some of the best musicians in the city, followed by generous refreshments.[89] He continued his journey on the following day towards Milan.[90]

Rè Britt.co consegnata all'Ill.mo Sig.r Gir. Belloni', 18 April 1727; SP 106/35, Ellis to James III, 19 April 1727.

[82] The two men had known each other since childhood at Saint-Germain, and Lord Tynemouth had joined the rising in Scotland in 1716.

[83] BL. Add MSS 31264, f. 284, Inverness to Gualterio, 25 January 1727.

[84] RA. SP 105/111, Ellis to Inverness, 2 April 1727; SP 105/140, James III to Ellis, 9 April 1727.

[85] BL. Add MSS 31264, ff. 327, 329, Inverness to Gualterio, 4 and 22 April 1727.

[86] Ghiselli, 4 May 1727.   [87] Ghiselli, 30 April 1727.

[88] WSRO. Goodwood MS 105/419, McSwiny to Richmond, 9 May 1727.

[89] Beaufort irritated James III by taking into his own service one of the cooks employed at the court, a Frenchman named Théophile Lesserteur, whose father had been master cook to Mary of Modena at Whitehall and Saint-Germain. It is not clear when or how this happened, though Beaufort's accounts refer to paying Lesserteur 'pour son voiage de Boulogne a Venise' and 'pour ses gages depuis le 1er Janvier 1727' (Badminton Archives Fm I/4/3, accounts with Dominique Dufour, 17 July 1727). The king commented that 'I don't intend to take Lesertur [sic] back into the family, tho he should have a mind to return to me' (RA. SP 112/28, James III to Ellis, 9 November 1727). In fact Lesserteur remained permanently in the employment of the Duke of Beaufort in England (Badminton Archives Fm I/4/13, accounts with Hoare's Bank, 1729–33; and Beaufort to Dufour, 23 April 1732), though he made visits to Saint-Germain (RA. SP 149/149, 150/89, 151/77, 180/142, Dicconson to Ellis, 28 October and 9 December 1731 and 27 January 1732, and to Edgar, 2 July 1735).

[90] Ghiselli, 1 May 1727. He noted that Beaufort paid for everything 'con monete d'oro'. Beaufort's visit to Bologna is not mentioned in Ingamells, *Dictionary*, p. 68, but is also referred to in RA. SP 112/160, rough notes by Ellis, undated [1727].

Shortly after these visits James III made arrangements for the court to spend a few weeks *en villeggiatura* in the countryside outside Bologna. It was at this time that he finally agreed to grant the queen her own separate household, and (probably advised by the principessa di Piombino, who planned to join the court in Bologna)[91] he now decided to receive her in the relative tranquillity of the countryside rather than in the centre of the city. The move from Rome to Bologna the previous year had been referred to, somewhat misleadingly, as a *villeggiatura*, but of course it was really no more than a move from one city to another. As James no longer had easy access to the Palazzo Apostolico at Albano, where he could enjoy a real *villeggiatura*, he needed to find an alternative. He selected the Villa Alamandini, which he had known since the previous autumn,[92] and which was available because its occupant (Girolamo Alamandini) had just died. It was very conveniently situated two miles to the east of the Porta San Vitale. Ghiselli noted on 28 May that the king had taken the 'delicious' villa for himself and the queen, with 'some other buildings nearby for his family'.[93]

The two princes left Bologna, accompanied by Lord Dunbar, Lady Nithsdale and their servants, on 4 June,[94] and the king followed them two weeks later.[95] While he was there he made detailed arrangements for the queen's new household, and was visited by Lord North and Grey, one of the leaders of the abortive Atterbury Plot.[96] When everything was ready he sent Lady Nithsdale to meet the queen in Rome and accompany her from the Convent of Santa Cecilia back to Bologna. Then, suddenly, just as he was preparing to welcome Clementina back after a separation of over seventeen months, the news reached Bologna that King George I had died at Osnabrück. On 5 July 1727, while Lady Nithsdale was with the queen in Rome,[97] James III hastily left Bologna and travelled north incognito to Lorraine, hoping that the time for his long-delayed restoration had finally arrived.[98]

---

[91] On 29 June 1727 Ghiselli noted that the principessa di Piombino came to Bologna and inspected both the Palazzo Monti and the Palazzo Caprara as possible residences.

[92] Frati, *Settecento a Bologna*, p. 133; WSRO. Goodwood MS 105/409, McSwiny to Richmond, 1 November 1726.

[93] Ghiselli, 24 and 28 May 1727.   [94] Ghiselli, 4 June 1727.

[95] SCA. BL 2/305/16, Mayes to Stuart, 7 June 1727; Ghiselli, 21 and 25 June 1727.

[96] BL. Add MSS 31255, f. 341, James III to Gualterio, 20 June 1727.

[97] NA. SP 85/16/f. 279, Stosch to Newcastle, 5 July 1727.

[98] BL. Add MSS 31262, f. 168, Dunbar to Gualterio, 5 July 1727.

The period from 1727 to 1729 was a significant turning point in the history of the Stuart court in exile. It was also at this time, following the peaceful accession of King George II, that James III seems to have resigned himself to the probability of a permanent exile in Rome, with all hope of a restoration transferred to his two sons in the event of a future Anglo-French war.

There are several reasons why the court changed. In the first place its size and expense were considerably increased. This process began with the establishment of a separate household for the queen in July 1727, and continued with the recruitment of additional staff to serve Prince Charles at the time of his seventh birthday in December 1727. During 1728, moreover, plans were made to entrust Prince Henry's upbringing to men when he was four years old in 1729, with the necessary additional servants recruited in anticipation.

There were also changes in the secretariat. It was at this time that James III stopped employing a secretary of state, and thenceforth entrusted all his correspondence to a private secretary and a clerk.

The national composition of the court altered at this time. Although it had employed servants of several nationalities (French, Italian, German and Swiss, in addition to the king's own subjects), the most senior posts and those in the secretariat had so far been reserved for the English, the Irish and the Scots. The establishment of a separate household for the queen and the death and retirement of some of the older servants began a slow but steady process whereby the more important posts were given to Italians and other foreigners.

The queen's household

During June 1727 Sir William Ellis drafted a paper in which he suggested that the queen's new household might be established at a cost of 3630 *livres* each month. He allocated 1000 *livres* for the queen's 'Table comprehending Chocholat, Coffee, and Thea, [and] table linnen', 1000 *livres* for the queen's personal spending money (to include her 'Cloaths, Jewels, lace, Pictures and body linnen, port of letters, station.ry ware, Books etc'), 500 *livres* for her 'Liveries, Horsemeal, Farrier, coaches, wheelright etc belonging to ye Stables' and 1130 *livres* for the salaries of her servants. There were to be twenty-two of them, including a lord chamberlain, two gentlemen, a confessor, a secretary, a physician, two *valets de chambre*, three dressers or chambermaids, a necessary woman, a sweeper, a cook or 'cookmaid', an assistant in the kitchen, a coachman, a postillion, a helper in the stables and four footmen. Ellis's paper identified how much he thought each of the servants should be paid, including 200 *livres* for the lord chamberlain, and 75 *livres* for each of the gentlemen.[1]

One obvious criticism of Ellis's proposed household is that it did not include any ladies of the Bedchamber, nor even any women of a status above that of chambermaid. Another criticism is that the proposed salaries of the gentlemen were too low to attract people of quality. The king therefore modified the proposal by adding two ladies of the Bedchamber, each with a monthly salary of 200 *livres*, and by increasing the monthly salaries of the gentlemen from 75 *livres* to 100 *livres*. He also gave the queen a second necessary woman. These changes, and some other minor modifications, increased the monthly salary bill from the 1130 *livres* proposed by Ellis to 1609 *livres*. To find this extra money, while keeping within the proposed budget, James decided that the cost of the queen's table should be reduced by making her pay for her chocolate, coffee and tea out of her pin money, and by making her employ the king's own servants in the kitchen.[2]

Most of the members of the queen's household, including her confessor (Father John Brown), her secretary (Robert Creagh), her physician (Dr Charles Maghie), her *valets de chambre* (Gottfried Rittel and François Decelles) and her chambermaids (Mary Fitzgerald, Isabella Gordon and Mary Rivers) were already working for her in Rome, and were to accompany her to Bologna. The king, however, needed to select a new lord chamberlain (renamed the first gentleman), two other gentlemen and two ladies of the Bedchamber. He gave the first post to Lord Nithsdale, who was already receiving 200 *livres* each month as a pension. The other four posts he gave to Bolognese aristocrats. The two gentlemen were marchese Fabio Albergati (whose father was one of the *anziani*) and conte Girolamo Formigliari (whose

[1] RA. SP Box 3/1/72, 'If a Family totally separate' by Ellis, undated but June 1727.
[2] RA. SP 108/19, 'List of the Queens Family, and Regulations relating to it', 4 July 1727.

family owned one of the opera houses). The two ladies were marchesa Lucrezia Legnani and contessa Ranuzzi.[3]

Both Fabio Albergati and Lucrezia Legnani were related by marriage to Cardinal Gualterio. Albergati was the brother-in-law of the cardinal's nephew.[4] Legnani had been brought up at Urbino where her aunt, Lucrezia Staccoli, was married to the brother-in-law of the cardinal's brother, Lord Dundee.[5] James III wrote to Gualterio on 28 June that 'the Marchesa Legnani . . . is witty and clever and is much esteemed and admired here, and you can be sure that the relationship she has to your family has made her find all the more favour in my eyes'.[6] It seems clear that the king intended to give his wife senior servants whose primary loyalty would be to him. Neverthless Clementina had finally obtained her own separate household, and a small group of attendants worthy of her royal status.

The 'List of the Queens Family, and Regulations relating to it' was signed by James III on 4 July, immediately before he left Bologna in his unsuccessful attempt to recover his thrones. It explained the duties of the gentlemen and the ladies as follows:

Lord Nithsdale will attend the Queen wherever she goes, will give her his hand, present people to her when she is out of her Bedchamber, and give such orders as are to be given to the two Italian Gentlemen, and in his absence Marq.s Fabio Albergati is to supply his place.

The two Gentlemen are always to attend the Queen abroad, and to attend in the Antechamber from the time the Queen returns in the afternoon till supper, and in the morning, from the hour that shall be appointed to them at night, till dinner.

The two Ladys will take their turns of waiting by days or weeks. She in waiting will present people to the Queen and in her bed chamber. They are both of them to attend the Queen when she goes out in the afternoon, if she pleases, and at least the Lady in waiting is to attend in the morning, to go to Church with the Queen when she goes.

The Valets de Chambre and the Livery men, are to be entirely under Lord Nithsdale. . .

The Queen is to have a Table of five Covers served Dinner and Supper. The Lady in waiting is always to eat with the Queen. The others to be such as the Queen pleases.

---

[3] According to Ghiselli (2 and 5 July 1727) the king originally selected Benedetto Vittori rather than conte Fomigliari, and contessa Fontana rather than contessa Ranuzzi.
[4] See Chapter 9, p. 182.   [5] Corp, *Jacobites at Urbino*, pp. 76–7, 182.
[6] BL. Add MSS 31255, f. 342, James III to Gualterio, 28 June 1727. See also BL. Add MSS 31263, f. 167, Dunbar to Gualterio, 28 June 1727 ('Marquis Fabio Albergati, qui outre beaucoup de merite personel a celui a present d'appartenir a V.E.'); and BL. Add MSS 31267, f. 75, Graeme to Gualterio, 2 July 1727.

There will be six coach horses, a Berlin and a Fourlone always at the Queen's disposal.

During my absence Sir William Ellis will order any of my servants to wait on the Queen or my children as occasion offers.[7]

The king's sudden departure from Bologna in 1727, like his departure from Rome in 1719, made it necessary to establish who was to be in charge during his absence. On the previous occasion James III had entrusted the management of the court to James Murray, now Lord Dunbar.[8] This time he left the management in the hands of several people, though Queen Clementina would be regarded as being in overall command. The queen's new household was under the authority of Lord Nithsdale. Those servants of the king who remained in Bologna were to be under Sir William Ellis. On the same day that he signed the regulations for the queen's new household, James also issued new warrants to Lord Dunbar, Sir Thomas Sheridan and Father Lawrence Mayes, confirming them as governor, under-governor and preceptor of the Prince of Wales, and to Lady Nithsdale confirming her as governess of the Duke of York.[9] The implication was clear. The families of the two princes were to be regarded as separate, and the queen was not to interfere with the arrangements made for the senior servants of her children.[10]

By this time Lady Nithsdale was in Rome, accompanied by Captain John O'Brien and a small staff of people to escort Clementina to Bologna.[11] Baron von Stosch recorded that the queen and Dorothy Sheldon came out of the Convent of Santa Cecilia on 3 July to dine with the principessa di Piombino, the principessa Pamphili and Lady Nithsdale.[12] The news then reached Rome that the king had left Bologna, but it was too late for Clementina's plans to be changed. She had agreed to go to Bologna, and the Pope had given her money for the journey. She left on 7 July, accompanied as far as the Porta del Popolo by the principessa di Piombino and the principessa Pamphili.[13]

---

[7] See note 2.   [8] Corp, *Jacobites at Urbino*, pp.125–6.   [9] RA. SP 108/14–17.

[10] For example, some people assumed that the queen would recall Andrew Ramsay to be Prince Charles's preceptor instead of Mayes. See Sylvie Mamy, *Lettere d'Antonio conti da Venezia a madame la comtesse de Caylus, 1727–29*, p. 159, 29 August 1727: 'Monsieur Ramsay se flatte-t-il de retourner avec [Jacques III] ... La princesse Sobieski [sic] est retournée avec son époux, et il me semble qu'elle protégeoit Mr de Ramsay.'

[11] NA. SP 85/16/f. 277, Stosch to Newcastle, 3 July 1727.

[12] NA. SP 85/16/f. 279, Stosch to Newcastle, 5 July 1727.

[13] BAV. Fondo Borgia Lat MS 565, f. 355, Foucquet's diary, 7 July 1727; NA. SP 85/16/f. 281, Stosch to Newcastle, 10 July 1727. Stosch said she left on 8 July, but Foucquet witnessed her departure on 7 July.

Queen Clementina arrived unannounced at the Villa Alamandini at one o'clock in the morning on Sunday 13 July.[14] On the following day she was shown the list of the members of her 'Family and Regulations relating to it'. She immediately objected to having to pay for her chocolate, coffee and tea out of her pin money, and sent Lord Nithsdale to complain to Sir William Ellis.[15] The latter reported that he had managed to persuade her to accept the arrangement by explaining how little money the king now had, particularly as the Pope had given her a separate annual income of 4000 *scudi*.[16]

There was, however, a much more serious problem to be overcome, because the queen had brought with her from Rome three servants whom the king had deliberately omitted from the list of her Family. They were Dorothy Sheldon, a chambermaid called Masson,[17] and a *valet de chambre* called James Duncan, who had previously been employed by Lady Southesk.[18] Dunbar wrote to Gualterio on 16 July: 'May God grant that the steps she has taken are pleasing to the King, but I will tell your Eminence in confidence that I am very much afraid that bringing Miss Sheldon and two other servants against His Majesty's express wishes will give a bad impression.'[19] An unsatisfactory compromise was soon arranged. The queen refused to part with Dorothy Sheldon and agreed to pay her out of her own money. Ellis reported to the king that he had told her that he 'could not put Masson, nor James Duncan on yr Ma.ties Establishment, they not being on the list signed by Yr Ma.tie'. When the queen insisted, Ellis was advised by Dunbar to let her have her way.[20]

When the *gonfalonier* and the *anziani* heard of the queen's arrival they quickly arranged for a formal embassy to be sent to welcome her.[21] The following day Clementina sent Albergati and Formigliari to thank them on her behalf, but surprised them by stating that for the time being she would remain at the Villa Alamandini and not actually visit Bologna at all.[22]

---

[14] RA. SP 108/76, Dunbar to James III, 14 July 1727; BL. Add MSS 31262, f. 170, Dunbar to Gualterio, 16 July 1727.

[15] RA. SP 108/74, Ellis to James III, 14 July 1727.

[16] RA. SP 108/111, Ellis to James III, 21 July 1727.

[17] It is possible that 'Masson' was actually Lady Misset, who had been with the queen in the Convent of Santa Cecilia.

[18] NA. SP 85/15/f. 512, Stosch to Newcastle, 8 December 1725.

[19] BL. Add MSS 31262, f. 170, Dunbar to Gualterio, 16 July 1727.

[20] RA. SP 108/111, Ellis to James III, 21 July 1727.

[21] ASB. Ass di Mag, Aff Div, b. 118, cap 20; and ASB. Senato Diari vol. 12, both 15 July 1727.

[22] ASB. Ass di Mag, Aff Div, b. 118, cap 20, 16 July 1727; Ghiselli, 26 July 1727.

The queen also cut herself off from the king's and the prince's servants at the villa. Ghiselli noted in his diary on 19 July that she 'continues to stay . . . inside Her room, almost always in Prayer', except for a daily visit to the nearby Church of the Croce del Biaccio.[23] According to Ellis she received a visit each day from three priests, who came to say masses for her.[24] Father Lawrence Mayes, who was evidently not one of the three, wrote at the beginning of August that 'she lives with us in ye Villa very retird: and receives no [other] visits'.[25]

The king at Avignon

By this time the king was living incognito in Lorraine at Frouard, north of Nancy.[26] When he left Bologna he had taken with him only nine people: his secretary of state and under-secretary (Sir John Graeme and James Edgar), three gentlemen (Alan Cameron, John Stewart and a new arrival, Captain William Hay), two of his *valets de chambre* (Thomas Saint-Paul and François Delaux), a cook (Ignace Faure) and a servant from the stables (Peter Jolly de Falvie).[27] He had also ordered Lord Inverness to leave his new home at Pistoia and join him en route – thereby risking a new rupture with the queen. In August, when it was clear that the hoped-for restoration would not take place, James instructed Inverness to return to Pistoia,[28] but decided himself to go to Avignon rather than Bologna, hoping to avoid having to return to the Papal States. If he could persuade the French court to let him remain in Avignon he would then invite the queen and the princes to join him there.[29]

The king rented a house in Avignon from the marquis de Villefranche,[30] and increased his small entourage by summoning Thomas Forster and his new Franciscan confessor, Father O'Callaghan, to join him.[31] But in

[23] Ghiselli, 19 July 1727, translated in Ascari, 'James III at Bologna', p. 30. For further references to the queen's devotions, see Ghiselli, 10 December 1727, 14 January and 5 June 1728.

[24] RA. SP 108/111, Ellis to James III, 21 July 1727.

[25] SCA. BL 2/305/18, Mayes to Stuart, 2 August 1727. See also Ghiselli, 13 August 1727.

[26] Frouard is on the left bank at the confluence of the rivers Moselle and Meurthe.

[27] BL. Add MSS 31262, f. 170, Dunbar to Gualterio, 16 July 1727; RA. SP 109/110, James III to Ellis, 25 August 1727. The servants left behind in Bologna were therefore available to serve the queen.

[28] BL. Add MSS 31264, f. 347, Inverness to Gualterio, 2 September 1727; BL. Add MSS 31262, f. 193, Dunbar to Gualterio, 3 September 1727.

[29] BL. Add MSS 31262, ff. 191, 194, Dunbar to Gualterio, 30 August and 6 September 1727.

[30] NA. SP 85/16/f. 303, Stosch to Newcastle, 6 September 1727.

[31] RA. SP 111/80, James III to Ellis, 16 October 1727; RA. SP 112/26, a list of the salaries and pensions paid at Avignon, November 1727 to February 1728. Father Antonio

October he changed his plans regarding the queen. Because the French court seemed reluctant to let him remain in Avignon permanently, he tried to strengthen his negotiating position by persuading Clementina and all her household to join him there immediately,[32] to be followed by the two princes and their servants, and all the rest of the king's own servants, the following spring.[33] Clementina refused, however, to leave Bologna and make the difficult journey across the Alps until she knew that the French had already agreed.[34]

The king was so keen to persuade Clementina that he made further concessions to her. He agreed that she should have her own surgeon (Dr James Hay) and her own equerry (Captain John O'Brien).[35] When Father John Brown fell ill and had to return to his convent at Fano, he also let her have both a new confessor (Father Cangiassi) and a chaplain (Father O'Brien).[36] And when he drew up the list of people who should accompany her to Avignon, and commented to Sir William Ellis that 'I have left out of the List Mrs Sheldon, Masson and Duncan', he added that he (Ellis) should 'not oppose if the Queen insists'.[37]

Clementina, however, was not to be persuaded. In the middle of October she finally left the Villa Alamandini and moved into the Palazzo Fantuzzi.[38] Dunbar informed Gualterio on the 15th that 'the Royal Household returned to Bologna two days ago and it seems it will spend the winter there'. He added that there was 'little evidence ... of good relations' between the king and the queen:

Not only is Miss Sheldon still here despite having come against the King's wishes, but she is actually lodging with the Queen in Her Majesty's apartment; I confess with much pain to Your Eminence that this and many other

Ragazzi, the king's previous confessor, was sent back to Rome. The king also asked Ellis to send his Garter ribbon and 100 touch-pieces to Avignon (RA. SP 112/86, Ellis to James III, 2 December 1727).

[32] BL. Add MSS 31262, ff. 197, 201, 203, Dunbar to Gualterio, 10, 24 and 28 September 1727; RA. SP 111/71, 79, 80, James III to Dunbar and Ellis, 16 October 1727; H.C. Stewart, 'The Exiled Stewarts [sic] in Italy, 1717–1807', *The Scottish Historical Society Miscellany*, VII, 3rd ser., vol. 35 (Edinburgh, 1941), pp. 55–130, at p. 101, James III to Lercari, 16 October 1727.

[33] RA. SP 111/80, 82, James III to Ellis, and note by James III, 16 October 1727.

[34] BL. Add MSS 31262, ff. 210, 212, Dunbar to Gualterio, undated and 25 October 1727; BL. Add MSS 31264, f. 353, Inverness to Gualterio, 31 October 1727; RA. SP 112/78, James III to Ellis, 9 November 1727; HMC, *9th Report*, part II appendix, p. 219, Atterbury to Keith, 17 November 1727.

[35] RA. SP 111/79, 'List of the Queen's Family', 16 October 1727.

[36] BL. Add MSS 31262, f. 185, Dunbar to Gualterio, 20 August 1727; RA. SP 110/47, Ellis to James III, 14 September 1727; RA. SP 111/80, James III to Ellis, 16 October 1727.

[37] RA. SP 111/80, James III to Ellis, 16 October 1727.

[38] RA. SP 102/87/70, Ellis to Read, 9 October 1727; Ghiselli, 12 October 1727.

circumstances that are too long to write here seem to me to promise nothing good, and that it looks as if the second outcome will be even worse than the first.[39]

The French court, under extreme pressure from George II, would probably not have permitted James III to remain at Avignon, but Clementina's refusal to leave Bologna effectively sabotaged his plans. James eventually realised that he had no choice but to return to the Papal States. He left Avignon on 20 December, and arrived in Bologna on 7 January 1728.[40] Father Lawrence Mayes observed that 'ye meeting of ye King and Queen was with all signs of love and tenderness'.[41] This was partly because each of them had made a concession: 'She sent Mrs Sheldon into a convent the day before the King arrived, and his Majesty in recompence of this condescendance took back a Valet-de-Chambre [James Duncan] that the Queen likes and that he had dismissed.'[42] The chambermaid called Masson is not mentioned again and seems to have left the court.

The reorganised court

The Stuart court in exile was now organised as it had been at Saint-Germain-en-Laye. The king, queen and Prince of Wales each had a separate household, or Family. The governess and servants of the Duke of York were regarded as temporarily part of the household of the queen, until the duke's upbringing was entrusted to men. The only significant difference, apart from the smaller size and the absence of senior courtiers, was that the king and queen shared some of the servants in the household below stairs.

Now that formal waiting had been reintroduced in the queen's Bedchamber and Chamber, James III felt obliged to appoint two grooms to wait in his own Bedchamber. They were both Scottish. Alan Cameron had been appointed a groom of the Bedchamber in Scotland in February 1716,[43] but since the abolition of formal waiting at Pesaro in March 1717 had remained at the court and eventually been regarded as one of the pensioners. He now resumed his duties, and was joined as groom of

---

[39] BL. Add MSS 31262, f. 208, Dunbar to Gualterio, 15 October 1727.
[40] Ghiselli, 10 and 14 January 1728; NA. SP85/16/f.358, Stosch to Newcastle, 17 January 1728.
[41] SCA. BL 2/313/5, Mayes to Stuart, 14 January 1728.
[42] HMC, *10th Report*, p. 166, Liria to Gordon, 22 February 1728. Dorothy Sheldon was sent to San Pietro Martire, the convent of Dominican nuns (Ghiselli, 10 January 1728).
[43] SCA. BL 2/207/17, L. Innes to T. Innes, 6 February 1716. Cameron's name is missing from the list of the grooms of the Bedchamber published in Corp, *Court in Exile*, p. 361.

the Bedchamber by Captain William Hay.[44] The other servants attached to the king's Bedchamber were his three *valets de chambre*, Thomas Saint-Paul, Felix Bonbled and François Delaux.

The king did not reintroduce formal waiting in his Chamber, but he did appoint another Anglican chaplain. This was the Revd Ezekiel Hamilton, who had previously been with him at Avignon and Pesaro, and had since then been serving the Duke of Ormonde.[45] The Stuart court now again provided Anglican ceremonies for the Protestant servants and visiting Grand Tourists, and James had already arranged for a Protestant cemetery to be opened at Bologna.[46] The king also employed a Scottish physician, Dr Robert Wright.[47]

The household below stairs, the table and the stables remained under the control of Thomas Forster as *maggiordomo*, and of Sir William Ellis as controller and treasurer supported by two Italian assistants (Pietro Marsi and Domenico Arnoux). The king and queen were served by a small group of two cooks, two confectioners, a baker, a scourer, and an assistant in the wine cellar.[48] In the stables the king and queen each had an equerry, a coachman and a chairman, seven postillions, seven footmen and one groom.[49]

Prince Charles's household consisted of his governor, under-governor and preceptor (Dunbar, Sheridan and Mayes), two gentlemen (John Stewart and John Constable, newly recruited from England), two *valets de chambre* (Michele Vezzosi and Pierre Ferbos, newly recruited

---

[44] Ruvigny, *Jacobite Peerage*, p. 224. Cameron's monthly salary as a groom of the Bedchamber had been 204*l.* 2*s.* 3*d.* (RA. SP Misc 34, November 1722), but his pension had been only 100 *livres* (RA. SP Box 3/81). Now that formal waiting was reintroduced, he was given a salary of 102*l.* 2*s.* 3*d.*, whereas Hay was given 100 *livres* (RA. SP 129/94, 136/53). Ellis explained on one occasion that James II and Queen Mary had 'made several retrenchments [at Saint-Germain], by certain proportions, as a 10th or a 7th part, or the like; wch occasioned such odd summs on the Establishm.t of Salaries', as 204*l.* 2*s.* 3*d.* (RA. SP 112/86, Ellis to James III, 2 December 1727).

[45] Corp, *Jacobites at Urbino*, pp. 19, 51, 147.

[46] Ghiselli, 14 May 1727. It was 'dietro alle mure di Galeria', on the north side of the city. Ghiselli refers to a Protestant burial service in his entry for 14 January 1728.

[47] He was the son of the minister at Culross (RA. SP 330/137, Wright to Edgar, 5 April 1752) and had worked in France and Holland before going to Rome (BL. Add MSS 31265, f. 190, Inverness to Gualterio, undated).

[48] Matthew Creagh and Jean-Baptiste Dupuis (cooks), Pierre Pecquet and Henry Read (confectioners), Jean Bouzier (baker), Magdalen Rebout (scourer) and Francesco Girelli (assistant).

[49] James Delattre and Sir John O'Brien (equerries), Edmund Butler and Angelo Salvatore (coachmen), Henry Kerby and Antoine Brun (chairmen). The postillions and footmen were mainly locally employed, and frequently changed. The grooms were Frank Ridge and Roger Ryan, old servants from Saint-Germain.

from France), an equerry and riding master (the chevalier Geraldin), a second equerry (Captain John O'Brien), a footman and a groom.[50]

The queen's household remained in 1728 as originally appointed the previous year, except that she had a new surgeon (James Murray, who had previously worked for the duc de Noailles at Saint-Germain) to replace James Hay, who had died.[51] Prince Henry was served by his governess (Lady Nithsdale), a chambermaid, a cook, a footman and a groom.[52]

During 1728 the king recruited two men destined to serve as the under-governors of Prince Henry when he reached the age of four and a half. They were to be under the authority of Lord Dunbar as governor, and it is striking that they both came from Saint-Germain. The first was Hugh Dicconson, whose brother William had been treasurer at Saint-Germain for many years.[53] The second was John Paul Stafford, who had been born at Saint-Germain, and whose mother had been both under-governess to the king himself and then governess to his sister, Princess Louise Marie.[54] These Catholics from Saint-Germain were probably acceptable to the queen.

The secretariat

By July 1727, when James III left Bologna, the secretariat employed three people: the secretary of state (Graeme), the under-secretary (Edgar) and Sir David Nairne, by then seventy-two years old. Nairne had been employed by the exiled Stuart court since 1689, and from 1713 to 1719 had been responsible for all the king's Catholic correspondence, independent of the secretary of state. Since 1719 he had been effectively demoted and made subordinate to Murray and then Inverness.[55] He longed to retire, but was afraid of losing his salary. The king, however, had regarded him as indispensable, particularly after the sudden

---

[50] Francis O'Neill and an Italian named Tomaso.

[51] RA. SP 102/87/130, Ellis to Dicconson, 9 March 1728.

[52] Respectively Mrs Grace Appleton, Richard Conway, Jacques Catillon and Domenico Pedrottini. In addition, Lady Nithsdale had two chambermaids, Mrs Cecilia Evans and Mrs Mary Lindsay, who also helped look after Prince Henry.

[53] There are many references to him in Corp, *Court in Exile* and *Jacobites at Urbino*. Their younger brother, Edward Dicconson, was a Catholic priest, who later became the Agent of the English Clergy in Rome (1737) and then a bishop (1740).

[54] His mother, Mary, who had died giving birth to him at Saint-Germain in 1700, had been married to John Stafford (vice-chamberlain to Queen Mary). He was himself the brother of Mrs Mary Plowden (see Chapter 7, p. 141) and later succeeded his nephew as 4th Earl of Stafford.

[55] Corp, *Jacobites at Urbino*, chapters 12 and 13; and above, Chapter 6, p. 128.

departure of Francis Kennedy in 1726. He was completely bilingual in English and French, and spoke Italian fluently. He also had a seemingly endless capacity for hard work.

A widower since 1715,[56] he had been obliged to leave his daughters in Paris, and had unsuccessfully begged the king to let them come to Rome to look after him in his old age. The king, however, knew that Nairne strongly disliked his favourites, Inverness and Dunbar, and suspected that he sympathised with the queen in demanding her own household. He had therefore refused to let them come. When James left Bologna he took with him both Graeme and Edgar, and told Nairne to handle any correspondence which came, under the supervision of Dunbar.

Once the king settled in Avignon, Nairne hoped that he would be summoned, like Forster and Father O'Callaghan, to join the king in the Hôtel de Villefranche. James, however, had other plans and wrote to Lord Dunbar: 'Tell Nairn [sic] that he must have patience to come with the gross baggage next spring.'[57] This prompted a protest from Lewis Innes, who wrote from Paris to urge the king to treat Nairne more fairly. James replied that he had burned Innes's letter, and added the following: 'Nairn [sic] stays in Italy till my children come here. I am far from having any objection to his Daughters going to him either there or here, the moment it is no expense to me.'[58]

The king, however, was not really willing to let them come, and by the summer of 1728 nothing had changed. Lewis Innes wrote again to protest: 'I cannot but humbly and earnestly recommend to your Majesty the case of an old faithfull servant Sr Da. Nairne, that in his old age he may not want bread, but that if your Majesty hath no further use for him, his pension may be continued to him.'[59] The king replied that ''tis true I have not for a long time been pleased with Nairn [sic] for some particulars, but that won't hinder me from continuing his pension to him'.[60]

Despite this, the king continued to refuse either to let Nairne return to France or to let him invite his daughters to look after him. In March 1729 he appeared to change his mind, and wrote to Nairne himself: 'I have no difficulty in allowing you to go into France, where I shall continue to you what I now give you as long as I am able, not doubting that you will behave yourself there in such a manner as to deserve the

[56] NLS. MS 14266, the list of his children at the end of Nairne's journal.
[57] RA. SP 111/71, James III to Dunbar, 16 October 1727.
[58] RA. SP 111/131, James III to L. Innes, 25 October 1727.
[59] RA. SP 118/137, L. Innes to James III, 2 August 1728.
[60] RA. SP 119/60, James III to L. Innes, 19 August 1728.

continuance of my protection.'[61] But he must have changed his mind, because Nairne remained in Italy without his daughters for another four and a half years.

A new development, however, at last permitted Nairne to retire. In the summer of 1728 Sir John Graeme informed the king that he would like to resign as secretary of state and move to France. James agreed to let him go, and asked him to visit Bishop Atterbury in Paris, to invite him to come to Bologna as his replacement. Atterbury's reply was categorical. He sent a message that he would only join the king if Lord Dunbar, like Lord Inverness, were to be sent away for good, and if the king would invite the Duke of Ormonde and the Earl Marischal to leave Spain and rejoin the court.[62] As James had no intention of dismissing Dunbar, this episode convinced him that he would never be able to appoint another secretary of state.

As a result the king decided to reorganise the structure of his secretariat. James Edgar was promoted from his position as under-secretary and henceforth became known as the king's private secretary, with a new clerk to assist him. This was Mathurin Jacquin, who had worked as private secretary to Cardinal Gualterio until his death in April 1728, and was therefore already privy to Jacobite secrets. James III arranged with Gualterio's nephew that Jacquin should join the Stuart court in Bologna at the end of October.[63] The consequence was that Nairne was finally allowed to retire (though not to leave the Papal States).

The reorganisation of the secretariat was partly possible because the volume of the king's correspondence had declined. But the decision to do without a secretary of state was also made because James III now decided to get political advice from a wider spectrum of people. In the years to come he would have a series of informal ministers. As most of these were Italian or French, this development should also be regarded as an integral part of the process, started by the establishment of the queen's household, whereby the Stuart court in exile became increasingly foreign.

---

[61] RA. SP 125/177, James III to Nairne, 16 March 1729.

[62] NA. SP 85/16/f. 447, Stosch to Newcastle, 19 August 1728; RA. SP 121/12, L. Innes to James III, 4 October 1728. It should be added that doubts were raised concerning Graeme's loyalty (Haile, *James Francis Edward*, pp. 326–7), but as he was later employed as James III's minister and James also gave him an earldom it is clear that the king did not share them (see Chapter 17).

[63] BL. Add MSS 20661, f. 39, James III to abbate Gualterio, 24 September 1728. Biblioteca Universitario d'Urbino, Fondo del Comune, b. 212, fasc. I, contains the annual letters sending New Year's greetings from James III to the *gonfalonier* of Urbino from 1720 to 1764. The letters are all written and signed by Nairne until 1728 (pp. 65–83), after which they are written and signed by Jacquin.

The pensioners

During the early 1720s the number of Scottish pensioners attached to the court in Rome had gradually reduced. In 1726, when James III went to Bologna, there were only twelve left. The king told them they could do as they pleased. Five followed the court to Bologna; seven remained in Rome.

The five who went to Bologna were Alan Cameron and Captain William Hay (both subsequently appointed grooms of the Bedchamber), Dr Robert Wright (subsequently appointed the king's physician), Lord Nithsdale (subsequently appointed the queen's first gentleman) and Charles Fleming. The latter's elder brother, the 6th Earl of Wigton, had no sons, so Fleming was his heir.[64] At some point while the court was at Bologna, Fleming returned to Scotland,[65] where he eventually (in 1743) succeeded his brother as 7th Earl.

The seven pensioners who remained in Rome were James Hay (appointed the queen's surgeon),[66] Colonel William Clepham, Francis Kennedy, Lord Kilsyth, Lord Southesk, Robert Watson and Lord Winton.[67]

Southesk and Kennedy, as we have seen, had been particularly critical of the king and his favourites, and openly supportive of the queen. Lady Southesk, though a Protestant, had even joined Clementina in the Convent of Santa Cecilia in Trastevere and become one of her closest confidantes. At the beginning of 1727 the Southesks and Kennedy decided to obtain a pardon from the government of George I and return to Scotland.[68] They eventually left Rome on 20 May,[69] and the departure of Lady Southesk was no doubt a factor in persuading the queen to accept a reconciliation with the king. With one exception, the other pensioners remained in Rome until the court returned there in 1729.

---

[64] SCA. BL 2/264/2, T. Innes to Stuart, 11 January 1724.
[65] He was in Brussels at the beginning of 1729 (SCA. BL 2/321/3, L. Innes to T. Innes, 25 January 1729).
[66] He entered the service of the queen in October 1726, and went to Bologna in June 1727 (NA. SP 85/16/ff. 159, 262, Stosch to Newcastle, 12 October 1726 and 7 June 1727).
[67] RA. SP Box 3/81, pensions paid in Rome, [October] 1726. (The king had stopped giving a pension to Lord Southesk.) See also SCA. BL 2/294/14, Stuart to T. Innes, 13 November 1726.
[68] NA. SP 85/16/ff. 217, 237, 251, Stosch to Newcastle, 22 February, 29 March and 3 May 1727.
[69] NA. SP 85/16/ff. 257, 259, Stosch to Newcastle, 17 and 24 May 1727; Tayler, *Seven Sons of the Provost*, p. 125. By that time Lord Southesk had already obtained his pardon, but Kennedy's was not obtained until the beginning of June (*Seven Sons of the Provost*, p. 126, St Clair to Baron Kennedy, 6 June 1727).

The exception was Lord Kilsyth, by then seventy-eight years old. He joined the court at Bologna in April 1728.[70]

The reduction in the number of pensioners at Bologna (when James III returned from Avignon in January 1728 there were none left) meant that the king could no longer call upon a group of extra gentlemen to attend him when he needed them. During 1728 he therefore invited four more people to join the court: two Scots, one Englishman and one Irishman. The Scots were George Abernethy (a friend of Lord Kilsyth)[71] and Thomas Arthur, who had taken part in the rising in 1715.[72] The Englishman was William Goring, whose father, Sir Henry, had been one of the leaders of the Atterbury Plot.[73] The Irishman was Captain Henry Fitzmaurice, previously of Clare's Regiment, whom the king had recruited at Avignon and whose uncle was the Bishop of Waterford and Lismore.[74] These new pensioners provided the king with an additional group of gentlemen, whom he needed now that both the queen and Prince Charles had been given their own gentlemen in attendance.

The cost of the court

This expansion of the court inevitably involved considerable additional expense. In 1726–7, before he went to Avignon, the king had been providing salaries and pensions for approximately 87 people, including those servants and pensioners who had remained in Rome. By 1728, after his return, this number had risen to 130,[75] an increase of 50 per cent, and at a total annual cost of 16,750 *scudi*. Sir William Ellis estimated that the king and queen's other expenses, including the payment of some pensions in France, but 'without any extraordinary monie, journies, sending expresses, or the like', amounted to about 33,250

---

[70] NA. SP 85/16/f. 395, Stosch to Newcastle, 24 April 1728.

[71] Abernethy and Kilsyth shared the same apartment in Rome (ASVR. Santi Apostoli, vols. 63 and 64, both unpaginated).

[72] Daniel Szechi, *1715: The Great Jacobite Rebellion* (New Haven, 2006), pp. 102–4, 204.

[73] There are many references to Sir Henry Goring (created Viscount Goring in 1722) in Cruickshanks and Erskine-Hill, *Atterbury Plot*. See also Ushaw College, Tyrrell Papers OS 2/B.83, R. Creagh to Tyrrell, 17 January 1729.

[74] His uncle was Richard Pierce (RA. SP 133/57, Pierce to James III, 29 January 1730). For the relations between Pierce and the Stuart court, see Edward Corp, 'The Irish at the Jacobite Court of Saint-Germain-en-Laye', pp. 143–56, in Thomas O'Connor (ed.), *The Irish in Europe, 1580–1815* (Dublin, 2001), at pp. 155–6.

[75] These figures are mainly based on RA. SP 103/50; 105/92; 108/19; 111/79 and 113; 123/21 and 37; 128/34; 129/94; Box 3/78, 81 and 84; Box 4/2/10; Box 4/4/39 and 135.

scudi, making a total of 50,000 *scudi*.[76] As the king's papal pension was much smaller than that, and anyway had not been paid since the first quarter of 1727, it is surprising that James III was able to find the necessary money to maintain his court.

During 1725 James's papal pension had been 16,000 *scudi*, or 4000 *scudi* each quarter. This had been reduced to 3000 *scudi*, of which 500 had been given directly to the queen, and then to 2500 *scudi*, of which 1000 had been given directly to the queen. No money at all was received at the beginning of July, nor at the beginning of October.[77] The effect on the king's finances was disastrous. When he found himself obliged to establish the queen's new household at the beginning of July 1727, just before going to Lorraine and then Avignon, he was already accumulating serious debts.

The king was obliged to sell some of his plate. There is an undated note listing silver and silver gilt, described as 'Argenti di Francia', 'Argenti di Germani', 'di Carlino' and 'di Firenze', 'sold by Mr [Girolamo] Belloni in year 1726 or 1727'.[78] Another note, of June 1727, states that 'all useless plate, esp[ecial]ly' some bequeathed by Cardinal Dada in 1719, was also to be sold to help pay the king's debts.[79]

The situation was helped by the reaction of the French and Spanish courts when they heard that Queen Clementina had agreed to leave the convent and rejoin her husband at Bologna. The French sent 12,000 *scudi* in July 1727,[80] and the Spanish sent an unspecified amount shortly afterwards.[81] This money was needed to help pay the king's debts. As Dunbar wrote to Gualterio at the end of September:

[The Pope] has not only reduced the King's pension to 10,000 *scudi* but ... His Holiness has given ... four to the Queen, so that the King will receive four thousand less in the future than he had when the Queen was fed at her own expense in the convent, and His Majesty will have to pay for the Queen's

---

[76] RA. SP 111/114, Ellis to James III, received 23 October 1727, enclosing SP 111/115, 'Settld payments made by the King yearly'. Also RA. SP 110/136, accounts of Ellis, undated (1727).

[77] Chapter 1, p. 32.

[78] RA. SP 112/164. According to RA. SP 112/163 the plate yielded 3581 *livres*.

[79] RA. SP 112/160. The sale of plate should not be exaggerated, because Ellis was specifically told not to sell various objects which he had suggested. They included the 'Table Plate and Kitchin Plate', 'among the Spanish plate some pieces as large dishes, a large basin, judgd useless', and 'ye gold covers' (RA. SP 112/161). In October 1728 Ellis arranged for inventories to be made of all the plate at the court (RA. SP 112/3–7 and 113/1), and these inventories include most of the objects shown in the earlier inventories. See Appendix F.

[80] BL. Add MSS 31262, f. 178, Dunbar to Gualterio, 30 July 1727.

[81] BL. Add MSS 31262, f. 181, Dunbar to Gualterio, 8 August 1727.

household as well, which on the understanding that the King had before leaving will amount to around eleven thousand *scudi* a year.[82]

During the second half of October 1727, while James was in Avignon, Pope Benedict made it known that he would resume the payment of the pension in January 1728 to cover the fourth quarter of 1727.[83] As the Pope had now settled on the queen a separate income of 4000 *scudi* per annum, he also agreed that the entire pension (2500 *scudi* each quarter) should be paid to the king. Moreover, he instructed the *Camera Apostolica* to give him the six months' arrears, with an additional 1000 *scudi*, making 6000 *scudi* in all.[84]

It was the resumption of the papal, French and Spanish pensions which enabled the king to pay for his greatly expanded court. There is a paper written by Ellis at about this time which identifies the king's other sources of income. It refers to 38,203 *scudi* from the king's *luoghi di monte* in both Rome and Bologna 'for ye whole year 1727 and the 4 l[ast] months of year 1726', and a small amount of rent from some vineyards and other properties in the Papal States. More money came from France, including 1000 *livres* from the Salts of Brouage on the Ile de Ré, 31,360 *livres* from *rentes* on the Hôtel de Ville in Paris (including 8860 from those which formed part of Clementina's dowry), and the 'overplus' of 2581 *livres* on the Colonels' List at Saint-Germain, making an annual total of 34,941 *livres*, or a little under 7000 *scudi*.[85] It was barely enough to maintain the expanded court, so the king economised by abolishing communal dining.[86] As James put it in March 1728, 'the truth is, were all my pensions pay'd, they would barely suffice for my necessary expence'.[87] But we should be careful not to exaggerate. A few weeks earlier the king had given a gala ball with 'bellissimi divertimenti' to celebrate Prince Henry's birthday, and later on he organised gala balls at the court for the nobility of Bologna to celebrate St George's Day and Prince Charles's eighth birthday.[88]

---

[82] BL. Add MSS 31262, f. 203, Dunbar to Gualterio, 28 September 1727.

[83] BL. Add MSS 31262, f. 212, Dunbar to Gualterio, 25 October 1727.

[84] See Chapter 1, p. 33.

[85] RA. SP 112/163, rough notes by Ellis, showing James III's income from various sources in Italy and France, 1727. For the Colonels' List, see Corp, *Court in Exile*, pp. 123, 132, 339.

[86] RA. SP 102/87/70, Ellis to Read, 9 October 1727; RA. SP 111/80, James III to Ellis, 16 October 1727; RA. SP 112/28, James III to Ellis, 9 November 1727; RA. SP 112/86, Ellis to James III, 2 December 1727. Apart from the queen and the people she invited to eat with her, there was a table for Dunbar, Sheridan, Mayes and Lady Nithsdale. Ellis and Nairne were given board wages.

[87] RA. SP 115/13, James III to O'Brien, 22 March 1728, quoted in Gregg, 'The Financial Vicissitudes of James III', p. 68.

[88] Ghiselli, 13 March and 24 April 1728, 5 January 1729.

The court in 1728

During January and February 1728 it became clear that good relations between the king and the queen would never be properly restored. Clementina became increasingly withdrawn, as James wrote to Inverness:

I proposed to her diverting herself in the Carnival, but she showed no inclination to it. She has taken no manner of amusement, not even taking the air, and when she is not at church or at table, is locked up in her room and sees no mortal but her maids and sons. She ... fasts to that degree that I believe no married woman that pretends to have children ever did. I am very little with her. I let her do what she will.[89]

This, of course, meant that the queen's ladies (marchesa Legnani and contessa Ranuzzi) and her gentlemen (Nithsdale, Albergati and Formigliari) had virtually nothing to do, and that the establishment of her separate household no longer seemed necessary. In April the principessa di Piombino came from Rome to try to help, and remained at the court for two months,[90] but it seems that nothing changed.

The fact was that the queen was deeply depressed, and had lost the only women to whom she felt she could turn – though she continued to visit Dorothy Sheldon in her convent from time to time.[91] Lady Southesk had returned to Scotland, Lady Misset had rejoined her husband in Spain. Legnani and Ranuzzi, by contrast, were appointed by the king. Meanwhile Lord Dunbar remained at the court, and kept in contact with Lord and Lady Inverness. In October 1727 Inverness had written to Gualterio in confidence from Pistoia that 'My Ld Dunbar was on a hunting party 20 miles from Bologna where I went alone to meet him and the Marquis Fabio Albergati'.[92] At the end of March 1728 Dunbar went to spend a few weeks with Lord and Lady Inverness at Pisa, and he spent a few months with them during that autumn.[93] Inverness was not physically present at the court, but his influence was still felt, and even

---

[89] RA. SP 114/116, James III to Inverness, February 1728, quoted in McLynn, *Prince Charles Edward Stuart*, p. 26. See also Ghiselli, 14 January 1728.

[90] NA. SP 85/16/f. 380, Stosch to Newcastle, 27 March 1728; Ghiselli, 10, 14, 21, 24, 25 April, 22 May, 5 and 12 June 1728. She lived in the Palazzo Boncampagni, not in the Palazzo Fantuzzi.

[91] Ghiselli, 24 April, 29 May, 31 July 1728.

[92] BL. Add MSS 31264, f. 353, Inverness to Gualterio, 31 October 1727.

[93] SCA. BL 2/313/7, 17, 20, Mayes to Stuart, 31 March, 3 November and 15 December 1728; Ghiselli, 24 April 1728. According to Stosch, Forster also went to meet Inverness (at Livorno) in the autumn of 1728 (NA. SP 85/16/f. 463, to Newcastle, 14 October 1728).

Albergati, one of the queen's own gentlemen, had been prepared to see him secretly with Dunbar.

This was all the more regrettable because the reorganised court at Bologna might have been a very much happier place, now that the king and queen had at last been reunited. The queen's married male servants from Rome had brought with them their wives and children, and the two royal princes, now seven and three years old, were growing up to the admiration of Bolognese society as a whole. The court had also been joined by the young daughter of Lord and Lady Nithsdale.

The Nithsdales had two children, whom they had not seen since 1716. Their son, Lord Maxwell, had been born in 1700, and their daughter, Lady Anne Maxwell, in 1710. In 1726 Lord Maxwell visited Italy on his Grand Tour, and brought with him his sixteen-year-old sister to live with her parents. They arrived in November 1726,[94] spent the winter and spring in Bologna, then visited Rome in May and June 1727,[95] after which Lord Maxwell returned home, leaving his sister at Bologna. By then Lady Anne was seventeen years old, an ideal age to serve Queen Clementina as her maid of honour. It was the first time the court had contained a noble family other than the Stuarts themselves since it had left Saint-Germain.[96]

During May James III again rented the Villa Alamandini, so that Clementina could spend the summer months there *en villeggiatura*.[97] He himself visited Venice, and then took Prince Charles to Parma, Colorno and Piacenza to see the Dowager Duchess of Parma.[98] Shortly after his return it is said that the queen had a miscarriage, followed by a false pregnancy during the autumn.[99] By 1729 it was apparent that the exiled court was unlikely to witness the birth of another Stuart prince or princess.

On a more positive note, James III's relations with the papacy continued to improve. Cardinal Ruffo had been replaced as Papal Legate by Cardinal Giorgio Spinola, who became a good friend and would often

---

[94] SCA. BL 2/289/3/2, Mayes to Stuart, 16 November 1726.

[95] NA. SP 85/16/ff. 255, 271, Stosch to Newcastle, 10 May and 21 June 1727.

[96] According to Ghiselli (13 March 1728) on one occasion Lord and Lady Nithsdale and their daughter gave 'una sontuosa cena' with 'sontuose sinfonie' in the Palazzo Ranuzzi-Cospi for marchesa Legnani, contessa Ranuzzi and Lord Dunbar.

[97] SCA. BL 2/313/11, Mayes to Stuart, 30 June 1728; Ghiselli, 1 and 29 May, 31 July 1728.

[98] McLynn, *Prince Charles Edward Stuart*, p. 27. During June the king also had two meetings with Lord Inverness, the first at Castel Franco and the second at the Villa Alamandini (Ghiselli, 12 and 26 June 1728).

[99] McLynn, *Prince Charles Edward Stuart*, p. 27; Ascari, 'James III at Bologna', pp. 30–1; Ghiselli, 14 and 25 April 1728.

socialise with James in Rome during the 1730s.[100] More important was the arrival of Cardinal Prospero Lambertini to be the new Archbishop of Bologna in October 1728.[101] The warm relations which James established with Lambertini were to be particularly beneficial when the cardinal was elected Pope, as Benedict XIV, in 1740.

Another development during the autumn of 1728 indicated that the king's relations with Pope Benedict XIII were now much better. James III had a high opinion of the chevalier Geraldin, the equerry and riding master of Prince Charles, and in 1727 had obtained for him a Commandership with the Grand Cross from the Grand Master of the Order of Malta.[102] In the summer of 1728 the position of Grand Prior of England became vacant, and the king persuaded the Grand Master to give the vacancy to Geraldin. The position had once been held by James III's illegitimate half-brother, the Duke of Albemarle (younger brother of the Duke of Berwick), and carried considerable prestige, but it necessitated going to Malta for the ceremony of installation. In September 1728 Geraldin went to Rome and obtained a special dispensation from Pope Benedict XIII, enabling him to take his vows as the new Grand Prior without having to travel to Malta and thus absent himself for an extended period from the court.[103]

The return to Rome

By the end of 1728 James III had decided that there was no longer any point in his remaining in Bologna. The queen had rejoined the court, his papal pension was being regularly paid, and his relations with the Pope seemed much better. He decided that the time had come to return to Rome. If he continued to stay at Bologna he knew that he might lose the Palazzo del Re, which had been left unoccupied for over two years. He also risked being away from the papal city at the time of the elderly Pope's death. He needed to be in Rome before the next conclave.

The king's plan was that the court should return to Rome in three stages. He would himself make the journey in February and ensure that

---

[100] BL. Add MSS 31262, f. 188, Dunbar to Gualterio, 27 August 1727; Ghiselli, 29 December 1727, 3 March 1728. See Chapter 12, p. 267.

[101] ASB. Senato Diari vol. 12, 3 October 1728.

[102] BL. Add MSS 31264, f. 320, Inverness to Gualterio, 26 March 1727. The Grand Master was Antonio Manoel de Vilhena. The king conducted the ceremony of investiture the following year in the presence of Ferreti, the Grand Prior of England, 'ed altri cavaglieri di tal' ordine' (Ghiselli, 22 May 1728).

[103] NA. SP 85/16/ff. 455, 459, Stosch to Newcastle, 16 and 30 September 1728; Ghiselli, 3 October 1728.

the Palazzo del Re was properly prepared and furnished for his wife and children. The two princes would then follow in April,[104] followed by the queen in May or June. The plan was subsequently modified because Prince Henry fell ill,[105] so he returned with his mother rather than with his brother.

The king arrived in Rome on 6 February and went to stay for two nights with the principessa di Piombino at the Villa Ludovisi while his apartment in the Palazzo del Re was prepared.[106] He brought with him most, though not all, of his own servants, and was also accompanied by Lord Dunbar and John Stewart.[107] This reflected James's recent decision to have ministers rather than a secretary of state.

The palazzo was furnished during March,[108] and the horses and heavy baggage arrived in April.[109] Meanwhile Queen Clementina had made arrangements for her aunt, the Dowager Duchess of Parma, to visit her in Bologna.[110] Sir Thomas Sheridan, who was responsible for bringing Prince Charles to Rome, wrote to the king on 16 April that he had delayed their departure by a few days because the queen wanted the duchess to 'see the Prince before he sets out'.[111] Prince Charles then left Bologna on 22 April,[112] accompanied by all his servants (except Dunbar and Stewart), and also by Alan Cameron, Thomas Arthur, Captain Henry Fitzmaurice and William Goring.[113] The party arrived at the Palazzo del Re at the end of the month.[114]

The rest of the court left Bologna in May 1729. The eight *anziani* formally visited the Palazzo Fantuzzi to say farewell to the queen on the 9th. The description of their embassy refers to their reception at the

---

[104] RA. SP Box 1/79, Regulations for the removal of the court from Bologna to Rome, by Arnoux, corrected by Ellis, April 1728.

[105] Ghiselli, 6 April 1729; *SPW*, p. 83, Lady Nithsdale to James III, 21 April 1729.

[106] Ghiselli, 5 February 1729; NA. SP 85/16/f. 500, Stosch to Newcastle, 10 February 1729.

[107] NA. SP 85/16/f. 502, Stosch to Newcastle, 17 February 1729.

[108] NA. SP 85/16/ff. 516, 519, Stosch to Newcastle, 24 and 31 March 1729.

[109] NA. SP 85/16/f. 526, Stosch to Newcastle, 21 April 1729.

[110] ASB. Senato Diari vol. 12, 21 April 1729. The duchess stayed in the Palazzo Zambeccari, not with the queen in the Palazzo Fantuzzi. See RA. SP Box 4/2/17, 18, 'Liste de ce qu'on aura besoin pr service de la Reyne, et l'arrivée de la Duchesse de Parme', April 1729; Ghiselli, 27 April 1729. The duchess gave Queen Clementina a present of 12,000 *scudi* (Ghiselli, 11 May 1729).

[111] *SPW*, p. 82, Sheridan to James III, 16 April 1729.

[112] The formal embassy to say farewell took place on 19 April 1729 (ASB. Senato Diari vol. 12).

[113] RA. SP Box 1/79, Regulations for the removal of the court from Bologna to Rome, April 1729.

[114] *SPW*, p. 84, Sheridan to Queen Clementina, 23 April 1729, and Queen Clementina to Prince Charles, 9 May 1729; NA. SP 85/16/f. 523, Stosch to Newcastle, 5 May 1729.

foot of the staircase by Albergati and Formigliari, and at the top by Nithsdale, who then conducted them to the queen's antechamber, where they waited until Clementina came out of her bedchamber to greet them.[115] The queen and the little duke left Bologna nine days later on 18 May, having been delayed by bad weather.[116] They were accompanied by all their own servants, and by the remaining servants of the king,[117] and reached the Palazzo del Re in Rome on 5 June. There they were greeted by the king, who immediately took the queen to the Palazzo Apostolico at Albano, where they were visited by Pope Benedict XIII.[118] They were both back in Rome by 13 June,[119] and finally reestablished in the Palazzo del Re for the first time since November 1725. Stosch, who was now again able to watch the court at close quarters, wrote to London that 'I have noticed that the household . . . is now more numerous than it was before they left Rome'.[120]

All that remained was to reallocate the accommodation within the palazzo to take account of the changes at the court. The queen had her own separate household, so the state apartment on the second floor was now described as the apartment of the queen rather than the joint apartment of the king and the queen.[121] It was there that Clementina continued to lead her life of relative seclusion, attended by Lucrezia Legnani, her chambermaids and her valets, with Nithsdale, Albergati and Formigliari available when necessary. Stosch was informed, with some exaggeration, that 'she now dislikes the English so much that it is only the Gentlemen and people from Bologna who approach her and to whom she entrusts her errands'.[122]

On the first floor the king decided that the apartment with the *loggetta*, previously occupied by Lord and Lady Inverness, should now be left

---

[115] ASB. Senato Diari vol. 12, 9 May 1729; Ascari, 'James III in Bologna', pp. 31–2. They returned the following day to take a formal farewell of Prince Henry (same references). See also Ghiselli, 11 May 1729. After the departure of the court the bridge connecting the Palazzo Fantuzzi and the Palazzo Ranuzzi-Cospi was destroyed (Ghiselli, 6 April 1729).

[116] *SPW*, p. 85, James III to Queen Clementina, 11 May 1729. According to Ghiselli (15 May 1729) the queen also visited Dorothy Sheldon in the Convent of San Pietro Martire to say a final farewell.

[117] RA. SP Box 3/1/78 and 84.

[118] NA. SP 85/16/f. 544, Stosch to Newcastle, 9 June 1729; *SPW*, p. 86, James III to Queen Clementina, 10 June 1729.

[119] *SPW*, p. 87, James III to Queen Clementina, 12 June 1729.

[120] NA. SP 85/16/f. 544, Stosch to Newcastle, 9 June 1729.

[121] ASV. PAC 983, no. 135/14, payments made by the *Camera Apostolica* for James III, 4 February 1729.

[122] NA. SP 85/16/f. 550, Stosch to Newcastle, 30 June 1729.

vacant.[123] It was used to provide accommodation for important visitors, but otherwise served as a constant reminder that James hoped his favourite might return. Various changes, however, had to be made because Prince Henry was about to be taken out of the hands of women and entrusted to his new under-governors, Hugh Dicconson and John Paul Stafford. The little boy was 'breeched' in June,[124] and then formally handed over to men at the age of four and a half in September 1729.[125] He was moved out of the nursery and given the apartment on the second floor of the north-east *palazzetta* which had previously been occupied by Lord Dunbar. The latter moved down to the apartment on the first floor of the north wing previously occupied by Thomas Forster. Forster moved into the apartment in the south-east *palazzetta* previously occupied by Sir David Nairne, who presumably found new accommodation somewhere outside the palazzo. Finally, Dicconson and Stafford, the new under-governors, were given accommodation in unspecified quarters, presumably on the second floor near the apartment of Prince Henry.[126]

[123] RA. SP 131/7, James III to Inverness, 1 October 1729.
[124] *SPW*, p. 87, James III to Queen Clementina, 12 June 1729.
[125] RA. SP 130/83, James III to L. Innes, 23 August 1729.
[126] ASV. PAC 983, no. 135/14, 4 February 1729; RA. SP 131/7, James III to Inverness, 1 October 1729; RA. SP 131/29, Edgar to Ellis, 5 October 1729.

Part III

Rome, 1729–1766

11 The Stuarts and the papacy: II

The relations between James III and the papacy were more cordial after 1730 than they had been during the previous decade. In part this was because of the personalities of the popes themselves, who strongly disapproved of the way Pope Benedict XIII had supported Queen Clementina against her husband.[1] In part it was because of changed political circumstances. The Spanish conquest of Naples in 1735 meant that Imperial troops were no longer a short marching distance from the Papal States. Also the Habsburg–Lorraine marriage of 1736 meant that James III's friend Duke Francis of Lorraine was now the husband of Charles VI's daughter and heiress, Maria Theresa. The papacy was therefore very much less afraid of offending the government in London by demonstrating its overt support for the Jacobite cause.

This was also the period when the two Stuart princes began to grow up and enter Roman society. Their popularity and the hopes they encouraged of an eventual restoration undoubtedly made the successive popes more generous in their treatment of the exiled royal family. Finally, the renewal of war between Great Britain and Spain in 1739, and between Great Britain and France in 1743 (and again in 1756), meant that the prospects of a restoration were for a time enormously improved. Indeed the two decades of the 1730s and 1740s were the heyday of the Stuart court in Rome, when the Palazzo del Re was at its most splendid and when the Stuarts themselves made their greatest impact on Roman society.

At the same time the popularity of the Grand Tour, bringing more and more British and Irish nobles and gentlemen to Rome, kept the Stuarts in regular contact with a generation of supporters born since James had left Saint-Germain. It also provided evidence for the papal court of the respect and support which the Stuarts still commanded within the British Isles.

---

[1] In the opinion of Pope Benedict XIV, 'Benoît XIII ... n'avait pas la première idée du gouvernement' (*Benoît XIV*, II, p. 282, to Tencin, 1 August 1753).

Clement XII, 1730–1740

In July 1730, after a conclave lasting more than four months, Cardinal Lorenzo Corsini was elected Pope Clement XII. In the following month his nephew, marchese Neri Corsini, who had previously served as the Tuscan envoy to London and Versailles,[2] was created a cardinal. Almost immediately the new pope and the new cardinal showed themselves to be active supporters of James III.

There were two questions waiting to be answered. Would Clement XII side with Queen Clementina in her determination that Lord and Lady Inverness should remain away from the court? And would he restore the 6000 *scudi* which his predecessor had deducted from James's annual pension? Both questions were answered before the end of the year.

In September 1730 the Pope sent Cardinal Corsini to speak to the queen and inform her that it was proper that James III should be master in his own family, and that she should drop her objections to the return of Lord and Lady Inverness. Clementina protested against this change of papal policy, and asked to see the Pope himself, but during an audience a few weeks later was plainly told that it was her duty to submit to her husband. After two months of silence she gave way, and told the king that she would not oppose the return of his favourites.[3]

As it turned out, Clementina was spared the unwelcome presence of Lord and Lady Inverness in the Palazzo del Re. Inverness himself travelled from Pisa to Rome in January 1731, but the weather was so bad that he left his wife behind, with instructions to follow him when conditions improved. Before that could happen, however, Inverness was told frankly by various English Jacobites that (as he put it himself) 'my remaining in Rome would be prejudicial to the King's interests, that I am even believed to be capable of betraying him'. Fortunately for the harmony of the court he accepted this advice and obtained James's agreement that he should return to Pisa, and make arrangements to live with his wife permanently at Avignon.[4] It was the ideal solution: the Pope now supported the king, and yet Inverness was to remain away from the court.

By the end of the year, Clement XII had also restored the king's pension. On 29 July he renewed the previous annual payment of

---

[2] NA. SP 98/32/f. 82, Stosch to Newcastle, 13 July 1730.

[3] Haile, *James Francis Edward*, pp. 336–8.

[4] *Ibid.*, p. 340; NA. SP 988/32/ff. 140, 142, Stosch to Newcastle, 4 and 11 January, 1 February 1731; Valesio, *Diario di Roma*, v, p. 327, 27 January 1731.

10,000 *scudi*,[5] and also gave James a present of a further 10,000 *scudi* to celebrate his election.[6] He told the king that he intended to resume payment of the extra 6000 *scudi* each year, but that the details still needed to be arranged.[7] Because the *Camera Apostolica* could not easily afford the additional payment, the Pope decided in December to provide it out of the income he himself received from the *Datario*.[8] Throughout the pontificat of Clement XII the restored annual pension of 16,000 *scudi* was then regularly paid to James III in quarterly instalments, thereby guaranteeing the financial stability of the exiled court.[9]

The court was in fact more than just financially stable during the 1730s, because Clement XII supplemented James III's regular pension with frequent gifts. Stosch recorded in May 1735 that 'the continual additional gifts of money ... that the Pope gives him from time to time ... are far larger than the ordinary pension'.[10] In October 1739 he was more specific, and reported to London that the additional money given to James by the Pope amounted to more than three times the regular pension of 16,000 *scudi*.[11] That seems to have been an exaggeration, but Stosch's letters do provide us with some details to support his claim.

For example, each time James III went to Albano for his *villeggiatura* he informed the Pope in advance of his intended absence from Rome. According to Stosch, the Pope then gave him a present which was much larger than what was needed to cover the cost of his journey: 10,000 *scudi* in autumn 1732, 3000 *scudi* in both spring and autumn 1733, 12,000 *scudi* in autumn 1734, and 6000 *scudi* in spring 1735.[12] In a letter of 1739 Stosch recorded that James III was normally given 3000 *scudi* for each *villeggiatura*,[13] so the larger amounts must have been exceptional. But as the king generally went to Albano at least twice each

---

[5] ASV. SS: Ingh 21, p. 248; ASR. Cam I: GT b. 550/f. 11.

[6] ASV. SS: Ingh 21, p. 255; ASR. Cam I: RMC b. 1077. The 10,000 *scudi* were brought to the Palazzo del Re by Cardinal Corsini himself (Valesio, *Diario di Roma*, v, p. 257, 4 August 1730).

[7] RA. SP 139/79, James III to O'Bryen, 20 September 1730.

[8] RA. SP 141/5, James III to O'Rourke, 16 December 1730; *Benoît XIV*, II, p. 60, Benedict XIV to Tencin, 23 September 1750.

[9] The payments from the *Camera Apostolica* are all recorded in ASR. Cam I: RMC b. 1077 to b. 1082. Those for 1730–1 and 1737 are also recorded in ASR. Cam I: GT b. 550/f. 11, b. 562/f. 8 and b. 628/f. 4. For the continued payments from the *Datario*, see NA. SP 98/37/f. 271, Stosch to Newcastle, 17 September 1735.

[10] NA. SP 98/38/f. 176, Stosch to Newcastle, 28 May 1735.

[11] NA. SP 98/41/f. 350, Stosch to Newcastle, 11 October 1739.

[12] NA. SP 98/32/ff. 442, 526, 577, Stosch to Newcastle, 27 September 1732, 16 May and 3 October 1733; NA. SP 98/37/ff. 162, 232, to Newcastle, 18 September 1734 and 4 June 1735.

[13] NA. SP 98/41/f. 346, Stosch to Newcastle, 27 September 1739.

year, we can regard these payments as providing an additional annual income of at least 6000 *scudi*, bringing the total to 22,000 *scudi*.

There are other payments mentioned by Stosch in his letters during the 1730s, some of unknown value,[14] others amounting to 34,000 *scudi* in total.[15] These, however, were only the payments given to the king himself. Stosch refers to a further 28,700 *scudi* given to Prince Charles[16] and another 13,600 *scudi* given to Prince Henry.[17] Other presents for the princes included 'relics covered with jewels'[18] and a magnificent gondola with eight oars 'covered in red damask with gold trimmings . . . for them to enjoy using on the lake at Albano'.[19]

In addition to the pension and all these extra payments, the *Camera Apostolica* continued to rent, maintain and furnish the Palazzo del Re. The rent remained at 1632 *scudi* per annum, but the annual amount spent on other things during the 1730s averaged an additional 1282 *scudi*.[20] During 1733 and 1734 the royal apartments were completely redecorated and refurnished, prompting Stosch to write in 1735: 'Pope Clement XII, more splendid than his predecessors, has just given an order to the *Camera Apostolica* to pay for him in advance everything he asks for, and anything else that he needs to maintain his household and family without having given him a fixed total sum of expenditure.'[21] Stosch was probably also thinking of the Palazzo Apostolico at Albano, where important improvements were carried out between 1735 and 1738.[22]

In addition to providing James III with a greatly increased income and maintaining both the Palazzo del Re and the Palazzo Apostolico at Albano, Clement XII gave him a permanent papal guard, something he had not had since the court left Urbino in 1718.

---

[14] NA. SP 98/32/ff. 475, 514, Stosch to Newcastle, 10 January and 4 April 1733; NA. SP 98/37/f. 404, to Newcastle, 22 September 1736.

[15] NA. SP 98/37/ff. 22, 27, 79, 198, 202, 307, Stosch to Newcastle, 16 and 23 January 1734, 24 April 1734, 22 January and 5 February 1735, 7 January 1736; NA. SP 98/41/f. 4, to Newcastle 12 January 1737.

[16] NA. SP 98/32/ff. 343, 361, 389, 475, 514, Stosch to Newcastle, 23 February, 12 April and 24 May 1732, 10 January and 4 April 1733; NA. SP 98/37/ff. 35, 135, 147, to Newcastle, 6 February, 24 July and 14 August 1734.

[17] NA. SP 98/32/ff. 475, 479, 514, 554, Stosch to Newcastle, 10 and 24 January, 4 April and 25 July 1733; NA. SP 98/37/f. 135, to Newcastle, 24 July 1734.

[18] NA. SP 98/32/f. 104, Stosch to Newcastle, 21 September 1730.

[19] NA. SP 98/32/ff. 267, 289, Stosch to Newcastle, 29 September and 27 October 1731.

[20] The details are all in ASR. Cam I: CDG b. 2017bis/13/14, 16 and 18; and ASV. PAC 984 and 985.

[21] NA. SP 98/37/f. 271, Stosch to Newcastle, 17 September 1735.

[22] In 1730–1 the *Camera Apostolica* spent 1220 *scudi* in renovating and cleaning the palazzo at Albano (ASR. Cam I: GT b. 553/f. 198, b. 561/f. 16, b. 567/f. 15). Another 573 *scudi* were spent in 1735–8 (ASR. Cam I: GT b. 610/f. 4, b. 615/f. 6, b. 638/f. 14).

In December 1731 Clement XII offered to provide James III with a company of soldiers to protect the Palazzo del Re, and even said that the king could nominate to join it any unemployed Jacobites whom he wished. James declined the offer,[23] but two years later an incident took place which made him change his mind.

On Christmas Eve, 1733, James was warned that there might be an attempt to kidnap the two princes during the coming night. He therefore sent Lord Dunbar to speak to Cardinal Corsini in the Quirinale and ask for a detachment of soldiers. Corsini responded by sending four Swiss Guards to protect the royal apartments within the Palazzo del Re, and twenty soldiers to clear the streets surrounding the palazzo and stop any unauthorised people entering either the Piazza dei Santi Apostoli or the Piazza della Pilotta. On Christmas Day Corsini informed marchese Girolamo Muti that part of the ground floor of his palazzo, opposite the east wing of the Palazzo del Re, would be commandeered and converted into a barracks for the detachment of soldiers, who would thenceforth permanently guard the Stuart court.[24] The Pope then gave orders that eight cuirassiers and a junior officer should be ready at all times to accompany the king and the princes, if required, whenever they left the Palazzo del Re.[25]

This arrangement was continued for the rest of the king's life, and when Charles de Brosses visited James III at the Palazzo del Re in 1739 he observed that 'the Pope's troops mount the guard there, as they do at Monte Cavallo [i.e. the Quirinale] and accompany him when he goes out'.[26] Within Rome itself – going for a walk or making a social visit or going to the opera – the eight cuirassiers and their officer were considered sufficient.[27] Travelling to and from Albano was felt to require a greater level of security. In May 1734 James III and his sons were attended on their *villeggiatura* by forty-five infantry

---

[23] NA. SP 98/32/f. 313, Stosch to Newcastle, 22 December 1731.

[24] Marchese Muti's family no doubt resented this intrusion. On 13 August 1734 Valesio noted in his diary that one of Muti's sons had fired an arquebus from an upper window at one of the soldiers guarding the east entrance to the Palazzo del Re (*Diario di Roma*, v, p. 717).

[25] Valesio, *Diario di Roma*, v, p. 654, 25 and 26 December 1733; NA. SP 98/37/ff. 16, 39, Stosch to Newcastle, 2 January and 20 February 1734; SCA. BL 3/7/8, Stuart to Carnegy, 31 December 1733: The Pope 'of late has hon.d [the king] with a guard as he had at Urbino as proper under pr[e]s[en]t circumstances'. The idea of employing Jacobites in the detachment of guards seems to have been dropped.

[26] Brosses, *Lettres d'Italie*, vol. II, pp. 76–7.

[27] NA. SP 98/37/ff. 27, 35, 43, Stosch to Newcastle, 23 January, 6 February and 6 March 1734.

soldiers and twelve cuirassiers.[28] The following year the Pope asked the king how many soldiers he would like. James said he needed sixty infantrymen, but that he could do without the cuirassiers,[29] so Clement XII arranged that he should be accompanied by the sixty foot soldiers during every future *villeggiatura*.[30] The presence of the papal guards was a visible daily reminder both of James's royal status and of the more active support he now enjoyed from the papal court.

Pope Clement XII's generosity towards James III requires some explanation, because it went far beyond the support provided by his three predecessors. It was certainly made possible by the very good relations which James established with the members of the Pope's family, which was related to that of Cardinal Salviati.[31] After his election Clement's nephews and nieces left their native Florence and established themselves in the Piazza Navona, to which Cardinal Corsini regularly invited the king and the two princes,[32] and where the Pope's nieces organised a series of balls in honour of Prince Charles.[33]

The most significant factor, however, seems to have been the influence of Sir Thomas Dereham, an English Jacobite who had lived in Florence since childhood, and who had been an intimate friend of the Pope and his nephew for many years.[34] As early as 1731 Stosch noted that Dereham was the principal confidant and counsellor of Cardinal Corsini[35] and that he was a great favourite of the Pope, attending his *lever* every morning.[36] As the years went by Dereham's influence at the papal court seems to have increased. In March 1733 Stosch commented that 'Sir Thomas Dereham is playing the part of Pope's favourite, and is extremely influential with Cardinal Corsini';[37] and in February 1737, when Corsini was nominated by James III to be the Cardinal Protector of Ireland, Stosch wrote that the cardinal was 'solely directed by

---

[28] Valesio, *Diario di Roma*, v, p. 695, 19 May 1734; NA. SP 98/37/f. 105, Stosch to Newcastle, 29 May 1734.

[29] NA. SP 98/37/ff. 265, 275, Stosch to Newcastle, 27 August and 1 October 1735.

[30] NA. SP 98/37/f. 408, Stosch to Newcastle, 6 October 1736; NA. SP 98/41/ff. 57, 177, to Newcastle, 17 June 1737, 2 June 1738; NA. SP 98/43/f. 50, to Newcastle, 11 June 1740.

[31] NA. SP 98/32/f. 188, Stosch to Newcastle, 3 August 1730.

[32] NA. SP 98/32/ff. 217, 241, Stosch to Newcastle, 26 June and 18 August 1731; Valesio, *Diario di Roma*, v, p. 620, 2 August 1733.

[33] NA. SP 98/32/ff. 303, 321, Stosch to Newcastle, 23 November 1731, 12 January 1732; Valesio, *Diario di Roma*, v, p. 566, 10 February 1733.

[34] For Dereham's biography, see Ingamells, *Dictionary*, pp. 292–3.

[35] NA. SP 98/32/f. 201, Stosch to Newcastle, 26 May 1731.

[36] NA. SP 98/32/ff. 257, 303, Stosch to Newcastle, 8 September and 23 November 1731.

[37] NA. SP 98/32/f. 494, Stosch to Newcastle, 7 March 1733.

Dereham's advice'.[38] The latter's influence was probably the key factor in obtaining so much support from the papacy during the 1730s. Dereham himself died in February 1739,[39] and was buried in the chapel of the English College in Rome,[40] but by then his work as a committed Jacobite had been accomplished. When Clement XII died the following year, Stosch commented that 'after he was elected to the Papacy ... and following the advice given him by his nephew, himself influenced by Sir Thomas Dereham, he did all he could for [James III]'.[41]

The king, however, had to make provision for the future, in the event of an eventual failure to achieve a restoration to his British thrones. He assumed that when he died his elder son, Prince Charles, would inherit his papal pension and the use of the Palazzo del Re. But he was worried about his younger son, Prince Henry, who would need both money and status. Specific documentary evidence is lacking, but it can be supposed that he broached the subject with Clement XII in 1732, when Henry was seven years old, and obtained the Pope's agreement that the prince might eventually become a cardinal.[42]

The agreement involved two things. The Pope would acknowledge formally that James III had the right as King of England to nominate cardinals, which meant that he might one day nominate his own son. And the Pope would issue a brief allowing Prince Henry (but not Prince Charles) to hold ecclesiastical benefices, offices and pensions, which meant that the prince might eventually become financially independent.

In January 1733 Clement XII agreed that Domenico Riviera, with whom James had become acquainted at Urbino, should be created a cardinal on the specific nomination of the king.[43] At exactly the same time Clement issued a brief in favour of Prince Henry,[44] indicating that the two questions were linked. In response to a letter from the king dated

---

[38] NA. SP 98/41/f. 12, Stosch to Newcastle, 9 February 1737.
[39] NA. SP 98/41/f. 265, Stosch to Newcastle, 16 February 1739.
[40] The monument was designed by Ferdinando Fuga, with sculpture by Filippo della Valle, and can still be seen in the chapel of the English College.
[41] NA. SP 98/43/f. 14, Stosch to Newcastle, 14 February 1740.
[42] There was a possible alternative, that Prince Henry might be elected King of Poland, but he was too young when the throne became vacant in 1733. See Corp, 'The Nomination of Cardinals by James III in Rome', pp. 159–60.
[43] NA. SP 98/32/ff. 477, 479, Stosch to Newcastle, 17 and 24 January 1733. The announcement was made in January, and the ceremony took place at the beginning of March (NA. SP 98/32/f. 508, to Newcastle, 14 March 1733).
[44] RA. SP 286/123, 'Ristretto di tutti li Brevi delli Papi Clemente 12° et Benedetto 14° a favore della Casa Reale per godere Benefiti Ecclesiastici et in specie una pensione di doppie 4^m sopra li Benefiti Ecclesiastici delle Spagne'; NA. SP 98/32/ff. 477, 479, Stosch to Newcastle, 17 and 24 January 1733. There were actually two briefs, both dated 5 January 1733. Prince Henry's copies are BAV. Vat Lat 15127.

7 January 1733, Lewis Innes wrote from Paris to express his satisfaction at 'the two marks . . . of the Pope's great goodness':

The Indult [i.e. brief] is as ample and of as great extent as it was possible to draw it . . . I beleeve ther will scarce be found an example of so comprehensive a Grant . . .

As to the other mark of the Pope's kindness . . . altho it be undoubtedly your Majesties Right, yet it is of importance to keep possession of it, and that it be obtaind by your Majesties own credit . . . I pray God to reward and preserve His Holyness [for his] . . . kindness.[45]

A few months later, at the request of James III, Prince Henry was confirmed by the Pope himself in the latter's private chapel within the Quirinale.[46]

Encouraged by Clement XII's support, James decided at the beginning of 1734 to revive the project to have his father beatified, the first step towards canonisation. The numerous miraculous cures attributed to the intercession of James II in 1701–3 had been witnessed and authenticated at the time,[47] but the project had been allowed to lapse, and by 1734 most of the people who had known James II at Saint-Germain had died. The king asked the Archbishop of Paris (Charles Gaspard de Vintimille)[48] to appoint a commission to interview the surviving witnesses, obtain written testimony and provide a new list of the miracles attributed to his father. The commission completed its work by the end of the year, and the Process was sent to Rome in January 1735.[49] Its arrival, however, coincided with the death of Queen Clementina.

Since December 1730, when she had agreed to the return of Lord and Lady Inverness, the queen had embarked on a rigid programme of religious devotions, giving charity to the poor and serving them in the hospitals. By the end of 1734 she had ruined her health by self-denial amounting to virtual starvation, but she had come to be regarded by the people of Rome as a saint: in the words of Valesio she lived an 'extremely

---

[45] RA. SP 159/6, Innes to James III, 26 January 1733.

[46] Valesio, *Diario di Roma*, v, p. 614, 12 July 1733; NA. SP 98/32/ff. 552, 554, Stosch to Newcastle, 18 and 25 July 1733.

[47] Bernard and Monique Cottret, 'La sainteté de Jacques II, ou les miracles d'un roi défunt', in Edward Corp (ed.), *L'autre exil: les Jacobites en France au début du xviiiᵉ siècle* (Montpellier, 1993), pp. 92–7.

[48] He had previously been Archbishop of Aix-en-Provence from 1708 to 1729, and had probably met James when the latter was at Avignon in 1716–17 and 1727.

[49] Geoffrey Scott, '"Sacredness of Majesty": The English Benedictines and the Cult of King James II', *Royal Stuart Papers*, XXIII (Huntingdon, 1984), pp. 9–10; Haile, *James Francis Edward*, p.353.

holy and exemplary life'.[50] Early in January 1735, when the Process for the beatification of James II was sent from Paris, it was obvious that she was dying. Special prayers were said for her in all the churches of Rome, but by the 11th her doctors had given up hope for her recovery. She died on the evening of Tuesday 18 January in her apartment on the second floor of the Palazzo del Re.[51]

On the following day her body was embalmed and dressed in the habit of a Dominican nun, and then taken in a procession of great splendour from the palazzo, via the Corso, to the Church of Santi Apostoli, where it was exposed in a private chapel under the protection of the Swiss Guards.[52]

Pope Clement XII now ordered that Queen Clementina should be given a state funeral with full royal honours, to be paid for by the *Camera Apostolica*.[53] It took place on Sunday 23 January, attended by thirty-two cardinals. Dressed in her robes as a queen, Clementina was placed in the nave of Santi Apostoli on a huge bier beneath a canopy surmounted by an enormous crown, designed by the Florentine architect Ferdinando Fuga. At the end of the service Clementina's body was carried through the streets of Rome on a bed of state, in a magnificent procession from Santi Apostoli to St Peter's Basilica at the Vatican. There, her royal robes were laid aside to reveal the nun's habit beneath, and she was buried within a coffin in the crypt.[54] The artist Giovanni Paolo Panini was ordered to attend the funeral and observe the procession, and produce large drawings which could be engraved to preserve the memory of these events.[55]

Shortly after the funeral Pope Clement XII decided that a monument to the queen should be erected within the Church of Santi Apostoli, with

[50] Valesio, *Diario di Roma*, v, p. 751, 11 January 1735. There is an illuminated vellum manuscript of a patent admitting Queen Clementina into the Roman Archconfraternity of the Most Holy Name of Mary, *c*.1731, in the National Library of Scotland. The armorial binding is reproduced in *The Double Tressure*, the Journal of the Heraldry Society of Scotland, no. 17 (1995), p. 29. See also SCA. BL 3/13/11, Stuart to G. Innes, 16 December 1734: 'the Queens strength of body is extreamly impaird, for she is near skin and bones'.

[51] Valesio, *Diario di Roma*, pp. 751–3, 11 to 18 January 1735; Haile, *James Francis Edward*, pp. 357–8.

[52] Valesio, *Diario di Roma*, v, pp. 753–4, 19 January 1735.

[53] ASV. PAC 1007 records all the funeral expenses, totalling 16,503 *scudi*.

[54] There is an account of the death and funeral of the queen (before the 'Ristretto de Pagamenti') in ASV. PAC 1007. See also Valesio, *Diario di Roma*, v, pp. 754–6, 21 to 27 January 1735; SCA. BL 3/19/5, Stuart to G. Innes, 27 January 1735; NA. SP 98/37/f. 202, Stosch to Newcastle, 5 February 1735; James Russel, *Letters from a Young Painter abroad to His Friends in England* (2 vols., London, 2nd edn, 1750), vol. II, pp. 58–71; and Fagiolo, *Corpus delle feste*, pp. 92–3.

[55] They are reproduced in Sharp, *Engraved Record of the Jacobite Movement*, pp. 109–10, nos. 197, 198; and Fagiolo, *Corpus delle feste*, p. 93.

a plaque above the entrance, and that an illustrated book should be written describing the funeral and the procession, with a short account of the life and miracles of the queen.

The monument was 'fixed on the second pilaster, on the right hand side after one has entered',[56] and was said to contain both the queen's intestines and her heart. In fact her heart was not there: James III wrote in November 1736 that 'what is called here the *Precordie* ... is ... buried in our Parish Church, and the Heart should naturally be there, but the Pope allowed me to take it, and I have it in my Chappel'.[57] The plaque above the church door stated, in Latin, that the queen was 'eminently distinguished for Piety to God, Charity to others, Denial to herself', and that 'Clement XII Pope, decreed these obsequies to be performed with all Royal Honours in Rome'.[58]

The writing of the book, published at the end of 1736 as *Parentalia Mariae Clementinae Magn. Britan., Franc., et Hibern. Regin Iussu Clementis XII Pont. Max*, was entrusted to Cardinal Vincenzo Gotti, who had been prior of the Dominican monastery in Bologna while the Stuart court had been in that city, and who had acted as the queen's spiritual adviser.[59] Although Gotti was credited with writing the entire book, James III recorded in a private letter that the account of the queen's life and miracles was actually written by Sir Thomas Sheridan.[60] The book was printed 'magnificently', with a frontispiece by Panini reproducing Meytens's portrait of the queen, and the Pope gave 200 of the copies to James to distribute among his friends and supporters.[61] Within a few days of its publication Cardinal Gotti visited the king and told him that another miracle had been performed in the name of the queen in one of the hospitals of Rome: 'a small piece of her clothing' had cured a woman who was 'ill with a dilated vein'.[62]

The honours paid to the queen, the numerous other funeral and memorial services for her in the churches of Rome[63] and the miracles

---

[56] Valesio, *Diario di Roma*, VI, p. 182, 31 October 1738; Russel, *Letters from a Young Painter*, vol. II, p. 69.

[57] RA. SP 191/90, James III to Innes, 11 November 1736.

[58] Haile, *James Francis Edward*, p. 358.

[59] Ghiselli, 15 May 1728; NA. SP 98/37/f. 251, Stosch to Newcastle, 23 July 1735.

[60] RA. SP 192/85, James III to Innes, 16 December 1736; RA. SP 195/102, Innes to James III, 15 April 1737.

[61] NA. SP 98/37/f. 424, Stosch to Newcastle, 1 December 1736. In his letter of 16 December 1736 (see note 60) James explained that the ones given to him were 'better bound' than the ones given to other people.

[62] NA. SP 98/37/f. 430, Stosch to Newcastle, 22 December 1736.

[63] Valesio, *Diario di Roma*, V, pp. 767, 769, 832, 26 February and 1 March 1735, 19 January 1736; NA. SP 98/37/f. 315, Stosch to Newcastle, 28 January 1736; NA. SP 98/41/f. 10, to Newcastle, 2 February 1737; Fagiolo, *Corpus delle feste*, pp. 93–6.

associated with her[64] convinced James III that the beatification of his father was no longer of pressing importance. It was better for his children to be the sons rather than the grandsons of a saint. The project to secure the beatification of James II continued, but it was not pursued with any vigour and was eventually dropped.[65]

By 1737 there was another problem which seemed more urgent: Freemasonry. It had developed in England during the seventeenth century as a fraternity primarily motivated by loyalty to the Stuart royal dynasty, but since 1715 had become split into two rival but overlapping groups: Jacobite Freemasons and Hanoverian Freemasons. The former group were at first dominant in continental Europe; the latter group, after a power struggle lasting from 1717 to 1723, were dominant in England.

The Jacobite lodges included Protestants, so the Hanoverians hoped to infiltrate and even take control of them on the Continent, and during the 1720s and 1730s they made considerable progress, helped by the fact that French foreign policy under Cardinal Fleury was pro-Hanoverian.

By 1737 the Jacobites still controlled the lodge they had founded in Rome, which was mainly Catholic but also admitted many Protestants. Meanwhile the Hanoverians had established an important lodge in Florence, which was mainly Protestant but admitted people of all religious beliefs, even atheists, so long as they supported the anti-legitimist principles embodied in the Whig revolutionary settlement of 1689. As the Corsini family had come from Florence, where Pope Clement XII had been the archbishop until his election in 1730, the existence of the lodge there was regarded by them as particularly objectionable. James III obviously agreed, but he was even more concerned by the news which arrived from France in the summer of 1737 that the Hanoverian Freemasons had succeeded in recruiting so many French Catholics that they had wrested control of the *Grande Loge de France* from the Jacobites.

In the winter of 1737–8 James asked the Pope to issue a bull which would condemn Hanoverian Freemasonry in Catholic Europe. Clement XII and Cardinal Corsini were keen to oblige the king, but reluctant to take a step which was overtly hostile to the Hanoverian régime in England and strongly opposed to the foreign policy of Cardinal Fleury. The condemnation was therefore drawn up in terms which were religious rather than political, and which did not make clear the distinction between acceptable Jacobite Freemasonry and unacceptable Hanoverian

---

[64] See Haile, *James Francis Edward*, p. 358, for a miracle associated with Queen Clementina as late as 1777.

[65] Scott, "'Sacredness of Majesty'", p. 10.

Freemasonry. To get what he wanted, James agreed that the Jacobite Freemasons within the Papal States would need thenceforth to be particularly circumspect.[66]

The bull *In Eminenti Apostolatus Specula* was signed by Clement XII for James III on 28 April 1738. It explained the reason for condemning Freemasonry as follows:

> in reflecting on the great ills that commonly come out of this kind of society or assembly, not only for the maintaining of peace in temporal states, but also for the saving of souls, and that they cannot in any way be in accord with civil and canon law . . . and for other just and reasonable causes known to Ourselves . . . we have decided and decreed that the said societies of Freemasons be condemned and prohibited.[67]

James's close friend the duc de Saint-Aignan, the French ambassador in Rome, reported to Versailles that 'the number of Protestants who principally form the society of Freemasons, the oath on the Bible that they are made to swear, and all that is dangerous in the unbreakable silence to which they commit themselves, are all circumstances which seem to have deserved the censures that the Pope pronounced against them'.[68] The purpose of the bull has often been misunderstood, because most historians have assumed that it was directed against all Freemasons, but at the time it was a particularly favourable gesture by the papacy on behalf of the exiled king. Baron von Stosch, an atheist, argued that the bull had primarily been influenced by Sir Thomas Dereham to put pressure on the Grand Duke of Tuscany to close the Hanoverian lodge in Florence.[69]

By 1738, when the bull against Freemasonry was issued, Pope Clement XII was eighty-seven years old and completely blind, dependent on his nephew Cardinal Corsini. At the beginning of the following year the two men once again obliged King James. The latter had for a long time wanted to nominate Archbishop de Tencin to be a cardinal, but his previous nominee, Cardinal Riviera, was still alive. Despite this, the Pope agreed that Tencin should also be created a cardinal in March 1739 on James's nomination.[70] A French courtier noted in

[66] Edward Corp, 'La Franc-Maçonnerie jacobite et la bulle papale *In Eminenti* d'avril 1738', *La règle d'Abraham*, 18 (Paris, 2004), pp. 14–15, 24–30.

[67] José-Antonio Benimelli, *Les archives secrètes du Vatican et la Franc-Maçonnerie* (2nd French edn, Paris, 2002), pp. 134–5.

[68] *Ibid.*, p. 144, Saint-Aignan to Fleury, 28 June 1738.

[69] NA. SP 98/41/f. 180, Stosch to Newcastle, 9 June 1738.

[70] Castries, *Scandaleuse Madame de Tencin*, pp. 173–5; NA. SP 98/41/f. 275, Stosch to Newcastle, 9 March 1739.

his diary that '[James III] has been shown a very particular favour on the subject of the position of cardinal which the pope is giving on his recommendation ... How has it come about that pretenders to a throne have two cardinalships in their giving, whereas real monarchs have only one?'[71] The answer was not difficult to ascertain. A precedent had been established which would permit James, if necessary, to nominate Prince Henry to be a cardinal without waiting for a vacancy.

Pope Clement XII died in February 1740. During the conclave to elect his successor, Stosch noted that 'according to a new plan of Card. De Tencin, his younger son [i.e. Prince Henry] will be created a Cardinal by the future Pontiff'.[72]

Benedict XIV, 1740–1758

The conclave of 1740 lasted six months. James III and Cardinal de Tencin nearly secured the election of Cardinal Riviera,[73] but in the end it was Cardinal Prospero Lambertini who was elected as Benedict XIV on 17 August 1740. He was well acquainted with the king, having lived in Rome during the early 1720s, and having been appointed Archbishop of Bologna in 1728, a few months before the Stuart court left the city. After the election James III went to see the new pope 'in Card. Corsini's cell, where he had dined, in order to enlist his support'. Benedict gave him a friendly reception, and said that 'he would always look upon him and his family with feelings of genuine affection'.[74]

One of Benedict's first acts, on 24 August, was to give James a gift of 10,000 *scudi* to celebrate his election,[75] and to renew the Stuart pension of 10,000 *scudi* per annum from the *Camera Apostolica*.[76] He soon discovered, however, that the papal finances were considerably overstretched and that retrenchments were necessary.[77] The cardinal in charge of the *Datario*, Pompeo Aldrovandi, suggested that he stop giving James both the additional 6000 *scudi* per annum and the generous presents whenever the king went to Albano for his *villeggiatura*, but Benedict refused to do

---

[71] René-Louis de Voyer, marquis d'Argenson, *Journal et Mémoires*, ed. E.J.B. Rathéry (9 vols., Paris, 1859–67), vol. II, p. 116, 18 March 1739.

[72] NA. SP 98/43/f. 54, Stosch to Newcastle, 25 June 1740. See also NA. SP 98/43/ff. 72, 74, to Newcastle, 27 August and 3 September 1740.

[73] Edward Gregg, 'The Financial Vicissitudes of James III in Rome', in Edward Corp (ed.), *The Stuart Court in Rome: The Legacy of Exile* (Aldershot, 2003), pp. 76–7.

[74] NA. SP 98/43/f. 72, Stosch to Newcastle, 27 August 1740.

[75] ASV. SS: Ingh 21, p. 255.

[76] *Ibid.*, p. 253; ASR. Cam I: RMC b. 1085.

[77] NA. SP 98/43/f. 78, Stosch to Newcastle, 17 September 1740.

either of these.[78] All he would accept was a reduction (by an unspecified number) in the soldiers guarding the Palazzo del Re and escorting James and his sons on their journeys to and from Albano.[79]

Nevertheless, the Pope asked marchese Girolamo Belloni, who was James III's banker in Rome, to give him advice how best to reform the administation of the *Camera Apostolica*.[80] As a result its system of accounting was restructured in 1743, when the department known as the *Depositeria Generale* was transferred to the *Monte di Pietà di Roma*.[81] This is important for any study of the Stuart court in Rome because the papal archives of the *Camera Apostolica* concerning the payment of the Stuart pension and the maintenance of the Palazzo del Re in Rome and the Palazzo Apostolico at Albano suddenly come to an end at this time.[82] We know that the pensions continued to be paid, and Benedict specifically said so in a letter of 1750,[83] but all we are left with are the archives of the *Computisteria Generale* recording the continued payment of the annual rent of 1632 *scudi* for the Palazzo del Re.[84] According to a letter which the Pope sent to the *maggiordomo* of the *Camera Apostolica*, James III was thenceforth to be given 600 *scudi* each year for the maintenance of the palazzo, to use as he wished, on the understanding that he could keep any money not spent.[85] As the average annual expenditure on maintaining the building was by then approximately 637 *scudi*, this represented a small retrenchment.[86]

---

[78] NA. SP 98/43/ff. 84, 96, 215, Stosch to Newcastle, 8 October and 19 November 1740, 30 September 1741; NA. SP 98/46/f. 49, to Newcastle, 5 May 1742; *Benoît XIV*, II, p. 60, Benedict XIV to Tencin, 23 September 1750.

[79] NA. SP 98/43/f. 84, Stosch to Newcastle, 8 October 1740; *Benoît XIV*, I, p. 470, to Tencin, 12 February 1749.

[80] Girolamo Belloni, *Scritture inedite e dissertazione 'del commercio'*, ed. Alberto Caracciolo (Rome, 1965), pp. 235–44.

[81] Maria Grazia Pastura Ruggiero, *La Reverenza Camera Apostolica e i suoi archivi, secoli xv–xviii* (Rome, 1984), unpaginated 'tavola fuori testo' at the end. The *Depositeria Generale* and the *Computisteria Generale* had both been supervised by the *Tesoriere Generale*.

[82] ASR. Cam I: RMC b. 1085 contains the payments of the pension in 1740–3. The last entry is dated 30 September 1743, recording the quarterly payment to Girolamo Belloni of 2500 *scudi* for the months of July to September of that year. The last payments for the maintenance of the Palazzo del Re are shown in ASR. Cam I: CDG b. 2017bis/13/19 and 20, and ASV. PAC 987; and for the maintenance of the Palazzo Apostolico at Albani in ASR. Cam I: GT b. 682, b. 683, b. 684 and b. 689.

[83] *Benoît XIV*, II, p. 60, to Tencin, 23 September 1750.

[84] ASV. PAC 5045 and 5220.

[85] ASV. PAC 987, no. 309/15, Benedict XIV to Girolamo Colonna, 18 December 1742.

[86] Exceptional expenditure, such as repairing the damage caused by a fire in the apartment of Lord Dunbar in October 1743, continued to be paid by the *Camera Apostolica* (ASV. PAC 988, no. 8/6; and ASV. PAC 5220, p. 8). In *Benoît XIV*, II, p. 60, to Tencin, 23 September 1750 the Pope stated that James received approximately 2500 *scudi* 'pour le loyer et l'ameublement du palais qu'il habite' (n.b. there is a misprint in the published edition, which shows 25,000 instead of 2500 *scudi*). This included 1632 *scudi* for the rent, 600 *scudi* for maintenance and an additional 268 *scudi* for exceptional expenditure.

By contrast, expenditure on James's residence at Albano, which belonged to the papacy, significantly increased after Benedict XIV became pope. The Palazzo Apostolico had originally been considered large enough for the *villeggiature* of James and his court, but as the two princes grew up and were attended by more servants, extra space was needed. In the autumn of 1740 Benedict agreed that an additional five houses, several rooms in the nearby Palazzo Costaguti, and a *rimessa* (hangar) for the guards should be rented by the *Camera Apostolica* each time the king went there.[87]

This arrangement, however, was no more than temporary. In October 1742 Benedict agreed that the Palazzo Apostolico should itself be expanded with the construction of a new wing. Stosch recorded that the Pope went to Albano to see 'the old Palace of the *Camera* . . . which is being demolished to build in its place another wing on the palace in which the King resides in order to provide him with more living-space'.[88] The front façade of the old palazzo was rebuilt, with a *cavalcavia* (enclosed bridge) projecting forward from the right-hand end to a completely new building.[89] The works were finished by the end of 1743, at a cost of 15,971 *scudi*, which also included the construction of a new road into Albano for the convenience of the Stuart court.[90] The interior decorations, paid for in 1747, cost 19,491 *scudi*, and the furniture another 3518 *scudi*.[91] At a time of financial retrenchment, the expansion of James III's residence at Albano was a particularly generous gesture by the Pope.

The explanation of Benedict XIV's generosity can be found in his private correspondence with Cardinal de Tencin. Two letters of March 1744 are worth quoting. On the 5th he wrote:

We are truly and sincerely attached to this royal house of Stuart, primarily for the advantage it brings to our sacred religion, secondly because the house has right and justice on its side, thirdly because the king and the princes his children are extremely pleasant with fine and rare qualities.[92]

Six days later he added:

Apart from that motive [i.e. religion] we have another reason to desire all sorts of good for the Prince of Wales; this is the good manners and pleasant looks

---

[87] ASR. Cam I: GT b. 659/f. 14, b. 682/f. 7.

[88] NA. SP 98/46/ff. 116, 120, Stosch to Newcastle, 20 October and 3 November 1742.

[89] These two buildings with their connecting *cavalcavia*, together with the ruins of the gate of San Severus on the left-hand side, formed the Piazza del Re (now called the Piazza Constituente).

[90] ASR. Cam I: GT b. 683/f. 8, b. 689/f. 8.

[91] ASV. SS: Ingh 21, pp. 258–60. According to Stosch, there was a 'nouveau Apartement', and various rooms were made 'plus commode' for the princes (NA. SP 98/53/f. 19, to Newcastle, 14 March 1747).

[92] *Benoît XIV*, I, p. 124, to Tencin, 5 March 1744.

of the prince and also the wisdom and gentle manner with which his father has always behaved here. In all the years he has been here, he has never caused the slightest difficulty to the government.[93]

In view of the problems caused by Queen Clementina in 1725–7, and the support she had then received from the papacy, this comment is particularly significant.

By 1740 Queen Clementina was remembered for the saintly life she had led in the last years before her death in January 1735. Benedict XIV does not seem to have offered any encouragement for the possible beatification of either James II or Clementina, but shortly after his election he devised a more visible method of honouring the Stuart queen.

As we have seen, Clement XII had arranged for Clementina to be buried in the crypt of St Peter's, and had commissioned a monument for her in the Church of Santi Apostoli. Benedict XIV now decided that a second and much larger monument should be erected within the Basilica of St Peter's itself, with her portrait 'worked in fine mosaic by the best craftsmen in Rome'.[94] James III was asked to select a portrait to be reproduced, and he chose the one by Martin van Meytens, already included in the *Parentalia*, which showed Clementina 'dressed as a queen'. But Cardinal Lanfredini, in charge of the *Fabbrica di San Pietro*, refused to accept it, insisting that the portrait was 'not really decent', and that the mosaic should show her 'dressed as a penitent, as indeed the saintly princess actually was'. The question had to be referred to Benedict XIV, who supported the king and publicly visited the *fabbrica* in March 1741 to order Lanfredini to accept the Meytens portrait.[95]

The monument, designed by Filippo Barigioni, with sculpture by Pietro Bracci and the portrait in mosaic worked by Pietro Paolo Cristofari, took two years to complete, at a cost of 18,000 *scudi*,[96] and was opened to the public in November 1742.[97] Two years later, in January 1745 (the tenth anniversary of her death), Benedict ordered that the queen's body should be removed from the crypt and taken up into the basilica. In a ceremony attended by twenty-five cardinals and 'a great many of the ... Nobility', the corpse was placed under a large canopy of state 'covered with a pall of gold tissue, over which were fixed two little angels, one holding a crown, the other a sceptre', while 'solemn music

[93] *Ibid.*, p. 126, to Tencin, 11 March 1744.
[94] NA. SP 98/43/f. 94, Stosch to Newcastle, 12 November 1740.
[95] Valesio, *Diario di Roma*, VI, pp. 444, 448, 18 February and 3 March 1741.
[96] *Benoît XIV*, I, p. 175, to Tencin, 23 January 1745.
[97] NA. SP 98/46/f. 135, Stosch to Newcastle, 8 December 1742. James III gave Barigioni 'un grand Medaillon d'or mis dans une Boete ornée du Portrait' of the queen (NA. SP 98/46/f. 147, to Newcastle, 29 December 1742).

was performed by voices and instruments', and then 'carried in a grand ceremony and deposited in the urn of porphyry' which forms part of the monument.[98] Pope Benedict wrote that 'the memory of such a pious queen, the king her good husband and her worthy children merited such an honour'.[99]

The Pope had meanwhile kept in mind that Prince Henry might need one day to become a cardinal. In 1742, when the prince was seventeen years old, and there seemed no immediate prospect of a restoration, rumours began to circulate in Rome that he might soon be promoted.[100] At the end of that year Pope Benedict made an arrangement with Father William Clark, the Scottish Jacobite confessor of the King of Spain, whereby James III would be permitted to receive an annual income of up to 12,000 *scudi*, payable from 'ecclesiastical rents from bishoprics, abbeys and canonrys in the kingdom of Spain', with the ability to 'pass them on to his sons'. The intention was that if Henry *were* to become a cardinal, then 'the transfer of the pension would be limited to the cardinal-duke alone'.[101] In January 1743 Baron von Stosch wrote to London that the king's servants in the Palazzo del Re 'are boasting ... that his younger son will be granted the Dignity' of becoming a cardinal.[102]

The plan was put temporarily aside when Great Britain and France declared war in 1743, and French help for a Stuart restoration once again became a possibility – for the first time for over thirty years. Prince Charles secretly left Rome to travel to France in January 1744, followed by Prince Henry in August 1745. In his private letters to Cardinal de Tencin the Pope described his regular meetings with James III, 'who is living between hope and fear',[103] and expressed his own hopes that Prince Charles would achieve a restoration after his landing in Scotland. Benedict gave 100,000 *scudi* to help finance the invasion attempt,[104] and allowed the king to raise a loan of another 100,000 *scudi* from the *Monte di Pietà di Roma*

---

[98] NA. SP 98/49/f. 145, Stosch to Newcastle, 26 January 1745; *Diario ordinario*, no. 4293, pp. 2–6, 30 January 1745; Russel, *Letters from a Young Painter*, vol. I, pp. 244–5, 16 May 1745; and Fagiolo, *Corpus delle feste*, p. 128.

[99] *Benoît XIV*, I, p. 175, to Tencin, 23 January 1745; NA. SP 98/49/f. 163, Stosch to Newcastle, 30 March 1745.

[100] NA. SP 98/46/ff. 83, 131, Stosch to Newcastle, 4 August and 1 December 1742.

[101] *Benoît XIV*, II, p. 72, to Tencin, 11 November 1750. Also *ibid.*, I, p. 184, to Tencin, 13 May 1745. Benedict's briefs of December 1742 authorising the arrangement are in RA. SP 286/123 and ASV. SS: Ingh 21, p. 281. They were supplemented by a further brief of March 1745 (same references, and ASV. Fondo Benedetto XIV 19, p. 201, York to Benedict XIV, 24 May 1751).

[102] NA. SP 98/46/f. 153, Stosch to Newcastle, 19 January 1743.

[103] *Benoît XIV*, I, p. 243, to Tencin, 2 February 1746.

[104] NA. SP 98/49/f. 207, Stosch to Newcastle, 31 August 1745.

on the security of jewels worth a great deal less than that.[105] 'We dearly love the Stuarts,' he commented at the beginning of 1746.[106]

When the news reached Rome that Prince Charles had been defeated at Culloden, the Pope shared in James III's disappointment and fears for the safety of his son, and when he heard that the prince had succeeded in avoiding capture and had returned to France he asked Louis XV to let him remain there permanently, perhaps at Saint-Germain: 'to see him come back . . . and go to Albano for his *villeggiatura*, as he did before he left, would cause us too much pain'.[107]

The failure of the Jacobite rising of 1745–6 revived the plan to make Prince Henry a cardinal, because James III and his younger son were now convinced that there would never be a Stuart restoration.[108] Prince Charles, by contrast, remained optimistic that French help might be forthcoming, so his brother remained with him in Paris for several months instead of immediately returning to Rome. This simple fact has misled Jacobite historians and all Stuart biographers into believing that the idea that Prince Henry should become a cardinal was a sudden decision, despite all the evidence to the contrary since 1733.[109] What made Prince Henry leave Paris and hasten back to see his father was not any new desire to become a cardinal, but rather some alarming news which he received in April 1747.

Since becoming Pope in 1740 Benedict XIV had created cardinals on two occasions. The first promotion was in September 1743, when Henry was still in Rome. It was then assumed that the prince would, if necessary, be included in the next promotion, but his continued absence from Rome, and the possibility that there might be another restoration attempt, obliged the Pope to go ahead without him. In a consistory on 10 April 1747 Benedict created eleven new cardinals, including one nominated by Louis XV (Frédéric-Jérome de La Rochefoucauld, Archbishop of Bourges) and one nominated by James III (Armand de Rohan-Soubise, coadjutor Bishop of Strasbourg).[110]

[105] *Benoît XIV*, I, p. 204, to Tencin, 25 August 1745.

[106] *Ibid.*, I, p. 245, to Tencin, 9 February 1746.

[107] *Ibid.*, p. 280, to Tencin, 9 November 1746.

[108] RA. SP 287/4, James III to Tencin, 29 August 1747; *Benoît XIV*, I, p. 421, to Tencin, 7 August 1748.

[109] Frank McLynn's comment that 'in December 1746 James raised, almost as an aside, the idea – no more than a *jeu d'esprit* at this stage – that Henry might like to consider becoming a Cardinal' is a typical example (*Charles Edward Stuart*, p. 328).

[110] James had actually wanted to nominate Lord Francis FitzJames, the Bishop of Soissons (and son of the 1st Duke of Berwick), but had been persuaded to nominate Archbishop de Rohan-Soubise instead, to please Louis XV (*Benoît XIV*, I, p. 195, to Tencin, 28 April 1745 and 3 May 1747; ASV. SS: Ingh 21, p. 289, James III to Benedict XIV,

When the news of this second promotion reached Prince Henry in Paris he was seriously alarmed. He knew that his father had the right to nominate a second cardinal, but he was afraid that he might have to wait several years until the next promotion. It was this that made him suddenly leave Paris and return to Rome, and ask his father to do what he could to help him. In June 1747, shortly after Henry's return, James III had a private meeting with the Pope in the Villa Barberini at Castel Gandolfo, and said he would like to nominate a second cardinal. Benedict XIV wrote on 14 June that 'he was very pressing that we should make the Duke of York a cardinal in the first consistory of July; we, considering that the Cardinal of Auvergne [Archbishop of Vienne] had just made a position vacant, that the creation of just one cardinal does not involve a promotion, that the person in question is very deserving and that *he would bring honour to us and to the Sacred College*, we had no difficulty in replying that we would do so with pleasure'.[111] Prince Henry was created a cardinal, and thenceforth known as the Cardinal Duke of York, at the beginning of July, in a ceremony which took place in the Sistine Chapel at the Vatican.[112] The Pope himself described the occasion: 'The king his father was in a private but covered gallery. At the moment when we gave him the cardinal's hat, the canons of the castles of Sant' Angelo and Monte Cavallo were fired for a second time. It was a very splendid occasion.'[113]

The rest of July was taken up with celebrations and receptions of various kinds, which Benedict ordered should be 'with all possible pomp and brilliance'.[114] At the beginning of August the Pope again expressed his favourable opinion of the Stuarts: 'Cardinal York ... continues to lead an exemplary life and is gaining the affection of everybody. One might also say that the king his father is in a way venerated.'[115]

As part of the celebrations Pope Benedict required all the cardinals living in Rome to illuminate the outside of their residences, and said that new cardinals on this occasion should in addition decorate their homes with a false façade, or *facciata*. James III explained to Cardinal de Tencin

---

5 April 1747; Philippe d'Albert, duc de Luynes, *Mémoires sur la cour de Louis XV*, ed. L. Dussieux and E. Soulié (17 vols., Paris, 1860–6), vol. VIII, p. 188, 21 April 1747.

[111] *Benoît XIV*, I, p. 331, to Tencin, 14 June 1747. My emphasis. For James III's letter of 9 June 1747 to Louis XV, see *ibid.*, p. 546.

[112] *Ibid.*, pp. 334, 337, to Tencin, 21 June and 5 July 1747; ASV. SS: Ingh 25, pp. 27, 31; *Diario ordinario*, no. 4674, 8 July 1747, pp. 2–12, and no. 4677, 15 July 1747, pp. 2–3, 6–10; Fagiolo, *Corpus delle feste*, p. 138; Alice Shield, *Henry Stuart, Cardinal of York and His Times* (London, 1908), p. 118; Pietro Bindelli, *Enrico Stuart, cardinale duca di York* (Frascati, 1982), p. 76. ASV. PAC 1058/no. 30 contains the payments for the gifts given by the Pope to Prince Henry on this occasion.

[113] *Benoît XIV*, I, pp. 338–98, to Tencin, 12 July 1747.   [114] *Ibid.*, p. 339.

[115] *Ibid.*, p. 342, to Tencin, 2 August 1747.

on 25 July, 'The Pope has revived an ancient custom of which I know neither the origin nor the use, which is that all new cardinals should put up what is called a painted façade on their houses, which must remain there for 40 days after they are made Cardinal. The Duke's one has only just been finished.'[116] The *facciata*, which was designed by Clemente Orlandi, took nineteen days to build and decorate, and cost 4481 *scudi*.[117] It was erected outside the new cardinal's apartment in the east wing of the Palazzo del Re, overlooking the Piazza della Pilotta, and remained in place until September 1747 (Fig. 18).[118]

While these celebrations were continuing James III was asked if he would like to nominate his son to be the Cardinal Protector of one of his three kingdoms. The present protectors, Cardinals Riviera (England), Lante (Scotland) and Corsini (Ireland), all offered to resign their positions to make way for him, but James said he had no wish to nominate his son, and asked them to continue. Pope Benedict hoped that Henry might become the Cardinal Protector of France, but neither the king nor his son wanted this either, so the matter was dropped.[119] The episode was useful, however, because it confirmed James III's right to choose the cardinal protectors of his three kingdoms. In the years which followed, he continued to nominate new cardinals and new cardinal protectors.

The relations between the Stuarts and the papacy were now complicated by the reports which reached Rome of the way Prince Charles was behaving and his reaction to the news of his brother's becoming a cardinal. Pretending that he knew nothing of the plans which had been developed since 1733, Charles told his father that Prince Henry was no longer his brother and that he never wanted to hear his name mentioned again.[120] Becoming ever more reckless in his behaviour after Great Britain and France made peace at Aix-la-Chapelle, and refusing to leave France when asked, he eventually had to be arrested, briefly imprisoned and then forcibly expelled from France

---

[116] RA. SP 285/187, James III to Tencin, 25 July 1747. See also NA. SP 98/53/f. 59, Stosch to Newcastle, 1 August 1747.
[117] RA. SP 288/164, a list of Cardinal York's expenses, 24 July to 31 December 1747. The details are shown in RA. SP Misc 40, p. 95. A further 2098 *scudi* were spent in recording the appearance of the *facciata* in an engraving by Claude-Olivier Gallimard. A painting was made after the engraving in 1748, bringing the total up to 5294 *scudi*.
[118] Corp, 'Location of the Stuart Court in Rome', pp. 197–9; Fagiolo, *Corpus delle feste*, p. 138. Cardinal Lante's *facciata* is shown in Fagiolo, p. 139.
[119] *Benoît XIV*, I, pp. 337, 346, to Tencin, 5 July and 23 August 1747. No new Cardinal Protector of France had been appointed since the death of Ottoboni in 1740 (NA. SP 98/53/f. 47, Stosch to Newcastle, 20 June 1747).
[120] McLynn, *Charles Edward Stuart*, p. 332.

Figure 18. *The 'facciata' of Cardinal York, July 1747*, 1748 (195.5 × 297 cm), by Pubalacci, Paolo Monaldi and Silvestri (Louis de Silvestre?). The *facciata* was erected on part of the east side of the Palazzo del Re, outside the apartment which had been occupied by Prince Henry on the second floor.

on the orders of Louis XV. Pope Benedict's letters are full of the sadness and irritation he felt when Prince Charles settled at Avignon without permission and caused endless problems for the papal vice-legate there. The Pope offered to let him live within the Papal States at Bologna, as he had no desire to see him return to Rome and cause trouble,[121] but Prince Charles declined the offer and embarked on the wandering life which was to continue for the next seventeen years.[122]

In Rome, by contrast, the relations between the Pope and Cardinal York were excellent. The following comment in a letter of May 1748 is typical of the Pope's attitude:

The ... Sacred College owes us much for having introduced Cardinal York who is an angel in human form and an example to Rome. He holds his own very well in the meetings to which we have sent him, always showing intelligence, speaking knowledgeably and modestly.[123]

In September 1748 Cardinal York was ordained a priest and given the Church of Santa Maria in Campitelli.[124]

Pope Benedict then set in motion a series of negotiations to provide him with an income from various lucrative benefices in France, Spain and Naples. In August 1750 he promised to appoint him to be the next Archpriest of St Peter's Basilica on the death of the present incumbent (Cardinal Annibale Albani);[125] in September 1750 he agreed to transfer the original annual Stuart pension of 10,000 *scudi*, paid by the *Camera Apostolica*, from James III to Cardinal York, so that it could continue after the king's death;[126] and in November 1750 he agreed that the Spanish income settled on the king in 1742 should now be transferred on his death to Cardinal York only, and not to Prince Charles.[127] These arrangements were partly inspired by the will which James was thinking of making at this time. His idea was to leave to Prince Charles all his

---

[121] *Benoît XIV*, I, pp. 453, 456, 463, 487, 491–2, to Tencin, 1 and 15 January, 12 February, 28 May and 11 June 1749.

[122] McLynn, *Charles Edward Stuart*, chapters 26–32.

[123] *Benoît XIV*, I, p. 404, to Tencin, 15 May 1748. A few days before he wrote this, Pope Benedict had given King James a present of 6000 *scudi* (*ibid.*, p. 401, to Tencin, 1 May 1748).

[124] Shield, *Henry Stuart*, p. 118; Bindelli, *Enrico Stuart*, p. 77.

[125] *Benoît XIV*, II, pp. 49, 60, 148, to Tencin, 12 August and 23 September 1750, 20 October 1751.

[126] *Ibid.*, pp. 60, 90, 148, 525, to Tencin, 23 September 1750, 3 February and 20 October 1751, 8 September 1756.

[127] *Ibid.*, p. 72, to Tencin, 11 November 1750. Also *ibid.*, p. 148, to Tencin, 20 October 1751, summarising all these arrangements.

income from his *rentes* in France, and to Cardinal York all his income in Italy and Spain.[128]

In the autumn of 1751, when James III and his younger son were still living together in the Palazzo del Re, Cardinal York was appointed Archpriest of St Peter's, as promised. The appointment carried with it a house in the Piazza della Sagrestia, beside the basilica,[129] but Henry did not intend to live in it. At this moment, however, a dispute arose between the king and the cardinal concerning the management of the household appointments at the Stuart court,[130] which resulted in a serious breach between them. Pope Benedict found himself obliged to do all he could to bring about a reconciliation between the two men, beginning by reminding the king that 'however great the affection felt by a son for his father, it is never as great as that felt by a father for his son'.[131]

As the weeks went by the relations between James and Henry became worse, and Benedict realised that all his efforts were in vain because, as he put it, 'unfortunately, we are dealing with two people who both have the English character'.[132] In February 1752 James III threatened to leave Rome and live somewhere else if his son would not give way,[133] which made Benedict fear that the cardinal would leave his father and live in the house he now had as Archpriest of St Peter's.[134] Eventually Cardinal York did move out of the Palazzo del Re, in July 1752, but instead of going to his own house he preferred to retire temporarily 'with the Fathers of the Mission at San Giovanni and San Paolo', while he looked for a palazzo of his own near the English College.[135]

The Pope did what he could to bring the two sides together, but he agreed that the king was right in wanting to maintain control over the household appointments, and that Cardinal York was being badly advised by his friends. This provoked Henry to leave Rome to take the waters at Nocera (near Foligno), saying that he would go on to Bologna and not return to Rome until his father had given way.[136] For his part, James told the Pope that if his son did return to Rome he would never consent to his living anywhere but the Palazzo del Re[137] and that, 'if his

[128] *Ibid.*, p. 90, to Tencin, 3 February 1751. For Cardinal York's letter to James III of 10 April 1751, renouncing his share of the income in France, see ASV. SS: Ingh 25, p. 68.
[129] *Benoît XIV*, II, p. 176, to Tencin, 22 March 1752; Shield, *Henry Stuart*, p. 145.
[130] See below, Chapter 15.   [131] *Benoît XIV*, II, p. 153, to Tencin, 24 November 1751.
[132] *Ibid.*, p. 160, to Tencin, 29 December 1751.
[133] *Ibid.*, p. 166, to Tencin, 2 February 1752.
[134] *Ibid.*, pp. 177, 184–5, to Tencin, 22 March and 3 May 1752.
[135] *Ibid.*, pp. 199, 200, 202–3, to Tencin, 12, 19 and 26 July 1752.
[136] *Ibid.*, pp. 203, 207, 208, to Tencin, 2, 16 and 23 August 1752.
[137] *Ibid.*, pp. 209, 213, to Tencin, 30 August and 13 September 1752.

son did take a separate palace, a plan that he could not prevent, it would be incumbent on him at least never to receive him, nor to see him, which he himself was determined to carry out'.[138]

Cardinal York remained at Bologna in the Palazzo Angelelli during the autumn of 1752 and eventually agreed to return to live in the Palazzo del Re, on condition that he should have 'real liberty, and among other things, to be able to sup on his own'.[139] He arrived back at the end of November[140] and was received by James III at the top of the grand staircase: 'the cardinal threw himself to his knees before the king and begged for his forgiveness. His kind father embraced him with tears in his eyes.' The cardinal then went to see Pope Benedict: 'We told him frankly what he must do so as not to make a public spectacle of himself again. He asked that we should write to the king assuring him of his absolute submission.'[141]

Relations between James III and Cardinal York thereafter remained strained but amicable, much to the relief of Pope Benedict. The incident did nothing to lessen the Pope's affection and respect for the king, but it made him realise that the cardinal was easily led and would make a bad administrator. In 1753 he gave Henry the Church of Santi Apostoli, and allowed him to hold it *in commendam* with Santa Maria in Campitelli.[142] He also remained very active in securing for him important ecclesiastical revenues in France and Spain. But he refused to consider him as a possible papal legate, and was not willing to make him a bishop.[143] 'The cardinal is a good priest,' he wrote, 'but he is very immature and ... very much needs paternal authority.'[144] James III wanted Benedict to give his son an office in the government of the Papal States, but Benedict felt that Cardinal York 'is not capable of it, nor will he ever be'.[145]

In 1756 the office of *vice-cancelliere* became vacant, and James III pressed Pope Benedict to give it to his son. The latter refused, saying that he had already made Cardinal York the Archpriest of St Peter's and had obtained for him large revenues, as well as the continuation of the Stuart pension from the *Camera Apostolica*. 'The cardinal is in truth a very pious young man, but incapable of holding responsibility or even of being helped,' he wrote.[146]

---

[138] *Ibid.*, p. 214, to Tencin, 20 September 1752.
[139] *Ibid.*, pp. 222, to Tencin, 25 October 1752. Also *ibid.*, pp. 223, 224, 226, to Tencin, 1, 8 and 15 November 1752.
[140] *Ibid.*, p. 228, to Tencin, 22 November 1752.
[141] *Ibid.*, p. 228, to Tencin, 29 November 1752.
[142] Shield, *Henry Stuart*, p. 152; Bindelli, *Enrico Stuart*, p. 85.
[143] *Benoît XIV*, II, pp. 416, 424, to Tencin, 4 June and 9 July 1755.
[144] *Ibid.*, p. 455, to Tencin, 19 November 1755.
[145] *Ibid.*, p. 466, to Tencin, 31 December 1755.
[146] *Ibid.*, p. 525, to Tencin, 8 September 1756.

In any event, Prince Henry's future in exile was now secure, as an important cardinal with a large income. But the same could not be said for Prince Charles, who had virtually severed all contact with his father and brother, had never returned to Rome, and had done nothing to cultivate any support at the papal court. His private life, moreover, including a conversion to Anglicanism during a visit to London, had scandalised his supporters in France and Spain. In November 1755, when James III was recovering from a bout of illness, Benedict admitted, 'In our case, if the king had died, we would have been at a loss to know if we should or should not recognise the prince ... as king like his father ... We hope that ... it will be our successor who has to cope with this matter.'[147]

Benedict XIV's wish was granted, and it was indeed left to his successor to deal with the problem. But his affection for the Stuarts remained with him until the end of his life. In April 1758, when he was seriously ill and had only a few weeks to live, he granted James III one final favour. Against his better judgement he appointed Cardinal York to be the *camerlengo* of the Sacred College of Cardinals.[148]

Clement XIII, 1758–1769

Cardinal Carlo Rezzonico, who had been consecrated Bishop of Padua in the Church of Santi Apostoli beside the Stuart court,[149] was elected Pope Clement XIII on 6 July 1758. According to the king's private secretary he always showed 'great love and attention' to both James and Cardinal York.[150] Nevertheless the king, who was now seventy years old, never developed with him the close relations he had enjoyed with his two predecessors.

Clement XIII renewed the Stuart pensions and agreed to go on renting the Palazzo del Re,[151] but his generosity was particularly directed to Cardinal York. He reappointed him as the *camerlengo*,[152] and in November 1758 personally consecrated him as Bishop of Corinth

[147] *Ibid.*, p. 455, to Tencin, 19 November 1755.
[148] Bindelli, *Enrico Stuart*, p. 89. This post should be distinguished from that of *camerlengo* of the Holy Roman Church. It was the latter who presided over a conclave to elect a new pope. The two posts are confused in Shield, *Henry Stuart*, p. 169.
[149] Fagiolo, *Corpus delle feste*, p. 126. The ceremony took place in March 1743.
[150] NLS. MS 14264, p. 99, Lumisden to Prince Charles, 16 January 1766.
[151] McLynn, *Charles Edward Stuart*, p. 471. The payments for the rent are recorded in ASV. PAC 5220.
[152] Shield, *Henry Stuart*, p. 170.

in partibus in a ceremony held in the Church of Santi Apostoli.[153] In February 1759 he allowed him to exchange Santi Apostoli, which he held *in commendam*, for the more prestigious Church of Santa Maria in Trastevere, and in July 1761 promoted him to be Bishop of Frascati.[154] His last gesture towards James III was to appoint his son to be the *vice-cancelliere* of the Church, with the use of the enormous Palazzo della Cancelleria, in January 1763.[155] In this way Clement XIII provided the exiled Stuarts with the security which James III had always hoped for, should there never be a restoration to the thrones of England, Scotland and Ireland.

It was at this time that any lingering hopes that there might be a restoration were completely extinguished. In October 1760 King George II died and was succeeded by his English grandson George III. In the following month James III made his will, asking to be buried in 'the Parish Church of the Holy Twelve Apostles under the place where the bowels of the late Queen our dearest Consort are already buried'. The will, of which the Pope was to be the sole executor, explained in detail how James's money and possessions were to be divided between his two sons, and how various Jacobite pensions were to be financed. Cardinal York was to receive very much less than Prince Charles, but James explained that the cardinal, so well provided for by the Church, would not object. In May 1762 he added a codicil 'for the greater advantage and conveniency of our dearest son Charles Prince of Wales and that the pensions . . . may be the more punctually and regularly paid'.

James was well aware that Prince Charles, who had still not returned to Rome, had made no overtures to the Pope, and that there was no guarantee that papal support would be continued after his own death. The prince might, therefore, have to depend on the generosity of the King of France. King James commented in his will, 'And as what we leave to the Prince in this our last Will and Testament is noways sufficient to afford him a decent maintenance even in exile we earnestly recommend to the generosity of his Most Christian Majesty the continuing to him at least the same marks of it which we have so long enjoyed.'[156] In May 1763 he sent a personal letter to Louis XV,

[153] *Ibid.*, p. 170; Bindelli, *Enrico Stuart*, p. 83. The banquet given by Clement XIII on this occasion for Cardinal York and seventy people, including nine other cardinals, with music performed by the Pontifical Chapel, is described in ASV. PAC 1048.

[154] Shield, *Henry Stuart*, pp. 170, 174; Bindelli, *Enrico Stuart*, pp. 85, 87.

[155] Shield, *Henry Stuart*, p. 180; Bindelli, *Enrico Stuart*, p. 87.

[156] ASV. SS: Ingh 25, pp. 109–12, the Last Will and Testament of James III, 21 November 1760; and pp. 128–9, the codicil of 26 May 1762.

expressing his gratitude for all the support he had received from France, and begging Louis to continue his protection for his two sons.[157]

By this time James III's health had been deteriorating for several years and it was clear that he did not have much longer to live. His death would then confront Clement XIII with the problem of whether or not to recognise Prince Charles as the next *de jure* king. In November 1763 this question became of pressing importance for two reasons: James's health declined again, so that he became virtually bed-ridden;[158] and George III's younger brother Edward, Duke of York, arrived in Genoa at the start of a Grand Tour of Italy.

The duke travelled incognito as the Earl of Ulster, but was received everywhere he went with the honours befitting his real rank. In April 1764, when he arrived in Rome for two weeks, he was well received by the Pope, who gave him various rich presents and a reception in the gardens of the Quirinale.[159] The presence of this man, such a short distance from the Palazzo del Re, and described in the papal archives as 'H.R.H. the Duke of York, Brother of the reigning King of England',[160] made it clear to everyone that serious consideration of Prince Charles's future status could no longer be delayed.

At the end of December 1764 the Pope summoned the cardinals to a meeting at the Quirinale to consider 'the ceremonial relations between the Cardinals and the Prince of Wales'. No decisions were reached at this point. Cardinal York argued the case in favour of recognising his brother. Some of the other cardinals, notably Alessandro Albani, were opposed.[161] The issue hung in the balance, and was still hanging when Prince Charles finally wrote to the Pope in October 1765 to say that he would return to Rome to ask for recognition as *de jure* monarch after the death of his father.[162]

During the hectic negotiations which followed, only one decision was taken. When James III eventually died he would not be buried as he had asked in the Church of Santi Apostoli. Pope Clement XIII was determined that he would be given a magnificent state funeral, with full royal honours as *de jure* King of England, Scotland, France and Ireland, and that he would be buried in the Basilica of St Peter's at the Vatican.

---

[157] ASV. SS: Ingh 25, p. 193, James III to Louis XV, 5 May 1763.

[158] James Dennistoun, *Memoirs of Sir Robert Strange ... and His Brother-in-Law Andrew Lumisden* (2 vols., London, 1855), vol. I, p. 218.

[159] Ingamells, *Dictionary*, p. 1034. The duke was in Italy from November 1763 to August 1764.

[160] BAV. Vat Lat 12432 ('Materie di Cerimoniale'), pp. 89–95.

[161] *Ibid.*, p. 11.   [162] McLynn, *Charles Edward Stuart*, p. 471.

12   James III, the Stuart princes and Roman society

When examining the Stuart court in Rome a clear distinction needs to be made between those courtiers who chose to join the entourage of the exiled royal family and those who were employed by it as salaried or pensioned servants. The most important members of the latter group have until now monopolised the attention of Jacobite historians and biographers, but it was with the former group that the Stuarts mixed and socialised. The nature of the court cannot be appreciated unless we begin by concentrating on the Italians, British and French who regularly attended James III and his family without having – or even wanting – an official post.

During the long period of thirty-seven years between the return of the court from Bologna in 1729 and the death of James III in 1766, the composition of this group obviously evolved. But so too did that of the royal family. These years can be divided into four phases.

From 1729 until 1738 the social life of the court mainly revolved around James III himself. Queen Clementina effectively withdrew into a life of good works and personal abstinence which culminated in her death in 1735, while Prince Charles and Prince Henry were still very young. The former, however, reached his thirteenth birthday at the end of 1733 and began slowly to enter society during the next few years.

It was not until Prince Henry also reached the age of thirteen, in March 1738, that the second phase began. The years from 1738 to 1745 were the heyday of the exiled court, when James III and his two popular sons made their greatest impact on Roman society, and provided regular entertainments for their friends and servants within the Palazzo del Re.

The phase came to an end when Prince Charles left Rome for France in 1744, followed by Prince Henry in 1745. James III, by then fifty-seven years old, retrenched the size of the court and restricted its entertainments, while awaiting the outcome of events in Scotland and England. The royal family was now represented in Rome by the king only.

The fourth and last phase began with the return of Prince Henry in 1747, and the latter's appointment to be a cardinal. In the years which followed, the king steadily withdrew from an active social life, while his younger son became increasingly involved with his ecclesiastical career. During the earlier years James III and his entourage had remained optimistic that the longed-for Stuart restoration would eventually take place. This last phase was influenced by the knowledge that no such restoration was possible, while James's mounting depression and deteriorating health reduced his contact with the people who were not his servants and advisers.

1729–1738

From the early 1720s until the 1750s the social life of James III and his family was recorded in the series of weekly letters which Baron von Stosch sent to one of the secretaries of state in London. The letters, which Stosch described as a 'kind of precise Journal' of the king's life,[1] are particularly useful for the period after the Stuart court returned from Bologna. They provide information about the king's daily routine, and about the people who visited the Palazzo del Re. They also tell us where the king went and whom he met. In particular they allow us to distinguish between those people in Rome who were effectively members of the Stuart court and those with whom James III and his family were merely on friendly terms.[2]

James's closest friend during the early 1730s remained the principessa di Piombino, who was frequently at the Palazzo del Re, and who joined the king in his box at the opera during the carnival seasons. When she died at the end of December 1733 she was assisted throughout her final illness by Queen Clementina. In her will she left all her plate to the king, valued at 66,000 *scudi*.[3]

James was also on particularly good terms with five of her daughters, principessa Giustiniani, principessa Barberini di Palestrina, the duchessa di Fiano, duchessa Salviati and the principessa di Santobuono. These five and their husbands regularly visited the Stuart court and socialised with the king. The duchessa Salviati was described on more than one

---

[1] NA. SP 98/32/f. 325, Stosch to Newcastle, 19 January 1732.

[2] Except where shown, all the information in this chapter has been taken from Stosch's weekly letters. The references are NA. SP 85/16 (1728–9), and NA. SP 98/32 (1730–4), 37 (1734–6), 38 (1735), 41 (1737–9), 43 (1740–1), 46 (1742–3), 49 (1744–6), 53 (1747–50), 58 (1751–2), and 61 (1753–7). Until February 1748 they were addressed to the Duke of Newcastle, thereafter to the Duke of Bedford until June 1751, then the Earl of Holderness until March 1754, then Sir Thomas Robinson until November 1754, then Henry Fox until December 1756 and finally William Pitt. To avoid unnecessary repetition, the reference of each letter will again be restricted to the folio number in the relevant volume.

[3] Stosch, 9 January 1734 (f. 20).

occasion as 'his favourite lady',[4] and principe Giustiniani as his closest friend among the Roman princes,[5] but all five couples are constantly mentioned in the letters.

The king was in regular contact with conte and contessa Bolognetti,[6] who had come from Bologna, and with duca and duchessa Strozzi; the duchessa became Queen Clementina's closest friend.[7] Two other people who could be fairly described as virtual members of the court were principe and principessa Borghese, who began to invite Prince Charles to go hunting on their estate at Mentana in 1736. James himself went hunting on the estates of principe Rospigliosi at Zagarolo and Macarese.[8]

Among the cardinals resident in Rome James was on particularly good terms with Cornelio Bentivoglio (who died in January 1733), Alamanno Salviati (who died in February 1733), Alessandro Falconieri (who died in January 1734, leaving the Stuarts 7000 *scudi* in his will),[9] Troiano Aquaviva and Gianantonio Davia, the Protector of England. But it was Domenico Riviera with whom he was closest. By the 1730s the king no longer employed a secretary of state, preferring instead to have a private secretary to deal with his correspondence and a series of ministers to give him advice. Cardinal Riviera was described as the 'Chief Minister' at the Stuart court by the end of 1736.[10]

According to Stosch, writing in 1731, all the cardinals resident in Rome were pro-Jacobite except the Imperial ambassador (Juan Alvaro Cienfuegos) and Alessandro Albani,[11] and virtually all of them could be relied on to visit the Palazzo del Re on fête days.[12] But so long as the Emperor Charles VI was the ruler of Naples and Sicily the Roman families with Neapolitan and Sicilian estates had to be cautious in their relations with King James. This changed in 1734 when Charles de Bourbon, Duke of Parma (son of Philip V of Spain and his second wife, Elisabeth Farnese), conquered Naples and established himself there as the King of the Two Sicilies. All the Roman nobles with Neapolitan and Sicilian estates were then obliged to pay homage to him as their new king, and Stosch recorded that 'since for the same reason they are

---

[4] Stosch, 21 January 1736 (f. 311); 29 December 1738 (f. 240).
[5] Stosch, 24 March 1736 (f. 329).
[6] They had inherited the Villa Alamandini in 1729.
[7] Stosch, 22 January 1735 (f. 98).
[8] Stosch, 4 May 1730 (f. 61); 7 and 14 May 1735 (f. 230, f. 172); 5 May 1736 (f. 353); 3 May 1739 (f. 294). The payments for James III's hunting at Macarese are recorded in ASV. Rospigliosi, vols. 262–5 (I am grateful to Michael Erwee for this reference).
[9] Stosch, 6 February and 17 April 1734 (f. 3, f. 63).
[10] Stosch, 26 January 1737 (f. 8).   [11] Stosch, 5 May 1731 (f. 187).
[12] Stosch, 18 April 1733 (f. 518).

obliged to treat [James III] in the same way, there is not a single important household in Rome that is not obliged to pay him court'.[13]

This particularly applied to the Colonna family, who were the king's neighbours in the Piazza dei Santi Apostoli. Principe Colonna was the Constable of the Kingdom of Naples, and it was therefore outside his palazzo that the *Festa della Chinea* continued to be held each summer from 1729 to 1733.[14] But although he and James were cousins and had enjoyed good relations during the 1720s, the Colonnas are never mentioned in Stosch's weekly letters during the same period. This changed after the Bourbon conquest of Naples and Sicily. The various members of the Colonna family then openly showed their support for James III and became regular visitors to the Palazzo del Re.[15]

Although it would clearly be an exaggeration to claim that someone was a member of the Stuart court simply because he or she socialised with James III, the people mentioned so far were in such regular contact with the king that they might fairly be regarded as part of his entourage. It must be remembered, however, that Rome also contained the papal court at the Quirinale. James met very regularly many people not mentioned here, including the nephews and nieces of Pope Clement XII, notably Cardinal Neri Corsini and Cardinal Giovanni Antonio Guadagni, and with Cardinal Pietro Ottoboni (the *vice-cancelliere* of the Church), none of whom can be regarded as part of his entourage at the exiled court. Sir Thomas Dereham acted as an unofficial ambassador from King James to the papal court. According to Stosch, he gave himself 'the airs of a Minister' and regarded himself as 'protector of the British nation'.[16]

In addition to Dereham, there were four of James III's own subjects, one English, one Scottish and two Irish, who attached themselves to him in the early 1730s. They were Charles Radcliffe, who succeeded as 5th Earl of Derwentwater in 1732, Lord Bourke, Lord William Drummond and a Jesuit priest named Leigh. All of them became permanent members of the court during the early 1730s.

Charles Radcliffe was a cousin of the king through his mother, who was married to the 2nd Earl of Derwentwater and was an illegitimate

---

[13] Stosch, 8 December 1736 (f. 426).
[14] Fagiolo, *Corpus delle feste*, pp. 72, 79, 83, 85, 88.
[15] From 1734 to 1737 principe Colonna ceased to be the Constable of Naples, so the *Festa della Chinea* was no longer held in front of James III's gallery. When Colonna was reappointed to the post he organised the *festa* in front of the Palazzo Farnese, which King Charles of the Two Sicilies had inherited from his mother (Fagiolo, *Corpus delle feste*, pp. 91, 105).
[16] Stosch, 28 November 1733 (f. 594); 27 November 1734 (f. 182).

daughter of Charles II. His two elder brothers, James and Francis (who died in 1715), lived for several years at the court of Saint-Germain, and his uncle William was a wealthy merchant with an apartment in the Palazzo Pamphili at the south-west end of the Piazza Navona.

Charles's brother James Radcliffe succeeded as 3rd Earl of Derwentwater in 1705, and had been attainted and executed in February 1716 for his part in the Jacobite rising of that year, leaving a two-year-old son (John, 4th Earl). Charles himself was also sentenced to be executed, but escaped abroad, and was probably with James III when the court was at Urbino.[17] In 1724 he married Charlotte Maria (née Livingstone), the widow of Thomas Clifford, and in her own right the Countess of Newburgh. In 1727, when the Stuart court was at Bologna, Radcliffe and his wife joined his uncle William in Rome, bringing with them Lady Newburgh's two daughters by her first marriage and their own baby son. By the time the court returned from Bologna they had one more son and two more daughters.[18]

The Radcliffes, because of their noble status, the family's sacrifice in the Jacobite rising and Charles's own connection with the Stuarts, became the leading family at the exiled court. They lived in the Piazza Navona, had independent financial means, and held their own *conversazioni* (described as 'brilliant')[19] in the Palazzo Pamphili, but they were very regularly at the Palazzo del Re and permanent members of the king's entourage, with a box beside his in the Teatro Aliberti.[20] Moreover, Lady Newburgh's daughters by her first marriage, Anne and Frances Clifford (the former described as 'very beautiful'),[21] were about twenty years old and an important addition to the social life of the court. Early in 1732 the news reached Rome that Radcliffe's young nephew John had died in England, which meant that Charles Radcliffe himself became the 5th Earl of Derwentwater. Later that year his uncle William died, leaving him all his money and property, valued at 200,000 *scudi*.[22]

Lord and Lady Derwentwater and their growing family (by 1734 they had seven children of their own), left the Palazzo Pamphili in 1735 and rented a palazzo near Trajan's column, in order to be closer to the Palazzo del Re.[23] The following year, however (and for reasons to be explained later), they left Rome and went to live in Paris.

[17] Corp, *Jacobites at Urbino*, pp. 47, 155.   [18] Ingamells, *Dictionary*, pp. 793–4.
[19] Stosch, 24 February 1731 (f. 159).   [20] Stosch, 19 January 1732 (f. 325).
[21] Stosch, 22 June 1730 (f. 78).
[22] Stosch, 12 September 1733 (f. 568); Ingamells, *Dictionary*, p. 794.
[23] Stosch, 21 May 1735 (f. 176).

Toby Bourke, described by Mary of Modena as an 'Irish gentleman of merit and good family',[24] was knighted by James III at Saint-Germain in 1705. His career does not need to be resumed here.[25] The key point is that he obtained the favour of the princesse des Ursins when she was all-powerful in Spain, and served as James III's ambassador to the court of Madrid from 1705 to 1713. He then continued to live there with his French wife and daughter Marianne until 1719, when a ship in which they were sailing in the Mediterranean was wrecked. He was saved, but his wife was drowned, and his daughter, then only eight years old, was captured by Algerian corsairs and taken to North Africa as a slave. Bourke ransomed her in 1726, and then took her to Italy to start a new life. After visiting Bologna, where James III gave him a peerage as Baron Bourke in February 1727,[26] he lived in Rome in a rented palazzo near the Trinità dei Monti.[27] When James returned to Rome in 1729, Bourke and his daughter, by then nearly eighteen years old, were said to 'be very frequent visitors' to the Palazzo del Re.[28] Marianne Bourke soon entered the convent of the Visitation nuns in Rome, while Bourke himself became one of the king's chief ministers, going to the Stuart court with great regularity, sometimes twice a day.[29] In the years which followed, Bourke, like Derwentwater, was in constant attendance on the king, until he eventually decided to return to Madrid in 1737.[30]

Lord William Drummond, a priest, was a younger son of the 1st Duke of Melfort. He lived in Rome from 1718 to 1727, during which time he was ordained and appointed Archpriest of the Basilica di Sant' Eustachio (east of the Piazza Navona). He returned to Rome at the beginning of 1732 to pursue a lawsuit concerning a priory that he held at Nantes. The case lasted for a year and a half, and during that period he was very regularly at the Stuart court, where he was known as the abbé Melfort.[31]

Leigh, whose Christian name is not mentioned by Stosch, was the son of an Irish merchant at Cadiz and had become a Jesuit.[32] He lived in

---

[24] Ruvigny, *Jacobite Peerage*, p. 20.
[25] See Micheline Kerney Walsh, 'Toby Bourke, Ambassador of James III at the Court of Philip V', in Cruickshanks and Corp (eds.), *Stuart Court in Exile*, pp. 143–53.
[26] Ruvigny, *Jacobite Peerage*, p. 20.
[27] Stosch, 2 and 16 December 1728 (f. 475, f. 480).
[28] Stosch, 17 February 1729 (f. 502).
[29] Stosch, 28 April and 28 July 1731 (f. 185, f. 233).
[30] Stosch, 4 and 18 May 1737 (f. 38, f. 45).
[31] RA. SP 104/141, Ellis to Inverness, 12 March 1727; RA. SP 114/4, Drummond to James III, recd 5 February 1728; RA. SP 151/9, James III to Duchess of Melfort, 9 January 1732; Stosch, 5 January and 2 February 1732 (f. 319, f. 335); RA. SP 225/31, Drummond to James III, 17 July 1740.
[32] Stosch, 23 January 1734 (f. 27); 6 August 1735 (f. 259); Ingamells, *Dictionary*, p. 592.

Rome from the beginning of 1734 (possibly earlier) until about 1738, though his arrival and departure were not recorded. In fact, very little is known about Leigh, but for four and a half years he was a constant member of the king's entourage, along with Derwentwater, Bourke and (for a shorter period) Drummond.

The Stuart court in Rome was much more than its salaried servants. It was these men, and the Italian aristocrats and cardinals already mentioned, who gave the court its quality. It must be emphasised, however, that it was the French, with whom he had been brought up, that were particularly favoured by James III. Whatever might have been thought or desired at Versailles, the successive French ambassadors to the papal court behaved as though they had also been sent as ambassadors to the exiled court of the Stuarts.

When James returned from Bologna, Cardinal de Polignac was still the French diplomatic representative in Rome. According to Stosch, writing in March 1729, Polignac preferred to support the king rather than carry out the orders he received from Versailles.[33] He was described as the 'intimate friend' of James III,[34] and in a letter of September 1731 Stosch reported that Polignac 'protected the interests [of James III] in every way he could during his stay in Rome'.[35]

Polignac was replaced in March 1732 by Paul-Hyppolite de Beauvilliers, the duc de Saint-Aignan, whom James III had known very well at the French court. Saint-Aignan was three and a half years older than James, but his elder half-brother, the duc de Beauvilliers, had been governor to James's cousins, the three grandsons of Louis XIV. His half-sister had married the marquis de Livry, *premier maître d'hôtel* (lord steward) at the French court, whose house (the Château du Rancy) James occupied when he left Saint-Germain in 1712.[36] Having served as *premier gentilhomme de la chambre* to the duc de Berri, Saint-Aignan was French ambassador to Berri's elder brother Philip V at Madrid from 1715 to 1718.

While he was in Madrid, Saint-Aignan had become friendly with Lord (then Sir Toby) Bourke, whom he now asked to select for him a palazzo in Rome to be the new French embassy. Bourke chose the Palazzo Bonelli because it was in the Piazza dei Santi Apostoli, immediately opposite the Palazzo del Re.[37] The Governor of Rome asked Bourke and Saint-Aignan to select a different residence, because the *sbirri*

---

[33] Stosch, 11 and 17 March 1729 (f. 510, f. 513).
[34] Stosch, 8 February 1731 (f. 156).   [35] Stosch, 1 September 1731 (f. 247).
[36] Corp, *A Court in Exile*, p. 282.   [37] Stosch, 1 September 1731 (f. 247).

(the papal police) patrolled the piazza at night, and no *sbirri* were allowed to pass in front of an embassy, but they refused to do so.[38]

Immediately after his arrival in March 1732 Saint-Aignan and his wife went to see James III and Queen Clementina.[39] In July Stosch reported that James III and Saint-Aignan were seeing each other very frequently, and that the French embassy was now 'always ... full of Jacobites', and that the ambassador was 'following each and every bit of advice' from Lord Bourke.[40] At the beginning of 1733 Saint-Aignan gave a great ball in the French embassy to celebrate Prince Charles's twelfth birthday.[41]

During 1733 James and Saint-Aignan continued to see each other almost every day, in the Palazzo del Re, the Palazzo Bonelli or the French Academy on the Corso. As Stosch put it in August, 'the Duc de Saint-Aignan talked with him in private for a long time, as he does everywhere'.[42] The following month he referred to 'the caresses and submissions which the Ambassador of France to Rome makes to him in public'.[43] The practical effect was that the French ambassador was accredited to the court of James III as much as he was to the court of the Quirinale.

Saint-Aignan maintained regular contact with Bourke, but he also established good relations with Lord Derwentwater and his family. In September 1733, for example, he went with his wife and children to see the Derwentwaters in the Palazzo Pamphili: 'This visit was made with a lot of show and affectation.'[44] When Derwentwater returned the visit he travelled in one of the king's coaches to emphasise his connection with the court.[45] Indeed, these cordial relations were very important for the reputation of the Stuart court because, as Stosch put it, they convinced the people in Rome that two-thirds of the people of England were pro-Jacobite.[46]

In October 1734 the duchesse de Saint-Aignan died, and her funeral was attended by both James and Clementina[47] – probably the queen's last public appearance before her own death two and a half months later. The deaths of their wives perhaps drew the two men even closer together. At any rate, during 1736, 1737 and 1738 they continued to see each other with great regularity, as did their children.

The Palazzo del Re welcomed any French people who visited Rome, such as the sons of the duc de Noailles and the duc d'Harcourt in

---

[38] Stosch, 8 December 1731 (f. 309).
[39] Stosch, 29 March and 5 April 1732 (f. 357, f. 359).
[40] Stosch, 19 July 1732 (f. 414).   [41] Stosch, 10 January 1733 (f. 475).
[42] Stosch, 29 August 1733 (f. 564).   [43] Stosch, 19 September 1733 (f. 570).
[44] Stosch, 10 October 1733 (f. 579).   [45] Stosch, 7 November 1733 (f. 586).
[46] Stosch, 16 January 1734 (f. 22).   [47] Stosch, 30 October 1734 (f. 174).

1736,[48] or Jean Philippe d'Orléans, the *grand prieur de France*, an illegitimate son of the Regent, in August 1734. Stosch recorded that on the latter occasion James gave a magnificent dinner for the *grand prieur* and all the French people who were in Rome at the time.[49]

One Frenchman who was constantly with the king was Bishop François Foucquet, the former Jesuit whom James had met during the early 1720s. Foucquet had been a missionary in China for over twenty-two years, spoke fluent Mandarin and taught the language to King James. A passing reference in one of Stosch's letters tells us that 'during the evening he [the King] passed the time speaking Chinese with the Prelate Fouquet [sic]'.[50]

Between 1729 and 1738 it was with these people that James III mainly mixed, when not dealing with the papal court at the Quirinale. On a typical day he would attend morning mass in the Church of Santi Apostoli or the Church of San Marcello, either side of the Palazzo del Re, perhaps preceded by mass in the Chapel Royal. He would then dine in his apartment with a group of friends, such as Bourke, Drummond, Giustiniani, Foucquet, Derwentwater, Saint-Aignan, Strozzi, Bolognetti, Leigh, Riviera, Salviati, Borghese or Colonna, with or without their wives.[51] In the afternoon he would walk or ride with his friends, most often at the Villa Borghese or the Villa Ludovisi (the home of the principessa di Piombino), but also at the Villa Patrizi (the home of Cardinal Riviera), the Villa Bolognetti or the Villa Montalto Negroni. He also liked to walk outside the walls, from the Porta Pia to the Porta del Popolo, or from the Porta del Popolo to the Ponte Molle. A favourite walk was up the Corso to the Porto del Popolo, and back home via the Piazza di Spagna, or the other way about. The rest of the day was, of course, devoted to his correspondence.

Occasionally the king would attend an important religious ceremony or some other significant occasion. During this period one such took place in September 1737, when Girolamo Vaini, principe di Cantalupe, was invested as a *chevalier de l'Ordre du Saint-Esprit* by the duc de Saint-Aignan in the Church of San Luigi dei Francesi. The prince's family came from Urbino and his father had been given both the Saint-Esprit and his princely title in 1696 on the recommendation of Mary of Modena, because he was pro-French at a time when most of the Italian nobles

---

[48] Stosch, 7 January, 18 February and 21 April 1736 (f. 307, f. 319, f. 345).
[49] Stosch, 4 September 1734 (f. 154).   [50] Stosch, 9 February 1739 (f. 262).
[51] RA. SP Misc 31 contains the details of all the menus for the king's 'diners' and 'soupers' during 1732–3. For the king's wine from the Côte Rôtie, see RA. SP 130/184 and 131/109; from Burgundy, see RA. SP 150/71, 111; and from elsewhere in France, probably Champagne, see RA. SP 151/77.

were pro-Austrian.[52] The ceremony of investiture was recorded in a painting by Pierre Subleyras, which shows James III and his sons observing the proceedings from a tribune to the right of the high altar.[53]

The most spectacular of the ceremonies remained the flooding of the Piazza Navona every August, when the successive Spanish ambassadors had a magnificent balcony, with a royal throne for James III, erected outside the Spanish church so that he and their other guests could watch the parade around the piazza. As the Spanish church was directly opposite Lord Derwentwater's apartment in the Palazzo Pamphili, where a similar balcony was decorated, the Stuarts and their courtiers could watch it from either side. It was noted that James III was generally accompanied by the duc de Saint-Aignan as well as by the Spanish ambassador, who from 1735 was his friend Cardinal Troiano Aquaviva.[54]

In the evenings James III frequently attended *conversazioni* and balls hosted by the princely families of Rome, especially during the carnival season. During the period from 1729 to 1738, however, he gave relatively little reciprocal hospitality within the Palazzo del Re. In January 1733, when the duc de Saint-Aignan and conte Bolognetti gave spectacular balls in their palazzi to celebrate Prince Charles's birthday,[55] James planned to give 'a great concert of music', but for some reason it was cancelled,[56] possibly because of the recent death of Innocenzo Fede, his master of the music.[57] Instead James invited all his friends to a performance of a new opera by Porpora (*Issipile*) at the Teatro Pioli (within the Palazzo Ruspoli on the Corso). As Stosch put it, 'he offered magnificent refreshments to a large number of Roman ladies and to all the Pope's relations at the Teatro Pioli, having hired at his own expense the whole upper gallery of the Stalls'.[58]

It was not until December 1736, when Prince Charles had his sixteenth birthday, that James began tentatively to offer evening entertainments in the Palazzo del Re. Stosch noted that on the 2nd 'in the

[52] Luynes, *Mémoires sur la cour de Louis XV*, vol. I, p. 15, 1 January 1737, note by the abbé de Pomponne.
[53] Fagiolo, *Corpus delle feste*, p. 99; Stosch, 30 September 1737 (f. 91). The painting is in the Musée des Beaux Arts de Caen.
[54] Stosch's letters every August and September, 1729–36 and 1738.
[55] Stosch, 17 January 1733 (f. 477).   [56] Stosch, 31 January 1733 (f. 482).
[57] RA. SP 158/41/16, certificate of Ippolito Desideri, SJ, recording the death of his cousin on Christmas Day, 29 December 1732.
[58] Stosch, 21 February 1733 (f. 488). See also Valesio, *Diario di Roma*, v, p. 566, 11 February 1733: 'Questa sera, essendo andato il re d'Inghilterra ad udire il dramma nel teatro Pioli, avendo ivi cenato, fece distribuire magnifici rinfreschi e quelli che erano nella platea, nelle quale vi era molta nobiltà.'

evening there was music in his appartment, attended only by his sons and his servants, and no foreigners other than Birx [Bourke], and the Prelate Ley [Leigh]'.[59] Two evenings later 'another cantata was sung in his palace, attended by the same Birx and Ley'.[60] On 5 February 1737 'in the evening he gave a Concert of Music, with only the Duke of Saint-Aignan's sons, the Prelate Ley, and other close friends present'.[61]

1738–1745

During the carnival season of 1738, shortly before Prince Henry celebrated his thirteenth birthday, James III decided that the time had come for the Stuart court to provide regular musical entertainments for Roman society. On 26 December 1737 he gave 'a grand concert of vocal and instrumental music', and announced that similar concerts would be given in the Palazzo del Re twice a week, on Mondays and Thursdays.[62] Stosch noted that the people invited on 2 January 1738 included the sons of the duc de Saint-Aignan and conte Bolognetti.[63]

These concerts were continued during the subsequent carnival seasons, sometimes once, sometimes twice a week, until the princes left for France in 1744 and 1745.[64] Charles de Brosses, who was in Rome between October 1739 and April 1740, stated that the concerts provided 'the best music in Rome' and that he himself never failed to attend them. The vocal music included cantatas and arias from recent operas. The instrumental music included sonatas and concerti.[65]

---

[59] Stosch, 15 December 1736 (f. 328).
[60] *Ibid.*   [61] Stosch, 16 February 1737 (f. 16).
[62] Stosch, 6 January 1738 (f. 125).   [63] Stosch, 13 January 1738 (f. 129).
[64] Stosch, 4 May 1743 (f. 198); 11 January and 29 December 1744 (f. 18, f. 139); 5 January and 16 March 1745 (f. 139, f. 159).
[65] Brosses, *Lettres d'Italie*, vol. II, p. 81. Brosses recorded the following incident in the same letter: 'Hier j'entrai pendant qu'on exécutait le fameux concerto de Corelli appelé Le Notte di Natale [opus VI, no. 8]; je témoignai d'avoir du regret de n'être pas arrivé plus tôt pour l'entendre en entier. Lorsqu'il fut fini et qu'on voulut passer à autre chose, le prince de Galles dit: "Non, attendez, recommençons ce concerto; je viens d'ouïr dire à M. de Brosses qu'il serait aise de l'entendre tout entier."' In another letter Brosses wrote that Metastasio's libretto of *Artaserse* 'est le plus fameux opéra italien' and explained that, having already heard the setting of the opera by Hasse, he was very keen to hear how one of its arias, 'Palido il sole', had been set to music by Vinci. However he found that Vinci's aria was no longer available in Rome ('ce morceau ne se trouve pas facilement'), where it had not been performed since 1731. When Prince Charles heard about this he had 'la bonté de me le donner', which implies that the music was part of the collection in the Palazzo del Re (*Lettres d'Italie*, vol. II, p. 314). Prince Charles later owned ninety cantatas in manuscript composed by Alessandro Scarlatti, some of them presumably inherited from his father. The prince's score of Feo, *Andromaca* (Valle, 1730) is in BL. Add MSS 243031 (Jane Clark, 'The Stuart Presence at the Opera in Rome', pp. 85–94 in Corp (ed.), *The Stuart Court in Rome*, at p. 91).

Prince Charles and Prince Henry were themselves both keen amateur musicians. According to Brosses, 'the young princes both have a passion for music, and are very knowledgeable about it; the elder boy plays the cello very well; the younger one sings Italian arias in a lovely little child's voice in the best of taste'.[66] Prince Charles was in fact less keen on music than his younger brother. In December 1741 it was observed that the former 'takes great delight in riding, hunting and other exercises; and the other, besides these, loves music ... and sings ... very well'.[67] A few weeks later James Edgar wrote that Prince Charles 'prefers the exercise and diversion of shooting', but nevertheless 'loves and understands music very well'.[68] As the years went by both princes became more accomplished. The duc de Luynes, who met them in France, testified that 'both princes are musicians. Prince [Charles] plays the harpsichord and the 'cello; the Duke of York loves music even more than his brother; he accompanied on the harpsichord ... really quite well .... He loves music passionately.'[69]

The Stuart court also provided concerts when it was at Albano. In the autumn of 1742 the princes themselves organised concerts in the Palazzo Apostolico 'almost every evening of the week', having brought there 'the principal musicians from Rome'. The concerts were attended by 'the chief members of the nobility of both sexes, and the courtier Prelates of the Pope'.[70]

In January 1739, one year after inaugurating the regular Stuart concerts, James III started to invite his friends to balls in the Palazzo del Re. On the 12th he gave 'a private ball in his palace for several ladies of his acquaintance', including 'the Corsini Princesses', principessa Santobuono, duchessa Salviati and contessa Bolognetti.[71] One week later he gave another, and the guests included the sons of the duc de Saint-Aignan, duchessa Salviati, contessa Bolognetti and the principe and principessa Santobuono.[72]

No further balls are mentioned during the carnival season of 1739, though they probably took place, but in 1740 Brosses recorded that the king arranged 'some public receptions for his young sons from time to time, inviting the ladies, and at which he appeared for an hour'. 'I have never seen a prince,' he added, 'entertaining a large circle of people with

[66] Brosses, *Lettres d'Italie*, vol. II, p. 81.
[67] Russel, *Letters from a Young Painter*, vol. I, p. 77, 2 December 1741.
[68] McLynn, *Charles Edward Stuart*, pp. 567–8, quoting RA. SP 239/71.
[69] Luynes, *Mémoires sur la cour de Louis XV*, vol. VII, pp. 461–2, 23 October 1746.
[70] Stosch, 20 October and 3 November 1742 (f. 116, f. 120).
[71] Stosch, 26 January 1739 (f. 248).   [72] Stosch, 2 February 1739 (f. 250).

so much grace and nobility'.[73] The balls continued in the following years. In both 1741 and 1742 they took place every Thursday throughout the carnival season, and Stosch described one of them as 'a grand ball' for 'the principal nobility of Rome'.[74] In 1745, after his brother had left, Prince Henry gave four balls during the carnival season 'with great splendour', at least one of which was followed by 'a grand supper'.[75]

The princes were, of course, invited to the concerts and balls held elsewhere. In January 1741 Prince Charles appeared at a 'public ball at the palazzo Pamphili in the Piazza Navona' wearing Scottish Highland dress: 'wearing the uniform of an officer of the Scottish Highlanders with a multi-coloured checked costume decorated with embroidery and different coloured jewels'.[76] In February of the following year he wore his Highland dress again at a 'public ball' in the Palazzo Bonelli, at which he had the first dance with the Countess of Strathmore, who was visiting Rome at the time.[77]

Prince Charles was able to develop his passion for hunting and shooting thanks to three of the king's friends among the Roman noble families, principe Borghese, the duca di Caserta and the principe Barberini di Palestrina. Borghese began by inviting Charles to hunt on his estate at Mentana (north of Rome) in December 1736, Caserta invited him for the first time to hunt at Cisterna (south-east of Rome) in December 1737, and Palestrina invited him to Palo (beside the sea) in May 1738. Thereafter Prince Charles, sometimes accompanied by Prince Henry, went hunting at Mentana, Cisterna and Palo every year until his departure for France in 1744.[78]

Although there was hunting in the woods around Albano, particularly at Nemi, James III never accompanied his sons to Mentana, Cisterna or Palo. This was partly because he hunted at Macarese as a guest of principe Rospigliosi, partly also because he preferred riding and walking. When he was at Albano he often attended mass in the Church of Santa Maria della Stella, but he liked to ride out to the Church of Santa Maria di Galero, south-east of Albano (between Ariccia and Genzano), or to go in his carriage to the Church of Santa Maria delle Grazie at Marino,

[73] Brosses, *Lettres d'Italie*, vol. II, p. 77.
[74] Stosch, 4 February 1741 (f. 130); 10 and 17 February 1742 (f. 12, f. 14).
[75] Stosch, 2 and 9 March 1745 (f. 147, f. 149).
[76] Stosch, 18 February 1741 (f. 136). See 23 February, 2 March and 16 August 1739 (f. 271, f. 273, f. 334).
[77] Stosch, 17 February 1742 (f. 14).
[78] Lord Elcho, who accompanied Prince Charles to Cisterna in January 1741, has left a description of the three days they spent there. See Alice Wemyss, *Elcho of the '45* (Edinburgh, 2003), p. 27.

north-west of Lake Albano, where his Colonna cousins had their summer palazzo. Going to Marino involved travelling along a track with overarching trees called La Galleria to Castel Gandolfo, and then around a large part of the spectacular lake. Once he was at Marino he could either go on to visit friends having their *villeggiatura* at Frascati, or return to see the Pope and anyone staying at the Villa Barberini or the Villa Cybo at Castel Gandolfo. The king then liked to get out of his carriage and return at least part of the way to Albano on foot, walking along La Galleria.

In Rome James's life had settled into a more regular pattern by the end of the 1730s. James Russel, who arrived in the city in January 1740, wrote that 'in his conversation' the king was 'good-natured, affable, and chearful':

He passes all his time in a very regular manner: rising early, he spends the morning in business, hears mass at a set hour, and dines at twelve. He often walks in the fine gardens at Rome, especially those of the Villa Borghese: in the evening he receives visits, sups at ten, and goes to bed about mid-night.[79]

Lord Elcho, who arrived in October 1740, wrote that the king 'went every day to mass' in the Church of Santi Apostoli, where a gallery was 'especially constructed' for his use 'during the great religious festivals, and where the French ambassador was always in attendance':

It was on his leaving the church that people paid him homage. After dinner he would make his devotions at the church of the Porta del Popolo, leaving it in a carriage[80] from which he would alight to take an hour's-long walk. In the winter he would go every evening to the Opera where ... the French ambassador never failed to pay him a visit.[81]

Charles de Brosses, who was in Rome during the winter of 1739–40, recorded more detailed information about the king's dining arrangements:

His table ... is always elegantly set with eleven places, for the ten people who normally eat with him. When Roman or foreign gentlemen come to pay court, he usually gets one of his officers to ask them to stay; however many stay, the same number of people from his own household go and dine at another table. I have never been there without being invited to stay.[82]

---

[79] Russel, *Letters from a Young Painter*, vol. I, p. 76.

[80] In 1738 James III commissioned 'un des plus magnifiques Carosses qui a eté jamais fait a Rome', to be given as a present to the Duke of Berwick. The latter died before it could be delivered, so the king perhaps kept it for himself (Stosch, 17 March and 16 June 1738 (f. 148, f. 182)).

[81] Wemyss, *Elcho*, pp. 26–8.   [82] Brosses, *Lettres d'Italie*, vol. II, pp. 77–8.

In another letter Brosses recorded that one of his fellow guests was principe Giustiniani, to whom James III paid particular attention.[83]

According to Brosses, 'his table is served with good honest food, with nothing luxurious', for these daily dinners.[84] Special guests, however, were given special treatment. In April 1740 Rome was visited by the prince de Craon, his wife and family. Craon was the chief minister of the Grand Duke of Tuscany and went out of his way to pay court to James III because, as Stosch wrote, he was obliged to James 'for having by his intercession obtained for him the rank of Grandee of Spain from King Philip V'. Craon and all his family became regular visitors to the Palazzo del Re to show their gratitude, and the king treated them as personal friends because he had stayed with them at Lunéville in 1713–15.[85] Stosch noted that 'the Prince de Craon ... continues to frequent his palace very assiduously',[86] and that James 'gave a superb dinner for the Prince and Princess de Craon, and their sons the Primate of Lorraine, and the Prince de Beauvau'.[87]

During the period 1738–45 James III's entourage remained approximately the same as in previous years. Some of his old friends died (Sir Thomas Dereham in 1739, Cardinal Davia in 1740, François Foucquet in 1741), but he remained in regular contact with Cardinal Riviera, Cardinal Aquaviva, the daughters and sons-in-law of the principessa di Piombino, the Bolognettis, the Strozzis, the Colonnas and the Borgheses. He was also on very good terms with the Corsini family, who moved from the Piazza Navona to the Palazzo Riario (renamed the Palazzo Corsini) in 1738.[88] In January 1740 Baron von Stosch sent to London a list of all the people who had visited the Palazzo del Re that New Year's Day.[89] It included thirty-two cardinals, all the people mentioned above, and a few new names, including abbate Vinciguerra (who became a particular friend of Prince Charles),[90] principessa Carbognano (married to one of the Colonnas), baronessa Cenci (a friend of Cardinal Corsini) and baronessa Testa Piccolomini.

The Testa Piccolomini family owned a villa at Frascati which was rented by successive French ambassadors for their *villeggiature*.[91]

---

[83] *Ibid.*, p. 105.
[84] James continued to serve Burgundy wines. See RA. SP 202/6 for 1737; and RA. SP 212/ 212 for 1739.
[85] Stosch, 24 April 1740 (f. 35).   [86] Stosch, 8 May 1740 (f. 39).
[87] Stosch, 29 May 1740 (f. 45).
[88] Stosch, 5 May and 15 September 1738 (f. 162, f. 210).
[89] Stosch, 10 January 1740 (f. 4).
[90] *Benoît XIV*, I, p. 226, Benedict XIV to Tencin, 24 November 1745.
[91] *Benoît XIV*, II, p. 471, Benedict XIV to Tencin, 14 January 1756.

In January 1745, when Baronessa Piccolomini gave birth to a son, the king agreed that the child might be baptised in the Chapel Royal of the Palazzo del Re, with Prince Henry as godfather. The service was conducted by Archbishop (later Cardinal) Ferdinando Maria de Rossi, the *vice-regente* of Rome, who soon afterwards became one of James III's closest friends.[92]

Now that Derwentwater, Bourke and Leigh had all left Rome, there were no longer any of James III's own subjects attached to his court, apart from his salaried servants and pensioners. However, the court had been joined by James FitzJames, the eighteen-year-old son and heir of the 2nd Duke of Berwick and Liria.

Berwick himself was not only a childhood friend, but also the eldest son of the king's half-brother. He had last visited the Stuart court when it had been at Bologna.[93] At the beginning of 1734 he was appointed to command the Spanish army sent to conquer Naples, and he stayed in the Palazzo del Re en route to take up his command.[94] Once the campaign was over he remained in Naples as the Spanish ambassador, and decided to send his eldest son to be educated in Rome under the protection of King James. The details were fixed during a visit which Berwick made to Albano in November 1736,[95] and the following February he returned to Rome with his son, who was placed in the Collegio Clementino.[96] Berwick then remained at the Palazzo del Re for nearly two months, before returning to his post at Naples in the second half of April.[97]

Berwick died in Naples at the beginning of June 1738, so his son James succeeded as the 3rd Duke. The latter then left the Collegio Clementino the following year and became permanently attached to the Stuart court for the next two and a half years. The duke dined with James III at the Palazzo del Re with great regularity, and did not return to Spain to look after his inheritance until July 1742.[98]

The king's closest friend at the end of the 1730s remained the duc de Saint-Aignan who, as Stosch put it in July 1739, 'continues his frequent conferences' with James 'more regularly than ever'.[99] In another letter a

---

[92] *Diario ordinario*, no. 4290, 23 January 1745, p. 3; Stosch, 2 February 1745 (f. 147).
[93] See Chapter 10, p. 186.
[94] Stosch, 20 and 27 March, and 3 April 1734 (f. 47, f. 51, f. 55).
[95] Stosch, 10 November 1736 (f. 418).
[96] Stosch, 9 and 16 March 1737 (f. 22, f. 24).
[97] Stosch, 27 April 1737 (f. 36). A few weeks later Berwick's half-brother, Lord Francis FitzJames, stayed with James III before and after visiting Naples: 27 May, 3 June and 5 August 1737 (f. 49, f. 53, f. 75). Two years later he was appointed Bishop of Soissons.
[98] Stosch, 28 July 1742 (f. 81).   [99] Stosch, 26 July 1739 (f. 326).

few weeks later he referred to the fact that the French embassy and the Palazzo del Re were at opposite ends of the Piazza dei Santi Apostoli:

> It is impossible to know exactly on which days and how frequently there are meetings between [James III] and the Ambassador of France, because without passing through the Antichambers he [Saint-Aignan] can come up the secret staircase right into his Cabinet by going through the palazzo Colonna, and the Convent of the Santi Apostoli, which is linked to it.[100]

During the summer of 1739 Archbishop de Tencin, who had been created a cardinal earlier that year on the nomination of James III, returned to Rome.[101] By then Pope Clement XII was not expected to live much longer, and the plan was that Tencin should replace Saint-Aignan as the French ambassador once the conclave had elected a new pope. Tencin went out of his way to show his support for the king, and became a very regular visitor to the Palazzo del Re. He stayed with James at Albano in October, and in the following month gave him 'a Public Dinner with full *Royal honours*'.[102] Stosch complained in December that 'almost every day of the year Cardinal de Tencin, either in public or in secret, has conferred with [King James] ... This goes too far, as if the Cardinal wanted all Rome to be forced to believe that the king his master [Louis XV] took the interests [of King James] very deeply to heart.'[103]

In February 1740 Pope Clement XII died and the king and his two sons went to St Peter's where, 'in a balcony especially prepared', they were able to watch his funeral service.[104] Then, during the conclave, James III had meetings every evening with Saint-Aignan, who transmitted his opinions to Cardinal de Tencin and Cardinal de Rohan (who had arrived from France).[105] Once the new pope had been elected, Saint-Aignan and Tencin continued 'always to give public marks of their attachment' to King James.[106] This continued until Saint-Aignan left Rome in the spring of 1741, followed by Tencin in the summer of 1742. Tencin's embassy came to an early end because he was recalled to join the *Conseil d'Etat* at Versailles.[107]

The open support of the French ambassadors, who behaved as though they were formally accredited to King James III, played a significant part in maintaining and even enhancing the standing of the Stuart court in Rome during these years. When Cardinal Fleury died in January 1743,

---

[100] Stosch, 9 August 1739 (f. 332).
[101] Castries, *Scandaleuse Madame de Tencin*, pp. 173–6.
[102] Stosch, 29 November 1739 (f. 364).   [103] Stosch, 13 December 1739 (f. 368).
[104] Stosch, 28 February 1740 (f. 18).   [105] Stosch, 13 and 20 August 1740 (f. 68, f. 70).
[106] Stosch, 17 September 1740 (f. 78).
[107] Castries, *Scandaleuse Madame de Tencin*, pp. 229, 232.

and England and France declared war, it was only natural that people in the papal city should feel increasing optimism about the prospects of a Stuart restoration. In fact, it was these men, Saint-Aignan and Tencin, rather than any of the king's own servants, who acted as his ministers. It is interesting to observe that Stosch once again referred to Cardinal Riviera as the king's 'Chief Minister' a few weeks after the departure of Tencin.[108]

The renewal of war between England and France, and the appointment of Tencin to the *Conseil d'Etat*, were not the only encouraging developments during the early 1740s. In February 1742 the news reached Rome that the Elector of Bavaria, whom James had known since they were both living in exile in France, had been elected to be the new Emperor Charles VII. To celebrate the event, James 'had his palace magnificently illuminated with great numbers of wax torches, and had bonfires lit in front of the door, to celebrate the Election of the new Bavarian Emperor who is his personal friend'.[109] The king repeated the spectacle for three consecutive nights in the autumn of 1744, when Louis XV recovered from a dangerous illness,[110] and again in June 1745 for two nights to celebrate the marriage of the Dauphin.[111] These years were undoubtedly the period when the court was at it most splendid.

1745–1747

In January 1744, just before Prince Charles left Rome, Baron von Stosch reported to London that the correspondent who provided him with a daily journal of the court's activities had died.[112] Although Stosch continued to obtain information from other sources, it was never so detailed, and his letters tell us less and less about James III's social life. We know about the king's meetings with his political advisers, but we lose track of his relations with the rest of his Roman entourage.

Yet we do have enough information to know that the short period from 1745 to 1747 represented an important turning point in the history of the Stuart court. The combined effect of worry, loneliness and disappointment seems at last to have broken James's spirit. He had for so long remained courageous and even optimistic in the face of much adversity,

---

[108] Stosch, 25 August 1742 (f. 92).
[109] Stosch, 10 March 1742 (f. 24). Ref. to his death, Stosch, 9 February 1745 (f. 149).
[110] Stosch, 6 October 1744 (f. 113).   [111] Stosch, 22 June 1745 (f. 187).
[112] Stosch, 18 and 25 January 1744 (f. 20, f. 22).

but now, in his late fifties, he could no longer cope with the strain. His health began to deteriorate and he became depressed.

The king's daily routine remained the same (morning mass, dinner with invited guests, afternoon walks), but he became increasingly withdrawn. The first indication was in May 1744, when Stosch recorded that 'he continues to remain very withdrawn in his palace'.[113] During the summer he remained 'so withdrawn',[114] and then in October he was overtaken by 'an extraordinary Melancoly'.[115] By January 1745 it was observed that he often felt faint, particularly when walking up stairs.[116] During the period 1745–7 these symptoms are referred to over and over again in Stosch's weekly letters. James began to excuse himself from attending important social functions,[117] and even began to talk of retiring to live at Assisi.[118]

The brief success of Prince Charles in Scotland naturally raised the king's hopes, but it also increased the strain on his nervous system. Then the news of the Battle of Culloden, the fear that Prince Charles might be captured, the relief when he returned safely to France, and the deep disappointment and irritation provoked by his unwise behaviour in Paris, combined to magnify James's mental decline. In October 1746 Stosch noted that the king 'is even more withdrawn and not really involved in conversation'[119] and that his 'melancoly . . . increases every day, and he speaks to almost no one'.[120]

James did what he could to put on a brave face. He organised a big reception in the Palazzo del Re each year to celebrate Prince Charles's birthday, and in August 1746 he appeared briefly to observe the flooding of the Piazza Navona.[121] But at the beginning of 1747 he received the news that his friend Lord Derwentwater had been captured and then executed in London. It was noted that, 'weighed down by misery', he had resolved to take no part in any of the 'entertainments of the carnival'.[122]

The impact on the Stuart court in Rome was of course considerable, because it ceased to be the major social centre that it had been in the previous years. Nevertheless James III did continue to welcome the most intimate members of his entourage. Duchessa Salviati, principessa Santobuono, duchessa Strozzi, principessa Borghese and their husbands are still occasionally mentioned in Stosch's weekly letters, though it is impossible to say how often James met them.[123]

---

[113] Stosch, 26 May 1744 (f. 73).   [114] Stosch, 1 September 1744 (f. 103).
[115] Stosch, 13 October 1744 (f. 115).   [116] Stosch, 5 January 1745 (f. 139).
[117] E.g. Stosch, 22 June 1745 (f. 187); 25 January 1746 (f. 259).
[118] Stosch, 14 September 1745 (f. 211).   [119] Stosch, 11 October 1746 (f. 337).
[120] Stosch, 25 October 1746 (f. 341).   [121] Stosch, 30 August 1746 (f. 325).
[122] Stosch, 14 February 1747 (f. 13).   [123] The Bolognettis are no longer mentioned.

What we do know is that during this period James created an informal council of Italian and French advisers, whom he saw regularly. The Italians included Cardinal Riviera, his 'Premier Ministre', Cardinal Aquaviva (until his death in March 1747), and Archbishop de Rossi, his 'very close friend'.[124] The French included abbé Claude-François de Canillac (chargé d'affaires after the departure of Cardinal de Tencin), Tencin's nephew Jean-Louis Guérin, known as the bailli de Tencin (the Maltese ambassador), and Archbishop (later Cardinal) Frédéric-Jérôme de La Rochefoucauld, the French ambassador in Rome from June 1745 to February 1748. Stosch's letters are full of references to the frequent and long political conferences which the king had with these men.

As usual it was with the French that James felt particularly at ease. Within two weeks of his arrival, La Rochefoucauld had developed 'a very close friendship' with the king.[125] According to the Pope the bailli de Tencin was 'the only one who has the entire confidence of the king, because Cardinal Riviera ... makes so many difficulties, is so ambiguous and so indecisive in his advice, that he is not much use to him'.[126] Nevertheless Stosch wrote that the king frequently occupied himself in his cabinet for long periods 'writing letters under the guidance of Cardinal Riviera his main adviser'.[127] The king's salaried servants, such as Lord Dunbar, delivered messages and no doubt gave advice from time to time, but it was his Italian and French counsellors who now filled the position at court once occupied by the secretary of state.

1747–1766

The return of Prince Henry from France, followed by his promotion to be a cardinal, revived the king's spirits and breathed new life into the Stuart court. It also resulted in one of the most spectacular celebrations ever witnessed by James III in Rome. Stosch reported on 18 July that the king

attended on two evenings running the magnificent vocal and instrumental music that Cardinal de Rochefaucoult [sic] gave in the Teatro Argentina, which had been decorated at his expense, to celebrate the marriage of the Dauphin to the Princess Royal of Saxony. This occasion had been postponed for a considerable time in order to celebrate the promotion of Cardinal Stuart at the same time.[128]

---

[124] Stosch, 27 December 1746 (f. 359).   [125] Stosch, 13 July 1745 (f. 193).

[126] *Benoît XIV*, I, p. 311, Benedict XIV to Tencin, 15 March 1747. A few weeks later Stosch described the bailli de Tencin as James's 'principal conseiller confident' (25 April 1747 (f. 33)).

[127] Stosch, 21 February 1747 (f. 15).   [128] Stosch, 18 July 1747 (f. 55).

Figure 19. A detail from *The Performance of a Serenata by Niccolò Jommelli in the Teatro Argentina on 12 July 1747*, 1747 (204 × 247 cm), by Giovanni Paolo Panini. James III can be seen on the right-hand side, in the triple box which he was given as King of England, Scotland and Ireland.

The music was a newly composed serenata *a quattro voci* by Niccolò Jommelli, and the theatre was decorated 'to look like a salon'.[129] James III wrote that the serenata 'was a great succes, and indeed it was the most magnificent, tasteful and best-arranged reception that I have ever seen'.[130] Panini's famous painting, which recorded the event, shows James III surrounded by his entourage in a triple box on the right-hand side of the auditorium (Fig. 19).[131]

A few days later the *facciata* was erected outside Cardinal York's apartment in the east wing of the Palazzo del Re.[132] When it was taken down in September the king and the new cardinal went via Assisi to visit the Santa Casa at Loreto, taking with them a silver bust of Prince Charles to be presented to the basilica there.[133] Shortly after their return

[129] *Benoît XIV*, I, p. 339, Benedict XIV to Tencin, 12 July 1747.
[130] RA. SP 285/148, James III to Bailli de Tencin, 18 July 1747. Also RA. SP 285/149, James III to Cardinal de Tencin, 18 July 1747: the fête 'étoit le plus beau spectacle que j'ai jamais vu, d'une magnificence et d'un bon gout extraordinaires'.
[131] The painting is in the Louvre. See also *Diario ordinario*, no. 4677, 15 July 1747, pp. 20–1; Fagiolo, *Corpus delle feste*, p. 139.
[132] See Chapter 11, p. 232.
[133] Stosch, 19 and 26 September 1747 (f. 71, f. 73); *Benoît XIV*, I, pp. 351, 355, Benedict XIV to Tencin, 20 September 1747; 4 October 1747; ASV. Fondo Benedetto XIV, 23, p. 234, 'Ricevimento delle Maesta Reali d'Inghilterra' at Assisi, 26 September 1747.

Cardinal York moved into the apartment on the second floor of the Palazzo del Re which had previously been occupied by the queen.[134]

In his new and much more spacious accommodation, and with a gallery overlooking the Piazza dei Santi Apostoli, the cardinal was able to hold a regular *conversazione*, to which he invited all the other cardinals, the noble families and the senior prelates of Rome. It was inaugurated in November 1747,[135] and provided musical entertainment as well as refreshments. At the end of December he celebrated his absent brother's birthday with 'a grand concert of vocal and instrumental music, attended by six Cardinals and many members of the nobility and prelacy'.[136]

For a while it looked as if the Stuart court had regained its former splendour, but the king himself remained deeply distressed by the behaviour of Prince Charles in Paris. By January 1748 he had reverted to an 'extraordinary sadness', and Stosch reported that Riviera and Rossi had tried and failed to lift his spirits.[137] At the end of the year, when the news arrived that Prince Charles had been arrested, briefly confined in the Château de Vincennes and then expelled from France, the king's depression became even more pronounced. It was made even worse by Prince Charles's provocative behaviour at Avignon.

During 1749, 1750 and 1751 Cardinal York continued to hold his regular *conversazioni*, and James III did his best to appear cheerful in public, sometimes joining the throng of people in his son's apartment above.[138] He also attended the most important ceremonies conducted

---

[134] ASVR. Santi Apostoli vol. 72, p. 89, a note added to the *Stati d'Anime* for 1747 concerning the second floor of the Palazzo del Re: 'Appart[amen]to Reale della Regina: Henry Duke of York, Cardinal, creato a 3 Lug[li]o.'

[135] *Benoît XIV*, I, p. 366, Benedict XIV to Tencin, 22 November 1747.

[136] Stosch, 9 January 1748 (f. 103). Now that Prince Henry was a cardinal it was necessary to determine various questions of ceremonial, and in particular to decide whether people should be allowed to sit in his presence during his *conversazioni* and concerts without having previously paid an official visit standing up. For the sensible compromise negotiated by James III, whereby those people who wished could be dispensed from making an official visit, see *Benoît XIV*, I, pp. 367, 371, 376, 378, Benedict XIV to Tencin, 29 November 1747; 13 December 1747; 3 and 10 January 1748. The ceremonial to be adopted for Prince Henry had always posed problems, because the cardinals had been willing to give precedence to Prince Charles only, whereas James III had wanted his two sons to be treated equally, as they would have been in England and France. It had been arranged back in 1730 that Prince Henry should take precedence over all the cardinals except the Cardinal Doyen, but that a distinction should be made between the two princes (Stosch, 3 August 1730 (f. 88); RA. SP 139/79, James III to O'Bryen, 20 September 1730). The first part of this compromise was renewed in 1747: Stosch, 27 June and 4 July 1747 (f. 49, f. 51).

[137] Stosch, 30 January 1748 (f. 109).

[138] Stosch, 21 February 1749 (f. 218); 1 January 1751 (f. 2).

by his son in the Church of Santa Maria in Campitelli,[139] as well as the reopening of the Porta Santa at St Peter's Basilica in December 1749.[140] Two years later he was present, as usual in a specially constructed balcony, to see his son installed as the Archpriest of St Peter's.[141] A week later he made what was probably his last appearance at a major fête, when the new French ambassador (the duc de Nivernais) rented the Palazzo Farnese to celebrate the birth of the duc de Bourgogne (the future Louis XVI). The great *sala* on the first floor was converted into a ballroom, with a stage at one end, and three tiers of boxes surrounding its other three sides. In the centre, facing the stage, the principal box was occupied by James III, with the ambassadors and most important people on either side. The two tiers of boxes above were occupied by the 'Princesses and Ladies',[142] including those whom Stosch described as 'the ladies of his suite, the Princesses [sic] Salviati, Corsini, Strozzi and Santobuono'.[143] For three consecutive nights James again ordered that the Palazzo del Re should be illuminated with flaming torches and lanterns ('torce, lanterooni, e facciole').[144]

A few weeks later the king lost his closest friend, duchessa Salviati. Reporting her death in January 1752, Stosch wrote that 'he appeared inconsolable in the days that followed'. She had been 'his friend and confidante for many years', and in the Palazzo Salviati on the Corso 'he was accustomed to spend every Friday afternoon in conversation with the cardinals ... and his main supporters'.[145] It was at this moment that James's dispute with his son over household appointments came to a head, resulting in Cardinal York's decision to move out of the Palazzo del Re in July 1752.

Although Prince Henry returned in November, and resumed his weekly *conversazione*, the king never fully recovered from this incident. He continued his regular routine – morning mass at Santi Apostoli, dinner with a few friends, a visit to a church in the afternoon, followed

[139] Stosch, 28 February 1749 (f. 220); 13 February 1750 (f. 322); Fagiolo, *Corpus delle feste*, pp. 144–5, 7 February 1750.

[140] Fagiolo, *Corpus delle feste*, pp. 143–4, which also reproduces the contemporary engraving showing James III in his box.

[141] *Diario ordinario*, no. 5358, 20 November 1751, pp. 5–8.

[142] *Diario ordinario*, no. 5361, 27 November 1751, pp. 22–34; Fagiolo, *Corpus delle feste*, p. 150.

[143] Stosch, 28 February 1749 (f. 220).

[144] *Diario ordinario*, no. 5361, 27 November 1751, p. 29.

[145] Stosch, 21 and 28 January 1752 (f. 107, f. 109).

by a walk outside the Porta del Popolo[146] – but from a social point of view the Stuart court seemed increasingly the home of an important cardinal rather than that of the exiled king.

In fact James had considerably reduced the size of his entourage and was seeing fewer people. Detailed documentary evidence is lacking, but we know that he was often ill and sometimes remained a recluse in his apartment. For example, Pope Benedict wrote in May 1754: 'Our good king of England keeps to his chamber; his sickness consists of a great melancholy and fatigue.'[147] Even when he went out he was now very different. In the summer of 1754 the Pope wrote again:

When he goes to the church of the Santi Apostoli, he no longer uses the wooden gallery, but a window in the convent that opens into the church. He attends divine office in his underclothes and a dressing-gown. It is the same when he goes out in his carriage, when he is wrapped up in a great cloak and he has the horses go very slowly because he says that every movement gives him pain.[148]

Although James III still had several years more to live, until the first day of 1766, it was at this time that his court effectively became Italian. Cardinal de La Rochefoucauld and the bailli de Tencin both left Rome at the beginning of 1748. The duc de Nivernais, who arrived as the new French ambassador in 1749, was a cousin and established a close working relationship with him, but he also left in 1752 and was not replaced for three years. From then on his counsellors were exclusively Italian.

Already in April 1751 Stosch had described Cardinal Silvio Valenti Gonzaga (the papal secretary of state) and Cardinal Corsini as his 'principal Counsellors and confidants, who run his affairs' now that Riviera was too old.[149] By the following year Cardinal Federico Marcello Lante was regarded as the man most likely to succeed Riviera as 'Chief Minister'.[150] In fact, James did not replace Riviera when he died at the end of 1752, preferring instead to take advice from Valenti Gonzaga, Corsini, Lante and his friend Rossi (created titular Patriarch of Constantinople in 1751). As Pope Benedict once put it, with some exaggeration, Valenti Gonzaga was 'the sole cardinal

---

[146] *Benoît XIV,* ii, p. 228, Benedict XIV to Tencin, 29 November 1752; Stosch, 12 March 1756.
[147] *Ibid.,* p. 341, Benedict XIV to Tencin, 29 May 1754.
[148] *Ibid.,* p. 348, Benedict XIV to Tencin, 3 July 1754.
[149] Stosch, 9 April 1751 (f. 30).   [150] Stosch, 17 March 1752 (f. 123).

in whom he has confidence ... but he is not always consulted and he [King James] does not do everything he says'.[151]

What matters, however, was that all of the king's counsellors were now Italian, and that the exiled Stuart court had ceased for most practical purposes to be English or French, let alone Irish or Scottish. As Stosch noted in January 1753, 'the Italians have at last got what they have long desired: to take over completely the administration of the political affairs ... [of the King]'.[152]

---

[151] *Benoît XIV*, II, p. 366, Benedict XIV to Tencin, 9 October 1754.
[152] Stosch, 5 January 1753 (f. 1).

13 The Stuarts and Italian music

After his return to Rome in 1729 James III continued to patronise the opera as an important way of maintaining his royal status. The opera houses provided a meeting place for all the great families in the city, and thus enabled him both to meet his friends and to be seen by the general public, including the British and Irish Grand Tourists. It provided a spectacular location in which to invite people to have supper in his box. And it allowed him to exercise his royal privilege (which only he and later his sons enjoyed) of giving people 'the satisfaction of asking for an aria to be repeated'.[1] The 1730 carnival season was particularly distinguished, and Stosch noted that James 'spends all his time at public performances and regularly has supper in his box':[2] '[he] is every day at the opera'.[3] Queen Clementina, by contrast, seems entirely to have stopped attending any of the performances.

The pattern was similar during the 1731 carnival. The king regularly attended the three theatres, and continued to have supper in the royal box,[4] while the queen remained behind in the Palazzo del Re. The year 1731 saw a novelty in that the Teatro Aliberti, for the first time in Rome, put on a season of opera in the spring as well as during the carnival. One of the two works was Vinci's enormously successful *Artaserse* (dedicated to Clementina in 1730), which was revived to meet popular demand.[5] Stosch noted that on 20 June James 'treated the Pope's nieces, nephews and Cardinal Corsini to a splendid supper in his box at the Teatro Aliberti'.[6] This was the first recorded occasion on which James III also

---

[1] NA. SP 98/46/f. 171, Stosch to Newcastle, 9 March 1743.
[2] NA. SP 98/32/f. 15, Stosch to Newcastle, 5 January 1730.
[3] NA. SP 98/32/f. 17, Stosch to Newcastle, 12 January 1730.
[4] NA. SP 98/32/f. 144, Stosch to Newcastle, 18 January 1731.
[5] De Angelis, *Il teatro Alibert*, p. 152.
[6] NA. SP 98/32/f. 217, Stosch to Newcastle, 26 June 1731. See also Valesio, *Diario di Roma*, IV, p. 371, 20 June 1731: 'nel teatro Alibert il dramma dell' *Artaserse*, recitatovi nell'anno scorso, e molto piacque; vi fu il re d'Inghilterra, che cenò nel palchetto assieme con le due dame Corsine e col cardinale Corsini'.

took his younger son, the Duke of York, then six years old, to the opera in Rome. In a letter of 4 July 1731 James wrote that 'the Duke is in great joy to sup with me to night at the Opera, which is indeed a very fine one'.[7]

Later the same year, 1731, a new opera house was built which was intended to equal the Aliberti. Briefly called the Teatro Cesarini, it was soon to be known as the Teatro Argentina (which it will be called here). We are fortunate to have some letters which refer specifically to James III's three boxes in the new theatre. Stosch recorded that on 28 November James 'went with the principessa di Piombino to see the building of Duke Cesarini Sforza's new theatre, to choose the three boxes he would like'.[8] In January 1732 he mentioned another mark of distinction: 'The Pope has given [to James III] three boxes in the best gallery in the theatre, which the Duke Cesarini has had rebuilt, and to honour him still further, they have made a communicating bridge to an adjacent house, over which [James III] will be able to enter his boxes without going up the ordinary staircase.'[9]

To illustrate the social importance attached by James to attending the opera, we might take the 1732 carnival season as an example. The operas performed that year were Vinci, *Didone abbandonata* and Giai, *Demetrio* at the Aliberti; Sarro, *Berenice* and Giacomelli, *Rosbale* at the Argentina; and Hasse, *Caio Fabricio* and Porpora, *Germanico in Germania* at the Capranica.[10] Stosch recorded the following visits:[11]

January 2 Aliberti
3 Aliberti (with the Pope's nieces)
7 Aliberti (with principessa di Piombino, Cardinal Carafa, Cardinal Salviati and Cardinal Banquieri)
13 Capranica (with Cardinal Bentivoglio)
14 Aliberti (with Prince Charles and Prince Henry)
15 Capranica (with principessa di Piombino)
16 Argentina (with Cardinal Salviati and Cardinal Carafa)
20 Capranica (with principessa di Piombino and Cardinal Bentivoglio) (the princes were at the Aliberti)
21 Capranica (with Prince Charles and Prince Henry)
22 Aliberti (with Prince Charles and Prince Henry)

[7] RA. SP 146/141, James III to Inverness, 4 July 1731.
[8] NA. SP 98/32/f. 309, Stosch to Newcastle, 8 December 1731.
[9] NA. SP 98/32/f. 325, Stosch to Newcastle, 19 January 1732.
[10] All the information about the operas performed in Rome and elsewhere is taken from Sartori, *I libretti italiani a stampa*.
[11] NA. SP 98/32/ff. 321, 325, 331, 335, 339, 341, 343, 351, Stosch to Newcastle, 12, 19, 23 January; 2, 9, 16, 23 February; and 8 March 1732.

23 Argentina
27 Capranica
28 Argentina
(29 Church of Santi Apostoli to hear Mass performed by the
    singers from the Capranica)
30 Capranica

February   3 Capranica
           4 Argentina
           5 Aliberti
           6 Capranica
           9 Capranica
          10 Argentina (with principessa di Piombino, principessa di
              Santobuono and Cardinal Spinola)
          13 Argentina
          14 Capranica
          16 Aliberti
          18 Capranica
          25 Aliberti

These were the visits to the opera of which Stosch, who was in Florence, was informed. He had to rely on receiving information from his correspondents in Rome and, as the latter did not always know, or note down, the names of the people with whom James shared his box and his supper, we must take this list as a minimum. But it is more than sufficient to illustrate not only James's enthusiasm for music but also the importance he attached to attending, and being seen to attend, the opera in Rome.

During 1732 the Aliberti put on a second spring season of operas (Porpora, *Issipile*, and Porta, *Lucio Papirio*), which coincided with the arrival in Rome of the duc de Saint-Aignan as the new French ambassador. Saint-Aignan reopened the question of opera boxes, and demanded parity with the Imperial ambassador (who had two). As a result of the ensuing arguments Pope Clement XII ordered that the theatre should be closed, and the season thus came to a premature end.[12] As neither the French nor the Imperial ambassador was willing to give way, the controversy dragged on, with the result that there was no carnival season in either 1733 or 1734.[13]

To compensate for this disappointment, Porpora's *Issipile* was performed privately in the Teatro Pioli, to which James III invited his friends

---

[12] NA. SP 98/32/f. 391, Stosch to Newcastle, 31 May 1732.
[13] De Angelis, *Il teatro Alibert*, p. 159; NA. SP 98/32/f. 467, Stosch to Newcastle, 13 December 1732.

on 11 February 1733.[14] A few weeks later the principe di Santobuono invited James to his palazzo to hear Faustina Bordoni, one of Handel's leading singers at the Royal Academy in London, who had been engaged to sing in the cancelled carnival season.[15]

The only opera presented in Rome in 1734 was a revival of Sarro's *Partenope* (dedicated to Clementina in 1724), which opened in February with new arias specially composed by Giovanni Costanzi. It was given in the newly opened Teatro Tordinona, where the ambassadors where obliged to buy their boxes.[16] James, however, was allocated the two best ones[17] and attended eight performances, two of them with his two sons.[18]

The problem of the opera boxes had still not been resolved when Clementina died at the beginning of January 1735, giving the Pope a new reason to cancel the season at the Tordinona.[19] According to Stosch, the duc de Saint-Aignan then organised for Prince Charles and Prince Henry 'a great concert of music, in which the principal members of the opera sang ... to compensate them, in a sense, for the fact that they had not been able to be present at the said operas because of the illness and death of their mother'.[20]

The only operas allowed in Rome that year were performed during the spring at the Tordinona and the Valle, another theatre where the ambassadors did not have their own boxes. The season was notable because it was the first during which operas by Pergolesi were put on in Rome, *La serva padrona* as an intermezzo at the Valle, and *L'Olimpiade* at the Tordinona. James returned from Albano especially to hear the first

---

[14] See Chapter 12, p. 249.

[15] NA. SP 98/32/f. 514, Stosch to Newcastle, 4 April 1733.

[16] NA. SP 98/37/f. 35, Stosch to Newcastle, 6 February 1734; Bianca Maria Antolini, 'Rome, 1730–1800', *New Grove Opera*, vol. IV, p. 27. The Tordinona, which had been destroyed in 1697, was rebuilt in 1732 on the orders of Pope Clement XII to provide a government-run theatre, where no boxes were allocated to ambassadors.

[17] NA. SP 98/37/f. 41, Stosch to Newcastle, 27 February 1734.

[18] NA. SP 98/37/f. 41 to f. 47, Stosch to Newcastle, 27 February to 20 March 1734. The theatres were briefly described by Charles de Brosses: 'A Rome, le théâtre ... construit par le comte Alibert ... est le plus grand, et passe pour le plus beau; c'est là que se fait ordinairement la grande tragédie. Le second est celui d'Argentina, carré d'un bout et rond de l'autre, moins grand que le précédent, mais mieux ramassé et contenant presque autant de monde, dans un plus petit espace. Celui de Tordinona à peu près de même forme est aussi très joli' (Brosses, *Lettres d'Italie*, vol. II, p. 289). The Tordinona, like the Valle and the Pace, had five tiers, whereas the Aliberti and the Argentina both had six. James III's box in the latter was situated on the first tier up, on the right-hand side as one looked at the stage (Lowell Lindgren, 'Rome, 1680–1730', and Antolini, 'Rome, 1730–1800', *New Grove Opera*, vol. IV, pp. 25–7).

[19] De Angelis, *Il teatro Alibert*, p. 159.

[20] NA. SP 98/37/f. 218, Stosch to Newcastle, 26 March 1735.

performance of the latter,[21] and then attended five further performances, one of them with his sons.[22]

It was similar in both 1736 and 1737. In the former year James III
attended ten performances of the two operas at the Tordinona, including
four of them with his sons;[23] in the latter he attended six performances of
the two operas, including five with his sons.[24] The 1737 season was
significant because it included an opera (*Temistocle*) by Gaetano Latilla,
which Prince Henry also attended on two further occasions without his
father or brother. Latilla was the first of the composers whom Henry
particularly patronised, and in 1740 he was described as the 'virtuoso del
duca di York'.[25]

It was not until September 1737 that Saint-Aignan gave way[26] and
Rome was able to have another carnival season of operas, this time at the
Aliberti, the Argentina and the Valle. But by way of compensation the
ambassador organised a spectacular concert every summer to celebrate
the feast of Saint-Louis, to which the Stuarts were always invited. Details
are lacking, but in 1733 there was a serenata *a due voci*, in 1735 a concert
featuring two of the finest singers from the papal choir (Pasqualigi and
Menicucci) and in both 1737 and 1739 serenatas by Giovanni Costanzi.[27] The Spanish ambassador (Cardinal Troiano Aquaviva) then also
began a series of spectacular annual concerts every November, to celebrate the birthday of the Queen of the Two Sicilies. Once again the
details are lacking, but there was a serenata *a tre voci* in 1738, and
another serenata by Costanzi in 1741.[28]

The long-awaited carnival season opened in January 1738 with two
new operas at the Aliberti, one of which (Logroscino, *Quinto Fabio*) was
dedicated to James III. We are not told if the Stuarts attended performances at the Argentina and the Valle, but the king did attend at least
five performances at the Aliberti, one of them with his sons, who also
attended two performances by themselves.[29] The season was notable

[21] RA. SP 179/158, Edgar to Innes, 1 June 1735: 'H.M. is come into Town to hear an opera that is here, and is, thanks to God, in very good health, as are also the Princes at Albano, whither H.M. is to return after tomorrow.'

[22] NA. SP 98/38/f. 180, Stosch to Newcastle, 11 June 1735; and 98/37/f. 244 to f. 251, his letters of 9 to 23 July 1735. James also attended two performances of Duni, *Nerone*.

[23] NA. SP 98/37/f. 307 to f. 321, Stosch to Newcastle, 7 January to 25 February 1736.

[24] NA. SP 98/41/f. 10 to f. 22, Stosch to Newcastle, 2 February to 9 March 1737.

[25] In the libretto of *Siroe*.

[26] NA. SP 98/41/f. 91, Stosch to Newcastle, 30 September 1737.

[27] NA. SP 98/32/f. 566; 98/37/f. 267; 98/41/f. 91, f. 340, Stosch to Newcastle, 5 September 1733; 3 September 1735; 30 September 1737; 6 September 1739.

[28] NA. SP 98/41/f. 234, Stosch to Newcastle, 8 December 1738; Hans Joachim Marx, 'Giovanni Battista Costanzi', *New Grove Music*, vol. VI, pp. 527–8.

[29] NA. SP 98/41/f. 131 to f. 144, Stosch to Newcastle, 20 January to 3 March 1738.

because on one evening the king's servants arrived to find that the 'gold trimming' and part of the 'red damask' had been stolen from his box, and these had later to be replaced by the *Camera Apostolica*.[30]

From 1739 to 1742 the king and his sons continued to attend with great regularity the operas at the Aliberti, the Argentina and the Capranica (which replaced the Valle) during each carnival season. The last opera dedicated to James III (Giacomelli, *Achille in Aulide*) and the first to Prince Charles were performed at the Argentina in 1739, while the first one to be dedicated to Prince Henry was performed at the Aliberti the same year. Thereafter there was an opera dedicated to Prince Henry and another one to Prince Charles each year, at the Aliberti in 1740, 1741 and 1743, and at the Argentina in 1742.[31] These dedications were a reflection of the number of times the princes now attended the opera. They attended 6 performances in 1741, 9 in 1742 and 16 in 1743, whereas the king attended 15 performances in 1741, 9 in 1742, and only 2 in 1743. As an indication of the princes' enthusiasm for opera, it is worth noting that they attended performances at the Aliberti (Cocchi, *Adelaide* and

---

[30] NA. SP 98/41/f. 139, Stosch to Newcastle, 17 February 1739. James's box at the Aliberti was described in 1730 as being decorated 'de damas a galons d'or' (NA. SP 98/32/f. 15, Stosch to Newcastle, 5 January 1730). This brief description, however, may be supplemented by a detailed entry in one of the Stuart inventories. It is useful because it demonstrates that James not only decorated his own boxes, but also removed the furnishings when he no longer needed them: 'Parati, e Mobile per li tre Teatri, cioè Argentina, Aliberti, e Valle, consistenti in 5 fregi di veluto cremisi tutti guarniti di trina, e frangia d'oro falso, e li parapetti, e fregi sopra de palchi. Altro fregio di amuerra cremisi ondato guarnito di frangia simile. Sette pezzi di damasco cremisi a opere diverse guarniti di trina come sopra, alcuna di quali grande ed altri picoli, due cuscinette ricop.ti di veluto per li parapetti delli palchetti, uno de quali senza guanize. Diversa frangia d'oro false, e gallone sud. per guarniz.e di detti palchi. 6 plachette scompagne. 4 tavollini e 2 cornocopie di ferro ordinarie assai. Altro paratino di tela stamp.ta con fonto per la pel Teatro Valle. 3 banchetti imbotiti ricoperti di tela rossa. Due cuscini per spaliera, 8 sediolette imbotite, e cio il tutto ricoperto di tela rossa in tutto' (Archivio Storico di Propaganda Fide, Stato Temporale Eredita del Card. Duca di York, Inventario Contessa [sic] d'Albany vol. 5, no. 83, 'Rendimento dei Conti Generale di tutto l'Asse Ereditario della Ch. Mem. Sig.ra Duchessa di Albania cessata da vivere in Bologna li 17 Novembre 1789', inherited by Cardinal York and concluded in July 1794, item 277. There is a copy of this inventory in ASR. Misc Famiglia: Stuart b. 170, part 2, f. 5).

[31] The operas dedicated to Prince Charles were: da Capua, *Vologeso re de' Parti* (Argentina, 1739); Latilla, *Le Amazzoni* (Aliberti, 1740); Bernasconi, *Demofoonte* (Aliberti, 1741); Leo, *Demetrio* (Argentina, 1742); and Cocchi, *Adelaide* (Aliberti, 1743). Those dedicated to Prince Henry were: Latilla, *Romolo* (Aliberti, 1739); Latilla, *Siroe* (Aliberti, 1740); Lampugnani, *Semiramide riconosciuta* (Aliberti, 1741); Manna, *Tito Manlio* (Argentina, 1742); and Terradellas, *Merope* (Aliberti, 1743). From 1741 to 1746 the Argentina was managed by conte Francesco Albergati, presumably a cousin of marchese Fabio Albergati, who had been one of Queen Maria Clementina's gentlemen (Antolini, 'Rome, 1730–1800', *New Grove Opera*, vol. IV, p. 27. See also Chapters 8 and 9). Stosch mentions two visits by Albergati to the Palazzo del Re (NA. SP 98/43/f. 94, to Newcastle, 12 November 1740; SP 98/46/f. 274, to Newcastle, 28 December 1743).

Terradellas, *Merope*) on 12, 13, 16, 17, 18, 19, 20, 21, 23, 24 and 25 February 1743. King James joined them on the 24th, so they had presumably persuaded him to hear the music which they appreciated so much.[32]

It was during these same years that regular concerts were organised by the princes in the Palazzo del Re, and that people began to notice that Prince Charles had become a proficient performer on the cello. This raises two significant questions. Who was the master of the music at the Stuart court, in charge of preparing the concerts? And who taught Prince Charles to play the cello? The answer to both questions seems to be Giovanni Costanzi, who was also patronised by the duc de Saint-Aignan and Cardinal Aquaviva.

Costanzi, described by the caricaturist Ghezzi as 'Giovannino del Violoncello, famoso sonatore di detto istromento',[33] was both a composer and a cellist, who entered the employment of Cardinal Ottoboni in 1721 as one of his chamber musicians. According to his biographers he remained in the service of Ottoboni (the Cardinal Protector of France) until the latter's death in 1740, after which he worked in some of the churches in Rome, eventually becoming *maestro di cappella* at St Peter's.[34] This, however, is misleading. As we have seen, he also occasionally worked for both the French and Spanish ambassadors, who were two of James III's closest friends.

There is a significant gap in Costanzi's operatic career. Between 1726 and 1729 he composed four operas, three of which were performed publicly. From 1744 to 1752 he composed several more. The gap between these two periods coincides exactly with the period between the return of the Stuart court from Bologna and the departure of Prince Charles for France. It is most likely that Costanzi continued to be formally employed by Cardinal Ottoboni, but that he also worked when required for the two ambassadors and for James III as well. There is no direct evidence from the 1730s that he worked for the Stuart court, but there is no evidence concerning any other musicians either. Costanzi's regular salary was paid by Ottoboni,[35] so he would have received only occasional

---

[32] NA. SP 98/43/f. 122 to f. 140 (1741); 98/46/f. 4 to f. 14 (1742); 98/46/f. 155 to f. 171 (1743).

[33] Stefano La Via, 'Il Cardinale Ottoboni e la musica: nuovi documenti (1700–1740), nuove lettere e ipotesi', in *Intorno a Locatelli*, vol. I, p. 477. The description is on a caricature dated 1728. There is another caricature dated 28 October 1727 (p. 474).

[34] La Via, 'Il Cardinale Ottoboni', pp. 373–4, 382, 406, 454, 473–8; Marx, 'Costanzi', *New Grove Music*, vol. VI, pp. 527–8, and *Grove Opera*, vol. I, p. 971.

[35] Costanzi's monthly salary was 8 *scudi*, increased to 10 *scudi* in December 1736 (La Via, 'Il Cardinale Ottoboni', p. 373).

payments from the Stuarts for each specific concert that he gave, no doubt taken from the privy purse of the king or one of the princes.

In November 1742, two and a half years after Ottoboni's death, James Edgar wrote that 'at night, after a day's strong fatigue, the Prince sits down and diverts himself at music for an hour or two ... and plays upon the bass viol [sic] very well, for he loves and understands music to a great degree. His brother ... sings, when he pleases, much better.'[36] A household list has survived from December 1742 which identifies Prince Charles's cello teacher, Prince Henry's singing teacher and the harpsichord player employed to support them both. They are shown as Giovanni Costanzi, 'Maître de la Basse de Viole du Prince'; Domenico Ricci, 'Musicien'; and Felice Doria, 'Maître de Clavecin'. Costanzi and Doria both received thirty *livres* (6 *scudi*) each month, whereas Ricci, a soprano castrato who had had a distinguished operatic career in Rome and elsewhere, received fifty *livres* (10 *scudi*).[37] Costanzi's signature on the list, confirming receipt of his salary, is identical to his signature as preserved in the Ottoboni papers.[38]

All three men continued to be employed by Prince Henry after he became Cardinal York. Ricci and Doria are included in the lists of his household in 1750–1,[39] and Costanzi is shown as still being a member of his orchestra.[40] A few years later Costanzi also became a member of his household[41] and was given accommodation in the Palazzo del Re.[42]

These, however, were not the only musicians patronised by Prince Henry. In 1740 Charles de Brosses noted that 'the taste changes frequently here. At the moment Latilla is in fashion in Rome. The opera *Siroës* [sic], which is on in the Teatro Aliberti, was composed by him.'[43] It was in the libretto of *Siroe*, which was dedicated to the fourteen-year-old

---

[36] McLynn, *Charles Edward Stuart*, p. 74, quoting RA. SP 245/42.

[37] RA. SP 246/111, 'Gages de la Famille du Roy pour Décembre 1742'. Costanzi's salary was the same amount as the pension previously paid to Innocenzo Fede until his death in 1732 (RA. SP 158/41, receipts for pensions paid in 1732). Domenico Ricci was a pupil of Gasparini, had sung regularly in Rome since 1724, and had appeared in all the operas staged at the Tordinona from 1735 to 1737.

[38] Compare RA. SP 246/111 with the reproduction of an account signed by Costanzi in March 1740 in La Via, 'Il cardinale Ottoboni', p. 408.

[39] RA. SP 312/107 and 319/183, the household of Cardinal York in October 1750 and March 1751.

[40] RA. SP 303/108, 'Lista dell'Accademia di S.A.R. Ema. il Sig.re Cardinale Duca d'Jork per il meso di Gennaro 1750'. Costanzi is one of ten names listed.

[41] M.J. Cryan, *Travels to Tuscany and Northern Lazio* (Vetralla, 2004), pp. 22–4, gives the names of all the members of the 'Famiglia Alta e Famiglia Bassa' of Cardinal York in 1764.

[42] ASVR. Santi Apostoli vol. 76, p. 71, *Stati d'Anime*, 1762.

[43] Brosses, *Lettres d'Italie*, vol. II, p. 314.

Prince Henry, that Latilla was described as 'virtuoso del duca di York'. That year witnessed the first performance in Rome (at the Argentina) of an opera by Niccolò Jommelli.

Jommelli's original biographer wrote (in a book published in 1785) that he was 'summoned to Rome in 1740 under the protection of Cardinal York'.[44] Prince Henry was, of course, not yet a cardinal, but this early patronage has been retained by one of Jommelli's most recent biographers who, referring to the year 1749, states that by then Prince Henry 'had been his patron for many years'.[45] No details of this patronage have survived, but Stosch did record both princes attending a performance of Jommelli's oratorio *Betulia liberata* at the Chiesa Nuova in March 1743.[46]

No operas were performed in Rome during the 1744 and 1745 carnival seasons because of an outbreak of plague in the Kingdom of Naples.[47] By 1746 both Prince Charles and Prince Henry had left Rome, and thus the series of operas dedicated to the two Stuart princes came to an end. It was not until the summer of 1747 that Prince Henry returned and was created a cardinal by Pope Benedict XIV. Two weeks after that, when Cardinal de La Rochefoucauld celebrated the marriage of the Dauphin and the promotion of the prince, it was Jommelli whom he commissioned to compose a serenata *a quattro voci*.[48]

Jommelli had had two operas performed in Rome while Prince Henry was in France, and he was now engaged by the Argentina to compose a new setting of *Artaserse* for the carnival season of 1749. Prince Henry, however, had decided, now that he was a cardinal, that he would no longer go to the opera. 'In spite of his taste for music,' commented Pope Benedict, 'the cardinal has never once appeared at the theatre, and will not do so.'[49] His patronage of composers, therefore, had to be transferred from the opera house to the church. During that same year he commissioned an oratorio from Jommelli, entitled *La passione di Gesù Cristo*, and also persuaded him to write music for the Church of Santa Maria in Campitelli. The composer continued to write operas, but 'in the early 1750s Jommelli's work gravitated towards sacred music'.[50]

[44] Saverio Mattei, *Memorie per servire alla vita del Metastasio ed elogio di N. Jommelli* (1785; facsimile edn, Bologna, 1987), p. 76.

[45] Marita P. McClymonds, 'Jommelli', *New Grove Music*, vol. XIII, p. 178.

[46] NA. SP 98/46/f. 173, Stosch to Newcastle, 16 March 1743.

[47] De Angelis, *Il teatro Alibert*, p. 164.

[48] Fagiolo, *Corpus delle feste*; *Diario ordinario*, no. 4677, 15 July 1747, pp. 15–21. This serenata is omitted in the articles by McClymonds on 'Jommelli' in both *New Grove Music*, vol. XIII, pp. 178–86, and *New Grove Opera*, vol. II, pp. 907–12.

[49] *Benoît XIV*, I, p. 464, Benedict XIV to Cardinal de Tencin, 12 February 1749.

[50] McClymonds, 'Jommelli', *New Grove Music*, vol. XIII, p. 178.

In November 1751 Cardinal York was appointed Archpriest of St Peter's, where Jommelli had recently been given the post of assistant *maestro di cappella*.[51] When Jommelli eventually left Rome in 1753 to pursue his operatic career, Cardinal York gave his post to Giovanni Costanzi, whom he then promoted to be the *maestro di cappella* when the incumbent (Pietro Paolo Bencini) died in 1755.[52]

By then Cardinal York had begun to patronise Baldassare Galuppi, whose operas were regularly performed at the Aliberti and the Argentina after 1747. In February 1754 his setting of *Siroe* was performed at the Argentina with the celebrated castrato Caffarelli in the title role. Because Cardinal York no longer attended the public theatres, he had to hear the opera privately. Stosch noted that 'Cardinal York went two days running to the home of Cardinal Gian Francesco Albani to hear the famous musician Caffariello [sic] sing'.[53] A few days later York persuaded his father to come to the final rehearsal (in the home of Cardinal Imperiali) of 'the music for the opera Siroe, which is destined for the Teatro Argentina'.[54]

Galuppi never had a church appointment in Rome, but when he was there 'he rehearsed masses and got up concerts' for Prince Henry in the Church of Santa Maria in Campitelli.[55] In 1755 he also composed a mass for him, and performed it in the church that July.[56] In January 1756 Stosch wrote that 'Cardinal York spends most of his time with the famous Buranello [i.e. Galuppi] the Chapel Master who recently came from Venice and to whom he gave a hundred Scudi for some musical compositions'.[57] Another work commissioned by Cardinal York during these years was a *Magnificat a sette voci*, composed in 1760 by the elderly Porpora.[58]

However, the composer who was most closely associated with the Stuart court during the last years of James III's life, when the king had stopped attending the opera, remained Costanzi. When James died in January 1766 it was Costanzi who provided the music both for the solemn requiem mass held in St Peter's and for another one in the church of the English College.[59] The composer's long connection with

---

[51]   According to McClymonds, 'Jommelli', *New Grove Opera*, vol. II, p. 907, Cardinal York was partly responsible for securing this post for him.

[52]   Marx, 'Costanzi', *New Grove Music*, vol. VI, pp. 527–8.

[53]   NA. SP 98/61/f. 117, Stosch to Holderness, 15 February 1754.

[54]   NA. SP 98/61/f. 119, Stosch to Holderness, 22 February 1754.

[55]   Shield, *Henry Stuart*, p. 142. Galuppi had operas performed in Rome in 1748, 1751, 1753, 1754, 1756, 1759 and 1762.

[56]   *Ibid.*, p. 167.   [57]   NA. SP 98/61/f. 317, Stosch to Fox, 16 January 1756.

[58]   The manuscript is in BAV. Vat. Mus. 583.

[59]   *Diario ordinario*, no. 7572, 11 January 1766, p. 11; no. 7581, 1 February 1766, p. 4.

the Stuarts was not terminated until his own death in 1778, when he bequeathed to Cardinal York his very large music library.[60]

In Chapter 4 of this work it was argued that the involvement of the Stuarts with Italian opera between 1719 and 1726 was significant not only for the musical life of Rome itself, but also because its ramifications were felt in London as well. This remained true for much of the period after 1729. The libretti of operas previously performed in Rome continued to be set to music by Handel and other composers in London,[61] and singers with known Jacobite connections, notably Farinelli, continued to perform in the English capital.[62] But as the years went by, and the repertoire of successful libretti became increasingly standardised, this became less significant. The Stuarts remained influential in Rome, but their impact on the operatic life of London certainly declined. Handel's borrowings from Jommelli might perhaps 'have acted as a potent Jacobite symbol to contemporary audiences',[63] but by the early 1740s many of the libretti dedicated to the Stuart princes in Rome had already been set to music in London.[64] Galuppi, for example, had already enjoyed considerable success in London before he ever came to Rome.[65]

By the 1750s, when James III and Cardinal York had mainly withdrawn from the operatic life of Rome,[66] and the Jacobite cause in

[60] Bindelli, *Enrico Stuart*, p. 127: 'Il 18 marzo 1778, avendo S. A. ereditato l'archivio di musica dal defunto celebre maestro di cappella Giovanni Costanzi' (Costanzi had died on 5 March 1778).

[61] The operas composed and pasticcios arranged by Handel which had previously been performed in Rome after 1727 were: *Ezio* (1731; Auletta, 1729), *Catone* (1732; Vinci, 1728), *Semiramide riconosciuta* (1733; Vinci, 1729) and *Caio Fabriccio* (1733; Hasse, 1732). These libretti had not been dedicated to the Stuarts, but Handel did arrange a pasticcio on the libretto dedicated to James III at Faenza (see Chapter 10): *Arsace* (1737; Orlandini, 1728).

[62] Edward Corp, 'Farinelli and the Circle of Sicinio Pepoli: A Link with the Stuart Court in Exile', *Eighteenth Century Music*, 2:2 (September 2005), pp. 311–19.

[63] *The Handel Institute Newsletter*, reporting on a paper delivered by Lowell Lindgren at the American Handel Society Conference at Santa Fe in March 2005. (I am grateful to Professor Xavier Cervantes for this reference.)

[64] The libretti included: *Demofoonte* (1741; Duni, 1737), *Demetrio* (1742; Pescetti, 1737) and *Merope* (1743; Broschi, 1737). In addition to these, there were others which had recently been set to music in London, but performed in Rome before that: *Siroe* (1740; Handel, 1728, and Hasse, 1736), *Semiramide riconosciuta* (1741; Handel pasticcio, 1733), *Adelaide* [*Lotario*] (1743; Handel, 1729).

[65] Dale E. Monson, 'Baldassare Galuppi', *New Grove Opera*, vol. II, p. 337: 'Galuppi arrived in London in October 1741 and supervised eleven opera productions over the next year and a half, including four original works.'

[66] According to Stosch, both James III and Cardinal York attended at least one performance at the Aliberti in January 1755 (NA. SP 98/61/f. 211, to Fox, 10 January 1755).

England was finished, any residual connection between operatic music from Catholic Italy and the exiled Stuarts had come to an end. Even *La passione di Gesù Cristo*, the oratorio commissioned by Cardinal York from Jommelli in 1749, could be performed in London in 1764 and 1770, and in Edinburgh in 1772, without having any notice taken of its political implications. The newspaper advertisement for the first performance in London declared that the work 'is too well known to every Person who has been in Rome, as well as to the Connoisseurs in Music, to stand in need of any Encomium on its Excellency'. It might possibly 'have conveyed a political as well as a religious message to any auditor who knew that it had been commissioned by a grandson of James II', but it is 'the only Italian oratorio' of which 'the complete score, including recitatives and treble accompaniments ... was printed in eighteenth-century London'.[67] It seems that the musical involvement of the Stuarts, which this chapter has attempted to recover from obscurity, was already largely forgotten by the time James III died in 1766.

---

[67] Lowell Lindgren, 'Oratorios Sung in Italian at London, 1734–82', pp. 513–52 in Paola Besutti (ed.), *L'Oratorio musicale italiano e i suoi contesti (sec. XVII–XVIII), atti del convegno internazionale a Perugia*, (Florence, 2002), at pp. 536–7.

14 The portraits of the Stuarts and their courtiers: II

Shortly after the return of the Stuart court to Rome James III received a request from some of his friends in France and England for portraits of his two sons.[1] The earlier portrait of Prince Charles painted by David in 1726 had been copied and engraved,[2] but the prince was now eight years old, and had changed. David's portrait of Prince Henry had been neither copied nor engraved, and Jacobites were naturally eager to know what he looked like.

The Duke of Bedford asked for a double portrait, but James observed that 'I could not send them to you both in one, without spoiling their likeness ... since there are none here who could paint such a picture ... well, that draw pictures like.'[3] He therefore commissioned David to paint separate companion portraits of the two princes. A pair would be displayed in the Palazzo del Re, available to be copied for distribution among the king's Italian friends. A replica pair would be sent to France to be copied by Belle before being sent to the Duke of Bedford.

David accepted the commission, but insisted on being given a substantial advance payment,[4] because his previous bill had been reduced two years earlier.[5] When the portraits were finished James was delighted with them and commented that they were 'very like'.[6] Two pairs were eventually sent to Paris, the first in October 1729,[7] the second in March

---

[1] Anne Oglethorpe to James III, 1 August 1729, referred to in RA. SP 130/85, James III to Anne Oglethorpe, 23 August 1729; RA. SP 130/59, James III to O'Bryen, 17 August 1729.

[2] See Chapter 4, p. 114; Corp, *King over the Water*, p. 64, fig. 49.

[3] RA. SP 130/85, James III to Anne Oglethorpe, 23 August 1729.

[4] RA. SP Misc 35, account book, August 1729: 'A David à bonconto di ritratti ... 500 livres.'

[5] See Chapter 4, p. 117.

[6] RA. SP Misc 35, account book, October 1729: 'A David pittore p. resto d'un suo conte di z. 191. 65/458l. 5s. 0d.'; RA. SP 131/181, James III to Innes, 8 November 1729; RA. SP 133/110, James III to Anne Oglethorpe, 17 January 1730.

[7] RA. SP 131/73, O'Bryen to James III, 17 October 1729; RA. SP 131/80, James III to Cholier, 18 October 1729.

1730.[8] The first of these pairs was then copied twice by Belle before being sent on to England,[9] so that three pairs were available for distribution in France.[10] The replicas for the Duke of Bedford had been painted without the Garter or the Thistle, to make it safer to smuggle them into England,[11] so Belle presumably added both orders to his own copies. Before they were sent on to England Bedford's pictures were engraved anonymously and without inscriptions in Paris,[12] and because there was no Garter sash to be taken into account these engravings were simply reversed. The result was that the buttons appeared on the wrong sides of the princes' coats.[13] An opportunity to rectify the mistake arose the following year when John Simon made a copy of these engravings in England, but he failed to do so. This was particularly annoying for the Stuarts because Simon reversed the incorrect engraving of the duke and actually took the trouble to transfer the buttons to the wrong side![14]

Despite this disappointment, James remained very pleased with the portraits themselves and asked David to provide copies until

[8] RA. SP 133/176, 177, James III's accounts, 3 January 1730: 'David Painter: 405 Livres'; RA. SP 133/16, Edgar to Cholier, 1 March 1730, and Edgar to Waters, 2 March 1730; RA. SP 134/189, Cholier to Edgar, 17 March 1730.

[9] RA. SP 131/131, O'Bryen to James III, 31 October 1729: 'Jay remis a Mr le belle les portraits des princes pour qu'il travaille incessament a en faire des copies. Je suis convenus de luy donner 100 livres par copie nayant pas voulus y travailler a moins, ainsy les quatres se monteront a 400 livres'; RA. SP 132/66, James III to O'Bryen, 23 November 1729: 'You will find inclosed an order for 400 Livres to pay the copies of my childrens pictures when they are made.'

[10] These three pairs were given to: Sir Christopher Nugent at Saint-Germain (RA. SP 130/59, James III to O'Bryen, 17 August 1729; RA. SP 130/183, Nugent to James III, 26 September 1729); Président Cholier at Lyon (RA. SP 131/171, O'Bryen to James III, 7 November 1729; RA. SP 132/128, Cholier to Edgar, 17 December 1729; RA. SP 133/16, Edgar to Cholier, 8 February 1730; RA. SP 134/87, Cholier to Edgar, 23 February 1730); and the princesse de Montauban, who was a niece of Anne Oglethorpe (RA. SP 135/15, James III to Anne Oglethorpe, 22 March 1730; RA. SP 136/7, Anne Oglethorpe to James III, 23 April 1730; RA. SP 136/110, James III to marquise de Mézières, 10 May 1730). John Ingleton was promised a pair, but there is no evidence in the Stuart Papers that he received either of the portraits (WDA. Epist. Var. 13/106, Ingleton to Mayes, 13 February 1730; WDA. Epist. Var. 13/114, Ingleton to Mayes, 7 May 1730). Copies of the paintings, by David or Belle, are in the National Portrait Gallery, London.

[11] RA. SP 130/85, James III to Anne Oglethorpe, 23 August 1729. The pictures were taken to England by Anne Oglethorpe (RA. SP 132/55, Anne Oglethorpe to O'Bryen, 20 November 1729).

[12] RA. SP 135/50, James III to O'Bryen, 29 March 1730; RA. SP 136/62, James III to O'Bryen, 2 May 1730. The engraving of the portraits cost 1000 livres (RA. SP, Waters's accounts, 1 July 1730).

[13] RA. SP 146/135, Dunbar to O'Bryen, 3 July 1731; RA. SP 167/172, Edgar to Sister Mary Rose Howard, 23 January 1734.

[14] Sharp, *Engraved Record*, pp. 111–12, nos. 204, 208; and pp. 123–4, nos. 259, 260.

1732.[15] This was possible because the original pictures made the princes look 'a little older than the life'.[16] The composition of the portraits of the duke remained the same, though in some of the later ones he looks a little older. The image of the Prince of Wales did not change, but in two of the later ones he is shown wearing armour instead of a coat.[17] In addition to the copies ordered by James III himself, David made copies for Lord Marischal and John Urquhart of Cromarty.[18]

In June 1730, when the originals of these portraits of the princes had been copied and engraved, James III decided that the time had come to resume making copies of the portraits by Meytens of himself and Clementina. These had been copied by Gill during 1727 and the beginning of 1728, but no more had been made after he had been told to stop,[19] and the people to whom they had been promised kept waiting. Now, two years later, the list of 'pictures promised' was revised[20] and expanded.[21] Letters

[15] A pair was sent to Sir Charles Wogan in 1732 (RA. SP 141/107, Edgar to Wogan, 8 September 1731; RA. SP 151/100, James III to Wogan, 31 January 1732; RA. SP 150/181, Edgar to Wogan, 1 March and 17 April 1732; RA. SP 152/135, Wogan to Edgar, 2 April 1732). The Stuart accounts for May 1732 include a reference to two pairs ordered by Maria Clementina: 'Depense della Reine: Payes au paintre pour quattre portraits de leur Altesses: 10. 0. 0' (RA. SP 155/176). As the name of the painter is not mentioned, and the price for the four pictures is so low (10 Spanish *pistoles* = 30 *scudi* = 150 *livres*), these copies were presumably not painted by David. Perhaps they were painted by William Mosman, who is known to have made copies of some of the Stuart portraits at this time (see below, note 18).

[16] RA. SP 131/181, James III to Innes, 8 November 1729. A recently discovered miniature shows Prince Henry as he really was in 1729, without being made a little older than the life (Christies, sale of Old Masters and British Pictures, July 2011).

[17] Examples of the paintings showing Prince Charles in armour (Corp, *King over the Water*, p. 70, fig. 56) and Prince Henry looking a little older are in the collection of the marquis de Villefranche.

[18] James Holloway, 'John Urquhart of Cromarty: A Little-known Collector of Roman Paintings', in David Marshall, Karin Wolfe and Susan Russell (eds.), *'Roma-Britannica': Art Patronage and Cultural Exchange in Eighteenth-Century Rome* (London and Rome, 2011), pp. 103–12. The copies made for Urquhart are in the Scottish National Portrait Gallery, Edinburgh, dated 1732: see Corp, *King over the Water*, pp. 68–9, figs. 54 and 55.

[19] Chapter 4, p. 116.   [20] RA. SP Box 4/2/11, 'Pictures promised', June 1730.

[21] RA. SP Box 4/2/9, 'Pictures promised', July 1730. The original list contained '2 Busts of ye King and one small picture, 6 Busts of ye Queen [and] 1 Picture of ye Prince'. '2 other Busts of ye King' were 'now added'. The busts of the king were for Bishop Bonaventura of Montefiascone, an unnamed person at Lucca, Nathaniel Mist in England and Monsieur de la Naye at Liège. The busts of the queen were for the Bishop of Montefiascone, the same unnamed person at Lucca, contessa di Sardi at Lucca, contessa Molza at Modena, Colonel O'Rourke in Vienna and Brigadier Macdonnell in Spain. The picture of the prince was for Sir Luke O'Tool, and was now to be a copy of David's recent portrait of 1729 instead of his earlier one of 1726.

were then sent out to inform some people that they would soon receive the portraits they had been expecting.[22]

It is not known who made these copies. Perhaps it was William Mosman, or even Gill if he was still in Rome. In any event the first ones were ready for despatch during August,[23] and others were sent in September.[24] When, in November 1730, Sir Charles Wogan asked for copies of David's portraits of the two princes, he was told 'to renew his request in that respect next autumn',[25] which indicates that whoever was employed to copy the Meytens portraits of the king and queen was not expected to be free to copy those of the princes by David until the following year.

Given the large number of copies made in 1727–8, and now in 1730–1, it is surprising that neither of Meytens's portraits of the king and queen was engraved at this time. One explanation might be found in an incident which took place at Avignon in December 1730. Jeremiah Broomer had retired from the court that autumn and decided to return to Saint-Germain-en-Laye.[26] He took with him 'a long box with a portrait of the Queen in it . . . which the King of Great Britain was sending . . . to Paris for Mr. Bell'. It is possible that this portrait was intended to be engraved in Paris, as well as copied by Belle. As it happened, Broomer died en route in Avignon, and all his possessions, including the portrait, were stolen.[27] The portrait therefore never reached Paris, and was neither copied by Belle nor (if that *was* the intention) engraved. We do not know what happened to it.

A portrait of the queen did reach Paris nearly four years later. In May 1734 Lewis Innes asked James III for portraits of the queen and the Duke of York, to be added to the collection in the Scots College at Paris: 'We want only these two to have all the Royal Family in this your own College.'[28] The two portraits were finished in August of that year, and

[22] RA. SP 138/18, Edgar to de la Naye, 1 July 1730; RA. SP 138/47, Molza to Edgar, 5 July 1730; RA. SP 138/85, O'Rourke to Ellis, 29 July 1730; RA. SP 139/21 and 22, Macdonnell to James III and Edgar, 6 September 1730.

[23] RA. SP 138/154, Molza to Ellis, 26 August 1730; RA. SP 139/31, Molza to Ellis, 9 September 1730.

[24] RA. SP 133/16, Edgar to Cholier and to Waters, 13 September 1730; RA. SP 139/144, Waters to Edgar, 3 October 1730.

[25] RA. SP 133/16, Edgar to Wogan, 25 November 1730.

[26] See below, Chapter 15, p. 315.

[27] RA. SP 141/87 and Box 4/2/24, memoir by Elizabeth Crane 'touchant les effets du Sieur Broomer, mort en Avignon', December 1730; RA. SP 141/129, Elizabeth Crane to Inverness, 15 January 1731.

[28] RA. SP 170/89, Innes to James III, 17 May 1734. Innes explained that 'your Majesty was so good as to send us that of his R.H. the Prince some years ago', presumably a reference to David's portrait of 1726, and added that 'it is now some years since your

sent to Paris during the autumn.[29] The one of the queen was probably another copy of the original by Meytens. It is just possible, however, that it might have been a new one by Domenico Muratori, which is now lost but known because it was engraved in Rome by Girolamo Rossi. That portrait, about which nothing is otherwise known, shows the queen pointing with her right hand to a crucifix, which she holds in her left hand and which rests on a table beside her royal crown.[30]

The portrait of Prince Henry must have been the last copy to be made of the one painted by David five years earlier, in 1729. Before it could be despatched to Paris James received another request for portraits, this time from London: 'As the Prince and Duke are the subjects of conversation, if I should be honoured with their pictures ... I can have them done [i.e. copied] without being discovered and would lend them to friends.'[31] It seems to have been this request that persuaded James that the time had come to replace the portraits of 1729. Edgar replied that portraits would be sent as soon as possible, but explained that 'there has not been originals done of them these 2 years [sic], and that this winter they are to sit again for their pictures'.[32] It was once again David who was commissioned to paint the new portraits. The one of the duke is similar to the earlier one of 1729, though his left hand is now placed on his hip and he wears a breastplate under his coat.[33] The Prince of Wales, by contrast, is shown looking over his right shoulder and wearing full armour, perhaps because he had been present earlier that year at the Siege of Gaeta.[34]

These were the last portraits that David painted for the Stuarts. It was while he was still working on them that Queen Clementina died in January 1735. The Pope ordered that her body should lie in state in the Church of Santi Apostoli, and then be taken to St Peter's for burial.

Majesty was graciously pleased to promise me Her Majesties picture'. The promise had actually been made before 1725 (RA. SP 81/66, Innes to Inverness, 9 April 1725; RA. SP 85/47, Innes to Inverness, 13 August 1725).

[29] RA. SP 171/94, James III to Innes, 5 July 1734; RA. SP 172/182, T. Innes to Edgar, 30 August 1734; RA. SP 175/5, Edgar to Innes, 10 November 1734; RA. SP 175/142, Innes to James III, 6 December 1734.

[30] Sharp, *Engraved Record*, pp. 108–9, no. 194. It is possible that this was the portrait displayed at the *Collegio di Propaganda Fide*. See NA. SP 98/37/f. 315, Stosch to Newcastle, 28 January 1736: 'on avoit placé le Portrait ... sous un Dais magnifique'.

[31] RA. SP 173/118, Cockburne to Edgar, 23 September 1734.

[32] RA. SP 174/171, Edgar to Cockburne, 3 November 1734. The use of the word 'originals' is interesting. It presumably refers to copies made by David himself, rather than copies made by other people. The portrait of the duke sent to the Scots College in Paris that very same month must have been copied by someone other than David.

[33] Corp, *King over the Water*, p. 70, fig. 58. The painting is at Ingatestone Hall.

[34] *Ibid.*, p. 70, fig. 57. The painting is at Ingatestone Hall.

As we have seen, he also commissioned Giovanni Paolo Panini to design the frontispiece of an illustrated book describing the funeral.[35] Panini's design has not survived, but it included a copy of Meytens's portrait of Clementina, as can be seen in the engraving by Girolamo Frezza.[36] Another book which described the queen's funeral included an engraving in reverse of Muratori's portrait of the queen, slightly different because she now holds the crucifix in both hands.[37]

The death of his wife apparently prompted James to commission a very large painting showing their marriage at Montefiascone in September 1719. James and Clementina are shown kneeling before Bishop Sebastiano Bonaventura in the presence of courtiers and attendant clergy. A sceptre and the crowns of their three kingdoms are prominently displayed on a cushion beside James's right knee, and an altar with large candlesticks can be seen behind the bishop. The portrait of Clementina seems to have been modelled on the early ones by Trevisani, whereas the one of James shows him in profile for the first time in any of his Italian portraits, other than those on his medals.[38] A smaller copy, which omits some of the spectators, still hangs in the sacristy of Montefiascone Cathedral, and was presumably given to the bishop at the time. There is also an engraving by Antonio Friz, based on the original painting, which includes some additional spectators. Unlike the original painting, it shows James putting the wedding ring on his wife's finger.[39]

The painting is traditionally attributed to Agostino Masucci, and it is always dated 1735, but there is no documentation in the Stuart Papers to confirm either of these suppositions. All that survives is a letter of May 1735 from Edgar to Waters in Paris: 'The Painter the King employs wants an ounce of ye Paint mentioned in ye enclosed paper. He says there is none good of it to be had in Rome and that the best is to be gott at Paris.'[40] As no other painting is known to have been painted for James III at this time, this letter could be referring to the picture of the marriage at Montefiascone, but the name of the painter is not given. Waters replied that he would do what he could 'to send you in the Packett an ounce of Matecot chiaro e scuro', but he observed that 'your

[35] Chapter 11, p. 222.
[36] *Parentalia Mariae Clementinae Magn. Britan., Franc., et Hibern. Regin Iussu Clementis XII Pont. Max* (Rome, 1736), frontispiece.
[37] *Epicedium pro immaturo funere Mariae Clementinae Magnae Britanniae etc Reginae* (Rome, 1738), opposite p. xv. This book also contains six other engravings of the queen, and one of the two princes as little angels, all of them imaginary (pp. lxxvii, lxxix, lxxxii–vii).
[38] Corp, *King over the Water*, p. 73, fig. 60. The painting is in the Scottish National Portrait Gallery, Edinburgh.
[39] Sharp, *Engraved Record*, pp. 213–14, no. 697.
[40] RA. SP 179/117, Edgar to Waters, 25 May 1735.

painter should have given you ye name in French, which he could easily have done in yt city. I know not whether Drugsters and Dealers in coulors will understand it, but I will get some painter to explain it if he can.'[41] A week later Waters sent two ounces of different sorts of 'Matecot'.[42] Given the significant amount of yellow in the painting it may well be that that was the colour wanted by the painter.[43] The correspondence therefore agrees with 1735 as the date of the painting, though (like the engraving) it makes no reference to Masucci.

There is, however, a portrait of Clementina, known only from an engraving by Sorello of 1737, which can definitely be attributed to Masucci. It too shows the queen kneeling in front of an altar. This time, however, she kneels immediately in front of it, with a breviary in her right hand. The sceptre and one of the crowns are on her right side, beside a cushion similar to that in the former painting, and a large candlestick has been placed beside her.[44] The existence of this engraved portrait gives further support to the attribution to Masucci of the large painting of the marriage.

These paintings were not the only Stuart portraits produced during the early 1730s. James seems to have been content to reissue from time to time the older medals which showed himself and Clementina. Thus he ordered fifty unspecified medals to be struck to mark the return of the Stuart court to Rome in 1729,[45] and told Ermenegildo Hamerani in 1730 to reissue the medal (*Providentia obstetrix*) which had commemorated the birth of the Prince of Wales.[46] But at the end of 1731 he commissioned Ottone Hamerani to produce a new medal, which showed the two princes in profile.[47] The obverse shows the eleven-year-old Prince Charles facing right, and states that *Micat inter omnes* (he shines in the midst of all). The reverse shows the six-year-old Prince Henry facing left, and describes him as *Alter ab illo* (the next after him).[48] The medal was clearly intended for circulation in England, as the princes are not identified, but it was presumably also distributed to friends and supporters in Italy. There is a note of

[41] RA. SP 180/42, Waters to Edgar, 14 June 1735.
[42] RA. SP 180/75, Waters to Edgar, 21 June 1735.
[43] The *Oxford English Dictionary* gives two relevant definitions of 'mastic': 'a shade of pale yellow', and 'a fine varnish used for varnishing pictures'. In the present context it seems more likely that the painter wanted the colour.
[44] Sharp, *Engraved Record*, p. 109, no. 195. See above, note 30.
[45] RA. SP 125/172, James III to Ellis, 16 March 1729.
[46] NA. SP 98/32/f. 61, Stosch to Newcastle, 4 May 1730. The king gave one of these medals to Bishop Foucquet on 30 April 1730 (BAV. Fondo Borgia Lat MS 565, f. 379).
[47] NA. SP 98/32/f. 325, Stosch to Newcastle, 19 January 1732.
[48] Noel Woolf, *The Medallic Record of the Jacobite Movement* (London, 1988), p. 87, no. 43.

June 1732 which gives the king's approval for one gold and twenty silver medals to be struck for the queen.[49]

Two more medals of the princes were struck in 1737, one in Rome by Ermenegildo Hamerani, the other in Venice by Agostino Franchi. They both show Prince Charles on the obverse, and Prince Henry on the reverse, with each of them facing right. The legends on the medal by Hamerani are *Hunc saltem everso iuvenem* (at least permit this youth [to repair the ruins of the age]) for Prince Charles, and *Triplicis spes tertia gentis* (the third hope of a triple nation) for Prince Henry.[50] Those on the medal by Franchi, by contrast, identify the princes as *Carolus Walliae Princ.* and *Henric. Dux Eborancensis*.[51]

Franchi's medal is particularly interesting because it was struck while the Prince of Wales was in Venice. It has been observed that 'the profile of Prince Charles ... can be shown to be identical' with a drawing made in Rome by Giles Hussey, 'with the exception of the back of the head':

Clearly Franchi based his portrait on Hussey's work. It would appear that he had no separate portrait of Henry to copy, and so made use of the same profile, but knowing Henry to be five years younger than his brother he weakened the chin and generally produced a chubbier effect.[52]

Some explanation is perhaps required of how Franchi obtained the drawing of Prince Charles.

It is already known that Hussey arrived in Rome towards the end of 1732 and acquired a considerable reputation as a portrait draughtsman, producing a series of profile heads in monochrome.[53] None of his biographers, however, has noticed that he was joined by one of his sisters, Mary Anne, who became a servant of Lady Nithsdale and lived in the Palazzo del Re.[54] This gave Hussey easy access to the Stuart princes, and helps explain the portraits of them which he produced in 1735 and 1736.

In 1737 Hussey left Rome and returned to England, but his sister remained at the court. The day before Prince Charles set out for Venice, at the end of April, she married William Turner, who was one of Prince Henry's *valets de chambre*.[55] Hussey had probably given the drawing to Prince Charles, and the latter had taken it with him to Venice.

---

[49] RA. SP 154/3, Edgar to Ellis, 3 June 1732.
[50] Woolf, *Medallic Record*, p. 90, no. 47. The medal was reissued in 1742 (NA. SP 98/46/ f. 47, Stosch to Newcastle, 28 April 1742).
[51] Woolf, *Medallic Record*, p. 89, no. 46.   [52] *Ibid.*, p. 89.
[53] Sheila O'Connell, 'Giles Hussey', in *Oxford Dictionary of National Biography* (Oxford, 2004), *Oxford*, vol. xxviii, pp. 985–6; Ingamells, *Dictionary*, p. 540.
[54] ASVR. Santi Apostoli vol. 65, *Stati d'Anime*, 1735, p. 91.
[55] ASVR. Santi Apostoli vol. 23, p. 49.

Presumably the prince did not own, or take with him, one of Hussey's companion portraits of his younger brother, but this connection would seem to explain how Franchi was able to obtain in Venice a drawing of Prince Charles which had been made by Hussey in Rome.

While Prince Charles was in Venice he sat for two identical pastel portraits by Rosalba Carriera. The original was sent to James in Rome; the replica was sent to Owen O'Rourke, the Jacobite diplomatic representative in Vienna.[56] Prompted by this, James agreed during that summer to commission two further pastels, of himself and the Duke of York, with copies in oils to be sent to O'Rourke.

The artist selected by James was Jean-Etienne Liotard, presumably because he had just produced a portrait of Pope Clement XII. James wrote that 'it is true I am very unwilling to sit for my Picture, but however I was prevailed upon lately to do so, to a very good Picture drawer who is now here'. He promised that 'there shall be a copy made of it, and of the Duke's picture also'.[57] These copies, which were made by Louis-Gabriel Blanchet, were finished in February 1738.[58]

As James thought highly of the new portraits he agreed to let Liotard make a third pastel portrait of the Prince of Wales, and a miniature, both of which were finished in December 1737.[59] When James compared it with the one done by Carriera he felt that Liotard's was 'the better likeness of the two', so he told Blanchet to make a copy in oils of this one as well,[60] which was finished in March 1738. All three oil copies were

[56] RA. SP 198/41, O'Rourke to James III, 22 June 1737; RA. SP 200/1, 113, James III to O'Rourke, 9 August and 7 September 1737; RA. SP 202/26, James III to O'Rourke, 15 November 1737; RA. SP Misc 38, account book, November 1737 ('Pagati per porta ... a Palazzo d'una Casetta d'un ritratto del Principe, venuto di Venezia'). Corp, *King over the Water*, p. 74, fig. 62. The pastel, which is in a private collection in Rome, was the last portrait to show Prince Charles with his own hair (RA. SP 199/166, Edgar to Tyrrell, 3 August 1737: 'the Prince is in great joy on acc.t of his hair being cut off this afternoon and his putting on a Wig. I was present at the operation'). A copy was made by Francesco Guardi in 1738 for Graf von der Schulenburg. It is now in a private collection in New York (Antonio Morassi, *Guardi: I dipinti* (Venice, 1975), vol. I, p. 348, no. 215, and vol. II, fig. 233. It should be added that the portrait by Rosalba Carriera described in Bernardina Sani, *Rosalba Carriera* (Turin, 2007), p. 288, no. 320 as showing James III in about 1730 is definitely *not* a portrait of the king.

[57] RA. SP 200/113, James to O'Rourke, 9 July 1737.

[58] RA. SP 202/26, 143, James III to O'Rourke, 15 November and 6 December 1737; RA. SP 202/106, O'Rourke to James III, 30 November 1737; RA. SP 203/18, James III to O'Rourke, 13 December 1737; RA. SP 203/145, O'Rourke to James III, 4 January 1738; RA. SP 205/110, James III to O'Rourke, 17 February 1738. For the portrait of Prince Henry, see Corp, *King over the Water*, p. 75, fig. 64. The painting is in the Scottish National Portrait Gallery, Edinburgh.

[59] RA. SP Misc 38, account book, December 1737: 'Pagati a Liotard 54 Zecchini per Tre Ritratti in Pastella del Re, Principe e Duca, et une miniatura del Principe: 553. 10.'

[60] RA. SP 203/56, James III to O'Rourke, 20 December 1737.

then sent to Vienna,[61] where they were shown to the Empress (the wife of Charles VI), who was known to be sympathetic to the Jacobite cause.[62]

In addition to these oil copies, James commissioned from Liotard a set of miniature copies of each of his pastels,[63] and Lord Dunbar commissioned two copies in enamel of the portrait of Prince Charles.[64] Other copies must have been made, because several sets of miniatures, and one of James III himself, were sent to France, Scotland and England during the rest of 1738.[65] In most of these pictures, none of which was engraved, the princes are shown with the Garter only and not the Thistle. None of Liotard's pastels has survived, and his portrait of James is known only from the miniature, which shows him facing right, and wearing a brown coat with gold buttons (Fig. 20).[66]

There seem to have been two reasons why Blanchet was chosen to copy the portraits by Liotard. The first is that David died in July 1737,[67] the very month during which James decided to commission

---

[61] RA. SP 205/134, James III to O'Rourke, 14 March 1738; RA. SP Misc 38, account book, March 1738: 'Pagati a M. Edgar Z.30 m. de d'ord. [del Re], Ritratti. Vienne: 150 livres'; RA. SP 206/104, O'Rourke to James III, 3 May 1738; RA. SP 206/156, James III to O'Rourke, 16 May 1738. The payments for the frame (to Santi, *falegname* and Vasselli, *indoratore*), are in RA. SP Misc 38, account book, April 1738. For the portrait of Prince Charles, see Corp, *King over the Water*, p. 75, fig. 65. The painting is in the Scottish National Portrait Gallery, Edinburgh.

[62] RA. SP 206/166, O'Rourke to James III, 17 May 1738: 'they were a day or two in her m.s closet, and she [said] . . . yt she had much satisfaction in seeing those pictures, yt she shewd them to both her daughters, and to the Duke of Lorraine, who all admired the beauty of the princes'.

[63] RA. SP Misc 38, account book, February 1738: 'Pagati a Liotard Z.100 m. 4 Ritratti in miniature del Re, Regina e Principi consegn.ti a Mr Edgar con le loro scattole.' It is worth noticing that Liotard also made a copy of a portrait of Clementina, presumably the one by Meytens.

[64] RA. SP Misc 38, account book, February 1738: 'Pagati a Liotard Z.75 p. due Ritratti del Principe en email a Milord Dunbar.'

[65] RA. SP 202/107, Smith to Edgar, 30 November 1737; RA. SP 205/131, Edgar to Villefranche, 20 March 1738; RA. SP 206/122, Edgar to T. Innes, 8 May 1738; RA. SP Misc 38, account book, November 1738, a payment for six miniatures, 350 livres; RA. SP 212/65, Pajot de Villiers to Edgar, received December 1738. Some of these miniatures were probably by Pompeo Batoni, and at least one of them also had the participation of Orsola Urbani. An inscription on the back of a miniature reads: 'Prin.e Henrico Benedetto Stuart a Roma da Orsola Urbani sotto Pompeo Battoni an.o 1738' (L.R. Schidlof, *La miniature en Europe aux 16ᵉ, 17ᵉ, 18ᵉ et 19ᵉ siècles* (Graz, 1964), vol. i, A–L, p. 522). The same miniature has recently been dated 1734 by Philip Mould Ltd, but the date on the back actually reads 1738, and the earlier dating is contradicted by all the evidence already cited here from the Stuart Papers.

[66] Corp, *King over the Water*, p. 111. There are two known sets of miniatures which include Liotard's portrait of James III.

[67] *I David* exhibition catalogue, p. 204. David went to Naples to work for King Charles, and died there in 1737 (Imma Ascione (ed.), *Lettere ai sovrani di Spagna*, ii, *1735–39* (Rome, 2002), pp. 118, 124–43, 234–5).

Figure 20. *James III*, 1737 (miniature), after Jean-Etienne Liotard.

the copies. The second is that James had known, or known of, Blanchet
for several years. The painter had been one of the first *pensionnaires* at
the Académie de France, which James had visited with increasing
frequency since December 1729, when Blanchet and others, including
Pierre Subleyras, had entertained him with a performance of Molière's
L'Avare.[68] By 1737 Blanchet and Subleyras had both graduated from
the Académie, but decided to remain in Rome, in lodgings which they

---

[68] Blanchet joined the Académie de France in 1728. The list of *pensionnaires* is given in
Olivier Michel and Pierre Rosenberg (eds.), *Subleyras, 1699–1749*, exhibition catalogue
(Paris, 1987), pp. 116–17. For the performance of *L'Avare*, see NA. SP 85/16/f. 608,
Stosch to Newcastle, 1 December 1729.

shared.[69] Given James's close relations with the duc de Saint-Aignan and the Académie de France,[70] it was natural that he should consider employing one of its graduates, and these two were the only painters among them who had not returned to Paris. We do not know why Blanchet rather than Subleyras was the painter selected. Perhaps they settled the matter between them. Or perhaps it was because Blanchet had just painted his successful portrait of Panini.[71] In any event, it was while Panini was painting the large canvas for the duc de Saint-Aignan, with James and his two sons shown in a prominent position in the Church of S. Luigi dei Francesi,[72] that Blanchet was commissioned to make his copies of the pastels by Liotard.

That same month, November 1737, James also commissioned Blanchet to produce two large full-length portraits of the princes, with the faces copied exactly from the pastels by Liotard, for the Duchess of Parma. They were both finished by the summer of 1738, when the princes were seventeen and thirteen respectively.[73] Blanchet's images of the princes are so similar to Liotard's that it is difficult to distinguish between them, particularly as the duke is shown wearing the same embroidered brown coat.[74] The only obvious difference is in the costume of the Prince of Wales, who now has an armour breast-plate over the embroidered red coat which he wears in the portrait by Liotard. The prince stands confidently, with his right hand placed on a helmet, his left hand on his hip (Fig. 21). The duke, by comparison, seems delicate and even timid, accompanied by a hound with its two front feet raised on a chair (Fig. 22). Both princes wear the Garter, but neither has the Thistle.[75]

In the following year, 1739, Blanchet was commissioned by William Hay (the king's *maggiordomo*) to paint another pair of portraits. They are similar to the previous ones, but the princes, who had matured in the

---

[69] Michel and Rosenberg (eds.), *Subleyras*, pp. 116, 120.   [70] Chapter 12.

[71] Blanchet's portrait of *Panini* was painted in 1736 (private collection).

[72] *The duc de Saint-Aignan giving the Cordon of the Saint-Esprit to Prince Vaini* in November 1737 (Musée des Beaux Arts, Caen). See Chapter 12, p. 248.

[73] RA. SP 206/159, Duchess of Parma to James III, 16 May 1738; RA. SP 207/19, James III to Duchess of Parma, 23 May 1738. Blanchet was paid 90 *zecchini* = 450 *lire* for each painting. The payments are all recorded in RA. SP Misc 38. For the portrait of Prince Charles he received 30 *zecchini* in November 1737, 7 in February 1738, 12 in April, and 42 when it was finished in May. (The extra *zecchino* was for the case.) For the portrait of Prince Henry he received 30 *zecchini* in May 1738, and 60 when it was finished in August. (An additional small payment was made for the case in September.)

[74] As Liotard's original pastels have not survived, it might be objected that this comparison is invalid, in that we are not actually able to compare Blanchet with Liotard, but only Blanchet with his own copies of Liotard.

[75] Corp, *King over the Water*, pp. 76–7, figs. 66, 67. The paintings are in the National Portrait Gallery, London.

Figure 21. *Prince Charles*, 1737–8 (190.5 × 141 cm), by
Louis-Gabriel Blanchet.

intervening year, are now shown to below the waist only. Because Hay
was Scottish, he insisted that the Thistle should be shown in a prominent
position on top of the *cordon bleu* of the Garter. Whereas the Prince of
Wales wears both orders over his armour (indeed the star is actually
welded on to his breastplate), the duke has his red coat open to show that
he is wearing both orders beneath it.[76] Once again these portraits were
not engraved.

The fact that these pictures were commissioned by William Hay is
interesting because it draws attention to the relative scarcity of known
Jacobite portraits painted in Rome during the ten years after the return

[76] *Ibid.*, p. 78, figs. 68, 69. The paintings are in Holyroodhouse, Edinburgh.

Figure 22. *Prince Henry*, 1738 (186 × 140.3 cm), by
Louis-Gabriel Blanchet.

of the court from Bologna in 1729. Lord Marischal commissioned a
small portrait of himself from Placido Costanzi in or about 1731.[77]
There is a caricature drawing of Lord William Drummond made in
1732 by Pier Leone Ghezzi.[78] And one of the Stuart inventories refers
to a portrait of Sir Thomas Sheridan.[79] But that is all. Then, in 1739, the

[77] The painting is in the National Portrait Gallery, London. Lord Marischal was in Rome
from July 1731 to March 1733. When he returned in 1736 he commissioned Costanzi to
paint *The Battle of Bannockburn* (NA. SP 98/37/f. 315, Stosch to Newcastle, 28 January
1736).

[78] Ingamells, *Dictionary*, p. 315. Ghezzi had previously made a caricature drawing of Lord
Southesk (*ibid.*, p. 880), another of Sir Thomas Dereham dated 1725 (*ibid.*, p. 293), and
two of James III, one of which is dated 7 January 1729 (Sotheby's, London, 10
December 1979, p. 82, n. 141).

[79] RA. SP 262/94, inventory of the possessions of Prince Charles left in Rome, 1744.

Figure 23. *Sir William Hay*, 1739 (62 × 48 cm), by Domenico Dupra. Having served as a captain in the Russian navy, William Hay was groom of the Bedchamber 1727–39, then *maggiordomo* in 1739–41 and 1744–51.

year that Hay commissioned Blanchet to paint the two princes, we get portraits of James Edgar, Dr James Irwin and William Hay himself painted by Domenico Dupra. All three men are shown facing right, with a cloak, but Hay's has fallen away from his right shoulder to show that he, as a former captain in the Russian navy, is wearing armour beneath it (Figs. 23, 24).[80]

These two portraits are part of a set of nine which show members of the Society of Young Gentlemen Travellers in Rome,[81] all of them painted by Domenico Dupra, perhaps with the assistance of his

[80] The paintings of Edgar, Irwin and Hay are in the Scottish National Portrait Gallery, Edinburgh. The portrait of James Edgar is referred to in SCA. BL 3/55/15, G. Innes to Grant, 21 December 1739.
[81] Chapter 16, p. 332.

Figure 24. *Dr James Irwin*, 1739 (62.9 × 48.5 cm), by
Domenico Dupra. Irwin was one of the king's physicians from
1729 until his death in 1759.

brother Giuseppe.[82] It is not known how or why Dupra was the
painter selected to produce all these portraits, but his work was
evidently appreciated because it resulted in some important commissions from James III.

By 1740 the political situation in both Great Britain and Europe as a
whole seemed increasingly favourable to the prospects of a Stuart restoration. Under these circumstances James felt that it was important that
new images of the handsome young princes should be made available, to
inspire both the loyalty of the dissatisfied in Great Britain and the

[82] It is not clear to what extent Domenico Dupra was assisted by his brother Giuseppe in
painting these nine portraits. One receipt for a Stuart portrait refers to 'i due Pitori
Dupra' (RA. SP 259/32, receipt by Edgar, 4 September 1744).

support of pro-Jacobites in France and Spain. As no new engravings had been circulated since 1730, James decided that the time had come to commission some new ones.

In 1740 Dupra painted two portraits each of the princes, and all four were strikingly successful. In the first pair both princes are shown in armour, with an ermine-lined red cloak. The picture of the prince has been lost and is only known from a slightly reduced copy. The one of the duke shows him holding a baton in his left hand and resting it on a table. In the second pair they are both holding batons in their right hands. The duke's armour extends to below his elbow, whereas the prince is wearing a breastplate (Figs. 25, 26). In all four the Garter and the Thistle are clearly visible on their chests.[83] James preferred the second pair, and ordered at least four copies to be made, as well as several pairs of miniatures.[84] The engravings were done in Paris by J. Daullé and J.G. Wille and are of outstanding quality. These portraits quickly established themselves as the official images of the princes, were copied by other engravers and very widely circulated in the years which followed, which coincided with the 'Forty-Five'.[85]

It was during 1740, while Dupra was painting these portraits, that it was decided to create the imposing monument to Queen Clementina in St Peter's. The monument was to contain a portrait of the queen reproduced in mosaic, and the *Fabbrica di San Pietro*, responsible for creating mosaics, asked James III to select the image to be included. The procedure was that the portrait would be copied in oils by a painter employed by the *fabbrica*, and then worked up from that into the mosaic for the monument.[86]

Not surprisingly, James chose the portrait by Meytens, which Panini had previously included in the frontispiece of the book describing her funeral. The copy was painted by Lodovico Stern, who finished it in

[83] Corp, *King over the Water*, p. 79, figs. 70–2. These paintings are all in private collections. A larger version of the lost portrait of Prince Charles, which might even be an original, is at Darnaway Castle.

[84] RA. SP Misc 38, account book. This records several payments during 1740: two portraits in February for 'M.P.' (40 *zecchini*), two more in February for 'Dame B—be' (30 *zecchini*), two more in April for the comte de Béthune (40 *zecchini*), two more, and one of the king, 'in piccolo' in April for James Kearney (45 *zecchini*), two more 'in miniatura' in July for 'B—y' (30 *zecchini*) and two more in August for Ralph Smith to send to England (30 *zecchini*). See SCA. BL 3/62/6, G. Innes to Grant, 7 March 1740: 'The pictures are all come, and Mr Waters wants only orders and an opportunity to send 'em.'

[85] Sharp, *Engraved Record*, pp. 112–14 and pp. 124–5.

[86] NA. SP 98/43/f. 94, Stosch to Newcastle, 12 November 1740. See Brosses, *Lettres d'Italie*, vol. II, pp. 241–3, for a detailed description of how this was done.

Figure 25. *Prince Charles*, 1740 (71.8 × 59.1 cm), by Domenico Dupra.

June 1740,[87] and then gave it to Pietro Paolo Cristofari, the *sovrain-tendente ai lavori del mosaico*,[88] who finished the mosaic in June 1741.[89] It was included in the monument when it was eventually unveiled in January 1745.[90]

Stern was not the only painter to copy the portrait of Clementina by Meytens during the summer of 1740. Prince Henry decided that he

[87] 'Registro degli Ordini della Rev. da Fabbrica di San Pietro', no. 22, p. 74, 21 June 1740. Stern was paid 40 *scudi*. (I am grateful to Peter Pininski for giving me photocopies of some of the pages in the 'Registro'.)

[88] *Ibid.*, no. 37, p. 78, 20 September 1740. Cristofari was given an advance payment of 150 *scudi*.

[89] *Ibid.*, no. 86, p. 94, 6 June 1741. Cristofari was given a further payment of 50 *scudi*. See above, Chapter 11, p. 228.

[90] *Benoît XIV*, I, p. 175, to Tencin, 23 January 1745.

Figure 26. *Prince Henry*, 1740 (71.8 × 59 cm), by Domenico Dupra.

would like a copy for himself, and commissioned Blanchet to paint one for him.[91] William Hay then asked Blanchet for another copy, of the same approximate dimensions as his 1739 portraits of the princes. To match those, Blanchet extended the original composition to show Clementina to below the waist, with her left hand resting on a crown. Although only a copy, Blanchet's is in fact the best known of the various versions of Meytens's portrait that have survived, and has consequently misled people into thinking that his was actually the original.[92]

While Blanchet was working on these two copies, his friend Subleyras was also painting the portrait of a Jacobite. His sitter was Countess

[91] RA. SP Misc 38, account book, August 1740: 'Pagati a Blanchet z.12 m.ta per copia del Ritratto della Regina p. il Duca: 60 livres.'
[92] Corp, *King over the Water*, p. 80, fig. 74. The painting is in a private collection.

Mahony (née Lady Anne Clifford), the twenty-five-year-old step-daughter of the 5th Earl of Derwentwater. Having lived for many years in Rome, she had gone with her parents to Saint-Germain-en-Laye, and married Count James Joseph Mahony in 1739. The portrait was painted in the summer of 1740, when she travelled via Rome to join her husband in Naples. The three-quarter-length portrait shows her seated, with a King Charles spaniel on her knee, no doubt a reference to the fact that Lord Derwentwater was a grandson of Charles II. Her white chemise ('[she] is wearing a négligée cut very low on the bust') is decorated with pink ribbons, and she has a bracelet on her left wrist with two rows of large pearls.[93]

During the following year William Hay was obliged to leave the court.[94] He settled at Sens in France, where there was a Jacobite community, but before leaving he gave enough money to his friend James Edgar to pay Blanchet to paint a new portrait of the king.[95] This was intended to complete his set and console him for his enforced departure. James was not willing to sit for a new portrait, but Edgar had in his possession a pen and ink drawing of James's head in profile, which he felt was a very good likeness. It had been drawn in January 1741 by Francesco Ponzone.[96] Edgar lent this drawing to Blanchet, who then used it (in reverse) to paint the new portrait. James wears a cloak over most of his chest, so the Thistle is obscured, but the Garter is the same as in Blanchet's 1739 portrait of the Prince of Wales. The picture is smaller than the other three in Hay's possession, because Blanchet had not been left enough money for a larger picture,[97] but in all other respects it was intended to be part of a set. Most notably, James is shown wearing a fashionable pointed glove on one of his hands only, as are the princes.[98]

Once Blanchet had finished with Ponzone's drawing, Edgar sent it to Paris to be given to the Duchess of Buckingham.[99] A copy had already

[93] *Subleyras*, pp. 264–5. The painting is in the Musée des Beaux Arts, Caen, and a copy of 1785 by Batoni is in the National Gallery of Scotland, Edinburgh. A companion portrait of Count Mahony, by Francesco de Mura, is in the Fitzwilliam Musem, Cambridge.

[94] See Chapter 16, p. 333.   [95] RA. SP 232/40, Edgar to Hay, 22 April 1741.

[96] The drawing is in the Royal Collection. Very little is known about Ponzone, who signed this profile 'Francesco Ponzone Milanese'. In 1741 he also made a sketch in Rome of Edward Holdsworth, a Jacobite tourist (Ingamells, *Dictionary*, p. 509).

[97] RA. SP 232/66, Edgar to Hay, 29 April 1741: 'I have given Mr Blanchet the 15 cequins you left with me with wch he was very well satisfyed.'

[98] Corp, *King over the Water*, p. 81, fig. 76. The painting is in the National Portrait Gallery, London.

[99] RA. SP 233/103, Edgar to Waters, 15 June 1741; RA. SP 234/85, Waters to Edgar, 4 July 1741.

been made in Rome showing the bust as well as the head,[100] and this was subsequently engraved in reverse in 1747, with a false inscription claiming that it was 'publish'd according to act of Parliament'. The engraving, which was made in England, is interesting because it has subsidiary images of the two princes based on the pen-and-ink profiles by Giles Hussey.[101]

At the beginning of 1742 James commissioned Dupra to paint a set of four portraits. The ones of the princes were reduced copies of those Dupra had already made in 1740. James now agreed to sit for his own portrait and Dupra, like Stern and Blanchet, made a copy of Meytens's portrait of Clementina. The dimensions were virtually the same as the oil copies by Blanchet of Liotard's 1738 pastel portraits of the princes, and it may be that they were intended to be interchangeable.[102] Dupra made several other copies of these portraits, and a smaller one of the new portrait of James himself was sent to Lord John Drummond.[103] In 1742 Dupra also painted two new portraits of the princes which James kept for himself. Both are half length and show an ermine-lined cloak over armour. Prince Charles looks over his right shoulder, and Prince Henry over his left.[104]

The creation and circulation of sets of four pictures showing all the members of the royal family, including Clementina, became quite frequent from this point onwards. The sets were most frequently in miniature, and the painter who was particularly employed to produce them was Veronica Telli, the sister of Lodovico Stern. Her earliest known miniatures are copies of the pastel portraits of the princes by Liotard, and dated 1743,[105] and she was employed again when Prince Charles was in Paris preparing to invade England.

[100] Corp, *King over the Water*, p. 80, fig. 75. The drawing is in the National Portrait Gallery, London.

[101] Sharp, *Engraved Record*, pp. 100–1, no. 158. A 'note in an 18th-century hand' on the copy of the engraving in the British Museum states that it was 'after a drawing from Life, in possession of Dr Irwin at Rome'.

[102] The paintings are in a private collection. When General Randall Macdonnell forwarded to the court a request for portraits of the king and the two princes, Edgar wrote to him in March that 'upon what you say of being commissioned by Madame Campiglio to seek the pictures of their R.R.H.H. for her, the King is very glad of the opportunity to do her a pleasure, so that H.M. has actually already ordered the Pictures to be done' (RA. SP 240/87, Edgar to Macdonnell, 3 March 1742). For the portrait of James III, see Corp, *King over the Water*, p. 82, fig. 77.

[103] RA. SP 244/69, Edgar to Drummond, 20 September 1742.

[104] The paintings are now in the Palacio da Liria, Madrid, where they are wrongly attributed to Joseph François Parrocel. They were apparently given by Cardinal York to the 4th Duke of Berwick. For the portrait of Prince Henry, see Corp, *King over the Water*, p. 111.

[105] The miniatures are at Drummond Castle.

In May 1744 Prince Charles asked to be sent miniature portraits of his father, mother and brother. He specified that he wished these miniatures to be done by Pompeo Batoni,[106] 'coppid from the likest pictures',[107] but James gave the commission to Veronica Telli instead.[108] Not wishing to disappoint his brother, Prince Henry then ordered Dupra in July to paint a new portrait of himself, holding a miniature of the Prince of Wales,[109] which was then copied in miniature by Batoni.[110] The duke disliked Batoni's copy, writing to his brother that 'Pompeo has at last finished my Picture, it is finely done, but to tell you the Truth it is not well copied from the Originall'. He therefore employed Telli to produce an alternative, intending to send to Paris the one he preferred.[111] In the end Prince Charles was sent the four miniatures by Telli, and not the one by Batoni: 'All the Pictures you ordered are at last finished. I am afraid you wont be very well pleased with any of them except mine, which is judged by everybody to be the likest thing that ever was done for me.' Prince Henry also sent his brother a profile which was perhaps copied from the one by Ponzone: 'As your Picture of the King is very unlike I reckoned you wou'd not

---

[106] For Batoni's very close (and hitherto unsuspected) links with the Stuart court during the 1730s, see Edward Corp, 'The Stuart Court and the Patronage of Portrait Painters in Rome, 1717–1757', pp. 39–53, in Marshall, Wolfe and Russell (eds.), 'Roma-Britannica', at pp. 46–7.

[107] RA. SP 257/60, Charles to Edgar, 25 May 1744: 'In my letter to the King, I desired his Majesty to be so good as to send me his Picture the Queens and the Duke in minature. I reccon you will have the direction of them, for which reason I write to you this letter for to desiere you to get them to be don by Pompeo, that's to say coppid from the likest pictures and to have them if possible all the three together, so that they may be put in a box (to explen myself) the King and Duke together and the Queen as it were in a picture in the same room, but I leve it to your judgment whether to have them so or all three separate.' Prince Charles's letter to James III of the same date is RA. SP 257/57.

[108] RA. SP 257/131, James III to Charles, 19 June 1744.

[109] RA. SP 257/133, Henry to Charles, 19 June 1744; RA. SP 258/12, Henry to Charles, 4 July 1744 ('I have sitt no less than four Owers for my Picture yt with a good deal of Patience, doing what I can to make it as like as you would wish'); RA. SP 258/60, Henry to Charles, 17 July 1744 ('I believe ... you will be pleased with my Picture for the Originall from whence it is to be copied tho' it be not quite finished yet it is as like as two droppes of water. I have sitt allready for it about 14 ours'); RA. SP 259/32, receipt by Edgar, 4 September 1744 ('Ho Ricevuto scudi quaranta m.ta per dare alli due Pitori Dupra, per un ritratto del Duca con in mano quello di S.A.R. il Principe').

[110] RA. SP 259/103, receipt from Batoni, 21 September 1744 ('Io sotto scritto confesso do aver ricevute dall Ill.m M. Marsi scudi venti, moneta, quale sono per una migniature fatta da me rapresentate il ritratto di S. Altezza Reale il Sig. Duca di Yiorche').

[111] RA. SP Box 1/98, Henry to Charles, 28 August 1744 ('the same person that has copied the other three Pictures for you, is actually copieing of mine, when it is finished, I shall send you the one that will be judgd most lick me').

be sorry to have a Profile of him that I had gott be made lately for myself; for it is finely done, and very like.'[112]

In the following year, after the prince had sailed to Scotland, the duke also went to Paris to request a French invasion of England. Like his brother he omitted to take any miniatures with him, so Telli was again employed by James. This time it was to make a set of four, including all the members of the family.[113] In the years which followed Telli continued to make these sets. Her portrait of the king was based on the one by Dupra of 1742; that of the queen was after the Meytens of 1725, recently copied by her brother as well as by Blanchet and Dupra; while for the pictures of the princes she used either the 1740 or the 1742 portraits by Dupra.[114]

So long as there was a serious prospect of a Stuart restoration these miniature portraits, like the engravings and the medals of the princes, continued to serve the practical political purpose of stimulating and maintaining loyalty to the exiled dynasty. The defeat of the Jacobite army at Culloden, however, made it clear that there never would be a restoration. This inevitably had consequences for the production of Stuart portraits. When Prince Henry ensured the future security of the family in Rome by becoming a cardinal, he commissioned several portraits which showed him in his robes, but they were inappropriate for circulation in England and Scotland. From this point onwards, therefore, the portraits produced at the exiled court were intended exclusively for display in the Palazzo del Re or for distribution to the friends and sympathisers of the Stuarts in Italy and France. Not many of these were needed.

Prince Henry was appointed a cardinal deacon in July 1747, and ordained a priest in September of the following year.[115] He commissioned two new portraits before his ordination, and two more after it. The first two were by Domenico Corvi and Blanchet. The second two were by Corvi and Anton Raphael Mengs. It is not known why or how Corvi and Mengs were selected.

---

[112] RA. SP Box 1/203, Henry to Charles, 18 September 1744. See also RA. SP 259/71, receipt by Edgar, 12 September 1744 ('J'ay Receu de Marsi la Somme de Soissante et deux ecus Pour quatre Portraits en miniature de la Maison Royale pour envoyer a S.A.R. le Prince scavoir 15 ecus pour chaque portrait et deux ecus pour la Boite'); RA. SP 259/90, James III to Charles, 18 September 1744.

[113] RA. SP 268/14, Edgar to Henry, 14 September 1745 ('The day after you parted from hence, I spoke to the King as you directed me, about yr great desire to have the four portraits of the royal family done in miniature, which H. M. very readily agreed to, so that as soon as your departure was public, I went to the Woman Painter and bespoke them').

[114] For Telli's miniature of James III, see Corp, *King over the Water*, p. 96, fig. 90.

[115] Chapter 11, pp. 231, 234.

In Corvi's first portrait of the cardinal, Prince Henry is shown three-quarter length seated at a table, holding a letter in his left hand and a quill pen in his right. Beyond the letter a bell can be seen, placed on some closed books. This portrait was painted in 1747 and engraved in Rome by Pietro Campana the following year.[116] Blanchet's portrait, painted in 1748, shows the cardinal standing full length, with his right arm outstretched before a draped curtain. He is beside a large and richly gilded chair and holds a biretta in his left hand.[117]

In Corvi's second portrait, Prince Henry is again shown seated at a table, though this time full length, holding a paper. The book is now open, with the bell placed beside it. The cardinal wears a richly jewelled cross on his chest, suspended from a string of pearls around his neck where once he had worn the Thistle. At his feet is a coronet representing Rome. The original portrait was painted in 1748, and apparently given to the brother of marchese Francesco Angelelli (the cardinal's *maestro di camera*), but many copies were also made, of which two half-lengths and five busts have survived.[118]

The painting by Mengs, which also dates from 1748, has been lost, but two copies have apparently survived,[119] as well as a most sensitive study in oils of his head and shoulders. The study is similar to the busts by Corvi, except that the cardinal is shown looking to the right instead of to the left.[120] The image was engraved the same year in Rome by Antonio Pazzi, as an illustration for *Effigies Cardinalium*, though not attributed to Mengs. The engraving shows a jewelled cross around the cardinal's neck, though none is shown in the sketch.[121] Like the one by Campana, it shows how relatively inferior the Roman engravers were, compared with the French.

It is possible that Mengs also painted a new portrait of James III, presumably to make a pair with his portrait of the cardinal, and perhaps to mark the king's sixtieth birthday in June 1748. Three

---

[116] Corp, *King over the Water*, p. 89, fig. 84. The painting is in the Wadsworth Atheneum, Hartford, Connecticut. It was presumably this portrait which was copied in miniature in the summer of 1747 and given to the papal master of ceremonies (NA. SP 98/53/f. 73, Stosch to Newcastle, 26 September 1747: 'une boete d'or avec son portrait').

[117] Corp, *King over the Water*, p. 88, fig. 80. The painting is at Darnaway Castle.

[118] *Ibid.*, p. 88, figs. 81, 83. The painting is in Holyroodhouse, Edinburgh. For the gift to Ottavio Angelelli, see Michael Levey, *The Later Italian Pictures* (London, 1964), p. 101, no. 652.

[119] The copies are in the Royal Castle (Ciechanowiecki Foundation), Warsaw, and the house of the Missionary Fathers, Cracow.

[120] Corp, *King over the Water*, p. 88, fig. 82. The painting is in the Musée Fabre, Montpellier.

[121] Sharp, *Engraved Record*, pp. 126–7, no. 272.

versions have survived. One is a bust and shows James looking to his left, with a crown above his raised right hand. He wears the Garter over a mole-coloured coat trimmed with gold lace, with the Thistle under it, though the St Andrew medal can be seen on his chest.[122] The other two are the same, but both show James three-quarter length and wearing armour. The king now holds a baton in his right hand, and the Thistle ribbon is shown around his neck below the sash of the Garter.[123] In each case the king's image is clearly derived from the earlier portrait by Dupra. In 1748 Mengs was only twenty years old and at the very beginning of his career, so he (like Blanchet) might well have accepted a prestigious commission which involved little originality. However, the dimensions of the bust are virtually the same as two of Corvi's busts of the cardinal, so it might perhaps be by the latter rather than by Mengs.[124]

In addition to these new portraits, there is also a set of four miniatures by Veronica Telli, signed and dated 1748, which includes one of Prince Henry as a cardinal. Her portraits of James and Clementina are still copied from the ones by Dupra and Meytens respectively, but she seems to have copied Blanchet's new portrait of Prince Henry as a cardinal deacon, and a French engraving of the Prince of Wales, who had been absent for over four years.[125]

In the autumn of 1747 Cardinal York commissioned Claude-Olivier Gallimard to make an engraving of the *facciata* which had been erected outside the north-east *palazzetta* of the Palazzo del Re. He then commissioned a large painting based on the engraving. The main difference between the engraving and the painting was that the latter – painted by three people in 1748 – included portraits of James III, the new cardinal and some of the Jacobite courtiers. Most of the picture, showing the *facciata*, part of the Palazzo del Re and the surrounding buildings, was painted by an unknown artist named Pubalacci. Nearly all the figures were added by Paolo Monaldi, then at the very beginning of his career as a painter of *bambocciate* (low-life figures). Finally the portraits of the king and the cardinal themselves were probably added by the third artist

---

[122] Corp, *King over the Water*, p. 91, fig. 85. The painting is in the National Portrait Gallery, London.

[123] *Ibid.*, p. 92, fig. 86. The painting is at Stonyhurst College.

[124] Steffi Roettgen, *Anton Raphael Mengs, 1728–79* (Munich, 1999), ex. 178, rejects the attribution to Mengs, and suggests that the portrait might have been painted by Benedetto Luti (who had died twenty-four years earlier, in 1724).

[125] They were sold to Asprey at Christie's, London in November 1967. One year before these miniatures were produced by Telli, 'un buste d'Argent du Portrait de son Fils ayné' was given by James III to the Casa Santa at Loreto (NA. SP 98/53/f. 71, Stosch to Newcastle, 19 September 1747).

called Silvestri (presumably an italianisation of Mengs's friend Louis de Silvestre).[126] Father and son are shown in profile, and behind the king can be seen two of his principal courtiers. One of them must certainly be his *maggiordomo*, William Hay, but there are several possible candidates for the other.

After 1748 there are very few references in the Stuart Papers to the commissioning of portraits. In January 1750 Cardinal York paid 100 *livres* for a miniature ('per un Ritratto in Miniatura ... per ... una Tabacchiera d'Oro'),[127] and in both 1750 and 1752 Carlo Costanzi engraved several intaglios showing the king's head.[128] There is also a payment to Blanchet in April 1752 of 24 *zecchini*, or 120 *lire*, for two pictures, one of the king and one of the cardinal, to be sent to Paris.[129] The relatively modest price suggests that the paintings must have been copies. In fact there are only two original portraits of James III and Cardinal York that have survived from the period 1748–65. There is a full-length which shows the elderly king in a formal pose, standing with a cloak opened up to reveal armour beneath. He wears both the Garter and the Thistle, while his right hand holds a baton resting beside the crown on a table. The king is now a very much older man, but the portrait still recalls the pictures by Mengs (or Corvi), though the painter remains unidentified (Fig. 27).[130] There is also a portrait of Cardinal York painted by Mengs in about 1756.[131] By the 1750s it seems that neither James III nor Cardinal York had any desire to commission many new portraits, being content to let their existing ones be copied when necessary. We do, however, have a pencil sketch of James which was drawn after his death in January 1766, while his body lay in state in the Church of Santi Apostoli. It shows his face and torso.

---

[126] Edward Corp, 'The *Facciata* of Cardinal York: An Unattributed Picture in the Scottish National Portrait Gallery', *Journal of the Scottish Society for Art History*, 15 (2010–11), pp. 33–8. Pubalacci was paid 150 *scudi* for painting the *facciata* and surrounding buildings, Monaldi was paid 200 *scudi* for painting most of the figures and Silvestri was paid a further 35 *scudi* for adding some of the figures, presumably those of the king and the cardinal (RA. SP Misc 40, p. 95, and a loose sheet of paper inserted in the same volume headed 'Nota delle Spese fatte per La Facciata per Servitio di A.A.R. Ema.').

[127] RA. SP 303/98, Cardinal York's household expenditure, January 1750.

[128] RA. SP 310/70, Prince Charles to Edgar, 25 August 1750; RA. SP 330/17, Hay to Edgar, 17 February 1752; RA. SP 330/150, Hay to Edgar, 7 April 1752.

[129] RA. SP 331/62, 'Conto Generale del Mese di April 1752'. It is interesting to note that during 1752 Blanchet was imprisoned for debt (*Subleyras*, p. 120).

[130] Corp, *King over the Water*, p. 92, fig. 87, where the portrait is wrongly attributed to Placido Costanzi. The painting is at Alloa Tower. For Costanzi's relations with the Stuart court, see Corp, 'Patronage of Portrait Painters in Rome', p. 47.

[131] The painting is in the National Portrait Gallery. For the attribution to Mengs, see Edward Corp, 'Prince Charles or Prince Henry ?', pp. 51–7, *The British Art Journal*, 10:2 (2009), at p. 55.

Figure 27. *James III*, 1757 (76 × 44 cm), by an unknown artist.

He wears a crown and has an orb placed on his left side.[132] The drawing is anonymous, but was perhaps made by one of the British artists in Rome at the time.

By the 1750s there was in fact a significant number of English and Scottish artists studying and working in the city. Andrew Lumisden (Edgar's under-secretary) is known to have recommended six Scottish pupils to Mengs, with whom he was in contact.[133] One of them, George Chalmers, painted an unfinished portrait of Lumisden himself in 1753.[134] The only British painter, however, to produce any portraits of the Stuarts after 1748 seems to have been Cosmo Alexander (later Chalmers's brother-in-law), who painted a set of four in 1749.[135]

Alexander, whose father had worked in Rome for the Duke of Mar in 1718, arrived in the city at the beginning of 1747 with a letter of recommendation to James Edgar.[136] The king told Edgar to give him ten *zecchini*, which seems to have been charity rather than payment for a painting.[137] It is not clear how Alexander then lived, but in 1749 he painted a portrait of the Earl of Winton, shortly before the latter's death. The elderly earl, who is shown without his wig, wears armour under his coat and rests his right elbow on a table beside him. In his right hand he holds a baton, presumably a reference to his military involvement in the rising of 1715–16.[138]

It was during the same year that Alexander painted his set of four Stuart portraits. The one of James III was after the recent one by Mengs (or Corvi). That of Clementina was based on her earlier portraits by both Trevisani and David. For the Prince of Wales he used a recent French engraving of one of Dupra's portraits of 1740, and for Cardinal

---

[132] The drawing is in the collection of the Master of Forbes.

[133] Ingamells, *Dictionary*, p. 617. See James Dennistoun, *Memoirs of Sir Robert Strange . . . and of his Brother-in-law Andrew Lumisden* (London, 1855), vol. I, p. 247, Lumisden to unspecified, 1753: 'A few months ago came from Dresden a Saxon painter called Mincks [Mengs] . . . He was formerly here.' For Lumisden's friendship with Mengs, see NLS. MS 14260, p. 58, Lumisden to Harper, 15 October 1760.

[134] Ingamells, *Dictionary*, p. 193.

[135] In 1749 James Russel's father asked him for portraits of James III and Cardinal York (Ingamells, *Dictionary*, p. 832). Russel painted a 'life-size' portrait of the cardinal and probably also another one of the king, neither of which have survived (private information in August 2010 from Dr Jason Kelly, editing the unpublished letters of James Russel for the Walpole Society).

[136] Ingamells, *Dictionary*, p. 12.

[137] RA. SP 285/14, James III to Marsi, 19 July 1747: 'Marsi donnera a Edgar diz zechins pour le Pere Magines et diz zechins pour un tel Alexandre jeune Peintre Ecossois, le tout de l'argent.'

[138] Tayler, *Stuart Papers*, opposite p. 276.

York he used the first (1747) portrait by Corvi. All four compositions were altered just enough to give an appearance of originality.[139]

During the years after the return of the court from Bologna in 1729 James III and his son commissioned approximately thirty original portraits and a considerably larger number of copies. Most of the original images are mentioned in the correspondence and accounts preserved in the Stuart Papers, but many are not, and are only known because they happen to have survived. We can, therefore, be sure that the present chapter is not exhaustive. Confirmation of this is to be found in the inventories of the possessions of the Duchess of Albany and Cardinal York, drawn up after their deaths in 1789 and 1807 respectively.

The inventory of the duchess, which contains items she had inherited from her father (Prince Charles), includes a pastel portrait of Queen Clementina and, significantly, a bronze bas-relief of James III about which nothing is known.[140] The inventory of Cardinal York, which contains items he had inherited from the duchess as well as his own collection, includes what appears to be a double portrait of himself and his brother: 'A small picture representing the portrait of the two boys of the Royal Family' (quadro piccolo rappresentante il ritratto di due ragazzi della Real Famiglia).[141]

There are also intriguing references in both the inventories to lost family group portraits. That of the duchess includes 'a large picture representing copies of Portraits of 5 members of the Royal Family'

---

[139] For the portraits of James III, Clementina and Prince Charles, see Corp, *King over the Water*, p. 96, fig. 91; p. 97, fig. 93; and p. 111. The paintings of the king and queen are in private collections. Those of Prince Charles and Prince Henry are, respectively, at Sizergh Castle and the Château de Versailles. There is a self-portrait of Cosmo Alexander painting his portrait of James III in a private collection (sold by Philip Mould Ltd in 2010).

[140] Archivio Storico di Propaganda Fide, Stato Temporale Eredita del Card. Duca di York, Inventario Contessa [sic] d'Albany vol. 5, no. 83, 'Rendimento dei Conti Generale di tutto l'Asse Ereditario della Ch. Mem. Sig.ra Duchessa di Albania cessata da vivere in Bologna li 17 Novembre 1789', inherited by Cardinal York and concluded in July 1794, items 190 and 60. The only known contemporary bas-relief of James III is the triple one by Andrea Pozzi (*c*.1747–8), which shows the king with his two sons in profile (private collection). According to an inventory of 1788 the English College in Rome had 'due piedistalli di pietra colorita, con due medagléone di pietra bianca colorita di Giacomo III Rè d'Inghilterra, e di Maria Clementina Subieschi sa moglie' (VEC. Scritture 47/22, 'Inventario di tutta la Mobilia esistente nel Ven. Collegio Inglese di Roma', 31 August 1788).

[141] ASR. Misc Famiglia: Stuart b. 171, f. 5, 'Copia dell'Inventario de Beni Ereditari della Ch. Me. di S.A.R. Em.a il Sig.e Card.l denominato Duca di York esistenti nel palazzo della Cancelleria', 18 July 1807.

(un quadro grande rappresentante 5 Figure della Famiglia Reale copia).[142] That of the cardinal includes both 'a picture representing the Royal Family of the Deceased Cardinal Duke' (un quadro rappresentante la Famiglia Reale del Defonto Card.e Duca) and 'another picture of the Family' (uno altro ritratto di Famiglia).[143] The mention of '5 Figure' suggests that the family portrait belonging to the duchess probably included the four Stuarts (James III, Clementina, Prince Charles and Prince Henry) and Louise of Stolberg, the wife of Prince Charles. If so, it must have been painted after their marriage, and would therefore fall outside the chronological period covered by the present study. It may well be that it is one of the two pictures referred to in the cardinal's inventory, but it cannot be the 'picture representing the Royal Family' (quadro rappresentante la Famiglia Reale), because the dimensions do not fit.[144] Whether this painting was commissioned by James III or Cardinal York we cannot tell, but it is the only group portrait of the Stuart royal family in exile which is known to have been painted in Rome. The loss of such a significant family portrait, which has left no trace in the contemporary archives, is a clear indication that the patronage of portrait (and other) painters by the Stuart court in Rome might have been even greater than this chapter has been able to demonstrate.

---

[142] See note 140, item 189. This is presumably the painting mentioned in an inventory of Prince Charles: 'quadro ... per traverso longo palmi 10 e largo palmi 8 [245 × 196 cm] con cornice liscia rappresentanti cinque ritratti della Casa Reale con un grosso cane' (RA. SP 496/167, 'Inventario delle due Camere chi esistono nell'Appartamento di S.M. a Roma, e spedito in Firenze', 11 August 1779. That inventory also refers to a 'quadri alti palmi 9 e largo palmi [220.5 × 171.5 cm] con cornice stretta rappresentantà due ritratti in piede della Casa Reale con due cani levrieri'.

[143] See note 141.

[144] The painting of the duchess is described as 'in misura di palmi 9 e 6' (220.5 × 147 cm), whereas the one belonging to the cardinal was 'di misura Palmi 7; e 3 per traverso' (171.5 × 73.5 cm), clearly a different shape and a different picture. The dimensions of the painting belonging to the duchess are given in another copy of her inventory (Archivio Storico di Propaganda Fide, Stato Temporale Eredita del Card. Duca di York, Inventario Contessa [sic] d'Albany vol. 4, no. 29, also item 189). Those of the painting belonging to Cardinal York are given in a note attached to the inventory by Angiolo Cesarini, Bishop of Milevi: 'nota di porzione nel mobilio di Roma scelto da' me'.

15   The composition of the court, 1729–1747

During the 1730s, after the return of the court from Bologna, the household was divided into four parts, or families, respectively serving the king, the queen, Prince Charles and Prince Henry. The servants in the household below stairs and the stables worked for all four.[1] Perhaps the most significant development at this time was the steady increase in the number of locally recruited Italians. Most of the senior posts continued to be occupied by people from England, Scotland, Ireland and France, but the kitchen, wine cellar, confectionary and stables were mainly staffed by Italians from the Papal States and (for reasons which are not clear) the Duchy of Milan.

The size of the court varied. In the early 1730s it employed and supported about 135 people, at an annual cost in salaries and pensions of approximately 16,420 *scudi*.[2] After the death of the queen in 1735 the number of people employed was slightly reduced, bringing the total cost of salaries and pensions down to about 16,000 *scudi*. As the princes grew up they were given extra servants, so the annual total rose to approximately 16,322 *scudi*. When the two young men went to France in 1744–5 the court was considerably retrenched. By the early 1750s, when Prince Charles was still away and Prince Henry had a separate household paid for out of his ecclesiastical revenues, the king employed and supported about 100 people at a total annual cost of approximately 10,500 *scudi*. With very few exceptions the amounts of the salaries and pensions, always recorded in *livres* rather than in *scudi*, remained the same as they had been when decided at Saint-Germain, Urbino and

---

[1] Except where shown, the description which follows is based on the lists of salaries and pensions in RA. SP (particularly 129/88, 130/193, 131/136, 131/137, 135/81, 136/45, 136/53, 137/39, 144/21, 151/107, 158/41, 167/44, 176/89, 184/161, 214/51, 215/5, 239/17, 246/111, 247/53, 254/137, 259/3, 259/133, 273/160, 280/3); the registers of baptisms, marriages and death for the parish of Santi Apostoli in ASVR. (vols. 12, 13, 23, 42); and the *Stati d'Anime* for the parish in ASVR. (vols. 65 to 70 and 72).

[2] At Bologna the court contained 130 people, and the annual cost of salaries and pensions was 16,750 *scudi* (see Chapter 10, p. 201).

Bologna.[3] One visitor noted in 1741 that 'the family live very splendidly and yet pay every body and ... are certainly in no want of money'.[4]

The steady increase in the number of Italians employed at the court can be identified by examining the approximate figures for the other nationalities. In 1730 there were 20 English, 22 Scots, 9 Irish, 17 French, 1 Pole and 1 Swiss, totalling 70. In the following years the number of non-Italians steadily declined: 62 in 1735, 57 in 1740, 38 in 1745, 29 in 1750, 19 in 1755, and only 14 in 1760.[5] Most people at the Stuart court spoke Italian, but there remained a group of anglophones surrounding the royal family. The princes, like their father, spoke English, Italian and French 'perfectly well',[6] though they normally spoke to the king in English.[7]

Most of the non-Italian servants were unmarried, widowed or at least no longer living with their spouses. Only four of the servants had come to Rome with wives of their own nationality: Lord Nithsdale, Gottfried Rittel (the queen's Polish *valet de chambre*), Dr James Irwin (physician) and Pierre Arnoux (chapel keeper). Four had already taken Italian wives,[8] and one had married someone of a different nationality.[9] The parish records include five Jacobite marriages which took place after the return of the court in 1729: Isabella Gordon (chambermaid to the queen) and Pietro Marsi (paymaster) in 1730, François Decelles (*valet de chambre* to the king) and the daughter of Gottfried Rittel (*valet de chambre* to the queen) in 1736, William Turner (*valet de chambre* to the duke) and Mary Anne Hussey (sister of the artist Giles Hussey) in 1737, James Duncan (*valet de chambre* to the king) and an Italian named Joanna Barbarossa in 1738, and Michele Vezzosi (*valet de chambre* to the prince) and Mary Lindsay (chambermaid to Lady Nithsdale) in 1739.[10] This was significant because, with the single exception of the Irwins (who lived in the parish of San Andrea delle Frate),[11] all of these

---

[3] Corp, *A Court in Exile*, pp. 118–23, 131–5; Corp, *Jacobites at Urbino*, pp. 152–3.
[4] Lady Mary Wortley Montagu to Wortley Montagu, 25 February 1741, quoted in Gregg, 'Financial Vicissitudes', p. 76.
[5] The detailed breakdown of these figures was as follows: *1735*: 17 English, 17 Scots, 9 Irish, 17 French, 1 Pole and 1 Swiss. *1740*: 12 English, 18 Scots, 9 Irish, 16 French, 1 Pole, 1 Swiss. *1745*: 11 English, 13 Scots, 3 Irish, 10 French, 1 Swiss. *1750*: 7 English, 11 Scots, 3 Irish, 7 French, 1 Swiss. *1755*: 6 English, 7 Scots, 2 Irish, 3 French, 1 Swiss. *1760*: 5 English, 5 Scots, 1 Irish, 2 French, 1 Swiss.
[6] Russel, *Letters from a Young Painter*, vol. I, p. 76.
[7] Brosses, *Lettres d'Italie*, vol. II, pp. 77–8.
[8] Domenico Arnoux (assistant to the paymaster), Felix Bonbled (*valet de chambre* to the king), Joseph Boulieux (cook), Bernhardt Nieriker (guard).
[9] Jean-Baptiste Dupuis (*maestro di casa di cucina*), whose wife was Irish.
[10] ASVR. Santi Apostoli vol. 23, pp. 12, 43, 49, 52, 53.
[11] Ingamells, *Dictionary*, p. 545.

couples lived within the Palazzo del Re. They, and a small number of married Italian servants, therefore ensured that the exiled court remained a balanced community, unlike at Urbino, where there had been virtually no women. By 1726 there were more than ten children living in the palazzo,[12] and three more were born in 1727–30. The Decelles then had nine children, all of whom survived, between 1737 and 1747, and the Duncans had six, four of whom survived, between 1739 and 1748. These thirteen, and two more born to the wife of Lord Dunbar's *valet de chambre* in 1736 and 1744,[13] meant that the Palazzo del Re in Rome, like the Château de Saint-Germain a few decades earlier, contained a significant number of children in addition to the Stuart princes.

The servants of the queen, 1729–1735

During the last five and a half years of her life, the queen continued to be served in her Bedchamber by the people who had returned with her from Bologna: marchesa Lucrezia Legnani (lady of the Bedchamber), Lady Anne Maxwell (maid of honour), her three chambermaids (Marie Rivers, Mary Fitzgerald and Isabella Gordon), her necessary woman, her washerwomen, and her three valets (Rittel, Decelles and Duncan). Her first gentleman remained the Earl of Nithsdale, supported by marchese Fabio Albergati and conte Girolamo Formigliari, while Robert Creagh continued to deal with her correspondence. All of these were, of course, Catholics. Very little changed. Lady Anne Maxwell married Lord Bellew in 1731 and left the court.[14] Isabella Gordon married Pietro Marsi in 1730 and remained. Albergati returned to Bologna in 1733 because he was underemployed.

During 1729 and 1730 the queen's confessor was Father Cangiassi, but it is not clear how long he remained in her service. It appears that he was replaced by (Saint) Leonardo da Porto-Maurizio.[15]

After the queen's death in January 1735 Lucrezia Legnani entered the service of the Dowager Duchess of Parma,[16] and Formigliari returned to Bologna. Decelles and Duncan became additional valets to the king. All the other servants were given pensions equal to the value of their salaries, and remained at the court for the rest of their lives.[17]

---

[12] See above, Chapter 6, p. 122.   [13] ASVR. Santi Apostoli vols. 12, 13.

[14] NA. SP 98/32/ff. 265, 275, 573, 577, Stosch to Newcastle, 22 September and 13 October 1731, 26 September and 3 October 1733.

[15] Michel and Rosenberg (eds.), *Subleyras*, p. 88.

[16] NA. SP 98/37/f. 275, Stosch to Newcastle, 1 October 1735.

[17] Gottfried Rittel's daughter was given most of the queen's clothes. The inventory is in RA. SP 192/179.

The servants of the Prince of Wales, 1729–1744

Until he reached his eighteenth birthday in December 1738 Prince Charles's upbringing continued to be supervised by his Scottish governor, Lord Dunbar, and by his Irish under-governor, Sir Thomas Sheridan. His education was entrusted to his English preceptor, Father Lawrence Mayes, though he also had an Italian tutor of Spanish descent for mathematics and geometry (Diego de Revillas) and studied astronomy and physics with the Bolognese physician Antonio Leprotti.[18] For more mundane matters he was looked after by his two *valets de chambre*, Michele Vezzosi (Italian) and Pierre Ferbos (French), possibly his former nurse Francesca Battaglia (Italian) and his washerwoman Marie Gouy (the Swiss wife of Lord Dunbar's *valet de chambre*). Apart from Dunbar, they were all Catholics.

The prince also had two equerries, the *grand prieur* Geraldin and Captain John O'Brien, both of whom were Irish Catholics. When Geraldin died in 1733 the king decided that he should be replaced by two English Catholics, Francis Strickland and George Carteret. At that time they were serving in the French army in Berwick's Regiment, but they were released by Berwick and arrived in Rome in December 1734, just before the death of the queen.[19] Both men had been brought up at Saint-Germain, where Strickland's parents had been treasurer and Bedchamber woman to Mary of Modena, and where Carteret's had been gentleman usher of the Black Rod and Bedchamber woman to Princess Louise-Marie.[20] In addition to his equerries the prince was served by two gentlemen, John Stewart of Bute, who was replaced in 1736 by one of the English pensioners, William Goring, and John Constable. Both of them were Catholics, as were his Italian coachman and groom, and his Irish footman (Francis O'Neill).[21] The prince seems to have developed

---

[18] For Revillas, see NA. SP 98/37/f. 273, Stosch to Newcastle, 24 September 1735, and *SPW*, p. 108, memorandum by Dunbar, 1742. For Leprotti, see William Eisler, 'The Construction of the Image of Martin Folkes (1690–1754)', pp. 5, 11. It is not known who was employed as the prince's confessor, but Michael MacDonogh, an Irish Dominican, is said to have held the post in 1729–30 (Thomas Burke, *Hibernia Dominicana* (1762), p. 504).

[19] RA. SP 167/114, James III to Dicconson, 12 January 1734; RA. SP 169/3, James III to Innes, 17 March 1734; RA SP 170/103, Berwick to James III, 20 May 1734; RA. SP 174/153, James III to Innes, 1 November 1734.

[20] Corp, *A Court in Exile*, pp. 362–4, 366.

[21] When Prince Charles went to the Siege of Gaeta in July 1734 he was accompanied by Dunbar and Sheridan, his father's confessor, Saint-Paul, Vezzosi and Ferbos, and 'quelques valets de chambre et pied'. Because Strickland and Carteret had not yet arrived, their places were taken by Goring and Fitzmaurice (NA. SP 98/37/ff. 137, 141, Stosch to Newcastle, 31 July and 7 August 1734).

harmonious relations with all his servants except Lord Dunbar, who happened to be the only Protestant among them.

At the end of 1738 the prince reached his majority, and Dunbar, Sheridan and Mayes relinquished their posts. Sheridan, however, was retained to become the prince's *maggiordomo*, responsible for overseeing all his servants. Three other changes are worth recording. Carteret died in February 1740, followed by O'Brien in November 1741 and Goring in February 1743.[22] It is not clear who was appointed to serve as the prince's new equerry, but Goring was replaced by Edward Stafford, the son of John Stafford (vice-chamberlain to Mary of Modena) by his second wife Theresa (Bedchamber woman to Mary of Modena and sister of Francis Strickland). Stafford was, of course, another Catholic.[23]

The servants of the Duke of York, 1729–1745

Prince Henry reached his age of majority in March 1743, and until then his upbringing was also supervised by Lord Dunbar as governor. At first he had two English under-governors, Hugh Dicconson (brother of the treasurer at Saint-Germain) and John Paul Stafford (half-brother of Edward Stafford), but when the latter resigned in October 1730, because he wished 'to retire from the world' and enter the Church,[24] he was not replaced. Henry's education, like that of his elder brother, was entrusted to Father Lawrence Mayes until the latter's retirement in 1739. He was replaced by Father Ildefonso, the rector of the *Collegio di Propaganda Fide*.[25] The duke also had two *valets de chambre*, Martin Floriot (French) and William Turner (English), and possibly his former nurse Teresa Keller (Italian), and Prince Charles's washerwoman. Apart from Dunbar, all these servants were Catholics.

There is no evidence that the duke had his own equerry or gentleman at this stage, so he presumably shared those attached to his elder brother, but he did have his own Italian coachman and groom, and his own French footman (Jacques Catillon, who had worked at the Stuart court

---

[22] RA. SP 220/144, James III to FitzJames, 19 February 1740; ASVR. Santi Apostoli vol. 42, p. 67, 18 November 1741; NA. SP 98/46/f. 163, Stosch to Newcastle, 16 February 1743.

[23] Edward Stafford and Francis Strickland were confused by Stosch, who referred to Francis Stafford (NA. SP 98/49/f. 65, to Newcastle, 28 April 1744). His mistake is repeated in McLynn, *Charles Edward Stuart*, pp. 83–4.

[24] RA. SP 139/23, James III to Innes, 6 September 1730. He succeeded his nephew as 4th Earl of Stafford in 1751.

[25] *SPW*, pp. 107–8, memorandum by Dunbar, 1742.

since 1703).[26] His household, like that of Prince Charles, was Catholic and cosmopolitan, though it contained no Irish.

Dicconson, the under-governor, died in January 1743, shortly before Prince Henry's eighteenth birthday.[27] He might perhaps have become the duke's *maggiordomo* had he survived, but instead the post was given to John Townley, an English Catholic who had visited the court a few years before.[28] Lord Dunbar, having been governor to one or both princes since 1725, then found himself unemployed on a pension.

The king's Bedchamber and Chamber, 1729–1747

During the 1730s and 1740s James III continued to be served by a very small group of people in his Bedchamber. They included his three French *valets de chambre* (Thomas Saint-Paul, Felix Bonbled and François Delaux), an Italian page of the backstairs (Andrea Ciareine) and two or three washerwomen. After the death of the queen he also employed two of her *valets de chambre* (Decelles and Duncan). This might in part have been because Saint-Paul was growing old, but also because François Delaux went into business as a merchant, trading between Languedoc and the Papal States.[29] By 1739 he was described as *cameriere giubilato*, with a salary reduced by a half.

The permanent servants attached to the king's Chamber were his spiritual and medical attendants. His confessors were all Italian: Father Antonio Ragazzi until his death in November 1732, then a Cordelier named Father Francarsi,[30] and by 1747 a Conventual Franciscan.[31] His chaplain was Father Lawrence Mayes (who also served as preceptor to the two princes). The Chapel Royal, where the king regularly heard mass and sometimes took communion 'with all his Roman Catholic Servants',[32] was cared for by a French sacristan (Pierre Arnoux). When the latter died in 1741[33] he was succeeded by Pietro Battaglia, a son of Prince Charles's wet nurse.

---

[26] His first job was *valet de chambre* to Lady Sophia Bulkeley. He had become a servant of the king by 1712 (Lart, *Jacobite Extracts*, vol. II, pp. 44, 114).

[27] RA. SP 249/80, E. Dicconson to Edgar, 28 April 1743.

[28] NA. SP 98/32/ff. 508, 516, Stosch to Newcastle, 14 March and 11 April 1733.

[29] The company was called Delaux-Guarinoni, and its papers are preserved in the Archives des Pieux Etablissements de France at Rome. Delaux was described by Cardinal de Tencin in 1741 as 'un marchand français, honnête homme, très protégé' by King James (Pialoux, 'Rome, théâtre des relations diplomatiques', p. 278).

[30] NA. SP 98/32/f. 484, Stosch to Newcastle, 7 February 1733

[31] *Benoît XIV,* II, p. 244, to Tencin, 14 February 1753.

[32] NA. SP 98/32/f. 473, Stosch to Newcastle, 3 January 1733. Stosch's letters contain many references to hearing mass in the Chapel Royal.

[33] ASVR. Santi Apostoli vol. 42, p. 67, 18 November 1741.

There were also Anglican chaplains to provide services in one of the rooms of the palazzo for the Protestant servants and pensioners. At first there were two chaplains. The Revd Daniel Williams was Welsh and died suddenly of an apoplexy in August 1733.[34] The Revd Ezekiel Hamilton, who was Irish, left the court in November of the same year.[35] They were replaced in June 1734 by the Revd Thomas Wagstaffe, the son of a nonjuring bishop in England.[36]

The king's doctors were always Scottish. They included Dr Charles Maghie (who died in November 1732), Dr Robert Wright and Dr James Irwin, who joined the court with his wife in 1729. The king's surgeon, confusingly called James Murray, like Lord Dunbar, had joined the court at Bologna in 1728.

The king had briefly reintroduced formal waiting in his Bedchamber while the court was at Bologna, because the queen had insisted on it in her own apartment.[37] But it does not seem to have lasted long. Alan Cameron, one of the grooms of the Bedchamber, died in November 1730.[38] The remaining groom, Captain William Hay, appears to have joined the pensioners as one of the gentlemen in attendance, to serve in the Chamber when required.

The secretariat, 1729–1747

As already stated, James III reorganised the secretariat at Bologna in 1728 after the departure of Sir John Graeme and the retirement of Sir David Nairne. Contrary to what is said in all Stuart biographies and books on Jacobitism, the king never again employed a secretary of state.[39] His secretariat consisted of James Edgar (Scottish), his private secretary, and Mathurin Jacquin (French), described variously as under-secretary or *commis*. The secretary of state had been paid 204*l*. 2*s*. 3*d*. each month; Edgar received 100 *livres*. Nairne, as secretary of the closet, had been paid 205*l*. 3*s*. 2*d*.; Jacquin received 80 *livres*. If Edgar and Jacquin were ill or unavailable, or needed help, the king called upon the services of an Irish pensioner, Captain Henry Fitzmaurice.[40]

---

[34] NA. SP 98/32/f. 560, Stosch to Newcastle, 15 August 1733; RA. SP 164/73, Innes to O'Bryen, 24 August 1733.
[35] See below, Chapter 16, p. 326.
[36] In May 1736 an Anglican clergyman called Black asked unsuccessfully to be appointed chaplain to the court (Ingamells, *Dictionary*, pp. 93–4).
[37] See above, Chapter 10, p. 195.
[38] NA. SP 98/32/ff. 114, 116, Stosch to Newcastle, 26 October and 2 November 1730.
[39] RA. SP 225/43, Edgar to Maclean, 21 July 1740.
[40] NA. SP 98/43/f. 98, Stosch to Newcastle, 26 November 1740.

The ministry, 1729–1747

It seems to have been generally overlooked by historians that James III replaced the office of secretary of state by the creation of an informal group of ministers whose role it was to give him political advice. As it was impossible to obtain a replacement of sufficient standing and experience to become secretary of state, the king preferred to rely on trusted friends and supporters who were already in Rome.

Cardinal Gualterio had been a *de facto* minister until his death in 1728, and to some extent his place was taken by Cardinal Davia until he died in 1740. But James mainly sought advice from the French and Spanish ambassadors, particularly the duc de Saint-Aignan (1732–41) and Cardinal Aquaviva (*c.*1735–47). A little later his chief advisers included Cardinal de Tencin (1739–42) and the latter's nephew Jean-Louis Guérin, the bailli de Tencin (1739–48). From time to time he consulted Lord Dunbar, but the latter was too anti-French to have much influence. When both princes had achieved their majority in 1743 Dunbar tended to be ignored and used for little more than running errands and delivering messages.[41]

Two men can be identified as perhaps fulfilling the role of chief minister. The first was the Earl Marischal, who arrived in June 1731.[42] Many Jacobites had hoped that either the Duke of Ormonde or the Earl Marischal, both of whom had established themselves in Spain, might be persuaded to join the court as secretary of state, but neither had been prepared to do so unless both Inverness and Dunbar were first sent away. Marischal finally agreed to come in 1731, when it was clear that Inverness would never return, even though Dunbar was still at the court. By then the post of secretary of state had been abolished. He stayed with James III as his principal minister until March 1733, when he left Rome because he detested Dunbar.[43] He was replaced by Cardinal Riviera, who remained the king's chief minister for nearly twenty years.[44]

The household below stairs, the table and the stables, 1729–1747

Whereas the king's Bedchamber and Chamber continued to be mainly British and French, the other departments of his household became increasingly Italian. Even the names of the departments and the

---

[41] This comment is based on numerous references in NA. SP 98/46 and 49.
[42] NA. SP 98/32/f. 233, Stosch to Newcastle, 28 July 1731.
[43] NA. SP 98/32/ff. 490, 494, 508, Stosch to Newcastle, 28 February, 7 and 14 March 1733.
[44] See above, Chapter 12, p. 242.

positions within them ceased to be English. Thus the kitchen became the *cucina*, controlled by the *maestro di casa di cucina*; the wine cellar became the *bottiglieria*, controlled by the *bottigliere* or *cantiniere*; the confectionary became the *credenza*, controlled by the *confetiere* or *credenuere*; and the stables became the *scuderia* and *stalla*, controlled by the *cavallerizzo* and *maestro di stalla*. Above these men was the *maggiordomo*, responsible for the household below stairs, the table and the stables.

The *maggiordomo* was always English or Scottish. Thomas Forster held the position from 1722 to 1736, when he retired and left the court.[45] He was succeeded by John Stewart (previously gentleman to the prince), who died in January 1739,[46] then Francis Strickland (previously equerry to the prince), who went to France in July 1744,[47] then William Hay (previously groom of the Bedchamber, and created a baronet in 1748).[48]

The numerous members of the household below stairs and the stables do not need to be identified, particularly as there was a relatively quick turnover in the subordinate positions. The *cucina* had for many years been controlled by an Irishman, Jeremiah Broomer, recruited by James II in 1689. He retired in September 1730,[49] and was succeeded in turn by two Frenchmen. The *capocuoco* until at least 1742 was another Irishman, Matthew Creagh, recruited at Saint-Germain, but the other cooks were all French and Italian.

The *cucina* was situated on the ground floor of the north-east *palazzetta*, beside the entrance facing the Palazzo Muti. The *bottiglieria* was on the south side, beside the entrance facing the Piazza dei Santi Apostoli. Until 1728 it was controlled by another Irishman recruited by James II in 1689 (Charles Macarty).[50] When he died he was succeeded for four years by a Welshman (David Lewis),[51] after which the *bottigliere* was always an Italian.

---

[45] Stosch believed that he left the court because he was very discontented with the king, though he did not say why (NA. SP 98/37/ff. 251, 365, to Newcastle, 23 July 1735 and 2 June 1736).

[46] ASVR. Santi Apostoli vol. 42, p. 57, 8 January 1739. The parish register states that the body was taken for burial to the chapel of the Scots College.

[47] *SPW*, p. 146, James III to Sheridan, 25 July 1746.

[48] NA. SP 98/53/f. 103, Stosch to Newcastle, 9 January 1748.

[49] NA. SP 98/32/f. 108, Stosch to Newcastle, 5 October 1730. He died in Avignon, on his way back to Saint-Germain (RA. SP 141/87, 129, memoir by Elizabeth Crane, December 1730, and Elizabeth Crane to Inverness, 15 January 1731).

[50] Macarty had a 'considerable [business] dealing in wine' and died in March 1728 (RA. SP 102/87/134, 135, Ellis to Helen Macarty, 20 March and to Dicconson, 23 March 1728).

[51] RA. SP 143/150, Lewis to Ellis, 13 March 1731. Lewis possibly entered the service of Lord Palmerston in 1732 (Ingamells, *Dictionary*, p. 599).

The *credenza*, situated on the ground floor of the *palazzo grande*, beside the entrance in the Via di San Marcello, was controlled by a Frenchman (Pierre Pecquet) who returned to Paris in 1730,[52] and an Englishman born at Saint-Germain (Henry Read) who served until at least 1742. His successor and all the other servants in the sub-department were Italian.

Finally the bakehouse, possibly situated beside the *cucina*, was controlled by a French baker (Jean Bouzier). When he left (or died) in 1730 or 1731 he was not replaced, so bread was then perhaps brought in from a *panetteria* outside.

The *scuderia* and *stalla*, part of which (called the *stalla grande*)[53] was at the north-west corner of the palazzo, on the angle of the Via di San Marcello and the Vicolo dell'Archetto, was controlled by two old servants from Saint-Germain: James Delattre (French: equerry, or *cavallerizzo*) and John Sheridan (Irish: riding purveyor, now called *maestro di stalla*). When Delattre retired in 1742 he was succeeded by an Italian, cavaliere Giuseppe Gigli from Lucca. Sheridan, who died in June 1729,[54] was also succeeded by an Italian, Camillo Dini. As the years went by all the remaining old servants from Saint-Germain were gradually replaced. Edmund Butler, the king's first coachman (now the *primo cocchiere*) retired in 1740/41 and was succeeded by Salvatore Mambretti. Henry Kerby, his chairman, returned to France in 1730,[55] while the remaining grooms and footmen all retired or died in the following years.[56]

The absence of both Prince Charles and Prince Henry meant that some of the servants in the household below stairs and the stables were no longer needed. In September 1745 the king sold some horses and laid off several servants in the stables.[57] In December 1746 he laid off several more and also reduced the number of people working in the *cucina*, the *bottiglieria* and the *credenza*.[58]

The servants in these sub-departments naturally guarded the three entrances to the Palazzo del Re, but they were joined in December 1733

---

[52] André Kervella, *La passion ecossaise* (Paris, 2002), pp. 465, 467.

[53] ASV. PAC 983, no. 135/14, payments made by the *Camera Apostolica* for James III, 4 February 1729.

[54] ASVR. Santi Apostoli vol. 42, p. 12, 23 June 1729.

[55] RA. SP 176/47, 'Estat des Pensions du Roy payées par Mr Waters à Paris, 1733'. (The name has accidentally been entered as Jacques, not Henri. His son, James Kerby, was in Rome.)

[56] This refers to Andrew Simms, Mark Manning and Roger Ryan.

[57] NA. SP 98/49/f. 211, Stosch to Newcastle, 14 September 1745; *Benoît XIV*, I, p. 211, to Tencin, 15 September 1745.

[58] NA. SP 98/49/f. 355, Stosch to Newcastle, 13 December 1746.

by the Swiss Guards appointed by the Pope.[59] The main entrance in the Via di San Marcello already had its own *guarda portone*. This was Bernhardt Nieriker (from Zurich) until his death in March 1746,[60] and then Josef Luither (from Luzern).

The salaries of all these servants were paid by Sir William Ellis, the cofferer of the household, and Pietro Marsi, the paymaster, assisted by a French clerk named Domenico Arnoux. When the court returned from Bologna the cofferer had independent responsibility and reported directly to the king. This changed when Ellis (by then known as the *tesoriere*) died in August 1732.[61] Pietro Marsi (now the *segretario*) and Domenico Arnoux (now the *computista*) continued to pay the salaries, but under the supervision of the *maggiordomo*.

The pensioners and recruitment

The servants employed in the *tesorerie* were also responsible for paying the pensions to those exiled Jacobites with no official posts who were attached to the court. These pensioners were an important group, partly because they provided the king with an entourage of his own subjects both in his Chamber and when he went out, and partly because they could be drawn on to fill any posts which became vacant. It was therefore important for the king to attract enough people to replace the original pensioners when they either died or left.

In 1729, apart from the retired servants (Nairne, Rodez and Lady Nithsdale), there were only two of the original pensioners still in Rome: the Earl of Winton and Viscount Kilsyth. Seven others had been recruited while the court was at Bologna: one Englishman (William Goring), four Scots (George Abernethy, Thomas Arthur, Alexander Cameron and Arthur Elphinstone) and two Irishmen (Captain Henry Fitzmaurice and Sir John O'Brien). Cameron left the court to become a Jesuit in 1731,[62] and Elphinstone (later 5th Lord Balmerino) returned to Scotland in 1734.[63] Abernethy and Arthur remained until they died during the 1740s. The others were all eventually given posts.

When the Earl Marischal joined the court in 1731 he brought with him two Scottish Protestants (Mark Carse and Charles Slezor) who

---

[59] See above, Chapter 11, p. 217.
[60] ASVR. Santi Apostoli vol. 42, p. 91, 19 March 1746.
[61] RA. SP 155/48, James III to Dicconson, 6 August 1732.
[62] NA. SP 98/32/f. 307, Stosch to Newcastle, 1 December 1731.
[63] He left Rome and went to Berne in 1733 (NA. SP 98/32/ff. 475, 482, Stosch to Newcastle, 10 and 31 January 1733). He returned to Scotland in 1734 (André Kervella, *Le mystère de la rose blanche* (Paris, 2009), p. 118).

remained as pensioners after his departure. Maurice Corbet, another Scot who had been serving in the Dutch army, joined a few years later.[64] Then, during the 1740s, the king recruited four English Catholics: Joseph Bulstrode, James Paston, Robert Fermor and Joseph Dormer. Bulstrode had previously lived with his father at Saint-Germain,[65] and Dormer had been serving in the Austrian army.[66] Paston (from Norfolk) and Fermor (from Somerset) were already voluntary exiles.[67] It is not known how they were recruited. David Fotheringham of Powrie, a Scot who had been in exile since 1716, was invited to join the court in 1747, but died within a few weeks of his arrival.[68]

The only under servant from Great Britain recruited during these years was a certain John Macpherson, who became a footman shortly before 1739. Presumably he went to Rome in order to ask for employment, and perhaps he was the person referred to on 9 November 1737 in the Pilgrim Book of the English College: 'a Scotchman from Paris who sayd he intended to get into the King's service'.[69] That book refers to a certain 'Edward Windell, a Yorkshireman, by calling a Farrier', who stayed at the college, was given some money by the king and then left to return home. The entry for 12 January 1737 records that 'he was sent for afterwards to come into the King's service but was departed from Leghorn before the letters arriv'd'.[70]

One reason why English, Scottish and Irish people came to Rome was to be touched by the king, to be cured of the king's evil (scrofula). The Pilgrim Books of the English College contain many such examples of all three nationalities between 1729 and the 1750s, both men and women, Protestants and Catholics, mainly but not exclusively from modest social backgrounds. The ceremonies took place in

---

[64] NA. SP 98/49/f. 87, Stosch to Newcastle, 7 July 1744.
[65] For Sir Richard Bulstrode, see Corp, *A Court in Exile*, pp. 360, 363. Joseph Bulstrode had accompanied the 14th Earl of Shrewsbury as tutor during his Grand Tour in 1739–40 (Ingamells, *Dictionary*, p. 858). He had joined the court by 1742 (Chiddingstone Castle, Bower MSS, James III to the Mother Superior of the Convent of the Infant Jesus at Paris, 31 January 1742). One of his brothers was a priest in the English College in Rome (VEC. Scritture 27/5/1, J. Bulstrode to Benedict XIV, 24 September 1749).
[66] NA. SP 98/53/f. 81, Stosch to Newcastle, 24 October 1747.
[67] For Paston, see Ingamells, *Dictionary*, pp. 744, 749; and NA. SP 98/49/f. 89, Stosch to Newcastle, 14 July 1744. For Fermor, a cousin of Townley, see Ingamells, *Dictionary*, p. 352.
[68] NA. SP 98/53/ff. 81, 85, 89, Stosch to Newcastle, 24 October, 7 and 23 November 1747; *SPW*, p. 214, James III to Prince Charles, 7 November 1747.
[69] VEC. Libri 292, p. 21, 9 November 1737.
[70] VEC. Libri 292, p. 15, 12 January 1737. The Pilgrim Book also records that a certain Ramsay became cook to Lord Nithsdale (p. 16, 2 May 1737) and a John Stroel became a servant to John Constable (p. 26, 1 August 1739).

the Chapel Royal of the Palazzo del Re, though at least two are recorded as having been conducted at Albano.[71] James III commented on one occasion that 'the evil ... is very common in this Country, so that I often touch people for it, and always have medals by me for that use'.[72]

The Protestants

By the 1730s there were very few Protestants at the court, and they met in 'a small chappel where the Congregation usually consisted of five or six, and sometimes a smaller number'.[73] Services were held very regularly, according to the Revd Ezekiel Hamilton even 'four times in one day', but preaching was not permitted.[74]

In 1729–30 there were only ten Protestants, in addition to the Anglican chaplains already mentioned. They included Thomas Arthur (pensioner), Alan Cameron (groom of the Bedchamber), Lord Dunbar (governor), James Edgar (secretary), Sir William Ellis (cofferer), Thomas Forster (*maggiordomo*), William Hay (groom of the Bedchamber), Dr James Irwin, Dr Charles Maghie and Dr Robert Wright. They were joined in 1731 by Lord Marischal, Mark Carse and Charles Slezor, and later by Maurice Corbet, but by 1743 there were only five left: Corbet, Dunbar, Edgar, Irwin and Wright. The others had all either died or left Rome. William Hay returned in 1744, and the Revd Thomas Wagstaffe continued to have a very small congregation. His main purpose was to demonstrate James III's continued commitment to religious toleration, and to provide services for visiting Grand Tourists.

Wagstaffe was also responsible for ensuring that the Protestants in Rome did not convert to Catholicism. On one occasion a Protestant at the court gave some money to a Catholic priest for masses to be said for the soul of William Goring, who had died a few years earlier. He received a letter from Wagstaffe complaining that 'so many among us ... have turned their back upon our Religion'. Paying for the masses was either a complete waste of money, or implied accepting the Catholic doctrine on Purgatory and showing an indifference to the distinction between truth (Anglicanism) and error (Catholicism).[75]

---

[71] VEC. Libri 292, pp. 5, 26, 10 October 1733 and 18 June 1739.
[72] RA. SP 179/132, James III to Innes, 28 May 1733.
[73] RA. SP 167/92, Hamilton to Edgar, 7 January 1734.
[74] RA. SP 166/16, Hamilton to Edgar, 6 November 1733.
[75] NLS. MS 14269, p. 2, Wagstaffe to Lumisden, 7 September 1752.

The allocation of space

As already explained, the king's apartment was on the first floor of the *palazzo grande*, with the queen's immediately above, and the two princes lived on the second floor of the north-east *palazzetta*, facing the Vicolo dell'Archetto and the Piazza Pilotta. Lord Dunbar had an apartment on the first floor of the north wing, extending from the grand staircase to the Via di San Marcello above the *stalla grande*. The *maggiordomo* (Forster) lived on the first floor of the south-east *palazzetta*, facing the Convent of Santi Apostoli and the back of the Palazzo Muti. The apartment with the *loggetta* on the first floor of the north-east *palazzetta*, facing the Piazza della Pilotta, was left vacant in 1729 so that Lord Inverness could occupy it if he returned to the court.[76] He lived there briefly in January 1731, after which the apartment became available for other people.

The first person to occupy it was the Earl Marischal, who arrived at the court five months after Inverness left. When he also left in 1733 it seems to have been reserved for important visitors whom the king wished to honour. They included the Duke of Liria in 1734, Inverness himself in 1736, Marischal in 1736 and 1737, the 2nd Duke of Berwick (i.e. Liria) and his son in 1737, the marquis de Villefranche in 1741, and the 3rd Duke of Berwick in 1742.[77]

Villefranche, who had provided accommodation for James III in Avignon in 1727,[78] also visited the king in 1731 when the apartment with the *loggetta* was occupied by Marischal. On that occasion it was necessary to organise an elaborate exchange of apartments (involving Bonbled, Constable, Dicconson, Jacquin and both O'Briens) to make room for him.[79]

The location and occupation of all the other apartments and rooms in the palazzo can be ascertained by examining the annual *Stati d'Anime*, but they are of uneven quality.[80] There are no lists between 1720 and 1727, and then not until 1735, after which the *Archivio Storico Vicariato di Roma* contain a list for virtually every year. The lists gradually become more and more detailed, and eventually describe the location of each

---

[76] See above, Chapter 10, p. 208.

[77] NA. SP 98/37/ff. 47, 315, 357; 41/ff. 20, 22; 43/ff. 154, 156; 46/f. 81, Stosch to Newcastle, 20 March 1734, 28 January and 12 May 1736; 2 and 9 March 1737; 1 and 8 April 1741; 28 July 1742; ASV. PAC 985, no. 234/11, payments by the *Camera Apostolica* for James III, 3 October 1737.

[78] NA. SP 98/43/f. 156, Stosch to Newcastle, 8 April 1741.

[79] NA. SP 98/32/ff. 175, 223, Stosch to Newcastle, 7 April and 11 July 1731; RA. SP 147/142, a list of items placed in the Wardrobe, 8 August 1731; RA. SP 148/11, apartment and room changes in the King's Palace, August 1731.

[80] See note 1.

servant's accommodation in considerable detail, though the handwriting of the priests is sometimes completely illegible! The list for April 1740, entitled 'Lista di quelli che stanno nel Rollo del Rè d'Inghilterra e che habitano in Palazzo di S.M.', is particularly useful because it was given to the local priests by someone at the court, probably Jacquin.[81] It contains the names of 56 servants, 9 wives, 1 husband, 17 children, 3 relations (mother-in-law and sisters-in-law), and 3 personal servants, making a total of 89, in addition to the king and his two sons. The apartment of the queen was left empty after her death.

All the other servants and pensioners, with their wives or husbands and families, and several of them with their own servants, lived in the surrounding area, though not necessarily in the same parish. They included George Carteret, James Delattre, William Hay, Dr James Irwin, James Murray, John Stewart and the Revd Thomas Wagstaffe among the servants; and George Abernethy, Thomas Arthur, Joseph Bulstrode, Mark Carse, John Constable, Maurice Corbet, Joseph Dormer, Robert Fermor, Henry Fitzmaurice, Lord Kilsyth, James Paston, Charles Slezor and Lord Winton among the pensioners. Lord and Lady Nithsdale lived within the palazzo, perhaps on the second floor above the apartment of Lord Dunbar.[82]

The king's apartment

Although the king's apartment was regularly maintained by the *Camera Apostolica*, we know very little about its actual appearance, apart from the ceilings already described. It was presumably similar to the apartments of the Roman princes and cardinals, with mirrors, tapestries and paintings[83] decorating the walls, and with a canopy, or *baldachino*, in the third antechamber (the Presence Chamber).[84] In 1732 the Pope gave the king 'two magnificent tables of rare marble',[85] though we are not told where they were placed. In the fourth antechamber (the Privy Chamber) there was a small card table 'of green velvet with gold braid', another one made of oak 'with spaces to attach dogs underneath', and a table made of walnut wood 'garnished with red morocco'. At that time the Bedchamber contained a bed with four 'green serge curtains edged with yellow'.[86]

---

[81] ASVR. Santi Apostoli vol. 68, a separate sheet of paper inserted between pages 2 and 3.
[82] ASV. PAC 984, no. 156/19, payments made by the *Camera Apostolica* for James III, October to December 1732.
[83] For example, Cardinal Davia bequeathed to James III 'le plus beau Tableau de sa Galerie' (NA. SP 98/43/f. 8, Stosch to Newcastle, 24 January 1740).
[84] NA. SP 98/41/f. 49, Stosch to Newcastle, 27 May 1737.
[85] NA. SP 98/32/f. 335, Stosch to Newcastle, 2 February 1732.
[86] RA. SP 150/180, a list of the king's furniture, 1732.

In January 1733 the king's Bedchamber was completely redecorated and furnished, with 'a rich bed and all the decorations for a chamber', costing 1370 *scudi*.[87] This was essential to keep the room as impressive as possible because James's guests had to pass through it to reach his gallery.[88] The room contained twelve chairs and a green damask sofa on which the king sat when receiving his guests,[89] so we may conclude that he had adopted French rather than English etiquette as regards access to his Bedchamber. And it was in these surroundings that James III began and ended each day, speaking French to his *valets de chambre*.

---

[87] NA. SP 98/32/f. 482, Stosch to Newcastle, 31 January 1733. Stosch was told that the new Bedchamber cost 12,000 *scudi*, but the correct figure can be found in the papal archives.

[88] In 1742 and 1743 the well-known painter Pier Leone Ghezzi was employed (with a gilder named Giacomo Marini) to decorate parts of the Palazzo del Re, including the fireplace and chimney in the king's Bedchamber (ASV. PAC 987, no. 304/1; PAC 5045, p. 65; ASR. Cam I: GDT b. 2017 bis/13/19/pp. 45, 58; b. 2017 bis/13/20/pp. 4, 5).

[89] ASR. Cam I: CDG b. 2017 bis/13/14/p. 1; and ASV. PAC 5044, p. 72. Both show that the bill for 1370 *scudi* was paid on 24 March 1733. See also HMC, *10th Report*, appendix, part VI, p. 229, Prince Charles to Marefoschi, January 1772, in which he says that it was his father's custom to be 'on the sofa' when receiving visitors.

16 Freemasons and factions within the royal household, 1729–1747

No account of the Stuart court in Italy would be complete if it did not emphasise the negative influence of James Murray, Earl of Dunbar. From his arrival at Urbino in 1718 until his final departure from Rome in 1747, Dunbar was the cause of friction and discontent among the household servants and pensioners, and even between members of the royal family. During the early 1730s a concerted effort was made to reduce his influence with the king and to bring about his downfall. It ended in complete failure. Not until the 1740s was James III finally convinced that he should rid himself of Dunbar's unfortunate influence.

There were two main objections to Lord Dunbar's presence at the court, in addition to his personal unpopularity. He was held partly responsible for the strained relations between the king and the queen. And he was regarded as a close ally of his brother-in-law, Lord Inverness, who was living in Avignon. So long as Dunbar remained at the court, it was felt that the opinions of Inverness continued to influence the king.

This was important because many of the leading Jacobites in exile had begun to regard Dunbar and Inverness as the two chief obstacles to a successful restoration. Unless the evil influence of both men could be removed they felt they were wasting their time and energies – they were 'tilting at windmills' – in trying to help James III recover his thrones.

There were also serious doubts about the loyalties of both Dunbar and Inverness. The latter's brother, the 8th Earl of Kinnoull, had sworn allegiance to both George I and George II, and was appointed British ambassador to Constantinople in 1729. Dunbar's elder brother, the 6th Viscount Stormont, had similarly sworn allegiance to both Hanoverian kings, while his younger brother, William, had begun a brilliant legal career in close contact with the Whig establishment in England, which would lead to his joining the government as solicitor-general in 1742. It is hardly surprising that the Jacobites viewed both Dunbar and Inverness with complete mistrust. The fact is that the reports of Baron von Stosch and those sent by the elder brother of Lord Inverness all arrived on the same desk at Whitehall.

The opponents of Dunbar were not necessarily a united group of people, but most of them happened to be Freemasons, and several of the Freemasons were Protestants. Some of the latter argued that the best hope, perhaps the only hope, of a Stuart restoration was for Prince Charles to renounce his father and convert to Anglicanism.

The Order of Toboso

In 1726, shortly after the separation of the king and queen, an organisation was created by the Jacobites in Spain called the Order of Toboso.[1] It purported to be a chivalric order, but was actually a club and probably a network of Freemasons. The so-called Grand Master was the Revd Ezekiel Hamilton, then chaplain to the Duke of Ormonde, and its members included the Earl Marischal and Mark Carse, all of whom were in Spain at the time. Whatever the original purpose of the group, the members of the order seem from the outset to have been hostile to both Lord Inverness and Lord Dunbar. Their principal aim was to persuade the king to dismiss those two counsellors and replace them with Ormonde and Marischal.

Once Lord Inverness had been obliged to resign, the members of the Order of Toboso began to join the court. In 1728 Hamilton himself was appointed one of the two Anglican chaplains at Bologna,[2] and he soon enrolled William Hay and John Stewart to be members of the order. The next success came in June 1731 when Lord Marischal arrived to be the king's principal minister, accompanied by Mark Carse. Each member of the order was given a ring with the inscription 'To a Fair Meeting on the Green'. In anticipation of Marischal's arrival, William Hay had two new rings made in Naples. In June 1731 they were presented to Prince Charles and Prince Henry, both of whom agreed to wear them and become patrons of the order.[3]

During the rest of 1731 and 1732 Hamilton, Marischal, Hay and Carse recruited new members, who included Lord Nithsdale and Lord Kilsyth, the two most senior Jacobites at the exiled court.[4] They also

---

[1] Steve Murdoch, 'Tilting at Windmills: The Order of Toboso as a Jacobite Social Network', in Paul Monod, Murray Pittock and Daniel Szechi (eds.), *Loyalty and Identity: Jacobites at Home and Abroad* (Basingstoke, 2010), pp. 243–64.

[2] See above, Chapter 10, p. 196.

[3] NA. SP 98/32/f. 213, Stosch to Newcastle, 12 June 1731; HMC, *10th Report*, p. 178, Hay to Gordon, 2 February 1732.

[4] It is possible that Forster and Geraldin were also members. See NA. SP 98/32/f. 221, Stosch to Newcastle; and HMC, *10th Report*, p. 184, Hamilton to the Knights of Toboso, 22 April 1734.

did what they could to influence the two princes against Dunbar. As early as November 1731 Marischal wrote that Prince Charles 'has already got the better of his Governors'.[5] Yet the king still continued 'his esteem and regard' for Dunbar.[6] Marischal informed Ormonde in May 1732 that 'such counsels prevail [here] as can not frankly be told to an honest man'.[7]

The members of the Order of Toboso gradually moved towards their goal. In October 1732 Marischal wrote confidentially to his brother that Dunbar was detested in Rome, and that an attempt was being made to remove him.[8] This came to a head early in 1733, when Ezekiel Hamilton submitted a paper to James III in which he asked him to dismiss the unpopular governor.[9] When the king refused, Lord Marischal decided to leave the court and return to Spain. He departed on 2 March,[10] leaving Hamilton and the other members of the Order of Toboso to battle against Dunbar without him.

Hamilton's position was fatally weakened by this episode, and Dunbar counter-attacked. The sudden death of the Revd Daniel Williams in August left Hamilton as the only Anglican chaplain at the court, and gave him a short reprieve, but in October the king ordered him to leave the Papal States, because 'His Majesty sees now with concern that the uneasyness of mind he [Hamilton] suffers is not like to cease, as long as he remains in this country'.[11] At first Hamilton refused to leave, so the king gave instructions that he 'should come no more to this palace, nor appear any further in his presence'.[12]

What followed shows only too clearly the limits to the authority of a king living in exile. Hamilton simply refused to obey. On 8 November he visited the Palazzo del Re while the king was at Albano and, according to Dunbar's 'Account of Hamilton's Disgrace', 'after having sent to notify to all His Majesty's Protestant servants that he was there, and finding that none of them appeared, being scandalized to the last degree at his behaviour, and having remained there for the space of two hours all alone, he thought fit to retire'.[13] The king was forced to appeal to the

---

[5] HMC, *9th Report*, Part II, p. 222, Marischal to Keith, 21 November 1731.
[6] HMC, *10th Report*, p. 178, Hay to Gordon, 2 February 1732. The words quoted actually referred to Inverness, but were equally applicable to Dunbar.
[7] HMC, *9th Report*, Part II, p. 222, Marischal to Keith, 6 May 1732, reporting what he had written to Ormonde.
[8] *Ibid.*, p. 22, Marischal to Keith, 30 October 1732.
[9] Ingamells, *Dictionary*, p. 447.
[10] NA. SP 98/32/ff. 490, 494, 508, Stosch to Newcastle, 28 February, 7 and 14 March 1733.
[11] RA. SP 165/189, Edgar to Hamilton, 23 October 1733.
[12] RA. SP 165/236, Edgar to Hamilton, 1 November 1733.
[13] RA. SP 142/114, undated.

Pope, and a few days later the Governor of Rome formally expelled Hamilton from the Papal States,[14] which left the court without an Anglican chaplain.

The quarrel between Hamilton and Dunbar had a profound effect on the twelve-year-old Prince of Wales, who had agreed to be a patron of the Order of Toboso. The prince hated Dunbar, and this impacted on his attitude towards his father who had appointed and now defended him. Stosch reported that 'he made all sorts of insults, and even wanted to kick his Governor . . . and threatened to kill him'.[15]

Encouraged by Prince Charles's attitude, Hamilton returned secretly to Rome in April 1734, but he was soon discovered staying 'in a vineyard outside the Porta del Populo', and once again expelled by the Governor of Rome at the king's request.[16] There is a curious document dated 22 April, just after he had been discovered and expelled, in which Hamilton suggested that Dunbar had applied to become a member of the Order of Toboso. The paper contains a vitriolic attack on Dunbar, who is accused of having been grossly dishonest when he lived in Scotland and England before 1718, of having been insolent to Queen Clementina since then, and of having been rude to the *grand prieur* Geraldin. The king regarded Hamilton as 'little better than a mad man',[17] and the final paragraph of the document seems to bear this out:

We therefore Don Ezekiel Hamilton, Grand Master of the most ancient, the most illustrious and most noble order of Toboso, for these and other just reasons to be produc'd in due time and place and specifyd more at large in a life that will soon be publish'd, have decreed by the advice and consent of our brethren, all true and valiant knights, that the said James Murray &c is unworthy to be admitted into our order or into the lowest and meanest employment belonging to it, that his company ought to be avoided by all honourable knights and worthy squires, that he ought to be condemned to admire himself, to laugh at his own insipid jests and to read his own dull and malicious poems; and the said James Murray &c is by these presents declared to be for ever incapable of any of the honours, rights, dignitys, privileges, preheminencys and authoritys belonging to the said order.[18]

The problem was, of course, that Hamilton's lack of credibility strengthened Dunbar's position with the king, and threatened to

---

[14] NA. SP 98/32/ff. 590, 594, 596, Stosch to Newcastle, 21 and 28 November, 5 December 1733.

[15] NA. SP 98/32/f. 577, Stosch to Newcastle, 3 October 1733. See also f. 582, to Newcastle, 24 October 1733.

[16] RA. SP 169/77, James III to O'Bryen, 21 April 1734; NA. SP 98/37/f. 85, Stosch to Newcastle, 1 May 1734.

[17] RA. SP 166/9, James III to O'Bryen, 4 November 1733.

[18] HMC, *10th Report*, p. 184, Hamilton to the Knights of Toboso, 22 April 1734.

undermine the relationship between James and his elder son. In June 1734 Hamilton wrote to advise Prince Charles to disavow his father's authority.[19] This was absurd and irresponsible, as there was nothing that the thirteen-year-old boy could have done. But it still further strained the relations between the prince and his governor, and by extension between the prince and his father.

Hamilton never returned to Rome, and spent the rest of his life in the United Provinces and the south of France, maintaining contact with both Marischal and Ormonde. The latter wrote to him on one occasion that 'I never doubted of your friendship, nor shall you have reason to doubt of mine'.[20] His surviving correspondence is full of hostile comments about both Inverness and Dunbar,[21] the latter of whom he accused (in a letter to the king) of being 'the Chief, if not the sole Obstacle to your Majesty's Restoration'.[22] The king's opinion was that 'Mr Hamilton's true character ... [is] now so little a secret, that anything that is known to come from him will be of little consequence'.[23] If anything, Dunbar's position with the king had been strengthened by the whole episode.

The Jacobite Lodge at Rome

On 19 December 1733, about a month after Hamilton's initial expulsion, Sir Thomas Dereham invited Lord Winton to discuss the situation over dinner with Antonio Leprotti (tutor to Prince Charles, but also personal physician to Pope Clement XII) and Martin Folkes, a secret Jacobite who had been Deputy Grand Master of the Grand Lodge of London.[24] The latter had just arrived in Rome, and was staying at an inn on the Corso called Giuseppe's,[25] run by a Jacobite named Joseph O'Neill. It was on this occasion that the decision was taken to found a lodge in Rome for Jacobite Freemasons, who would hold their meetings at Giuseppe's.

Assemblies of Freemasons had already been taking place in Rome for several years – though we have no specific information about them,[26]

---

[19] McLynn, *Charles Edward Stuart*, p. 43.

[20] HMC, *10th Report*, p. 492, Ormonde to Hamilton, 9 May 1737.

[21] *Ibid.*, pp. 467–519. Inverness and Dunbar were 'the two foxes' (p. 468), and 'the Brethren of the Par Ignobile Fratrum' (pp. 478, 481, 505). Dunbar was 'a Man without Truth and Honour, and who is not to be trusted even in the smallest Matter' (p. 519).

[22] *Ibid.*, p. 493, Hamilton to James III, 11 June 1737.

[23] ASV. SS: Ingh 21, p. 214, Edgar to Goddard, 25 January 1737.

[24] Eisler, 'Construction of the Image of Martin Folkes', p. 12.

[25] Ingamells, *Dictionary*, p. 366.

[26] Pierre Pecquet, the yeoman confectioner, was a Freemason (Kervella, *Passion Ecossaise*, pp. 465, 467).

other than the fact that they admitted both Jacobites and visiting Hanoverians. Baron von Stosch, himself a Freemason who had attended what he chose to call 'those mysterious assemblies', wrote on 2 January 1734 (two weeks after Dereham's dinner party) that the Jacobite and Hanoverian masons no longer wished to meet together,[27] and gave that as the reason for the creation of the exclusively Jacobite Lodge. The new lodge was soon joined by Mark Carse, William Hay and John Stewart, members of the Order of Toboso.

Lord Dunbar was never apparently a Freemason, and had not therefore attended the meetings which included both Jacobites and Hanoverians. The creation of an exclusively Jacobite lodge, containing his leading opponents at the court, meant that he would not have been admitted even if he had applied for membership. The prime purpose of the Jacobite Lodge was no doubt to pursue the ideals and ceremonies of Freemasonry, but it also became a meeting place for the people who disliked Lord Dunbar. Lord Winton was a member, as probably also was Lord Nithsdale. The lodge was then joined by Henry Fitzmaurice, Dr James Irwin and Charles Slezor, and it welcomed any Grand Tourists visiting Rome who were known to be Jacobites. One of them was Sir Marmaduke Constable, first cousin to Lord Derwentwater and later the husband of Lord Nithsdale's granddaughter. It appears that Derwentwater was regarded as the Grand Master of all Jacobite Freemasonry, in France as well as Rome.[28]

We know nothing about the lodge in 1734 because the minute book for that year has not survived, but in April 1735 it was joined by William Howard, Viscount Andover, the 21-year-old son and heir of the Earl of Suffolk and Berkshire. On the 16th Stosch reported that Andover and other visiting Jacobites (notably Sir Thomas Twisden and the Revd Richard Younger) were openly meeting Lord Nithsdale and the other servants of James III.[29] By the beginning of May Andover was in contact with both Lord Derwentwater and Sir Thomas Dereham, and had had a very long conversation with James III himself.[30] He was then elected Master of the Jacobite Lodge.

During May it was noted that Andover spoke 'often, and very familiarly' with Prince Charles,[31] and that he was in contact with Lord Bourke,

---

[27] NA. SP 98/37/f. 16, Stosch to Newcastle, 2 January 1734.

[28] The Jacobite Lodge in Rome is analysed in Edward Corp, 'La Franc-Maçonnerie jacobite et la bulle papale *In Eminenti* d'avril 1738', *La règle d'Abraham*, 18 (2004), pp. 13–44.

[29] NA. SP 98/37/f. 224, Stosch to Newcastle, 16 April 1735.

[30] NA. SP 98/37/f. 228, Stosch to Newcastle, 2 May 1735.

[31] NA. SP 98/37/f. 172, Stosch to Newcastle, 14 May 1735.

through whom 'intrigues that one wants to hide from [Dunbar] normally pass'. He also gave 'a splendid dinner' for Stewart, Bourke and several other courtiers.[32] This contact continued throughout June, with Andover regularly meeting the king, the princes and Lord Derwentwater.[33] In July, when the time came for him to leave Rome and return to England, he arranged to say a public farewell to the king outside the Porta del Popolo.[34]

The first meeting of the lodge after the departure of Andover took place at Giuseppe's on 16 August, with John Cotton (heir to Sir Robert Cotton of Gedding, Huntingdonshire) as the new master. It was attended by (among others) Hay, Irwin, Slezor, Stewart and Winton, and involved a supper as well as the usual masonic ceremony.[35] Earlier that week Hay had a public quarrel with Dunbar in which they were only prevented from coming to blows by the intervention of others.[36]

Two further meetings took place at Giuseppe's in September, with Charles Slezer and John Stewart as the two wardens. During that same month Henry Fitzmaurice, one of the masons, was given the Grand Cross of the Order of Saint-Louis by the duc de Saint-Aignan, with 'a grand dinner for 18 people', most of whom were members of the Jacobite court.[37]

We do not know about James III's attitude towards the Jacobite Lodge, but we may assume that it was at least sympathetic both because of his friendship with Lord Derwentwater and with the master of the lodge, Lord Andover, and also because all non-Jacobites or pro-Hanoverians were specifically excluded. Moreover, it included his own servants and pensioners, one of whom had just been honoured by the French ambassador. But Carse, Hay, Irwin and Slezor were all Protestants, and the Roman Inquisition was concerned about heresy, and about the possibility of the masonic lodges being used for illegal Protestant ceremonies. On 20 December the members of the Inquisition deliberated what to do: 'After a report had been made about certain gatherings which were strongly suspected of heretical views, and which were usually held in a certain rented property on the Corso ... their

[32] NA. SP 98/38/f. 174, Stosch to Newcastle, 21 May 1735.
[33] NA. SP 98/38/ff. 180, 192, Stosch to Newcastle, 11 and 25 June 1735; NA. SP 98/37/ f. 238, to Newcastle, 2 July 1735.
[34] NA. SP 98/38/f. 204, Stosch to Newcastle, 30 July 1735.
[35] The minute book covering the period 16 August 1735 to 20 August 1737 was published by William James Hughan in *The Jacobite Lodge at Rome, 1735–7* (Torquay, 1910), pp. 37–52. The editorial comments are full of mistakes, but the book's authenticity is proved by the inclusion of two facsimile pages.
[36] NA. SP 98/37/f. 263, Stosch to Newcastle, 20 August 1735.
[37] NA. SP 98/37/f. 273, Stosch to Newcastle, 24 September 1735.

Eminences said that the landlord of the property, called Giuseppe, should be imprisoned.'[38]

The Inquisition, however, knew that it could make no arrests without the agreement of the king, so it published a decree forbidding any further meetings. John Cotton and Dr Irwin wisely kept away, but Carse, Fitzmaurice, Slezor, Stewart and Winton all went to Giuiseppe's on 27 December. On the following day the Inquisition ordered that Joseph O'Neill, 'known commonly as Giuseppe', should be imprisoned. It also decided that Irwin's valet should be arrested and forced to reveal what he knew about the Freemasons.[39]

Cardinal Pico (the Bishop of Albano) was sent to obtain the king's agreement to these arrests. James III, who of course disliked the Hanoverian Freemasons and who was perhaps concerned about the behaviour of his Protestant subjects, gave his consent on 4 January, and both men were arrested.[40] That same evening Slezor (deputy master), Carse, Fitzmaurice, Stewart and Winton, this time with Irwin but without Joseph O'Neill, met at Giuseppe's on the Corso. Perhaps they did this without the king's knowledge and agreement, but perhaps not.

Dr Irwin's valet was soon released,[41] presumably because the inquisitors soon realised that the Jacobite Freemasons posed no threat, but it was then the turn of the valets of visiting Hanoverian Freemasons to be arrested. Stosch reported that 'as some are released, others are arrested ... The motive is that the Roman Inquisition is determined to discover the Freemasons' secret, and not daring to lay hands on the masters, they hope to find out about it from the servants.'[42] On 4 February the Inquisition published a notice that it would arrest some of the servants of British Grand Tourists to discover the locations and membership of the masonic lodges in Rome.[43] It was, of course, the Hanoverian lodges with which the Inquisition was now concerned.

Although no longer suspect, the Jacobite Lodge needed to find new premises. At the end of February 1736, shortly after the death of Mark Carse, it met at a place described as 'chez Dion', and thereafter at an inn called the *Tre Re* in the Strada Paolina (near Santa Maria Maggiore). In April Lord Winton was elected to succeed Cotton as master, and in

---

[38] M.A. Morelli Timpanaro, *Tomasso Crudeli Poppi, 1702–1745*, vol. I (Florence, 2003), p. 42, quoting the Archivio della Congregazione del Sant' Ufficio (ACSU), 20 December 1735. (I am grateful to William Eisler for this reference.)

[39] Morelli Timpanaro, *Tomasso Crudeli*, p. 42, quoting ACSU, 28 December 1735.

[40] *Ibid.*, p. 43, quoting ACSU, 4 January 1736.

[41] NA. SP 98/37/f. 315, Stosch to Newcastle, 28 January 1736.

[42] NA. SP 98/37/f. 313 [sic], Stosch to Newcastle, 4 February 1736.

[43] NA. SP 98/37/f. 317, Stosch to Newcastle, 11 February 1736.

May James III appointed one of the wardens (Stewart) to be his *maggiordomo*. The membership of the lodge varied, as Grand Tourists came and went, but Winton, Slezor, Stewart, Fitzmaurice, Hay and Irwin continued to attend the meetings. In fact, it is worth observing that Dunbar and Edgar were the only senior male Scottish servants of the king who were not Freemasons. The absence of Edgar can be explained by his constant attendance on the king, so the implication seems to be that the lodge was opposed to Lord Dunbar's influence at the court. That hypothesis is strengthened by the fact that Lord Andover is known to have been in friendly contact with both Ezekiel Hamilton and the Order of Toboso.[44]

We should not suppose, however, that the Jacobite Freemasons were a united body. Lord Derwentwater, who was probably the Grand Master of all Jacobite Freemasons, left Rome in June 1736 to support the Jacobites in Paris who were losing control of the *Grande Loge de France*. At the first election to be held in Paris after his arrival he was elected its Grand Master on 27 December. Six days later, on 2 January 1737, Lord Winton signed the minute book of the Jacobite Lodge in Rome as Grand Master rather than Master. This separation from the Jacobite Freemasons under Lord Derwentwater in France seems to have been resented, and five days later he was warned by John Stewart (junior warden) via Charles Slezor (senior warden) that someone was planning to have him murdered. It is hard to imagine who that might have been, but Winton reported the fact to James III in the following letter:

Were I treated as a gentleman, I would not have the occasion to inform your Majesty how little respect is given to those of your following in this place (wich in consequence falls upon your Majesty) by the message sent me from Mr Steuart [sic] by Mr Slezer on the 7th instant, threatening me with murder without any reason and which is not to be neglected either in jest or earnest ... If those about your Majesty would have ventured to inform your Majesty of this, I would not have troubled your Majesty with it, and wish that their refusal upon this and several other occasions do not give occasion the Enemys of your Majesty's Person and Family to say it proceeds from your being surrounded with favourites, flattering and ignorant, who always has been and will be the ruine of Kings and Princes and of all other persons that trust in them. I hope your Majesty will take this in your serious consideration and give satisfaction to me and all honest men.[45]

It is difficult to know how to interpret this letter, and whether or not the 'flattering and ignorant' favourites included Dunbar. At any rate, James Edgar sent the following brief reply:

[44] HMC, *10th Report*, p. 466, Andover to Hamilton, 4 December 1736.
[45] *SPW*, p. 274, Winton to James III, 14 January 1737.

The King having read your letter, Commands me tell you in answer to it that he thinks you ought to take it well of Mr Stewart his informing you of what he heard. That he is sorry you are uneasy. That he cannot but recommend it to you to live quietly and peaceably with your neighbours ... which is the only way he thinks will bring you out of your present embarras.[46]

Winton, Slezor, Stewart, Fitzmaurice and Hay all attended the lodge on 23 January, and a few weeks later Fitzmaurice was attacked near the Church of San Marcello by some of the *sbirri*: 'after a great fracas, and after he had defended himself, they let him escape to his master's palace nearby'. This incident is also difficult to interpret, but Stosch believed that the *sbirri* 'would never have dared to commit such an attack' without the connivance of someone at the court.[47]

It is unlikely that the Jacobite Lodge could have exerted much influence to weaken the position of Lord Dunbar, though the latter appears to have been concerned about its activities.[48] But the divisions within the lodge itself surely reduced any chance of doing this still further. The Jacobite Lodge was then sacrificed by James III in April 1738, when he persuaded Pope Clement XII to issue the bull *In Eminenti* condemning Hanoverian Freemasonry. This bull was not directed at all Freemasonry, but only at the Hanoverian lodges which admitted atheists as well as heretics, and which were spreading in Italy and elsewhere in Catholic Europe.[49] Nevertheless it was agreed at the court that it would be safer to stop holding masonic meetings in Rome. In January 1739 the Pope issued a further decree offering money to anyone who revealed the secrets of Freemasonry and threatening the death penalty for anyone found participating in its assemblies.[50] During the same month Stewart died and Hay, who succeeded him as *maggiordomo*, then created with Irwin an organisation called the Society of Young Gentlemen Travellers in Rome.[51] This was clearly the Jacobite Lodge under another name, but by avoiding any suggestion of Freemasonry they were able to greet and sup with Jacobite Grand Tourists with impunity.

---

[46] *SPW*, p. 275, Edgar to Winton, no date given.

[47] NA. SP 98/41/f. 24, Stosch to Newcastle, 16 March 1737.

[48] In a letter of 8 January 1738 (RA. SP 203/163, quoted in French translation in Kervella, *Mystère de la rose blanche*, p. 182), Dunbar tried to find out the secret of Freemasonry from O'Bryen, alleging that it was the two princes who wanted to know about it.

[49] See note 28.

[50] NA. SP 98/41/ff. 250, 262, Stosch to Newcastle, 2 and 9 February 1739; Kervella, *Mystère de la rose blanche*, p. 202. In March the Inquisition burned in the Piazza Minerva a book entitled *Relation apologique et historique de la Société de Francs Massons* (Dublin, but really Paris, 1738): NA. SP 98/41/f. 275, Stosch to Newcastle, 9 March 1739.

[51] The name is taken from the portraits of its members (including Hay and Irwin) painted by Domenico Dupra.

The fall of Dunbar

By the end of the 1730s neither the Order of Toboso nor the Jacobite Lodge had weakened Dunbar's position with the king. In 1736 he had been able to organise an extended visit to the court by Lord Inverness.[52] An unexpected development in 1741 seemed to strengthen Dunbar. In April of that year William Hay suddenly picked a quarrel for no apparent reason with Thomas Arthur, until then an intimate friend. He then did the same with another member of the court, and on both occasions drew his sword within the Palazzo del Re.[53] James III felt obliged to order him to leave the court and go to France. The letter to Hay, in which the king expressed his regret at having to do this, added that 'you know my good opinion of you, and how much I approved of the kindness The Prince has for you'.[54] Hay was succeeded as *maggiordomo* by Francis Strickland.

Although his enemies at the court gradually disappeared (Stewart in 1739, Hay in 1741, Slezor in 1742), Dunbar found himself faced with a much more formidable opponent after 1739. He was disliked and regarded as anti-French by Cardinal de Tencin. In February 1740 Stosch informed London that since Tencin's arrival the king 'defies … Dunbar, who is always being sent out of the household on one pretext or another, when the Cardinal brings to the Audiences … English people who support him'.[55] Tencin left Rome in 1742, and by then Dunbar's position had finally been undermined. In March 1743 Prince Henry achieved his majority and Dunbar ceased to have a specific role at the court. He continued as one of the king's ministers, but was much less influential than Cardinal Riviera, and was often used principally for sending messages and talking to people on the king's behalf. Canillac, the French chargé d'affaires, described him in January 1744 as 'one of the most anti-French people I know'.[56] With Great Britain and France once again at war, and Prince Charles going to Paris to obtain French help, Lord Dunbar was finally discredited. It had taken nearly thirty years for James III to come round to the point of view of nearly everyone

---

[52] NA. SP 98/37/ff. 357, 386, Stosch to Newcastle, 12 May and 4 August 1736. Inverness had converted to Catholicism in the winter of 1731–2 (RA. SP 151/21, Innes to James III, 14 January 1732).

[53] RA. SP 231/198, 'Project of a letter about Mr Hay', 12 April 1741; RA. SP 232/54, Edgar to Murray of Broughton, 27 April 1741.

[54] RA. SP 231/187, James III to Hay, 9 April 1741.

[55] NA. SP 98/43/f. 14, Stosch to Newcastle, 14 February 1740. Also ff. 10, 27, to Newcastle, 31 January and 27 March 1740.

[56] *Benoît XIV*, I, p. 117, Canillac to Amelot, 11 January 1744.

at the court. In 1746 he described Dunbar as 'the person of all at Rome ... the least agreeable to me'.[57]

When Prince Charles went to France in 1744 he was joined by his *maggiordomo*, Sir Thomas Sheridan. Shortly afterwards the king discovered that his own *maggiordomo*, Francis Strickland, had been trying to persuade the prince to join the Church of England.[58] James informed his son that Strickland was a 'wicked man': 'whenever your eyes are opened to him, you wont I am sure allow a disciple or prosolite of his to come near you'.[59] Strickland was ordered to leave the court and go to Avignon, whence he joined Prince Charles in Paris and eventually accompanied him and Sheridan to Scotland.[60] To replace Strickland, the king recalled Dunbar's enemy William Hay to resume his duties as *maggiordomo*.

Lord Dunbar finally left the court in April 1747. No longer consulted by the king, and outspoken in his support of Prince Charles's irresponsible behaviour in Paris after returning from Scotland, Dunbar's presence in Rome was no longer welcome.[61] He left on 8 April and settled in Avignon with his sister, Lady Inverness, who had been widowed since 1740.[62] At last, the influence of John Hay and James Murray, respectively Lords Inverness and Dunbar, which had been such a destructive influence on the exiled court and the entire Jacobite movement since 1717, was at an end.

---

[57] *SPW*, p. 176, James III to Prince Charles, 25 July 1746. Dunbar had been given a share of the income from the Salts of Brouage, so he was financially secure (see Chapter 9, note 66).

[58] Shield, *Henry Stuart*, p. 49.

[59] *SPW*, p. 176, James III to Prince Charles, 25 July 1746.

[60] *SPW*, p. 148, Sheridan to James III, 14 August 1746.

[61] *Benoît XIV*, I, p. 311, to Tencin, 15 March 1747; NA. SP 98/53/ff. 23, 25, Stosch to Newcastle, 21 and 28 March 1747.

[62] *JCR*, p. 31, Graeme to Edgar, 26 September 1740. Lady Inverness visited her brother at the court from the end of May until October 1740 (NA. SP 98/43/ff. 50, 86, 88, Stosch to Newcastle, 11 June, 15 and 22 October 1740). It was while she was there that her husband died in Avignon.

17 The decline of the court, 1747–1766

The defeat of Prince Charles's army at Culloden, followed by the collapse of the Jacobite rising in Scotland, convinced James III that there never would be a Stuart restoration, and that his court would remain in Rome until he died. The exiled Stuart court entered a slow but inevitable decline.

When Prince Henry was created a cardinal in 1747 he was given his own household of about forty people. They were all Italian, with the single exception of a sweeper, named William Barber. It was arranged that Henry, who would live with his father in the Palazzo del Re, would have his own servants in the Bedchamber, the Chamber and the stables, but that he would eat his meals with the king and use the latter's servants in the household below stairs (*cucina, bottiglieria* and *credenza*).[1]

There was, however, an important innovation at the court. Whereas the king was content to be waited on in his Chamber by his gentlemen pensioners, Cardinal York was given a *maestro di camera* to take formal charge of the ceremonies in his new apartment on the second floor of the *palazzo grande*, previously occupied by the queen. As a special concession, Pope Benedict XIV allowed York to employ a priest in this role.[2] The man selected was Father Leigh, the Irishman whom James III had favoured during the 1730s. Authority within the court was consequently divided between the *maggiordomo*, who served the king, and the new *maestro di camera*, who served the cardinal.

The household of the king

There is little that needs to be said about the servants of the king during this final phase.[3] In 1749 two of James's French *valets de chambre*

---

[1] RA. SP 308/117, 312/107, 315/10 and 319/183 give the household of Cardinal York in 1750 and 1751. They can be compared with the list for 1764 published in Mary Jane Cryan, *Travels to Tuscany and Northern Lazio* (Vetralla, 2004), pp. 22–4.

[2] *Benoît XIV*, I, p. 332, to Tencin, 14 June 1747.

[3] The king's household during the 1750s can be seen in the lists of salaries and pensions in RA. SP 308/115, 309/156, 312/108 and 109, 315/3, 319/181, 331/58, Box 3/69, 369/25, 370/35.

(Saint-Paul and Decelles) died.[4] They were replaced by an Italian (Filippo Adami). Father Lawrence Mayes, the king's chaplain, also died that year.[5] He too was replaced by an Italian (Father Marcolini). In 1752 his equerry, cavaliere Giuseppe Gigli, was transferred to the household of Cardinal York and replaced by another Italian, conte Bernardini.[6] By contrast, when Mathurin Jacquin, the French under-secretary, died in 1750 he was replaced by Andrew Lumisden, a Scottish Protestant who had served Prince Charles in Scotland and had come to Rome the previous year in search of employment.[7]

The most important development was the arrival in October 1747 of Daniel O'Bryen, who had served for many years as James III's ambassador to the court of France. O'Bryen was given an Irish peerage as Earl of Lismore, and invited to replace Dunbar as one of the king's ministers – *not* as secretary of state, as always alleged.[8] The problem for Lismore, however, was that the king consulted other people, such as Cardinal Riviera, Cardinal Valenti Gonzaga, Archbishop de Rossi and Henry Fitzmaurice, and that he (Lismore) was not given the confidence he expected. To compensate for this, he tried to take control of all the king's household, and thus he came into rivalry with Sir William Hay, the *maggiordomo*.

Lismore was absent from the court for much of 1749, on a protracted visit to France,[9] but when he returned the rivalry between him and Hay seems to have built up. In April 1751 Hay decided to retire and return to France. He was replaced by don Antonio Escudero, not an Italian but a Spaniard! Pope Benedict informed Cardinal de Tencin:

he has only had with him an elderly Protestant Englishman [sic] who was serving as his *maggiordomo* and for whom he has now substituted the Grand Prior of Navarre, knight of the Order of Malta, a Spaniard, who will keep him company on his knees in the churches as much as he wants and who will not tire him much with his chatter when they are out in the carriage as he is a true old-fashioned Spaniard in his piety and gravity.[10]

---

[4] Shield and Lang, *King over the Water*, p. 131; ASVR. Santi Apostoli vol. 42, p. 108, 5 April 1749.

[5] ASVR. Santi Apostoli vol. 42, p. 109, 24 August 1749.

[6] *Benoît XIV*, II, p. 185, to Tencin, 3 May 1752.   [7] Ingamells, *Dictionary*, p. 616.

[8] *SPW*, pp. 213, 247, James III to Prince Charles, 7 November 1747, and to Graeme, 20 November 1759.

[9] Argenson, *Journal et mémoires*, vol. V, p. 483, 24 May 1749; and vol. VI, p. 102, 22 December 1749.

[10] *Benoît XIV*, II, p. 151, to Tencin, 21 April 1751. The *maggiordomo* was expected to accompany the king as though he were the first gentleman of the Bedchamber (NLS. MS 14260, p. 89, Lumisden to Pazzagli, 7 May 1761).

Escudero, who was inevitably an isolated figure at the court, was no match for Lismore, and was quickly discontented with his position, confiding to the Pope in November of the same year that he would like to retire, 'being unable to live amidst such annoyances'.[11] When he eventually did resign in July 1753 he was much more specific, and gave as his reason that he could no longer 'bear the despotism of Lord Lismore at this court'.[12] He was replaced by John Constable, who was given a knighthood.

The household of Cardinal York

The 'annoyances' to which Escudero referred also concerned the household of Cardinal York. They began in August 1749 when Henry dismissed James III's friend Father Leigh, his *maestro di camera*,[13] and replaced him with a young priest of his own age called Giovanni Lercari.

We need to be cautious, because the available sources reveal very little, but it seems probable that Cardinal York was homosexual, and that he and Lercari were attracted to each other. As the cardinal was bound to reveal his feelings to his confessor, this latter's influence naturally assumed considerable importance. If he granted the cardinal absolution for his sinful thoughts and desires (or even actions), then the relationship with Lercari might prosper. If he did not, then the cardinal might have to find another *maestro di camera*.

The confessor was Father Ildefonso, a Piarist who had been appointed by the king to be Prince Henry's tutor in 1739. He was the rector of the *Collegio di Propaganda Fide*, where Lercari's brother was the secretary. Ildefonso seems to have granted absolution to Cardinal York, who not only continued to employ Lercari but also invited other people of whom the king disapproved to his apartment in the Palazzo del Re.

In September 1751 James III asked Pope Benedict XIV to expel Ildefonso from Rome, on the grounds that he was alienating Cardinal York from his father. The Pope agreed to do this.[14] When the cardinal was told what had happened he was very upset. He reluctantly agreed to have no further dealings with Ildefonso. What really worried him, however, was whether or not he would be allowed to retain Lercari as his *maestro di camera*.[15]

---

[11] *Benoît XIV*, II, p. 151, to Tencin, 17 November 1751.
[12] *Ibid.*, p. 281, to Tencin, 25 July 1753. Also *ibid.*, p. 338, to Tencin, 8 April 1754.
[13] Shield, *Henry Stuart*, p. 144.
[14] *Benoît XIV*, II, pp. 130, 139, to Tencin, 21 July and 8 September 1751.
[15] *Ibid.*, pp. 151, 153, to Tencin, 17 and 24 November 1751.

It appears that the new confessor, who was rector of the college at Albano and, like Ildefonso, a member of the Order of Piarists, was no improvement from the king's point of view. Cardinal York sent for him two or three times each day 'because of the scruples which tormented him',[16] and the new confessor put his mind at rest. In January 1752 James therefore demanded that both Lercari and the confessor should be dismissed, whereupon his son replied that 'he could not live without these two people'.[17]

Lercari had the good sense to offer his resignation, but Cardinal York refused to accept it, so the king ordered Lercari never again to enter the Palazzo del Re. Henry was furious, but he was told by the Pope that he should give way and accept that Lercari's further employment at the court was impossible.[18]

The king then set about trying to find a new *maestro di camera*, while his son ostentatiously met and spent hours with Lercari outside the palazzo.[19] Various people were considered for the post,[20] which was eventually accepted in May by marchese Francesco Angelelli of Bologna, whose younger brother Roberto was already serving as one of the cardinal's priests.[21] The Pope commented that 'the present system in this palace [the Stuart court] is a total separation of the two households ... The cardinal enjoys his own ecclesiastical revenues; the King has given him carriages and eighteen horses whose fodder he pays for, and he has dressed his servants ... The son will remain in the palace without paying rent and will continue to have his food provided.'[22]

The king ordered Angelelli to have no dealings with Lercari, but unwisely told his son that he could now see his former *maestro di camera* if he wished to do so.[23] The result was disastrous. According to Pope Benedict, Lercari began to behave with 'the most insulting arrogance and disdain',[24] and James III soon realised that Lercari still had the same authority at the court as if he were still employed as *maestro di camera*.[25]

---

[16] *Ibid.*, pp. 244–5, to Tencin, 14 February 1753.

[17] *Ibid.*, p. 166, to Tencin, 2 February 1752.

[18] *Ibid.*, pp. 169–70, to Tencin, 16 February 1752; NA. SP 98/58/f. 115, Stosch to Holderness, 18 February 1752.

[19] *Benoît XIV*, II, pp. 171, 172, 176, 183, 186, to Tencin, 23 February, 1 and 22 March, 26 April and 10 May 1752. In March Cardinal York gave Lercari a silver drinking cup (NA. SP 98/58/f. 121, Stosch to Holderness, 10 March 1752).

[20] The candidates included marchese Baldassini, duca Caffarelli, conte Fogliani and conte Viviani (*Benoît XIV*, II, pp. 178, 180; NA. SP 98/58/f. 131, Stosch to Holderness, 21 April 1752; RA. SP 331/120, James III to Mahony, 18 May 1752).

[21] *Benoît XIV*, II, p. 187, to Tencin, 17 May 1752. For Angelelli's brother, see note 1.

[22] *Ibid.*, p. 185, to Tencin, 3 May 1752.   [23] *Ibid.*, p. 187, to Tencin, 17 May 1752.

[24] *Ibid.*, pp. 200–1, to Tencin, 19 July 1752.   [25] *Ibid.*, p. 199, to Tencin, 12 July 1752.

In July 1752 Cardinal York moved out of the Palazzo del Re and went to live with 'the Fathers of the Mission at San Giovanni and San Paulo', stating that he would not return unless he could keep his new confessor and see Lercari there whenever he wanted. This was too much, and the Pope expelled Lercari from Rome, ordering him to go to his family home at Genoa.[26]

Cardinal York responded by himself leaving Rome, saying he would not return until Lercari was allowed back.[27] After a while he went to stay at Bologna in the Palazzo Angelelli, where he was taken in hand by his hostess, who persuaded him to return to Rome. The Pope reported that this was due to 'the very strong and very serious representations made to the cardinal by the marchesa Angelelli, sister-in-law of his *maestro di camera* and at whose home he is staying in Bologna, on the subject of the general disapproval and discredit that his conduct towards his father was provoking'.[28]

Cardinal York returned to live in the Palazzo del Re in November 1752. He was met by James III at the top of the grand staircase, and apologised in the *sala* (Guard Chamber). It was agreed that he would thenceforth dine and sup separately in his own apartment, though his food would be prepared by the king's servants in the household below stairs.[29]

In March 1753 Henry agreed to accept as his new confessor the secular priest of the Church of San Biagio della Pagnolta in the Via Giulia.[30] By August the new confessor (in the Pope's words) had 'put his conscience in the state it should be in regard to scruples'.[31] But King James steadfastly refused to permit Lercari to return, and Pope Benedict made it clear he would never do anything against the king's wishes.[32]

By 1753 James III was deeply depressed. Both his sons – though in different ways – had disappointed him, and he knew that the Jacobite cause was finished. But as the king grew older he began to accept what he could not change, and the following year saw harmony restored between father and son. Pope Benedict wrote that 'the son has completely forgotten young Lercari whose place has now been taken by Cardinal Gian Francesco Albani'. He referred to 'this new friendship whose ardour knows no limits'.[33] The king and cardinal went to Albano together in the autumn of 1754, but the latter returned once a week to

[26] *Ibid.*, p. 202, to Tencin, 26 July 1752.   [27] *Ibid.*, p. 203, to Tencin, 2 August 1752.
[28] *Ibid.*, p. 223, to Tencin, 1 November 1752.
[29] *Ibid.*, pp. 224, 228–9, to Tencin, 8 and 29 November 1752.
[30] *Ibid.*, p. 250, to Tencin, 7 March 1753.   [31] *Ibid.*, p. 284, to Tencin, 8 August 1753.
[32] *Ibid.*, pp. 267, 282, 358, to Tencin, 23 May and 1 August 1753, 4 September 1754.
[33] *Ibid.*, p. 362, to Tencin, 25 September 1754.

see Albani, 'who, according to the present whim, occupies young Lercari's place'.[34] That autumn the king finally gave his consent that Lercari should be allowed to return.[35]

The last years

From the king's point of view, there was one good thing which emerged from the quarrel with his son: he himself became friendly with a Venetian nobleman named Georgio Maria Lascaris, who became his chief adviser.

Lascaris was a Theatine who was employed by the Congregation of Propaganda Fide in Poland, and was rewarded by being made a bishop *in partibus*. While he was there he had also undertaken various tasks for James III connected with the inheritance of Prince James Sobieski. In 1748 he returned to Rome and was said to be 'continually with the King of England'. When Cardinal York was appointed Archpriest of St Peter's he selected Lascaris to be his vicar.[36] The latter took up his post in June 1752, shortly before the cardinal left the Palazzo del Re.

Although Lascaris was an ecclesiastical subordinate of Cardinal York, and in no other way connected with the Stuart court, he began to mediate between the cardinal and King James, pointedly telling the former that it was a dishonourable thing for someone (i.e. Lercari) to drive a wedge between a father and his son.[37] When Henry left Rome the king was obliged to take his *villeggiatura* at Albano by himself, so he asked Lascaris to accompany him there.[38] James used him to negotiate the return of Cardinal York from Bologna, and increasingly employed him as a secretary to deal with his correspondence.[39] Cardinal Riviera had recently died, and Lascaris filled the void he had left. Before long Lascaris had become minister and secretary as well as friend to the deeply depressed king.

Before the arrival of Lascaris, James had been consulting Henry Fitzmaurice.[40] In January 1753 the latter was said to 'complain bitterly to his friends' that the king 'hardly listens to his advice any more, since the Prelate Lascaris is now the only one favoured, to the exclusion of all

[34] *Ibid.*, p. 366, to Tencin, 9 October 1754.
[35] *Ibid.*, p. 369, to Tencin, 30 October 1754.
[36] *Ibid.*, pp. 191–2, to Tencin, 7 June 1752.   [37] *Ibid.*, p. 203, to Tencin, 2 August 1752.
[38] *Ibid.*, p. 216, 27 September 1752.
[39] *Ibid.*, pp. 220, 222, 224, 18 and 25 October, 8 November 1752. In August 1752 James III summoned Lord Lismore's son to Rome to be employed as a secretary. Because the king now relied on Lascaris, Lismore's son was soon told to return to France (Shield, *Henry Stuart*, pp. 153–4).
[40] NA. SP 98/58/ff. 125, 131, Stosch to Holderness, 24 March and 21 April 1752.

his old servants'.[41] When Fitzmaurice complained to the king he was given 'a strong reprimand',[42] and sent away from the court. He died a few weeks later.[43]

By 1754, therefore, the Stuart court contained two separate households, sharing the same servants in the household below stairs. Cardinal York and his Italians were mainly situated on the second floor, with Angelelli as *maestro di camera*. The king occupied the first floor, and was served principally by Sir John Constable as *maggiordomo*, five gentlemen pensioners (Bulstrode, Corbet, Dormer, Fermor and Paston)[44] and conte Bernardini, his equerry, under the effective control of Lord Lismore as *palatii prefectus*.[45] In the secretariat James Edgar and Andrew Lumisden worked as useful scribes and corresponded with the Jacobites in France and elsewhere. But Lascaris enjoyed all the king's 'confidence to the exclusion of all others in the household',[46] and managed the difficult task of working for both James III and his son. He was 'his confidant *and* the cardinal's vicar at San Pietro'.[47]

By this time the king's health had begun to deteriorate. He was looked after day and night by Antonio Rossi, previously a footman who was now his *guardia fissa* (carer), and slept in one of the rooms of his apartment.[48] In May 1755 he dozed off before dinner and found himself unable to speak properly when he woke up.[49] In the months which followed he gradually recovered, but then had several fainting fits, accompanied by fever.[50] In March 1757 the Pope granted him a special bull allowing him to drink chocolate before attending mass, so that he would not collapse during the service.[51]

---

[41] NA. SP 98/61/f. 1, Stosch to Holderness, 5 January 1753.

[42] NA. SP 98/61/f. 9, Stosch to Holderness, 2 February 1753.

[43] He was already ill, and was said to have been sent to the Convent of San Matteo where he died 'dans un âge fort avancé' (NA. SP 98/61/ff. 13, 25, Stosch to Holderness, 16 and 30 March 1753).

[44] Lord Nithsdale had died in 1744, followed by Lady Nithsdale in 1749 (ASVR. Santi Apostoli vol. 42, pp. 82, 108, 16 February 1744 and 22 April 1749). Lord Winton had died in 1749 (Ingamells, *Dictionary*, p. 1013).

[45] This is the description in the parish register when he died (ASVR. Santi Apostoli vol. 42, p. 167, 6 November 1759).

[46] NA. SP 98/61/f. 109, Stosch to Holderness, 18 January 1754.

[47] *Benoît XIV*, II, p. 424, to Tencin, 9 July 1755.

[48] This can be seen in the annual *Stati d'Anime*, starting in 1752: ASVR. Santi Apostoli vols. 72 (p. 271), 73 (pp. 43, 90), 74 (pp. 36, 84, 123), 75 (pp. 32, 77, 119), 76 (pp. 32, 71, 80), 77 (p. 89).

[49] *Benoît XIV*, II, p. 415, to Tencin, 28 May 1755.

[50] *Ibid.*, pp. 455, 457, 465, 477, 477–8, to Tencin, 12 and 19 November, 24 December 1755, 4 and 11 February 1756; NA. SP 98/61/f. 329, Stosch to Fox, 27 February 1756.

[51] ASV. Fondo Benedetto XIV 27/f. 26, 'Indultum Jacobo III Magnae Britanniae regi suscipiendi eucharistiam, de spiritualis directoris consilio, etiamsi non sit jejunus', 24 March 1756; NA. SP 98/61/f. 345, Stosch to Fox, 23 April 1756.

The king's declining health made it necessary to determine who should be his medical adviser. Back in 1750 both James and Henry had decided to rely on Dr Laurenti, the Pope's personal physician, rather than either Dr Irwin or Dr Wright: 'both of them entrusted to him the care of their health; they have had experience of the two English doctors [sic] in their service, of whom one is ignorant and the other too hasty'.[52] In 1755 the Pope wrote that the king's gradual improvement was thanks to Laurenti, 'whose advice the king has always followed, despite the arguments put up by the English doctor [sic] to everything that our man suggested and in particular to a second bleeding which saved the king'.[53] The 'English' doctor was James Irwin, because Robert Wright had left Rome in 1752.[54]

The argument over bleeding the king was resumed in February 1756 when James had another attack of fever. Irwin was opposed, but Laurenti insisted, 'saying that bleeding was the only hope'. Irwin eventually gave way, and the king's health improved.[55] The episode revealed the extent to which James had come to rely on his Italian friends and advisers rather than the Jacobites attached to his court. For the next three years his health improved, and Lumisden noted in May 1759 that the king 'now goes abroad regularly to take a little exercise'.[56]

By 1759, when the king was seventy years old, there were only eleven of his own subjects still attached to his court: five English, five Scottish and one Irish. The English were Sir John Constable (*maggiordomo*), the Revd Thomas Wagstaffe (Anglican chaplain) and three pensioners: Joseph Dormer, Robert Fermor and James Paston. The Scots were James Edgar (secretary), Andrew Lumisden (under-secretary), Dr James Irwin (who died in February 1759),[57] James Murray (surgeon) and one pensioner: Maurice Corbet. The Irishman was Lord Lismore.

In November 1759 Lismore died,[58] leaving the king without a single British or Irish minister. James III wrote to invite Sir John Graeme, who had been his secretary of state in 1727–8, to return from France 'to assist me, as he [Lismore] did, in quality of minister, but without the title of

[52] *Benoît XIV*, ii, p. 65, to Tencin, 14 October 1750. Also *ibid.*, p. 341, to Tencin, 29 May 1754.
[53] *Ibid.*, p. 457, to Tencin, 19 November 1755. Also *ibid.*, pp. 415–16, to Tencin, 28 May 1755.
[54] RA. SP 330/127, Wright to Edgar, 5 April 1752; RA. SP 331/37, Lady Ramsay to Edgar, 23 April 1752.
[55] *Benoît XIV*, ii, p. 478, to Tencin, 11 February 1756; NA. SP 98/61/ff. 325, 327, Stosch to Fox, 13 and 20 February 1756.
[56] NLS. MS 14260, p. 2, Lumisden to G. Murray, 10 May 1759.
[57] Ingamells, *Dictionary*, p. 545.
[58] ASVR. Santi Apostoli vol. 42, p. 167, 6 November 1759.

Secretary of State'. He added: 'You will have an apartment in the house with a scrivener and two horses at your disposal; and tho' I am no more able to eat but alone, you shall have your table, in one shape or another.'[59] Graeme accepted, was given a Scottish peerage as Earl of Alford, and arrived in February 1760.[60]

A few weeks later James III 'was seized with a severe cold, attended with a fever and convulsive cough'. The cough was 'so violent' that he was not expected to recover, and Cardinal York gave him extreme unction.[61] But he did recover, having been confined to his Bedchamber throughout the summer. Lumisden noted in August that he still did 'not yet find himself in a condition to go abroad'.[62] Despite the presence of Cardinal York on the second floor, the exiled Stuart court in the Palazzo del Re was only a shadow of its former self. Servants were laid off from both the household below stairs and the stables.

In October the English-born George III succeeded peacefully as the new king of Great Britain and Ireland, and James III decided to make his will. It was witnessed by two gentlemen pensioners (Robert Fermor and Joseph Dormer) and by the paymaster (Pietro Marsi), and dated 21 November. It stipulated that annual pensions should be paid after his death to fifteen of his closest servants. They included Lord Alford (600 *scudi*); Sir John Constable (*maggiordomo*: 400); James Edgar (secretary: 400); Andrew Lumisden (under-secretary: 200); Maurice Corbet (pensioner: 200); James Murray (surgeon: 100); Felix Bonbled, Francesco Cassiani and Filippo Adami (*valets de chambre*: 100 each); Joseph Foullon and Pietro Pelli (unknown: 100 each); Salvatore Mambretti (*primo cocchiere*: 100); Father Bartolomeo Sabbatini (confessor: 100); Giuseppe Rè (*credenziere*: 100); and Domenico Arnoux (*computista*: 100).[63] In a codicil of 26 May 1762 five of these people (Corbet, Bonbled, Mambretti, Sabbatini and Arnoux) were eliminated,[64] for

---

[59] *SPW*, p. 247, James III to Graeme, 20 November 1759. See also *SPW*, p. 251, James III to Prince Charles, 3 March 1760: 'My health is much in the same state in which it has been a long while … and I have now, besides the accidentail ail of my convulsive cough, which generally lasts me a long while.'

[60] *SPW*, p. 249, Alford to Prince Charles, 20 February 1760.

[61] NLS. MS 14260, p. 43, Lumisden to G. Murray, 20 May 1760; Shield, *Henry Stuart*, p. 172.

[62] NLS. MS 14260, p. 55, Lumisden to G. Murray, 19 August 1760.

[63] ASV. SS: Ingh 25, pp. 109–12, the Last Will and Testament of James III, 21 November 1760.

[64] ASV. SS: Ingh 25, pp. 128–9, the codicil to James III's will, 26 May 1762. Lumisden explained on 24 March 1767 that 'the late King after making his codicil added nothing to the capital in the *luoghi di monti*. The annuities he left, together with the mancia [i.e. tax], were calculated exactly to exhaust the interest of that fund' (NLS. MS 14261, p. 39, to Alford).

reasons which are unclear, and four and a half months later James Edgar was also removed because he died.[65]

In October 1762 James III had a stroke and was partially paralysed. For a second time he was expected to die but recovered, this time with little memory, and without the ability to speak properly.[66] By 1763 he was unable to get out of bed.[67] His chief concern was the future of Prince Charles, who had still not returned to Rome and faced the real prospect that he might not be recognised as king by Pope Clement XIII.[68]

The Stuart court effectively ceased to function in 1763–4, before the king himself actually died. In January of that year Cardinal York was appointed *vice-cancelliere* of the Church, with the enormous Palazzo della Cancelleria as his new residence. He moved out of the Palazzo del Re early the following year,[69] followed by Lord Alford, who returned to France in the spring.[70] The queen's apartment on the second floor was again deserted, and the king's on the first floor no longer operated as any kind of social centre. James was visited by his son and Lascaris, and his still voluminous correspondence was opened, read and written for him by Lumisden, who had succeeded Edgar and moved into the latter's small apartment beside the king's cabinet.[71]

Death came relatively quickly at the end of 1765. On 24 December Lumisden informed Alford that the king 'has entirely lost his memory', but that he 'seems to be pretty much in his ordinary low situation'.[72] Three days later 'he had an attack of fever, attended with a fainting fit, [but] he remained calm'. Then, on 1 January 1766 after dinner, 'he had a relapse, that carried him off' at a quarter past nine in the evening. 'Notwithstanding his long illness,' wrote Lumisden, 'his death was a surprise on us.'[73]

[65] RA. SP 414/10, Flyn to Lumisden, 17 October 1762.

[66] Shield, *Henry Stuart*, p. 179.

[67] Dennistoun, *Memoirs of Sir Robert Strange*, vol. I, p. 219, Lumisden to Mrs Fotheringham, 21 August 1764.

[68] In October 1758 the king sent Lumisden on a mission to persuade Prince Charles to return to Rome. He was unsuccessful and himself returned in May 1759 (*SPW*, pp. 231–7, 246; Dennistoun, *Memoirs of Sir Robert Strange*, vol. I, pp. 181–2).

[69] Shield, *Henry Stuart*, p. 180.

[70] Dennistoun, *Memoirs of Sir Robert Strange*, vol. I, pp. 140, 179.

[71] *Ibid.*, vol. I, pp. 202, 301, 179 [sic], Lumisden to Isabella Strange, September 1762 and January [1764], and to an unspecified person, early 1764.

[72] *Ibid.*, vol. II, p. 75, Lumisden to Alford, 24 December 1765.

[73] NLS. MS 14264, p. 91, Lumisden to Prince Charles, 2 January 1766.

When James III was a boy the Stuart court in exile had included hundreds of English, Scottish and Irish followers. When he died on New Year's Day in 1766 there were only seven relatively minor servants left, four English (Bulstrode, Constable, Wagstaffe and Paston), and three Scots (Corbet, Lumisden and Murray).[74]

---

[74] Dormer died at the beginning of 1765 (Ushaw College, Tyrrell Papers OS 2/B.76, Lumisden to Tyrrell, 3 January 1765); and Fermor replaced Gigli as equerry in the household of Cardinal York in February 1765 (Ingamells, *Dictionary*, p. 352).

Conclusion

Time is the great enemy of dethroned royalty. If no restoration can be achieved within a certain number of years, perhaps about fifty, then a dynasty which has been deposed and exiled must lose its appeal and even its interest within the country which it formerly ruled. Over the years new loyalties will have been developed to the rival dynasty or régime, and new generations will have grown to maturity indifferent to what went before. If no restoration is achieved, then the exiled family seems doomed to an inevitable and protracted irrelevance and decline, unable to relinquish its legitimate claims, yet confronted by the hostility of its *de facto* heirs, and exposed to the scorn of contemporary society. Such was to be the ultimate fate of the exiled Stuarts.

It is very difficult for the historian to estimate how optimistic the Stuarts actually were as to their eventual restoration. Circumstances varied a great deal from year to year, and from decade to decade, and anyway appearances had to be maintained. But there is reason to believe that until the 1720s they expected, and sometimes even assumed, that they would be restored, and that they did not lose hope until the late 1740s. Throughout that period they maintained the faith that they, like Charles II in 1660, would one day return to their kingdoms.

The three generations of the exiled Stuart royal family reacted in different ways. James II resigned himself to a life of permanent exile in 1696, after the failure of the second Franco-Jacobite attempt to invade England. But he assumed that his son, the Prince of Wales, would one day be restored. In 1701, when the prince succeeded his father, and was recognised by the kings of France and Spain, and by the Pope, as King James III, the political and dynastic situation in Europe certainly favoured a restoration. The War of the Spanish Succession renewed French military support for the Jacobite cause, Queen Anne had no living heir, and the Tory party seemed as committed to the legitimate dynasty as it was to the Protestant religion. Many, if not most, people in Great Britain and continental Europe expected, or feared, that

346

King James III *would* succeed his half-sister, perhaps after an invasion, probably after her death.

Of course things did not turn out as expected, and the Elector of Hanover succeeded as King George I, but the history of the years 1714 to 1722, from the unexpected death of Queen Anne to the failure of the Atterbury Plot, is one of renewed optimism and bitter disappointments. As late as 1727, when George I died, James III still had hopes of finally succeeding to his thrones. His failure on that occasion seems to have convinced him that he, like his father, would never regain them. But Stuart hopes were not abandoned: they were passed on to the next generation. They felt that once James's elder son was old enough to command an army of invasion, during some future Anglo-French war, it was possible that he might one day be restored.

It was this belief that the Stuarts would eventually be restored, some-how, sooner or later, which encouraged Louis XIV and then six succes-sive popes to give them their support. In other words, it was assumed that supporting James III and his son made good political sense, and was in the long-term interests of France and the Catholic religion. The secret to understanding the generous treatment accorded to the exiled court, and thus its real significance during a period of extended exile, lies in considering popular perceptions abroad rather than political and military calculations in England or Scotland.

Yet such optimism could not be maintained indefinitely. Prince Charles was born in December 1720. The moment for a final decision, therefore, had to be at some time during the mid-1740s. If no Anglo-French war had broken out by then, it would become too late to think seriously of a Stuart restoration. Alternatively, if such a war had broken out, and an invasion attempt were then to fail, all hope of a restoration would have to be abandoned. This logic must have been clear to most contemporaries, and was certainly obvious to James III himself. Thus the defeat of the Jacobite army at Culloden in 1746, and the peace treaty between Great Britain and France at Aix-la-Chapelle two years later, destroyed all hopes that the Stuarts would ever be restored. James III knew that he would end his days living in exile as a guest of the Pope in Rome.

People in the papal city did not at first appreciate the significance of the failure of the Jacobite rising of 1745–6. The overt support of the French and Spanish ambassadors, running counter to, and sometimes even contradicting or negating, the official policies of their govern-ments, helped perpetuate the belief in Rome that the Stuarts might eventually be restored. There is an interesting letter written by James III to a former French ambassador in 1747, over a year after the defeat of the Jacobite army at Culloden. James writes that there could no longer be any question of his family ever being restored, but comments that the Italians seemed incapable of understanding or accepting this.[1] By the 1750s, however, when James began to withdraw from public life, it was generally accepted that the extended exile of the Stuarts was now permanent.

Defeat did not result in dishonour. James was always treated as a king, and this reminds us that the status of *de jure* monarchy in the early modern period was not dependent on the actual possesssion and administration of territory. Although their circumstances were otherwise totally different, the experience of James III in Rome can perhaps be compared to that of Queen Christina of Sweden, who had also lived there in the seventeenth century and was always treated as a monarch. Moreover the exile of the Stuarts was exceptional, in that the host government never recognised the Hanoverians as either *de facto* or *de jure* kings of Great Britain. Even Louis XIV had eventually had to recognise William III and Anne as *de facto* monarchs. The six popes who welcomed James III never extended any similar recognition to either George I or George II. And so long as that remained the case, as it did until 1766, the Stuarts were able fully to maintain their royal status – even when it became clear that they would never be restored.

The final tragedy for the Stuarts was that Prince Charles, unlike his father and brother, was unwilling to accept defeat. After his return from Scotland he behaved in Paris with increasing recklessness until he had to be arrested, briefly imprisoned, and then forcibly expelled from France by Louis XV. In the years which followed he became an alcoholic, wandered from place to place, behaved badly, and mistreated both his servants and the various women who entered his life. He refused to be reconciled with his father, who never saw him again, and ostentatiously stayed away from Rome. James III begged him to return, but he would not. In 1762, when James was ill and bed-ridden, he sent his final appeals:

My chief aim is to draw you if possible out of the hidden, and I may say, ignominious life you lead ... Will you not run straight to your father? ... There is no question of the past, but only of saving you from utter destruction for the future. Is it possible you would rather be a vagabond on the face of the earth than return to a Father who is all love and tenderness for you?[2]

---

[1] RA. SP 287/4, James III to Tencin, 29 August 1747.
[2] McLynn, *Charles Edward Stuart*, p. 462. The quotations are from letters of January and September 1762.

When James III died Charles had still not returned. His protracted absence, and his notorious alcoholism, had succeeded in alienating opinion in Rome, and in particular that of Pope Clement XIII.

On 7 January 1766 James III was given a state funeral in the Church of Santi Apostoli. The service was taken by his friend Lascaris, and the music was composed and conducted by Giovanni Costanzi.[3] Andrew Lumisden briefly described what happened in a letter written later the same day:

> Last night his body was carried to the Church of the Twelve Apostles, which is ornamented in the most magnificent manner; and this morning the solemn obsequies were performed there in the presence of the Pope and Cardinals. Amidst an infinite concourse of people, his body has been carried to St Peter's with the utmost pomp.[4]

The events were recorded in a specially printed pamphlet,[5] and in two large engravings. The first shows the king's lying-in-state inside the church; the second the procession from Santi Apostoli to St Peter's,[6] where James was buried in a large tomb in the crypt.[7]

Although Prince Charles had still not returned to Rome, he was known to be on his way, and the question of whether or not to recognise him as King of England, Scotland and Ireland could no longer be delayed. After a period of intense negotiations, Pope Clement XIII called together a specially appointed congregation of ten cardinals, from which Cardinal York was excluded, to consider the matter. It met on 14 January at the Quirinale. Prince Charles was to be given the use of both the Palazzo del Re and the Palazzo Apostolico at Albano, with the papal pension which his father had enjoyed, but the congregation voted by nine to one not to recognise him as king. His entourage would no longer be regarded as a royal court in exile.[8]

The news was taken to Prince Charles by Lumisden, who met him on the road south of Florence.[9] The prince was accompanied by three Scottish gentlemen, John Hay of Restalrig, Adam Urquhart and Lachlan Mackintosh, by his Scottish *valet de chambre*, John Roy Stuart, and by

[3] *Diario ordinario*, no. 7572, 11 January 1766, p. 11.

[4] Dennistoun, *Memoirs of Sir Robert Strange*, vol. I, p. 223, Lumisden to Strange, 7 January 1766.

[5] *Relazione della infermità, morte, solenni essequie, e trasporto di sua maestà Giacomo III re della Gran Bretagna, occorse in Roma a' di 7 gennaro 1766*, 8 pages.

[6] They are reproduced in Sharp, *Engraved Record*, pp. 101–2, nos. 161, 162; and Fagiolo, *Corpus delle feste*, pp. 176–7. The second engraving was actually a reworking of the plate originally produced in 1735 for the funeral procession of the queen.

[7] ASV. PAC 1008 contains all the 'pagamenti fatti per il Funerale'.

[8] McLynn, *Charles Edward Stuart*, pp. 471–9.   [9] *Ibid.*, p. 477.

some servants. Lumisden informed him that the queen's apartment on the second floor of the *palazzo grande* had been prepared for him, and wrote back to Cardinal York on 21 January that 'there must be a bed in the apartment for Stuart, and beds somewhere else for two of the King's domestics, besides beds for three gentlemen, and a servant that attends Mr Hay'.[10] Even if Prince Charles was not to be recognised as king, he would still become the master of the Palazzo del Re, able to decide which of his father's servants would be retained and which would be provided with accommodation.

Meanwhile the Jacobites in Rome, including his brother, Cardinal York, determined to welcome Prince Charles as their legitimate king. On 24 January, one day after the prince arrived, the members of the English College performed a second funeral service in their chapel, again with music by Costanzi,[11] to which he was invited. The rector of the college was Charles Booth, whose father (also Charles) had been groom of the Bedchamber at Saint-Germain and *maggiordomo* at Urbino. Booth and the rector of the Scots College, who both welcomed Prince Charles as though he were king, were swiftly dismissed by the Pope and banished from the Papal States.[12] The papal guard, which had protected the Palazzo del Re since December 1733, was withdrawn, and in May the royal coat of arms was taken down from above its entrance.[13] This in itself perhaps symbolises the end of the royal court.

Prince Charles lived in the Palazzo del Re from 1766 to 1774, when he went to Florence. He appointed Hay of Restalrig to be his *maggiordomo* in the place of Sir John Constable[14] (who nevertheless continued to live in the palazzo),[15] and he retained Lumisden as his secretary. He also kept the Revd Thomas Wagstaffe and James Murray the surgeon. Otherwise the only British people in his household were the Scots who had come with him. The rest of his servants were Italians who had previously been employed by his father.[16] The three pensioners, Bulstrode, Paston and Corbet, remained in Rome, but no longer frequented the palazzo.

It was not a happy household, because Prince Charles was frequently drunk. Lumisden, who wanted to leave Rome and only remained out of

---

[10] Dennistoun, *Memoirs of Sir Robert Strange*, vol. II, p. 89, Lumisden to York, 21 January 1766.

[11] *Diario ordinario*, no. 7581, 1 February 1766, p. 4.

[12] Dennistoun, *Memoirs of Sir Robert Strange*, vol. II, p. 94, Lumisden to Dunbar, 15 April 1766.

[13] McLynn, *Charles Edward Stuart*, pp. 479, 482. Josef Luither continued to be employed as *guarda portone*.

[14] Dennistoun, *Memoirs of Sir Robert Strange*, vol. II, p. 102

[15] ASVR. Santi Apostoli vol. 78, p. 25 and p. 134, *Stati d'Anime*, 1767 and 1771.

[16] RA. SP Box 3/68 shows the household of Prince Charles in *c.*1769–70.

a sense of duty,[17] wrote in January 1767 that 'I have lived for many years in a sort of bondage, but I may name these twelve months past a mere slavery'.[18] In another letter he referred to 'the fatigue and disagreeable scenes' which he had experienced since the return of Prince Charles.[19]

The situation steadily deteriorated during 1767 and 1768. Mackintosh left in January 1767, and in August Lumisden wrote that the prince no longer lived 'with any degree of decency'.[20] Nevertheless the following month he 'increased the number of his valets de chambre, by taking two of the late King's into his service'. They were Felix Bonbled, who had worked at the court since before Charles was born, and Francesco Cassiani, who had joined it before Charles went to France. They must have been deeply shocked by the contrast between their old and their new masters.

The strains in the Palazzo del Re came to a head in December 1768. According to his biographer, the prince 'had done little [that year] but drink', and 'his drunken rages increased in intensity'. In a scene which has often been described, Prince Charles dismissed Hay of Restalrig, Lumisden and Urquhart for trying to stop him attending the performance of an oratorio while drunk.[21] The three Scots were replaced by four Italians,[22] but John Roy Stuart, the *valet de chambre*, was promoted to be *maggiordomo*.[23] That appointment, made while Sir John Constable was still living in the palazzo, indicated the depth to which the household of Prince Charles had sunk in only three years.

The visiting Grand Tourists, who had once been drawn to the Stuart court as an attractive social venue and as a surrogate British embassy, now viewed the entourage of the prince with scorn, and had no communication with it.[24] Even before the death of James III most British Protestants had shown 'an extreme remisness in attending at worship',[25] but now they completely kept away. When Wagstaffe died in December

---

[17] Dennistoun, *Memoirs of Sir Robert Strange*, vol. I, p. 225, Lumisden to Mrs Strange, 7 January 1766. Also *ibid.*, vol. II, p. 90, to Strange, 12 February 1766.

[18] *Ibid.*, vol. II, p.107, Lumisden to Mrs B.Strange, 20 January 1767. Also NLS. MS 14261, pp. 40, 47, 53, Lumisden to Mackintosh, 25 March 1767, to Mrs Strange, 18 April 1767, and to Alford, 28 April 1767.

[19] NLS. MS 14261, p. 43, Lumisden to Alford, 31 March 1767.

[20] NLS. MS 14261, p. 88, Lumisden to Fotheringham, 25 August 1767.

[21] McLynn, *Charles Edward Stuart*, p. 485. They left Rome in April 1769 (Dennistoun, *Memoirs of Sir Robert Strange*, vol. II, pp. 120–2).

[22] NLS. MS 14262, p. 27, Lumisden to Mackintosh, 14 March 1769. Lumisden was himself replaced by the 3rd Lord Caryll in 1772 (McLynn, *Charles Edward Stuart*, p. 492).

[23] Dennistoun, *Memoirs of Sir Robert Strange*, vol. II, p. 103.

[24] NLS. MS 14261, p. 37, Lumisden to Alford, 17 March 1767.

[25] NLS. MS 14260, p. 58, Lumisden to Harper, 15 October 1760.

1770 Lumisden rightly wrote from Paris to his friend Murray in Rome that 'there will be no question I am persuaded of a successor to him'.[26]

The Italianisation of the household of both James III and Prince Charles needs to be emphasised, because it meant that they stopped employing people who like themselves were living in exile. The Stuart court at Saint-Germain, Bar-le-Duc, Avignon and Urbino, and also at Rome at first, had been genuinely a court in exile. The great majority of the people employed and supported by it were English, Scots and Irish who were political exiles, having taken up arms against the victorious government in London, or been outlawed for escaping abroad to follow King James. But whereas many people had joined the court after the rising of 1715–16, bringing a new group of exiles to supplement the dwindling number of earlier members, only one person (Lumisden) joined it after the rising of 1745–6.

King James III and his children themselves remained political exiles because of their hereditary royal status, but by the 1730s and 1740s this was less and less the case with their servants and pensioners. Jacobites born abroad were not exiles, particularly if one of their parents was foreign of if they themselves married someone who was Italian or French; nor were Catholics from England or Scotland or even Ireland who chose to emigrate to live in Italy; nor were French servants who had followed their employer to the Papal States, or had gone there for some other reason. And, most obviously, one would not use the term 'exile' for the Italians who were locally employed and who actually dominated the court numerically. The Stuart court in exile was therefore steadily transformed into the court of the exiled Stuart.

James III had difficulty recruiting servants from among his own subjects, but after 1746–7 he seems to have largely given up trying, contenting himself with being served even in senior positions by people – Italians and one Spaniard – whose only loyalty to him was purely that of a paid servant towards his master. Edmund Burke, writing in 1771, commented that Prince Charles 'is deserted by the whole world and by himself, [and] has, as I am told, not so much as a single Scotch, English or Irish footman about him'.[27] The second part of that comment was by the 1740s as true for James III as it was for his son.

It is important to remember that it was this final phase which shaped the popular perception of the exiled court in Rome, just as it did that of the court at Saint-Germain. Both courts, and particularly the latter, were truly regal and maintained on a relatively lavish scale, employing

---

[26] NLS. MS 14262, p. 133, Lumisden to Murray, 29 December 1770.
[27] McLynn, *Charles Edward Stuart*, p. 486.

many people and patronising both painters and musicians. Yet both courts ended in political failure and decline, which contributed to a complete loss of public memory. Leaving aside contemporary Whig propaganda, which understandably sought to minimise and misrepresent the exiled courts, in both cases it was the final years which were remembered, not the spectacular and optimistic ones which preceded them. At Saint-Germain the French pension fell into arrears after the death of Louis XIV, the succession of George I meant that credit became difficult to obtain and the failure of the rising of 1715–16 resulted in the arrival of many new exiles needing to be supported. The result was a few final years of impoverishment.[28] In Rome the collapse of Jacobite prospects after Culloden, the increasing ill-health of James III during the 1750s and the disastrous behaviour of Prince Charles similarly combined to obscure the reality of what the court had been during its first twenty-five or thirty years.

In their justly celebrated biography of James III, published in 1907, Alice Shield and Andrew Lang described the Palazzo del Re as 'a very dreary little Court', and added that 'it was just as it had been at St. Germains'.[29] Now that we have a much greater understanding of what the Stuart court had been like at Saint-Germain, this comment is bound to provoke an immediate riposte. The Château de Saint-Germain was a large and impressive royal palace, and the Jacobite court there was far from dreary. In some ways the court at Rome was indeed 'just as it had been' there. The Palazzo del Re was large enough for the court, the royal apartments were lavishly decorated and furnished, and the social life within them was magnificent.

Unfortunately for the historical record, neither of the two buildings has survived in any condition which permits us today to appreciate what the court would have looked like. Most of the apartments within the Château de Saint-Germain were destroyed during the 1790s, when it was turned into a political prison. The few that remained were destroyed in the 1860s when the five corner pavilions were knocked down and the château was converted into a museum of old stones and other prehistoric antiquities – which it still is today.[30] The Palazzo del Re underwent a similar transformation, and the deterioration actually started during the lifetime of Prince Charles.

Although the *Camera Apostolica* continued to pay the rent, and the building continued to be called the Palazzo del Re, the additional 600 *scudi* per annum given to James III to cover the costs of maintenance and

---

[28] Corp, *A Court in Exile*, p. 315.   [29] Shield and Lang, *King over the Water*, p. 402.
[30] Corp, *A Court in Exile*, pp. 351–8.

repairs[31] was withdrawn, leaving Prince Charles to pay for those him-self.[32] It is likely that the condition of the building began to deteriorate between 1766 and 1774. Prince Charles then went away to live in Florence for eleven years, from 1774 until the end of 1785, during which period the royal apartments were left completely unoccupied and unmaintained. It was a sign of extreme papal generosity that the *Camera Apostolica* continued to pay the rent each year for a building which the prince was not even using.[33] Eventually, in December 1785, Charles returned to Rome shortly before his sixty-fifth birthday, and remained there until his death in January 1788.

The building had originally been owned by marchese Giovanni Battista Muti, who had bequeathed it in 1730 to his daughter Ginevra, the wife of marchese Giovanni Battista Sacchetti.[34] She still owned it in 1766, but died in 1779 and left it to one of her relations, monsignore Giuseppe Casali.[35] In 1788, after the death of Prince Charles, the building was therefore renamed the Palazzo Casali. It must have been very dilapidated, because it had to be completely vacated[36] so that major works could be carried out, before it could be handed back. The papal archives record that the *Camera Apostolica* continued renting it for another entire year, and that the necessary works carried out during that time cost a further 1759 *scudi*.[37] In 1790 Casali and five others moved into what had been the king's apartment, a certain marchesa Vittoria del Cinque moved into the former queen's apartment and the rest of the building was rented out: to ten people in the north-east *palazzetta*, two more in the south-east *palazzetta*, and a further eight with seven children elsewhere.[38] The entire ground floor was partitioned off, divided up and rented out as shops,[39] as it has remained to the present day.

It was probably at this time that the king's gallery was divided into two unequal parts, that the decoration of the larger part was replaced with a neoclassical design of no distinction, and the window facing the Via di San Marcello was blocked. Further building works took place during the nineteenth century, particularly during the 1830s and 1840s. They

---

[31] See Chapter 11, p. 226.
[32] To compensate the owner of the building for the anticipated deterioration, the annual rent was increased from 1632 *scudi* to 1696 *scudi*. ASV. PAC 5220 records all the payments from 1743 to 1769, with a note (p. 179) explaining the reason for the increase.
[33] ASV. PAC 5223 records all the payments from 1775.
[34] ASR. Cam I: CDG b. 2017 bis/ff. 13/14/pp. 1, 3, 9–10.
[35] ASV. PAC 5223, pp. 40–6.
[36] ASVR. Santi Apostoli vol. 81, pp. 16, 18, *Stati d'Anime*, 1788 and 1789.
[37] ASV. PAC 5223, pp. 17–19.
[38] ASVR. Santi Apostoli vol. 81, p. 14, *Stati d'Anime*, 1790
[39] ASVR. Santi Apostoli vol. 82, no. 524, *Stati d'Anime*, 1792.

involved the suppression of all the painted ceilings and the repositioning of the doors in the king's apartment, the destruction of the chapel and the complete obliteration of the queen's apartment. Circulation within the palazzo was terminated, as the two *palazzetti* and the *palazzo grande* were all cut off from each other, and even partitioned within themselves to provide self-contained apartments and offices. Finally, an additional floor was added at the top, destroying the balance of the *palazzo grande* as seen from the Piazza dei Santi Apostoli.[40] Meanwhile the name of the building changed, to reflect the changing ownership: Casali became Savorelli, and then Balestra.[41]

We are thus deprived of any sense of what would have confronted the Grand Tourists of the early and mid eighteenth century – as we are also at Saint-Germain. Even the name of the building has become misleading, because it is now often referred to in the way it was before 1719, despite the fact that the adjacent building in the Piazza della Pilotta is also called the Palazzo Muti. The only entrance to the palazzo is the one on the south side from the Piazza dei Santi Apostoli. On the left as one enters there is a marble plaque bearing an Italian inscription which states:

There lived in this palazzo Henry, Duke later Cardinal of York who, surviving son of James III of England, took the name of Henry IX. In him in the year 1807 the House of Stuart expired.

Prince Henry did indeed live there for about thirty-four years, before moving to the Palazzo della Cancelleria in 1764, and he was the last legitimate descendant of the Stuarts in the male line. But the fact that James III also lived there for forty-four years, and that Prince Charles lived there for about thirty years, is completely ignored – like so much else connected with the Stuart court in Rome.

---

[40] These comments are based on my visits to the king's apartment and to the location of the queen's apartment within the Palazzo del Re in 2005. See also ASR. Collezione Disegni e Piante I, c. 87, no. 562, which includes the ground plans of the palazzo in 1870.

[41] The name 'Palazzo Balestra' is still shown above the entrance on the south side.

Appendix A   The household servants

(This list is restricted to the more senior servants and to those of British or Irish birth, and gives their monthly salaries, where known, in *livres*, on the right. It does not include the servants of servants. The Protestants are indicated with an asterisk*.)

Bedchamber	*l. s. d.*
Groom	
Alan Cameron, 1727–30 (died in service in Nov)*	102.02.03
William Hay, 1727–39*	100.00.00
Yeoman of the robes	
James Rodez, by 1692 to 1729	78.10.07
Valet de chambre / cameriere / lacchè	
Thomas Saint-Paul, 1709–49 (died in service)	78.10.07
Gerald Fitzgerald, 1711–21/22 (died in service)	78.10.07
Felix Bonbled, 1716–66	78.10.07
Pierre Bouffer, at least 1719–20	78.10.07
François Delaux, by 1722 to 1739	78.10.07
1739–1750s (*giubilato*)	39.05.00
François Decelles, 1735–49	78.10.07
James Duncan, 1735–59	78.10.07
Francesco Cassiani, by 1742 to 1766	78.10.07
Filippo Adami, by 1749 to 1766	78.10.07
Guardia fissa	
Antonio Rossi, by 1752 to 1766	35.00.00
Garçon de backstairs / bailleur / garzone del bakstaid	
Andrea Ciareine, by 1730 to 1744	35.00.00
Lorenzo De Angelis, 1744–66	30.00.00
Washerwoman / *blanchisseuse* / *lavandara*	
Catherine Macane, 1719 to at least 1742	20.00.00
Mrs Tomson, by 1722 to at least 1739	20.00.00
Theresa Kerby, at least 1729	unknown
Anne O'Neill, 1735 to at least 1756	30.00.00

Chamber	l. s. d.
Confessor	
Father John Brown, 1717–21	unknown
Father Antonio Ragazzi, by 1721 to 1732 (died in Nov)	unknown
Father O'Callaghan, 1727–8	unknown
Father Francarsi, 1733–?	unknown
'Un réligieux conventuel de Saint-François', at least 1747	unknown
Father Bartolomeo Sabbatini, by 1760 to ?	unknown
Chaplain / *prélat du palais*	
Father Lawrence Mayes, 1726–49 (died in service in Aug)	120.00.00
Father Marcolini, at least 1755–6	unknown
Chapel keeper / *sagrestano*	
Pierre Arnoux, by 1726 to 1741	25.00.00
Pietro Battaglia, 1741–7	15.00.00
Anglican chaplain	
Revd George Barclay, 1717–26*	35.00.00
Revd Patrick Cowper, 1717–26*	35.00.00
Revd Ezekiel Hamilton, 1728–33 (expelled)*	80.00.00
Revd Daniel Williams, 1728–33 (died in service)*	50.00.00
Revd Thomas Wagstaff, 1734–66*	100.00.00
Physician / *médecin*	
Dr Charles Maghie, 1709–32 (died in service)*	100.00.00
Dr Robert Wright, by 1729 to 1752 (left Rome), 1755	100.00.00
Dr James Irwin, 1729–59 (died in service)	100.00.00
Surgeon / *chirurgien* / *chirurgo*	
James Murray, 1728–66	60.00.00
Master of the music	
Innocenzo Fede, 1687–1732 (died in service)	30.00.00

Secretariat	l. s. d.
Secretary of state	
Duke of Mar, 1716–19 (resigned and left Rome)*	471.09.06
Earl of Inverness, March 1725–April 1727 (resigned and left court)*	204.02.03
Sir John Graeme, May 1727–August 1728 (left Rome)*	204.02.03
Acting secretary of state	
James Murray, Feb 1719–Feb 1721 (left Rome)*	200.00.00
John Hay, Feb 1721–March 1725*	204.02.03
Secretary of the Closet	
Sir David Nairne, 1713–28 (retired in Aug)	205.03.02

Secretariat	l. s. d.
Under-secretary	
John Paterson, 1716–19 (resigned and left Rome)★	60.00.00
Robert Creagh, Feb–Sept 1719	60.00.00
Francis Kennedy, Sept 1719–July 1725 (resigned)★	60.00.00, then 100.00.00
Thomas Sheridan, Jan 1721–Sept 1725	60.00.00, then 100.00.00
James Edgar, July 1725–Aug 1728★	100.00.00
Latin secretary	
Father Lawrence Mayes, by 1720	*see* Chaplain
Secretary	
James Edgar, Aug 1728 to 1762 (died in service)★	100.00.00
Andrew Lumisden, 1762–6★	100.00.00
Clerk / *commis* / under-secretary	
Mathurin Jacquin, 1728–50	80.00.00
Andrew Lumisden, 1750–62	50.00.00

Ministry	l. s. d.
(The ministers were not paid, except where shown. The dates are only approximate.)	
Cardinal Filippo Antonio Gualterio, 1717–28 (died in office)	
Cardinal Gianantonio Davia, 1728–40 (died in office)	
Lord Bourke, 1729–37 (left Rome)	
Earl Marischal, 1731–3 (left Rome)★	
Paul-Hyppolite, duc de Saint-Aignan, 1732–41 (left Rome)	
Cardinal Domenico Riviera, 1733–52 (died in office)	
Cardinal Troiano Aquaviva, 1735–47 (died in office)	
Cardinal Pierre de Tencin, 1739–42 (left Rome)	
Jean-Louis Guérin, bailli de Tencin, 1739–44, 1745–8 (left Rome)	
Earl of Dunbar, 1743–6★	250.00.00
Archbishop (later Cardinal) Frédéric-Jérome de La Rochefoucauld, 1745–8 (left Rome)	
Cardinal Federico Marcello Lante, *c.* 1746–66	
Archbishop (later Cardinal) Ferdinando de Rossi, *c.* 1746–66	
Cardinal Silvio Valenti Gonzaga, *c.* 1746–66	
Cardinal Neri Corsini, *c.* 1746–66	
Captain Henry Fitzmaurice, 1747–53 (died in office)	100.00.00
Earl of Lismore, 1747–59 (died in office)	250.00.00
Bishop Georgio Maria Lascaris, 1752–66	
Earl of Alford, 1760–3 (retired; left Rome in 1764)	250.00.00

Treasury	*l. s. d.*
Cofferer / *tesoriere*	
Sir William Ellis, 1698–1732 (died in service)★	59.14.06
Paymaster / *secretaire* / *segretario*	
Pietro Antonio Marsi, 1726–66	110.00.00
Clerk / *assistant* / *computista*	
Joseph Martinash, by 1717 to 1722 (died in service)	25.00.00
William Watkins, 1722–7 (left Rome)	25.00.00
Domenico Arnoux, 1727–64	50.00.00
	(by 1760:
	60.00.00)

The Household below stairs, the table and the stables	*l. s. d.*
Maggiordomo / *intendant de la maison*	
John Hay, 1718–Oct 1722★	100.00.00
Thomas Forster, Oct 1722–May 1736 (left Rome)★	100.00.00
John Stewart, 1736–9 (died in service in Jan)	100.00.00
William Hay, 1739–41 (left Rome in April)★	100.00.00
Francis Strickland, 1741–4 (left Rome in July or Aug)	100.00.00
Sir William Hay, 1744–51 (baronet in Jan 1748)★	100.00.00
Don Antonio Escudero, Grand Prior of Navarre, 1751–3	100.00.00
(resigned and left court in July)	
Sir John Constable, 1753–66 (baronet in Sept 1753)	(by 1757:
	125.00.00)
Kitchen / *cucina (portone in facciata à Muti)*	
Yeoman of the kitchen / *maestro di casa di cucina* / *scalco* / *écuyer*	
de la cuisine / *intendant de la cuisine* /*maître d'hôtel*	
Jeremiah Broomer, 1689–1730 (returned to France)	98.10.07
Jean Baptiste Dupuis, 1734–42 (died in Jan 1743)	98.10.07
Giuseppe Generat, 1742–50s	98.10.07
Pietro Pelercha, in 1759	unknown
Cook / *cuisinier* / *cuoco* / *capocuoco*	
Matthew Creagh, 1727 to at least 1742	64.13.09
Simon Oliver, at least 1737–40	75.00.00
François Lafon, by 1742 to 1745 (left Rome)	75.00.00
Joseph Boulieux, at least 1750–52	50.00.00
Assistant / *sottocuoco*	
Matthew Creagh, 1696–1727	27.06.00
Théophile Lesserteur, by 1717 to 1727	25.00.00
Richard Baines, by 1718–20 (died in service)	25.00.00
Jean-Baptiste Dupuis, by 1722 to 1734	25.00.00
James Miner, by 1715 to 1727	15.00.00
Alexis Morelli, at least 1728–30	20.00.00

The Household below stairs, the table and the stables	*l. s. d.*
Maître rôtisseur / rosticciere	
Pierre Garnier by 1742 to 1750s	50.00.00
Garçon de la cuisine / garzone della cucina	
Richard Conway, by 1717 to 1729	30.00.00
Ignace Faure, 1727 to at least 1742	30.00.00
Wine cellar / *bottiglieria (portone in facciata à Santi Apostoli, mano sinistra)*	
Yeoman of the wine cellar / *officier de la paneterre / boutillier / bottigliere / cantiniere*	
Charles Macarty, 1689–28 (died in service)	64.13.09
David Lewis, 1728–33	unknown
Giovanni Battista Cantina, 1733 to at least 1750	50.00.00
Andrea Landuzzi, by the 1750s	unknown
Loreto Tei, 1759	unknown
Pietro Del Oro, 1759–64	unknown
Garçon de la cave / ballieur / garzone della cantina	
Francesco Girelli, 1718–1750s	20.00.00
Bakehouse	
Baker / *boulanger*	
Jean Bouzier, by 1722 until at least 1730	40.00.00
Confectionary / *office des fruits / credenza (portone in facciata à Santi Apostoli)*	
Yeoman confectioner / *confiturier / confetieri / credenziere*	
Pierre Pecquet, 1715–30 (returned to France)	44.13.09
Henry Read, 1730 to at least 1742	44.13.09
Giuseppe Rè, by 1739 to 1766	50.00.00
Confectioner / *confetieri*	
Henry Read, 1719–30	30.00.00

Stables / *stalla / scuderia*	*l. s. d.*
Equerry / *cavallerizzo*	
James Delattre, 1704–42	117.12.10
Sir John O'Brien, 1728–34	60.00.00
Cavaliere Giuseppe Gigli, by 1742 to 1752	100.00.00
Conte Bernardini, 1752 to at least 1757	100.00.00
Riding purveyor / *maréchal / maestro di stalla*	
John Sheridan, 1707–29 (died in service)	95.16.08
Camillo Dini, by 1729 to 1750s	50.00.00
1st Coachman / *1er cocher / primo cocchiere*	
Edmund Butler, by 1713 to at least 1740/41	52.05.00
Coachman / *cocher / cocchiere*	
Salvatore Mambretti, by 1728 to 1762	35.00.00
Chairman / *porteur de chaise / corriere / cadola*	
Henry Kerby, by 1693 to 1730 (returned to Saint-Germain)	52.05.00
Antoine Brun, 1716–50s	35.00.00
Massimo Carafa, 1722–?	unknown

Stables / *stalla* / *scuderia*	*l. s. d.*
Footman / *valet de pied* / *laquais*	
Andrew Simms, 1695 to at least 1739	36.08.00
Nicolas Prévot, by 1710 to at least 1722	36.08.00
Jacques Catillon, 1712–27 and 1739–40	36.08.00
John Morice, by 1717 to at least 1720	36.08.00
Francesco Mesi, by 1717 to 1724 (died in service)	36.08.00
James Kerby, by 1728 to at least 1742	36.08.00
John Macpherson, at least 1739–40	36.08.00
Francis O'Neill, by 1739 to ?	36.08.00
Groom / *palfrenier*	
Frank Ridge, by 1695 to at least 1728	31.07.00
Nicholas Clark, by 1696 to 1726 (died in service)	31.07.00
Mark Manning, by 1699 to 1729	31.07.00
Roger Ryan, 1705 to at least 1731	31.07.00
Postillon / *postiglione*	
Ryan Cornell, at least 1720	31.07.00
Thomas Barty, at least 1720	31.07.00
Garçon d'ecurie / *garzone di stalla*	
Michael Maguill, at least 1729–30	20.00.00
Harbourer of the deer	
Peter Jolly de Falvie, by 1709 to 1729/30	27.13.07
Guards (portone in facciata à San Marcello)	
Guarda portone	
Bernhardt Nieriker, 1719–46 (died in service)	60.00.00
Josef Luither, 1746–66	60.00.00
Albano	
Guardarobba	
Gio. Batta Evangelista, 1721–31 (assassinated)	30.00.00
Stefano Marchesi, by 1739 to 1750s	35.00.00
Madame Cantini, 1750s	35.00.00

Queen's Bedchamber, 1719–1735	*l. s. d.*
Lady / *dama d'onore*	
Mrs Marjory Hay, 1719–22*	200.00.00
Marchesa Lucrezia Legnani, 1727–35	200.00.00
Contessa Ranuzzi, 1727–9	200.00.00
Woman / *dama*	
Eleanor, Lady Misset, 1719–20, 1721–2, 1725–8	100.00.00
Dorothy Sheldon, 1725–8	unknown
Maid of honour	
Lady Anne Maxwell, 1727–31	unknown

Queen's Bedchamber, 1719–1735	*l. s. d.*
Chambermaid / *cameriera*	
Mrs Mary Fitzgerald, 1719–35	50.00.00
Isabella Gordon, by 1720 to 1735 (Mrs Marsi in Jan 1730)	50.00.00
Mrs Mary Rivers, by 1726 to 1735	73.15.00
Necessary woman	
Mrs Margaret Baines, 1719–35	25.00.00
	(by 1735:
	35.00.00)
Mrs Sarah Maguirk, 1719–?	15.00.00
Mrs Shaw, 1719–before 1727	15.00.00
Mrs Levieux, by 1722–before 1727	15.00.00
Washerwoman / *blanchisseuse* / *lavandara*	
Catherine Macane, 1719–35	25.00.00
Mrs Anna Doyle, by 1722–before 1727	40.00.00
Mrs Tomson, by 1722 to 1735	20.00.00
Anne O'Neill, 1729–35	30.00.00
Mender and marker of linen	
Mrs Anne Prévot, 1719–26/27	unknown
Valet de chambre / *cameriere*	
Gottfried Rittel, 1719–35	78.10.07
Michele Vezzosi, 1719–25	78.10.07
François Decelles, by 1725 to 1735	78.10.07
James Duncan, 1726–35	78.10.07
Servant	
Alexander Gordon, 1719–35	15.00.00
Sartore	
Joseph Weber, 1719–20	unknown

Queen's Chamber, 1719–1735	*l. s. d.*
First gentleman / *primo gentiluomo*	
Earl of Nithsdale, 1727–35	200.00.00
Gentleman / *gentiluomo*	
Marchese Fabio Albergati, 1727–33	100.00.00
Conte Girolamo Formigliari, 1727–35	
Clerk / *commis*	
Robert Creagh, 1719–35	50.00.00
Confessor	
Father John Brown, 1719–27 (left court in Oct)	unknown
Father Cangiassi, at least 1727–30	unknown
Father Leonardo da Porto Maurizio, 1730–5?	unknown

Queen's Chamber, 1719–1735	*l. s. d.*
Chaplain	
Father O'Brien, 1729–30	unknown
Physician	
Dr Charles Maghie, 1726–32*	100.00.00
Dr Robert Wright, 1727–35	100.00.00
Surgeon	
Dr James Hay, 1726–8 (died in service)	50.00.00
James Murray, by 1728 to 1735	50.00.00

Prince of Wales, 1721–1725	*l. s. d.*
In charge	
Eleanor, Lady Misset, Jan–Feb 1721	unknown
Mrs Lois Hughes, Feb 1721–March 1722	unknown
Dorothy Sheldon, March 1722–Sept 1725	unknown
Chambermaid / *cameriera*	
Mrs Grace Appleton, by 1722 to 1725	50.00.00
Wet nurse	
Mrs Lois Hughes, Jan to Feb 1721	unknown
Wet nurse, then dry nurse	
Mrs Francesca Battaglia, Feb 1721–Sept 1726	30.00.00

Prince of Wales, 1725–1744	*l. s. d.*
Governor	
Earl of Dunbar, Sept 1725–Dec 1738*	250.00.00
Under-governor	
Sir Thomas Sheridan, Sept 1725–Dec 1738	100.00.00
Maggiordomo	
Sir Thomas Sheridan, 1738–44	100.00.00
Gentleman	
John Stewart, 1726–36	100.00.00
John Constable, 1728–43	80.00.00
William Goring, 1736–43 (died in service)	100.00.00
Edward Stafford, 1743–4	80.00.00
Preceptor / *precettore*	
Andrew Ramsay, Jan to Nov 1724	unknown
Father Lawrence Mayes, July 1726–1738	120.00.00
Valet de chambre / *cameriere*	
Michele Vezzosi, 1725–44	78.10.07

Prince of Wales, 1725–1744	_l. s. d._
Pietro Ferbos, by 1728 to 1744	78.10.07
Blanchisseuse	
Marie Gouy, by 1735 to 1744	40.00.00
	(by 1742:
	50.00.00)
Equerry and riding master	
Chevalier Nicholas Geraldin, Grand Prior of England, 1726–33	100.00.00
Equerry / _écuyer_	
Captain John O'Brien, 1726–41 (died in service)	60.00.00
Francis Strickland, 1734–41	60.00.00
George Carteret, 1734–40 (died in service)	60.00.00
Footman / _valet de pied/lacchè_	
Francis O'Neill, 1726 to before 1739	36.08.00

Duke of York, 1725–1729	_l. s. d._
Governess	
Countess of Nithsdale, Nov 1725–29	200. 00. 00
In charge	
Dorothy Sheldon, March to Nov 1725	unknown
Eleanor, Lady Misset, Nov 1725	unknown
Chambermaid / _cameriera_	
Mrs Grace Appleton, 1725–9	50.00.00
Wet nurse, then dry nurse	
Mrs Teresa Keller, 1725–6	15.00.00

Duke of York, 1729–1745	_l. s. d._
Governor	
Earl of Dunbar, June 1729 to March 1743*	250.00.00
Under-governor	
Hugh Dicconson, June 1729–43 (died in service)	100.00.00
John Paul Stafford, June 1729–30 (resigned)	100.00.00
Maggiordomo	
John Townley, 1743–5	100.00.00
Gentleman	
John Constable, 1743–5	80.00.00

Duke of York, 1729–1745	*l. s. d.*
Preceptor	
Father Lawrence Mayes, 1729–39	120.00.00
Father Ildefonso, 1739–43	unknown
Valet de chambre / cameriere	
Martin Floriot, 1729–45	78.10.07
William Turner, 1729–45	78.10.07
Blanchisseuse	
Marie Gouy, by 1735 to at least 1744	40.00.00
	(by 1742:
	50.00.00)
Equerry and riding master	
Chevalier Nicholas Geraldin, Grand Prior of England, 1729–33	100.00.00
Equerry / *écuyer*	
Captain John O'Brien, 1729–41 (died in service)	60.00.00
Francis Strickland, 1734–41	60.00.00
George Carteret, 1734–40 (died in service)	60.00.00
Footman / *valet de pied / lacchè*	
Jacques Catillon, 1727 to before 1739	36.08.00

Music teachers to the princes	*l. s. d.*
Dancing master / *maître à danser*	
Jean Arnaux, by 1725 to 1745	45.00.00
Maître de clavecin	
Felice Doria, by 1742 to 1745	30.00.00
Maître de la basse de viole / sonatore di violoncello	
Giovanni Battista Costanzi, by 1742 to 1745	30.00.00
Singing teacher / *musicien*	
Domenico Ricci, by 1742 to 1745	50.00.00

Pensioners	*l. s. d.*
Peers	
William Livingston, 3rd Viscount Kilsyth, 1716–33*	200.00.00
James Livingston, 5th Earl of Linlithgow, 1716–23*	200.00.00
William Maxwell, 5th Earl of Nithsdale, 1719–27, 1735–44	200.00.00
Winifred (née Herbert), Countess of Nithsdale, 1719–27, 1729–49	200.00.00

Pensioners	*l. s. d.*
James Carnegie, 5th Earl of Southesk, 1716–25*	200.00.00
George Seton, 5th Earl of Winton, 1716–49	200.00.00
Gentlemen	
Joseph Bulstrode, 1742 to at least 1757	100.00.00
Joseph Dormer, 1747–65	100.00.00
Robert Fermor, by 1746 to 1765	100.00.00
Charles Fleming, 1716–26	100.00.00
Thomas Forster, 1716–22*	100.00.00
David Fotheringham, 1747: his son until 1750*	100.00.00
William Goring, 1728–36*	100.00.00
William Hay, 1726–7*	100.00.00
Cavaliere Pontelli, by 1757 to ?	100.00.00
John Paul Stafford, 1728–9	100.00.00
James Paston, by 1742 to 1766	75.00.00
Officers and others	
Captain Collier, 1716 to before 1726*	72.10.00
Thomas Arthur, 1728–42*	60.00.00
Alexander Cameron, 1729–31	60.00.00
Mark Carse, 1731–6*	60.00.00
Colonel William Clepham, 1716–29*	60.00.00
Maurice Corbet, by 1739 to at least 1760	60.00.00
Arthur Elphinstone, 1729–33	60.00.00
Captain Henry Fitzmaurice, 1727–47	60.00.00
Charles Slezor, by 1734 to 1742*	60.00.00
George Abernethy, 1734 to at least 1746*	50.00.00
Major John Cockburne, 1716 to before 1726*	45.00.00
Charles Forbes, 1716 to before 1726*	45.00.00
Captain John O'Brien, by 1722 to 1726	45.00.00
George Abernethy, 1728–33*	37.10.00
James Hay, 1718–27*	35.00.00
James Edgar, 1716–25*	30.00.00
Robert Watson, 1718–29*	15.00.00
Relicts	
Widow Browne, 1726–33	30.00.00
Helen Macarty, 1728–?	30.00.00
Frances Kerby, 1730–5	25.00.00
Former servants of the king	
Baldassare Artema (ex-*valet de chambre*), 1716 to before 1726	78.10.06
Alan Cameron (ex-groom of the Bedchamber), 1717–27	100.00.00
Francis Kennedy, 1725–7*	100.00.00
Sir David Nairne, 1728–33	205.03.02
James Rodez, 1729–39	78.10.07
James Delattre, 1742–50	117.12.10
Father Lawrence Mayes, 1743–9	120.00.00
Former servants of the queen	
Mary Fitzgerald, 1735–50s	50.00.00
Isabella Gordon-Marsi, 1735–50s	50.00.00

Pensioners	*l. s. d.*
Marie Rivers, 1735–50s	73.15.00
Margaret Baines, 1735–50	35.00.00
Gottfried Rittel, 1735 to at least 1742	78.10.07
Alexander Gordon, 1735 to at least 1742	15.00.00
Robert Creagh, 1735–9	50.00.00
Former servants of the prince and duke	
Francesca Battaglia, 1725–50s	30.00.00
Grace Appleton, 1729–55	50.00.00
Teresa Keller, 1729–50s	15.00.00
John Constable, 1745–53	80.00.00

Newly recruited English, Scottish and Irish
servants in Rome after 1720

(The ones who had previously lived at Saint-Germain are marked
  with an asterisk*.)

Recruited by 1721	Dr Robert Wright
1721	Lady Misset
	Mrs Lois Hughes
	Thomas Sheridan*
1722	William Watkins*
	Dorothy Sheldon*
	Mrs Grace Appleton*
1724	Andrew Ramsay
1726	John Stewart
	Mary Rivers
	Captain John O'Brien
	William Hay
	James Duncan
1727	Dr James Hay
	Father O'Callaghan*
	Captain Henry Fitzmaurice
1728	John Constable
	William Goring
	Thomas Arthur
	Revd Daniel Williams
	Revd Ezekiel Hamilton
	James Murray*
	George Abernethy
	Lady Anne Maxwell
1729	William Turner
	Father O'Brien

Newly recruited English, Scottish and Irish
servants in Rome after 1720

	Hugh Dicconson
	John Paul Stafford*
	Sir John O'Brien
	Alexander Cameron
1731	Earl Marischal
	Mark Carse
By 1734	Charles Slezor
1734	Revd Thomas Wagstaff
	Francis Strickland*
	George Carteret*
By 1739	Maurice Corbet
	John Macpherson
By 1742	James Paston
1742	Joseph Bulstrode*
1743	Edward Stafford*
	John Townley
By 1747	Robert Fermor
1747	Father Leigh
	Earl of Lismore
	Joseph Dormer
	David Fotheringham
1750	Andrew Lumisden
1760	Earl of Alford

Appendix B Jacobite honours and titles

One problem facing any king in exile is how to reward people for their loyalty and faithful service. An obvious way of doing this is to grant knighthoods and hereditary titles. Yet if this is done too liberally the value of such honours will inevitably be eroded. James III's policy was to give a restricted number of knighthoods, baronetcies and peerages, but to insist that most of them were kept secret.

The Order of the Garter

James gave the Garter to Prince Charles a few days before his second birthday, in December 1722.[1] He also gave it to Prince Henry at some time before 1729, when the four-year-old boy is shown wearing it in his earliest surviving portrait.[2] As royal princes it was important that they should be seen to be knights of the most important English order of chivalry.

Only four other people are known to have been given the Garter after the court was established in Rome: the 5th Duke of Hamilton in 1723, the Duke of Wharton in 1726, the Duke of Liria in 1727 and the Earl of Lismore in 1747.[3] As Hamilton was living in Great Britain his Garter remained secret.[4]

In 1723 the marquise de Mézières (née Oglethorpe) asked the king to give the Garter to her son-in-law, the prince de Montauban.[5] James had recently obtained from Lord Lansdowne an 'authentick' paper about the rules of the Order of the Garter 'in the very hand of Garter King of Arms himself' in London.[6] He sent a refusal to the marquise, explaining that the question of giving the honour was not as simple as she thought, and that he would only do so if he were to receive a request signed personally by the Regent of France. Otherwise, he said, he would never give the Garter to a foreigner.[7]

---

[1] RA. SP 64/58, James III to Lansdowne, 27 December 1722.
[2] See Chapter 14, p. 278.   [3] Ruvigny, *Jacobite Peerage*, p. 193.
[4] RA. SP 84/11, warrant signed by James III and sent to Paris on 4 August 1723.
[5] RA. SP 67/18, marquise de Mézières to James III, 10 May 1723.
[6] RA. SP 57/117, Lansdowne to James III, 5 February 1722.
[7] RA. 67/112, James III to marquise de Mézières, 27 June 1723.

One reason for not doing so was because a foreigner might not give it precedence. The Duke of Berwick had both the Garter and the *Saint-Esprit*, and annoyed James III and the Jacobites in France by wearing the *cordon bleu* of the Garter under his coat and the *cordon bleu* of the *Saint-Esprit* over it.[8] When he died in 1734 his widow asked the king what she should do with his Garter collar. She offered to send it to Rome, so that it could be given to her stepson the Duke of Liria, now the 2nd Duke of Berwick.[9] But she really hoped that her own son, Lord Charles FitzJames, now the 4th duc de FitzJames, might be created a Knight of the Garter, so that she could keep it and give it to him. A lengthy correspondence ensued, during which James III made it clear that he would not give the Garter to the new duc de FitzJames because, sooner or later, he would probably receive the *Saint-Esprit*. The collar was therefore given to the 2nd Duke of Berwick (Duke of Liria) who was already a Knight of the Garter.[10] The sons of the 1st Duke of Berwick, although naturalised in Spain and France, were not regarded as foreigners.

The Order of the Thistle

Apart from Prince Charles and Prince Henry, who were given the Thistle at the same time as the Garter, seven people are known to have been given the most important Scottish order of chivalry: Lord Dillon in 1722, the 5th Duke of Hamilton in 1723, Lords Marischal, Inverness, Nithsdale and Dunbar in 1725, and the 3rd Duke of Perth in 1739.[11] Those given to Hamilton and Perth remained secret because they were living in Great Britain.

---

[8] RA. SP 171/128, James III to L. Innes, 13 July 1734; RA. SP 174/38, L. Innes to James III, 11 October 1734.

[9] BL. Add MSS 38851, ff. 177, 186, James III to the Duchess of Berwick, 19 September 1734 and L. Innes, 22 September 1734. (The letters were removed at some point from the Stuart Papers.)

[10] The correspondence lasted from 1 November 1734 to 16 August 1735, and can be seen in RA. SP 174/153, 163; 175/72, 157; 178/26, 72; 179/49, 182; 180/14, 104, 133; 181/6, 92, 172. The only known portrait of the 2nd Duke of Berwick, attributed to Louis-Michel Van Loo, shows him in his robes as a Knight of the *Toison d'Or* (Palacio da Liria, Madrid). There is a bust copy (dated 1737) showing the duke wearing armour, with the *Toison d'Or* suspended from a red ribbon around his neck (Museo dell'Accademia Etrusca, Cortona). In neither of them is he shown wearing any insignia of the Order of the Garter.

[11] Ruvigny, *Jacobite Peerage*, p. 194. When Marischal arrived in Rome in 1731 it was noted that he wore the St Andrew medal of the Thistle (NA. SP 98/32/f. 233, Stosch to Newcastle, 28 July 1731), but it is not shown in his portrait painted in Rome in 1733, attributed to Placido Costanzi (NPG 522). Yet he wore it when he left Rome in 1733 and went to Venice (NA. SP 98/32/f. 510, Stosch to Newcastle, 21 March 1733).

Baronetcies and other knighthoods

After 1719 James III created at least 27 baronets: 4 English, 11 Scottish and 12 Irish.[12] It is not known how many knighthoods were given. But the general rule was clear. All these honours were to be kept secret unless the recipients were serving at the exiled court (like Sir David Nairne, Sir Thomas Sheridan, Sir John Graeme, Sir William Hay and Sir John Constable), or were living in exile (like Sir Charles Wogan, Sir John Forrester, Sir Timon Connock and Sir Andrew Ramsay).

Most of these honours were given when there was still hope of an eventual restoration. In February 1750 the king rejected a request from an Irishman who wanted to be made a baronet in the following way:

I should be very glad to gratify you in that and in all other respects, but this is really not the time for granting such sort of empty favours, and as a few days ago I actually refused one of the same kind to a gentleman considerable in his own country and who joined the Prince in person when he was in Scotland. So that my rule of not granting such favours just at this time is general and without exception.[13]

Peerages

Apart from those given to his own sons, James III created thirty-three peerages after 1719, but insisted on even stricter rules of secrecy. The only ones which were made public were the earldoms given to Dillon, Inverness, Dunbar, Lismore and Alford. Dillon was the king's representative at the court of France; the other four were serving with the king in Rome. The fact of living in exile was not regarded as a sufficient reason for a peerage to be publicly acknowledged. The Duke of Mar was given an Irish dukedom in 1722, and the Earl of Inverness was elevated to be a duke in 1727, but both titles remained secret.[14]

As an illustration we might take the example of Sir John Cameron of Lochiel, who was created Baron Lochiel in 1717. King James wrote to Prince Charles in 1747:

I remark and take well of you that you do not ask directly of me to declare Lockyel's Tittle, for after what I had already writ to you on such matters, you could not but be sensible that those were things I could not do at this time; were

---

[12] Ruvigny, *Jacobite Peerage*, pp. xv–xviii.

[13] RA. SP 304/77, James III to Wogan, 23 February 1750. There is some confusion concerning Wogan, because there is evidence that he was made a baronet after rescuing Princess Clementina in 1719 (Ruvigny, *Jacobite Peerage*, p. 187).

[14] Ruvigny, *Jacobite Peerage*, pp. xv–xviii.

I now to declare all the latent Patents (which are in great number) and which it would be highly improper to do, I should please but one, and disgust a great many other deserving people, and in Lockyels case, I should particularly disoblige the other Clanns, who have all Warrants as well as he. Neither is Lord Lismore's case a precedent for others, since his Tittle had not been declared without he had come here to be about me in the way he is in. Lockyel's interest and reputation in France will make him more considered there than any empty Tittle I could give him.[15]

There was another reason for keeping secret the 'empty' titles of Jacobites living abroad. Some of them had been sold to people who might not otherwise have been given them. In this way the king raised money, and the people who purchased the peerages made a long-term investment in the confident expectation of an eventual restoration. For example, Sir Peter Redmond was a wealthy Irish merchant in Lisbon who had been made a baronet in 1717. Four years later he wrote to the king and asked to be made a baron in exchange for money. James wrote to the Duke of Ormonde:

I am far from being fond of making peers on such bargains but I think in the present case nothing is to be neglected which can get us any money since as matters stand our all depends on that Article. I therefore send you the enclosed lines for Sir Peter for you to forward to him, and I would have you at the same time propose to him the sending you of six thousand Crowns, adding that in consideration thereof I have authorised you to give him my promise of making him an Irish Baron after you have received the money. O'Brien at Malaga ... might very likely be also induced to advance a sum of money and there may be for aught I know others either in Portugal or Spain able and willing to do as much.

James added that any such transactions would have to be done 'without noise' and only when 'one can be very sure of the secret'. But it was obvious that 'any who lends money will no doubt expect some recompense', and the king told Ormonde that 'there can never be any difficulty in promising in my name to repay, any sum so lent, double after my restoration'.[16] It was this long-term prospect which interested Redmond. When promising to keep the matter secret, the latter admitted that 'the fewer that know it, the more convenient for my affairs at present'.[17]

[15] *SPW*, p. 213, James III to Prince Charles, 7 November 1747.
[16] RA. SP 54/102, James III to Ormonde, 11 August 1721.
[17] RA. SP 55/40, Redmond to James III, 14 October 1721.

Appendix C Money paid for Stuart portraits

The payments shown below, made by James III and his family, were all for oil paintings on canvas, except where specified. The list is not complete, but it includes all the payments recorded in the Stuart Papers, and mentioned in Chapters 5 and 14. As most of the payments were for more than one picture, the main list is preceded by a short one showing the ten single most expensive paintings:

Pubalacci, Monaldi and Silvestri, *The Facciata of Cardinal York* (1748)	1925 *livres*
David, *The Baptism of Prince Charles* (1725)	603 *livres*
David, *Prince Charles* (1726–7)	502 *livres*
Meytens, *James III* (1725) and *Queen Clementina* (1725)	500 *livres* each
David, *Prince Charles* (1729) and *Prince Henry* (1729)	479 *livres* each
Blanchet, *Prince Charles* (1737–8) and *Prince Henry* (1738)	450 *livres* each
Trevisani, *James III* (1720) and *Queen Clementina* (1720)	418 *livres* each

The rates of exchange between the four currencies used varied from year to year, but the following provides a very rough guide:

1 (Spanish) *pistole* = 16 *livres* 15 *sols* 0 *deniers*
1 *scudo* = 5 *livres*
1 *zecchino* = 5 *livres*
1 pound sterling = 4 *scudi* = 20 *livres*

In many cases the Stuart Papers record the payment for a portrait in more than one currency. However, the first item in the list has been converted into *livres* by the author for the purpose of comparison.

	livres	pistoles	scudi	zecchini
Pubalacci, Monaldi and Silvestri, *Facciata* of *Cardinal York* (1748)	(1925.00.00)		385.00	
Meytens, *King* and *Queen* (1725) (100 *zecchini* each)	1000.00.00			200.00
David, *Prince* and *Duke* (1729)	958.05.00			191.65
Trevisani, *King* and *Queen* (1720) (25 *pistoles* each)	837.05.00	50.0		
Fratellini, *King* and *Queen* (1728)		40.0		
Fratellini, *King*, *Queen*, 2 of *Prince*, *Duke*: pastels (1729)		40.0		
David, *Baptism* (1725)	603.00.00	36.0		
Liotard, *King*, *Prince* and *Duke*: pastels; and *Prince* miniature (1737)	553.10.00			
David, *King* and *Prince* (1723) (20 + 10 *pistoles*?)	502.10.00	30.0		
David, *Prince* (1726/27) (reduced from 40 *pistoles*)		30.0		
Liotard, *King*, *Queen*, *Prince* and *Duke*: miniatures (1738)				100.00
David, *King* and *Queen* (1723) (three-quarter + bust)	485.15.00	29.0		
Blanchet, *Prince* (1737–8)	450.00.00			90.00
Blanchet, *Duke* (1738)	450.00.00			90.00
David, *Prince* and *Duke* (1730) (2 pairs of copies)	405.00.00			
Belle, *Prince* and *Duke* (1729) (2 pairs of copies)	400.00.00			
Liotard, *Prince* and *Duke*: miniatures on enamel (1738)				75.00
David, copies of *King* and *Queen* (1724) (unknown number)	351.15.00	21.0		
Batoni and others, 6 miniatures (1738)	350.00.00			
Pesci, *King* (1721)	335.00.00		67.00	
David, copies of *King* and *Queen* (1724) (unknown number)	318.05.00	19.0		
Telli, *King*, *Queen*, *Prince* and *Duke*: miniatures (1744) (15 *scudi* each)			60.00	
Dupra, *Prince* and *Duke*, and miniature of *King* (1740) (copies)				45.00
David, 2 miniatures of *Queen* (1727) (reduced from 16 *pistoles*)		12.0		
Pesci, *King* (1721)	200.10.00		40.20	
Dupra, *Prince* and *Duke* (1740)				40.00
Dupra, *Prince* and *Duke* (1740) (copies)				40.00
Stern, *Queen* (1740)			40.00	
Dupra, *Duke* holding a miniature of *Prince* (1744)			40.00	
Pesci, *Queen with Prince* (1722)	166.05.00		33.50	

	livres	pistoles	scudi	zecchini
David, 10 pictures (copies?) (1720) (1 *pistole* each: miniatures?)	166.05.00	10.0		
David, 2 three-quarter copies of *Prince* (reduced from 12 *pistoles*)		10.0		
Unknown, *Prince* and *Duke* (1732) (2 pairs of copies)		10.0		
Blanchet, *King*, *Prince* and *Duke* (1738) (copies)	150.00.00			
Dupra, *Prince* and *Duke* (1740) (copies)				30.00
Dupra, *Prince* and *Duke* miniatures (1740)				30.00
Dupra, *Prince* and *Duke* (1740) (copies)				30.00
David, copy of *Duke* (1727) (reduced from 10 *pistoles*)		6.0		
David, *Duke* (1726/27) (reduced from 12 *pistoles*)		6.0		
David, *Lady Inverness* (1726–7) (reduced from 10 *pistoles*)		6.0		
Unknown, a picture for the Chapel altar (1723)	131.00.00			
Batoni, *Duke* miniature (1744)			20.00	
Blanchet, *King* and *Duke* (1752)	120.00.00			24.00
Unknown, *Duke* miniature (1750)	100.00.00			
Gill, *King*, *Queen* and *Prince* (1727) (1 *pistole* and 2 *filippi* each)	83.15.00	5.0		
David, *Queen* (1727)	83.15.00	5.0		
Blanchet, *King* (1741)				15.00
David, *Prince* (1726)	67.00.00	4.0		
David, bust copy of *Prince* (1726–7) (reduced from 6 *pistoles*)		4.0		
Pesci, small *King* (1721)	66.05.00		13.40	
Pesci, small *Queen* (1721)	66.05.00		13.40	
Blanchet, *Queen* (1740) (copy)	60.00.00			12.00
Gill, *King* and *Queen* (1727) (1 *pistole* and 2 *filippi* each)	55.16.00	3.1		
Pesci, miniature of *King* (1721)	50.05.00	3.0		
Pesci, miniature of *Queen* (1721)	50.05.00	3.0		
Casalini Torelli, *Prince* (1727)	40.00.00			
David, two pictures (copies?) (1720) (1 *pistole* each: miniatures?)	33.05.00	2.0		
David, two copies of *Queen* (1728) (1 *pistole* each)	33.05.00	2.0		
David, miniature copy? (1726)	22.00.00	1.1		

Appendix D Portraits of the Jacobite courtiers painted in exile

Lady Anne Clifford (Countess Mahony) (1739–40, 100 × 74.5 cm), by Pierre Subleyras (Caen, Musée des Beaux Arts: copies by Domenico Cherubini, 1778, at Madrid, Academia San Fernando, and by Pompeo Batoni, 1785, in a private collection)

James Murray, Earl of Dunbar (1719, 101.6 × 76.2 cm), by Francesco Trevisani (Scone Palace)

James Edgar (1739, 18.6 × 15 cm), by Domenico Dupra (Scottish National Portrait Gallery 3360)

Charles Fleming (later 7th Earl of Wigton) (c.1716, 73 × 61 cm), by Alexis-Simon Belle (private collection)

William (later Sir William) Hay (1739, 62 × 48 cm), by Domenico Dupra (Scottish National Portrait Gallery 1565)

John Hay, Earl of Inverness (1724, 96.5 × 76.2 cm), by Francesco Trevisani (Lord Kinnoull)

John Hay, Earl of Inverness (1740, 90 × 100 cm), marble medallion possibly by Filippo della Valle (Avignon, Musée Calvet)

Marjory Hay, Countess of Inverness (1719, 101.6 × 74.9 cm), by Francesco Trevisani (Scone Palace)

Marjory Hay, Countess of Inverness [as Diana, with a bow and arrow] (1723, 97.7 × 76.2 cm), by Antonio David (Scone Palace: copy in a private collection)

Marjory Hay, Countess of Inverness [as Flora, with flowers] (1723, 96.5 × 76.2 cm), by Antonio David (Lord Kinnoull)

Dr James Irwin (1739, 62.9 × 48.5 cm), by Domenico Dupra (Scottish National Portrait Gallery 1598)

George Keith, 10th Earl Marischal (1716, 124.5 × 99.1 cm), by Pierre Parrocel (Scottish National Portrait Gallery 311)

George Keith, 10th Earl Marischal (c.1733, 44.2 × 32.1 cm), attributed to Placido Costanzi (National Portrait Gallery 522)

George Keith, 10th Earl Marischal (1752), by Cosmo Alexander (private collection)

Francis Kennedy (*c.* 1727–8), a miniature attributed to John Alexander (private collection: reproduced in H. Tayler, *The Seven Sons of the Provost*, opposite p. 102)

John Erskine, Duke of Mar (1718, 74 × 61 cm), by Francesco Trevisani (Alloa Tower)

Frances, Duchess of Mar, and Her Daughter Lady Frances Erskine (1719, 135 × 97.5 cm), by Francesco Trevisani (Alloa Tower)

Sir David Nairne (1714, 76.2 × 63.5 cm), by Alexis-Simon Belle (private collection)

James Carnegie, 5th Earl of Southesk (1726, 31.7 × 22.2 cm), a caricature drawing by Pier Leone Ghezzi (Scottish National Portrait Gallery 2452)

James Seton, 5th Earl of Winton (1749), by Cosmo Alexander (private collection: reproduced in A. and H. Tayler, *The Stuart Papers at Windsor*, opposite p. 276)

There are portraits of Lord and Lady Nithsdale painted in Scotland by Sir John de Medina, now at Traquair House (reproduced in Flora Maxwell Stuart, *Lady Nithsdale and the Jacobites* (Traquair House, 1995), respectively p. 25 and the front cover). The same book reproduces an undated and unattributed pencil drawing of Lady Anne Maxwell (p. 139).

Appendix E A Stuart pretender

There is a drawing by Pier Leone Ghezzi which has the following inscription:

Ritratto dell'Inglese soprannome La Reginella che si fingeva essere il Rè Giacomo Stuardi d'Inghilterra, fatto da mè Cav.re Pierro Leone Ghezzi il di – 10 – settembre 1728.[1]

[Portrait of the Englishman nicknamed 'La Reginella' [little queen] who was pretending to be King James Stuart of England, done by me Cavaliere Pierro Leone Ghezzi on 10 September 1728.]

The drawing shows a young man with his own hair (i.e. without a wig) of perhaps thirty to thirty-five years of age. In September 1728 James III was thirty years old and living in Bologna, having been absent from Rome for two years. Who was this Stuart pretender? According to Ghezzi he was an Englishman, and of approximately the same age as the king. But how could he have been pretending to be James III when the latter was so well known in the Papal States?

A partial answer is provided by two letters preserved among the Stuart Papers, both of them in Italian and sent to James III from Genoa by a man who signed his name as 'Giacomo Stuardo'. The first is dated 8 May 1736. Stuardo informs the king that they share a 'common lineage', and asks to be allowed 'to enter the presence of Your Majesty'. He states that he has 'Stuart blood', and describes himself as 'a Prince so close to You because of the lineage'.[2] The second letter, dated 15 August 1739, implies that his request was unsuccessful: 'I never succeeded in finding a shelter under the charitable shadow of Your patronage.' In this letter Stuardo describes himself as James III's cousin, and again begs to 'have the chance to humble myself in Your presence' in order to 'explain the

---

[1] It is in the Albertina at Vienna (Inv. 1259, 24.8 × 17.8 cm). The date could be read as 1708 rather than 1728, but the latter date seems more likely.

[2] RA. SP 187/42. In this letter Stuardo states that he has contacted Lord Inverness, and that he is sure that the latter 'has already presented to You my concerns and explained my pitiful condition'.

deepest feelings of my heart'.[3] We do not know for sure whether or not he was received by the king. It seems, however, that Ghezzi was misinformed when he wrote that the man was pretending to be King James himself. But could he have been James's cousin? Who might his parents have been?

Once again we have a partial answer, this time in the correspondence of Baron von Stosch. Four years later, in November 1743, the latter reported that a man had arrived in Rome from Naples calling himself 'Prince Jacques Stuard'. He claimed to be a bastard son of King Charles II, though he was believed actually to be a Neapolitan named 'Jacques Origo'.[4] He was arrested on the orders of Pope Benedict XIV and imprisoned in the Castel Sant' Angelo. When interrogated he produced a large Stuart family tree, some large seals bearing the Stuart coat of arms, various patents, and some (unspecified) insignia of the Order of the Garter. He was threatened with various punishments, but persisted in his claim and was eventually banished from the Papal States in February 1744. All his papers, seals and insignia were confiscated.[5]

While he was in prison the man sent an engraving of 'B. Catharina Elisca Adurna Januensis Vidua' to James III, and begged his continued protection in a note written in Italian by a scribe, but which he signed as 'Giacomo Stuardo CB'. In the note he claimed to be a son of Charles II, and therefore a cousin of James III.[6] As Charles II had died in 1685, over three years before the birth of James III, he was claiming to be at least fifty-nine years old.

It is not known when the Stuart pretender (if such he was) died. But there is an undated copy of his will in a folder of papers otherwise devoted to the inheritance of Cardinal York in 1807.[7] At the beginning of the will 'Giacomo Stuardo' states that he drew it up 'in questa città di Nap[oli] infirmo nel letto, mà p[er] la Dio gratia sano di mente, et in rectissimi sensi, considerando il pericolo imminente di mia morte'. He evidently believed that he really was a Stuart bastard because there, on his deathbed, he repeats his claim to be a 'figlio naturale di Carlo Secondo Stuardo Potentissimo'. There is no indication of how he came to be living in Naples rather than England or Genoa, and his claim is not strengthened by his reference to being procreated by 'Maria Stuardo

[3] RA. SP 216/140. In this letter Stuardo states that 'the Duke of Ormonde is now helping me', and hopes that 'thanks to his honourable intercession You will be so clement to protect and defend me'.
[4] NA. SP 98/46/ff. 262, 264, Stosch to Newcastle, 23 and 30 November 1743.
[5] NA. SP 98/46/f. 268, Stosch to Newcastle, 7 December 1743; NA. SP 98/49/ff. 16, 18, 35, Stosch to Newcastle, 4 and 11 January, and 3 March 1744.
[6] RA. SP Box/1/125.   [7] ASR. Misc Famiglia: Stuart b. 172, f. 3.

della famiglia delli Baroni di San Marzo'. He gives his date of birth as 19 February 1669, and entrusts his wife (Teresa Corona) and children to the protection of James III. Given the date of his birth we may assume that he probably died during the 1740s or 1750s. The man might well have sincerely believed himself to be a bastard of Charles II, but it seems highly unlikely that he really was one. It remains a mystery as to how and why this undated copy of the will ended up in a file of papers concerning Cardinal York.

Appendix F The personal possessions of James III

In his Last Will and Testament, King James III stated that he wanted his personal possessions to be divided between his two sons.[1] They consisted of his money invested in both France and Italy, the insignia of the orders of the Garter and the Thistle, his family portraits, his jewels, his plate, his coaches, his horses, his pictures, his books, his furniture and personal objects and his papers. This note concerns those of the king's possessions which are known to have survived.

The orders of the Garter and the Thistle

James III specified in his will that the insignia of the two orders should be left to Prince Charles:

And whereas we have at present in our custody two Collars called of SS. one with diamonds the other without, two medals of the Garter one set with rubies and diamonds and the other with diamonds alone, with a small medal of the Order of St Andrew set with small diamonds, with some other small medals of the same orders . . . we leave the above-mentioned Collars [and] jewels . . . to our dearest son the Prince of Wales.

After the death of Prince Charles in 1788 the most important of these items were inherited by Cardinal York, who then bequeathed two of them to the Hanoverian Prince of Wales, later George IV, in 1807. Their despatch to England was delayed because of the war, but the Great George with diamonds suspended from the collar of the Order of the Garter arrived in 1813, followed two years later by the small medal of the Order of the Thistle. These two (the collar and Great George, and the medal) were deposited in Edinburgh Castle in November 1830, and have remained there ever since.[2]

---

[1] ASV. SS: Ingh 25, pp. 109–12, the Last Will and Testament of James III, 'at our Court of Rome', 21 November 1760.

[2] 'The Stuart Jewels – their Travels and Travails', transcript of a lecture delivered by Stephen Patterson of the Royal Collection to the Jewellery History Society on 23 September 2008, and kindly communicated by him to the author.

The medal of the Garter with diamonds, the Lesser George, was inherited in 1788 by Prince Charles's illegitimate daughter, the Duchess of Albany, from whom it passed to his estranged wife, the Countess of Albany, and then a dealer, before being purchased by Lord Wellesley in 1811. It has been in the possession of the Dukes of Wellington since 1843. Although not in its original condition, it is the medal which was worn by Charles I when he was executed in 1649, and is therefore now referred to as the 'Scaffold George'.[3]

The king's family pictures

James III's 'family pictures big and small' were also bequeathed to Prince Charles, and many of them have survived: they are discussed in Chapters 5 and 14. Most of them were inherited by Cardinal York in 1788 and 1789, and they are mentioned in the inventory of his possessions drawn up after his death.[4]

Cardinal York left his collection of family portraits to his friend Angiolo Cesarini, Bishop of Milevi, who in turn left them to his niece, contessa Caterina Malatesta, in 1817. They were then sold by the latter's husband, conte Sigismondo Malatesta, during the 1840s.[5]

The family portraits which had remained at Saint-Germain, and which the king seems to have forgotten about, were dispersed during and after the French Revolution.[6]

The king's jewels

Although we do not have a list of the king's jewels, we know that they also were to be left to Prince Charles:

---

[3] Gerald Wellesley, 7th Duke of Wellington, 'The Scaffold George of Charles I', *The Antiquaries Journal*, 33:3, 4 (July–October 1953), pp. 159–68.

[4] The inventory of the Duchess of Albany, dated 20 April 1790, is in Archivio Storico di Propaganda Fide, Stato Temporale del Card. Duca de York, Inventario Contessa [sic] d'Albany vol. 5. (There is a copy in ASR. Misc Famiglia: Stuart b. 170/2/f. 5). The inventory of Cardinal York, dated 18 July 1807, is in ASR. Misc Famiglia: Stuart b. 170/f. 5, 'Inventario de Beni Ereditari della ... Cardinale ... Duca di York esistenti nel palazzo della Cancelleria'. For the portraits which have not survived, see Chapter 14, pp. 305–6.

[5] Peter Lole, 'The Bequests of the Cardinal King, Henry IX', *The Jacobite*, 110 (Winter 2002), pp. 10–16; Corp, 'Conclusion', in *Stuart Court in Rome*, p. 165.

[6] For the family portrait by Largillière, see Corp, *King over the Water*, p. 35 (quoting from Agnes Strickland, *Lives of the Queens of England*, vol. IX: *Mary of Modena* (London, 1846), p. 313. There are references to other portraits in Strickland on pp. 236, 333). For the family portrait by Mignard, see Elizabeth Mortimer, 'A Portrait of James II and his Family by Pierre Mignard' (MA thesis, Courtauld Institute of Art, 1986).

And whereas for greater security we have deposited in the Monte della Pieta of this city a box of jewels the lock of which is sealed with our seal we here declare that all the jewels contained in the same box belong to our dearest son the prince above mentioned except that portion which was formerly mortgaged by the republick of Poland to the Family of Sobieski.

The only jewel which is known to have survived is a ruby ring which was worn by both Charles II and James II at their coronations. It was bequeathed by Prince Charles to Cardinal York, and then by the latter to the Prince of Wales in 1807. It also has been on deposit in Edinburgh Castle since 1830.[7]

The Polish crown jewels, which had been mortgaged to the Sobieski family, were inherited by Prince Charles from Queen Clementina, but the 'Republick of Poland' had the right to redeem them during a period of fifty years, after which they would become the absolute property of the Stuarts. The jewels had still not been redeemed when Poland was partitioned in the late eighteenth century. They were sold and dispersed during the 1790s, but the great Sobieski Sapphire, which Cardinal York had mounted in his bishop's mitre, was bought from a dealer for the Royal Collection and is now mounted on the reverse side of the Imperial State Crown.[8]

The king directed that all his other possessions in Italy, 'whether plate coaches horses pictures books ready-money and moveables of any kind whatsoever', should become the property of Cardinal York.

The king's plate

The Stuart court in exile commissioned a large amount of gold, gilt and silver plate during the early 1690s.[9] The only gold items were three complete *couverts*. The gilt included two caddinets, four other complete *couverts*, thirty-five plates, and various accessories, including two salts, a mustard pot, two salvers and a cup. As the years went by the balance of the collection formed in the 1690s was inevitably changed. It remained at Saint-Germain until the autumn of 1718, when it was eventually packed up and sent to the newly established Stuart court

---

[7] See note 2.
[8] McLynn, *Charles Edward Stuart*, pp. 104–6; Kathryn Barron, '"For Stuart blood is in my veins" (Queen Victoria). The British monarchy's collection of imagery and objects associated with the exiled Stuarts from the reign of George III to the present day', pp. 149–64 in Corp (ed.), *The Stuart Court in Rome*, at p. 151.
[9] Corp, *A Court in Exile*, p. 110; Corp, 'James II and James III in Exile: The English Royal Table in France and Italy, 1689–*c.*1730', in Leonor d'Orey (ed.), *European Royal Tables – International Symposium Acts* (Lisbon, 1999), pp. 112–20.

in Rome.[10] By then the thirty-five gilt plates had been melted down, but in compensation there was a noticeable increase in the number of gilt accessories.[11] As a generalisation, it may be said that at Saint-Germain James III had only gold and gilt items on his table, but that in Rome the accessories were gold and gilt and the plates were mainly silver.

These Stuart commissions were supplemented by gifts from other people. The most important came in 1719 from Cardinal D'Adda and King Philip V of Spain. When the cardinal died in Rome in January 1719 he bequeathed all his plate to James III.[12] The gift from Philip V was received when James was in Spain. It consisted of a complete service for the king's table: various salts, salvers, *couverts*, dishes and plates, including some which were described as *entrée* plates and *entremêt* plates.[13]

Certain items were clearly kept and used over a very long period – notably the gold *couverts*;[14] the gilt caddinets of the king and the queen,[15] the gilt salts (the basic symbol of state and royalty in England), and a large silver basin and ewer for the ceremonial washing of hands. Others were gradually melted down, so that the precious metal could be used for other purposes.[16] The only object which is still in existence today is a silver *ecuelle*, or porringer, with its cover,[17] which belonged to Queen Clementina.[18]

Mary of Modena had a large collection of porcelain, but it was not used at Saint-Germain during the dinners and suppers, as the royal table was only laid with plate. In Rome, by contrast, the Stuarts did have

[10] Corp, *Jacobites at Urbino*, pp. 50, 120, 193–4.
[11] Inventories of the plate belonging to the Stuarts in RA. SP Misc 33, pp. 147–53, February 1719; RA. SP 99/114–120, 16–18 November 1726; and RA. SP 123/80–8, 28 July–3 August 1729.
[12] RA. SP Misc 33, p. 145. James III had most of it melted down, but retained 12 complete gilt *couverts* and some other items, which are shown in the inventories of 1726 and 1729 (RA. SP 99/118; 123/80, 85).
[13] RA. SP 99/117, 118; RA. SP 123/84, 85.
[14] RA. SP 123/85. The king's gold *couvert* is also referred to in RA. SP 97/100, receipt by Saint-Paul, 28 September 1726.
[15] Prince Charles was given a gold caddinet (RA. SP 123/86).
[16] For example, 12 thin silver trencher plates which had belonged to Mary of Modena were melted down in 1725 to make a writing box (RA. SP 72/18, receipt by Ellis, 5 January 1724; RA. SP 88/16, note by Ellis, 11 December 1725).
[17] It measures 28 cm over the handles and weighs 727 grams, and is included in RA. SP 99/118 and 123/85.
[18] It was included as exhibit no. 520 in the *Royal House of Stuart* exhibition at the New Gallery, London, in 1889, auctioned by Sotheby's in London on 12 May 1996 (lot 101), and auctioned again on e-Bay on 21 November 2002. It is presumably the same as the silver *ecuelle* made by Angelo Spinazzi which was auctioned by Sotheby's at Gleneagles on 29 August 2000 (Godfrey Evans, 'The Acquisition of Stuart Silver and Other Relics by the Dukes of Hamilton', pp. 131–48 in Corp (ed.), *The Stuart Court in Rome*, at pp. 132, 145).

porcelain on their table. A large consignment in 'cases ... of a very considerable size' was received by sea from France in the summer of 1722.[19] Later on, James III also commissioned (or was given) some Vincennes porcelain. There is a very fine broth basin with cover and stand bearing his arms, dated *c.*1748–52, now in the Royal Collection.[20]

The king's pictures

James III had a collection of paintings in the Palazzo del Re and in the Palazzo Apostolico at Albano. According to the inventories of 1726–7 the ones in Rome were at that time mainly grouped together in three rooms. Two of these were in James's apartment, in some private cabinets beyond his bedchamber on the first floor; the other was in the bedchamber on the second floor. There were twenty-eight pictures in the two rooms below and eleven 'great pictures' in the bedchamber above.[21] The collection would obviously have been expanded during the following forty years, but we have no information to identify individual pictures, many of which would anyway have been Stuart family portraits. We may assume, however, that there were portraits of other people, and we know that there was one of Pope Clement XI, presumably by David,[22] and another of Benedict XIV, said to be by Batoni.[23] These pictures, like the family portraits, were all inherited by Angiolo Cesarini and then dispersed.

The king's books

Cardinal York added to the collection of books which he inherited from his father, and eventually gave his entire library to the seminary at Frascati. The books have been in the Vatican since 1944, and are fully discussed in *La biblioteca del Cardinale*, published in 2007.[24] Some of

---

[19] BL. Add MSS 20303, f. 102, Hay to Gualterio, undated (July 1722); BL. Ass MSS 31265, f. 235, Hay to Gualterio, undated (July 1722). See also the porcelain listed in RA. SP Misc 33, p. 147.

[20] Barron, 'The British Monarchy's Collection of Imagery and Objects Associated with the Exiled Stuarts', pp. 149–64 in Corp (ed.), *The Stuart Court in Rome*, at p. 160.

[21] RA. SP 98/131 and 106/79. See Corp, *King over the Water*, p. 92.

[22] According to the inventory of 1807 (see note 4), there was a portrait of 'Papa Albani' in Cardinal York's *Camera del Baldacchino*.

[23] Tayler, *SPW*, p. 32.

[24] Edited by Marco Buonocore and Giovanna Cappelli, and published in Rome in 2007 to accompany an exhibition at Frascati from December 2008 to January 2009. (The book is lavishly illustrated, but unfortunately includes some portraits on pp. 132, 177, 183, 208 and 240 which do not, as alleged, show Cardinal York, and another on p. 181 which does not, as alleged, show his brother, Prince Charles.) There is a useful discussion of

James III's books, however, are preserved elsewhere, and several are in the Royal Collection. They include the so-called *Sobieski Book of Hours* (*c.*1420–5), which had belonged to Queen Clementina; an illuminated French Book of Hours, produced in Paris *c.*1500; and a French *Missal* of 1655. There is also an *Office de la Semaine Sainte* of 1715, with the binding of Mary of Modena, which was given by the Duchess of Albany to the duc de FitzJames and is now in Paris in the private collection of one of the latter's descendants.

The king's moveables

The catalogue of the *Royal House of Stuart* exhibition mounted at the New Gallery in London in 1889 contains only seven items, other than portraits and papers, which were said to have belonged to James III. They were a gold ring (with an intaglio chalcedony portrait of Mary Queen of Scots, no. 335); an ivory casket which had previously belonged to James I (no. 1105); a sword which had previously belonged to James II (no. 784); another sword (no. 1133); a pair of silver spurs (no. 624); a small ivory snuff-mill (no. 1086); and a pair of brass taper stands (no. 567). There were also pieces of Garter ribbon which had allegedly been worn by the king (nos. 515, 1090). The present whereabouts and even authenticity of these items is unknown.

The king's papers

The archives of the Stuart court in Rome are now at Windsor Castle and have been amalgamated to form a single collection. But in his will James III divided them into two categories. The first group was for Prince Charles:

And whereas in the beginning of the year 1744 when the Prince left Rome we had a great number of papers by us which may be hereafter of some use to him we have already deposited the said papers in the English College of this city to be at his disposal after our decease, and we shall take proper measures that his letters to us with the copies of ours to him whether already writ or which may be hereafter written should . . .

---

the most important items from Cardinal York's library in Bindelli, *Enrico Stuart*, pp. 126–8, 132–7. The books inherited from James III include two sixteenth-century Books of Hours (BAV. Vat Lat 14935, 14936), a Polish prayer book of 1685 (BAV. Vat Lat 15144) and *The Variation of the Armes, and Badges of the Kings of England . . . until this present Yeare*, presented by James Terry (Athlone Herald of Arms) to the Prince of Wales at Saint-Germain-en-Laye in 1697 (BAV. Vat Lat 14937).

At this point the bottom of the manuscript in the Vatican Secret Archives has been torn, and the rest of the sentence has been lost. We may assume, however, that the king's correspondence with his elder son, like the papers in the English College, was given to Prince Charles when he returned to Rome in 1766. The archives were then taken to Florence in 1774, and left there when the prince returned to Rome in 1785. They were inherited by the Duchess of Albany, and eventually sent to Carlton House in 1813.

The second category of Stuart Papers is referred to in the manuscript of the king's will immediately after the missing part:

> ... for the other papers we may have by us as they can be of no use to the Prince we have already otherwise disposed of them.

This laconic comment is unhelpful, but there is no reason to doubt that the papers had been entrusted to Cardinal York, and taken by him from the Palazzo del Re to the Palazzo della Cancelleria. After his death in 1807 they were inherited by Angiolo Cesarini, and were also sent to Carlton House, in 1817.[25]

Four possessions of Queen Clementina

In his will James III identified four important items which Queen Clementina had bequeathed to her elder son in 1735, and which were not therefore to be regarded as part of his own possessions:

> And we also declare that we have in our custody the following effects which belong to the Prince viz. a vase of topaze in the shape of a boat the price of which is not well known, a toilette of several pieces of plate which belonged to the late Queen our most dear and honoured Mother, a priez Dieu which was given to her by the late King of France Louis the XIV. And a cabinet curiously wrought with several pieces of enamel with some small jewels. We here declare that the same effects belong to the Prince.

These four items are shown in an inventory of Prince Charles's possessions in 1744, which states that at that time they were still in the queen's apartment.[26]

The toilet set had been taken from Saint-Germain to Urbino in 1718, and given to Queen Clementina the following year.[27] The prie-dieu,

---

[25] For the story of how the two groups of papers reached England, see A. and H. Tayler, the introduction to *SPW*; and Marion F. Gain, 'The Stuart Papers at Windsor', *Royal Stuart Society Papers*, XVII (London, 1981).
[26] RA. SP 262/94.   [27] Corp, *A Court in Exile*, p. 357.

which had been given to Mary of Modena by Louis XIV in 1689,[28] had been brought to Rome in 1723.[29] Both of them, like the topaz vase and the cabinet, have disappeared without trace.

Conclusion

The fact that James III had no legitimate grandchildren, and that his family had no settled residence, inevitably resulted in the dispersal of his possessions. So too did the upheavals caused by the revolutionary wars which broke out shortly after the deaths of Prince Charles and the Duchess of Albany, and during the last years of Cardinal York. Many of James's possessions must still exist, without their provenance being established. There may be others in private collections which are believed to have been owned by James III and which might emerge in the future – perhaps even prompted by this brief examination. For the time being we are left with the many family portraits, and with a small but important group of objects.

[28] *Ibid.*, p. 101.   [29] RA. SP 69/113, Ellis to Hay, 18 October 1723.

Appendix G Family trees

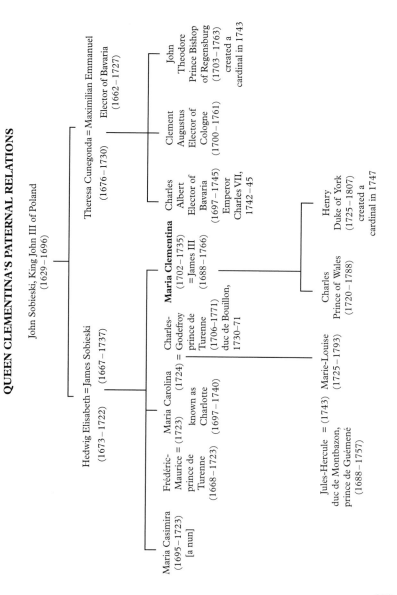

QUEEN CLEMENTINA'S PATERNAL RELATIONS

John Sobieski, King John III of Poland
(1629–1696)

Theresa Cunegonda = Maximilian Emmanuel
(1676–1730)   Elector of Bavaria
                                        (1662–1727)

Hedwig Elisabeth = James Sobieski
(1673–1722)   (1667–1737)

John
Theodore
Prince Bishop
of Regensburg
(1703–1763)
created a
cardinal in 1743

Clement
Augustus
Elector of
Cologne
(1700–1761)

Charles
Albert
Elector of
Bavaria
(1697–1745)
Emperor
Charles VII,
1742–45

Maria Casimira
(1695–1723)
[a nun]

Frédéric-
Maurice = (1723)
prince de
Turenne
(1668–1723)

Maria Carolina
(1724)
known as
Charlotte
(1697–1740)

Charles-
Godefroy = (1724)
prince de
Turenne
(1706–1771)
duc de Bouillon,
1730–71

Maria Clementina
(1702–1735)
= James III
(1688–1766)

Jules-Hercule = (1743)
duc de Montbazon,
prince de Guémené
(1688–1757)

Marie-Louise
(1725–1793)

Charles
Prince of Wales
(1720–1788)

Henry
Duke of York
(1725–1807)
created a
cardinal in 1747

QUEEN CLEMENTINA'S MATERNAL RELATIONS

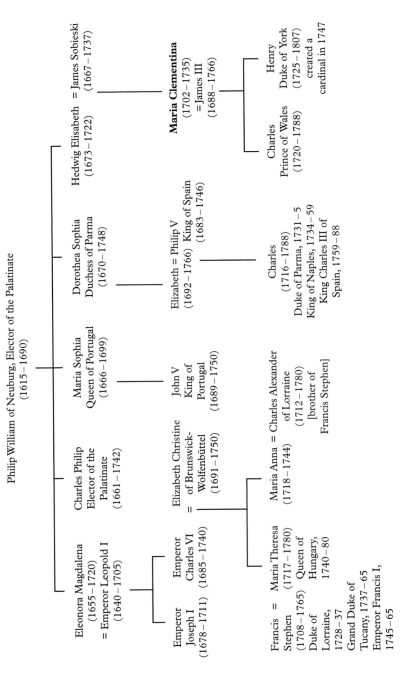

THE FAMILY OF THE DUKE OF BERWICK

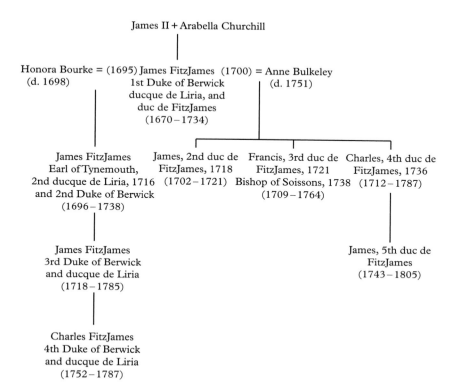

James II + Arabella Churchill

Honora Bourke = (1695) James FitzJames (1700) = Anne Bulkeley
(d. 1698)   1st Duke of Berwick   (d. 1751)
                   ducque de Liria, and
                   duc de FitzJames
                   (1670–1734)

James FitzJames   James, 2nd duc de   Francis, 3rd duc de   Charles, 4th duc de
Earl of Tynemouth,   FitzJames, 1718   FitzJames, 1721   FitzJames, 1736
2nd ducque de Liria, 1716 (1702–1721)   Bishop of Soissons, 1738 (1712–1787)
and 2nd Duke of Berwick   (1709–1764)
(1696–1738)

James FitzJames   James, 5th duc de
3rd Duke of Berwick   FitzJames
and ducque de Liria   (1743–1805)
(1718–1785)

Charles FitzJames
4th Duke of Berwick
and ducque de Liria
(1752–1787)

Sources and bibliography

It should be noted that all the manuscript and printed sources which are quoted in the text have been translated for the convenience of the reader into English, but that the original languages have been retained in the footnotes. It should also be noted that many of the manuscript sources in Great Britain, notably the Gualterio Papers (British Library), the correspondence of Stosch in the State Papers (National Archives), the Tyrrell Papers (Ushaw College) and the Stuart Papers (Royal Archives) are written in French, not English. The manuscript sources in Italy are mainly written in Italian, though some also are in French and English.

PRIMARY SOURCES: MANUSCRIPTS

Badminton, Duke of Beaufort's Archives, Fm 1/4/3, 13
Bologna:
  Archivio di Stato di Bologna
    Assunteria di Magistrati, Affari Diversi b. 27, 116, 118
    Senato Diario vol. 12
  Biblioteca Communale Archiginnasio
    MS B.3996
  Biblioteca Universitaria
    Avisi Secreti di Francesco Ghiselli, MS 770, vols. 91, 92
Chichester, West Sussex County Record Office, Goodwood MS 105
Chiddingstone Castle, unsorted Bower MSS
Durham, Ushaw College, Tyrrell Papers, OS 2/B
Edinburgh:
  National Library of Scotland
    Lumisden Papers, MS 14260, 14261, 14262, 14264, 14269
    Nairne's Journal, MS 14266
  Scottish Catholic Archives, Blairs Letters 2, 3

London:
  British Library, Gualterio Papers, Add MSS 20292, 20298, 20302, 20303,
    20305, 20308, 20310, 20313, 20330, 20467, 20533, 20661, 31255,
    31262–7
  National Archives, Stosch letters
    State Papers, Rome, 85/13, 14, 15, 16
    State Papers, Florence, 98/32, 37, 38, 41, 43, 46, 49, 53, 58, 61
  Westminster Diocesan Archives
    Epistolae Variorum (Mayes Papers) vols. 7, 8, 9, 10, 11
    MSS Archiv. Westmon. vol. XL
    Paris Seminary Papers
Oxford, Bodleian Library, Rawlinson MSS D. 1180, 1181, 1183, 1185
Rome and Vatican City:
  Archivio di Stato di Roma
    Camerale I: Conti della Depositeria Generale b. 2017 bis
    Camerale I: Giustificazione di Tesoriere b. 438, 444, 449, 457, 458,
      459, 460, 509, 524, 532, 553, 561, 567, 610, 615, 638, 659, 661,
      662, 669, 682, 683, 684, 689
    Camerale I: Registro de' Mandati Camerale b. 1066, 1068, 1069,
      1070, 1074, 1077, 1082, 1085
    Collezione Disegni e Piante 1, c. 87, no. 562
    Misc. Famiglia Stuart, b. 170, 171
  Archivio Segreto Vaticano
    Archivio Rospigliosi, 262, 264
    Fondo Benedetto XIV, 19, 23, 27
    Palazzo Apostolico Computisteria, 854, 982 to 988, 1007, 1008,
      1048, 1058, 5044, 5045, 5220, 5223
    Segretario di Stato: Inghilterra 21, 25
  Archivio Storico di Propaganda Fide
    Stato Temporale Eredita del Cardinale duca di York
      Cause Diverse 1, 2, 3, 4
      Giustificazioni 1, 3, 4, 5, 11
      1807 1, 2
      Inventario contessa d'Albany 3, 4, 5
  Archivio Storico Vicariato di Roma
    Santi Apostoli vols. 12, 13 (Battesimi)
    Santi Apostoli vols. 22, 23 (Matrimoni)
    Santi Apostoli vols. 41, 42, 43 (Morti)
    Santi Apostoli vols. 57–82 (Stati d'Anime)
  Biblioteca Apostolica Vaticana
    Fondo Borgia, Lat MS 565 (the diary of François Foucquet)
    Vat. Lat. 12432 (Materie di Cerimoniale)

British School at Rome
  The Papers of Diego de Revillas, Envelope F
Scots College
  Archives vol. 4
  Venerable English College
    Libri 283, 292
    Scritture 3, 27, 46, 47, 48, 50
Urbino, Biblioteca Universitaria, Fondo del Comune, Rep III and b. 167
Windsor, Royal Archives, Stuart Papers
  Vol. 41 onwards
  Misc 16–35
  Box 1, 2, 3, 4, 5, 7

PRIMARY SOURCES: PRINTED FROM MANUSCRIPTS

Argenson, René-Louis de Voyer, marquis d'. *Journal et Mémoires*, ed. E. J. B. Rathéry (9 vols., Paris, 1859–67), vols. II, V, VI.

Belloni, Girolamo. *Scritture inedite e dissertazione 'del commercio'*, ed. Alberto Caracciolo (Rome, 1965).

Benedict XIV, Pope. *Correspondance de Benoît XIV*, ed. Emile de Heeckeren (2 vols., Paris, 1912).

Brosses, Charles de. *Lettres d'Italie* ed. Frédéric d'Agay (2 vols., Paris, 1986).

Caesar, Mary Frewan. *The Journal of Mary Frewan Caesar*, ed. Dorothy B.T. Potter (Lampeter, 2002).

Conti, Antonio. *Lettere d'Antonio Conti da Venezia a Madame la Comtesse de Caylus, 1727–29*, ed. Sylvie Mamy (Venice, 2003).

Historical Manuscripts Commission, *9th Report*, part II, appendix (London, 1884). [Correspondence of the Earl Marischal]

Historical Manuscripts Commission, *10th Report* (London, 1885). [Correspondence of Admiral Gordon and of Ezekiel Hamilton]

Historical Manuscripts Commission, *10th Report*, appendix, part VI (London, 1887). [Stuart Papers]

Historical Manuscripts Commission, *Stuart Papers* (London, 7 vols., 1902–23), vols. IV, V, VII.

Lettere ai Sovrani di Spagna, II, *1735–39*, ed. Imma Ascione (Rome, 2002).

Leyburne, Bishop. *Bishop Leyburne's Confirmation Register of 1687* (North West Catholic History Society, Wigan, 1997).

Luynes, Philippe d'Albert, duc de. *Mémoires sur la cour de Louis XV*, ed. L. Dussieux and E. Soulié (17 vols., Paris, 1860–6), vols. I, VII, VIII.

Maintenon, madame de, and the princesse des Ursins. *Correspondance de madame de Maintenon et de la princesse des Ursins*, ed. Marcel Loyau (Paris, 2002).

Tayler, Henrietta (ed.). *The Jacobite Court at Rome in 1719* (Edinburgh, 1938).

Tayler, Alistair and Henrietta (eds.). *The Stuart Papers at Windsor* (London, 1939).

Valesio, Francesco. *Diario di Roma*, IV, *1708–28*, ed. Gaetano Scana, (Milan, 1978).
Diario di Roma, V, *1729–1736*, ed. Gaetano Scana, (Milan, 1979).
Diario di Roma, VI, 1737–1742, ed. Gaetano Scana, (Milan, 1979).

PRIMARY SOURCES: CONTEMPORARY PRINTED BOOKS

Chracas, Francesco (publisher). *Diario ordinario,* published weekly in Rome from 1719 onwards, 'presso S. Marco al Corso'.
De Rossi, Domenico. *Studio d'architettura civile, libro primo: Sopra gli ornamenti di porte e finestre* (Rome, 1702).
De Rossi, Giambattista. *Palazzi diversi nel'alma città di Roma* (Rome, 1638).
Epicedium pro immaturo funere Mariae Clementinae Magnae Britanniae etc Reginae (Rome, 1738).
Murray, John. *Genuine Memoirs of John Murray, Esq, Late Secretary to the Young Pretender . . . in a Letter to a Friend* (London, 1747).
Parentalia Mariae Clementinae Magn. Britan., Franc., et Hibern. Regin Iussu Clementis XII Pont. Max (Rome, 1736).
Relazione della infermità, morte, solenni essequie, e trasporto di Sua Maestà Giacomo III re della Gran Bretagna, occorse in Roma a' di 7 gennaro 1766 (Rome, 1766).
[Rialton, Viscount] *A Letter from an English Traveller at Rome to His Father of the 6th of May 1721* (London, 1721).
Russel, James. *Letters from a Young Painter Abroad to his Friends in England* (2 vols., London, 2nd edn, 1750).
Specchi, Alessandro. *Il nuovo teatro delle fabbriche et edifici in prospettiva di Roma moderna* (Rome, 1699).

SECONDARY SOURCES

Andrieux, Maurice. *La vie quotidienne dans la Rome pontificale au XVIIIe siècle* (Paris, 1962).
Antinori, Aloisio. 'Il palazzo Muti Papazzurri ai Santi Apostoli nei secoli XVI e XVII: Notizie sull'attività di Giovanni Antonio de Rossi, Carlo Fontana e Carlo Francesco Bizzaccheri', in *Architettura: processualità e trasformazione,* proceedings of the international conference, Rome, Castel Sant'Angelo, 24–7 November 1999, ed. Maurizio Caperna and Gianfranco Spagnesi (Rome, 2002), pp. 439–46.
Antolini, Bianca Maria. 'Rome, 1730–1800', in *New Grove Dictionary of Opera,* vol. IV, pp. 25–7.
Ascari, Maurizio. 'James III in Bologna: An Illustrated Story', *Royal Stuart Papers,* LIX (London, 2001).
Barbier, Patrick. *Farinelli: Le castrat des lumières* (Paris, 1994).
Bartolucci, Anna Fucili. 'Urbino e gli Albani', pp. 441–8 in Franco Battistelli, ed., *Arte e cultura nella provincia di Pesaro e Urbino dalle origini a oggi,* (Venice, 1986).
Batorska, Danuta. 'Grimaldi and the Galleria Muti-Papazzurri', *Antologia di belli arti,* 7/8 (1978), pp. 204–15.

Benimelli, José-Antonio. *Les archives secrètes du Vatican et la Franc-Maçonnerie* (2nd French edn, Paris, 2002).

Bevan, Bryan. *King James the Third of England* (London, 1967).

Bindelli, Pietro. *Enrico Stuart, cardinale duca di York* (Frascati, 1982).

Bowron, Edgar Peters. *Pompeo Batoni* (London, 1985).

Bugliosi, Chiara. *Itinerario storico archeologico artistico di Albano Laziale* (Albano, 1989).

Candé, Roland de. *Vivaldi* (Paris, 1967, 2nd edn 1994).

Caracciolo, Alberto. *L'Albero dei Belloni: una dinastia di mercanti del Settecento* (Bologna, 1982).

Castries, René de la Croix, duc de. *La scandaleuse Madame de Tencin, 1682–1749* (Paris, 1986).

Cavazzoni Zanotti, G.P. *Storia dell'Accademia Clementina* (Bologna, 1739).

Clark, Jane. 'The Stuart Presence at the Opera in Rome', pp. 85–94 in Edward Corp (ed.), *The Stuart Court in Rome: The Legacy of Exile* (Aldershot, 2003).

Corp, Edward. *The King over the Water: Portraits of the Stuarts in Exile after 1689* (Edinburgh, 2001).

Edward Corp (ed.). *The Stuart Court in Rome: The Legacy of Exile* (Aldershot, 2003).

Edward Corp. *A Court in Exile: The Stuarts in France, 1689–1718* (Cambridge University Press, 2004).

The Jacobites at Urbino: An Exiled Court in Transition (Basingstoke, 2009).

'James II and James III in Exile: The English Royal Table in France and Italy, 1689–c.1730', pp. 112–20 in Leonor d'Orey (ed.), *European Royal Tables – International Symposium Acts* (Lisbon, 1999).

'The Irish at the Jacobite Court of Saint-Germain-en-Laye', pp. 143–56 in Thomas O'Connor (ed.), *The Irish in Europe, 1580–1815* (Dublin, 2001).

'Farinelli and the Circle of Sicinio Pepoli', *Eighteenth Century Music* 2:2 (September 2005), pp. 311–19.

'Maintaining Honour during a Period of Extended Exile: The Nomination of Cardinals by James III in Rome', pp. 157–69 in Martin Wrede and Horst Carl (eds.), *Zwischen Schande und Ehre: Erinnerungsbrüche und die Kontinuität des Hauses* (Mainz, 2007).

'*La Senna festeggiante* Reconsidered: Some Possible Implications of Its Literary Text', pp. 231–8 in Francesco Fanna and Michael Talbot (eds.), *Antonio Vivaldi, passato e futuro* (Venice, 2009).

'Prince Charles or Prince Henry ?', *The British Art Journal* 10:2 (2009), pp. 51–7.

'The Location of the Stuart Court in Rome: The Palazzo del Re', pp. 180–205 in Paul Monod, Murray Pittock and Daniel Szechi (eds.), *Loyalty and Identity: Jacobites at Home and Abroad* (Basingstoke, 2010).

'The *Facciata* of Cardinal York: An Unattributed Picture in the Scottish National Portrait Gallery', *Journal of the Scottish Society for Art History*, 15 (2010), pp. 33–8.

'The Stuart Court and the Patronage of Portrait-Painters in Rome, 1717–1757', pp. 39–53 in D.R. Marshall, S. Russell and K. Wolfe (eds.), *'Roma-Britannica': Art Patronage and Cultural Exchange in Eighteenth-Century Rome* (London and Rome, 2011).

'La Franc-Maçonnerie jacobite et la bulle papale *In Eminenti* d'avril 1738', *La règle d'Abraham* no.18 (Paris, 2004), pp. 13–44.

Cottret, Bernard and Monique. 'La sainteté de Jacques II, ou les miracles d'un roi défunt', pp. 92–7 in Edward Corp (ed.), *L'autre exil: Les Jacobites en France au début du XVIIIe siècle* (Montpellier, 1993).

Crespi, L. *Felsina Pittrice. Vite de' Pittori Bolognesi* (Bologna, 1769).

Cruickshanks, Eveline, and Howard Erskine-Hill. *The Atterbury Plot* (Basingstoke, 2004).

Cryan, M.J. *Travels to Tuscany and Northern Lazio* (Vetralla, 2004).

De Angelis, Alberto. *Il teatro Alibert o Delle Dame, 1717–1863* (Tivoli, 1951).

Delaméa, Frédéric. '*Giustino*, Vivaldi's Last Roman Triumph', booklet to accompany the recording of *Il Giustino* by Il Complesso Barocco, conducted by Alan Curtis (EMI Records, Virgin Classics, 2002), pp. 10–12.

Dennistoun, James. *Memoirs of Sir Robert Strange . . . and His Brother-in-law Andrew Lumisden* (2 vols., London, 1855).

Donati, Fedora Servietti. 'Sua Maestà britannica a Bologna e il Palazzo del Rè, anno 1728', *Strenna Storica Bolognese*, 30 (1980), pp. 332–46.

Doran, John. *Mann and Manners at the Court of Florence, 1740–1786* (2 vols., London, 1876).

Dulon, Jacques. *Jacques II Stuart, sa famille et les Jacobites à Saint-Germain-en-Laye* (Saint-Germain, 1897).

Eisler, William. 'The Construction of the Image of Martin Folkes (1690–1754): Art, Science and Masonic Sociability in the Age of the Grand Tour', *The Medal* 58 (Spring, 2011), pp. 4–29.

Ewald, A.C. *The Life and Times of Charles Edward Stuart* (2 vols., London, 1875).

Fagiolo, Marcello (ed.). *Corpus delle feste a Roma*, vol. II: *Il Settecento e l'Ottocento* (Rome, 1997).

Frati, Lodovico. *Il Settecento a Bologna* (Bologna, 1923).

Gibson, Elizabeth. *The Royal Academy of Music, 1719–1728: The Institution and Its Directors* (New York and London, 1989).

Graziani, Irene. *La bottega dei Torelli: Da Bologna alla Russia di Caterina la Grande* (Bologna, 2005).

Gregg, Edward. 'The Jacobite Career of John, Earl of Mar', pp. 179–200, in Eveline Cruickshanks (ed.), *Ideology and Conspiracy: Aspects of Jacobitism, 1689–1759* (Edinburgh, 1982).

'The Financial Vicissitudes of James III in Rome', pp. 65–83 in Edward Corp (ed.), *The Stuart Court in Rome: The Legacy of Exile* (Aldershot, 2003).

Guthrie, Neil. ' "A Polish Lady": The Art of the Jacobite Print', *1650–1850: Ideas, Aesthetics and Inquiries in the Early Modern Era*, 14 (2007), pp. 287–312.

Haile, Martin. *James Francis Edward, The Old Chevalier* (London, 1907).

Harris, Ellen T. 'With Eyes on the East and Ears in the West: Handel's Orientalist Operas', *Journal of Interdisciplinary History*, 36:3 (Winter, 2006), pp. 419–43.

Hogwood, Christopher. *Handel* (London, 1984).

Holloway, James. 'John Urquhart of Cromarty: A Little-known Collector of Roman Paintings', pp. 103–12 in David Marshall, Karin Wolfe and Susan Russell (eds.), *'Roma-Britannica': Art Patronage and Cultural Exchange in Eighteenth Century Rome* (London and Rome, 2011).

Hughan, William J. *The Jacobite Lodge at Rome, 1735–7* (Torquay, 1910).

Hunter, David. 'Senesino disobliges Caroline, Princess of Wales, and Princess Violante of Florence', *Early Music* 30 (May 2002), pp. 215–23.

Ingamells, John. *A Dictionary of British and Irish Travellers in Italy, 1701–1800, Compiled from the Brinsley Ford Archive* (New Haven and London, 1997).

Kerney Walsh, Micheline. 'Toby Bourke, Ambassador of James III at the Court of Philip V', pp. 143–53, in Eveline Cruickshanks and Edward Corp (eds.), *The Stuart Court in Exile and the Jacobites* (London, 1995).

Kervella, André. *La passion écossaise* (Paris, 2002).

Le mystère de la rose blanche (Paris, 2009).

Lamy, Gabriella. 'Des jardiniers Saint-Germanois au service de Louis XV puis de Marie-Antoinette au Petrit Trianon: Claude (1705–1784) et Antoine (1734–1807) Richard', *Bulletin des amis du vieux Saint-Germain*, 44 (2007), pp. 103–15.

Lart, C.E. *The Parochial Registers of Saint-Germain-en-Laye: Jacobite Extracts*, vol. II (London, 1912).

La Via, Stefano. 'Il Cardinale Ottoboni e la musica: nuovi documenti (1700–1740), nuove lettere e ipotesi', pp. 319–526 in Albert Dunning (ed.), *Intorno a Locatelli: Studi in occasione del tricentenario della nascita di Pietro Antonio Locatelli (1695–1764)* (2 vols., Lucca, 1995), vol. I.

Letarouilly, Paul-Marie. *Les edifices de Rome moderne* (Paris, 1860; rev. edn Novara, 1992).

Levey, Michael. *The Later Italian Pictures in the Collection of Her Majesty the Queen* (London, 1964).

Lionnet, Jean. 'Innocenzo Fede', in *New Grove Dictionary of Music and Musicians*, vol. VIII, pp. 634–5.

Lindgren, Lowell. 'Oratorios Sung in Italian at London, 1734–82', pp. 513–52 in Paola Besutti (ed.), *L'oratorio musicale italiano e i suoi contesti (sec. XVII–XVIII), atti del convegno internazionale a Perugia* (Florence, 2002).

'Rome', in *New Grove Dictionary of Music and Musicians*, vol. XXI, p. 629.

'Rome, 1680–1730', in *New Grove Dictionary of Opera*, vol. IV, pp. 25–7.

Lo Bianco, Anna, and Angelo Negro (eds.). *Il Settecento a Roma,* exhibition catalogue (Rome, 2005).

Marshall, David R., Susan Russell and Karin E. Wolfe (eds.). *'Roma-Britannica': Art Patronage and Cultural Exchange in Eighteenth-Century Rome* (London and Rome, 2011).

Marx, Hans Joachim. *Arcangelo Corelli, Historisch-Kritische Gesamtausgabe des Musikalischen Werke* (Cologne, 1980).

'Giovanni Battista Costanzi', in *New Grove Dictionary of Music and Musicians*, vol. VI, pp. 527–8.

'Giovanni Battista Costanzi', in *New Grove Dictionary of Opera*, vol. I, p. 971.

Masson, Pierre-Maurice. *Madame de Tencin, 1682–1749* (Paris, 1909; new edn Geneva, 1970).

Mattei, Saverio. *Memorie per servire alla vita del Metastasio ed elogio di N. Jommelli* (1785; facsimile edn Bologna, 1987).

McClymonds, Marita P. 'Niccolò Jommelli', in *New Grove Dictionary of Music and Musicians*, vol. XIII, pp. 178–86.

'Niccolò Jommelli', in *New Grove Dictionary of Opera*, vol. II, pp. 907–12.

McLynn, Frank. *Prince Charles Edward Stuart* (London, 1988).

Michel, Olivier, and Pierre Rosenberg (eds.). *Subleyras, 1699–1749*, exhibition catalogue (Paris, 1987).

Miller, Peggy. *A Wife for the Pretender* (London, 1965).

Monson, Dale E. 'Baldassare Galuppi', in *New Grove Dictionary of Opera*, vol. II, p. 337.

Morassi, Antonio. *Guardi: I dipinti* (2 vols., Venice, 1975).

Morelli Timpanaro, M. A. *Tomasso Crudeli Poppi, 1702–1745*, vol. I (Florence, 2003).

Murdoch, Steve. 'Tilting at Windmills: The Order of Toboso as a Jacobite Social Network', pp. 243–64 in Paul Monod, Murray Pittock and Daniel Szechi (eds.), *Loyalty and Identity: Jacobites at Home and Abroad* (Basingstoke, 2010).

Neveu, Bruno. 'A Contribution to an Inventory of Jacobite Sources', pp. 138–58 in Eveline Cruickshanks (ed.), *Ideology and Conspiracy: Aspects of Jacobitism, 1689–1759* (Edinburgh, 1982).

New Grove Dictionary of Music and Musicians, 2nd edn, ed. Stanley Sadie and John Tyrrell (29 vols., London, 2001).

New Grove Dictionary of Opera, ed. Stanley Sadie (4 vols., London, 1992).

O'Connell, Sheila. 'Giles Hussey', in *Oxford Dictionary of National Biography* (Oxford, 2004), vol. XXVIII, pp. 985–6.

Pantanella, Rossella. 'Palazzo Muti a piazza SS. Apostoli residenza degli Stuart a Roma', *Storia dell'arte*, 84 (1995), pp. 307–15.

Pascoli, Lione. *Vite de' pittori, scultori, ed architetti moderni* (Rome, 1730; facsimile edn 1933).

Pedley, Mary. 'The Manuscript Papers of Diego de Revillas in the Archive of the British School at Rome', *Papers of the British School of Rome*, LIX (London, 1991), pp. 319–24.

Pialoux, Albane. 'Rome, théâtre des relations diplomatiques', *Revue d'histoire diplomatique*, 118 (2004).

Piperno, Franco. ' "Su le sponde del Tebro": Eventi, mecenati e istituzioni musicali a Roma negli anni di Locatelli. Saggio di cronologia', pp. 793–877 in Albert Dunning (ed.), *Intorno a Locatelli: Studi in occasione del tricentenario della nascita di Pietro Antonio Locatelli (1695–1764)* (2 vols., Lucca, 1995), vol. II.

Ricci, Corrado. *I teatri di Bologna nei secoli XVII e XVIII* (Bologna, 1888).

Robert, Laurent. *Chatou et Croissy-sur-Seine: Villégiatures en bordure de Seine* (L'inventaire générale des monuments et des richesses artistiques de la France, Paris, 1993).

Roettgen, Steffi. *Anton Raphael Mengs, 1728–79* (Munich, 1999).

Ross, Janet, and Nelly Erichsen. *The Story of Lucca* (London, 1912).

Roversi, Giancarlo. *Palazzi e case nobili del '500 a Bologna* (Bologna, 1986).

Ruggiero, Maria Grazia Pastura. *La reverenza Camera Apostolica e i suoi archivi, secoli XV–XVIII* (Rome, 1984).

Ruvigny et Raineval, Melville Henry Massue, marquis de. *The Jacobite Peerage* (Edinburgh, 1904).

Sani, Bernardina. *Rosalba Carriera* (Turin, 2007).

Sartori, Claudio. *I libretti italiani a stampa dalle origini al 1800* (6 vols. and 2 vols. of Indici, Cuneo, 1990–94).

Schiavo, Armando. *Il Palazzo della Cancelleria* (Rome, 1963).
Schidlof, L.R. *La miniature en Europe aux 16ᵉ, 17ᵉ, 18ᵉ et 19ᵉ siècles*, I (Graz, 1964).
Scott, Geoffrey. ' "Sacredness of Majesty"; The English Benedictines and the Cult of King James II', Royal Stuart Papers, XXIII (Huntingdon, 1984).
Sharp, Michael. 'Jacobite and Anti-Jacobite Medals', *Royal Stuart Papers*, LXXIV (London, 2008).
Sharp, Richard. *The Engraved Record of the Jacobite Movement* (Aldershot, 1996).
Shield, Alice. *Henry Stuart, Cardinal of York and His Times* (London, 1908).
Shield, Alice, and Andrew Lang. *The King over the Water* (London, 1907).
Spiriti, Andrea, and Simona Capelli (eds.). *I David: Due pittori tra Sei e Settecento*, exhibition catalogue (Milan, 2004).
Stewart, H.C. 'The Exiled Stewarts in Italy, 1717–1807', *The Scottish Historical Society Miscellany* VII: ser. 3, vol. 35 (Edinburgh, 1941), pp. 55–130.
Szechi, Daniel. *The Jacobites: Britain and Europe, 1688–1788* (Manchester, 1994).
    1715: The Great Jacobite Rebellion (New Haven and London, 2006).
Talbot, Michael. Booklet to accompany the recording of *La Senna festeggiante* and *Gloria e Imeneo* by the King's Consort conducted by Robert King (Hyperion Records, 2002), p. 10.
Talbot, Michael, and Paul Everett. 'Homage to a French King: Two Serenatas by Vivaldi (Venice, 1725 and ca. 1726)', the introduction to Antonio Vivaldi, *Due Serenata*, facsimile edn (Venice, 1995).
Tayler, Henrietta. *Lady Nithsdale and Her Family* (London, 1939).
    The Seven Sons of the Provost (London, 1949).
Vitali, Carlo. 'Da "schiavottielo" a "fedele amico": lettere (1731–1749) di Carlo Broschi Farinelli al conte Sicinio Pepoli', *Nuova rivista musicale italiana* **26**:1 (1992), pp. 1–36.
Wemyss, Alice. *Elcho of the '45* (Edinburgh, 2003).
Whipple, E.E. *A Famous Corner of Tuscany* (London, 1928).
Woolf, Noel. *The Medallic Record of the Jacobite Movement* (London, 1988).

UNPUBLISHED THESES

Marinelli, Giuseppe. 'L'architettura palaziale romana tra Seicento e Settecento. Problemi di linguaggio. Un approccio filologico: la testimonianza delle incisioni dello "Studio d'architettura civile"; una verifica sistematica: il palazzo Muti Papazzurri alla Pilotta' (Università Sapienza di Roma, no date shown, but after 1990).
Taylor, Carole M. 'Italian Operagoing in London, 1700–1745' (Syracuse University, 1991).
Wortley, Clare Stuart. 'Stuart Portraits' (unfinished and ed. after her death by Henrietta Tayler, 1948).

Index